Public Sector
Labor Relations

Public Sector Labor Relations

Analysis and Readings

David Lewin
Columbia University

Peter Feuille
University of Illinois

Thomas A. Kochan
Massachusetts Institute of Technology

John Thomas Delaney
Columbia University

Lexington Books
D.C. Heath and Company/Lexington, Massachusetts/Toronto

Library of Congress Cataloging-in-Publication Data

Public sector labor relations.

  Rev. ed. of: Public sector labor relations/
David Lewin. 1977.
  Includes index.
  1. Collective bargaining—Government employees—
United States. 2. Trade-unions—Government employees—
United States. 3. Employee-management relations in
government—United States. I. Lewin, David, 1943–
II. Lewin, David, 1943–   Public sector labor
relations.
HD8005.6.U5P83   1988   331.89'041353   82–64038
ISBN 0–669–17125–5 (alk. paper)
ISBN 0–669–12893–7 (pbk: alk. paper)

Published simultaneously in Canada
Printed in the United States of America
Casebound International Standard Book Number: 0–669–17125–5
Paperbound International Standard Book Number: 0–669–12893–7
Library of Congress Catalog Card Number: 82–64038

The paper used in this publication meets the minimum requirements of
American National Standard for Information Sciences—Permanence of
Paper for Printed Materials, ANSI Z39.48–1984. ∞™

88 89 90 91 92 8 7 6 5 4 3 2 1

Contents

Preface

In addition to a new title, the third edition of *Public Sector Labor Relations: Analysis and Readings* has undergone several other important changes. First, regarding content, the book now contains twenty-five reading selections, compared to thirty-seven in the first edition and thirty in the second edition. Ten of the twenty-five readings are new to this book but, like the others, were originally published elsewhere, in scholarly and professional journals and as portions of books and monographs.

Second, each of the chapter introductions has been completely rewritten to take account of new developments, issues, public policies, and especially published research that has appeared since 1981, when the second edition was published. This includes part III of the book, which now features an updated police collective bargaining exercise and a teacher grievance case.

Third, the three original authors of the book have been joined by Professor John Delaney of Columbia University's Graduate School of Business. As before, the undertaking and completion of this edition of the book reflect a fully collaborative effort. Each author prepared the written material for and edited the reading selections in the chapters for which he was responsible. These were then reviewed and modified as required by the other authors. Lewin bore primary responsibility for chapters 3 and 6; Feuille for chapter 5, the bargaining exercise, and the grievance case; Kochan for chapter 4; and Delaney for chapters 2 and 7. Chapters 1 and 8 reflect contributions from and a blending of the views of the four authors.

Fourth, this edition of the book has a new publisher, Lexington Books, a division of D.C. Heath and Company. We are grateful to Bruce Katz of Lexington Books for his encouragement and assistance in the completion and publication of the third edition of *Public Sector Labor Relations: Analysis and Readings*. At the same time, we wish to acknowledge the support and friendship of Tom and Ann Horton of Thomas Horton and Daughters, Inc., the publisher of the first and second editions.

Despite all these changes, the third edition of this book is similar to the previous editions in several key respects. A common complaint about books of readings is that they rarely are constructed to give teachers and students coherent perspective on the subject matter at hand. A further alleged short-coming of collections of readings is that they often overcondense or truncate reading selections, thereby providing only bits and pieces of the relevant material to the reader. We have sought to avoid these deficiencies by integrating the topics chosen for inclusion, the textual materials and reading selections, and the readings contained in each chapter and subdivision thereof. Further, in most cases we have reprinted as full a version as possible of the original selection. Perhaps most important, all this material is organized into three main sections: background and overview, collective bargaining processes, and collective bargaining outcomes. These correspond to what we believe are the key dimensions of public sector labor relations: setting, process, and outcome.

Also as in previous editions, we integrate to the extent possible research on public sector labor relations with research drawn from the private sector. This is most clearly apparent in the authors' introduction to each chapter, and this material should help readers make judgments about the similarities and differences between public sector and private sector labor relations. Additionally, the collective bargaining exercise and grievance case, both drawn from real world public sector labor–management relationships, permit students to apply and observe experientially some of the concepts and processes discussed in this book.

The reader will probably note that we have contributed more written material to some chapters than to others, and also that the material and readings are arranged according to topical subdivision in some but not all chapters. This is a result of our conscious strategy in writing and organizing the materials to overcome gaps in the literature. In some topic areas, the gaps were substantial (though less so than in 1981 when the second edition of the book was published); in others the gaps were relatively small and/or the existing literature hung together reasonably well. Hence, we purposely chose to be responsive to this diversity in our own writing and editorial efforts, rather than to design an artificially uniform organizational format for the book.

We continue to believe that this book is well suited to courses in public sector labor relations, where it can serve as a basic textbook, and to courses in private sector collective bargaining and labor–management relations, where it can serve as a companion volume to other textbooks. However, by drawing from a broad base of public sector labor relations research, including one article that deals with aspects of the Canadian experience in this area, we hope to broaden the appeal of this book beyond those who are particularly interested in governmental collective bargaining. Specifically, the concepts, analytical frameworks, research designs, empirical findings, and policy implications contained in the following pages, together with the explicit recognition throughout of the economic, political, legal, and organizational forces that affect public sector bargaining processes and outcomes, commend the book to those interested in public management and administration, urban studies, personnel and human resource management, organizational behavior, and of course, industrial relations.

Publication of this book would not have been possible without the gracious permission of many individuals and organizations to reprint the reading selections contained herein. In addition to the authors, who are individually identified in the Contents and in the readings, we wish explicitly to acknowledge our appreciation to the following: *The Arbitration Journal,* The Association of Labor Mediation Agencies, The Brookings Institution, D.C. Heath and Company, *Industrial and Labor Relations Review, Industrial Relations,* Industrial Relations Research Association, New York State School of Industrial and Labor Relations, Cornell University, Plenum Press, and *The Review of Economics and Statistics.*

In sum, we hope that this third edition of *Public Sector Labor Relations: Analysis and Readings* serves the purpose of pulling together in a single volume the key issues, concepts, and research findings pertaining to contemporary public sector labor relations. It was the absence of such a volume that originally motivated us to prepare this book; the reactions of teachers and students to the first two editions were instrumental to our decision to produce a third edition. The wisdom of that decision will once again depend on the extent to which teachers and students find the book to be a useful learning tool.

David Lewin
Peter Feuille
Thomas A. Kochan
John Thomas Delaney

1
Background and Overview

Objectives and Focus of the Book

By the late 1980s, roughly a quarter-century of experience with "modern" collective bargaining had accumulated in the American public sector. During this period unionism advanced to the point where well over one-third of all public employees and about 45 percent of full-time public employees belonged to labor unions and employee associations—membership rates that far surpassed those prevailing in private industry.[1] Collective bargaining became a widespread mechanism for determining terms and conditions of public employment, and individual states continued to experiment with various forms of legislation to regulate labor relations and dispute resolution in the public sector.

Readers of the two previous editions of this book will recall that we identified a first and a second generation of public sector bargaining in the United States, which roughly corresponded to the 1960s and the 1970s, respectively.[2] The first generation featured an expansive economic climate, rapidly growing public employment, and a political environment that strongly supported public sector unionism and bargaining rights. The second generation, in contrast, witnessed taxpayer revolts, a shrinking public sector, and a political climate that supported restrictions on union activities and a hard bargaining stance on the part of public managers.

Can it fairly be said that, in the 1980s, the United States is experiencing a third generation of public sector bargaining? If so, what are its leading characteristics? Although we believe a generational interpretation of the evolution of public sector labor relations can be carried too far—which is a way of saying that we are not fully convinced that a third generation is upon us—the 1980s seem to feature a more pronounced emphasis on the performance and productivity of public services and public employees.

Consider, for example, recent initiatives to require competency testing of public school teachers, create master teacher positions, provide teacher performance "bonuses," and raise entry-level pay to attract higher quality teachers.[3] Or consider public sanitation service, where rapid technological change, especially automation, together with major job restructuring, has brought about a smaller, more productive public work force. (See the Lewin reading in chapter 4). Indeed, in sanitation and in several other public services the specter (or fact) of privatization has contributed strongly to the heightened emphasis on the performance of governments as service providers.[4]

From one perspective, these and related developments appear to threaten public employee unionism and collective bargaining. In the 1980s, unquestionably, some legislatures have sought to circumscribe public employees' unionism and bargaining rights, and some public employers have sought (and achieved) bargaining givebacks and other concessions. Certainly, no recounting of key public sector labor relations developments of the 1980s could overlook the firing of striking federal air traffic controllers by President Reagan and the subsequent demise of the Professional Air Traffic Controllers' Organization (PATCO). (See the discussion and readings about this event in chapter 4.)

From another perspective, however, the 1980s emphasis on the performance, productivity, even competitiveness, of the public sector provides new opportunities for public unionists and bargainers. Consider how leaders of the National Education Association (NEA) and the American Federation of Teachers (AFT) have adopted the teacher competence issue as one of their own and used it to strengthen their respective organizations. Unionized clerical and professional employees, sanitation workers, police, and other groups of public employees have joined with public managers to negotiate a variety of cooperative labor agreements that, for example, establish joint committees to deal with work performance, job design, quality of working life, and organizational communications. Further, in the 1980s some states, such as Ohio and Illinois, have enacted public sector bargaining legislation where none previously existed. Thus, it is not at all clear that the heightened emphasis on the performance and productivity of government poses fundamental threats to public employee unionism and bargaining; to the contrary, both seem very much alive.

Whether or not the reader agrees with our judgment call on this matter, the central objectives of the third edition of this book remain the same as those of the previous editions: to present and assess the state of knowledge concerning the key issues and problems of public sector bargaining by drawing on some of the leading research completed to date. Additionally, however, we will pose a number of unanswered questions that we believe will confront policymakers and practitioners in the years ahead and which therefore merit closer attention by researchers. Our approach is based on the premise that in order to make accurate judgments and recommendations about labor relations phenomena, we must first understand the variables that shape labor relations events and the implications of altering one or more of these variables. Consequently, we stress the need for an overall conceptual framework for analyzing, interpreting, and placing in perspective the many interrelated aspects of a collective bargaining system.

The material in the following chapters is organized within the context of the overall analytical framework presented here, and is intended to introduce the reader to collective bargaining in government. In each chapter, we first try to outline the central issues of interest that have been identified either by researchers or by practitioners. In a research sense, this amounts to identifying the major dependent variables in each area. Second, we attempt to specify, where appropriate or possible, the underlying factors that shape these events; that is, we outline the explanatory or independent variables that have been identified in each area. Third, we attempt to identify important public policy issues in each area. Fourth, we address the key decisions that unions and employers must make in meeting the challenges facing them in each of the areas. Finally, we offer a summary assessment of the current state of knowledge and research in each area, along with a suggested agenda for future research and discussion. Thus, while a rich blend of conceptual, policy, and descriptive material is included in this book in order to give the reader a balanced exposure to the field, the text and readings also reflect our goal of advancing the state of research and thinking about public sector collective bargaining.

The three core concepts in the framework used to organize the material in this book are the environment or context of union–management relations, the nature of the bargaining process, and the outcomes or impacts of that process. This general conceptual framework is portrayed in figure 1–1. We will briefly outline the substance of these concepts in order to set the stage for the chapters to follow.[5]

We begin by examining the environmental contexts of the bargaining process. In the private sector, the role of the economic environment has been

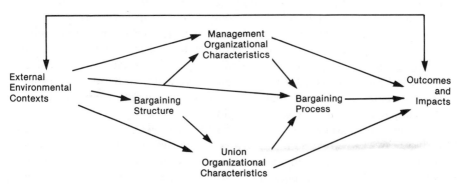

Figure 1–1. The Conceptual Framework

extensively analyzed, both theoretically and empirically. Product and labor market constraints, employer ability to pay, labor costs as a percentage of total costs, demand elasticities, and the like have all played a prominent role in explaining the behavior of the parties in bargaining and the outcomes of the bargaining process. Consequently, it behooves us to examine the nature of the economic context of bargaining in the public sector.

The legal environment—that is, public policy—has also been assigned an important role in studies of private sector collective bargaining. In public sector bargaining research, however, the role of public policy occupies an even more prominent place, largely because of the diversity of federal, state, and local policies in this area. This diversity provides a potential laboratory for debate, experimentation, and evaluation of policy alternatives. Consequently, we will examine the nature and development of the diversity of policy frameworks for bargaining in government, and will attempt to place the role of public policy in a broader perspective.

The evolution of bargaining in the public sector has forced both researchers and practitioners to pay greater attention to the role of the political environment in which bargaining takes place. Although the notion that the political context plays a role in shaping the behavior of the parties to bargaining is certainly not new, the fact that the public employer—in contrast to the private employer—is primarily a political institution has markedly increased the attention given to this aspect of the environment. We believe that the political nature of government is the key feature from which flow most of the important differences between public and private sector labor relations. Hence, the readings throughout the book reflect our belief in the centrality of this aspect of the bargaining environment.

In the past few years, labor and management professionals have become increasingly aware of the impacts that shifts in the demographic makeup of society exert on their bargaining relationships. The declining enrollments in public schools (which may be reversed in the 1990s); the economic resurgence of the northeastern states and economic stagnation of some Sunbelt states; and the changing racial and ethnic composition of urban areas, especially those where new immigrants congregate, have altered the demand for public services, influenced the resources available for collective bargaining, and increased the importance of the human resource and productivity provisions found in bargaining agreements. Therefore, we will treat these demographic characteristics as an additional dimension of the environment and discuss their impacts on collective bargaining in government.

From our treatment of the environmental contexts, we move inward to the structural and organizational factors that are important to understanding the nature of the bargaining process and bargaining outcomes in the public sector. The concept of *bargaining structure* has generally been treated in private sector research by addressing the question of the appropriate bargaining unit. This overall policy issue can be broken down into three questions:

1. What is the impact of centralized versus decentralized bargaining structures?
2. What is the impact of broad versus narrow bargaining units?
3. What is the appropriate bargaining status for supervisory and managerial employees?

Most of the research in the public sector has ignored the first question, principally because there has been very little experience in state and local governments with centralized (multiemployer or coalitional) bargaining structures. The second question is especially relevant, however, for those states and cities that have multiple sets of bargaining units and that maintain personnel and budget-making policies that cut across these units. Consequently, we will examine the advantages and disadvantages of alternative ways of structuring bargaining relationships. Because of the belief that supervisors in the public sector differ in their functions and responsibilities from their private sector counterparts, controversy persists over the appropriate bargaining rights for public sector supervisors. We will examine these arguments and, again, seek to identify the relevance of alternative policy options for the process and outcomes of bargaining.

The importance of the employer's organizational characteristics in shaping the process and outcomes of bargaining has received more attention in the public than in the private sector. Most of the literature has focused on the difficult problem of adapting governmental structures and decision-making processes to the requirements of collective bargaining. Although this is a problem that faces all employers when bargaining arrives on the scene, the political nature of public employers and the traditions of separation of powers, representative government, and multiple points of access to decision makers increase the magnitude of the problem for the public employer. For example, there is no objective formula by which a city government can decide how much of a voice in labor relations matters should be given to the mayor, the city council, the city attorney, the civil service commission, and so on. In fact, for many public jurisdictions during the initial period of bargaining, the most important problem may be deciding who is the employer for labor relations purposes. Experience has also shown that this is not just a transitory problem that withers away as the bargaining relationship matures. Instead, the question of who has the power to speak for and commit management to a decision in public sector bargaining continues to be a "normal" part of the politics of the decision-making process. Consequently, most of the material dealing with management as an actor in collective bargaining focuses on these types of problems and their impacts on bargaining process and outcomes.

The labor relations context and bargaining structure materials in chapters 2 and 3 set the stage for analyzing the more visible of our three core concepts: the characteristics of the bargaining process itself, including the resolution of negotiating impasses and the outcomes or impacts of bargaining. We introduce the material on the interaction process in chapter 4 by reviewing some of the bargaining process concepts that are found in the private sector literature. Then we suggest how some of these notions need to be adapted to be consistent with the bargaining process that is evolving in public jurisdictions in the United States. Specifically, we focus on the notion that, in contrast to the bilateral paradigm of the private sector, bargaining in the public sector tends to take on multilateral characteristics because of the numerous management interests and the political nature of the public employer. Next we examine how the bargaining process becomes transformed as the scope of issues discussed broadens to include those of interest not only to public employees and their employers, but to other groups in the community as well.

Because the function of the negotiations process is to resolve differences between employers and employees, we devote a substantial portion of our analysis of the bargaining process to the means used in the public sector to accomplish this end. Thus, in chapter 5 we examine the legal status and the normative arguments regarding the right to strike as well as the procedural mechanisms—mediation, fact-finding, and various forms of arbitration— that have been used to resolve negotiating disputes. In particular, we focus on the compatibility—or lack of it—between the incentives to engage in good faith bargaining and the availability of various impasse procedures.

The research on alternatives for resolving negotiation impasses provides a logical link to an analysis of the final set of dependent variables in our framework—namely, the outcomes and impacts of bargaining. Ultimately, policymakers, union and management practitioners, and researchers must struggle with two general questions in this area:

1. What determines the kinds of outcomes that are achieved in bargaining in the public sector?
2. What are the impacts of these outcomes on the goals of the parties and the larger society?

In this section we will not only examine the traditional impact-of-wages research, but will also discuss and include in the text studies that attempt to isolate the determinants of both wage and nonwage bargaining outcomes within a unionized context. This second approach essentially investigates the environmental, structural, organizational, and procedural factors that determine variations in outcomes under collective bargaining. The material in chapters 6 and 7 further illuminates the diversity of impacts and outcomes across thousands of bargaining relationships and underscores the difficulty of assigning proof of causality to particular independent variables.

Our final chapter features a look backward at the earlier chapters with an eye toward evaluating the state of public sector bargaining research. In chapter 8 we ask, "What have we learned from all of this research, what have we yet to learn, and how can we narrow the gaps in existing knowledge?" We close our reading material by discussing the implications that public sector research and practice may have for the study and practice of collective bargaining in general.

In the supplementary material at the end of this book, we attempt to go beyond the usual book of text and readings by providing readers with opportunities to get their feet wet. Specifically, we have included a negotiation exercise involving a city government and a police union and a grievance arbitration case set in a public school district. The exercise and the case enable students to apply some of the conceptual material presented in this book to the experiences of negotiating a new public sector labor agreement and resolving a dispute that arises out of the interpretation of an existing labor agreement.

The Authors' Perceptions

Since our interpretation and analysis of the issues examined in this book will be affected by our values and by our views of the current stage of development of public sector collective bargaining, we owe the reader a sketch of our perceptions of the governmental labor relations arena, circa 1987. At a basic level, we are committed to the right of public employees to form, join, and involve themselves in unions in order to participate via collective bargaining and other political processes in decisions that affect their work lives. For more than fifty years, the bedrock principle of our national labor policy has been that private sector employees have the right to participate in an organized manner in the decisions that affect their employment. We have yet to encounter any compelling reasons that public employees should not also enjoy similar rights. Therefore, this book contains very little material dealing with the appropriateness of collective bargaining for public employees[6] but, rather, contains a great deal of material dealing with the appropriate shape of public sector collective bargaining systems.

We currently see public sector bargaining moving toward a third phase or generation of development. Compared to the first two developmental phases, the third generation is characterized by five interrelated factors:

1. A mixed economic environment that features some elements of fiscal strain and some elements of economic expansion.

2. A mixed political environment in which some governments are characterized by aggressive managements, others by aggressive unions.

3. Continuing challenges to the effectiveness of dispute settlement procedures.

4. Improvement in the relative and real wage position of public employees.

5. An increasingly assertive general public that wants more efficiency in government and more input into key decision processes, but is less willing to support public services with increased tax burdens.

The third and fifth of these factors have been apparent since the mid-1970s; the others are of more recent vintage.

The Economic Environment of Collective Bargaining

During the 1960s, the economic environment of public sector bargaining was vibrant and expansionary. Public employment grew rapidly, and public employees experienced an era of catch-up wage increases. The 1970s, in contrast, were characterized by frequent economywide recessions, high inflation, and a pronounced economic and social decline of many U.S. cities. Indeed, several prominent cities—for example, New York City in 1975 and Cleveland in 1979—experienced imminent or actual bankruptcy, engendering ripple effects on other cities in the associated regions. The industrial centers of the Northeast and Midwest, in particular, lost jobs both to their surrounding suburbs and to the lower tax and faster growing Sunbelt states. This meant that cities that had experienced the greatest degree of public employee militancy in the 1960s and early 1970s had to negotiate new labor agreements during the 1970s under the constraint of severe fiscal stress. Moreover, measures like California's Proposition 13, enacted in 1978, and Massachusetts's Proposition 2½, enacted three years later, attested to the widespread public desire for reduced or at best constant tax levies. It was no surprise, then, that public employees suffered relative and real wage losses during the 1970s.

The economic environment of public sector bargaining in the 1980s cannot be as readily or as single-mindedly characterized as that of the 1960s or 1970s. On the one hand, the proportion of gross national product (GNP) represented by public expenditures rose to record highs in the 1980s under the Reagan administration; several northeastern and some midwestern states experienced major, even dramatic, economic recoveries; and several large state and city governments found themselves with budget surpluses.[7] On the other hand, public employment as a proportion of total economywide employment continued to decline (to about one-sixth), several formerly prosperous southern and Sunbelt states experienced economic downturns and conflicts over taxes, and competition from the private sector for the delivery of "public" services continued to grow.[8] Putting these contrasting developments together, it appears that in the 1980s government and union officials face an economic environment in which citizens are demanding demonstrable and measurable performance improvement in the delivery of public services, greater citizen involvement in decisions about the financing of public services, and increased use of private sector–like incentives and pricing systems—if not the private sector itself—in the "production" and delivery of public services. Nevertheless, we judge this type of economic environment to be consistent with the observed fact that public employee pay increases during the 1980s (specifically through 1986) have, on average, exceeded inflation as well as private sector pay increases. We examine the basis for this judgment in chapter 6.

Changing Structures of Political Influence

The deteriorating financial position of state and local governments in the 1970s led to a decline in the political influence of public sector labor unions relative to the influence of other interest groups. Even politicians who earlier had been elected with labor support found it possible to take a hard-line, fiscally conservative approach to collective bargaining with their public employees. As examples, the Democratic governors of the states of California, New York, Connecticut, and Massachusetts and the mayors of such cities as New York, Seattle, Boston, and Philadelphia all adopted positions that effectively reduced the political access or influence of the public sector unions that had helped put them in office.[9]

In the 1980s the influence of public employee unions has undergone at least a mild resurgence. Public employee unions were instrumental in the enactment of public sector bargaining laws in the states of Illinois and Ohio, the former under a Republican administration, and also played important roles in the election of Democratic governors in Massachusetts, New York, and Texas, and in numerous mayoral races. Yet, several state and municipal election campaigns of the 1980s also featured candidates of both major parties taking strong fiscal control positions, some of them explicitly focused on labor cost containment and the reduction of union power.[10]

We believe that the bargaining processes that evolved during the first and second generations of governmental collective bargaining and that have continued into the third generation of such bargaining have accurately been described as multilateral in nature—that is, involving the interplay of diverse interest groups rather than simply conforming to the bilateral dichotomy of labor versus management. Some observers have argued that a bilateral decision-making structure and process based on the private sector bargaining model would so insulate the public bargaining process from the public interest and from the normal political process (one characterized by the interplay of multiple interest groups and multiple access points) that the democratic principles on which government is based would inherently be destroyed or weakened (see, for example, the Wellington and Winter reading in chapter 2). Other observers, however, have argued that the political process infringed on the integrity of the collective bargaining process because power within the management structure was shared among diverse and often conflicting interest groups in a way that provided an incentive for labor unions to play one interest off against another. The result of this situation of dispersed management power and internal management conflict was that much of the bargaining between union representatives and those management officials who held the crucial decision-making power occurred away from the formal negotiating table. A whole new vernacular grew up for this practice—end runs, backdoor deals, two bites at the apple, double-dipping, and so on.

In practice, it appears that although the bilateral negotiations process has grown in importance throughout the several generations of public sector bargaining, enough potential for multilateral bargaining has been maintained to preserve the ability of politicians to intervene in the process when their critical interests are perceived to be at stake. Since labor costs are the biggest single controllable item in state and local government budgets, politicians have sometimes turned to a hard-line bargaining policy as one means of dealing with their economic problems. This strategy partly reflects economic necessity and partly a reaction or backlash to the perceived excesses of bargaining settlements that were negotiated during the first generation, especially in the areas of pensions and other fringe benefits. During the 1960s and the early 1970s, it was politically expedient and sometimes necessary for elected officials to agree to wage and fringe benefit improvements without regard for the funding consequences of these agreements. Because employment levels were expanding at a rapid rate during that period, the full financial implications of settlements negotiated during the first generation only later began to be felt.

However, the harder line stance toward public employees that became more popular among elected officials during the second generation of public sector bargaining also partly reflected simple political expediency. Whether or not actual budgetary conditions necessitated a hold-the-line approach, many politicians benefited politically from publicly endorsing a hard-line strategy. In other words, although the formal bargaining process continues to be the dominant mechanism for exchanges between public unions and public employers, economic pressures and public opinion changes have often caused politicians to become more actively involved in labor relations matters in ways that have reduced or altered union influence. In some instances, these stiffening managerial postures have, in turn, resulted in increased bargaining turmoil (see the material in chapter 5). This may be less true of the 1980s than it was of the 1970s, but it appears to be a persistent characteristic of public sector labor relations.

Challenges to Dispute Resolution Procedures

The first two generations of collective bargaining were marked by great expectations of finding effective ways to structure a good faith bargaining process without the right to strike—an arrangement that directly contradicted private sector practice and conventional wisdom. Public policymakers created impasse procedures as alternatives to the strike, and these procedural experiments generally were acclaimed as successful.[11] Such claims by both practitioners and researchers continue today, and empirical evidence largely supports some of them. In most jurisdictions that have been studied, the empirical data show that a majority of disputes were settled by the parties without relying on impasse procedures. Furthermore, the studies tend to show that almost all of the disputes that went to impasse resulted in settlement at some nonbinding step—for example, mediation or fact-finding. The remaining disputes tended to be resolved through some combination of further negotiations, arbitration, unilateral determination by the employer, or strike. Although public employee strikes are outlawed in most jurisdictions, they are permitted in some—but usually only after other dispute resolution mechanisms have been exhausted. Throughout the 1960s and 1970s, the incidence of strikes was much lower in government than in industry. In the 1980s—for which, unfortunately, few comprehensive data are available— public sector strikes may have occurred more frequently than private sector work stoppages. In any case, those public sector strikes that have occurred have tended to be of relatively short duration.[12]

There are some signs on the horizon, however, that may ultimately upset the earlier favorable predictions of the effectiveness of public sector dispute resolution procedures. First, we have witnessed a progression from mild forms of third-party intervention to stronger forms of third-party determination. For example, most of the early statutes provided for mediation, perhaps followed by fact-finding with recommendations. Then, in the late 1960s and early 1970s, several states amended their procedures to provide for the compulsory arbitration of police and firefighter bargaining impasses. Most of the legislative choices were for conventional binding arbitration, but in the late 1970s and early 1980s a number of states opted for a different form of third-party determination that has been labeled *final offer* arbitration. Second, there is some evidence of a growing reliance on mediation, fact-finding, and arbitration by other employee groups, especially teachers. Data from New York State jurisdictions and the Canadian federal service, for instance, indicate that the parties have gone further into impasse procedures in a larger proportion of negotiations in recent years than was true earlier.[13] A third development that may suggest trouble is that the parties to the most experienced and professional bargaining relationships and the ones in the most difficult bargaining environments are the heaviest users of impasse procedures.

In essence, they have experienced the "narcotic effects" predicted by the critics—that public sector managers and union officials will become addicted to using the impasse procedures as a painless means of avoiding the hard bargaining necessary to reach direct agreement. The parties in the largest cities with the most politicized union–management relationships and the most difficult economic problems have a much higher rate of reliance on impasse procedures than do the parties in smaller jurisdictions. Thus, the former appear to be dependent on these procedures as part and parcel of their negotiations processes. These developments have raised an important and difficult question: Is there some sort of natural half-life for dispute resolution procedures after which the parties learn how to incorporate the procedures into their bargaining strategies and ultimately cause the procedures to become less effective over time?

In general, dispute resolution procedures performed reasonably well during the first two generations of public sector bargaining. This is particularly encouraging when the contrasting economic-political environments of the first and second generations are taken into account. The third generation of public sector bargaining, however (if, indeed, we are in a third generation), features further development of strong dispute resolution systems (that is, ones ending in arbitration) and, as noted earlier, a growing emphasis on the productivity of public services and on the use of the private sector as an alternative to public services. Whether public sector dispute resolution procedures will continue to meet the challenges posed by these economic and political characteristics of the public sector bargaining environment is an exceedingly important question for future observation and research.

Ebb and Flow of Relative and Real Wages

As suggested earlier, during the first generation of bargaining the average public employee experienced catch-up wage increases that, in many cases, put him or her ahead of private sector counterparts doing comparable work (although, as the chapter 6 readings suggest, it is not clear that unionism and collective bargaining were exclusively or even primarily responsible for these relative wage gains).[14] At the same time, the fringe benefit packages of public employees also expanded at a faster rate than seemed to be the case in the private sector.

During the second generation of public sector bargaining, the gains of the first generation proved difficult to match. The constrained economic and political environments made it much harder to improve wage and fringe levels at a rate that the rank-and-file public employee union member had come to expect. Public managers learned that they could successfully resist union demands in bargaining, and they became increasingly willing to do so. As a consequence, public employee pay and benefit gains during the 1970s trailed those achieved by their private sector counterparts. Moreover, the relatively high rates of inflation experienced during the 1970s, especially the late 1970s, meant that public employees also suffered substantial real wage losses during that period.[15]

To this point in the 1980s, public employees appear to have once again gained pay advantages over their private sector counterparts. This stems not so much from large bargaining settlements in the public sector—public sector pay and benefit settlements averaged about 5 percent annually between 1981 and 1986—as from the very modest rates of pay increase that characterized private sector bargaining settlements during the first half of the 1980s.[16] Further, the continuing diminution of inflation during the 1980s has meant that the average public employee has attained real pay increases in public sector bargaining. Nevertheless, the rising forces of competition that have so markedly affected private sector pay settlements have also been felt in the public sector, where they take such forms as contracting out, technological change, consolidation of certain services, increased use of part-time personnel, and an overall decline in the proportion of public employees in the nation's work force. Consequently, although public employees in general appear to have improved their relative and real wage positions during the 1980s, the gains may well have accrued to a smaller public sector work force than existed during the first and second generations of public sector bargaining. Put differently, increases in public employee wage (and benefit) rates during the 1980s do not necessarily translate into corresponding increases in the public sector wage bill.

The challenge to governmental pay-setting processes during the remainder of the 1980s and into the 1990s will be to provide pay levels and pay increases that do not threaten the fiscal soundness of governments, that are responsive to external market and internal equity considerations, and that at least in part reward employee performance and individual or group productivity. In other words, the long-run problem is one of finding workable bases for financing public employee pay and benefits, improving the services provided to the community, and preserving the viability of public sector bargaining.

The Assertive Public

The inherent nature of public sector bargaining gives the public—or, more realistically, various public groups—the right to exert their influence over bargaining issues that are perceived to affect their vital interests. The economic and political trends summarized earlier, along with the dominant public sentiment against big government, high taxes, and poor services, have increased the desire of a number of these interest groups to assert themselves in collective bargaining decision making. Some of these efforts have been indirect, as, for example, through sponsorship of state referenda to limit or reduce the size of property taxes. Others have taken the form of general efforts to pass and/or enforce open meeting or "sunshine" laws that require bargaining sessions and dispute resolution procedures to be open to the public. Still others have taken a more direct approach, including requests for public seats at the bargaining table.

In addition to the role of community or taxpayer interest groups, various federal agencies and the judicial branch of government have asserted their roles in one or another area of public sector labor relations and human resource management. This is manifested, for example, in the areas of equal employment opportunity and affirmative action, extension of the Fair Labor Standards Act to the public sector, comparable worth in pay determination, and public employee rights to privacy and access to personal files. The public interest(s) in public sector labor relations thus appear not merely to have persisted, but to have expanded over time.

Further, the role of state governments and the federal government as sources of revenue for (or bankrollers of) major city governments appears to be shifting. Whereas this role expanded during the first two generations of public sector bargaining, and was spurred in particular by the fiscal crisis that threatened several prominent cities during the 1970s, it seems to be contracting during the 1980s. Most critical, perhaps, in this regard are the impending actions of the federal government to reduce budget deficits, which imply reductions in federal-to-state and state-to-local government revenue sharing.[17] At a minimum, the reduced dependence of local governments on outside sources of revenue raises the specter of a more pressing financial environment for public sector bargaining. The silver lining of this fiscal cloud, however, may be that the direct parties to public sector bargaining may come to have greater control of their own and their communities' destiny.

In short, the mixed directions and potential combined effects of these external forces impinging on public sector bargaining must continually be assessed by the direct parties to bargaining as they attempt to fashion workable labor relationships. Whether public sector labor and management will, by and large, respond to these forces by pursuing new cooperative arrangements or by relying on more traditional adversarialism remains to be seen. In any case, neither public management nor public unionists can ignore the numerous public interest groups that can vitally affect the public sector bargaining process and bargaining outcomes.

Labor Relations Research, Personal Preferences, and Policy Implications

One of the purposes of this book is to assess some of the research into governmental labor relations. Accordingly, we close this introductory chapter by offering some suggestions to help the reader evaluate the material in this book—including, of course, our own writing—with a more critical eye.

Research Considerations

In this book the reader will encounter a large number and variety of evaluative statements assessing the shape of relationships among labor relations variables. In chapter 2, for example, Wellington and Winter argue that the full transplant of private sector collective bargaining into the public sector will give government unions too much power vis-à-vis other interest groups. As another example, in chapter 5 Feuille argues that final offer arbitration has less of a chilling effect on the incentive to bargain than does conventional arbitration.

The reader should assess these types of evaluative statements along several dimensions. First, how carefully specified are the variables being researched? For instance, are such workhorse phrases as "too much power" or "the chilling effect" given some reasonably precise meaning, or are they stated in vague and general language? Precise definition and specification permit more careful measurement and stronger conclusions than does the use of open-ended concepts, but such precision may run the risk of abstracting from operational issues and problems. Second, it is necessary to distinguish between associational and causal relationships. For example, the fact that a high public sector wage or benefit level coexists with an aggressive public sector union does not necessarily mean that the union is responsible for the high wage or benefit. Such causality may exist, but first it is necessary to control for the other variables influencing wage and benefit rates. Further, research into social phenomena—especially those connected with power-based adversarial interactions—usually cannot be accomplished via controlled experiments (as chemists might perform in their laboratories); as a result, it is very difficult to isolate the effect of one variable (say, conventional arbitration) on another (say, wage or benefit rates).[18]

Third, one of the recurring themes in this book is the need for the reader to be aware of the diversity among thousands of public sector union–management relationships. This diversity necessarily limits the validity of sweeping generalizations about labor relations phenomena, and is especially true when one considers negotiating and impasse resolution practices and bargaining outcomes.[19] Similarly, the research process itself is constrained by time, effort, and financial scarcity and hence is based on informal or formal *sampling* of the entire population of such phenomena. Therefore, the reader needs to consider the scope of the data that are presented and the extent to which the data support generalizations. Researchers always face the temptation to expand the scope of their conclusions, and the reader should pay careful attention to possible inconsistencies between an author's conclusionary reach and the limits of his or her data.

Fourth, the reader should consider the relationship between the research issue being investigated and the data that are used. Because research is costly, there is a tendency for researchers to rely on readily available data. We have witnessed, for example, more "chilling effect" studies that compare the proportions of arbitrated and negotiated settlements than studies that directly measure the parties' movements or compromising behavior in negotiations. Thus, the reader may profitably ask whether the kind of data that are used are sufficient to answer the research issues being addressed and, further, what other kinds of information might provide better answers to these research questions.

Personal Preferences

A fifth dimension involves the interpretive latitude that exists in most of the writing in this area. The public sector labor relations literature continues to contain authoritative opinions, conventional wisdom, logical arguments, case studies, classification studies, and ad hoc surveys. The research methods used are often more informal and implicit than formal and explicit, although the trend is clearly toward the latter. Substantively, this literature consists of writings about various facets of human interactions over scarce resources in adversarial contexts where the outcomes of these interactions may be valued quite differently by different writers. Moreover, the literature is replete with such conclusions as "arbitration (or fact-finding or supervisory bargaining) is working well," unaccompanied by any standard of comparison, thereby leaving the reader to ask, "Working well compared to what?"

We make these points not to condemn the authors of the existing literature but, instead, to caution the reader that there is considerable room for personal preferences to influence researchers' (and other parties') conclusions. For instance, there are no precise formulae by which one can conclude that unions have "too much" or "too little" power or that the parties rely "too heavily" on arbitration. A given body of information may be interpreted in contrary fashion—one person's unit fragmentation is another's employee democracy. Similarly, only the very rare researcher or writer can be totally divorced from any normative opinion on these research topics, given that most of the topics are related to the allocation of scarce resources that may have a substantial impact on human welfare. In sum, most writers have considerable latitude to interpret the data they report, and their interpretations can be affected by their own preferences or values.[20]

Policy Implications

Public sector collective bargaining tends to increase the visibility and societal impact of government acting in its government-as-employer role relative to its government-as-regulator role. This is because public sector bargaining is a process of governmental decision making that allocates a variety of scarce public resources. The importance of the bargaining process to the government-as-employer role has resulted in considerable policy attention to the shape of the bargaining process, as can be seen most clearly in the attempts of various jurisdictions to regulate carefully the resolution of negotiating impasses. In general, we can say that the structure, process, and outcomes of public sector bargaining are closely connected with expressions of public sector labor relations policy.

The close connection between practices and policy creates an incentive for researchers and writers in the field to discuss the policy implications of their research. Although this is a wholesome tendency to the extent that their research is germane to policy issues, we urge the reader to evaluate carefully any policy implications or conclusions encountered in these (and other) readings. As we have noted, it is difficult to isolate the effect on bargaining of a single policy variable. In addition, it is often difficult to specify policy recommendations without some rank ordering of societal or policymakers' preferences (as, for example, avoiding strikes, encouraging the incentive to bargain, and so forth). As a result, the reader should check to see whether a writer's public policy implications (where offered) are supported by his or her data or whether these implications appear to be based on criteria other than empirical research (such as conventional wisdom, logical argument, or personal preference). In sum, we encourage the reader to be cognizant of the limits as well as the contributions of research to public sector labor relations policy.

Notes

1. See Leo Troy and Neil Sheflin, *Union Sourcebook: Membership, Structure, Finance, Directory* (West Orange, N.J.: Industrial Relations Data Information Service, 1985); David Lewin, "Public Employee Unionism in the 1980s: An Analysis of Transformation," in Seymour M. Lipset, ed., *Unions in Transition* (San Francisco: Institute for Contemporary Studies, 1986), pp. 241–264; and John F. Burton, Jr., "The Extent of Collective Bargaining in the Public Sector," in Benjamin Aaron, Joseph R. Grodin, and James L. Stern, eds., *Public-Sector Bargaining* (Washington, D.C.: Bureau of National Affairs, 1979), pp. 1–43.

2. David Lewin, Peter Feuille, and Thomas A. Kochan, *Public Sector Labor Relations: Analysis and Readings,* 1st ed. (Sun Lakes, Ariz.: Horton and Daughters, 1977), and 2nd ed. (1981).

3. See, for example, National Commission on Excellence in Education, *A Nation at Risk* (Washington, D.C.: U.S. Government Printing Office, 1983).

4. Lewin, "Public Employee Unionism," pp. 251–255.

5. This book is not intended to serve as a basic collective bargaining text. We have included very little material dealing with private sector labor relations practices,

union history, administration, and so on. For more comprehensive treatments of collective bargaining in the United States, see Neil W. Chamberlain and James W. Kuhn, *Collective Bargaining,* 3rd ed. (New York: McGraw-Hill, 1986); Daniel Q. Mills, *Labor–Management Relations,* 3rd ed. (New York: McGraw-Hill, 1986); John A. Fossum, *Labor Relations: Development, Structure, Process,* rev. ed. (Dallas: Business Publications, 1982); and Thomas A. Kochan, *Collective Bargaining and Industrial Relations: From Theory to Policy and Practice* (Homewood, Ill.: Irwin, 1980).

6. Three works that do question the appropriateness of "compulsory collective bargaining" in government are Sylvester Petro, "Sovereignty and Compulsory Public-Sector Bargaining," *Wake Forest Law Review* 10 (March 1974), pp. 25–165; Ralph de Toledano, *Let Our Cities Burn* (New Rochelle, N.Y.: Arlington House, 1975); and Robert S. Summers, *Collective Bargaining and Public Benefit Conferral: A Jurisprudential Critique* (Ithaca, N.Y.: New York State School of Industrial and Labor Relations, Cornell University, 1976).

7. Charles Brecher and Raymond D. Horton, "Retrenchment and Recovery: American Cities and the New York Experience," *Public Administration Review* 45 (March–April 1985), pp. 267–274.

8. James L. Perry and Timlynn T. Babitsky, "Comparative Performance in Urban Bus Transit: Assessing Privatization Strategies," *Public Administration Review* 46 (January–February 1986), pp. 57–66.

9. Brecher and Horton, "Retrenchment and Recovery." A particularly dramatic example in this regard comes from Seattle, where in 1975 the firefighters' union tried to have Mayor Wes Uhlman removed from office after he dismissed the fire chief. In the subsequent recall election, Uhlman amassed a far larger victory margin than he had in his 1973 election, when he had the active support of the firefighters' union. See Bureau of National Affairs (BNA), *Government Employee Relations Report,* no. 613 (July 6, 1975), pp. B4–B5. In another example, California Governor Jerry Brown embraced the property tax cuts and spending limitations required by Proposition 13, which was approved by the state's voters in June 1978, Brown's reversal of his initial anti–Proposition 13 stance was bitterly opposed by public sector union leaders, who had endorsed and otherwise strongly supported him in the 1974 California gubernatorial campaign.

10. See BNA, *Government Employee Relations Report,* no. 626 (October 6, 1975), pp. 21–25, for a special report on shifting public opinion regarding public employee unions. See also Josh Barbanel, "Complications in Municipal Bargaining," *New York Times,* January 12, 1985, p. 1, and "Shortsighted Management of City Government," *New York Times,* February 21, 1985, p. 21.

11. For a review of the early impasse procedure studies, see Thomas P. Gilroy and Anthony V. Sinicropi, "Impasse Resolution in Public Employment: A Current Assessment," *Industrial and Labor Relations Review* 25 (July 1972), pp. 496–511. For a more recent appraisal, see Paul F. Gerhart and John E. Drotning, "The Effectiveness of Public Sector Impasse Procedures: A Six State Study," in David B. Lipsky, ed., *Advances in Industrial and Labor Relations,* vol. 2 (Greenwich, Conn.: JAI Press, 1985), pp. 143–195.

12. See Lewin, "Public Employee Unionism," pp. 246–248.

13. Thomas A. Kochan, Mordechai Mironi, Ronald G. Ehrenberg, Jean Baderschneider, and Todd Jick, *Dispute Resolution under Fact-finding and Arbitration: An*

Empirical Evaluation (New York: American Arbitration Association, 1979), and John C. Anderson, "Arbitration in the Canadian Federal Public Service," in Lewin, Feuille, and Kochan, *Public Sector Labor Relations,* 2nd ed., pp. 326–344.

14. Nor is it clear when public employees in various jurisdictions achieved parity with or surpassed their private sector counterparts. Some literature suggests that the catch-up occurred prior to unionization and the introduction of formal collective bargaining into government. See the Fogel-Lewin article in chapter 6 as well as Sharon P. Smith, "Pay Differentials between Federal Government and Private Sector Workers," *Industrial and Labor Relations Review* 29 (January 1976), pp. 179–197, and Economic Development Council of New York City, Inc., *Looking Ahead in New York City: Reducing the 1975–76 Budget Gap in New York City* (New York: EDC, April 1975).

15. For evidence on this point, see the discussion in chapter 6 and the data sources cited therein.

16. See Daniel J.B. Mitchell, "Shifting Norms in Wage Determination," *Brookings Papers on Economic Activity 2* (Washington, D.C.: Brookings Institution, 1985), pp. 575–599, and Mitchell, "Understanding Union Wage Concessions, *California Management Review* 29 (Fall 1986), pp. 95–108.

17. See, for example, "Local Officials Seek to Shield Urban Aid from Deficit Cuts," *Congressional Quarterly Weekly Report,* January 25, 1986, p. 140.

18. For an early but still relevant critique of the public sector bargaining literature, especially the "union power" thesis, see David Lewin, "Public Employment Relations: Confronting the Issues," *Industrial Relations* 12 (October 1973), pp. 309–321. See also David Lewin and Peter Feuille, "Behavioral Research in Industrial Relations," *Industrial and Labor Relations Review* 36 (April 1983), pp. 341–360.

19. For further elaboration of the diversity thesis, see David Lewin, Raymond D. Horton, and James W. Kuhn, *Collective Bargaining and Manpower Utilization in Big City Governments* (Montclair, N.J.: Allenheld Osmun, 1979). Note that the diversity of private sector labor relationships is also considerably greater than is generally recognized.

20. See, for example, Peter Feuille, "Analyzing Compulsory Arbitration Experiences: The Role of Personal Preferences, Comment," *Industrial and Labor Relations Review* 28 (April 1975), pp. 432–435, and Mark Thompson and Jaimes Cairnie, "Reply," in the same issue of this journal, pp. 435–438.

Part I
Collective Bargaining
Processes

2
Labor Relations Contexts

T he external environment has a powerful influence on labor relations. It affects the structure, process, and outcome of bargaining. Moreover, in the public sector, the impact of environmental contexts is amplified because public employers are ultimately responsible to voters, including unionized public employees. In this chapter we address several overlapping aspects of the public sector environment that influence the practice of labor relations. First, we discuss some specific characteristics of public employers and public employment that affect labor relations outcomes. Then we examine three aspects of the environment that shape public sector labor relations: the economic-financial context, the legal context, and the political context. Because substantial interactions occur among these environmental contexts and public employer characteristics, we caution that this division of the environment, though convenient, is somewhat arbitrary.

It is noteworthy that the environmental contexts have changed dramatically over the past two decades. The changes caused collective bargaining to become a fact of life in the public sector. Further, many union–management relationships have reached maturity, and public sector labor relations have experienced relative stability in the 1980s. This is in stark contrast to the turmoil that has characterized private sector union–management relationships since the late 1970s. Historically, however, bargaining stability in the United States has not been long lived. Thus, it seems inevitable that a different pattern of public sector labor relations will emerge over time, partly in response to environmental developments. The onset of different labor relations patterns may be signaled by changes in the environmental contexts.

The Nature of the Public Sector

Among the many differences that exist between the public and private sectors, two background characteristics affecting public employers are particularly important. First, management power in the public sector is diffused across different branches of government and public officials. As Derber has noted, management responsibility for bargaining in the public sector "is generally divided or shared, and the formal responsibility often differs from the actual."[1] This situation is explained by several factors. Our government is organized into three branches (executive, legislative, and judicial) across several levels (federal, state, and local). Authority to make and implement policy is distributed across government levels and specialized agencies or bodies that are created by government branches. Thus, negotiated agreements between a public agency and a union may need to be approved subsequently by an elected executive and a legislature.

The requirement that collective bargaining contracts be approved by the executive or legislative branches has handicapped public management officials at various times. For instance, research has reported cases where mayors or councils have negotiated agreements with specific public employee unions without including a representative of management from the public agency involved on the city bargaining team.[2] This creates an enormous potential for making bargaining mistakes, one that has been fulfilled in various localities.[3] Although the exclusion of management representatives from negotiations is rare today, the sheer number of officials and agencies that may become involved in the bargaining process can make public sector bargaining very complex.

The diffusion of power is also influenced by the appropriations process in the public sector. Specifically, public employers often obtain their funding from several sources, and some revenue may be restricted to certain purposes. Thus, other levels or branches of government often have oversight responsibilities regarding a public agency's expenditures. The oversight function serves to provide higher levels of government with the authority to become involved in negotiations or to review union contracts. Further, the role of politics and appointed government labor relations professionals in the bargaining process can make public sector negotiations time consuming. The ensuing complexity of the process also makes it unclear where the accountability lies for the negotiation of "bad" contracts.

Second, public employers are ultimately responsible to an electorate, and public employees make up a large bloc of voters. At one extreme this can mean that public employees will elect favorable bosses and throw out any official with whom they find disfavor. In reality, it means that public employees can have substantial political power in some cases—and that power can lead to bargaining gains. The presence of other interest groups, concerned about labor relations and other issues, usually serves to weaken public employees' political power, particularly when a position favored by public employees necessitates an increase in taxes. Nevertheless, the fact that public employees vote can affect the labor relations strategies chosen by public employers.

Together, these two factors suggest the difficulties and complexity inherent in public sector bargaining. Management fragmentation can lead to confusion and inconsistency in labor relations decisions. The self-interest expressed by union members in their voting behaviors has the potential to influence public employers' decisions at the expense of other citizens. These structural characteristics do not typically arise in the private sector. Yet, in combination with other environmental contexts, they shape the essence of public sector labor relations.

The Economic-Financial Context

Economic Forces

In this section we discuss some of the economic sources of power on which private sector unions draw to achieve gains through collective bargaining, and then assess the relevance of these factors to the public sector. Next, we examine the sources of and trends in revenues available to state and local governments. Finally, we examine the longer term financial prospects for public employers, and we identify some potential problems and important research questions.

Most theories of the economic sources of power of private sector unions rely primarily on Alfred Marshall's four principles of the derived demand for labor. According to Marshall, unions will be most powerful when the following conditions are present: (1) the demand for the final product is inelastic; (2) labor is a strategic factor in the production process; (3) labor costs are a small percentage of total costs; and (4) the supply of alternative factors of production is inelastic (that is, the price of alternatives to union labor in the production process, such as capital or nonunion labor, rises rapidly as more of these factors are used).[4]

The public sector presents a mixed picture for labor regarding the Marshallian conditions. First, because public employers are often monopolies in the localities they serve, it has been argued that the demand for public sector labor is inelastic, or insensitive to increases in price. This belief has led some scholars to conclude that collective bargaining is not appropriate in the public sector as, they assert, the inelastic demand for labor will force the public to pay any price demanded for union-produced public services. The initial reading in this section, by Wellington and Winter, presents the most forceful and classic articulation of this argument. Wellington and Winter's theory, however, is not completely consistent with available data. In this regard, table 2–1 presents a summary of the estimated wage elasticities of demand for public employees that have been reported in several studies. The coefficients in the table represent the percentage reduction in employment that would occur if employee wages were raised by 1 percent. The elasticities reported in

Table 2-1
Estimates of Wage Elasticities of Demand for Public Employees

	States, 1958–1969[a]	States, 1958–1969[a]	States, 1929–1973[a]	States, 1968–1974[a]	States, 1967–1976[a]	School Districts, 1976–1977[b]	Cities, 1971–1980[c]	Cities, 1977–1982[d]
Police	−0.01 to −0.35	−0.29	x	x	x	x	−0.26 to −.050	−1.13
Fire	−0.23 to −0.31	−0.53	x	x	x	x	x	−1.28
Streets and highways	−0.44 to −0.64	−0.09	x	x	x	x	x	−1.66
Sanitation	−0.40 to −0.56	−0.23	x	x	x	x	x	−1.92
Public welfare	−0.33 to −1.13	−0.32	x	x	x	x	x	x
Hospitals	−0.30 to −0.51	−0.30	x	x	x	x	x	x
Public health	−0.26 to −0.32	−0.12	x	x	x	x	x	x
Natural resources	−0.39 to −0.60	−0.39	x	x	x	x	x	x
General control and financial administration	−0.09 to −0.34	−0.28	x	x	x	x	x	x
Education	−0.08 to −0.57	−1.06	x	−0.57 to −0.82	−0.89	−0.40	x	x
Noneducation	x	−0.38	x	x	x	x	x	x
All categories	x	x	−0.53	x	x	x	x	x

[a]Studies summarized in Ronald G. Ehrenberg and Joshua L. Schwarz, "Public Sector Labor Markets," in Orley Ashenfelter and Richard Layard, eds., *Handbook of Labor Economics*, forthcoming, table 3.

[b]Stephen A. Woodbury, "The Scope of Bargaining and Bargaining Outcomes in the Public Schools," *Industrial and Labor Relations Review* 38, no. 2 (January 1985), footnote 31, pp. 206–207.

[c]John Delaney, Peter Feuille, and Wallace Hendricks, "The Regulation of Bargaining Disputes: A Cost–Benefit Analysis of Interest Arbitration in the Public Sector," in David B. Lipsky and David Lewin, eds., *Advances in Industrial and Labor Relations*, vol. 3 (Greenwich, Conn.: JAI Press, 1986), p. 107.

[d]Jeffrey Zax and Casey Ichniowski, "The Effects of Public Sector Unionism on Pay, Employment, Department Budgets, and Municipal Expenditures," paper presented at NBER Conference on Public Sector Unionism, Boston, August 1986, footnote 10.

the table display some interesting patterns. Across most of the studies, a conclusion echoed by several investigators seems to hold: "In the main [the results] suggest that demand curves for labor in the [state and local government] sector are inelastic. However, the estimated elasticities do not appear to be substantially lower in absolute value than . . . private sector wage elasticities. . . ."[5] This conclusion partly supports Wellington and Winter's contention by revealing a generally inelastic demand for public workers. It is not clear what the finding means, however, given that the elasticities of demand in the public sector resemble those existing in the private sector.

The table also shows that demand elasticities vary considerably over time and across public employee functions. Moreover, the recent estimates reported by Zax and Ichniowski suggest that the demand for public workers has become much more elastic over time. For example, their analysis of data for the years 1977–1982 suggests that a 2 percent reduction in employment occurs for each 1 percent rise in sanitation workers' wages. This finding meshes with an earlier study that revealed that demand elasticities varied across states having high and low population densities.[6] A stronger trade-off between wages and employment was evidenced between high- and low-density states for many public occupational categories. As unionization was much more likely in high-density states, the results, in combination with Zax and Ichniowski's findings, suggest that public sector unions may not be as powerful as Wellington and Winter have suggested.

The most comprehensive studies of public sector demand elasticities analyzed data covering the 1950s and 1960s, a period when U.S. public employment at all levels increased by almost 50 percent. In contrast, between 1969 and 1977 public employment rose by 20 percent, although federal sector employment fell by 4 percent. Since 1977 there has been essentially no growth in public employment, and layoffs have become more common, particularly in municipalities facing fiscal crises (for example, New York City and Cleveland in the 1970s). Given these overall employment trends, the magnitude of the demand elasticities estimated by Zax and Ichniowski should come as no surprise.

The data, especially for the latest years, suggest the existence of a wage–employment trade-off. Thus, although the inelasticity of demand as a source of union power may have been important in the first generation of public employee bargaining, it appears to have withered over time. As of the early 1980s, economic forces appear to place substantial constraints on union compensation demands. Although it is likely that these economic constraints will fluctuate somewhat over time, their existence casts doubt on Wellington and Winter's assertion that an unchanging inelastic demand for government services would provide unions with permanent and excessive bargaining power. Evidence suggests that union strength fluctuates over time, partly in response to changing environmental conditions.

Regarding the second condition, the strategic position of labor in the production process varies considerably in the public sector. Labor would seem to have much more power in essential services, such as public safety, than in other services, such as parks departments. But it is difficult to assess accurately the overall degree of essentiality of labor in the public sector, because public employees perform diverse functions, and even the most essential employees are not irreplaceable. For instance, although the services performed by police, firefighters, and perhaps transit and sanitation workers are essential—providing a source of power to their unions—the services of library workers, college faculty or teaching assistants, and many general white-collar workers are less essential. Teachers, snow plow drivers (essential in January, dispensable in June), and other occupations fall somewhere in the middle range of essentiality. Although this source of union power would seem to vary across public sector occupations, it is constrained by other factors. Essential employee strikes are uniformly prohibited across the states, although some states do allow nonessential workers to strike (as we discuss in chapter 5). Also, one study has documented an increasing use by elected officials of the militia to replace striking employees, particularly essential employees.[7] Thus, the degree of essentiality is an unclear and unpredictable source of employee power.

The public sector provides a clear picture regarding the third Marshallian condition. The high percentage of total government expenditures accounted for by labor costs places a substantial constraint on the bargaining power of public employees. In 1982, for instance, payroll costs made up almost 60 percent of state and local government expenditures.[8] More important, within local government, those employee groups that are most highly unionized and militant—police, firefighters, teachers and sanitation workers—are in the most labor-intensive services. Wage increases for these employees therefore have relatively large impacts on the total costs of their departments, and any government efforts to cut costs will require stringent resistance to union demands for wage increases in the most labor-intensive functions. As a result, from the perspective of economics, this source of union power should, in the long run, act to hold down rates of increase in public employees' wages and benefits.[9] (Evidence of the union impact on public sector compensation is presented in chapter 6.)

The fourth condition involves the replacement of union labor with capital or with other workers. The service orientation of the public sector makes it more difficult to substitute capital for labor than is possible in the private sector, although there is limited evidence that such substitutions have occurred in sanitation services.[10] Other evidence suggests that public employers substitute one group of workers for another to cut costs (for example, police civilian employees have taken over many clerical jobs that were formerly held by police officers) and that certain public functions have been contracted out to the private sector.[11] Nevertheless, the labor-intensive nature of most public services has generally caused productivity growth in public employment to be lower than productivity growth in the private sector. Thus, wage improvements based on productivity gains are constrained in government.

In addition to the Marshallian conditions, the extent of employer concentration in a private sector industry has been mentioned as a source of union power. The underlying theoretical argument for this is that wages are not a competitive issue in monopolistic markets, where employers can simply pass on increased costs to customers without losing market share. Because, as noted earlier, public employers are often monopolists, and because there is no economic market clearing price for public sector services, there has been a debate over unions' ability to achieve monopoly rents.[12] The other side of this issue is that governments may be monopoly employers—monopsonists—and that this may affect compensation levels. Recent evidence suggests that where public employers possess monopsony power, they use it to pay lower wages and benefits to workers, other things being equal.[13] In combination with the potential contracting out of public services to the private sector, therefore, there is little evidence suggesting that the monopolistic nature of public product markets serves to increase public employee power and raise public sector costs.

At first glance, the economic characteristics of public employment suggest a mixed prognosis for the long-term strength that public employee unions will be able to exercise in collective bargaining with their employers. On the one hand, the essential nature of certain public services, coupled with the sometimes inelastic demand for public services, should act in the unions' long-run favor. On the other hand, the labor intensity of most public services, the productivity constraints inherent in public employment, and government efforts to substitute lower paid workers for unionized employees should offset any general accumulation of union power. Moreover, as noted earlier, there is evidence that public employers have occasionally used the militia to substitute for striking public employees, and the demand for public workers appears to have grown more elastic over time. As a result, the economic factors seem to suggest that union power fluctuates over time and across public occupations—a finding resembling the private sector situation. If so, then the arguments of Wellington and Winter and others opposing unions in the public sector are seriously weakened. Evidence reveals that the economic characteristics of the public sector do not provide unions with substantial power on a consistent basis. Indeed, this view will be reinforced by an analysis of the more specific financial problems of state and local governments.

Financial Forces

In order to assess the financial conditions of state and local governments, it is first necessary to understand where these governments obtain their revenues.

Tables 2–2 and 2–3 present an overall picture of the sources of revenue for state and local governments respectively, for fiscal years 1977, 1981, and 1983. The data in the tables suggest several noteworthy points. State governments, for example, tend to rely most heavily on sales taxes, federal aid, and personal income taxes as sources of general revenues (as opposed to restricted revenues, such as insurance trust funds—derived from required payroll and employer taxes—which must be expended for specific purposes). Local governments obtain more than half their revenues from state aid and property taxes. The table does not show that federal aid to local (but not state) governments increased rapidly during the 1970s as the federal revenue sharing program expanded. Since 1977, however, federal aid to both state and local governments has declined proportionally. Moreover, federal revenue sharing is slated to expire in fiscal year 1987, and, in the words of House Budget Committee Chairman William Gray, most federal aid programs to states and municipalities are currently on "the termination and funeral list."[14] As of late 1986, a total of about $8 billion in aid to cities and states was slated for elimination, and further cuts were likely in fiscal 1988.[15] Thus, a major source of revenue to states and localities is threatened. If these major cuts are carried out, then state and local governments will likely have to cut services or raise revenues through other means, or both.

In addition to the revenues provided by higher levels of government, state and local governments raise funds through the imposition of taxes, various user fees, and short- and long-term borrowing. The data in tables 2–2 and 2–3 suggest that the proportion of state and local government revenue derived from taxes declined slightly between 1977 and 1983. User fees and charges, in contrast, rose steadily over time. Government borrowing trends are more difficult to discern, however, as they tend to move cyclically (for instance, borrowing increased rapidly in the 1960s and slowed dramatically in the 1970s). Also, state and local government borrowing is generally restricted by legislation and constitutional provisions (such as balanced budget requirements). Because we are not attempting to present a comprehensive analysis of public finance, we turn to an examination of the relationship between collective bargaining by local government employees (where most public sector bargaining occurs) and government finances.

The major constraints on local government revenues come from: (1) the tax base of the community, (2) the willingness of the public or politicians to vote for tax increases, (3) constitutional or other legal restraints imposed by federal and state governments on the revenue-raising powers of local governments, and (4) constraints on the borrowing capacity of governments based on their credit ratings.

The key to the strength of a community's tax base is that employment influences the revenue-generating potential of property taxes. For example, a 1974 study of New York City suggested that various industries generated

Table 2–2
Sources of Revenue for State Governments, Fiscal Years 1977, 1981, and 1983

Source of Revenue	1977 Dollars[a]	(%)	1981 Dollars[a]	(%)	1983 Dollars[a]	(%)
Federal aid	45,938	(22.5)	67,868	(21.8)	68,986	(19.3)
State aid	—	—	—	—	—	—
Local aid	2,737	(1.3)	2,918	(0.9)	3,742	(1.1)
Property taxes	2,260	(1.1)	2,949	(0.9)	3,281	(0.9)
Income taxes						
Individual	25,493	(12.5)	40,895	(13.2)	49,789	(13.9)
Corporate	9,174	(4.5)	14,143	(4.6)	13,153	(3.7)
Sales taxes	52,362	(25.6)	72,751	(23.4)	83,895	(23.5)
Charges and miscellaneous	20,106	(9.8)	37,636	(12.1)	46,312	(13.0)
Insurance trust	32,365	(15.8)	48,041	(15.5)	61,971	(17.3)
Other revenue	14,040	(6.9)	23,627	(7.6)	26,532	(7.4)
Total	204,475	100.0	310,828	100.0	357,661	100.0

Sources: Adapted from The Tax Foundation, Inc., *Facts and Figures on Government Finance*, 20th, 22nd, and 23rd biennial editions (New York: The Tax Foundation, 1979, 1983, 1986), p. 19, table 7 (FY 1977); p. 23, table 11 (FY 1981); p. a13, table A11 (FY 1983).
[a]Dollars are in millions. Percentages may not add to 100 because of rounding.

Table 2–3
Sources of Revenue for Local Governments, Fiscal Years 1977, 1981, and 1983

Source of Revenue	1977 Dollars[a]	(%)	1981 Dollars[a]	(%)	1983 Dollars[a]	(%)
Federal aid	16,637	(8.5)	22,427	(7.8)	21,021	(6.2)
State aid	60,311	(30.7)	89,017	(30.9)	98,378	(29.1)
Local aid	—	—	—	—	—	—
Property taxes	60,275	(30.7)	72,020	(25.0)	85,824	(25.4)
Income taxes						
Individual	3,752	(1.9)	5,531	(1.9)	5,340	(1.6)
Corporate	—	—	—	—	1,105	(0.3)
Sales taxes	8,232	(4.2)	13,220	(4.6)	16,352	(4.8)
Charges and miscellaneous	27,237	(13.9)	50,960	(17.7)	65,998	(19.5)
Insurance trust	2,783	(1.4)	5,388	(1.9)	7,393	(2.2)
Other revenue	17,093	(8.7)	29,271	(10.2)	36,510	(10.8)
Total	196,321	(100.0)	287,834	(100.0)	337,921	(100.0)

Sources: Adapted from The Tax Foundation, Inc., *Facts and Figures on Government Finance*, 20th, 22nd, and 23rd biennial editions (New York: The Tax Foundation, 1979, 1983, 1986), p. 19, table 7 (FY 1977); p. 23, table 11 (FY 1981); p. a13, table A11 (FY 1983).
[a]Dollars are in millions. Percentages may not add to 100 because of rounding.

tax revenue on a per employee basis in the following decreasing order: (1) finance, insurance, and real estate; (2) wholesale trade; (3) manufacturing; (4) retail trade; (5) transportation and communications; and (6) services.[16] In general, this finding suggests an interesting note, as the service sector is the most rapidly growing sector of the economy. Further, since the 1970s there has been a movement of jobs from the highly unionized Frostbelt to the relatively nonunion Sunbelt. Also, many jobs have moved from the central cities of the Northeast and North Central regions to the suburbs. This decline of jobs has a two-pronged effect. On the one hand, the shrinkage of the tax base reduces the revenues available to central cities. On the other hand, because the population does not decline as rapidly as jobs are lost and because individuals with higher incomes are more likely than individuals with lower incomes to relocate, the need for city services does not diminish correspondingly. In some cases, the need for social services increases. Thus, cities in the Frostbelt have been left with a smaller tax base but a greater need for public services.

Such trends, however, are not geographically specific. In fact, partly as a result of the influx of individuals searching for jobs, general economic stagnation, and the recent drop in the price of oil, many Sunbelt states have been suffering a decreasing revenue base, whereas some northern cities—notably New York City and Boston—have experienced growth. These factors should serve to point out that, although city revenues are cyclically sensitive, the demand for city services is not. Periods of recession and inflation, in combination, have caused the price of public services to grow beyond the point where the tax base can finance them in many areas. As collective bargaining by public employees generally increases public employer costs,[17] this suggests that bargaining cities must find ways to raise revenues from declining or stagnating tax bases.

One way to raise revenues is to increase tax rates. Such action, however, has recently run into problems on two fronts. Although no systematic data are available, anecdotal evidence suggests that public employers, especially in Frostbelt cities, have reached or are approaching their tax and debt limits. In New York State, for example, both New York City and Yonkers were placed in forms of state receivership during the 1970s to oversee local decision making in order to avoid default, and the next five largest cities—Buffalo, Rochester, Syracuse, Albany, and Binghamton—were pushing against their constitutional tax limits. Such severe financial difficulties are not confined to New York, as the default by Cleveland and the financial difficulties of the states of Illinois, Michigan, and Ohio and the cities of Memphis and New Orleans, to name a few, have caused great concern. Moreover, on the second front, although tax rates and city financial well-being vary considerably, it is clear that U.S. taxpayers have become increasingly resistant to tax increases.

Since June 1978, when California voters passed Proposition 13, which reduced property taxes, a host of other tax and government spending initiatives have been placed before voters. Table 2–4 shows that at least 59 referenda went before the voters in 27 states on these issues between 1978 and 1984.[18] The data suggest that tax limitation initiatives were successful in the 1978 elections but enjoyed diminishing success in subsequent elections. One reason for the decreased success in later years seems to be organized opposition by business and community leaders concerned about the maintenance of a basic level of state services.[19] This finding suggests a mixed conclusion about tax and spending initiatives. The measures have succeeded in general, but they have not been automatically approved by voters. Further, it is noteworthy that voter turnout in these races has generally been relatively low (averaging about 40 percent), suggesting that the public does not have more interest in them than in elections generally. On the other hand, tax initiatives continue to be put before voters, and many, if passed, promise to have dramatic effects on public employment, wages, and/or services.

These tax problems have forced many local governments to turn to debt financing, user fee imposition, and public service cuts. Although debt financing is limited by state constitutions and federal legislation, the credit ratings of cities have generally remained favorable over the past decade.[20] Part of the reason for this, however, was the availability of aid from higher levels of

Table 2–4
Tax and Spending Restriction Referenda, 1978–1984

State	1978		1980		1982		1984	
	Pass	Fail	Pass	Fail	Pass	Fail	Pass	Fail
Alabama	PTL	—	—	—	—	—	—	—
Alaska	—	—	—	—	SSL	—	—	—
Arizona	SSL	—	—	PTL	—	—	—	SSL
Arkansas	—	STR	—	—	—	—	—	—
California	PTL	—	—	—	—	—	—	PTL
Colorado	—	SSL	—	—	PTL	—	—	—
Connecticut	—	—	—	—	—	—	—	—
Delaware	—	—	—	—	—	—	—	—
DC	—	—	—	—	—	—	—	—
Florida	—	—	—	—	—	—	—	—
Georgia	—	—	—	—	—	—	—	—
Hawaii	SSL	—	—	—	—	—	—	—
Idaho	PTL	—	—	—	—	—	—	STR
Illinois	PTL[a]	—	—	—	—	—	—	—
Indiana	—	—	—	—	—	—	—	—
Iowa	—	—	—	—	—	—	—	—
Kansas	—	—	—	—	—	—	—	—
Kentucky	—	—	—	—	—	—	—	—
Louisiana	—	—	—	—	—	—	—	SSL
Maine	—	—	—	—	ITI	—	—	—

Table 2–4 (Continued)

State	1978 Pass	1978 Fail	1980 Pass	1980 Fail	1982 Pass	1982 Fail	1984 Pass	1984 Fail
Maryland	—	—	—	—	—	—	—	—
Massachusetts	PTL	—	PTL	STL	—	—	—	—
Michigan	PTL	PTL	—	PTL TLM	—	—	—	TLM
Minnesota	—	—	—	—	—	—	—	—
Mississippi	—	—	—	—	—	—	—	—
Missouri	PTL	—	STL	—	—	—	—	—
Montana	—	TLM	ITI	—	—	—	—	—
Nebraska	—	SSL	—	—	—	—	—	—
Nevada	PTL	—	STL STL	PTL	STL	STL NTX	STR	PTL
New Hampshire	—	—	—	—	—	—	—	—
New Jersey	—	—	—	—	—	—	—	—
New Mexico	—	—	—	—	—	—	—	—
New York	—	—	—	—	—	—	—	—
North Carolina	—	—	—	—	—	NTX	—	—
North Dakota	STL	—	—	—	—	—	—	—
Ohio	—	—	—	TLM	—	—	—	—
Oklahoma	—	—	—	—	—	—	—	—
Oregon	—	PTL PTL	—	PTL	—	PTL PTL	—	PTL
Pennsylvania	—	—	—	—	—	—	—	—
Rhode Island	—	—	—	—	—	—	—	—
South Carolina	SSL	—	TLM	—	—	TLM	—	—
South Dakota	TLM	—	—	PTL	—	—	—	—
Tennessee	—	—	—	—	—	—	—	—
Texas	PTL	—	—	—	PTL	—	—	—
Utah	—	—	—	PTL STR	—	—	—	—
Vermont	—	—	—	—	—	—	—	—
Virginia	—	—	—	—	—	—	—	—
Washington	—	—	—	—	—	STR	—	—
West Virginia	—	TLM	—	—	PTL	—	—	—
Wisconsin	—	—	—	—	—	—	—	—
Wyoming	—	—	—	—	—	—	—	—

Sources: Austin Ranney, "Referendums and Initiatives," [title varies slightly across years] *Public Opinion,* November–December 1978, pp. 26–28; February/March 1981, pp. 40–41; December–January 1983, pp. 12–14; December–January 1985, pp. 15–17.

Notes: PTL = Property tax limitation measure;
     STL = State tax limitation measure;
     SSL = State spending limitation measure;
     STR = Sales tax reduction measure;
     ITI = Index state income tax;
     TLM = Tax law modification (e.g., require voter approval of tax increases, change amount of majority support required to pass tax increase, etc.);
     NTX = Impose some type of new tax.
[a]Advisory only—not binding.

government—aid that, as we have noted, is currently in jeopardy. Moreover, some changes imposed by the Tax Reform Act of 1986 may place new restrictions on the types of tax-exempt bonds that localities may issue. Thus, local governments may be forced to pay higher interest rates in future offerings in order to attract investors. These factors could serve to reduce cities' creditworthiness in the future, suggesting that, if municipal finances get tighter in the future, it is likely that higher user fees for various services will be imposed and that government services will be reduced.

In sum, all the financial characteristics reviewed here reinforce the view that the economic-financial context of the public sector does not provide public employee unions with a consistent ability to achieve wage and benefit gains. Moreover, the bleak revenue picture on the horizon may suggest a coming crisis in public sector labor relations when localities become unable to improve employees' compensation. Evidence suggests that the economic-financial context will place substantial constraints on public sector collective bargaining in the foreseeable future, and that this will present a stark contrast to the expansionary economic context that characterized the public sector as collective bargaining emerged and developed.

Notes

1. Milton Derber, "Management Organization for Collective Bargaining in the Public Sector," in B. Aaron, J. Grodin, and J. Stern, eds., *Public-Sector Bargaining* (Washington, D.C.: Bureau of National Affairs, 1979), p. 81.

2. Hervey A. Juris and Peter Feuille, *Police Unionism* (Lexington, Mass.: D.C. Heath, 1973), pp. 62–65.

3. David T. Stanley with Carole L. Cooper, *Managing Local Government under Union Pressure* (Washington, D.C.: Brookings Institution, 1972), p. 28.

4. These factors are summarized in Albert Rees, *The Economics of Trade Unions*, rev. ed. (Chicago: University of Chicago Press, 1977), pp. 66–69.

5. Ronald G. Ehrenberg and Joshua L. Schwartz, "Public Sector Labor Markets," National Bureau of Economic Research Working Paper no. 1179 (1983), p. 34.

6. Orley C. Ashenfelter and Ronald G. Ehrenberg, "The Demand for Labor in the Public Sector," in D. Hamermesh, ed., *Labor in the Public and Nonprofit Sectors* (Princeton, N.J.: Princeton University Press, 1975), pp. 55–78.

7. James B. Jacobs, "The Role of Military Forces in Public Sector Labor Relations," *Industrial and Labor Relations Review* 35, no. 2 (January 1982), pp. 163–180.

8. The exact figure was 57.1 percent. See Municipal Finance Officers Association, *The State and Local Government Fiscal Almanac* (Chicago: Municipal Finance Officers Association, 1982), table 1, p. 4.

9. It should be noted that this is the most controversial of the Marshallian conditions. Information on the controversy may be found in Rees, *The Economics of Trade Unions*, note 4, p. 68.

10. David Lewin, "Technological Change in the Public Sector: The Case of

Sanitation Service," in Daniel B. Cornfield, ed., *Workers, Managers, and Technological Change: Emerging Patterns of Labor Relations* (New York: Plenum, 1986).

11. See Lewin, "Technological Change"; James Ferris and Elizabeth Graddy, "Contracting Out: For What? With Whom?" *Public Administration Review* 46, no. 4 (July–August 1986), pp. 332–344; and John Delaney, Peter Feuille, and Wallace Hendricks, "The Regulation of Bargaining Disputes: A Cost-Benefit Analysis of Interest Arbitration in the Public Sector," in David B. Lipsky and David Lewin, eds., *Advances in Industrial and Labor Relations,* vol. 3 (Greenwich, Conn.: JAI Press, 1986), pp. 83–118.

12. See Rees, *The Economics of Trade Unions,* note 4, pp. 86–89.

13. See James Luizer and Robert Thornton, "Concentration in the Labor Market for Public School Teachers," *Industrial and Labor Relations Review* 39, no. 4 (July 1986), pp. 573–584; John Thomas Delaney, "Unionism, Bargaining Spillovers, and Teacher Compensation," in David B. Lipsky, ed., *Advances in Industrial and Labor Relations,* vol. 2 (Greenwich, Conn.: JAI Press, 1985), pp. 111–142.

14. See "Local Officials Seek to Shield Urban Aid from Deficit Cuts," *Congressional Quarterly Weekly Report,* January 25, 1986, p. 140.

15. The $8 billion is calculated from projected cuts in revenue sharing ($4.54 billion), community development block grants ($3.12 billion), and urban development action grants ($330 million). See ibid., pp. 140–141.

16. Roy W. Bahl et al., *Taxes, Expenditures and the Economic Base* (New York: Praeger, 1974).

17. See the discussion and references in chapters 6 and 7.

18. The referenda reported in table 2–4 may understate the total number of tax and spending limitation issues because of the difficulty inherent in defining referenda and because referenda on the ballot in off-year elections are not included.

19. See Austin Ranney, "Referendums and Initiatives," *Public Opinion,* January 1985, pp. 15–16.

20. See Susan Schwochau, Peter Feuille, and John Delaney, "The Resource Allocation Effects of Mandated Relationships," unpublished paper, 1987.

The Limits of Collective Bargaining in Public Employment

Harry H. Wellington
Ralph K. Winter, Jr. *

In the area of public employment the claims upon public policy made by the need for industrial peace, industrial democracy, and effective political representation point toward collective bargaining. This is to say that three of the

*Yale University. Reprinted from Harry Wellington and Ralph K. Winter, Jr., *The Unions and the Cities* (Washington, D.C.: Brookings Institution, 1971), pp. 12–32.

four arguments that support bargaining in the private sector—to some extent, at least—press for similar arrangements in the public sector.

Government is a growth industry, particularly state and municipal government. With size comes bureaucracy, and with bureaucracy comes the sense of isolation of the individual worker. His manhood, like that of his industrial counterpart, seems threatened. Lengthening chains of command necessarily depersonalize the employment relationship and contribute to a sense of powerlessness on the part of the worker. If he is to share in the governance of his employment relationship as he does in the private sector, it must be through the device of representation, which means unionization.[1] Accordingly, just as the increase in the size of economic units in private industry fostered unionism, so the enlarging of governmental bureaucracy has encouraged public employees to look to collective action for a sense of control over their employment destiny. The number of government employees, moreover, makes it plain that those employees are members of an interest group that can organize for political representation as well as for job participation.[2]

The pressures thus generated by size and bureaucracy lead inescapably to disruption—to labor unrest—unless these pressures are recognized and unless existing decision-making procedures are accommodated to them. Peace in government employment too, the argument runs, can best be established by making union recognition and collective bargaining accepted public policy.[3]

Much less clearly analogous to the private model, however, is the unequal bargaining power argument. In the private sector that argument really has two aspects. The first is affirmative in nature. Monopsony[4] is believed sometimes to result in unfair individual contracts of employment. The unfairness may be reflected in wages, which are less than they would be if the market were more nearly perfect, or in working arrangements that may lodge arbitrary power in a foreman, that is, power to hire, fire, promote, assign, or discipline without respect to substantive or procedural rules. A persistent assertion, generating much heat, relates to the arbitrary exercise of managerial power in individual cases. This assertion goes far to explain the insistence of unions on the establishment in the labor contract of rules, with an accompanying adjudicatory procedure, to govern industrial life.[5]

The second, or negative, aspect of the unequal bargaining power argument relates to the social costs of collective bargaining. As has been seen, the social costs of collective bargaining in the private sector are principally economic and seem inherently limited by market forces. In the public sector, however, the costs seem economic only in a very narrow sense and are on the whole political. It further seems that, to the extent union power is delimited by market or other forces in the public sector, these constraints do not come into play nearly as quickly as in the private. An understanding of why this is so requires further comparison between collective bargaining in the two sectors.

The Private Sector Model

Although the private sector is, of course, extraordinarily diverse, the paradigm is an industry that produces a product that is not particularly essential to those who buy it and for which dissimilar products can be substituted. Within the market or markets for this product, most—but not all—of the producers must bargain with a union representing their employees, and this union is generally the same throughout the industry. A price rise of this product relative to others will result in a decrease in the number of units of the product sold. This in turn will result in a cutback in employment. And an increase in price would be dictated by an increase in labor cost relative to output, at least in most situations.[6] Thus, the union is faced with some sort of rough trade-off between, on the one hand, larger benefits for some employees and unemployment for others, and on the other hand, smaller benefits and more employment. Because unions are political organizations, with a legal duty to represent all employees fairly,[7] and with a treasury that comes from per capita dues, there is pressure on the union to avoid the road that leads to unemployment.[8]

This picture of restraints that the market imposes on collective bargaining settlements undergoes change as the variables change. On the one hand, to the extent that there are nonunion firms within a product market, the impact of union pressure will be diminished by the ability of consumers to purchase identical products from nonunion and, presumably, less expensive sources. On the other hand, to the extent that union organization of competitors within the product market is complete, there will be no such restraint and the principal barriers to union bargaining goals will be the ability of a number of consumers to react to a price change by turning to dissimilar but nevertheless substitutable products.

Two additional variables must be noted. First, where the demand for an industry's product is rather insensitive to price—that is, relatively inelastic—and where all the firms in a product market are organized, the union need fear less the employment–benefit trade-off, for the employer is less concerned about raising prices in response to increased costs. By hypothesis, a price rise affects unit sales of such an employer only minimally. Second, in an expanding industry, wage settlements that exceed increases in productivity may not reduce union employment. They will reduce expansion, hence the employment effect will be experienced only by workers who do not belong to the union. This means that in the short run the politics of the employment–benefit trade-off do not restrain the union in its bargaining demands.

In both of these cases, however, there are at least two restraints on the union. One is the employer's increased incentive to substitute machines for labor, a factor present in the paradigm and all other cases as well. The other restraint stems from the fact that large sections of the nation are unorganized and highly resistant to unionization.[9] Accordingly, capital will seek nonunion labor, and in this way the market will discipline the organized sector.

The employer, in the paradigm and in all variations of it, is motivated primarily by the necessity to maximize profits (and this is so no matter how political a corporation may seem to be). He therefore is not inclined (absent an increase in demand for his product) to raise prices and thereby suffer a loss in profits, and he is organized to transmit and represent the market pressures described above. Generally he will resist, and resist hard, union demands that exceed increases in productivity, for if he accepts such demands he may be forced to raise prices. Should he be unsuccessful in his resistance too often, and should it or the bargain cost him too much, he can be expected to put his money and energy elsewhere.[10]

What all this means is that the social costs imposed by collective bargaining are economic costs; that usually they are limited by powerful market restraints; and that these restraints are visible to anyone who is able to see the forest for the trees.[11]

The Public Sector Model: Monetary Issues

The paradigm in the public sector is a municipality with an elected city council and an elected mayor who bargains (through others) with unions representing the employees of the city. He bargains also, of course, with other permanent and ad hoc interest groups making claims upon government (business groups, save-the-park committees, neighborhood groups, and so forth). Indeed, the decisions that are made may be thought of roughly as a result of interactions and accommodations among these interest groups, as influenced by perceptions about the attitudes of the electorate and by the goals and programs of the mayor and his city council.[12]

Decisions that cost the city money are generally paid for from taxes and, less often, by borrowing. Not only are there many types of taxes but also there are several layers of government that may make tax revenue available to the city; federal and state as well as local funds may be employed for some purposes. Formal allocation of money for particular uses is made through the city's budget, which may have within it considerable room for adjustments.[13] Thus, a union will bargain hard for as large a share of the budget as it thinks it possibly can obtain, and even try to force a tax increase if it deems that possible.

In the public sector, too, the market operates. In the long run, the supply of labor is a function of the price paid for labor by the public employer relative to what workers earn elsewhere.[14] This is some assurance that public employees in the aggregate—with or without collective bargaining—are not paid too little. The case for employer monopsony, moreover, may be much weaker in the public sector than it is in the private. First, to the extent that most public employees work in urban areas, as they probably do, there may often be a number of substitutable and competing private and public employers in the labor market. When that is the case, there can be little monopsony power.[15] Second, even if public employers occasionally have monopsony power, governmental policy is determined only in part by economic criteria, and there is no assurance, as there is in the private sector where the profit motive prevails, that the power will be exploited.

As noted, market-imposed unemployment is an important restraint on unions in the private sector. In the public sector, the trade-off between benefits and employment seems much less important. Government does not generally sell a product the demand for which is closely related to price. There usually are not close substitutes for the products and services provided by government, and the demand for them is relatively inelastic. Such market conditions are favorable to unions in the private sector because they permit the acquisition of benefits without the penalty of unemployment, subject to the restraint of nonunion competitors, actual or potential. But no such restraint limits the demands of public employee unions. Because much government activity is, and must be, a monopoly, product competition, nonunion or otherwise, does not exert a downward pressure on prices and wages. Nor will the existence of a pool of labor ready to work for a wage below union scale attract new capital and create a new, and competitively less expensive, governmental enterprise.

Even if a close relationship between increased economic benefits and unemployment does not exist as a significant deterrent to unions in the public sector, might not the argument be made that in some sense the taxpayer is the public sector's functional equivalent of the consumer? If taxes become too high, the taxpayer can move to another community. While it is generally much easier for a consumer to substitute products than for a taxpayer to substitute communities, is it not fair to say that, at the point at which a tax increase will cause so many taxpayers to move that it will produce less total revenue, the market disciplines or restrains union and public employer in the same way and for the same reasons that the market disciplines parties in the private sector? Moreover, does not the analogy to the private sector suggest that it is legitimate in an economic sense for unions to push government to the point of substitutability?

Several factors suggest that the answer to this latter question is at best indeterminate, and that the question of legitimacy must be judged not by economic but by political criteria.

In the first place, there is no theoretical reason—economic or political—to suppose that it is desirable for a governmental entity to liquidate its taxing power, to tax up to the point where another tax increase will produce less revenue because of the number of people it drives to different communities. In the private area, profit maximization is a complex concept, but its approximation generally is both a legal requirement and socially useful as a means of allocating resources.[16] The liquidation of taxing power seems neither imperative nor useful.

Second, consider the complexity of the tax structure and the way in which different kinds of taxes (property, sales, income) fall differently upon a given population. Consider, moreover, that the taxing authority of a particular governmental entity may be limited (a municipality may not have the power to impose an income tax). What is necessarily involved, then, is principally the redistribution of income by government rather than resource allocation,[17] and questions of income redistribution surely are essentially political questions.[18]

For his part, the mayor in our paradigm will be disciplined not by a desire to maximize profits but by a desire—in some cases at least—to do a good job (to implement his programs), and in virtually all cases by a wish either to be reelected or to move to a better elective office. What he gives to the union must be taken from some other interest group or from taxpayers. His is the job of coordinating these competing claims while remaining politically viable. And that coordination will be governed by the relative power of the competing interest groups. Coordination, moreover, is not limited to issues involving the level of taxes and the way in which tax moneys are spent. Nonfinancial issues also require coordination, and here too the outcome turns upon the relative power of interest groups. And relative power is affected importantly by the scope of collective bargaining.

The Public Sector Model: Nonmonetary Issues

In the private sector, unions have pushed to expand the scope of bargaining in response to the desires of their members for a variety of new benefits (pension rights, supplementary unemployment payments, merit increases). These benefits generally impose a monetary cost on the employer. And because employers are restrained by the market, an expanded bargaining agenda means that, if a union negotiates an agreement over more subjects, it generally trades off more of less or less of more.

From the consumer's point of view this in turn means that the price of the product he purchases is not significantly related to the scope of bargaining. And since unions rarely bargain about the nature of the product produced,[19] the consumer can be relatively indifferent as to how many or how few subjects are covered in any collective agreement.[20] Nor need the consumer be concerned about union demands that would not impose a financial cost on the employer, for example, the design of a grievance procedure. While such demands are not subject to the same kind of trade-off as are financial demands, they are unlikely, if granted, to have any impact on the consumer. Their effect is on the quality of life of the parties to the agreement.

In the public sector the cluster of problems that surround the scope of bargaining are much more troublesome than they are in the private sector. The problems have several dimensions.

First, the trade-off between subjects of bargaining in the public sector is less of a protection to the consumer (public) than it is in the private. Where political leaders view the costs of union demands as essentially budgetary, a trade-off can occur. Thus, a demand for higher teacher salaries and a demand for reduced class size may be treated as part of one package. But where a demand, although it has a budgetary effect, is viewed as involving essentially political costs, trade-offs are more difficult. Our paradigmatic mayor, for example, may be under great pressure to make a large monetary settlement with a teachers' union whether or not it is joined to demands for special training programs for disadvantaged children. Interest groups tend to exert pressure against union demands only when they are directly affected. Otherwise, they are apt to join that large constituency (the general public) that wants to avoid labor trouble. Trade-offs can occur only when several demands are resisted by roughly the same groups. Thus, pure budgetary demands can be traded off when they are opposed by taxpayers. But when the identity of the resisting group changes with each demand, political leaders may find it expedient to strike a balance on each issue individually, rather than as part of a total package, by measuring the political power of each interest group involved against the political power of the constituency pressing for labor peace. To put it another way, as important as financial factors are to a mayor, political factors may be even more important. The market allows the businessman no such discretionary choice.

Second, public employees do not generally produce a product. They perform a service. The way in which a service is performed may become a subject of bargaining. As a result, the nature of that service may be changed. Some of these services—police protection, teaching, health care—involve questions that are politically, socially, or ideologically sensitive. In part this is because government is involved and alternatives to governmentally provided services are relatively dear. In part, government is involved because of society's perception about the nature of the service and society's need for it. This suggests that decisions affecting the nature of a governmentally provided service are much more likely to be challenged and are more urgent than generally is the case with services that are offered privately.

Third, some of the services government provides are performed by professionals—teachers, social workers, and so forth—who are keenly interested in the underlying philosophy that informs their work. To them, theirs is not merely a job to be done for a salary. They may be educators or other "change agents" of society. And this may mean that these employees are concerned with more than incrementally altering a governmental service or its method of delivery. They may be advocates of bold departures that will radically transform the service itself.

The issue is not a threshold one of whether professional public employees should participate in decisions about the nature of the services they provide. Any properly run governmental agency should be interested in, and heavily reliant upon, the judgment of its professional staff. The issue rather is the method of that participation.

The Theory Summarized

Collective bargaining in public employment, then, seems distinguishable from that in the private sector. To begin with, it imposes on society more than a potential misallocation of resources through restrictions on economic output, the principal cost imposed by private sector unions. Collective bargaining by public employees and the political process cannot be separated. The costs of such bargaining, therefore, cannot be fully measured without taking into account the impact on the allocation of political power in the typical municipality. If one assumes, as here, that municipal political processes should be structured to ensure "a high probability that an active and legitimate group in the population can make itself heard effectively at some crucial stage in the process of decision,"[21] then the issue is how powerful unions will be in the typical political process if a full transplant of collective bargaining is carried out.

The conclusion is that such a transplant would, in many cases, institutionalize the power of public employee unions in a way that would leave competing groups in the political process at a permanent and substantial disadvantage. There are three reasons for this, and each is related to the type of services typically performed by public employees.

First, some of these services are such that any prolonged disruption would entail an actual danger to health and safety.

Second, the demand for numerous governmental services is relatively inelastic, that is, relatively insensitive to changes in price. Indeed, the lack of close substitutes is typical of many governmental endeavors.[22] And, since at least the time of Marshall's *Principles of Economics,* the elasticity of demand for the final service or product has been considered a major determinant of union power.[23] Because the demand for labor is derived from the demand for the product, inelasticity on the product side tends to reduce the employment–benefit trade-off unions face. This is as much the case in the private as in the public sector. But in the private sector, product inelasticity is not typical. Moreover, there is the further restraint on union power created by the real possibility of nonunion entrants into the product market. In the public sector, inelasticity of demand seems more the rule than the exception, and nonunion rivals are not generally a serious problem.

The final reason for fearing a full transplant is the extent to which the disruption of a government service inconveniences municipal voters. A teachers' strike may not endanger public health or welfare. It may, however, seriously inconvenience parents and other citizens who, as voters, have the power to punish one of the parties—and always the same party, the political leadership—to the dispute.

All this may seem to suggest a sharper distinction between the public and private sectors than actually exists. The discussion here has dealt with models, one for private collective bargaining, the other for public. Each model is located at the core of its sector. But the difference in the impact of collective bargaining in the two sectors should be seen as a continuum. Thus, for example, it may be that market restraints do not sufficiently discipline strike settlements in some regulated industries or in industries that rely mainly on government contracts. Indeed, collective bargaining in such industries has been under steady and insistent attack.

In the public sector, it may be that in any given municipality—but particularly a small one—at any given time, taxpayer resistance or the determination of municipal government, or both, will substantially offset union power even under existing political structures. These plainly are exceptions, however. They do not invalidate the public–private distinction as an analytical tool, for that distinction rests on the very real differences that exist in the vast bulk of situations, situations exemplified by these models.

Notes

1. See *Final Report of the Industrial Commission,* p. 805; C. Summers, "American Legislation for Union Democracy," *Modern Law Review* 25 (1962), pp. 273, 275.

2. For the "early" history, see S. Spero, *Government as Employer* (Carbondale: Southern Illinois University Press, 1948).

3. See, for example, *Governor's Committee on Public Employee Relations, Final Report* (Albany: State of New York, 1966), pp. 9–14.

4. Defined by the authors as a buyer's monopoly in which the terms and conditions of employment are generally below those that would exist under perfect competition (eds.).

5. See N. Chamberlain, *The Union Challenge to Management Control* (New York: Harper, 1948), p. 94.

6. The cost increase may, of course, take some time to work through and appear as a price increase. See A. Rees, *The Economics of Trade Unions* (Chicago: University of Chicago Press, 1962), pp. 107–109. In some oligopolistic situations the

firm may be able to raise prices after a wage increase without suffering a significant decrease in sales.

7. *Steele v. Louisville & Nashville Railroad Co.,* 323 U.S. 192 (1944).

8. The pressure is sometimes resisted. Indeed, the United Mine Workers has chosen more benefits for less employment. See generally M. Baratz, *The Union and the Coal Industry* (New Haven: Yale University Press, 1955).

9. See H. Cohany, "Trends and Changes in Union Membership," *Monthly Labor Review* 89 (1966), pp. 510–513; I. Bernstein, "The Growth of American Unions, 1945–1960," *Labor History* 2 (1961), pp. 131–157.

10. And the law would protect him in this. Indeed, it would protect him if he were moved by an antiunion animus as well as by valid economic considerations. See *Textile Workers Union of America v. Darlington Manufacturing Co.,* 380 U.S. 263 (1965). Of course, where fixed costs are large relative to variable costs, it may be difficult for an employer to extricate himself.

11. This does not mean that collective bargaining in the private sector is free of social costs. It means only that the costs are necessarily limited by the discipline of the market.

12. See generally R. Dahl, *Who Governs? Democracy and Power in an American City* (New Haven: Yale University Press, 1961). On interest group theory generally, see D. Truman, *The Government Process: Political Interests and Public Opinion,* 3rd printing (New York: Alfred A. Knopf, 1955).

13. See, for example, W. Sayre and H. Kaufman, *Governing New York City: Politics in the Metropolis* (New York: Russell Sage, 1960), pp. 366–372.

14. See M. Moskow, *Teachers and Unions* (Philadelphia: University of Pennsylvania, Wharton School of Finance and Commerce, Industrial Research Unit, 1966), pp. 79–86.

15. This is based on the reasonable but not unchallengeable assumption that the number of significant employers in a labor market is related to the existence of monopsony. See R. Bunting, *Employer Concentration in Local Labor Markets,* (Westport: Greenwood, 1982), pp. 3–14. The greater the number of such employers in a labor market, the greater the departure from the classic case of the monopsony of a single employer. The number of employers would clearly seem to affect their ability to make and enforce a collusive wage agreement.

16. See generally R. Dorfman, *Prices and Markets* (Englewood Cliffs, N.J.: Prentice-Hall, 1967).

17. In the private sector what is involved is principally resource allocation rather than income redistribution. Income redistribution occurs to the extent that unions are able to increase wages at the expense of profits, but the extent to which this actually happens would seem to be limited. It also occurs if unions, by limiting employment in the union sector through maintenance of wages above a competitive level, increase the supply of labor in the nonunion sector and thereby depress wages there.

18. In the private sector the political question was answered when the National Labor Relations Act was passed; the benefits of collective bargaining (with the strike) outweigh the social costs.

19. The fact that American unions and management are generally economically oriented is a source of great freedom to us all. If either the unions or management decided to make decisions about the nature of services provided or products manu-

factured on the basis of their own ideological convictions, we would all, as consumers, be less free. Although unions may misallocate resources, consumers are still generally able to satisfy strong desires for particular products by paying more for them and sacrificing less valued items. This is because unions and management generally make no attempt to adjust to anything but economic considerations. Were it otherwise, and the unions—or management—insisted that no products of a certain kind be manufactured, consumers would have much less choice.

20. The major qualification to these generalizations is that sometimes unions can generate more support from the membership for certain demands than for others (more for the size of the work crew, less for wage increases). Just how extensive this phenomenon is, and how it balances out over time, is difficult to say; however, it would not seem to be of great importance in the overall picture.

21. R. Dahl, *A Preface to Democratic Theory* (Chicago: University of Chicago Press, 1956), p. 145.

22. Sometimes this is so because of the nature of the endeavor—national defense, for example—and sometimes because the existence of the governmental operation necessarily inhibits entry by private entities, as in the case of elementary education.

23. A. Marshall, *Principles of Economics,* 8th ed. (New York: Macmillan, 1920), pp. 383–386.

The Legal Context

State and Local Government Labor Relations

Unlike private sector labor relations, which are regulated at the national level, public sector unionism and bargaining are governed by state laws. Since 1959, when Wisconsin adopted the first public employee bargaining law, numerous states have passed labor relations legislation covering various government workers. The passage of such laws was rapid from the mid-1960s through the early 1970s but has been sporadic since then. Much modification of state bargaining laws has occurred, however, especially regarding the right to strike, and impasse resolution procedures (treated in chapter 5). By 1986 at least thirty-seven states had enacted legislation requiring public employers to bargain or meet and confer with at least some public sector occupational group.[1] Further, there are few remaining state laws prohibiting public sector collective bargaining, although such prohibitions were pervasive in the early 1960s.

Recent research has suggested that the legal environment governing public sector bargaining has a substantial impact on the extent of public sector unionization and the process and outcome of negotiations.[2] Bargaining laws, impasse resolution procedure requirements, and legislated strike rights, individually and in combination, aid employees in obtaining better bargaining outcomes.[3] These findings have contributed to an academic debate regarding whether unionization leads to the passage of bargaining laws, or the reverse, and whether increased unionization or an employee-favorable legal environment leads to more favorable wages and working conditions. Kochan, who conducted the initial investigation into this area, used scaling, correlation, and regression techniques to examine the impact of various economic, political, and industrial relations factors on the comprehensiveness of state public sector bargaining statutes.[4] His results suggested that the states that have passed the most comprehensive legislation tend to be more industrialized, have higher levels of per capita income, spend more per capita on public services, and have a longer history of innovating with legislation in other policy areas than do other states. These findings suggest that there were systematic environmental pressures that contributed to the passage of public sector bargaining laws during the 1960s and early 1970s. Although Kochan's analysis did not address the legal environment issue in its entirety, it has served as a basis for more comprehensive investigations.

In the second reading of this chapter, Saltzman analyzes the relationship between teacher unionism and bargaining laws. His investigative interviews and empirical analysis pick up where Kochan left off; they suggest generally that some threshold level of bargaining activity is necessary to stimulate the passage of a bargaining law, which in turn causes a large increase in unionization and bargaining. Further, Saltzman's identification of a complex relationship has been reinforced by Ichniowski's similar findings in a study of municipal police departments.[5] Although further research on some aspects of the unionization–bargaining law relationship is needed, Saltzman's careful institutional and empirical examination provides substantial insight into the phenomenon.

The relationship between bargaining laws and bargaining outcomes has also been the subject of recent analyses. The general finding of these studies is that bargaining under a law leads unionized employees to achieve better bargaining outcomes than are achieved when these employees bargain without the aid of a law.[6] Moreover, the dispersion in bargaining outcomes within a state is less where bargaining laws exist than where there is no bargaining legislation.[7] This suggests that the passage of bargaining laws permits unionized employees generally to negotiate more favorable bargaining outcomes than occur where no law exists. In other words, the bargaining power of a specific public employee group is less important in achieving favorable bargaining outcomes where a law exists than where no law exists. A bargaining law, therefore, is union bargaining power. A more complete explanation of these relationships, however, awaits more comprehensive research. In particular, it will be interesting to ascertain the extent to which separate, specific provisions in public sector bargaining laws affect negotiated settlements. Also, it would be interesting to examine the interactions among the changing economic and financial characteristics described earlier in the chapter and bargaining laws and outcomes.

The enactment of public sector bargaining legislation does not guarantee its survival. Like other types of legislation, it is subject to alteration through the political process. This is particularly true of any statutory provisions that deal with impasse procedures. In the second reading of this section, Kochan describes the interplay of political forces at work in New York State during the late 1970s, which resulted in an amendment to the state's Taylor Law that, among other things, eliminated fact-finding but renewed the provision authorizing compulsory interest arbitration of police and firefighter labor disputes. Kochan shows how the various union and management organizations used the results of an independent research study of the effectiveness of the Taylor Law's impasse procedures selectively to support their own respective positions and oppose those of others with regard to amending the law. In particular, Kochan concludes that "it was the political power of the police and firefighters that provided the votes needed to insure that some form of arbitration would be extended." Finally, Kochan's discussion of the political power of public sector unions and employers provides a useful bridge to our general discussion of the political context of public sector labor relations in the next section.

It should be further noted that legislation on matters other than bargaining will influence state and local government labor relations. Laws governing, among other things, financial arrangements (such as limitations on state and local taxing authority, tax rates, or tax composition); political issues (such as the authority of state civil service systems, or restrictions on union political activities); and legislative controls on numerous issues (such as pensions, insurance plans, and union security arrangements) affect the bargaining process and bargaining outcomes. Some of these legal constraints may be eased (formally or otherwise) as bargaining develops in government, but others may be tightened. In fact, changes in other laws that are implemented without consideration of potential labor relations impacts may cause labor–management problems. For example, taxing or spending restrictions enacted subsequent to the expansion of bargaining rights could cause public employee strikes, legal or illegal. And, potentially more important, the myriad constraints vary from state to state and even across local governments within states. Thus, close attention must also be paid to the governmental entity in question and to its relations with other levels of government in order to gain an appreciation of the impact of the legal constraints on bargaining.[8]

An important legal issue that has received varying levels of support and opposition over time involves the potential enactment of national legislation governing the unionization and bargaining rights of state and local government employees. Although many unions prefer the current situation, where state laws govern public employee bargaining rights, some unions strongly support the implementation of a national law regulating state and local employee bargaining.[9] Partly in response to union lobbying, several bills covering public sector bargaining have been introduced into Congress during the past two decades. These bills have proposed various regulatory approaches, including an extension of the National Labor Relations Act to cover public employees, specific statutes regulating public employee bargaining rights, and legislation establishing specific minimum public employee bargaining rights that could be expanded by state law. It is noteworthy, however, that none of these bills has ever received serious consideration, and that virtually no effort has been made during the Reagan presidency even to raise this issue.

Despite circumstances that make a national public sector law unlikely to be enacted in the near future, a recent legal development could resurrect the possibility of such law. In the past, when the support for a national public sector law seemed stronger, there was an overriding concern about the constitutionality of such legislation. An indirect test of the probable fate of federal collective bargaining legislation for state and local government employees was provided by the U.S. Supreme Court in a 1976 decision that declared unconstitutional an extension of the national Fair Labor Standards Act to cover municipal governments.[10] That decision was generally viewed as indicating that a national public sector bargaining law would be similarly unconstitutional. Very recently, however, the Supreme Court has overturned its earlier decision regarding the extension of the Fair Labor Standards Act,[11] and this prevailing view may again suggest that a national public sector bargaining law would pass constitutional muster. Thus, although the likelihood of the passage of such a law is still very low, the Supreme Court has kept the possibility alive.

Federal Sector Labor Relations

Our discussion so far has dealt only with the legal framework for collective bargaining in state and local governments. That framework, however, gives us almost no information about the legal context regulating the bargaining rights of employees of the federal government—a subject that merits consideration. The first limited endorsement of bargaining rights for federal employees came with the signing of Federal Executive Order (EO) 10988 by President John F. Kennedy in 1962. Seven years later this original order was superseded by EO 11491, which was in turn amended on several occasions during the 1970s. The Civil Service Reform Act, which was signed into law in late 1978, formalized many parts of the amended EO 11491 and provided for the first time a unified, statutory basis for federal sector labor relations.[12] In brief, among other things, the act:

1. Protects the rights of employees to join or not join labor organizations

2. Establishes (a) the Federal Labor Relations Authority (FLRA), a three-member body appointed by the president, to administer the law's provisions dealing with organization, representation, and bargaining rights; (b) the Federal Service Impasses Panel, a seven-member entity within and appointed by the FLRA, to resolve negotiating impasses by taking "whatever action is necessary" (usually mediation, followed by fact-finding with recommendations); and (c) that the assistant secretary of labor for labor–management relations has responsibility for administering standards of conduct for federal labor organizations, particularly in the areas of internal democracy and financial integrity

3. Provides procedures for exclusive representation and national consultation rights for employee organizations (to consult on agencywide personnel policies)

4. Specifies the scope of bargaining and enumerates management rights

5. Requires the negotiation of grievance procedures

6. Requires the approval of all labor agreements by the top agency administrator

7. Enumerates a list of unfair labor practices for employee and employer organizations

One of the major differences between the Civil Service Reform Act and most state public employee bargaining statutes or the National Labor Relations Act is that wages, fringe benefits, civil service provisions, certain union security arrangements, and many agency personnel and other policies and practices are specifically excluded from the scope of federal sector bargaining. Despite these limitations, unionization and collective bargaining have spread to approximately 50 percent of all General Schedule (white-collar) employees and to over 80 percent of all Wage Grade (blue-collar) employees in the federal service. (Employees of the quasi-public U.S. Postal Service bargain under separate statutory authority—the Postal Reorganization Act of 1970—and are about 90 percent organized.)

Not surprisingly, the most controversial issue arising from the federal sector legal context regards the continuation of the bargaining scope restrictions that were initiated by the earlier executive order system. Federal employee unions have continually and actively tried to get Congress to remove the restrictions.[13] The ill-fated PATCO strike of 1981 was an attempt by the air traffic controllers' union to circumvent these restrictions.[14] Although in this book we focus primarily on state and local government labor relations, the continuing debate among management and union officials, policymakers, and neutrals about proper federal sector labor relations policies could cause new developments to occur in this area after the end of the Reagan presidency.

Notes

1. See Robert G. Valletta and Richard B. Freeman, "The NBER Public Sector Collective Bargaining Law Data Set," unpublished paper, 1986.

2. See, for instance, Casey Ichniowski, "Public Sector Union Growth and Bargaining Laws: A Proportional Hazards Approach with Time-Varying Treatments," NBER Working Paper no. 1809 (1986); Richard B. Freeman and Robert G. Valletta, "Does the Legal Environment Affect the Public Sector Labor Markets?" unpublished paper, 1986; Peter Feuille and John Thomas Delaney, "Collective Bargaining, Interest Arbitration, and Police Salaries," *Industrial and Labor Relations Review* 39, no. 2 (January 1986), pp. 228–240; and John C. Anderson, "The Impact of Arbitration: A Methodological Assessment," *Industrial Relations* 20, no. 2 (Spring 1981), pp. 129–148.

3. Ibid. See also Gregory M. Saltzman, "Delayed but not Denied: The Enactment of Public-Sector Bargaining Legislation in Ohio and Illinois," unpublished paper, 1986; John Thomas Delaney, "Strikes, Arbitration and Teacher Salaries: A Behavioral Analysis," *Industrial and Labor Relations Review* 36, no. 3 (April 1983), pp. 431–446; John Thomas Delaney, "Impasses and Teacher Contract Outcomes," *Industrial Relations* 25, no. 1 (Winter 1986), pp. 45–55.

4. Thomas A. Kochan, "Correlates of State Public Employee Bargaining Laws," *Industrial Relations* 12, no. 3 (October 1973), pp. 322–337.

5. Saltzman, "Delayed but not Denied," and Ichniowski, "Public Sector Union Growth."

6. See Saltzman, "Delayed but not Denied"; Delaney, "Impasses and Teacher Contract Outcomes"; Richard B. Freeman, Casey Ichniowski, and Harrison Lauer, "Collective Bargaining Laws and Threat Effects of Unionism in the Determination of Police Compensation," NBER Working Paper no. 1578 (1985).

7. See Delaney, ibid.; John Delaney, Peter Feuille, and Wallace Hendricks, "Police Salaries, Interest Arbitration, and the Leveling Effect," *Industrial Relations* 23, no. 3 (Fall 1984), pp. 417–423.

8. For an early, but still relevant, analysis of these constraints in Michigan jurisdictions, see Charles Rehmus, "Constraints on Local Governments in Public Employee Bargaining," *Michigan Law Review* 67 (March 1969), pp. 919–930.

9. See Marick F. Masters and John Thomas Delaney, "Union Legislative Records During President Reagan's First Term," *Journal of Labor Research* 8, no. 1 (Winter 1987), pp. 1–18.

10. See *National League of Cities v. Usery,* 426 U.S. 833 (1976).

11. See *Garcia v. San Antonio Metropolitan Transit Authority,* 469 U.S. 528 (1985).

12. See Bureau of National Affairs, "The Civil Service Reform Act," *Government Employee Relations Report,* Reference File 171 (Washington, D.C.: Bureau of National Affairs, December 4, 1978), pp. 21:1001–21:1059, esp. 21:1041–21:1055.

13. See the reading by Masters included in this chapter.

14. See Herbert R. Northrup, "The Rise and Demise of PATCO," and the comment on that study, reprinted in chapter 4.

Bargaining Laws as a Cause and Consequence of the Growth of Teacher Unionism

*Gregory M. Saltzman**

In the past thirty years, millions of public employees have either joined unions or forced the transformation of existing public employee associations into unions, and many states have enacted legislation extending the union rights of public employees. Neither of these important developments, however, was anticipated by most industrial relations scholars, and neither has been fully explained, even retrospectively. To assist the search for such an explanation, this study examines the growth of collective bargaining by public school teachers and the enactment of teacher bargaining laws.[1] Its central focus is what Burton called "the most tantalizing question about the growth of public sector bargaining," namely, how important were changes in bargaining laws as a cause of the growth of bargaining?[2]

Two conflicting answers have been offered to that question. On the one hand, many teacher union leaders and school board representatives have claimed that bargaining laws were very important. Most of the seventy practitioners interviewed for this study,[3] for example, pointed to the enactment of laws establishing a duty to bargain as the single leading reason for the spread of teacher bargaining.[4] They argued that such laws reduce the will and ability of public employers to resist the unionization of employees and that, to a lesser extent, these laws directly stimulate employee interest in bargaining. These practitioners also claimed that antiunion laws, or even an absence of prounion laws, significantly hinder the growth of bargaining.

On the other hand, some scholars have argued that bargaining legislation has only a small effect on the extent of bargaining. In comments on the private sector, Dunlop asserted that although the Wagner Act prevented the destruction of unions during depressions, it played only a minor role in the initial organizing of workers.[5] More recently, Burton contended that the laws enacted in the 1960s and 1970s giving public employees the right to bargain "were no more important than several other factors" in explaining the growth of public sector bargaining.[6] He added that "in some instances, the enactment of favorable legislation was as much a result of membership growth as a cause of it."[7] This latter claim implies that part of the apparent impact of bargaining legislation should be attributed to the preexisting strength of public employee unions.

*Brandeis University. Reprinted from *Industrial and Labor Relations Review* 38, no. 3 (April 1985), pp. 335–351.

Empirical analysis is needed to choose between these interpretations. Accordingly, this study presents estimates of the impact of changes in bargaining laws on the extent of teacher bargaining and the impact of changes in the extent of teacher bargaining on the nature of bargaining laws. The study also estimates the impact on bargaining coverage and on bargaining laws of other explanatory variables that are important, not only as controls but also in their own right. Finally, the paper concludes with comments on public policy and potential union strategy.

Previous Studies

Although there have been many qualitative studies of the development of teacher unionism and many econometric studies of union growth in general, there have been few econometric studies of the growth of teacher unionism or the enactment of public sector bargaining laws. Among the few are a paper by Moore, which analyzes the growth of teacher organizations and teacher bargaining coverage, and papers by Kochan and by Moore and Newman, which analyze the enactment of public sector bargaining laws.[8] The object of the present study is to improve upon those three papers by using a larger data set, additional explanatory variables (e.g., employment concentration, the extent of patronage in public employment, and Democratic party strength), and—most important—different dependent variables.

This reading distinguishes, for example, between those teacher organizations that are trade unions and those that are not. Moore's models of teacher union growth, on the other hand, use dependent variables that include all members of the two major teacher organizations for the period beginning in 1919. These organizations are the American Federation of Teachers (AFT), an openly declared trade union affiliated with the AFL-CIO, and the National Education Association (NEA), a professional association that shuns the label "union" but has become increasingly like one. Many AFT locals, however, used to be "friends of the labor movement" clubs, while NEA affiliates often were (and, in some parts of the South, still are) primarily educational lobbying groups, social clubs, or company unions. Grouping these organizations together with real teacher unions makes it difficult to interpret Moore's regression results because the reasons for joining a social club, for example, may be entirely different from those for joining a union.[9] To avoid this inappropriate grouping of dissimilar local organizations, this paper uses as a dependent variable the extent of teacher bargaining coverage, which is a better measure of teacher unionization than is membership in the AFT or NEA.

Second, this reading takes into account the irreversibility of changes in the extent of teacher bargaining and the nature of teacher bargaining laws.

Few school boards have terminated existing bargaining relationships, and few courts or legislatures have taken away legal bargaining rights already granted—even when environmental conditions have become much less favorable to unions than they were when the teacher organizations established their bargaining role. This irreversibility complicates the relationships among the variables, much as the irreversibility of hard boiling an egg complicates the relationship between the consistency and temperature of the egg (which, once hard boiled, remains so—even if it is subsequently refrigerated).

The regression models of bargaining legislation presented by Moore and Newman and by Kochan do not adjust for the existence of this hard-boiled egg effect. They used values of the explanatory variables in 1970 and 1972, respectively, to explain the nature of teacher bargaining laws in the same year. But for states where the bargaining laws had already been enacted in the 1960s, the nature of bargaining laws was a predetermined variable by 1970 or 1972; the laws reflected the social, economic, and political environment at the time of enactment, and not necessarily the environment in subsequent years. This paper, unlike the previous studies, uses *changes* in the extent of bargaining or the nature of bargaining legislation as a dependent variable. For example, 1970 values of the explanatory variables are used to explain changes taking place that year in the type of bargaining law, and not to explain the type of law already in effect.

A third difference between this paper and the previous studies concerns how bargaining laws are categorized. The Kochan and the Moore and Newman papers did not classify the laws for some states according to their own stated classification criteria. For example, both listed New Hampshire as having no public sector bargaining law, whereas in fact New Hampshire had a law authorizing but not requiring public employers to bargain. The classifications used here are based on a direct review of every relevant statute and court decision rather than on secondary legal sources.

The classification system used here better meets Kochan's aim of indicating the relative "extent to which the policies provide for a formalized bargaining relationship."[10] Kochan's scoring system gives the same weight to important and unimportant features of labor laws, which results in such anomalies as higher scores for Alabama and Texas (which *prohibit* bargaining by teachers) than for Colorado (which at that time had no statutes or supreme court rulings clarifying the legal status of bargaining, but did have teacher bargaining contracts in effect). The Moore and Newman classification system avoids giving *higher* scores to laws that actually are less favorable to bargaining; but because its categories are relatively broad, it still assigns to the same category states that prohibit bargaining and states that do not specify whether bargaining is legal but allow it on a de facto basis. Distinguishing between such dissimilar legal situations would result in a better classification system. Therefore, this paper subdivides two of the Moore and Newman bargaining law categories in order to provide more homogeneous groupings.

Table 1
Trends in Teacher Bargaining Coverage and Legislation in the United States, 1960–1977

Year	Percentage of Teachers Covered by Collective Bargaining Contracts	Number of States Requiring School Boards to Bargain
1960	0	0
1962	3	1[a]
1964	6	1
1966	12	5
1968	23	9
1970	34	18
1972	44	22
1974–1975	56 (1975)	27 (1974)
1976	63	30
1977–1978	65 (1977)	31 (1978)

Note: Sources described in "The Data and the Dependent Variables" section of the text.

[a]Whether the 1962 law, enacted in Wisconsin, established a duty to bargain was subject to dispute. In 1966 an administrative agency ruled, by a two to one vote, that it did not (*William E. Moes and City of New Berlin*, 61 LRRM 1487, Wisconsin Employment Relations Board, 1966). Nevertheless, the law is included here because it had other features that promoted the spread of bargaining. Specifically, it provided for enforcement by an administrative agency, prohibited unfair labor practices, and established an impasse resolution procedure.

Variables Affecting the Extent of Teacher Bargaining

The percentage of teachers in the United States covered by collective bargaining contracts increased substantially in the late 1960s and 1970s, as indicated in table 1. Ideally, a general theory of union growth would provide the basis for specifying the variables that led to this increase. Unfortunately, existing theories did not predict the upsurge of public employee unionism beginning in the 1960s and cannot fully explain it retrospectively. Particularly surprising to most researchers was that the wave of unionization in the public sector encompassed not only traditionally union-prone blue-collar workers, but also white-collar professional, and supervisory workers such as schoolteachers and principals. In view of their lack of predictive power, previous theories seem to be poor guides for selecting explanatory variables. Instead, it seems more appropriate here to adopt John R. Commons's approach of developing a model based on observation.[11] Thus, the variables used to explain the extent of teacher bargaining coverage are derived from the opinions of the practitioners I interviewed and the findings of previous studies. These variables are grouped into the six categories that follow.

Teacher and School Characteristics

Two major changes in the postwar period are the substantial increases from 1950 to 1970 in the percentage of male teachers (*MALE*) and in the average size of schools and school systems (*SCLSIZE* and *SYSSIZE,* measured in thousands of teachers per school building or per school system, respectively). Although the effects of the feminist movement and the rising fraction of women with long-term commitments to market employment may eventually eliminate male–female differences in the propensity to unionize, many previous studies have found that men are more likely to be organized.[12] Thus, the increase in the number of male teachers may have contributed to the rise of teacher bargaining.

The increase in the average size of schools and school systems should have a similar effect.[13] There are five main reasons for this. First, large schools are more likely to have a "critical mass" of militant teachers who reinforce each other's activism. Second, in large schools, teachers are more difficult for principals to monitor and therefore have more latitude to engage in union activities. Third, large school systems present attractive organizing targets for unions because there are economies of scale in providing representation services. Fourth, teachers in large school systems can more credibly threaten to strike for recognition because it is harder to replace large groups of strikers. Finally, large school systems have bureaucratic rule making and less personal contact between teachers and top administrators, which means that collective rather than individual bargaining is more effective in influencing employment conditions.

Labor Market Conditions

Teachers' real and relative earnings declined during World War II but rose steadily from the late 1940s to the late 1960s.[14] Thus, the claim by many practitioners that teachers became militant because of "bad salaries" is a plausible explanation for the teacher strikes of the late 1940s. But why did teachers become militant in the mid-1960s, when wages were better than ever before? Despite the improvements in teacher salaries, many teachers still resented earning less than some blue-collar workers. Moreover, the shortage of secondary teachers in the first half of the 1960s[15] and the availability of attractive employment alternatives during the Vietnam boom not only brought pay increases but also may have unleashed latent militancy among teachers by giving them the power to win strikes and engage in union activity without fear of losing their jobs.

The growth of bargaining should therefore be negatively related to the aggregate unemployment rate for the state in the previous year (*UNEMPL*). (Lagged values are used since union activists are most vulnerable to employer coercion when the organizational campaign is just getting started, which is often a year before teachers win representation rights.) The relationships with teachers' relative earnings $(RLPAY)$[16] and the rate of growth in teacher employment over the preceding four years $(GROWTH)$[17] are unclear, however, since low relative earnings and reduced or negative employment growth suggest both the economic grievances that spur militancy and the weak market position that forestalls it.

Membership of Other Unions

Although the percentage of employees belonging to unions grew for the public sector in the late 1960s and the 1970s, that for the labor force as a whole declined. Nevertheless, the labor movement remained strong in many states. The membership of all unions in a state should be positively related to the extent of teacher bargaining in that state because the labor movement often gave teachers political support.[18] The membership of public employee groups other than teachers should be particularly important, if only as an index of prevailing attitudes toward public sector bargaining. Thus, teacher bargaining should be positively related to the fraction of the population belonging to unions $(UNION)$ and to the fraction of noneducational state and local public employees belonging to the American Federation of State, County, and Municipal Employees $(AFSCME)$.[19]

Attitudes toward Unions

Prevailing attitudes toward unions should affect both teachers' demand for bargaining rights and the willingness of school boards to grant them. One direct measure of these attitudes is the voting record of members of Congress, who presumably tend to vote in accordance with the preferences of their constituents. Teacher bargaining coverage thus should be positively related to the average rating by the AFL-CIO's Committee on Political Education (COPE) of each state's delegation to the U.S. House of Representatives, divided by the average COPE rating for the House as a whole $(COPE)$.

Bargaining coverage may be related to two indirect measures of attitudes toward unions. The first is the level of economic development, which varies considerably by region. In particular, the South has traditionally been less developed. Marshall argued that Southerners tend to resist unions because they see them as a barrier to attracting industry.[20] This resistance to unionism may carry over to the public sector, particularly if allowing public sector bargaining leads to tax increases that may drive away investment.[21] Hence, bargaining coverage should be positively correlated with real state per capita income $(INCOME,$ measured in thousands of 1967 dollars).

A second indirect measure of attitudes toward unions is urbanization.

According to several of the practitioners interviewed, urban areas tend to be more prounion, so there may be a positive relationship between the fraction of the population living in urbanized areas (*URBAN*) and the extent of teacher bargaining.

The Previous Extent of Bargaining

The expected *change* in the extent of bargaining may depend upon the previous extent of bargaining (CB_{t-1}). When teacher bargaining is getting started, bargaining by some teachers may facilitate the spread of bargaining to other school systems in the same state because it provides an example for other teachers to imitate and because, in states where the legal status of bargaining is not clear, it may overcome the argument of school boards that bargaining is illegal. On the other hand, if bargaining is already extensive, the remaining school systems without bargaining may be the most difficult to organize. Furthermore, there is a strictly mechanical effect: the extent of bargaining cannot exceed 100 percent. Therefore, the expected increase in teacher bargaining should first rise, then fall, with the previous extent of bargaining.

Public Policy Changes

State laws governing public sector labor relations changed substantially during the past three decades. The trend toward the legalization of bargaining began in the late 1950s. Subsequently, state laws regulating bargaining by teachers and other public employees became progressively more like the private sector National Labor Relations Act. More and more state laws not only allowed but required public employers to bargain with majority representatives, established administrative agencies to enforce prohibitions of unfair labor practices, and gave public employees powerful weapons for inducing management concessions (either the right to strike or compulsory interest arbitration).

By all accounts, the extent of teacher bargaining should be positively related to the prior enactment of laws mandating bargaining with majority representatives (*MLAW2, MLAW4,* and *MLAW77,* dummy variables indicating, respectively, the enactment of a law in the preceding two years, enactment two to four years earlier, and a law on the books in 1977). The strength of this relationship, however, is in dispute: weak according to the practitioners. The extent of bargaining should also be positively related to the prior enactment of statutes or issuance of decisions by state appeals courts expressly permitting bargaining (*PLAW*)—such as the 1966 ruling in the *Board of Education of City of Chicago* case in Illinois; but it should be negatively related to laws banning representation elections (*ELAW*)—such as the 1965

Winton Act in California—and laws and court decisions expressly banning bargaining (*BLAW2,* indicating enactment in the prior two years, and *BLAW-old,* indicating enactment more than two years before)—such as the 1977 ruling in the *County Board of Arlington* case in Virginia.[22]

Factors Influencing the Nature of Teacher Bargaining Laws

What, in turn, explains the behavior of the state legislators and appeals court judges who effected these changes in bargaining statutes and case law?[23] The following factors may be important.

Bargaining Coverage and Union Membership

The growing strength of public employee unions may be not only an effect but also a cause of public policy changes. As public employee unions gain strength, politicians will become more sensitive to their demands. (Bargaining laws, however, may also be enacted to control public employee strikes rather than to strengthen public employee unions, which suggests a different interpretation of any positive relationship between the strength of public employee unions and the enactment of public sector bargaining laws.) The overall membership of the labor movement may also affect the nature of public policy. Thus, the enactment of prounion laws should be positively related to the lagged fraction of teachers covered by collective bargaining agreements (CB_{t-1}), the lagged change in that measure of teacher bargaining coverage (ΔCB_{t-1}), AFSCME membership (*AFSCME*), and total union membership (*UNION*).

Attitudes toward Unions

Relative COPE ratings (*COPE*), the level of economic development (*INCOME*), and urbanization (*URBAN*) may be positively related to the prospects for prounion public sector bargaining laws. The reasons for these associations are the same as those for the postulated associations with the extent of teacher bargaining.

Democratic Party Gains

Teacher bargaining laws are most likely to become more prounion just after the Democratic party makes gains in state legislative and gubernatorial elections. Such legal changes are especially likely if the Democratic gains cause a change in control of state government. These changes in Democratic strength can be measured by two variables: first, the change in the percentage of seats held by Democrats in the house of the legislature where the Democrats were weaker (%DEM); and, second, the change in the number of centers of power (the state senate, the state assembly, and the governorship) controlled by the Democratic party (#DEM).

Note that the variables used here measure *changes* in Democratic party strength, not *levels*. Using levels could be misleading because of the absence of a two-party system in much of the South prior to the 1970s. Thus, while a large Democratic majority might imply a liberal state legislature in most regions, that might not be the case in the South, where most legislators, liberal or conservative, were affiliated with the Democrats. Using *changes* in Democratic party representation provides a more accurate measure of the ebb and flow of liberal strength because it excludes one-party states where the Democrats always won all the seats.

The Extent of Political Patronage

Public policy concerning bargaining may depend on the strength of the civil service system. Several practitioners told me that where patronage is extensive, politicians oppose granting bargaining rights. Often, one of the first things workers seek when they win bargaining rights is protection against arbitrary discharge. This protection, however, would undermine patronage-based political machines, because public employees would no longer have to work on political campaigns in order to keep their jobs. Therefore, states with a high proportion of public employees protected by a civil service merit system (*MERIT*) may be more likely to enact prounion public sector bargaining laws.

Regional Patterns

Sharkansky has shown that state governments tend to adopt policies similar to those in neighboring states because public officials are more likely to consult their counterparts in nearby states and because neighboring states often have many socioeconomic characteristics in common.[24] Although some of these socioeconomic characteristics are controlled for in this model, residual regional effects may still remain. The regional pattern in bargaining laws can be measured by four variables indicating the fraction of contiguous states in various categories just prior to the lawmakers' decision: the fraction banning bargaining (*BFRAC*), mandating bargaining (*MFRAC*), with a more prounion law (*HIFRAC*), and with a less prounion law (*LOFRAC*).

Previous Bargaining Laws

Finally, the probability that teacher bargaining laws will become more prounion should be lower in a state with a law that already satisfies most union concerns. If that state does change the law, however, then the new law will probably be more prounion than new laws in other states. These relationships can be captured with six dummy variables indicating the prior law category (*CAT1* through *CAT6*).

The Data and the Dependent Variables

The preceding discussion suggests a list of variables that potentially explain the extent of teacher bargaining coverage and the nature of teacher bargaining laws. Aggregate statewide data were obtained for most of the variables for ten different years: for the bargaining coverage model, biennially from 1960 to 1972, plus 1975, 1976, and 1977; and for the bargaining law model, biennially from 1959–1960 to 1977–1978. Values for most of the variables could be readily calculated from a variety of published sources,[25] but deriving the data for bargaining coverage and bargaining laws was considerably more complex.

For teacher bargaining coverage, the main problem was obtaining accurate data for the periods before 1966 and after 1972. Published data are available for the period from 1966 to 1972,[26] but deriving data for subsequent years required extensive calculations using the 1975, 1976, and 1977 Census of Governments tapes;[27] and data for the period from 1960 to 1965 (when teacher bargaining was still unusual) had to be obtained from scattered published reports, archival materials, and interviews. By contrast, the raw data for teacher bargaining law variables—statutes and major court decisions—are always published; but these statutes and court decisions had to be located and interpreted. Bargaining laws were grouped into the six mutually exclusive categories shown in table 2. The categories are ordered: the higher the category, the more prounion the law.[28]

The bargaining coverage and bargaining law models each had two dependent variables, one measuring changes, the other levels. These dependent variables were: (1) the annual change in the fraction of teachers in each state covered by collective bargaining agreements (ΔCB), (2) the fraction of teachers in each state covered by collective bargaining contracts in 1977 (*CB77*), (3) the probability that a state's bargaining law would change to a higher category in the particular biennium [$Pr(\Delta LAW)$], and (4) the category of law just after the change in category (*LAW*). Note that since $Pr(\Delta LAW)$ can vary only between zero (indicating that it would not change to a more prounion category in the particular biennium) and one (indicating that it would change), it may be more realistic to postulate that the relationship in the $Pr(\Delta LAW)$ regression is logistic rather than linear.

A further assumption was that a simultaneous equation model was not appropriate. Since legislative changes are seen as both a cause and an effect of the spread of teacher bargaining, simultaneous equation bias could be a

Table 2
Categories of Teacher Bargaining Laws

1.	*BLAW*	Collective bargaining by teachers expressly prohibited.
2.	*NOLAW*	No statute or generally applicable court ruling concerning the right to bargain (although there may be laws prohibiting strikes, permitting or mandating informal consultation with teachers, etc.).
2a.	*ELAW*	Subset of category 2 in which secret ballot representation elections were banned; these statutes were obtained by the NEA in a few states in the 1960s for the purpose of thwarting AFT efforts to gain exclusive bargaining rights in big cities.
3.	*PLAW*	Law expressly permits bargaining with teacher organizations.
4.	*MLAW* (CAT 4)	Law mandates bargaining with teacher organizations representing a majority of teachers in the school system.
5.	*MLAW* (CAT 5)	Category 4 plus an administrative agency to determine bargaining units and enforce a prohibition of unfair labor practices.
6.	*MLAW* (CAT 6)	Category 5 plus either compulsory interest arbitration or a protected right to strike.

Note: In none of the first five categories are strikes protected; in many cases, states in these categories explicitly prohibit public employee strikes.

problem. The practitioners interviewed, however, claimed that these forces operate with a lag; that is, a change in teacher bargaining laws affects the extent of bargaining only after a delay of some months or even years, and vice versa. Lagged values of the other dependent variable, however, are predetermined variables.[29] Since all the explanatory variables are either exogenous or predetermined, a simultaneous equation model is not appropriate.

The four equations were estimated using four different sets of observations. District of Columbia data were included in the regressions for bargaining coverage but not in those for bargaining laws since no D.C. data were available for several key political variables. Data for ten biennial cross-sections were used in estimating the ΔCB and $Pr(\Delta LAW)$ equations;[30] data for 1977 for the *CB77* equation;[31] and data for the fifty-two cases between 1959 and 1978 where the law category changed for the *LAW* equation.

Bargaining Coverage Regressions

Regression estimates of the bargaining coverage models, equations 1 and 2, are presented in table 3. The major finding from these regressions is that changes in bargaining laws had a stronger association with the subsequent spread of bargaining than did any of the other explanatory variables. In particular, the enactment of laws mandating bargaining with majority representatives typically led to a rapid and substantial increase in the fraction of

Table 3
Determinants of Teacher Bargaining Coverage, 1960–1977

Independent Variables	Equation 1: Annual Change in the Percentage of Teachers in Each State Covered by Collective Bargaining Contracts, 1960–1977 (ΔCB)		Equation 2: Percentage of Teachers in Each State Covered by Collective Bargaining Contracts in 1977 (CB77)	
	Coefficient	(t-Ratio)	Coefficient	(t-Ratio)
Bargaining laws (dummy variables):				
Law mandating bargaining				
Enacted 0–2 years ago (*MLAW2*)	0.164***	(16.99)		
Enacted 2–4 years ago (*MLAW4*)	0.065***	(6.62)		
In effect in 1977 (*MLAW77*)			0.329***	(6.90)
Law permitting bargaining (*PLAW*)			0.193*	(2.45)
Law banning representation elections (*ELAW*)	−0.040	(1.94)		
Law banning bargaining				
Enacted 0–2 years ago (*BLAW2*)	−0.076**	(3.09)		
In effect at the time (*BLAWold*)	−0.018	(1.95)	−0.165*	(2.38)
Teacher/school characteristics:				
Fraction of teachers male (*MALE*)	0.128*	(2.54)	2.136***	(5.71)
Teachers per school (*SCLSIZE*)	1.030**	(2.60)	5.700*	(2.07)
Teachers per school system (*SYSSIZE*)	0.002	(0.84)	0.068***	(4.19)
Labor market conditions:				
Growth in teacher employment (*GROWTH*)	−0.069**	(2.69)	−0.359	(1.46)
Lagged unemployment rate (*UNEMPL*)	−0.095	(0.81)		
Membership of other unions:				
AFSCME membership (*AFSCME*)	0.025	(1.20)		
Attitudes toward unions:				
Relative COPE ratings (*COPE*)	−0.004	(0.71)		
Real per capita income (*INCOME*)	0.018**	(3.26)	0.129**	(3.37)
Control variables:				
Lagged extent of bargaining (CB_{t-1})	0.109***	(3.34)		
Lagged extent of bargaining squared $[(CB_{t-1})^2]$	−0.187***	(5.70)		
Constant	−0.074***	(4.12)	−0.913***	(5.44)
R^2	0.563		0.920	
Number of observations	510		51	

Note: ΔCB regression based on data for each state for 1960–1977; CB77 regression based on data for 1977 only.

*Significant at the 5% level (two-tailed test).

**Significant at the 1% level (two-tailed test).

***Significant at the 0.1% level (two-tailed test).

teachers covered by collective bargaining contracts. All three mandatory bargaining law variables, *MLAW2, MLAW4,* and *MLAW77,* had positive coefficients, indicating a positive relationship with increases in the extent of bargaining (ΔCB) and the extent of bargaining in 1977 (*CB77*). Moreover, these coefficients were all significant at the 0.1 percent level. Most important, however, they had large magnitudes, indicating that mandatory bargaining legislation had a great impact on the extent of teacher bargaining. This impact was greater than that of any other explanatory variables in the model.

The key role of bargaining legislation is demonstrated by calculating how much a nonlegal variable must change to have the same impact on bargaining coverage as does the enactment of a mandatory bargaining law. The coefficients for equation 1 indicate that the enactment of a law requiring school boards to bargain with majority representatives leads, within four years, to an increase of 0.229 (out of 1.00) in the fraction of teachers covered by collective contracts. (This is the sum of the coefficients for *MLAW2* and *MLAW4.*) The variable in equation 1 with the next greatest impact, *INCOME* (measuring real per capita income), would have to rise by $12,800 to bring the same increase in the extent of bargaining as a mandatory law passed four years earlier. But the standard deviation for *INCOME* was only $717 and its range for the two decades considered was only $4,622, so the actual variations in income had a much smaller impact on bargaining coverage than did the enactment of a mandatory bargaining law.

The coefficients for equation 2 indicate that the expected fraction of teachers covered by collective contracts in 1977 was 0.329 higher in states that had laws mandating bargaining with majority representatives. The explanatory variable with the next largest impact was *MALE,* the fraction of teachers who were male, which would have to rise by 0.16 to have the same effect on the extent of bargaining in 1977. Although this increase in *MALE* is less extreme than a $12,800 increase in *INCOME,* it is still large: the standard deviation for *MALE* in 1977 was only 0.07. Thus, particularly in equation 1, but also in equation 2, mandatory bargaining laws emerge as the most important factor explaining the growth of teacher bargaining. In other words, this finding tends to refute Burton's claim that changes in legislation were no more important a cause of growth in bargaining than were several other factors.

Furthermore, the estimated coefficients may understate the impact of mandatory bargaining laws on medium and smaller school systems. This can be seen by comparing the date when formal collective bargaining began in large school systems to the date when legislation establishing a duty to bargain was enacted. The data in table 4 show that 39 percent (37 of 95) of the large and very large school systems (those with full-time equivalent instructional staffs of more than 2,500 in 1977), and 55 percent of the teachers in those systems (325,906 of 594,782), started bargaining before the enactment

Table 4
Timing of Mandatory Bargaining Legislation and the Start of Teacher Bargaining: Large and Very Small School Systems Compared

Employment Stratum[a]	When Formal Bargaining Started	Total Systems		Total Staff	
		Number	(%)	Number	(%)
5,000 +	Before mandatory law	20	57	263,748	69
	After mandatory law	10	29	80,948	21
	No bargaining yet				
	In state where bargaining is banned	5	14	38,170	10
	In state where bargaining is not banned	0	0	0	0
	Total	35	100	382,866	100
2,500– 5,000	Before mandatory law	17	28	62,158	29
	After mandatory law	20	33	69,212	33
	No bargaining yet				
	In state where bargaining is banned	15	25	50,503	24
	In state where bargaining is not banned	8	13	30,043	14
	Total	60	100	211,916	100

Note: Includes all school systems with 2,500 or more full time equivalent instructional staff, based on figures from the 1977 Census of Governments. Data for when teacher bargaining started were obtained from *Negotiation Agreement Provisions* (Washington, D.C.: National Education Association, 1966–1967, 1968–1969, and 1970–1971 editions), and from the 1975, 1976, and 1977 Census of Governments tapes. Where necessary, these sources were supplemented by referring to various issues of the BNA *Government Employee Relations Report* and by telephone interviews with various state and local affiliates of the NEA and the AFT. Data for when the statutes mandating bargaining with majority representatives was enacted were obtained from the relevant session laws volume.

[a]Full-time equivalent instructional staff per school system in 1977.

of bargaining legislation. The magnitudes and statistical significance of the legislation coefficients, even when these large systems were included in the sample, suggests that the estimated impact of legislation would be even greater if small and medium school systems were considered alone.[32]

Additional evidence of the differential impact of legislation by size of school system is provided by comparing the timing of the onset of bargaining for the two different strata shown in table 4: very large school systems (instructional staffs of 5,000 or more) and large school systems (those with instructional staffs of 2,500 to 5,000). In the very large school systems, 69 percent of the teachers were represented in formal collective bargaining before mandatory bargaining legislation was enacted; but in large school systems, only 29 percent were thus represented. Moreover, among the very large school systems, only an explicit legal ban on teacher bargaining (such as that in a 1947 Texas statute) has sufficed to forestall bargaining indefinitely. Among the large school systems, by contrast, 14 percent of the teachers were in states with no such prohibition and nevertheless did not have collective bargaining (as of 1982). These clear differences between large and very large school systems indicate that the smaller the school system, the more teachers need mandatory bargaining laws to secure bargaining rights. Presumably, this generalization would apply with even greater force to medium and small school systems, where teachers have a less effective strike threat.

Other results of the bargaining coverage regressions were largely as predicted. Increases in the extent of bargaining and a greater extent of bargaining in 1977 were positively associated with laws expressly permitting bargaining (*PLAW*), the fraction of teachers who were male (*MALE*). The average number of teachers per school (*SCLSIZE*) and per school system (*SYSSIZE*), the fraction of noneducational state and local government employees belonging to AFSCME (*AFSCME*),[33] and real per capita income in the state (*INCOME*). Increases in the extent of bargaining and a greater extent of bargaining in 1977 were negatively associated with laws banning representation elections (*ELAW*), laws banning bargaining (*BLAW2* and *BLAWold*), the lack of alternative employment opportunities (*UNEMPL*), and the rate of growth of teacher employment (*GROWTH*). Most of these associations were statistically significant at the 5 percent level or better. Note that the negative coefficient for *GROWTH* implies that teachers are more likely to win bargaining rights when a deteriorating market position makes them angry, rather than when an improving market position makes them powerful.[34]

In addition, increases in the extent of bargaining were significantly and positively associated with the lagged extent of bargaining, CB_{t-1}, and significantly and negatively associated with $(CB_{t-1})^2$; the maximum increase occurred when about 29 percent of teachers had previously been covered by collective bargaining contracts. Perhaps, after a third of the teachers in a state have won contracts, the easily organized teachers have all been organized. Alternatively, after that level of organization, a backlash against teacher bargaining may begin to outweigh the increased awareness of the benefits of bargaining.

The bargaining regressions produced one unexpected result. The union membership variables (*AFSCME* and *UNION*) were insignificant, as was the direct measure of labor's political influence (*COPE*). This finding suggests that once there were controls for other explanatory variables, there was no relationship between the extent of teacher bargaining and labor movement strength.[35] This result is difficult to explain. Nevertheless, the bargaining coverage models seemed to provide a good fit: R^2 was about 0.57 for equation 1 and 0.92 for equation 2.

Bargaining Law Regressions

Regression results for the bargaining law models, equations 3 and 4, are presented in table 5. Equation 3 gives the expected probability that a state's bargaining law will change to a more prounion category in a given biennium, while equation 4 gives the expected category of bargaining law at the time the law changes.[36] Logit estimates are presented in equation 3, although the magnitude and statistical significance of the coefficients were greater in the linear probability model. But since the assumption of linearity is unreasonable in this case, the logit results seem preferable.

The bargaining law regressions show that the extent of bargaining had only a minor impact on the passage of bargaining laws. As the results for equation 3 indicate, the probability of prounion changes in teacher bargaining laws was higher where teacher bargaining had been spreading rapidly; but the coefficient for the spread of bargaining variable (ΔCB_{t-1}) had a more modest magnitude and a less impressive level of statistical significance than the mandatory bargaining law variables did in the bargaining coverage regressions. Moreover, the category of bargaining law enacted was actually *lower* where teacher bargaining previously was extensive, an unexpected result indicated by the negative coefficient of CB_{t-1} in equation 4. These results tend to support the claim that legal changes are more cause of bargaining coverage changes than an effect.

Several of the remaining explanatory variables had a significant impact on the enactment of bargaining laws. Prounion laws were more likely where (1) AFSCME and the labor movement as a whole had substantial membership, (2) real per capita income was high, (3) the Democrats had made gains in the most recent state government elections, especially in control of the governorship or one or both legislative houses, (4) few government jobs were subject to patronage, and (5) few neighboring states had enacted laws banning bargaining, but many had enacted laws mandating it. The best predictor of more prounion laws was the fraction of neighboring states mandating bargaining with majority representatives $(MFRAC)$, the coefficients for which had large magnitudes.

Another result was the pattern of coefficients for the variables controlling for the previous category of legislation. As one proceeds from category 1 (least favorable to unions) to category 6 (most favorable), the coefficients become algebraically smaller in equation 3 and algebraically larger in equation 4. Thus, as expected, states that already have prounion laws are less likely to change their laws to a more prounion category; but if they change them at all, the new law is likely to be more prounion than new laws in other states.

Some unexpected results were (1) the limited usefulness of AFL-CIA COPE ratings as a predictor of prounion laws ($COPE$ was deleted from the

Table 5
Determinants of the Nature of Teacher Bargaining Laws, 1959–1978

Independent Variables	Equation 3: Probability of Change To Higher Law Category, This Biennium [Pr(ΔLAW)]		Equation 4: Category of Law Just after the Change in Category (LAW)	
	Coefficient	(t-Ratio)	Coefficient	(t-Ratio)
Bargaining coverage/union membership:				
Lagged change in teacher bargaining coverage (ΔCB_{t-1})	3.883*	(2.03)		
Lagged extent of teacher bargaining coverage (CB_{t-1})			−1.801*	(2.05)
AFSCME membership (AFSCME)	2.769*	(2.56)	2.022	(1.98)
Union membership (UNION)			11.81*	(2.05)
Attitudes toward unions:				
Real per capita income (INCOME)	0.878*	(2.25)	0.736*	(2.05)
Urbanization (URBAN)	−1.303	(1.47)	−1.738*	(2.20)
Political characteristics:				
Change in minimum Democratic party strength in either house of state legislature (%DEM)	2.863	(1.55)		
Change in Democratic party control of governorship and legislative houses (#DEM)	0.204*	(2.14)		
State jobs not subject to patronage (MERIT)	2.828**	(2.98)	0.679	(0.97)
Law pattern of contiguous states:				
Fraction banning bargaining (BFRAC)	−3.337*	(2.11)		
Fraction mandating bargaining (MFRAC)	3.403**	(2.82)	1.731**	(3.07)
Fraction with a more prounion law (HIFRAC)	−1.407	(1.33)		
Fraction with a less prounion law (LOFRAC)	3.747**	(3.11)		
Prior law category (dummy variables):				
Banned bargaining (CAT1)	0.659	(0.50)	−1.386	(1.27)
Banned representation elections (CAT2a)	0.262	(0.27)		
Permissive law (CAT3)	−2.911**	(2.85)	0.600	(1.28)
Mandatory law (CAT4)	−3.902***	(4.36)	1.254*	(2.15)
Mandatory law (CAT5)	−6.533***	(4.61)	1.506	(1.77)
Mandatory law (CAT6)	13.73*	(2.34)		
Constant	−0.168*	(2.34)	0.504	(0.49)
Log-likelihood ratio/R^2	−119.25 (LLR)		0.544 (R^2)	
Number of observations	500		52	

Note: Pr(ΔLAW) regression based on data for each state for 1959–1960 to 1977–1978; logit results reported. LAW regression based on data for 52 cases where law category changed.

*Significant at the 5% level (two-tailed test).

**Significant at the 1% level (two-tailed test).

***Significant at the 0.1% level (two-tailed test).

regressions for failing to be significant at the 50 percent level); (2) the negative coefficient for the extent of urbanization (*URBAN*), indicating that less urbanized states were more likely to get prounion laws; and (3) the signs of the coefficients for two of the four legal pattern variables, *HIFRAC* and *LOFRAC,* which indicated that a state's bargaining law was more likely to change to a more prounion category if few neighboring states were previously in higher (more prounion) categories and if many neighboring states were in lower (less prounion) categories. There may be some omitted variable that causes a state to have a more prounion bargaining law than its neighbors; this variable may also increase the probability that the law will change to a higher category. The effect of this omitted variable may outweigh any tendency of courts and legislatures to imitate the behavior of their counterparts in neighboring states.[37]

Conclusions

The relationship between the growth of teacher bargaining coverage and collective bargaining laws is complex. Typically, teachers in large cities start bargaining prior to the enactment of bargaining legislation. This bargaining is one, but not the most important, factor leading to the subsequent adoption of bargaining laws. Once these laws are enacted, however, they provide a major impetus to further union growth, and bargaining quickly spreads to the suburbs, medium and smaller cities, and rural areas. Causality runs in both directions, but bargaining laws appear to have a much greater impact on the extent of bargaining than the extent of bargaining has on bargaining laws.

Although bargaining laws were the key factor leading to the growth of bargaining, other variables were also important. Male teachers and teachers in large employment units, for example, were more likely to start bargaining than female teachers and those in small units. These findings may have implications for the potential for organizing private sector white-collar workers, but the implications are tentative because two important variables could not be incorporated into the bargaining coverage model. The first is rival unionism, a spur to organizing, which has been unusually intense in public education. The second is management resistance to unionization, which may be less in public education than in the private white-collar sector.

The best predictor of the nature of bargaining laws was the fraction of neighboring states that had enacted mandatory bargaining legislation. Elimination of political patronage, higher levels of economic development, Democratic party gains, and higher membership in AFSCME also furthered the enactment of prounion bargaining laws.

What does the future hold? The substantial impact of bargaining laws on bargaining coverage suggests that the enactment of federal legislation giving state and local public employees the right to bargain would greatly facilitate the spread of bargaining by teachers and other public employees in states where bargaining activity is now sparse. Whether such a law is enacted depends in part on a variable that could not be incorporated into the quantitative model, namely, the degree of cooperation among the various public employee organizations. But the prospects for such cooperation, and hence for more prounion public sector bargaining laws, may be dimmed by the continued rivalry between the AFT and the NEA.

Notes

1. Restricting the focus to a homogeneous group such as teachers effectively holds many variables constant.

2. John F. Burton, Jr., "The Extent of Collective Bargaining in the Public Sector," in Benjamin Aaron, Joseph Grodin, and James L. Stern, eds., *Public-Sector Bargaining* (Washington, D.C.: Bureau of National Affairs, 1979), p. 36.

3. I interviewed 22 officers and staff members of the American Federation of Teachers (AFT), 24 officers and staff members of the National Education Association (NEA), 13 management representatives, and 11 others. Although many of those interviewed played leading roles in the unionization of teachers, an effort was made to obtain a variety of perspectives by interviewing persons ranging from AFT President Albert Shanker to rank-and-file members of teacher organizations. The emphasis on AFT and NEA personnel reflects the focus of this study, namely, the activities of teacher organizations. For a list of those interviewed and further details of the interview process, see Gregory M. Saltzman, "The Growth of Teacher Bargaining and the Enactment of Teacher Bargaining Laws," Ph.D. dissertation, Department of Economics, University of Wisconsin, 1981, pp. 358–368.

4. Some of the statutes also established election machinery to determine representation and prohibit employer discrimination against union activists. The effect that is attributed to the duty to bargain might therefore have sometimes resulted, at least in part, from these other statutory provisions. In many cases, however, the statutes they cited had merely established the duty to bargain and omitted the other provisions when they were first enacted.

5. John T. Dunlop, "Comments" on Irving Bernstein's "Growth of American Unions, 1945–1960," *Labor History* 2, no. 3 (Fall 1961), pp. 361–363.

6. Burton, "The Extent of Collective Bargaining," pp. 15, 36–37.

7. Ibid., p. 15.

8. William Moore, "An Analysis of Teacher Union Growth," *Industrial Relations* 17, no. 2 (May 1978), pp. 204–215; Thomas Kochan, "Correlates of State Public Employee Bargaining Laws," *Industrial Relations* 12, no. 3 (October 1973), pp. 322–337; William Moore and Robert Newman, "A Note on the Passage of Public Bargaining Laws," *Industrial Relations* 14, no. 3 (October 1975), pp. 364–370.

9. R.M. Blackburn made a similar point in a study of British bank clerks, arguing that one should consider both organizational membership and organizational

character when measuring the extent of unionization. He cited collective bargaining activity as a hallmark of a union. See *Union Character and Social Class* (London: Batsford, 1967), pp. 10, 18–19, 28.

Admittedly, some public employee organizations that do not engage in collective bargaining nevertheless influence the terms and conditions of employment for their members by use of political action. They therefore could be reasonably defined as labor unions. But in the absence of good data indicating which local teacher organizations have used political action to regulate employment conditions to a significant degree, the analysis here excludes methods of job regulation other than collective bargaining.

10. Kochan, "Correlates of State . . . Laws," p. 323.

11. John R. Commons, *The Economics of Collection Action* (New York: Macmillan, 1950), chap. 10, "Methods of Investigation," esp. 136–137.

12. For example, see William Moore and Robert Newman, "On the Prospects for American Trade Union Growth: A Cross-Section Analysis," *Review of Economics and Statistics* 57, no. 4 (November 1975), pp. 435–445.

13. This hypothesis is supported by Bain (who found that white-collar workers in Britain were more likely to be organized when they were employed in large work groups) but not by the studies of private sector certification elections reviewed by Heneman and Sandver (which found negative relationships between unit size and the union victory rate). See George Bain, *The Growth of White-Collar Unionism* (Oxford: Clarendon Press: 1970), pp. 72–81; and Herbert Heneman III and Marcus Sandver, "Predicting the Outcome of Union Certification Elections: A Review of of the Literature," *Industrial and Labor Relations Review* 36, no. 4 (July 1983), pp. 537–559.

14. Real earnings are listed in *Historical Statistics of the U.S. from Colonial Times to 1970* (Washington, D.C.: U.S. Bureau of the Census, 1975), part 1, p. 375. Earnings compared to the wages earned by 2,000 hours of nonfarm unskilled labor are reported in Peter Lindert and Jeffrey Williamson, "Three Centuries of Inequality" (Madison, Wisc.: University of Wisconsin, Institute for Research on Poverty, Discussion Paper 333–376, March 1976), p. 66.

15. Joseph Kershaw and Roland McKean, *Teacher Shortages and Salary Schedules* (New York: McGraw-Hill, 1962), pp. 79–115.

16. *RLPAY* was calculated by dividing the average nine month salary of teachers in a state by 50 × the average weekly earnings in that state of production workers in manufacturing. Ideally, relative earnings would also be measured using a group more comparable to teachers than are production workers; but data disaggregated by state and spanning the two decades studied are not available for other groups. In any case, teachers do compare their wages to those of blue-collar workers; and many teacher unions have organized and mobilized their members for strikes by citing the higher earnings of blue-collar workers with less than high school educations.

17. Ideally, growth in teacher employment would be measured over the preceding year rather than over the preceding four years, but during the 1960s, data on the number of teachers employed were available only biennially. Furthermore, the unreliability of these data (as indicated by discrepancies between figures from the NEA and those from the U.S. Office of Education) made it difficult to obtain an accurate measure of changes over a two-year period because percentage changes in reported figures might reflect minor errors in the data more than actual changes in employment.

Therefore, *GROWTH* was measured over a period of four years so that actual changes would be relatively large compared to errors in the data.

18. Jack Stieber, *Public Employee Unionism* (Washington, D.C.: Brookings Institution, 1973), pp. 108–110.

19. Membership in public sector unions other than AFSCME might also be important, but data were not available on other unions. In any case, AFSCME represents far more noneducational state and local government employees than any other union. Thus, AFSCME membership is a reasonable proxy for the overall size of the NEA's and AFT's potential public sector allies.

20. F. Ray Marshall, *Labor in the South* (Cambridge, Mass.: Harvard University Press, 1967), pp. 319–320.

21. Daniel Gallagher, "Teacher Bargaining and School District Expenditure Levels," *Industrial Relations* 17, no. 2 (May 1978), pp. 231–237; and Stanley Benecki "Municipal Expenditure Levels and Collective Bargaining," *Industrial Relations* 17, no. 2 (May 1978), pp. 216–230.

22. *Chicago Division of Illinois Education Association v. Board of Education of City of Chicago*, (Ill. App. Ct. 1966) 222 N.E. 2d 243; *Commonwealth of Virginia v. County Board of Arlington County*, (Va. S. Ct 1977) 232 S.E. 2d 30.

23. In Florida, the state supreme court not only effected changes in case law but virtually compelled the state legislature to enact a collective bargaining statute. This action was based on the court's controversial interpretation of the "right-to-work" provision of the 1968 revision of the Florida constitution, which the court construed as granting public employees the right to bargain. See *Dade County Classroom Teachers Association v. the Legislature of the State of Florida*, 269 So. 2d 684 (Florida, 1972). The legislature enacted a bargaining statute two years later, when it appeared that their continued inaction might lead to a state supreme court edict establishing compulsory interest arbitration. See BNA *Government Employee Relations Report*, no. 551, April 22, 1974, pp. B12–14.

24. Ira Sharkansky, *Regionalism in American Politics* (Indianapolis: Bobbs-Merrill, 1970), pp. 3–4.

25. Values of the variables for each state were computed from data in the following sources: (1) *MALE, SCLSIZE, SYSSIZE,* and *GROWTH* from U.S. Office of Education, *Statistics of Public Elementary and Secondary Day Schools* (title varies) and NEA, *Estimates of School Statistics*; (2) *UNEMPL, INCOME, URBAN, #DEM,* and *%DEM* from *Statistical Abstract of the U.S.; (3) RLPAY* from *Estimates of School Statistics* and U.S. Bureau of Labor Statistics (BLS), *Employment and Earnings*; (4) *UNION* from BLS, *Directory of National Unions and Employee Associations,* and U.S. Bureau of the Census, *Current Population Reports*; (5) *COPE* from *Congressional Quarterly Weekly*; (6) *MERIT* from Council of State Governments, *Book of the States;* and (7) *AFSCME* from data obtained from Prof. Leo Troy of Rutgers University. Note that all fractions and rates (*MALE, GROWTH, UNEMPL, AFSCME, UNION, URBAN, MERIT, CB77, AFTFRAC, BFRAC, MFRAC, HIFRAC,* and *LOFRAC*) were expressed as decimal fractions ranging from 0.0 to 1.0. ΔCB was also expressed as a decimal fraction, although it had negative values in those cases where extent of bargaining declined (as in Virginia in 1977, when collective bargaining was banned by court order).

26. Growth of Teacher Contracts, 1966–1973," *NEA Negotiation Research Digest*, January 1974, pp. 15–16.

27. The Census of Governments tapes are based on questionnaires mailed to all state and local governments every five years (including 1977) and to a sample of state and local governments in other years. The questionnaires cover not only labor relations but also such topics as government finances. For a summary of the results for the labor relations questions and more information about the survey techniques, see U.S. Bureau of the Census, *Labor–Management Relations in State and Local Governments, 1977 Census of Governments* 3, no. 3 (Washington, D.C.: Government Printing Office, 1979).

I manually verified the Census of Governments data for about 1,000 cases (all school systems with instructional staffs, of 1,000 or more, and those systems in which the tapes for different years gave contradictory information) by checking printed tables published by the NEA and, in some cases, by telephoning the appropriate state and local affiliates of the AFT and the NEA. Based on these comparisons, the data from the Census of Governments tapes were corrected for about 300 cases.

28. Bargaining law categories 4, 5, and 6 (shown in table 2) were grouped together in the *MLAW* category to explain changes in the fraction of teachers covered by union contracts. In part, this grouping was needed because the dependent variable was limited. Most states enacted laws in stages, with the category 5 or 6 laws coming only after most teachers had made use of a category 4 law to win bargaining rights. In many cases, therefore, no further increases in bargaining coverage were possible when the category 5 or 6 law was enacted because bargaining coverage had already virtually reached the maximum limit of 100 percent.

A second reason for grouping the three categories was that the practitioners interviewed thought that the additional provisions of categories 5 and 6 (an administrative agency to enforce a prohibition of unfair labor practices, and either compulsory arbitration or the right to strike) had little independent effect on the number of teachers covered by union contracts. Of course, the administrative agency and the ULP ban could be much more important for organizing in an industry where management fights unionization; and even in public education, arbitration or the right to strike could significantly affect bargaining outcomes.

29. But where there is serial correlation in the error term, lagged endogenous variables are not predetermined and ordinary least squares estimates of the parameters will be inconsistent. [See Robert Pindyck and Daniel Rubinfeld, *Econometric Models and Economic Forecasts,* 2nd ed. (New York: McGraw-Hill, 1981), p. 193.] The appropriateness of OLS thus depends on the absence of serial correlation, but in a pooled cross-section/time series model such as that presented in equations 1 or 3, one might expect serial correlation between the error terms for a given state in successive years. Because the Durbin-Watson test for serial correlation was not designed for pooled cross-section/time series regressions, an alternative test had to be devised. For both equation 1 and equation 3, I regressed the residuals for 1962–1978 on the lagged residuals for the same state and tested for the significance of the relationship between them. The relationship between the residuals and the lagged residuals was statistically insignificant, suggesting that there was no serial correlation and that OLS was appropriate.

30. Before the data were pooled, two hypotheses were tested: first, that the intercepts were the same for all states, and second, that they were the same for all years. An *F*-test failed to reject these hypotheses at approximately the 5 percent level or better.

31. Estimation using the entire set of observations from 1960–1961 to 1977–1978 was also attempted, but this pooled cross-section/time series approach could not be used because of a severe problem of autocorrelation. This autocorrelation arose because unexplained jumps in bargaining coverage are perpetuated in subsequent years.

32. Unfortunately, data for two of the variables (*MALE* and *SCLSIZE*) are not available separately for all of the large school systems for the entire twenty-year period, so that it was not possible to exclude the large school systems from the sample and to estimate separate bargaining coverage regressions for the small and medium systems alone.

33. Arguably, *AFSCME* is an endogenous variable that depends on the same factors that influence the growth of bargaining. Therefore, since including the variable *AFSCME* might obscure the effects of the truly exogenous variables. Equation 1 was also estimated with the variable *AFSCME* deleted. Because the coefficients and t-ratios for the legal variables changed very little, the findings concerning the impact of legislation on the extent of bargaining stand. The results after deleting *AFSCME* indicate, however, that if *AFSCME* is endogenous, table 3 may have overstated the importance of *COPE* and understated the importance of *SCLSIZE* and *SYSSIZE*.

34. The teacher union breakthrough in New York City during the period 1960–1962 may be an exception. This organizing campaign was led by junior high and, to a lesser extent, high school teachers just at the time when the baby boom generation was hitting the secondary schools, giving secondary school teachers a strong labor market position.

35. Indeed, preliminary regressions showed that these variables were sometimes insignificant even at the 50 percent level. Following Draper and Smith, all variables that failed to meet that significance level for a particular equation were deleted before the final regressions were run. See N.R. Draper and H. Smith, *Applied Regression Analysis* (New York: Wiley, 1966), pp. 167–169. The variables *URBAN* and *RLPAY* were also deleted on these grounds, although these deletions should be less surprising. Many of the reasons urbanization was supposed to facilitate the spread of bargaining (large schools and school systems, strong unions, and high income) were controlled for by other variables. Similarly, the expected effect of high relative pay for teachers was hard to predict, even leaving aside the complications arising from the endogeneity of teacher earnings.

36. The bargaining categories in equation 4 are ordinal, not cardinal, so that a multinomial logit model or discriminant analysis would be more appropriate than ordinary least squares. Unfortunately, these more sophisticated approaches require the estimation of a separate set of parameters for all but one of the categories and there are too few observations to allow this. Therefore, equation 4 was estimated by ordinary least squares, with cardinality of the dependent variable simply assumed. (These are the results shown in table 5). Equation 4 was also estimated after the ordinal dependent variable was transformed to an interval variable by means of *z*-scores; results were very similar.

37. It also could be argued that the legal pattern variables, like *AFSCME*, are not truly exogenous and should be deleted from the models. When this was done, the signs of the coefficients remained the same. The coefficient of ΔCB_{t-1} remained modest, while that of CB_{t-1} remained negative, so that the conclusions concerning the effect of bargaining coverage on bargaining laws still stand.

The Politics of Interest Arbitration

*Thomas A. Kochan**

An amendment to Section 209 of the New York State Public Employees Fair Employment Act (commonly known as the Taylor Law) extending compulsory interest arbitration for police officers and firefighters until July 1, 1979, was signed into law by Governor Hugh Carey on June 7, 1977.

The amendment eliminated fact-finding; required a record of the hearing, if requested by the parties; and stipulated that the arbitration panel consider statutory criteria and specify the basis for its findings in interest arbitration cases. Judicial review of the award was also provided for in the amendment.

Three years before the passage of the amendment, Dr. Thomas A. Kochan of the New York State School of Industrial and Labor Relations at Cornell University began a study, sponsored by the National Science Foundation, to evaluate the relative merits of fact-finding and arbitration as dispute settlement techniques. The conclusions and recommendations of that study were presented to policymakers and union and management officials in New York State in December 1976 at a symposium organized by the New York State Public Employment Relations Board.

In the following months, the study became the focal point for debate among police and firefighter unions, public officials, and neutral groups over the pending legislation. Several parties relied on the report in an attempt to influence the final form of the amendment.

The following is an account of the events leading up to the passage of the legislation, in which the research study played a central role. The author describes the positions of the unions and such organizations as the New York Conference of Mayors and the New York State Public Employer Labor Relations Association, as well as of the New York State Public Employment Relations Board and the governor, in the debate.

This reading is part of a larger study, "Dispute Resolution under Fact-finding and Arbitration: An Empirical Evaluation," which was published by the American Arbitration Association in 1978.

When discussions began about the possibility of amending Section 209 of the New York State Public Employees Fair Employment Act, both the police and firefighter unions in New York State took the initial position that the

*Massachusetts Institute of Technology. Reprinted from *The Arbitration Journal* 33, no. 1 (March 1978), pp. 5–9.

arbitration statute should be extended for an additional experimental period without alterations. In a memorandum outlining its position, the New York State Fire Fighters Association presented four arguments in support of extension without modification.[1] First, the firefighters argued that there was a better chance of preserving labor peace with arbitration than without it. To support this position, they pointed to the report on interest arbitration that had been presented to them at the New York State Public Employment Relations Board Symposium in December 1976. They cited the finding in that report that no strikes had occurred under the arbitration statute, along with the more qualitative statement that strike pressures had been building up prior to the enactment of the arbitration amendment. Information that no firefighter strikes had occurred up to that time in thirteen states with binding arbitration, compared to a number of strikes in states without arbitration over the last three years, was also used to support this argument.

Second, the union cited the report's finding that there were no significant increases or decreases in the size of wage settlements due to the arbitration statute. Third, the firefighters pointed out that the research showed that 60 percent of the arbitration awards were unanimous and that, where arbitration broke down, it was mainly due to a lack of commitment on the part of city governments to collective bargaining and arbitration. Fourth, the union emphasized the finding that arbitration had no more of a chilling or a narcotic effect than there had been under procedures before the passage of the arbitration statute.

The positions of the police and firefighters were probably best summarized in the comments made at the PERB symposium by the presidents of the New York State Fire Fighters Association and the New York State Police Conference. Robert Gollnick of the firefighters said,

> We concur with the use of binding arbitration for one simple reason: it's a terminal point, something we've never had before, something we desperately need. . . . We're already meeting, selecting committees of the New York State Professional Fire Fighters, looking into select strike plans in the event the arbitration laws are not renewed. We're also going to be sitting down with our brothers in the Police Conference and maybe having a joint select committee in select cities for strikes in the event the arbitration laws are not renewed. It's our only alternative. Without arbitration we have to have the right to strike. If we don't have the right to strike we're going to violate the law and do it anyway.[2]

Similarly, Al Scaglione of the Police Conference summarized his organization's position as follows:

> . . . if you take away binding arbitration and do not give us the right to strike, let me tell you the leadership of our State organization, the leadership

of our locals, will not be able to contain their membership. There will be a revolt regardless of what direction the leadership goes. And the only thing that can keep peace is the continuance of binding arbitration.[3]

The New York Conference of Mayors

In contrast, the official position adopted by the New York Conference of Mayors was that the arbitration amendment should be allowed to expire. The Conference of Mayors also referred to the report and used many of its conclusions to support its arguments. For example, the conference's major comment on the report was that:

> While the findings [of the report] are notable, some recommendations are questionable. The major conclusion is that compulsory arbitration should be continued with some modifications. The Conference of Mayors does not agree. Nor do we believe that the study's findings sustain that conclusion.[4]

Like the New York State Fire Fighter Association's position paper, the Conference of Mayors' paper cited the report's conclusions regarding the lack of strikes under the arbitration statute and the comment in the report that the return to fact-finding might result in the eruption of pressures that were building up prior to the passage of the arbitration amendment. Unlike the firefighters, however, the Conference of Mayors noted the report's statement that the potential for work disruptions was based on a subjective interpretation of interview data which was not documented by any quantitative evidence. The conference concluded:

> In other words, the author acknowledges that his recommendations to continue the arbitration statute for police and firefighters cannot be documented by any statistical evidence. The people of this state would hope that the legislature would not make a judgment upon such a limited finding.[5]

In addition to the police and firefighters' unions and the Conference of Mayors, many other individuals and groups that used the report focused on this single finding and interpretation regarding the likely impact on labor peace of alternative procedures. This was perhaps one of the least significant findings of the research since, as the Conference of Mayors' paper pointed out, it was a subjective or qualitative interpretation of comments based on conversations with union and management representatives interviewed in the project rather than a fact based on quantitative evidence. Almost every group used this statement in the report to support whatever position it advocated. Those who were in favor of extending arbitration used it to argue that the arbitration statute in fact deterred strikes. Those who advocated going back to the fact-finding procedure used it to argue that there was no evidence one way or the other that the two procedures differed in their effectiveness as a strike deterrent.

The Conference of Mayors' paper went on to make seven other points in support of its position, most of which were either based on data contained in the report or were rebuttals or criticisms of the report's conclusions and recommendations. Specifically, the conference (1) questioned the importance of the finding that negotiated settlements were not significantly different from settlements achieved through arbitrated awards, (2) suggested that arbitration had not been effective as a dispute resolution procedure because the rate of impasses had increased, (3) argued that the lack of deviation between fact-finding recommendations and arbitration awards raises the question about the worth of arbitration "in light of the invasion of both home rule and authority of elected officials to establish budgets and set local real property taxes," (4) questioned whether the added costs of arbitration were worthwhile, given the fact that the report had found that there were no significant differences in wage settlements due to arbitration, (5) suggested that it was improper to take away the right of labor and management to say no in collective bargaining and turn this right over to generally inexperienced neutrals, (6) questioned whether the previous record under fact-finding was bad enough to warrant changing the statute, and (7) pointed to the lack of any analysis of the effects of police and fire arbitrated wage levels on the economic costs of other city employee settlements.[6]

New York State Public Employer Labor Relations Association

The most severe criticism of the report's recommendations was contained in the position paper prepared by the New York State Public Employer Labor Relations Association (NYSPELRA). Like the Conference of Mayors, this group advocated allowing the arbitration amendment to expire.

> Some observations were made [in the report] which NYSPELRA fully support. However, on the more substantive and crucial question of interest arbitration, we believe the study has some major deficiencies. . . . Despite the fact that the . . . study found a 13 to 18% increase in the number of impasses with the new procedure, [it] recommends continuing some form of arbitration. This type of reasoning (or lack thereof) is not, unfortunately, an isolated instance in the report.
>
> The report cites ineffective collective bargaining in some jurisdictions prior to the arbitration amendment and states that this ineffectiveness continued in these jurisdictions under arbitration. It then says that this problem can not be attributed to arbitration; it omits pointing out that it cannot be

attributed to fact-finding/legislative hearing either, and provides no evidence that it can be. Yet, [the report] says that returning to fact-finding/legislative hearing appears to be inadvisable. There is absolutely no concrete evidence anywhere in the report to substantiate that opinion.[7]

The group went on to take issue with a number of other conclusions contained in the report. Again, it focused on the paragraph discussing strikes. It also disagreed with the conclusion that there was not a greater chilling effect under the arbitration statute than had been present under fact-finding. It relied on its own experiences to substantiate its claim.

The members of NYSPELRA work "in the trenches" daily. We have had to work within the impasse procedures. That experience had led us to the inevitable conclusion that binding arbitration has been a deterrent to good faith collective bargaining rather than an encouragement to it.

We believe that the arbitration process has not only had a chilling effect upon bargaining, but that chilling effect has in many instances spilled over into the bargaining with other units who have said there is no point in settling (bargaining) until their brothers in police and/or fire get their arbitration award. . . . For these reasons, we strongly urge PERB to recommend that the 1974 amendment relating to binding interest arbitration be allowed to expire with the consequent restoration of a fair, consistent, impasse procedure which recognizes and honors the democratic system within which that procedure must take place and which is an encouragement to collective bargaining rather than a deterrent.[8]

The Governor's Proposal

The director of the Office of Employee Relations for the State of New York, Donald Wollett, outlined the position of the governor at the PERB Symposium. His recommendation was to maintain the tripartite arbitration system with one very fundamental change. The arbitration decision would only be binding on the union, while the legislative body in the municipality would have the option of reviewing the arbitration decision and either approving or rejecting it. The position developed by the governor's representative was based partly on a general philosophical opposition to interest arbitration and partly in response to the dilemma identified in the report due to the role of judicial review of tripartite arbitration decisions. For example, at the PERB symposium Wollett said that

Three or four weeks ago I was in Chicago for a meeting sponsored by the American Bar Association on public sector labor relations. And there was a good deal of talk about binding interest arbitration, which is the focus of this conference. And one of the experts, a law professor from the University of

Wisconsin, described people who do not have any doubts, serious doubt, about the constitutional legitimacy and the political wisdom of binding arbitration as "thoughtful, enlightened, and emancipated." And I suppose that means that people who do have those doubts are "thoughtless, unenlightened, and unemancipated." So I want to identify for you at the outset where I'm coming from: I'm a member of that "thoughtless, unenlightened, and unemancipated" group, because I do have serious doubts about the constitutional legitimacy and, more importantly, the wisdom of binding arbitration, whether it involves the uniformed services or whether it involves other kinds of occupational groups in the public sector.[9]

Wollett went on to comment on a number of the report's research findings. His principal focus was on the discussion of the problems a court has in judging the reasonableness of an arbitration award arrived at through negotiation in a tripartite arbitration panel. While he indicated that he had no objections to the mediation-negotiation-arbitration process that was identified as being common to this statute, he agreed that courts not only would have a difficult time reviewing these decisions, but went one step further by arguing that since these arbitration decisions are essentially political decisions, the courts should not be reviewing them. Instead, he felt that the appropriate body to review political decisions was the legislative body in the community.

PERB's Recommendation

After the symposium was completed, the New York State PERB also made public its recommendations on the statute. Following considerable debate by the three members of the PERB board, the board unanimously recommended continuation of the arbitration statute without modification. The following quote from PERB's recommendation summarizes the reasons underlying its position:

1. The three year experiment was really more limited than the passage of three years would imply. The first year was largely used in litigation of the constitutionality question and the cut off date for the [study] was about a year before the experiment's scheduled expiration date of June 30, 1977. In addition, the time during which the experiment took place occurred in one of the most difficult periods of New York State financial history—a period when voluntary settlement was most difficult and any dispute resolution system would have been severely tested. This was not a good time for any kind of experiment with a new system.

2. In spite of a few difficult situations in controversial awards: a. The system provided finality of resolution; b. The arbitration wage awards were, generally speaking, in line with negotiated settlements. In fact, the wage

awards averaged about one and one-half percent less than the negotiated agreements; c. Although there were three minor instances of slow down, there were no police or fire work stoppages; d. Judicial review, albeit limited, has been declared to be available.

3. The experiment should be permitted to continue for a longer period in order to provide a more representative experience base.[10]

The Legislative Process

After each of the above groups formulated its initial positions, the governor introduced a bill to implement his proposal for revising the arbitration statute. The police and firefighters, in turn, introduced a bill into the legislature that called for continuation of the statute without modification. These bills were referred to various committees. No public hearings, however, were held on either. Instead, the various interest groups began an intensive lobbying campaign with individual members of the state legislature. Meanwhile, additional summaries of the report were furnished to members of the legislature and their staffs. Several months before the June 30, 1977, expiration date, intensive negotiations began between representatives of the governor's office and several key legislative leaders after it became clear to the legislators and to the governor that the police and firefighters had sufficient votes in both houses of the legislature to pass their bill providing an extention of the arbitration amendment without modifications.

The governor, however, was still publicly committed to vetoing an extension and was still advocating his proposed revisions. After several meetings between representatives of the governor and legislative leaders, a compromise bill emerged. This bill provided for continuation of the arbitration statute for two years, eliminated fact-finding as an intermediate step in the impasse procedure, provided that the parties share the costs of arbitration, and added a statement to the section dealing with the criteria for arbitration decisions that required the arbitrators to consider not only comparability of wages, but also the level of such fringe benefits as health insurance, leave policies, pensions, and holidays. The proposed bill also tightened the language on how these criteria were to be used by replacing the phrase "arbitrators may consider the following criteria" with language indicating that arbitrators "shall" consider these criteria. Furthermore, the initial compromise stipulated that the decisions of the State Court of Appeals on judicial review of the arbitration statute would be considered to be the appropriate scope of judicial review under the new amendment. Finally, this compromise bill required that a transcript of arbitration proceedings be kept and required the neutral arbitrators to appear in court if the award was subjected to judicial review.

This compromise proved to be unacceptable to several parties. The major objections came from PERB. Specifically, PERB objected to having the neutral arbitrator appear in court to defend his or her award under judicial review. Therefore, this draft proposal was further amended by dropping the requirement for a transcript and the provision providing for arbitrators to appear in court. This compromise bill was then introduced into the legislature and was passed by an overwhelming margin in both houses.

After the bill was passed by the legislature, but before the governor had signed it into law, the New York State Court of Appeals, the highest court in the state, issued a decision that upheld an arbitration award rendered in the case involving the City of Buffalo and the Buffalo police.[11]

This award had been overturned by a lower court in the state and thus the court of appeals reversed the lower court's decision. In its decision, the court of appeals made the statement that even though it felt that the legislation was less than well conceived, the court could not find evidence in the record presented to it that the decision did not have a substantial basis in the record or was arbitrary or capricious. Therefore, even though it was clear from the language used in the decision that the court felt that, given the economic problems of the city of Buffalo, the arbitration award was too high, it had no recourse but to uphold the award. This decision caused the governor to have some last-minute reservations about signing the bill. After considerable additional pressure was applied by the police and firefighter unions, however, the governor signed the bill into law. It called for a two-year extension, with modifications in the language on the decision criteria, the elimination of fact-finding, and cost sharing by the parties.[12]

In the message accompanying his signature, the governor made the following comments to indicate the reasons why he signed the bill. Essentially, the intent of these comments was to provide some legislative history for future consideration in interpreting the intent of the arbitration amendments.

> In my Annual Message to the Legislature, I proposed the enactment of legislation subjecting these arbitration determinations to legislative review, in order to assure appropriate political accountability. Legislation to require such review was included in my Budget Bill dealing generally with public employee labor relations (S.1337/A.1637). That bill did not receive favorable consideration by the Legislature.
>
> This bill before me is the product of discussions between Donald H. Wollett, Director of Employee Relations, and the Legislative Leaders, the purpose of which was to consider alternatives to the mere extension of existing provisions of law, in the absence of some requirement that arbitration determinations be subject to meaningful judicial, if not legislative, review.
>
> This bill tightens the standards and procedures in the compulsory arbitration process, so that the review of arbitration determinations by the courts henceforth will be meaningful.

Just yesterday, the Court of Appeals, in *City of Buffalo v. Rinaldo,* noted two defects in the present law. According to the Court: "The source of judicial power to review findings . . . is not to be found in the statute which itself is completely silent on the matter, but rather in the requirements of due process."

The Court also stated: "The statute, the wisdom of which it is for others to decide, vests broad authority in the arbitration panel to determine municipal fiscal priorities within existing revenues [and to] determine that a particular increase in compensation should take precedence over other calls on existing or even diminishing municipal revenues."

The bill before me corrects both of these defects.

First, the standard for judicial review that was developed by the Court of Appeals in the case of *Caso v. Coffey,* i.e., that the arbitrators' awards "are to be measured according to whether they are rational or arbitrary and capricious" remains unchanged. However, the source of judicial power to review arbitral findings and arbitral awards no longer generates solely from the requirements of due process; the statute itself now requires judicial review.

Second, the question of whether the arbitrators' work was rational or arbitrary and capricious is to be answered in terms of how well they carried out the statutory mandate to consider, among other things, the financial ability of the public employer and the comparative levels of compensation (including fringe and retirement benefits) currently enjoyed by the employee affected, and, where the statutory criteria point in different directions, to specify the basis for choosing one over the other.

These changes impart to the Courts the wisdom of the Legislature that judicial review must be strengthened so that it operates as an effective safeguard against arbitral abuses. This bill is intended to narrow the expansive authority accorded to arbitrators by the Court of Appeals in *City of Buffalo v. Rinaldo* and to make it clear that arbitrators must make findings with respect to each statutory criterion which the parties put in issue, that each such finding must have an evidentiary basis in the record, and that the arbitrators must specify in their final determination what weight was given to each finding and why.

I am aware of the concern of local government officials, many of whom have expressed opposition to *any* extension of compulsory arbitration, that compulsory arbitration may operate so as to place unreasonable financial burdens on local governments. Legislative review of arbitration determinations would, I believe, directly address that concern.

I am persuaded, however, that the enactment of this bill constitutes an improvement in the statutory provisions for compulsory arbitration. I am not convinced that a statutory structure such as the Taylor Law, which envisions a collective bargaining system for public employees, should mandate compulsory arbitration. For that reason, and in light of the fact that this bill provides for additional experimentation for just two years. I expect that there will be a continuation study of how the system actually works, so that we will have as complete a picture as possible before 1979 when we will again be faced with the decision of whether to continue, modify, or eliminate the experimental arbitration procedures.[13]

Impact of the Research

Did this research have a significant impact on the legislative debate and its final outcome? Readers will have to draw their own conclusions. It is clear, however, that the research did stimulate and focus the debate over the statute around the report's findings, conclusions, and recommendations. In the final analysis, however, it was the political power of the police and firefighters that provided the votes needed to insure that some form of arbitration would be extended. Once the political balance of power was clarified, the negotiations among the critical parties revolved around the question of what shape the arbitration procedures would take. It was at this point that the report's recommendations had their greatest substantive impact on the future of the law.

Overall, the most accurate assessment of the short-run effects of the report was that each interested party felt compelled to rationalize its public position on the policy issue in terms of the findings of this research. Either the parties used findings that were favorable to their position to document support for their views or they challenged the findings and conclusions and recommendations of the study where their position differed from those contained in the report. Thus, this research did not change any of the positions of the interest groups in any significant way. Rather, the interest groups used the research to support positions that reflected their philosophical and partisan viewpoints.

Almost all the attention given to the report during the legislative debate focused on specific conclusions and recommendations concerning the effects of the change from fact-finding to arbitration and on the changes that the report advocated in the arbitration procedure. Very little attention was given to the latter half of the report in which there was a discussion of the longer run deterioration in the performance of collective bargaining since the passage of the Taylor Act. In many respects, these longer run findings were more important than were specific findings regarding the marginal effects of the change from fact-finding to arbitration. It remains to be seen whether some of the longer run concerns raised in the report are given any attention in the future.

Notes

1. "Memorandum in Support of Extending Compulsory Arbitration for Fire and Police" (unpublished document, no date). See also *The Proceedings of the Sym-*

posium on Police and Firefighter Arbitration in New York State, December 1–3, 1976 (Albany: New York State Public Employment Relations Board, 1976), pp. 29–32.

2. *Symposium Proceedings,* pp. 29–30.

3. *Symposium Proceedings,* p. 41.

4. New York Conference of Mayors and Municipal Officials,"Position Paper—Compulsory Arbitration," March 1977 (unpublished document), p. 1.

5. Ibid., p. 2.

6. Ibid., pp. 2–6.

7. *Symposium Proceedings,* pp. 221–222.

8. *Symposium Proceedings,* pp. 223–224.

9. *Symposium Proceedings,* p. 129.

10. *Symposium Proceedings,* p. 213.

11. *City of Buffalo v. Rinaldo,* No. 414, New York Court of Appeals, June 6, 1977.

12. Senate Bill S-5859 and Assembly Bill A-8466, signed June 7, 1977.

13. "Memorandum filed with Senate Bill No. 5859-A." Governor Hugh Carey, State of New York Executive Chamber, June 7, 1977, pp. 1–2.

The Political Context

As Kochan's reading in the last section illustrates, politics plays a crucial role in public sector bargaining because public employers are typically governmental units whose decisions are ultimately shaped by political forces. Similarly, David Truman has demonstrated that political interest group access is the predominant mode of influence in the decision-making processes of government.[1] According to Truman, an interest group, in order to have an impact on government decisions, must develop political access to key decision makers and then use that access effectively. These realities of the political process suggest that public sector bargaining is inherently political.

Although scholars have generally accepted Truman's premises, some have grown concerned about their implications for public sector bargaining. The issue arises of whether public employee unionism is compatible with democracy. In other words, concern exists that public employee unions could become stronger than any countervailing interest groups and thus able to impose their will regarding wages, benefits, and the like on the government and the public. This concern, however, has been presented primarily through theoretical and philosophical arguments. Wellington and Winter, Robert Summers, and Clyde Summers, among other scholars, have used such arguments to raise objections to public employee collective bargaining. In the first reading of this section, Cohen takes issue with these arguments. Cohen does not conclude that public employee unionism and bargaining necessarily reduce a preexisting democratic condition or retard a potential rise in the level of democracy. He cautions that, in the absence of public employee bargaining, the governmental decision-making process does not necessarily operate according to a pure democratic ideal. There are a variety of possible distortions of this process, as reflected in one-party dominance, low voter turnout in elections, and the superior position of power that one or another interest group may occupy in the political process. Further, he observes that the evidence from the late 1970s demonstrates that public officials and various interest groups are effectively able to counter the demands and ostensible dominance of public employee unions. From this perspective, the rise of organized public employees and the spread of collective bargaining in the public sector may indeed be countervailed by the public will, as expressed through political channels. Therefore, Cohen contends, unionized public workers do not pose as substantial a threat to political democracy as others have claimed.

The evidence of time is also on Cohen's side in this argument. Casting theory and philosophy aside, the fact is that about two-thirds of the states have enacted bargaining laws covering some public sector group, that only a few bargaining laws have ever been declared unconstitutional by state courts, and that legislatures have in no case rescinded a bargaining law that was passed at an earlier time. It is doubtful that this situation would exist if public employee bargaining permitted unions to dominate other interest groups in the political process, partly because less than 20 percent of the work force is unionized. Further, collective bargaining has not caused widespread municipal bankruptcies, nor have strikes (legal and illegal) by public employees led to mayhem across the United States. As a result, bargaining has become an accepted practice.

At the same time, considerable evidence exists that public sector bargaining is multilateral. That is, the organization of government, with various levels of elected officials (executives and legislators) and appointed administrators, provides unions with multiple access points during negotiations. Unions have used this lack of a unified management organizational structure to achieve bargaining gains.[2] This underscores an inherent conflict that exists between the two highly valued goals of (1) developing an efficient bilateral negotiations process in which management acts as a unified team and the union applies pressure through formal negotiations and (2) maintaining multiple points of access required for an effective democratic decision-making process. This conflict poses a dilemma in public sector bargaining and lies at the heart of most discussions of the role of politics in bargaining

The presence of this conflict, however, does not ensure bargaining outcomes that are favorable to unions. It has often simply been assumed that unions use political action to augment their bargaining activities, and that the political action succeeds. The second reading in this section illustrates that such assumptions are not always true. Masters's paper about the political action (and, to a lesser extent, the bargaining activities) of federal employee unions reveals some interesting facts. Despite a limited scope of bargaining, which leaves many crucial workplace decisions to the discretion of Congress—a situation that calls for enhanced political action—the three unions studied by Masters emphasized bargaining activities. Notwithstanding that emphasis, their success at the bargaining table was quite limited, overshadowed only by their complete lack of success in the political arena. For various reasons, including limited bargaining rights, the nature of congressional politics, and the national issues arising in Washington, D.C., federal employee unions have not grown disproportionately powerful. In fact, they are relatively weak.

Other public sector unions have achieved greater political and bargaining success at the state and local levels. Yet, unions have not come to dominate other groups in the political process. The study of federal employee unions, in fact, illustrates the ability of other organized interest groups to oppose union positions successfully. Even though unions may achieve particular political and bargaining successes at one or more points in time, they also suffer defeats at other points in time. Thus, although public sector bargaining involves a substantial political element, the political process has never guaranteed any person or group continual success.

Notes

1. David Truman, *The Government Process: Political Interests and Public Opinion* (New York: Knopf, 1955).
2. See Thomas A. Kochan, "A Theory of Multilateral Collective Bargaining in City Governments," *Industrial and Labor Relations Review* 27, no. 4 (July 1974), pp. 525–542; Thomas A. Kochan, "City Government Bargaining: A Path Analysis," *Industrial Relations* 14, no. 1 (February 1975), pp. 90–101.

Does Public Employee Unionism Diminish Democracy?

*Sanford Cohen**

Current pessimistic evaluations of public sector unionism are reminiscent of the earlier criticisms of private sector unionism, bluntly summarized in Lindblom's assertion that unions were destroying the competitive price system.[1]

*University of New Mexico. Reprinted from *Industrial and Labor Relations Review* 32, no. 2 (January 1979), pp. 189–195.

The ensuing debate over the economic impact of private sector unions produced no obvious consensus at the time, but many students of the subject were apparently satisfied with a rebuttal that posited the impossibility of showing that unionism was responsible for a diminution of price competition in a market already far removed from the competitive model. Judging from the journal literature, however, one now senses a general acceptance of the proposition that there is some incompatibility between collective wage determination and a condition of continuing price stability: union wage policy may not have destroyed the competitive price system, but it certainly is viewed as being troublesome.

Contemporary criticism of public sector unions is focused more on their political than their economic consequences, the general thesis being that a private power center operating inside the government skews the results of the normal political process and thereby diminishes democracy. These criticisms have caused some unease among students of industrial relations who, by and large, had not previously questioned the wisdom of the spread of collective bargaining to the public sector. When those criticisms are carefully examined, however, I believe one must conclude that, as in the earlier controversy over private sector unionism, today's critics of public sector unionism have a point but there is something more to be said. This comment represents an effort to suggest the character of the "something more."

The Criticisms

In the literature considering the consequences of unionism, it is possible to identify two distinct analytical traditions. One, along the approaches of such scholars as Selig Perlman and Frank Tannenbaum, examines the philosophy, psychology, and broad goals of union members and leaders to determine where a particular union movement should be placed along a spectrum of ideologies.[2] The other, with roots that reach back at least to Henry Simons, is preoccupied with the labor market behavior of union organizations and, on the basis of that behavior, decides whether unions contribute to or interfere with a proper functioning of markets.[3]

With only slight modification, that description can apply to the contemporary contention over the consequences of public sector unions. On the one hand, those unions can be analyzed in terms of a broad family of variables that shed light on where the unions might be placed on some prodemocracy–antidemocracy scale. On the other hand, the analysis might be limited to the question of whether the quantum of power that now rests with public sector unions changes the preunion distribution of power to the extent that certain public decision-making processes (especially those at local levels of government) are less democratic than heretofore.

The differentiation suggested here is significant in that conclusions about the consequences of unionism are obviously conditioned by the selection of an analytical approach. The more prominent attacks on public sector unions fall into the second of the two analytical traditions, and it is important to note at the outset the limited perspective of that analysis and to express a caution concerning policy inferences drawn from that perspective. In the private sector, for example, one might conclude from a purely economic analysis that union wage behavior has contributed to price inflation and, consequently, that union bargaining power should be limited by appropriate policy measures. A more comprehensive analysis might suggest, however, that on balance, labor organizations have been stabilizing institutions in an era of considerable social instability. Although the latter conclusion does not directly rebut the former, it does suggest an important consideration for policymakers, who should consider the full consequences of their determinations.

The most cogent of the arguments that question the compatibility of public sector bargaining and the democratic process are those by Wellington and Winter and by Summers.[4] Following Dahl,[5] Wellington and Winter describe the normal American political process as one with a high probability that an active, legitimate group can effectively make itself heard at some crucial stage in the process of decision making. They conclude that public sector unions, able to combine the power to withhold labor with the usual methods of political pressure, possess a disproportionate share of effective power in the decision-making process and thus "skew the results of the 'normal' political process."[6] This conclusion is derived from a series of propositions:

1. Citizen consumers, faced with a public employee strike, are likely to be seriously inconvenienced given the absence of any substitute for most government services;

2. The citizenry, consequently, will place enormous pressure upon a mayor for a strike settlement.

3. Under these circumstances, it is difficult if not impossible for a mayor to give weight to the longer run fiscal implications of union demands.

4. The mayor will, then, defer to the general pressure for a settlement, a politically safe course since "few citizens can decipher a municipal budget or trace the relationship between today's labor settlement and next year's increase in the mill rate."[7] Furthermore, the cost of a settlement may be borne by a constituency—the state or nation—much larger than that represented by the mayor.

5. Given these considerations, the union's fear of a long strike, which is the major check on union power in the private sector, is not a factor in the public sector.

On the basis of the scenario traced here, Wellington and Winter conclude that the political process had been radically altered and that interest groups with priorities different from those of unions are apt to be less successful in their pursuit of government revenues than are the unions with power to interrupt services.

Summers also concludes that "public sector employee bargaining is, on balance, probably not good for society, and especially not good in a field such as public school education. . . ."[8] But while the general thrust of his contention is similar to that of Wellington and Winter, his position rests less on the assumption of union strength derived from the strike or the threat to strike. The mere existence of public employee bargaining is sufficient proof of a diminution of democracy for Summers, because such bargaining requires the sharing of public authority with private bodies.[9] This is particularly true when public sector bargaining occurs pursuant to statute, since public employing bodies are then obliged by law to share decisional authority with entities not subject to the control of or accountable to the public for the positions they take.[10] Thus, Summers contends, even when the outcomes under bargaining do not differ significantly from those reached in the absence of bargaining, there is an adverse impact on the democratic process, which is intended to afford opportunities for "process values" such as public participation as well as for public control of decisional processes. Insofar as bargaining short circuits, blocks off, or diminishes public participation, it limits the realization of process values.[11]

While Wellington and Winter and Summers do not explicitly exclude federal level collective bargaining from their analyses, their references to the federal area are sparse and apparently they are not seriously exercised about what occurs at that level. In fact, the federal model would seem to answer the larger portion of their objections to public employee bargaining. The strong proscription of strikes, the delimitation of the negotiable issues, and the final authority of the government to determine disputes over negotiability reduce the scope of bargaining in the federal sector to boundaries compatible with what Wellington and Winter and Summers would recommend.[12] Given those limits on bargaining in the federal service and the prevailing processes of decision making within the federal bureaucracy, it would be difficult to argue that collective bargaining for federal employees has had a significant effect on democratic processes, and the writers under review here do not do so.

It is more difficult to explain the absence in their works of direct references to state employees, for a number of the points made about local bargaining would appear to apply at the state level. One can only speculate about this gap, but clearly it is the public employee strike these writers find most objectionable, and perhaps the relative rarity of strikes by state employees accounts for their preoccupation with bargaining in local government.

Wellington and Winter further limit their analysis by distinguishing between strikes over monetary issues and those involving nonmonetary matters, and they describe their analysis as valid for the former but not necessarily for the latter. They maintain that in disputes over nonmonetary issues, intense concern on the part of well-organized interest groups opposed to a union would buttress a mayor in his resistance to union demands; yet, even in this situation, when rank and file back their union leadership, pressures for a settlement from the general public would, in time, become irresistible.

Summers does not make the monetary–nonmonetary distinction. His analysis is focused on the public schools, in which nonmonetary personnel issues are actually most likely to touch sensitive policy questions: class size, preparation periods, tenure, and teaching loads, for example, are matters of both working conditions and educational policy. Furthermore, although not monetary subjects in the sense of having a direct relationship to wages and fringe benefits, such issues usually have significant cost implications.

Vulnerable Assumptions

Conclusions about the relationship between collective bargaining by public employees and the condition of democracy generally rest upon assumptions about the nature of union power, public attitudes, and the behavior of public officials in impasse situations. The validity of the conclusions expressed obviously depends on the accuracy of the assumptions made. Considering first the issue of union power, we may ask whether unions operating in the public sector are, in fact, the power juggernauts described by Wellington and Winter and Summers. To the extent that they have overstated the case, their arguments lose force.[13]

These writers admit that public employee unions do not always win their strikes or achieve all their demands. Yet, the reasons for the union failures are not clear from their arguments. If, like their private sector counterparts, public sector unions win some and lose some, there must exist some limits on their power that are not identified in the analyses summarized earlier. In short, the Wellington-Winter and Summers arguments per se are unable to accommodate the experience of union defeat or retreat or, more generally, any instance of unions settling for less than what they would prefer. As examples of union defeats in the public sector accumulate, the picture of these unions as an irresistible force becomes flawed and the logic of an inherent inconsistency between public sector bargaining and the expression of public preferences through democratic processes becomes less persuasive. The Wellington-Winter position is especially vulnerable on this score since one is not led inevitably to the conclusion that the political process has been skewed when one finds that there *are* mayors concerned more about future budget integrity than current labor peace.

Although relatively recent in vintage, the Wellington-Winter and Sum-

mers arguments are oddly archaic in tone, perhaps because they present paradigms that were more relevant during the heady times of the 1960s and early
1970s than they are today. There have now been several examples of public
officials in major metropolitan centers—New York, Seattle, San Francisco,
and Atlanta, for example—standing firm against what they considered excessive union demands. Adding to these the numerous examples of industrial
relations confrontations in smaller communities with results that do not confirm the Wellington-Winter and Summers hypotheses on union power, we
find a variegated pattern of union power, which is not easily summarized in
simple expressions of union dominance.[14]

According to the Wellington-Winter model, the public is concerned
exclusively with a restoration of interrupted services regardless of settlement
cost. Summers sees the public more as a blackmail victim with no choice but
to pay up when essential services are cut off by work stoppages. Similarly,
both analyses represent public officers as inevitably buckling under to union
power plays on the basis of their reading of public preferences.

The Wellington-Winter and Summers assumptions are defensible in
describing a particular period in the history of public sector unionism,
although even for that period they may have neglected some important considerations. On the basis of more recent history, however, the longer run
validity of their assumptions must be questioned.

During the large-scale emergence of municipal employee unionism in the
1960s, illegal strikes were frequent, essential services were interrupted with
unpleasant consequences for the public, and many of the settlements reached
were fiscally unsound. The unions—at least some of them—appeared to have
acquired a type of power that did indeed skew the results of the normal political process. But can these experiences from the formative period of a new
system of municipal industrial relations be extrapolated as a continuing
pattern? If not, current conclusions about the long-run impact of public
employee unions on the democratic process become conjectural.

Historically, union thrusts into new territory (industrial, geographical,
or occupational) have been attended by conflict manifested through strikes
and general disorder. Thus, some of the disruption that occurred can
be attributed to the normal turmoil of a new union penetration. However,
this turmoil touched the public more directly than does the typical labor–
management impasse. Unaccustomed to seeing garbage pile up, the schools
closed, and uniformed officers on picket lines, the public understandably
pressured its elected officials to deal effectively with what it perceived as
emergencies—in other words, to settle the strike. Concurrent with much of
the rise of the public employee unions, furthermore, the state of the economy
facilitated such settlements in that municipalities and school districts enjoyed,
or at least thought they enjoyed, some play in their budgets.

The situation has changed, of course. Almost everywhere, local governments are in financial straits, the public is much less likely to panic in the face of service interruptions, and public officials are less reluctant to take tough bargaining stances than they were only a few years ago. Public and official reaction to a particular union action, consequently, is less predictable than Wellington and Winter suggest, and the ultimate effect of public employee bargaining on democracy is less discernible.

The Summers Model

On the basis of the general tenor of his arguments, the response Summers would likely make to the considerations expressed above can be anticipated: the fact that unions in the public sector do not always prevail is not significant. So long as private groups not accountable to the public share in decisional authority, democracy has been diminished.

In so arguing, Summers assumes a clear-cut dichotomy between democratic procedures before and after the onset of collective bargaining. Prior to collective bargaining, public employing bodies are considered broadly democratic; when bargaining begins, this condition is diminished.

The situation, of course, is not as neat as this and Summers admits as much when he notes that "in prebargaining days, local, state and federal bureaucracies were sometimes unresponsive to the public will, and in some law-making processes at some of these levels, powerful interest groups frequently had (and continue to have) disproportionate say."[15] In such circumstances, however, Summers argues that the remedy is not to create still more powerful interest groups such as unions to diminish democracy even further.

The argument at this point, however, has taken a subtle turn. It is one thing to contend that public employee unions have diminished a preexisting democratic condition and another to presume that they inhibit a potential rise in the level of democracy in situations where the democratic will is otherwise stifled. In the case of unionization of employees within an insensitive bureaucracy, the appearance of a union does not necessarily make the unresponsive bureaucracy more unresponsive. What it necessarily does, according to Summers, is to diminish the possibility for improvement by piling a new layer of insensitivity to public interest on top of an existing one.

This conclusion requires the assumption that unionization of a group of employees affects no variables in an institutional power structure other than that of employee power. It is not difficult, however, to conceive of situations in which an organizing process breaks the bureaucratic shield so as to enlarge the possibilities to general public influence.[16] In such cases, unionization will have improved the democratic condition. Summers's error on this point is that of treating possibilities as certainties.

It is clear, however, that the main concern of Summers is with those situations in which a union enters a public institution that is sensitive to and affected by close and frequent public contact. His model is public education, which he visualizes as reflecting the public will through various types of public participation in decision making and frequent elections of school board members. In his vision, the unionization of teachers reduces democracy in the schools by limiting the reach of the general public voice.

To the extent that democracy is measured by its conformity to the populistic model described by Summers, public employee bargaining does indeed limit democracy since such bargaining inevitably will determine some matters outside the arena subject to direct and immediate public influence. The validity of Summers's conclusions, however, depends upon the realism of both his model and his concept of democracy. If either can be tenably questioned, his conclusions must be adjudged to be possibilities rather than inevitable results.

First, a question of fact. In the typical school district, is there a flourishing townhall democracy that monitors and controls the operations of the schools in a significant way? Summers provides no supporting evidence on this point and contrary evidence exists: school board meetings, although tumultuous on occasion, ordinarily play to empty halls. In addition, the 7 percent voter turnout in the 1977 New York City community school board elections does not bespeak a vigorous grass-roots democracy in a city afflicted with severe problems in public education. Although 7 percent may be a low turnout for this type of election, the percentages achieved elsewhere are not impressive.[17]

Even if we assume an active citizenry at the school district level, is it not necessary to acknowledge the constraints on their influence from sources other than unions? Consider, for example, the role of the state legislature in local school finance and the towering influence of the colleges of education in determining what is taught and how it is taught. The political condition modified by the appearance of unionism is more complex than Summers's model suggests.

Waiving these considerations, we are left with the fundamental question of how to determine whether a specific institutional change—the unionization of public employees—has affected the democratic process so as to make it less democratic. If, as Summers presumes, union–management negotiations preempt the exercise of effective public influence on significant matters of public policy, there should be little objection to his conclusions. It is necessary to ask, however, following Dahl's formulation, whether collective bargaining in public agencies reduces the probability that active and legitimate groups can make themselves effectively heard at some crucial stage in the decision-making process.[18] Clearly, public employee bargaining may force changes in the processes through which nonunion groups express themselves, and the direct town-hall type of participation that Summers sees in the area of public education may have suffered from the advent of public employee unions. Democracy is diminished, however, only if alternative avenues for effective influence by nonunion groups are not available. Since alternative avenues for political action obviously are available,[19] the residual question goes to the matter of their effectiveness, leading us full circle to the Wellington-Winter argument of why public sector bargaining diminishes democracy—not because the general public is unable to express itself politically, but because unions in that sector possess a disproportionate share of political influence.

Conclusions

Experience will provide the ultimate test of the Wellington-Winter hypothesis. The record to date, however, while not conclusive, provides some basis for challenging their position. Writing in a popular magazine that has not been unfriendly to public sector unions, one observer concludes: "For the past few years . . . the challenge for the public employee unions has been to cope with a backlash against their continued success and public be damned attitudes. . . . In many . . . cities, municipal unions have been settling for little or no increase in wages and benefits. In some localities, an antiunion stance has measurably enhanced the popularity of politicians."[20]

In short, the public has been expressing itself on the matter of public sector unions in ways Wellington and Winter and Summers would approve, and it appears to be doing so effectively. If it is the public will, expressed through one political channel or another, that ultimately determines how much and in what ways public sector bargaining affects the general processes of democracy, the problem presented by such scholars as Wellington and Winter and Summers need not be especially worrisome.

Notes

1. Charles E. Lindblom, *Unions and Capitalism* (New Haven: Yale University Press, 1949), p. 4.

2. Selig Perlman, *A Theory of the Labor Movement* (New York: Augustus M. Kelly, 1949), and Frank Tannenbaum, *The Labor Movement: Its Conservative Functions and Social Consequences* (New York: G.P. Putnam's Sons, 1921).

3. Henry Simons, *Economic Policy for a Free Society* (Chicago: University of Chicago Press, 1948), chap. 6.

4. Harry H. Wellington and Ralph K. Winter, "The Limits of Collective Bargaining in Public Employment," *Yale Law Journal* 78, no. 7 (June 1969), pp. 1123–1127; Wellington and Winter, *The Unions and the Cities* (Washington, D.C.: Brookings Institution, 1971); and Robert S. Summers, *Collective Bargaining and Public Benefit Conferral: A Jurisprudential Critique* (Ithaca, N.Y.: Institute of Public Employment, New York State School of Industrial and Labor Relations, 1976.

Given the volume of literature on the politics of public employee bargaining, it is surprising that so little meets the arguments of Wellington-Winter and of Summers head on. The lack of response to Summers's thesis is especially surprising in view of the uncompromising character of his attack against public sector bargaining. Studies that raise doubts about the significance of the union impact on public sector wages, though not directed explicitly at Wellington and Winter or at Summers, can be interpreted as a challenge to their conclusions about the power of unions in that sector. Such studies, however, do not deal directly with the question that clearly preoccupies Wellington-Winter and Summers: the question of the power of unions to prevail in their contests with public employers. In any event, public sector wage impact studies present an inconclusive picture. See David Lewin, "Public Sector Labor Relations: A Review Essay," in Lewin, Peter Feuille, and Thomas A. Kochan, eds., *Public Sector Labor Relations: Analysis and Readings* (Glen Ridge, N.J.: Thomas Horton and Daughters, 1977), p. 375.

Although there are many references in the literature to a possible collision between public sector bargaining and democratic processes, very few writers appear to be exercised about the possibility. In his essay, "Public Employee Bargaining: A Political Perspective," Clyde Summers, for example, admits that collective bargaining in the public sector "constitutes something of a derogation from traditional democratic principles" (Lewin, Feuille, and Kochan, *Public Sector Labor Relations,* p. 49). Nevertheless, he concludes that basic characteristics of public employment justify a specially structured political process such as collective bargaining for making certain government decisions.

The explicit issues of whether public sector collective bargaining diminishes democracy can—Wellington-Winter and Summers would say "should"—be examined independently of questions about the economic impact and general desirability of public sector unionism.

5. Robert A. Dahl, *A Preface to Democratic Theory* (Chicago: University of Chicago Press, 1956), p. 145.

6. Wellington and Winter, "The Limits of Collective Bargaining," p. 1123.

7. Ibid., p. 1125.

8. Summers, *Collective Bargaining,* p. xi.

9. Ibid., p. 4.

10. Ibid.

11. Ibid., p. 7.

12. "Labor–Management Relations in the Federal Service," Executive Order 11491, as amended, 1975.

13. Although Summers does not base his case primarily on the power of unions to interrupt services, the union-led strike is by no means insignificant in his analysis. His monograph is laced, for example, with references to the "extraordinary leverage" of the union (p. 47), which has and knows it has the public "over a barrel" (p. 7). For Wellington and Winter, union power expressed through the strike is important in a critical way given their assumptions of the behavior of municipal officers in the face of a strike or strike threat.

14. A 1976 police strike in Las Cruces, New Mexico, for example, is noteworthy in that the strike, which ended disastrously for the union, was followed shortly thereafter by an unsuccessful union effort to influence the outcome of a municipal election. The point, of course, is that unions operating both within and outside of the government may be ineffectual in both locations. See Sanford Cohen and Christian

Eaby, "The Beginnings of Public Employee Unionism in New Mexico," unpublished manuscript (available on request).

15. Summers, *Collective Bargaining,* p. 2.

16. My point here is that the organizing process is something of a public event which exposes a bureaucracy to general view, with the possible result that it appears to be more within the reach of public pressures for basic changes. In a way, Wellington and Winter suggest this in their conclusions about the generation of pressure on a mayor in the course of a work stoppage. If such pressure is as irresistible as Wellington and Winter suggest, why would it not be effective when applied for other purposes?

17. *New York Times,* June 5, 1977, Section IV, p. 6. Comprehensive studies of voter participation in school board elections are rare. All writers who refer to the matter, however, state that the turnout is usually low. See, for example, Frederick Wirt and Michael Kirst, *The Political Web of American Schools* (Waltham, Mass.: Little, Brown, 1972), p. 63; Thomas Eliot, *Governing America, The Politics of a Free People* (New York: Dodd, Mead, 1946), p. 895; Thomas Dye, *Politics in States and Communities* (Englewood Cliffs, N.J.: Prentice-Hall, 1973), p. 438. Dye, who makes reference to "that small band of voters who turn out for school board elections," estimates that, on the average, less than one-third of the eligible voters bother to cast ballots in school elections.

18. Dahl, *A Preface to Democratic Theory,* p. 145.

19. Such avenues would include direct appeal to the appropriate political and administrative officials, expressions of preference through referenda on tax levies, support of antiunion candidates in school board and other elections, lobbying at budget hearings in the state legislature, and appeal through the media for support of particular positions. Summers, incidentally, appears to have given no consideration to the possibility that, in a particular union–public–management impasse, public sympathy might be with the union, and that the impasse could open possibilities for a democratic expression of grass-roots opinion that might not otherwise exist. This, of course, has occurred. See Robert U. Anderson et al., "Support Your Local Police—On Strike?" *Journal of Police Science and Administration* 4, no. 1 (March 1976), pp. 1–8.

20. Roger M. Williams, "The Clamor over Municipal Unions, *"Saturday Review,* March 5, 1977, p. 14.

Federal Employee Unions and Political Action

Marick F. Masters[*]

Unions have long engaged in political action to attain their objectives. Political action by unions has been viewed as particularly important to unions in the public sector, however, because elected officials are *employers* as well

[*]University of Pittsburgh. Reprinted from *Industrial and Labor Relations Review* 38, no. 4 (July 1985), pp. 612–628.

as *regulators* of the body politic.[1] Especially at the federal level, elected officials have maintained extensive control as employers, thereby causing political decision making to be a keen concern of federal employees.

Researchers investigating public sector labor relations have often spoken of the ripe incentive this employment relationship creates for the political action of public employee unions generally, and federal unions especially. Recent studies conclude that through organized political action, public sector unions, particularly at the federal level, have used the political process to reap economic rents. But despite the widespread recognition of these unions' interest in political decision making, few studies have directly examined the political activities and influence of federal employee unions.

The purpose of this reading is to narrow this research gap by examining the political activities and legislative records of the three largest nonpostal unions representing federal employees: the American Federation of Government Employees (AFGE), the National Federation of Federal Employees (NFFE), and the National Treasury Employees Union (NTEU).[2] Although postal unions appear to be quite active politically, they are excluded from this study because they operate under a statutory framework that permits bargaining over wages and most other conditions of employment.

This study is intended to focus on unions that operate in the white- and blue-collar sectors of the federal government in which collective bargaining is relatively circumscribed and the incentive for political action is therefore presumed high. The principal research issues are the extent to which these unions have engaged in various political activities and the degree of their success in achieving their legislative objectives. Data were obtained from various public records, union periodicals, and interviews with key union lobbyists and congressional staff members.

Background and Issues

Since the early 1960s, unionism has grown considerably at all levels of government and has continually aroused controversy among policymakers and scholars alike. Wellington and Winter triggered much of the contemporary scholarly debate over the potential economic and political clout of public sector unions.[3] Focusing mainly on local and state governments, they argued that the full transplant of labor relations policy from the private to the public sector would result in these unions gaining excessive power vis-à-vis their employer. More specifically, they theorized that the relative lack of economic market constraints on public budgeting, coupled with the politically unsettling consequences of strikes by public employees, makes it comparatively easy for public sector unions to exercise economic and political leverage. Although several studies have challenged the assertion that unions are stronger in the public sector than in the private, at least one recent study has lent some empirical support to the Wellington and Winter thesis[4]. Thus, the debate over this controversial thesis remains unresolved.

By denying employees the right to strike, to bargain over wages and other economic conditions, and to negotiate union security arrangements, labor relations policy in the federal government has been cited as "compatible with what Wellington and Winter . . . would recommend" in order to prevent public sector unions from acquiring undue power.[5] Perhaps for this reason, few studies have systematically examined federal sector labor relations, although numerous observers have noted that these unions have limited bargaining power.[6]

In the political arena, on the other hand, federal employee unions have not been viewed as weak. They have allegedly been quite active in politics because of the considerable authority over major employment matters maintained by elected congressional and executive officials.[7]

In fact, recent studies have concluded that these unions have successfully skewed the distribution of federal resources in their favor largely because of their organized political strength. For example, extending the wage determination study by Smith,[8] Bellante and Long find that federal employees receive substantial economic rents in the form of higher wages and fringe benefits because of certain institutional political processes, including union political action. From a public choice theoretical perspective, they argue that politicians behave as vote maximizers and thus engage continually in coalition building to increase their chances of reelection. Because public employees are often an important part of political coalitions, elected officials appeal to these potential voters by offering various economic benefits such as wages above the market level.

Politicians may incur political costs as a result, for example, by raising taxes to pay for these economic rents, but those costs are supposedly mitigated because the cost of taxes is distributed over many voters in contrast to the concentrated benefits being extended to public employees. Furthermore, the public's awareness of the connection between these benefits and their taxes may be minimal, thus sheltering politicians from voter retaliation.[9] The basis for this "strong union" thesis at the federal level is evidence of organized political action. Public employees' ability to take advantage of the vote-maximizing behavior of politicians, of the diffused tax system, and of voter ignorance "is increased by the kinds of political activities engaged in by public employee unions and associations."[10]

Arguing from assumptions similar to these, Bennett and Dilorenzo conclude that "a substantial amount of the resources of public employee unions are devoted to political activities" and that public employees therefore "earn sizable rents, especially at the federal level."[11] More specifically, they aver that through various political activities, including lobbying, the AFGE and

NFFE have blocked the contracting out of services, such as ship repair, from the federal sector to presumably more efficient private firms.[12]

Unfortunately, the studies just cited that investigate the potential political power of federal employee unions inadequately address three important issues. First, what kinds of political activities do federal sector unions undertake? Second, to what extent do they engage in these activities? Several researchers have assumed that these unions engage extensively in a host of orchestrated political actions, but few, if any, have empirically documented this assumption.[13] Third, how successful are federal unions in the legislative arena? Which of their attempts to influence legislation have met success and which have failed?

Data

As noted earlier, the unions examined in this analysis are the AFGE, NFFE, and NTEU—the unions that have represented the largest number of employees in the General Schedule (GS) and Wage Grade (WG) systems of the federal government since 1976.[14] The AFGE represented 695,984 employees in 1980; the NFFE, 136,312 employees; and the NTEU, 108,364.[15] Altogether, the three represented over 75 percent of the nearly 1.25 million GS and WG employees belonging to exclusively recognized units. Nonetheless, given the lack of compulsory membership clauses in the federal sector, the membership of these unions fell far short of these representational totals.

This study focuses on the 1977–1981 period, for two reasons. First, information on political action undertaken before that time is scarce. Many of the union personnel interviewed had no union experience before 1977, and some in fact were employed by their union for only part of this period. Second, many observers at the time viewed the 1977–1980 period as an era of growing union power.[16] In 1977 Jimmy Carter assumed the presidency with an overwhelmingly Democratic Congress. Organized labor in general was confident about its political future and initially anticipated the opportunity to obtain many long-desired legislative goals, such as labor law reform. The Carter years thus provide a unique opportunity to examine unions' political activity at a time when they could expect a favorable return from their efforts. The year 1981 is also included in the study because union lobbyists had indicated to the author that several important legislative developments occurred in that year and that those developments were the result of political trends begun during the Carter years.

Data were obtained from various sources. Qualitative data on the range of the unions' political pursuits were obtained from union periodicals and from interviews with key union political personnel. Seven professional union lobbyists (that is, full-time lobbyists who are appointed rather than elected to their jobs), among others, were interviewed on this issue in November 1981: three at AFGE; three at NTEU; and one at NFFE. The interviews were conducted at the unions' Washington, D.C., headquarters in a semistructured format and lasted ninety minutes, on average.

Unfortunately, quantitative data on most of the unions' political activities are unavailable. The unions do not itemize or publish their expenditures on most political activities, such as political education or voter registration drives, nor do they categorize their internal finances along broad functional lines to define such efforts as legislative or political ones. It is therefore difficult to determine the unions' total commitment of resources to political purposes. There are sufficient quantitative data from two government sources, however, to make inferences about general resource commitments. The Federal Election Commission's so-called D Indexes for the 1977–1978 and 1979–1980 election cycles contain information on labor political action committee (PAC) contributions to the campaigns of candidates for federal office. From those indexes, one can determine the extent to which federal unions have pursued the increasingly influential tactic of campaign financing. Union PAC contributions in general more than doubled between 1974 and 1980, and federal employee unions participated in that development to varying degrees.

The unions' LM-2 financial disclosure reports filed with the U.S. Department of Labor provide the other source of quantifiable data. In these reports, unions are required to itemize the disbursements (salaries and expenses) made to union employees who earn $10,000 or more annually. The AFGE's and NFFE's disclosures also itemize the employees' occupations, thus allowing calculations of their financial commitment to political personnel. The NTEU does not itemize by occupation, but through interviews, plus information in the *Washington Representatives 1982: Who Does What for Whom in the Nation's Capital,* I was able to identify NTEU's political personnel and thereby calculate its personnel commitment as of roughly 1980.[17]

Data on the unions' legislative achievements were collected from two sources. The unions' legislative scoreboards, which report the votes of legislators on selected issues, were examined for the period studied. These scoreboards, typically published in the union's national magazines shortly before general elections, offer a quantitative measure of unions' support for specific legislation. But because they ignore the qualitative differences among issues, they can yield misleading results. This study also focuses, therefore, on three legislative issues that union interviewees and union periodicals identified as particularly important to all three unions: the Federal Service Labor–Management Relations statute (Title VII of the 1978 Civil Service Reform Act); pay comparability decisions; and the 1981 Omnibus Budget Reconciliation Act. All of these had had far-reaching consequences for the unions studied and for most federal employees. The first defined the legal rights and responsibilities of the unions as bargaining agents in the federal sector. Annual pay comparability decisions affect the pay levels of roughly 1.6 million GS employees. Finally, the 1981 Budget Act set pay levels for GS and WG employees and also altered the retirement benefits for federal retirees.

The principal sources of information employed to investigate these three issues were union periodicals, and interviews with union political staff. The seven union lobbyists interviewed in 1981 were interviewed again in April 1982 regarding those issues that were within their lobbying experience or expertise. In particular, they were asked to identify their unions' legislative goals during 1977–1981 and to discuss the action Congress eventually took on each issue. Also, four staff members of the Committee on Post Office and Civil Service of the House of Representatives were interviewed in that same month to shed further light on the unions' legislative record.[18]

Empirical Evidence

Strategies and Tactics

In terms of the kinds of political activities they pursue, the AFGE, NFFE, and NTEU behave similarly to organized labor as a whole, engaging in activities designed to influence "public policy—rather than party politics per se."[19] Broadly speaking, they have taken two paths to influence public policy: electoral activities and lobbying. More specifically, they attempt to influence the outcome of federal elections, mainly congressional elections; and they lobby to influence more directly the actions of officials, once elected.

To achieve their electoral goals, the federal unions have engaged in three broad strategies: assisting candidates, educating union members and the general public, and mobilizing voters. To assist candidates, they have issued endorsements, made financial campaign contributions, and arranged for special communications between office seekers and voters. To inform potential voters about candidates and issues, the unions have resorted to a number of devices. They have communicated extensively on electoral events through written forums, especially their national magazines. The AFGE and NTEU have also established grass-roots legislative-political committees; the NFFE has established local legislative liaisons. These committees form a network through which electoral and other information is exchanged between the union member and the national offices. Further, the AFGE and NTEU in particular have held numerous local and regional political workshops. And each of the unions has installed telephone hotlines to better inform their members.

Finally, the unions have encouraged voter registration and get-out-the-vote drives. It is difficult to determine the extent of these unions' commitment to such drives, largely because they are undertaken at the local level where data are hard to collect. In addition, it should be noted that the effective use of voter mobilization drives by these unions may be hindered by the 1939 Hatch Act—a complicated piece of legislation that essentially denies federal employees the right to participate in a number of partisan political activities, including partisan voter registration and get-out-the-vote drives. Although it is unclear whether the act applies to federal employee unions as well as to their individual members, the unions have undoubtedly acquired and exercised the de facto right to engage in certain partisan activities, such as endorsing Democratic candidates and contributing money through PACs to Democratic candidates.[20] On the other hand, because federal employees as individuals are clearly forbidden by the act to participate in partisan voter mobilization efforts, their unions are deprived of an important means to influence elections. Moreover, because the Hatch Act is very difficult to interpret, it creates much uncertainty in the minds of federal employees over what is a legally permissible political activity.[21] This uncertainty may discourage some federal employees from participating in nonpartisan voter mobilization activities that are actually permissible under the act.

The unions studied here pursue three basic strategies to influence elected officials in their deliberations. Information regarding the unions' preferences is continuously channeled to these officials through a variety of means, including testimony and constituent visits. Also, union leaders try to arouse the members' interest in important legislative debates through the same forums as those used for electoral purposes. Their ultimate goal is for their members to pressure elected officials through letter-writing campaigns and organized demonstrations, among other activities. The third strategic approach to lobbying, forming interunion networks, or coalitions, dovetails with the other two with the objective being to coordinate educational efforts or pressure tactics. In 1978, for example, the three unions joined a twenty-six group coalition, the Fund for an Assured Independent Retirement, to resist legislation that would reduce federal retirees' benefits. More commonly, the unions form ad hoc lobbying arrangements among themselves or with other groups to support or oppose pending legislation of mutual concern.

Resource Commitments

The Federal Election Campaign Act (FECA) of 1971, as amended, permits labor organizations (as well as other organizations and groups, such as corporations) to form political action committees to raise money for campaign financing. The Hatch Act of 1939, it should be noted, does not prohibit federal employee unions from forming PACs. Under the FECA, unions may not contribute members' dues money to candidates for federal office, but they may raise money voluntarily from their members for so-called "segregated funds," or PACs.[22] This PAC money may in turn be contributed to federal candidates within certain limits. Although, as noted earlier, campaign financing is not the only electoral activity engaged in by federal unions, it is used in this analysis as a proxy for all electoral resource commitments, since quantitative data are generally unavailable on the other types of electoral behavior.

Federal Election Commission records on congressional campaign contributions, which are complete for the 1977–1978 and 1979–1980 election cycles, reveal that the AFGE and NFFE contributed to congressional campaigns in both cycles. Somewhat surprisingly, the NTEU did not make PAC contributions in 1977–1978; its National Executive Board did not decide to form a PAC until 1979. The AFGE and NFFE contributed $91,666 and $2,975, respectively, to congressional candidates in 1977–1978. In 1979–1980, the AFGE, NFFE, and NTEU contributed $140,905, $23,550, and $94,325, respectively.

These data therefore show that of the three unions, the AFGE has made the greatest use of campaign contributions as a strategy, but it is difficult to conclude whether these figures represent a comparatively large or small commitment. For this analysis, these unions' contributions were compared to the contributions of all labor organizations funding PACs.[23] In terms of total dollars contributed, the AFGE ranked twenty-fifth (of 71 unions) and twenty-second (of 81 unions) in the 1977–1978 and 1979–1980 cycles, respectively.[24] The NFFE ranked sixty-first in 1977–1978 and forty-eighth in 1979–1980. The NTEU ranked twenty-seventh in 1979–1980.

Because those rankings are influenced by the variation in size of the unions funding PACs, a per-member PAC contribution was also calculated for each union with a PAC in both cycles. A calculation made using union membership data from the *Directory of National Unions and Employee Associations, 1977* (and 1979) and using interviews with union staff showed that the AFGE's per-member contribution (PMC) was 35 cents and 53 cents for the respective cycles; the NFFE's was 6 cents and 46 cents respectively; and the NTEU's figure was at $1.35 for 1979–1980. In comparison to other unions, the AFGE's PMC was exceeded by 25 other unions in 1977–1978 and by 23 other unions (excluding the NTEU) in 1979–1980. The NFFE's was exceeded by 58 (excluding the AFGE) and 27 other unions (excluding the AFGE and NTEU) in the respective cycles.

Also, although the NTEU ranked ninth in 1979–1980, its PMC of $1.35 in that year was much lower than that of the leading union—the Marine Engineers Beneficial Association. With a membership of 32,000, MEBA donated $32 per member in 1979–1980. The Air Line Pilots Association, with a membership of 68,000, attained a PMC of over $4 in that cycle. In short, whether measured by aggregate or per-member PAC contributions, these three unions have committed relatively limited resources to congressional campaigns.

For the AFGE, NFFE, and NTEU to lobby Congress continuously and organize grass-roots political efforts, they need sizable legislative-political staff at the national office.[25] The extent to which they employ such a staff is a function of both their internal finances and their priorities. The occupational breakdowns provided in the AFGE's and NFFE's financial-disclosure reports illustrate the unions' functional priorities. Table 1 shows that the two largest occupational groups reported by the AFGE in fiscal years 1977–1980 were national representatives and labor relations professionals, such as contract specialists, labor–management advisors, and organizing specialists.[26] The AFGE's professional political staff is relatively small. The table also demonstrates similar priorities at the NFFE. Its two largest occupational groups were national representatives and legal professionals. In fact, the NFFE did not employ a full-time legislative director until 1979.

The limited resources devoted to political professionals is further evidenced by the proportionate expenditures to these employees. Proportionate expenditures to AFGE's and NFFE's political professionals were paltry, never having exceeded 5 percent of gross disbursements in the four years.

As noted earlier, the NTEU does not itemize the occupations of its staff. But data obtained from the *Washington Representatives 1982* directory[27] and interviews with union staff revealed the amount of resources the union devoted to full-time political professionals in its 1980 fiscal year (October 1, 1979 to September 30, 1980). In that year, the NTEU employed six full-time professionals (three full-time lobbyists, two legislative liaisons, and a PAC director), who together received 13 percent of the NTEU's itemized personnel disbursements. Interviewees indicated that the largest personnel group at the NTEU was the forty-person legal staff, whose function was to serve the bargaining and contract administration needs of the NTEU's members. It was emphasized that providing such labor relations service had long been the NTEU's top priority.

At this point, two cautionary notes about the personnel data are appropriate. First, despite the fact that they show the union's relative commitment of personnel to political and labor relations service, the data undeniably understate the unions' political resource commitments. In each union, several nonpolitical staff members assist the political staffs when needed. For instance, the NTEU's general counsel plays a role in drafting technical legislation the union may be promoting before Congress. In addition, the unions' top national officers also participate; lobbyists at each union indicated that their union presidents were intimately involved in key political actions. Furthermore, the unions may also combine their lobbying resources with those of other organizations. The AFGE in particular receives assistance from its affiliation with the AFL-CIO, which frequently offers lobbying aid.

Second, although the data suggest that staff at these federal unions function primarily as labor relations rather than political agents, they do not permit a broad comparison of the unions' personnel commitment. Without a

Table 1
Professional Political Employees of Two Federal Unions

Fiscal Year[a]	Union	Two Largest Occupational Groups (Excluding Secretarial)[b]	Professional Political Employees[c]	Gross Expenditure to Itemized Employees (in millions)	Percentage of Gross Personnel Expenditures to Itemized Political Employees[d]
1977	AFGE	National Reps. (81), Labor Relations/Personnel (22)	3	$4.9	1.9
1977	NFFE	National Reps. (10), Legal (4)	1	.6	2.5
1978	AFGE	National Reps. (79), Labor Relations/Personnel (26)	5	5.7	2.7
1978	NFFE	National Reps. (28), Legal (4)	1	1.1	1.4
1979	AFGE	National Reps. (76), Labor Relations/Personnel (28)	5	5.8	3.1
1979	NFFE	National Reps. (20), Legal (4)	1	1.0	1.5
1980	AFGE	National Reps. (75), Labor Relations/Personnel (29)	7	6.3	3.3
1980[e]	NFFE	National Reps. (16), Legal (5)	2	1.0	4.6

Source: Union LM-2 financial-disclosure reports filed annually at the U.S. Department of Labor. For more comprehensive information on the unions' overall personnel resources over a longer period of time, see Marick F. Masters, "Federal-Employee Unions: Bargaining or Political Agents?" *Journal of Collective Negotiations in the Public Sector* 13, no. 3 (1984), pp. 191–202.

[a] AFGE's fiscal year corresponds with the calendar year. The NFFE's fiscal year runs from July 1 to June 30. Thus, NFFE's 1980 fiscal year extended into 1981.

[b] The numbers in parentheses refer to the number of employees itemized in each occupational group.

[c] Employees who are full-time, nonelected, legislative experts and PAC directors.

[d] It should be noted that when the salaries of secretaries were excluded from the total personnel disbursements, these percentages did not change much. In fact, the percentage of expenditures to political professionals never exceeded 3.8 percent for the AFGE (excluding secretarial salaries); and it never exceeded 4.7 percent for the NFFE (excluding secretarial salaries).

[e] It should be added that the NFFE had not increased its legislative political staff as of April 1982, but the AFGE added one lobbyist in 1981.

major interunion examination of political personnel, it is difficult to conclude whether the unions' lobbying staffs are relatively large or small. In the early 1980s, for example, the United Steelworkers employed seven registered lobbyists,[28] and the Washington-based Political Affairs Division of the National Education Association (NEA) employed five professional staff members.[29] But much of the NEA's lobbying is done at the state and local levels. Any comparison of union lobbying efforts that is based solely on the number of Washington-located political professionals must be made with caution. Future research should obviously be directed toward a comprehensive interunion study on lobbying. Nonetheless, based simply on the absolute sizes of political staff, it is possible to conclude that the federal unions studied here have committed limited resources to developing political influence. As one NFFE lobbyist said, it is difficult for a legislative staff of two to pursue more than a few of the many important federal employee issues before the Congress at any particular time.

Legislative Record

The extent to which federal unions received favorable congressional treatment during the years 1977–1981 is extremely difficult to measure. Congress deals with a multitude of issues important to these unions, and the unions' stated legislative objectives reflect this scope.[30] Further, in the rough-and-tumble of Capitol Hill, no legislative outcome is necessarily interpretable in positive or negative terms. Nonetheless, one way to establish a quantitative measure of the unions' legislative record is by examining their legislative scoreboards. These scoreboards, which are published in union periodicals, present the "right" or "wrong" votes cast by legislators on selected issues. The scoreboards also chart whether the union's policy positions were adopted on these congressional roll calls.

The AFGE published scoreboards for 1977, 1978, 1979–1980, and 1981; the NTEU, for 1977–1978 and 1979–1980; and NFFE for 1979–1980 (it did not begin to publish those records until it employed a full-time legislative director). As shown in table 2, the results generally indicate a strong measure of congressional support before 1981, with the House and Senate accepting union positions in most cases and with high percentages of voting support evident in most scoreboards, especially those in the House.

These results are misleading for several reasons, however. Many of the so-called right votes were cast on matters only marginally acceptable to the unions. For example, the NTEU recorded as right votes against a proposal to delete the federal labor statute from the 1978 Civil Service Reform Act. But the NTEU at the same time was adamantly opposed to many of the key provisions in the statute. Also, the scoreboards do not weight the issues

Table 2
The Legislative Scoreboard Records of Three Federal Unions, 1977–1981

Congress	Union	Recorded House and Senate Victories[a]		Percentage of Favorable Votes Cast in House and Senate Roll Calls	
		House	Senate	House	Senate
95th Congress[b] (1977)	AFGE	8–1 (6)	5–2 (4)	61	57
(1978)	AFGE	8–2 (6)	3–6 (5)	53	48
(1977–1978)	NTEU	5–1 (0)	— —	66	—
(1977–1978)	NFFE	— —	— —	—	—
96th Congress (1979–1980)	AFGE	5–2 (4)	5–4 (6)	55	51
(1979–1980)	NTEU	4–1 (2)	5–1 (2)	69	58
(1979–1980)	NFFE	4–2 (1)	4–2 (3)	49	59
97th (1981)	AFGE	0–9 (7)	2–3 (2)	44	52

Sources: Congress Union periodicals. The AFGE published its scoreboards in *The Government Standard;* the NTEU, in *The Bulletin;* and the NFFE, in *The Federal Employee.*

[a]The numbers in parentheses in these two columns are the number of nonfederal employee issues (and issues broader than strictly federal employee concerns) included in the scoreboards. For example, the first entry in parentheses under House votes indicates that six of the nine votes concerned issues broader than or separate from strictly federal employee issues.

[b]The AFGE published separate scoreboards for the 1st and 2nd sessions (1977 and 1978), respectively, of the 95th Congress.

selected for scoring in terms of lobbying priorities, and they ignore legislative decisions at the committee level. Often, the unions experience their greatest setbacks in committee. In 1978, for example, the House Post Office and Civil Service Committee rejected a union-supported agency shop provision that was part of the proposed labor relations act for the federal sector.

Furthermore, several issues on which votes are cast are not strictly federal employee issues and interest a wide range of other groups. For example, many of the votes identified in table 2 touched on broad socioeconomic issues, such as appropriations for OSHA, the Equal Rights Amendment, and labor law reform. It is obviously very difficult to tie the outcomes of these legislative issues to federal employee union political preferences and activities.

It should therefore come as no surprise to learn that although these quantitative data present a generally favorable legislative record, they run counter to the qualitative assessment of union lobbyists and officials. Most lobbyists and officials of the federal employee unions have complained—in private and in public—that their legislative fortunes dwindled throughout the 1977–1981 period on issues of major economic and organizational import. The 1981 congressional testimony of AFGE's president, Kenneth Blaylock, exemplifies this sentiment:

> I don't think federal workers have ever faced a more troubled period than we face today. I travel all over this country talking with federal workers, and each day brings additional evidence that gains made by workers over the past 20 years are being rolled back.[31]

The reason for this frustration can be found by analyzing the outcomes of the legislative debates over Title VII of the 1978 Civil Service Reform Act, pay comparability decisions for federal employees made under the 1970 Federal Pay Comparability Act, and the 1981 Omnibus Budget Reconciliation Act. These outcomes affected the rights or benefits, or both, of most federal employees, and hence the legislative debates were the target of as intensive lobbying by these three unions as they could muster. Although these debates were too complex and lengthy to be treated fully here, a brief comparison between the unions' stated preferences, obtained from congressional records and interviews, and the legislative outcomes presents a strong case against the theory that these unions consistently achieve their political goals on bread-and-butter issues.

It is important to note that, beginning with the Title VII debate, these unions had long sought not only a statutory basis for collective bargaining in the federal service, but a statutory basis to their liking. Before the implementation of Title VII in 1979, federal labor relations operated under a highly restrictive Executive Order arrangement,[32] according to which unions were denied many of the major rights (such as to negotiate wages) extended to the private sector. Employees were permitted, however, to organize and negotiate over selected personnel matters. The unions' objective in 1978 was to replace this executive system with a more flexible statutory one.

Although the three unions failed to agree upon a unified lobbying strategy, they all focused on reform in four areas: scope of bargaining; union security; dispute resolution; and labor relations administration (see table 3). The NTEU proposed the most sweeping changes, proposing a vastly broadened scope of bargaining, an optional strike provision, a mandatory agency shop, and an independent federal labor board. The AFGE and NFFE, although ideologically sympathetic to these proposals, scaled down their recommendations for practical political reasons. In essence, they sought the best changes that would arouse the least opposition. But, as table 3 reveals, the unions' provisions, except those pertaining to administration, were generally rejected by Congress, which essentially codified the preexisting executive order. Hence, on those matters that would have entailed a significant redistribution of power, the unions' preferences were defeated. Although an independent Federal Labor Relations Authority was created and the unions achieved success in some other less significant aspects of Title VII, the thrust of federal labor policy on this subject was essentially unchanged.

The evidence on federal pay comparability decisions presents an even more disappointing situation from a union standpoint. The 1970 Federal Pay Comparability Act requires that the pay of GS employees be comparable to the pay of private sector workers.[33] To achieve this objective, the law requires that a *presidentially* appointed pay agent recommend to the president pay comparability adjustments on an annual basis. In forming these recommendations, the agent is to consider the views of a five-union Federal Employee Pay Council (FEPC). If the agent's proposed adjustments are accepted by the president, they may be implemented without congressional approval; however, the act permits presidents to submit alternative recommendations in cases of "national emergency or economic conditions affecting the general welfare." These so-called alternative plans may be vetoed by either body of Congress.

Although the 1970 Comparability Act was intended partly to reduce the politics associated with such pay decisions in the past, politics have nonetheless intruded into the process. The rule rather than the exception has been for presidents to submit alternative plans postponing or reducing the pay agent's recommendations. During the 1977–1981 period, Presidents Carter and Reagan recommended pay increases substantially below their agents' recommendations on four of five occasions (see table 4). And despite the intensive lobbying efforts of federal unions, Congress did not veto these adjustments. In fact, the unions were so angered that they jointly resigned from the FEPC in 1978. In that year, in an effort to control spending and inflation, President Carter had stated that he would propose a 5.5 percent pay hike regardless of the agent's recommendations.[34]

Table 3
Union Lobbying Priorities and Congressional Outcomes Concerning the Federal Service Labor–Management Relations Statute

Issue	Provisions of the Executive Order	Union Preferences for Provisions to Replace Executive Order			Provisions Adopted by Congress
		NTEU Preferences	AFGE Preferences	NFFE Preferences	
Scope of bargaining	Negotiations permitted over personnel policies and practices, excluding pay and other benefits, and governmentwide regulations. Also, a management rights clause forbade bargaining over the direction, assignment, and discipline of employees.	No management rights clause. Negotiable terms and conditions to include "pay practices, fringe benefits . . . work procedures, job classifications . . . assignments . . . , union security . . . ."	No management rights clause. Negotiable terms and conditions to include "pay practices, work hours and schedules; overtime practices, safety; promotion . . . seniority . . . ."	No management rights clause. Everything negotiable except statutes, governmentwide regulations, and controlling agreements at a higher agency level.	Management rights clause retained. Bargaining precluded over pay practices, other benefits, and governmentwide regulations.
Union security	All forms of union security arrangements are impermissible.	Mandatory agency shop for all employees in exclusively recognized bargaining units.	Mandatory agency shop for all employees in exclusively recognized units.	Fair representation fee elections in which employees would vote on whether they wanted a mandatory fee assessment for all members of a bargaining unit.	All forms of union security barred.
Impasse resolution	Strikes prohibited. Binding arbitration allowed if both parties agree and Federal Service Impasses Panel (FSIP) agrees.	Optional strike provisions. Unions would have to choose between making a fact finder's recommendation final or advisory. If the former, unions would	It is an unfair labor practice for a labor organization "to call or engage in any illegal strike."a Parties may agree, without FSIP approval, to binding arbitration.	Strikes illegal. Union officials allowed unlimited "official time" to negotiate in lieu of a strike, thereby creating an incentive to management to bargain in good faith.	Strikes illegal. FSIP must approve binding arbitration. "Official time" restraints lifted.

	be barred from striking even if they disagreed with the recommendations. If the latter, they could strike if they were unwilling to accept the recommendations.				
Administrative structure	Federal Labor Relations Council (FLRC)—made up of the secretary of labor, the director of the Office of Management and Budget, and the chairman of the Civil Service Commission—had a policy guidance role. The assistant secretary of labor (ASOL) for labor–management relations had authority over such matters as unit determination and certification elections.	Three-member, independent Federal Employee Relations Board to absorb functions of FLRC and ASOL.	Three-member, independent Federal Labor Relations Authority (FLRA) to absorb functions of FLRC and ASOL.	Three-member, independent FLRA to absorb functions of FLRC and ASOL.	Independent, three-member FLRA created with authority previously lodged in FLRC and ASOL.

Note: Information on the unions' lobbying priorities and preferences was obtained from interviews and congressional testimony in the cases of the AFGE and the NTEU. The NFFE lobbyist who was interviewed was not employed by NFFE at the time of the Title VII debates; therefore, NFFE's preferences were obtained from congressional testimony and union periodicals. The specific provisions preferred by the unions were discussed fully in U.S. Congress, House, Committee on Post Office and Civil Service, Subcommittee on Civil Service, *Hearings on Improved Labor–Management Relations in the Federal Service*, 95th Cong., 1st sess., April 21, 26, May 3, 10, 1977.

[a] One might thus presume that there was such a thing as a legal strike. In his legislative testimony, however, AFGE President Kenneth Blaylock stated that other statutes prohibit federal employees from striking. See U.S. Congress, House, Committee on Post Office and Civil Service, Subcommittee on Civil Service, *Hearings on Improved Labor–Management Relations in the Federal Service*, 95th Cong., 1st sess., April 21, 1977, p. 37.

Table 4
Presidential and Congressional Action under the Federal Pay Comparability Process, 1977–1981

Year	Pay Agent's Pay Increase Recommendations	President's Alternative Pay Recommendations	Congressional Action on President's Plan
1977	7.0%	—	—
1978	8.4%	5.5%	Accepted 5.5%
1979	10.4%	7.0%	Accepted 7.0%
1980	13.5%	9.1%	Accepted 9.1%
1981	15.1%	4.8%	Accepted 4.8%

Sources: Data for 1977–1980 are from U.S., Congress, House, Committee on Post Office and Civil Service, *Current Salary Schedules of Federal Officers and Employees Together with a History of Salary and Retirement Annuity Adjustments,* 96th Cong., 2d sess., December 31, 1980. Data for 1981 are from various congressional documents.

The debates over the 1981 Omnibus Budget Reconciliation Act centered on President Reagan's attempt to slash the expected massive growth in federal spending, and it thus posed multiple threats to federal employees. The president insisted on a $40 billion cut in expenditures for fiscal year 1982 (October 1, 1981, to September 30, 1982).[35] His overall recommendation was strongly dependent on specific cutbacks in several federal employee benefits. Specifically, he proposed to cap the GS and WG pay increase at 4.8 percent (in contrast to the agent's 15 percent–plus recommendation for GS employees); reform the pay comparability process to reduce future benefits; annualize the semiannual cost-of-living allowance (COLA) for federal retirees; and reform the federal worker's compensation plan to reduce benefits.

The Reagan administration was somewhat flexible as to where to make the $40 billion budget cuts, but it was wedded to the aggregate reduction. The debate over specific cuts thus became redistributive in nature. If federal employee benefits were restored by Congress, cuts would have to be made elsewhere. As the debate unfolded, it became clear that the most pressing Reagan demands on federal employee issues pertained to the monetarily most significant 4.8 percent pay cap and the annualized COLA. (The pay cap and COLA recommendations were estimated to save $4.26 billion and $500 million, respectively, in fiscal year 1982.[36]) Union lobbyists accordingly focused their efforts on those two proposals, which would affect 2 million federal employees and 1.5 million federal annuitants.

The unions were unable to prevent Congress from capping pay or annualizing the retirees' benefits, although Congress rejected the president's proposals on workers' compensation reductions. Although the budget reconciliation package had been based on the assumption that Congress would adopt the pay reform plan Reagan had submitted, Congress did not enact the plan.[37]. The adopted House–Senate conference report on reconciliation did recommend, however, that future pay increases be held to a level commensurate with the increases that would have been allowed under the reform plan.

Considered together, these results indicate that the unions' legislative record is at best mixed on these major controversies. Congress rejected those union preferences that involved the highest stakes. As a result, federal employees have continued to work under a circumscribed labor relations system and have suffered substantial reductions in levels of pay increases and future benefits.

Factors Contributing to Union Setbacks

Union lobbyists and congressional staffers commented extensively on the unions' legislative setbacks, citing several explanatory reasons in common. The lobbyists were displeased with the legislative record they had achieved during this period, although they believed that they had done the best job possible under extremely difficult circumstances.

Among the reasons they gave for their poor record, the most important was the public's negative attitude toward many of the nation's major institutions, including government and organized labor, and public employees, especially federal employees. Partial evidence of this sentiment was revealed in a 1977 Gallup poll, which had reported that two-thirds of the American public believed federal employees were overpaid and underworked in comparison with their private sector counterparts.[38] More broadly, government at all levels was blamed for high rates of inflation, unemployment, and taxation. As a result, the electorate moved in a conservative direction during this period, and conservative Republicans scored impressive victories in the 1978 and 1980 elections.

At the same time, organized labor's political fortunes, which are strongly linked to Democratic successes, were waning. Attempts to reform the National Labor Relations Act, to adopt a common-situs picketing bill, and to secure other social and economic legislation favored by labor were defeated.[39] For these reasons, union lobbyists and congressional staffers argued that it had become more politically acceptable and feasible to hold down federal pay and restrict the potential bargaining power of federal unions.

The second major contributing factor was the alleged conservatism of Presidents Carter and Reagan. Union lobbyists and congressional staffers blamed much of the legislative disappointments on the efforts of these two officials to capitalize on the antigovernment sentiment of the nation. Carter, in particular, was faulted for being an unexpected political nemesis of labor. One lobbyist said, "Carter was not a real Democrat. He did not understand the labor movement, and he thought like a manager."

A third explanation lay in the unions' limited political resources. The small size of the three unions restricted their direct voting power in most congressional districts. Although representing almost a million potential voters, they claimed less than half as dues-paying members during this period. In 1980, for example, the AFGE reported 250,000 members; the NFFE, 50,000; and the NTEU, 70,000.[40] Partly because of this free-rider problem, the unions could not afford to hire large political staffs. This, coupled with their small memberships, limited their visibility and support outside the House Post Office and Civil Service Committee.[41] Moreover, congressional staffers indicated that most legislators were indifferent or hostile to federal unions.

Another limitation lay in the unions' intraorganizational and interorganizational disunity, which was illustrated during the Title VII debates. As noted earlier, the unions had failed to develop a common legislative proposal. And while the AFGE had agreed to support the broader civil service reform package, despite its opposition to many Title VII provisions, the NFFE and NTEU opposed the entire effort. Furthermore, the AFGE itself was bitterly divided on this issue, with the leadership pitted against the membership. In a controversial decision, AFGE president Blaylock agreed to lobby for Carter's overall civil service reform plan if the president recommended that a federal labor statute be incorporated into the plan. Although Blaylock disagreed with many aspects of the statute Carter eventually proposed, he supported the thrust of the overall reform plan while also lobbying for changes in the proposed labor relations statute. Finally, the AFGE's membership, meeting in convention in 1978, passed a resolution that their leadership stop their proreform lobbying.[42]

More broadly, the splintered nature of the labor movement in the federal service has sapped these unions' organizational—and thus their political—strength. The AFGE, NFFE, and NTEU have followed different organizing strategies, and they have competed vigorously among themselves for additional members; they also have different organizational philosophies, with the NTEU preferring a more centralized form of representation than the others.[43] Furthermore, the unions are divided on the basis of their affiliation to the AFL-CIO, with the AFGE belonging to the federation and the NFFE and NTEU jealously guarding their organizational independence.

In sum, the lobbyists and staffers interviewed argued that these three unions, for reasons noted, have lacked the capacity to overcome the powerful forces of public opinion and presidential animus. They implied that the unions' legislative fortunes have been contingent on variables essentially beyond their control, such as public opinion toward government employees and the election of conservative presidents. Although they have attained some legislative successes, these successes as well as the defeats have occurred for reasons above and beyond the political efforts of these unions.

Conclusions

Two basic conclusions may be drawn from the preceding analysis. First, although the three largest nonpostal unions in the federal sector engage in an impressive variety of political pursuits, the small size of their professional political staffs strongly suggests that these unions lack the organizational tools to coordinate effective political action on a continual basis. That conclusion is bolstered by the modest involvement of these unions in electoral campaign financing. All three unions clearly place preponderant emphasis on their labor relations functions. Further, their small memberships raise doubts as to the likely significance of their political role even if they substantially altered their organizational priorities.

Second, the unions' legislative records are at best mixed, especially on the issues that have dominated their lobbying efforts. Their scoreboards reveal a generally positive record for the period in question, but these quantitative results are misleading. On matters involving the significant redistribution of resources—both power and financial—within the federal service, these unions have suffered legislative setbacks. They have lacked the political strength to offset the negative attitudes that appear to exist toward public employees in general and their unions in particular.

Although it is hazardous to make generalizations from a small-sample study, three inferences may be tentatively drawn. One is that the common assumptions about the extensive political activities and power of federal employee unions deserve reevaluation. Federal unions have made modest resource commitments to political action, and they have suffered major legislative defeats. Although federal employees may reap certain economic rents over and above their private sector counterparts, it is difficult to conclude that those rents accrue from their political activities and power. Future studies that associate such rents with political action by federal unions should either empirically document such an association or identify the real sources of pay and fringe benefit premiums in the federal sector. It may be that those premiums are more the result of bureaucratic administration and the budgetary process than of union political action.

The second inference is that the willingness of elected officials to respond favorably to the legislative preferences of federal unions—and perhaps other public employee unions—may vary considerably across different kinds of issues and under different environmental circumstances. As a more general proposition, it may be that in the face of negative public and presidential attitudes, federal unions are politically weak on redistributive issues. Under different circumstances, the unions might receive more positive treatment under public policies, but that still would not demonstrate a causal link between their political activities and legislative outcomes. There is evidence, for example, that legislative pay decisions have been relatively less favorable to federal employees in recent years than in the late 1960s and early 1970s, when budget deficits were not as high and thus were less politically important to elected officials.[44]

Finally, this analysis raises the question whether the federal unions' political activities are capable of yielding significant public-policy benefits to the unions themselves. Individually, the unions may not have reached the "critical mass" of resources—in terms of membership size, political unity, political staff, and external coalitions—they need to overcome powerful environmental obstacles. If so, they may want to consider merging more seriously than they have in the past. On the other hand, these unions—individually or jointly—may be incapable of resisting these environmental forces, no matter how great their collective political commitment. If this is the case, federal employee unions may want to consider whether even their current low level of political investment has been worthwhile.

Notes

1. For a discussion of the employer and regulator functions in the public sector, see Peter Feuille, "Selected Benefits and Costs of Compulsory Arbitration," *Industrial and Labor Relations Review* 33, no. 1 (October 1979), pp. 64–76.

2. The AFGE, NFFE, and NTEU are the largest nonpostal unions in the federal government in terms of the number of federal employees they represent as exclusive bargaining agents. Throughout this reading, the terms *federal unions, federal employee unions,* and *federal sector unions* are used interchangeably.

3. Harry H. Wellington and Ralph K. Winter, Jr., *The Unions and the Cities* (Washington, D.C.: Brookings Institution, 1971).

4. For evidence that the union–nonunion pay differential has often been smaller in the public sector than in the private, see Daniel J.B. Mitchell, "The New Climate: Implications for Research on Public Sector Wage Determination and Labor Relations," in Industrial Relations Research Association, *Proceedings of the 1983 Spring Meeting,* Honolulu, March 16–18, 1983 (Madison, Wisc.: IRRA, 1983), p. 477. On the other hand, for a study supporting the Wellington and Winter thesis, see Linda N. Edwards and Franklin R. Edwards, "Wellington-Winter Revisited: The Case of Municipal Sanitation Collection," *Industrial and Labor Relations Review* 35, no. 3 (April 1982), pp. 307–318.

5. Sanford Cohen, "Does Public Employee Unionism Diminish Democracy?" *Industrial and Labor Relations Review* 32, no. 2 (January 1979), p. 191.

6. See, for example, Douglas M. McCabe, "Problems in Federal Sector Labor–Management Relations under Title VII of the Civil Service Reform Act of 1978," in Industrial Relations Research Association, *Proceedings of the 1982 Spring Meetings,* Milwaukee, April 28–30, 1982 (Madison, Wisc.: IRRA, 1982), pp. 560–565.

7. This argument is made by Don Bellante and James Long in "The Political Economy of the Rent-Seeking Society: The Case of Public Employees and Their Unions," *Journal of Labor Research* 2, no. 1 (Spring 1981), pp. 4, 12. See also James T. Bennett and Thomas J. DiLorenzo, "Public Employee Unions and the Pri-

vatization of 'Public' Services," *Journal of Labor Research* 4, no. 1 (Winter 1983), pp. 33–34, 42; Neil W. Chamberlain, Donald E. Cullen, and David Lewin, *The Labor Sector,* 3rd ed. (New York: McGraw-Hill, 1980), p. 203; Peter Feuille and John C. Anderson, "Public Sector Bargaining: Policy and Practices," *Industrial Relations* 19, no. 3 (Fall 1980), p. 321; James W. Singer, "The Limited Power of Federal Worker Unions," *National Journal,* September 30, 1978, pp. 1547–1551. Singer discusses the presumably high political profile of these unions and attributes it to the unions' limited bargaining rights and power.

8. Sharon Smith, "Pay Differentials between Federal Government and Private Sector Workers," *Industrial and Labor Relations Review* 29, no. 2 (January 1976), pp. 179–197.

9. The argument of rational voter ignorance is made by Anthony Downs, *An Economic Theory of Democracy* (New York: Harper and Row, 1957), pp. 258–259.

10. Bellante and Long, "Political Economy," p. 4.

11. Bennett and DiLorenzo, "Public Employee Unions," p. 42.

12. For a discussion of the importance of contracting out to federal unions, see Paul D. Staudohar, "Contracting Out in Federal Employment," *Government Union Review* 2 (Spring 1981), pp. 3–10.

13. Gerhart has contributed an important analysis of political action within public employee unions, but he focused on the local level and ignored federal sector unions. See Paul F. Gerhart, *Political Activity by Public Employee Organizations at the Local Level: Threat or Promise?* (Chicago: International Personnel Management Association, 1974). Gerhart examined the types and effects of political activities undertaken by state and local unions in forty-one local jurisdictions.

14. The GS and WG systems cover white- and blue-collar employees, respectively. The GS system covers over 1.5 million workers and is administered under the Federal Pay Comparability Act of 1970. The WG system covers over 400,000 workers and is administered under a different pay statute prescribing that these workers earn a "prevailing wage." Both statutes, however, have as one of their objectives ensuring parity between private and federal sector pay. GS employees are more heavily represented in unions than are WG employees.

15. See U.S. Office of Personnel Management, *Union Recognition in the Federal Government* (Washington, D.C.: U.S. Government Printing Office, 1980).

16. For a discussion of union optimism during this period, see Rex Hardesty, "The '76 Elections: A Watershed Victory," *American Federationist* 83 (December 1976), pp. 1–7.

17. Arthur C. Close, ed., *Washington Representatives 1982: Who Does What for Whom in the Nation's Capital* (Washington, D.C.: Columbia Books, 1982).

18. Staff members of this House committee were interviewed because the committee is one with which the unions have some of their closest political relationships. The Senate has not had a standing committee comparable to the House Committee on Post Office and Civil Service since 1977, when, in a controversial decision, the Senate abolished its standing Post Office and Civil Service Committee and transferred its functions to the Senate Governmental Affairs Committee, which has a jurisdiction much broader than the former committee's. Also, since the Republicans won control of the Senate in 1980, the unions' relationship to the entire Senate body and the Governmental Affairs Committee has deteriorated.

19. Charles M. Rehmus, "Labor as a Pressure Group," in Charles M. Rehmus

and Doris B. McLaughlin, eds., *Labor in American Politics: A Book of Readings* (Ann Arbor: University of Michigan Press, 1967), p. 12. It should be mentioned that Rehmus was not suggesting that labor had ignored electoral politics but, rather, that it had generally abandoned any serious interest in establishing an independent labor party. Federal employee unions, too, have expressed no serious interest in an independent labor party, although the AFGE and the NTEU are closely allied with the dominant ideology of the Democratic party.

20. For a discussion of the Hatch Act and its applicability to federal employees and their unions, see Marick F. Masters and Leonard Bierman, "The Hatch Act and the Political Activities of Federal-Employee Unions: A Need for Legislative Reform," *Public Administration Review* 45, no. 4 (July–August 1985), pp. 518–526. Although the applicability of the Hatch Act to federal employee unions is a complicated legal question beyond the scope of this reading, it should be noted that the act has not been applied to those unions in recent decades. As a result, those unions have been free to engage in partisan political activities denied to federal employees as individuals.

21. For a discussion of the complexity of the Hatch Act, see Henry Rose, "A Critical Look at the Hatch Act," *Harvard Law Review* 75 (January 1962), pp. 510–526.

22. For a discussion of the 1971 Federal Election Campaign Act, as amended, see Edwin M. Epstein, "Labor and Federal Elections: The New Legal Framework," *Industrial Relations* 15, no. 3 (October 1976), pp. 257–274.

23. For a discussion of interunion variation in PAC contributions, see Marick F. Masters and John Thomas Delaney, "Interunion Variation in Congressional Campaign Support," *Industrial Relations* 23, no. 3 (Fall 1984), pp. 410–416.

24. A table presenting those figures is available upon request to the author.

25. For a discussion of competing economic theories and their implications for federal union lobbying activity, see Marick F. Masters, "Federal-Employee Unions: Bargaining or Political Agents?," *Journal of Collective Negotiations in the Public Sector* 13, no. 3 (1984), pp. 191–202.

26. National representatives in the federal unions perform a variety of functions primarily aimed at serving the collective bargaining and contract administration needs of local unions or chapters. They thus help provide an organizational liaison between the national unions and their locals.

27. Close, *Washington Representatives 1982,* p. 471.

28. Ibid., pp. 515–516.

29. This information on the NEA's legislative-political staff is from a letter to the author from Kenneth F. Melley, NEA Political Affairs Director, dated September 25, 1981.

30. According to the unions' constitutional procedures, union conventions, which meet biennially, establish the unions' legislative priorities through adopted resolutions. Although these priorities form the unions' formal agenda, they are generally too broad and ambitious to be realistic. Nonetheless, they reflect the range of union concerns. For an example of the unions' stated priorities, see the September 10, 1981, issue of the NTEU's *The Bulletin,* which published the convention's legislative resolutions.

31. U.S. Congress, House, Committee on Post Office and Civil Service, *Hearings on Budget Reconciliation,* 97th Cong., 1st sess., May 13, 14, 19, 20, and 21, 1981, p. 346.

32. For a discussion of the history of federal labor relations, see Murray B. Nesbitt, *Labor Relations in the Federal Government Service* (Washington, D.C.: Bureau of National Affairs, 1976). For an excellent resource on the legislative history of Title VII, see U.S., Congress, House, Committee on Post Office and Civil Service, *Legislative History of the Federal Service Labor–Management Relations Statute, Title VII of the Civil Service Reform Act of 1978,* 96th Cong., 1st. sess., November 19, 1979.

33. Federal Pay Comparability Act of 1970, P.L. 91-653, 91st Cong., H.R. 13000, January 8, 1971. For a comprehensive discussion of the pay comparability process, see U.S., Congress, House, Subcommittee on Compensation and Employee Benefits, Committee on Post Office and Civil Service, *Hearings on Pay Reform Act of 1979,* 96th Cong., 1st sess., October 9 and November 15, 1979.

34. *Government Employee Relations Report,* April 17, 1978, p. 8.

35. For an examination of the president's proposals, see U.S., Congress, House, Committee on the Budget, *First Concurrent Resolution on the Budget Fiscal Year 1982,* 97th Cong., 1st sess., April 16, 1981.

36. Ibid.

37. Under the budget process established by the 1974 Congressional Budget and Impoundment Control Act, Congress need not enact specific legislative proposals in setting spending targets or in making recommendations for subsequent fiscal years. Nevertheless, Congress may and does assume the enactment of legislation in setting those targets. In the case of the pay reform plan, Congress failed to pass the plan but the adopted budget conference report proposed that post–fiscal year 1982 pay comparability decisions would be consistent with those that would result from the president's original plan.

38. The Gallup poll was taken between May 20 and 23, 1977. See George H. Gallup, *The Gallup Poll/Public Opinion, 1972–1977* (Wilmington, Del.: Scholarly Resources, 1978).

39. See Marick F. Masters and John Thomas Delaney, "The AFL-CIO's Political Record, 1974–1980," in Industrial Relations Research Association, *Proceedings of the Thirty-fourth Annual Meeting,* Washington, D.C., December 28–30, 1981 (Madison, Wisc.: IRRA, 1982), pp. 351–359.

40. These union membership figures were estimated by many of the union staff interviewed in the study. The figures for the AFGE and the NFFE also correspond with those reported in U.S. Bureau of Labor Statistics, *Directory of National Unions and Employee Associations, 1979,* BLS Bulletin 2079 (Washington, D.C.: U.S. Government Printing Office, 1980), pp. 28–29. The NTEU membership is not reported in there.

41. Congressional staff members indicated that the House Post Office and Civil Service Committee was the major source of legislative support in Congress for the federal unions. The members of Congress serving on this committee were generally presumed to have a strong interest in federal employees, with many being sympathetic to the unions' position. A comparable situation did not exist in the Senate, according to union lobbyists, because of that body's Republican control in 1980 and because it did not have a standing committee dealing solely with federal employee issues.

42. The American Federation of Government Employees, *The Government Standard,* September 1978, p. 5.

43. For a brief discussion of the federal unions as institutions, see James L. Stern,

"Unionism in the Public Sector," in Benjamin Aaron, Joseph R. Grodin, and James L. Stern, eds., *Public-Sector Bargaining* (Washington, D.C.: Bureau of National Affairs, 1979), pp. 54–62.

44. It is interesting to note that the ratios of federal pay to private pay declined during the 1970s, although federal pay remained higher. Mitchell has suggested that this fact, plus others, may be reason to call for a "renewed agenda" in research on public sector wages. See Mitchell, "The New Climate," pp. 473–479.

3
Labor Relations Structure

Bargaining Units

By and large, the U.S. industrial relations system features decentralized collective bargaining. This is especially so in the public sector, where multi-employer bargaining is virtually unknown (except for the single case reported by Feuille, Juris, Jones, and Jedel later in this chapter) and where government employees enroll in and are represented by a wide variety of labor organizations. In the 1980s, as in the 1970s and 1960s, collective bargaining agreements are negotiated between single employers and single unions, with several and sometimes many such agreements in force in a specific government at any point in time. This is not to deny the existence, and in some cases the pervasiveness, of pattern setting or information exchanges with respect to collective bargaining within and among governments. Rather, it is to affirm the reality that the structure of public sector (and, increasingly, private sector) collective bargaining has been and at present is highly decentralized.

At the same time, the reader should recognize that the growth of unionism and bargaining in government is a little more than two decades old, that public sector bargaining laws were almost nonexistent before the 1960s, and that from a historical perspective the parties to bargaining have had a relatively limited experience. As noted earlier, it is even more recently that public employers and organized public workers entered into second and third generations of collective bargaining that featured more constrained economic and political environments than existed earlier. If the economic and political climates become even more restrictive, public employers and public employees may attempt to structure new relationships, both with their counterparts and with each other, and this may alter the structure of public sector bargaining. Such an outcome is far from certain, however, for it would require individual governments and unions to subordinate their particular interests to a larger joint interest. This is something that they may be unwilling to do or legally prohibited from doing, and that has occurred only rarely in response to portending bankruptcy or other major environmental threats.

Nevertheless, and in light of recent fundamental changes in private sector bargaining structures, this discussion underscores the limited experiential base of bargaining in government and reinforces the notion that the structure of bargaining is not an immutable characteristic of public sector labor relations.

Like other aspects of governmental labor relations, the structure of bargaining is dependent on the interests, preferences, and characteristics of labor and management, which in turn are influenced by the economic, legal, and political characteristics of the immediate environment (recall figure 1–1 in chapter 1). As the latter continue to change over time, they should give rise to modifications of certain dimensions of bargaining structure in government. For example, some observers have argued that changing fiscal, political, and demographic factors may bring about a centralized statewide structure of teacher bargaining in place of local or regional school district bargaining. Whether this will actually occur in one or more states in the 1980s and beyond is problematic, but whatever changes do occur in the structure of public sector bargaining can and should be chronicled and analyzed by interested observers and members of the research community.

Despite the comparatively short history of public sector bargaining in the United States, important issues have emerged that are germane to the topic of bargaining structure; it is to these issues that the materials in this chapter are addressed. Perhaps the key issue in this regard is the determination of the bargaining unit and, relatedly, the role of supervisory personnel in public organizations.

The bargaining unit is that entity to which a specific group of employees belongs for purposes of representation in negotiations with management. The public sector, like the private, overwhelmingly follows the principle of exclusive representation in the determination of bargaining units. This means that one and only one labor organization may represent an employee group for purposes of collective bargaining, provided the group has in fact voted for (or otherwise convinced the employer of the efficacy of) such representation. The principle of exclusive representation, which imposes on labor organizations the duty to represent all employees in the bargaining unit whether or not they are members of the union, is a peculiarly American institution, a cornerstone of public and private sector labor laws.[1]

Decisions about the composition of bargaining units typically are made by administrative agencies that are statutorily created to administer one or another bargaining law. The National Labor Relations Board has jurisdiction over the private sector in this regard, and comparable agencies occupy equivalent roles in state and local governments. (The Federal Labor Relations Authority performs this function in the federal sector.) Those states that authorize collective bargaining for public employees, which by the mid-1980s totaled about three-fifths of all states, usually invest a public employee relations board or commission with the power to determine bargaining units. In making such decisions, the administrative agencies establish a fundamental characteristic of—a direct influence on—subsequent bargaining relationships. Hence, these agencies must carefully consider their decisions in determining bargaining units, especially the criteria used to make such decisions.

How broad or narrow should public sector bargaining units be? There is no simple answer to this question. A study of seven public jurisdictions and the federal sector concluded that "the 'community of interest' standard is the most widely used in unit determination" but also that this standard is the one "most open to differing interpretation."[2] As an example, the Michigan Labor Mediation Board found that

> Community of interests [sic] is determined by a number of factors and criteria, some of which are as follows: similarity of duties, skills and working conditions, job classifications, employee benefits, the amount of interchange, a transfer of employees, the integration of the employer's physical operations, the centralization of administrative and managerial functions, the degree of central control of operations, including labor relations, promotional ladders used by employees, and supervisory hierarchy and common supervision.[3]

In a court case involving a local school district and a teachers' union in New Jersey, the supreme court of that state added to the considerations that may be encompassed under the community of interest standard:

> . . . the possible effect on employee–employer relations if the employees involved are admitted to one unit. They decide whether the group involved will operate cohesively as a unit; whether the unit will probably be effective in the public quest for labor peace. Community of interest has been regarded as identity of interest. An important consideration is whether the employee sought to be included in the unit is one from whom the other employees may need protection; whether his inclusion will involve a potential conflict of interest.[4]

It is generally the case that, for purposes of representation and bargaining, the professional worker's community of interest is not shared with that of the nonprofessional. Similarly, white-collar workers typically do not regard themselves as sharing common interests with blue-collar workers. In both the public and private sectors, these differing interests often give rise to separate, narrow bargaining units, even when blue-collar and white-collar workers or professionals and nonprofessionals are represented by the same union.

More specific distinctions between employee groups may be made, of course, especially in the public sector, where individual governments usually employ a more diverse, heterogeneous work force, occupationally speaking, than even the largest, private employers. And, although some public employee unions might wish to represent the widest possible array of government workers, they may be prevented from doing so by the distinct, often conflicting, interests that exist among employees of the public work force and members of individual unions and associations. For example, Stieber has pointed out that the American Federation of State, County, and Municipal Employees (AFSCME), the second largest public employee labor organization in the United States, with some 1.1 million members who are employed in a wide variety of occupations, prefers a city- or countywide unit of non-uniformed blue-collar workers, with a separate unit for white-collar personnel.[5] The AFSCME has such an arrangement with the city of Philadelphia, but in New York City, as a result of the local bargaining statute and decisions of the Office of Collective Bargaining (OCB), which administers the law, this union has many units of nonuniformed blue-collar and white-collar employees.

Unions that have members in both the public and private sectors (known as mixed unions), such as the Service Employees International Union (SEIU), the Laborers' International Union (LIU), and the International Brotherhood of Teamsters, are much less likely than the AFSCME to be designated as the exclusive representative in city- and countywide bargaining units. The SEIU typically has units composed of custodial and janitorial workers, hospital and other institutional workers, and social workers; the LIU generally represents low-skilled employees in, for example, street and highway maintenance; and the Teamsters union has been interested primarily in representing truck drivers, equipment operators, and equipment maintenance workers.[6] In the uniformed services, the trend has been toward separate labor organizations to represent police, fire, and sanitation personnel, with superior officers in the police and fire services represented in bargaining by other organizations. This results in narrow or single-occupation bargaining units. The same is generally true of nurses' labor organizations, such as the American Nurses Association (ANA), and of teachers' labor organizations, such as the American Federation of Teachers (AFT) and the National Education Association (NEA)—although the ANA and the AFT in particular have been involved in disputes over the inclusion of paraprofessional nurse and teacher aides, respectively, in their bargaining units.

The diversity of views displayed by these various labor organizations, reflecting a multiplicity of relatively narrow communities of interest, suggests that a public employer will negotiate with at least several distinct unions and bargaining units, rather than an all-encompassing organization or unit. As labor relationships continue to develop in the public sector, smaller bargaining units may merge with larger ones and employers may be more readily able to achieve their commonly articulated goal of dealing with broader units. A leading example of such a development occurred in New York City municipal government, where during the 1980s the number of bargaining units declined dramatically, from 405 to 80 (see the Lewin-McCormick reading later in this chapter).[7] At present, however, the wide variety of unions and bargaining units found in most American governments is a major characteristic and determinant of the decentralized structure of collective bargaining in the public sector.[8]

A key issue in the structuring of public sector collective bargaining—namely, the bargaining status of supervisory personnel—is addressed in the first reading in this section, by Hayford and Sinicropi. In the private sector, supervisors are excluded from coverage of the Taft-Hartley Act. Employers need not recognize organizations of supervisors or bargain with them, although they may choose to do so voluntarily. Consequently, few labor agreements are negotiated between supervisors and private employers.

In contrast, supervisory personnel in the public sector frequently bargain on a formal basis with the governments that employ them. This occurs, in part, because "the demarcation between various functions, supervisory responsibilities, and management and employee rights is more obscure [in government] than in conventional manufacturing employment."[9] In other words, public sector supervisors, even more than their private sector counterparts, are the proverbial "men [and women] in the middle."[10] Often they perceive themselves as supervisors in name only, and therefore seek to define their positions and job rights more explicitly through unionism and collective bargaining.

On this issue, as on many others, public sector labor organizations display a diversity of views. Some employee associations, including those in the federal service (for example, the American Federation of Government Employees), prefer supervisors to be included with nonsupervisory personnel in the largest possible bargaining unit.[11] Others, such as the AFSCME and the SEIU, seek and often do represent supervisory personnel, but in units separate from those for nonsupervisory employees. Still other labor organizations of teachers, police patrol officers, firefighters, and sanitation personnel generally prefer not to represent supervisors. In a few instances, as in the case of the ANA, unionists oppose management attempts to identify supervisors and exclude them from a bargaining unit on the grounds that such personnel do not really perform supervisory functions and the underlying motivation of management is to reduce union power.

The relative newness of public sector unionism and bargaining also must be considered in analyzing the presence of supervisor–employer labor negotiations in government. Again, comparison with the private economy is instructive. There, supervisors were accorded full representation and bargaining rights under the Wagner Act of 1935 and retained those rights for twelve years. Only with the passage in 1947 of the Taft-Hartley amendments to the Wagner Act were supervisors excluded from coverage of federal labor legislation. As collective bargaining continues to evolve in government, and if the emergent emphasis on the performance and productivity of public services widens and deepens, greater pressures may develop for the restriction, if not the outright elimination, of supervisory bargaining rights.

The phenomenon of supervisory bargaining in government is also due in part to supportive public policy statutes. As the reading by Hayford and Sinicropi points out, supervisors are accorded at least some bargaining rights in almost all the state and local public jurisdictions that they examined. Among those states, only Iowa explicitly excludes supervisors from coverage of its public sector bargaining law. The rest generally authorize supervisory bargaining, with the common proviso that supervisors be in separate bargaining units (but not separate unions) from nonsupervisory personnel. A few state laws exclude so-called bona fide supervisors from collective bargaining coverage.[12] Hayford and Sinicropi's discussion of this issue illuminates some of the problems encountered in structuring public sector labor relations when large numbers of government employees hold supervisory job titles but do not actually perform supervisory work. Finally, the authors contrast the permissive policies of state and local governments in relation to supervisory bargaining rights with the considerably more restrictive practices of the federal government that developed under Executive Order 11491 and were subsequently codified by the Civil Service Reform Act (of 1978).

Notes

1. See Derek C. Bok, "Reflections on the Distinctive Character of American Laws," *Harvard Law Review* 84 (April 1971), pp. 1394–1463.

2. Richard S. Rubin, *Public Sector Unit Determination, Administrative Procedures and Case Law* (Washington, D.C.: U.S. Department of Labor, Labor–Management Services Administration, 1979), p. 8.

3. As quoted in ibid., p. 3. See *City of Warren,* Michigan Labor Mediation Board Case no. R65-H30, January 18, 1966, p. 37.

4. As quoted in Rubin, *Public Sector Unit Determination,* p. 9. See *Board of Education, Town of West Orange v. Wilton,* 57 N.J. 404, 273 A.2d 44 (1971).

5. Jack Stieber, *Public Employee Unionism: Structure, Growth, Policy* (Washington, D.C.: Brookings Institution, 1973), pp. 140–141.

6. Ibid., pp. 141–142.

7. New York City Office of Collective Bargaining, "OCB News," February 6, 1980, p. 3. Note also that when forming new public sector bargaining laws or when facing newly organized public workers, policymakers and management officials may attempt to structure a few broad bargaining units. For an example in higher education, see David Lewin, "The Politics of Collective Bargaining Legislation for Public Higher Education in California," *Proceedings of the Thirty-second Annual Winter Meeting of the Industrial Relations Research Association* (Madison, Wisc.: IRRA, 1980), pp. 145–154.

8. Data on the size, composition, and distribution of bargaining units in state and local government can be found in U.S. Bureau of the Census, *1982 Census of Governments, Preliminary Reports:* vol. 3. *Public Employment* (Washington, D.C.: U.S. Government Printing Office, 1984). For the federal government, bargaining unit data are given in U.S. Office of Personnel Management, *Union Recognition in the Federal Service* (Washington, D.C.: U.S. Government Printing Office, 1980).

9. David Lewin, "Public Employment Relations: Confronting the Issues," *Industrial Relations* 12 (October 1973), p. 319.

10. On this point, see a classic article by Fritz J. Roethlisberger, "The Foreman: Master and Victim of Double Talk," *Harvard Business Review* 23 (Spring, 1945), pp. 283–298.

11. See Stieber, *Public Employee Unionism,* pp. 142–143. For a discussion of federal sector policy in this area, see Rubin, *Public Sector Unit Determination,* pp. 28–29.

12. Stieber, *Public Employee Unionism,* pp. 138–148, and Rubin, *Public Sector Unit Determination,* p. 29.

Bargaining Rights Status of Public Sector Supervisors

Stephen L. Hayford
*Anthony V. Sinicropi**

One of the most significant problems in public sector labor relations concerns the status and role of supervisors in the collective bargaining structure. Indicative of the confusion prevalent are the variety of postures taken by parties to the bargaining process. Some legislatures have favored excluding supervisors from bargaining units, while others have given them total representation rights. State labor relations agencies have also offered decisions going both ways. Some in public management, which has traditionally excluded all supervisory personnel from bargaining units, recently advocated the right to strike for public employees if supervisory exclusion is the quid pro quo. Unions and public employee organizations typically contend that all but a few "bona fide" supervisors be included in bargaining units. Finally, supervisors themselves have demonstrated a Jekyll and Hyde personality on the question.

This state of confusion does not exist in the private sector, where supervisors possess no right to join bargaining units with other employees or to

*Virginia Polytechnic Institute and State University and University of Iowa, respectively. Reprinted from *Industrial Relations* 15, no. 1 (February 1976), pp. 44–61.

form units of their own for bargaining purposes. However, supervisors in the public sector have not been subject to uniform and predictable treatment, a condition explained by several factors:

1. The public sector is not regulated by a singular preemptive federal statute, but by a patchwork of state laws, governors' executive orders, attorney general opinions, municipal ordinances, and a federal executive order—all of which offer variations reflective of the peculiarities of each jurisdiction.

2. Public sector bargaining, a relatively new phenomenon, has yet to achieve the stability of the private sector's nearly four decades of experience. Indeed, public sector bargaining, no more than fifteen years old, is only now gaining widespread acceptance and understanding.

3. Perhaps most important is the matter of the definition of supervisor, the rights granted such an employee, and the manner in which provisions are interpreted and applied. In the private sector, the definition is delineated in one statute—the Labor Management Relations Act (LMRA). Supervisors are excluded from coverage,[1] and a single administrative agency, the National Labor Relations Board (NLRB), is left to determine whether a class of workers and/or a group of jobs is supervisory. In the public sector, each state that has enacted public employee bargaining legislation and the federal government, through Executive Order (EO) 11491, have their own definition of supervisor (if such a definition is specified).

Although there are some marked differences between state statutes, as they relate to the definition of supervisor, there is a general and overriding consistency in such definitions—with some exception they resemble the one found in the LMRA. The real distinction in treatment seems to result from the addition of qualifying language and from interpretations by administering agencies. It is these differences on which our investigation will focus.

Analytical Framework

Our analytical framework allows for concise categories within which policies toward supervisors in selected jurisdictions can be placed. Four major categories were chosen:

1. *Exclusion—All Supervisors:* Jurisdictions where all supervisors are excluded from any form of statutory[2] bargaining rights protection.

2. *Exclusion—Bona Fide Supervisors:*[3] Jurisdictions where only bona fide supervisors are excluded from bargaining. In these governmental units many employees who have been classified by the public employer as supervisors have not been so categorized by the respective administrative agencies for the purpose of the statutes.

3. *Full Bargaining Rights—Autonomous Units:* Jurisdictions where supervisors have statutory rights comparable to rank-and-file employees but are separated into autonomous bargaining units.

4. *Meet and Confer—Autonomous Units:* Jurisdictions where there is statutory protection for supervisors in units separate from rank-and-file employees but without an employer obligation to bargain with them.

Table 1 represents a compilation of the statutory treatments afforded supervisors in each jurisdiction discussed in this study. The information there will serve as the basis for discussion.

Federal Government Policy

Although federal collective bargaining under Executive Order 11491, as amended, has no binding authority on state and local jurisdictions, it has influenced state and local policy. It is therefore important to analyze the federal government's policy toward supervisors and collective bargaining.

The assistant secretary of labor for labor–management relations is responsible for the interpretation and application of the Executive Order.[4] His decisions are subject to review by the Federal Labor Relations Council (FLRC) when major policy issues are presented or where in the council's judgment it appears that a "capricious or arbitrary decision" has been made.[5] The Assistant Secretary and the FLRC have often been concerned with the question of supervisory bargaining rights. Although the Council considers the uniqueness of each federal employment relationship under EO 11491, it nevertheless has shown an inclination to act consistent with NLRB policies.

A comparison of the provisions of EO 11491 with those of EO 10988 illustrates the parallel between the evolvement of the bargaining rights status of supervisors in the federal public sector and the private sector. Executive Order 10988, like the National Labor Relations Act (NLRA), did not contain any language relating to the bargaining rights status of supervisors. The only reference to supervisors present in the 1962 EO was a provision requiring that supervisors who evaluated the performance of other employees not be placed in the same bargaining units with such employees.[6] As with the NLRA, EO 10988 was eventually amended with the addition of language that both defined the term *supervisor* and specified the bargaining rights status of such individuals.

The August 1969 Report of the Study Committee appointed to recommend modifications in EO 10988 urged, among other changes, that supervisors be excluded from the coverage of the new EO.[7] This recommendation was incorporated in EO 11491 with the inclusion of six provisions that have acted to bring the bargaining rights status of supervisors in the federal public

Table 1
Bargaining Rights Status of Supervisors in Selected Jurisdictions

Jurisdiction	Statutory Definition of Supervisor	Bargaining Rights Status of Supervisors	Unit Placement of Supervisors	Additional Statutory Provisions
Private sector	Sec. 2(11)—Labor Management Relations Act[a]	None	—	—
Federal government	Sec. 2(c)—Executive Order 11491, consistent with LMRA definition	None	—	Sec. 24—E.O. 11491 "Savings Clause"
Iowa	Sec. 4(2)—Public Employment Relations Act, consistent with LMRA definition[b]	None	—	—
Wisconsin	Sec. 111.81(19)—State Employment Relations Act[c] Sec. 111.70(1)(a)—Municipal Employment Relations Act, consistent with LMRA definition	Only bona fide supervisors excluded from coverage	Less than bona fide supervisors in rank-and-file units	Sec. 111.81(3)(d) State Employment Relations Act[d]
Oregon	Sec. 243.650(14)—Public Employee Collective Bargaining Law, consistent with LMRA definition[e]	Only bona fide supervisors excluded from coverage	Less than bona fide supervisors in rank-and-file units	—
Connecticut	Sec. 7-471(2)—Municipal Employee Relations Act[f]	Only bona fide supervisors excluded from coverage	Less than bona fide supervisors in rank-and-file units	—
Hawaii	Sec. 89-2(18)—Collective Bargaining in Public Employment Law, consistent with LMRA definitions	Full bargaining rights	Autonomous units; less than bona fide supervisors in rank-and-file units	—
Minnesota	Sec. 179.63(9)—Public Employee Labor Relations Act, consistent with LMRA definition[g]	Full bargaining rights	Autonomous units; less than bona fide supervisors in rank-and-file units	Sec. 179.71(3) Public Employee Labor Relations Act

Massachusetts	No definition in statute	Full bargaining rights	Autonomous units; less than bona fide supervisors in rank-and-file units	—
New York	No definition in statute	Full bargaining rights	Autonomous units; less than bona fide supervisors in rank-and-file units	—
Michigan	No definition in statute	Full bargaining rights	Autonomous units; less than bona fide supervisors in rank-and-file units	—
Pennsylvania	Sec. 301(6)—Public Employee Relations Act, consistent with LMRA definition	Meet and confer rights	Autonomous units; less than bona fide supervisors in rank-and-file units	—

[a] ". . . any individual having authority, in the interest of the employer, to hire, transfer, suspend, layoff, recall, promote, discharge, assign, reward, or discipline other employees, or responsibly to direct them, or to adjust their grievances, or effectively to recommend such action, if in connection with the foregoing the exercise of such authority is not of a merely routine or clerical nature, but requires the use of independent judgment."

[b] This section also excludes as supervisory employees all school superintendents, assistant superintendents, principals, and assistant principals.

[c] In this section the definition of supervisor is prefaced by the phrase ". . . any individual whose principal work is different from that of his subordinates. . . ."

[d] This section allows WERC to consider petitions for the formation of two statewide units of supervisors (professional and nonprofessional).

[e] In this section the definition of supervisory employee is followed by the phrase, "However, the exercise of any function of authority enumerated in this subsection shall not necessarily require the conclusion that the individual so exercising that function is a supervisor. . . ."

[f] This section stipulates that in making a determination of supervisory status the board shall consider, among other criteria, whether the principal functions of the position are characterized by not fewer than two of the following: (a) certain management control duties; (b) duties that are distinct and dissimilar from those of subordinates; (c) exercising judgment in grievance adjustment and personnel and contract administration; and (d) participating in the establishment and implementation of performance standards. (paraphrased)

[g] Section 179.63(9a) defines "supervisory employee" as "the administrative head and his assistant" when it refers to "a municipality, municipal utility, police or fire department."

sector into substantial compliance with the status of such employees in the private sector under the LMRA.[8]

Section 2(b) of EO 11491 excludes from the definition of employee anyone serving as a "supervisor."[9] An exhaustive review of recent decisions by the assistant secretary and the FLRC discloses a restrictive approach to the issue of supervisory bargaining rights. This restrictive approach is based on an expansive interpretation of the EO's definition of *supervisor.*

In the leading case on the supervisory issue, *China Lake Naval Weapons Center,* the FLRC chose to take a "disjunctive" view of the Section 2(c) definition of supervisor. Under the policy established in this case, an individual is a supervisor if he possesses the authority to perform *any* of the functions enumerated in Section 2(c) in a manner requiring independent judgment.[10] The presence of higher level review of a supervisor's decisions does not detract from the authority that supervisor possesses.[11] This disjunctive interpretation of the supervisor definition is identical to the policy position of the NLRB and the federal courts under the Labor Management Relations Act.[12]

In related cases the council has held that:

1. In the determination of supervisory status under Section 2(c), it is immaterial whether the employee in question carries out his function(s) in a formal or informal manner.[13]
2. *The duties of the employee,* not the number of subordinates, determine supervisory authority.[14]
3. It is not necessary that an individual's subordinates be "employees" under the Executive Order for him or her to be deemed a supervisor.[15]

It is evident from this account that the FLRC has adopted an expansive interpretation of the supervisory definition contained in EO 11491 and thereby has placed considerable constraints on the bargaining rights of all supervisors. The FLRC explains its posture:

> Section 2(c) must be interpreted in a manner consistent with the realities of the exercise of authority in the federal sector. If only those individuals who possessed the unqualified authority to promote, or to make the final decision at the last stage of a grievance procedure were considered supervisors, only top officials would be supervisors and there would be no lower level supervisors in the federal sector. We see no basis for adopting such a strained interpretation of Section 2(c).[16]

The promulgation of EO 11838 in February 1975 ended much of the speculation as to the possibility of a major shift in the federal government's position on the supervisory bargaining rights issue. The one area left unresolved by recent amendments to EO 11491 and the decisions discussed here is that of the proper policy regarding representation of supervisors by unions in grievance and appeals procedures. In a June 1973 decision the assistant secretary held that a supervisor cannot choose to have a union represent him in such a proceeding.[17] As the FLRC has not heard this or any similar case, the matter remains unresolved. In its October 1974 report to the president (which was the basis for EO 11838), the FLRC maintained that the issue of the representation of supervisors by unions in grievance and appeals procedures outside of those sanctioned by EO 11491 (that is, Civil Service and agency procedures) is a question of "management policy for determination by the Civil Service Commission working with agencies concerned."[18]

These findings demonstrate that supervisors in federal employment face the continued prospect of a highly constrained bargaining rights status. Thus, in the context of our analytical framework, federal government treatment of supervisory personnel can be placed, with only very minor exception, in the category "Exclusion—All Supervisors."

Supervisors in State and Local Employment

In contrast to the uniform policy enforced under the federal Executive Order, the comprehensive public employee bargaining statutes[19] enacted by the several states present varying standards for determining the bargaining rights status of supervisors. The four categories noted are used in analyzing these statutes and their application. Although all comprehensive state statutes are not fully considered, a sampling of those typifying each category is reviewed.

Exclusion—All Supervisors

Of the sixteen states (by the authors' count) which have enacted comprehensive public employee bargaining legislation,[20] only Iowa's Public Employment Relations Act of 1974 appears to exclude completely supervisors from its coverage, without any modifying qualifications or additional related statutory language. Section 4(2) of the Iowa law provides that, among other groups, "any supervisory employees" are to be excluded from coverage. The act's definition of "supervisory employee" parallels the definition of *supervisor* found in the LMRA.

The Iowa statute's definitions section also enumerates specific supervisory positions excluded from bargaining. Section 4(2) includes the proviso that "all school superintendents, assistant superintendents, principals, and assistant principals shall be deemed to be supervisory employees." This enumeration approach is at variance with the majority of state statutes in that it relies on job titles rather than on job content or responsibilities to determine bargaining rights status. Interestingly enough, reference in the Iowa statute to specific job titles (other than agency chief executive officers) is limited to public education positions.

Since the Iowa law was not fully operational until July 1, 1975, there is a dearth of interpretive decisions on the supervisory issue by the Iowa Public Employment Relations Board (PERB). However, the language of the statute as it refers to supervisory employees is clear and leaves the Iowa PERB little, if any, discretion on this question, especially in the public education area. Iowa, by virture of the language of its Public Employment Relations Act, clearly falls in the category "Exclusion—All Supervisors."

Exclusion—Bona Fide Supervisors

The policy approaches developed by Wisconsin, Connecticut, and Oregon best exemplify the treatment that excludes from bargaining rights protection only bona fide supervisors. Wisconsin's State Employment Relations Act of 1971 removes from the definition of "employee" those "employees who are performing in a supervisory capacity."[21] The act uses the standard definition of supervisor derived from the LMRA with the addition of the phrase ". . . any individual whose principal work is different from that of his subordinates. . . ."[22] The Wisconsin Municipal Employment Relations Act of 1971 does not exclude supervisors from its coverage;[23] it also permits "law enforcement and firefighting supervisors" to form separate units for bargaining purposes.[24] Despite these differences in language, the Wisconsin Employment Relations Commission (WERC) has interpreted and applied both these statutes in a consistent manner.

In recent decisions dealing with the supervisory issue WERC has frequently drawn a distinction between "working foremen"[25] or "lead workers,"[26] who are not excluded from the statutes' protection, and "supervisors," who are excluded. The WERC has held that to be deemed a supervisor for the purposes of the state's bargaining laws, an employee must exercise sufficient supervisory authority (essentially the requirement of authority to hire, discharge, discipline, and the like, in a manner requiring independent judgment) over people, rather than directing an activity (for example, a nursing care plan) or performing administrative duties.[27] In addition, the commission, in making this delineation between "working foremen" and "supervisors," has relied heavily on the statutory requirement that a supervisor's principal work must differ from that of his subordinates. Finally, the commission has held that the frequency with which an employee performs the requisite supervisory functions enumerated in the act will not be a major consideration in determining such an employee's status.[28]

Both Oregon and Connecticut's public employee bargaining laws allow the administrative agencies to exercise a great deal of discretion in determining whether supervisory employees should be allowed to bargain collectively.

Oregon's statute, revised in 1973, specifically excludes supervisors from its definition of "employee."[29] However (in addition to the standard definition), the Oregon law defines "supervisory employee" further with the phrase, ". . . the exercise of any function of authority enumerated in this subsection shall not necessarily require the conclusion that the individual so exercising that function is a supervisor within the meaning of (this 1973 Act)."[30] The Oregon Public Employment Relations Board has not promulgated any major policy decisions under this provision. However, the policy reflected by the language of the Oregon statute seems similar to that developed by the Wisconsin Employment Relations Commission.

Connecticut's Municipal Employee Relations Act (MERA) of 1965, as amended in 1975, does not explicitly exclude supervisors from its coverage. Section 7-471(2) of that statute grants to the State Board of Labor Relations the power to determine whether a supervisory position is covered by the act. In making the determination of whether a supervisory position should be excluded from coverage, the board is instructed to consider, among other criteria, whether the principal functions of the position are characterized by not fewer than two of the following: performing of certain management control duties, performing such duties as are distinct and dissimilar from subordinates' work, exercising judgment in grievance adjustment and personnel and contract administration, and participating in the establishment and implementation of performance standards for subordinates.

The Connecticut board has made it clear that supervisors who do not meet at least two of the criteria established by Section 7-471(2) will, in most cases, not be excluded from MERA coverage. The trend in Connecticut is clearly toward inclusion of many individuals with supervisory titles under the state's public employee bargaining statute.[31] In general, the Connecticut board, with some exception,[32] has not placed supervisors deemed to fall under the protection of the MERA in separate units with nonsupervisory employees.[33]

It appears that both the Wisconsin Commission and the Connecticut Board have consistently required definitive evidence that the statutory definitions of supervisor are satisfied before deeming an employee to be a supervisor. The frequent appearance of the terms *working foremen, lead man,* and *lead workers* and the inclusion of such individuals in rank-and-file bargaining units in both WERC and board decisions indicates that neither automatically concludes that an employee classified as a supervisor by title or otherwise is a supervisor for the purpose of the states' public employee bargaining statutes. Therefore, the practice seems to indicate that several much less than bona fide supervisors have been placed in the same classification with rank-and-file employees and granted bargaining rights protection. The operative statutory provisions in Wisconsin, Oregon, and Connecticut and the interpretation and application of these provisions acts to place those states in the category "Exclusion—Bona Fide Supervisors."

Full Bargaining Rights—Autonomous Units

The states of Hawaii, Minnesota, Massachusetts, New York, and Michigan, either through explicit statutory language or through the interpretive decisions of their administrative agencies, grant full bargaining rights to supervisors in autonomous bargaining units. Hawaii and Minnesota specifically provide for bargaining units made up exclusively of supervisors. Hawaii's public employee statute of 1970, as amended 1975, divides all covered public employees into thirteen statewide units, including units of "supervisory employees in blue collar positions," "supervisory employees in white collar positions," and "educational officers and other personnel of the department of education under the same salary schedule."[34] The statute incorporates the prototype definition of "supervisory employees."[35] These provisions have been implemented with few clarifying interpretations by the Hawaii Public Employment Relations Board (PERB), and one prescribed supervisory unit is reported to be formed and engaged in bargaining with the state.[36]

Minnesota's Public Employee Labor Relations Act states that "supervisory and confidential employees, principals and assistant principals may form their own organizations."[37] Section 179.63.(9) defines "supervisory employee" in the standard manner. Section 179.63.(9a) defines "supervisory employee" as "the administrative head and his assistant" when it refers to "a municipality, municipal utility, police or fire department." Finally, Section 179.71(3) requires that for the Director of Mediation Services (who makes the initial unit determination decisions under the act) to deem an employee to be a supervisor, he must find that such employee "may perform or effectively recommend a majority of the functions referred to in Section 179.63, subdivisions 9 or 9a. . . ." Therefore, one can conclude that under the Minnesota statute a broad range of supervisory personnel, bona fide and otherwise, are granted full collective bargaining rights.

The Minnesota Public Employment Relations Board (PERB), in reviewing decisions of the Director of Mediation Services, has often used language similar to that of the Wisconsin commission. Employees who "performed some functions or effectively recommended actions that could be considered supervisory" have been held to not be "supervisory employees" for the purposes of the act.[38] The Director of Mediation Services and the PERB have declined to exclude from nonsupervisory units those employees whom they characterized as "working foremen"[39] or "lead men."[40] This interpretive language, analogous to that of the Wisconsin Employment Relations Commission, and the provisions cited here of that statute, indicate that Minnesota follows a policy of including less than bona fide supervisors in units of rank-and-file employees.

The New York and Massachusetts public employee bargaining laws make no reference to supervisory employees. However, both statutes do exempt "managerial employees" from coverage by bargaining rights provisions. The Massachusetts and New York statutes exclude from coverage employees who participate in policy formulation, or are required on behalf of the public employer to assist in preparation for or conduct of collective bargaining, or have a major role in either personnel management or contract administration.[41]

The Massachusetts law became effective on July 1, 1974; hence, there are few interpretive decisions by the Massachusetts Labor Relations Commission (MLRC). In its major decision involving the supervisory issue, the commission indicated a "strong preference" for placing bona fide supervisors in autonomous bargaining units.[42] In the same manner as Minnesota's PERB, the MLRC has established a policy of placing less than bona fide supervisors in the same units with rank-and-file employees.[43]

The New York Public Employee Relations Board (PERB) has interpreted the "managerial employee" exclusion contained in the Taylor Law of 1967, as amended in 1974, so as to bar from collective bargaining only employees who have an important role in one of the three areas mentioned (that is, only "managerial" employees are excluded from the Taylor Law's coverage). The board has asserted that "some responsibilities involving the administration of collectively negotiated agreements and personnel administration are more indicative of supervision than management."[44] Thus, New York's PERB appears to follow a policy of depending not on job titles but, rather, on actual authority exercised.

As to policy formulation provisions, the New York PERB, in upholding a decision by the Director of Public Employment Practices and Representation, has held that, "To be meaningful, the concept of policy formulation must be applied not at the lowest operating unit of the employer . . . but at a level of responsibility sufficiently high to encompass a discrete department or agency. . . ."[45] Thus, much of the supervisory activity that might arguably be characterized as policymaking does not necessarily exclude a supervisor from the statute's grant of bargaining rights if that activity occurs on a subagency or subdepartmental level. This policy position, along with a PERB ruling that the Taylor Act's definition of "employee" does not exclude supervisors, appears to grant bona fide supervisors collective bargaining rights identical to those of rank-and-file employees.

The New York PERB's policy as to the unit placement of supervisors is essentially the same as that established in Minnesota and Massachusetts. Bona fide supervisors are placed in autonomous bargaining units, while less than bona fide supervisors are included in the same units with rank-and-file employees.[46]

The Michigan Public Employment Relations Act of 1965, as amended in 1973, which does not cover state civil service employees, has been interpreted by the Michigan Employment Relations Commission (MERC) and the

Michigan Court of Appeals so as to include supervisors under its statutory protection.[47] In a manner similar to its counterparts in New York and Massachusetts, MERC has held (in accordance with Section 423.213 of the act) that only public employees in policymaking "executive" positions are excluded from bargaining.[48] A long line of consistent decisions by MERC in unit determination cases reflects a policy of establishing exclusive supervisory units based on the appropriate unit criteria contained in the act.

Thus, the Hawaii and Minnesota statutes afford supervisors bargaining rights that act to place those states in the category "Full Bargaining Rights—Autonomous Units." Michigan, Massachusetts, and New York, by virtue of interpretive decisions by their respective administrative agencies, fall into the same category.

Meet and Confer—Autonomous Units

Pennsylvania's Public Employee Relations Act of 1970 is unique. Although it sanctions formation of "separate, homogenous units" of supervisory employees, it obligates the public employer only "to meet and discuss" with organizations of supervisors.[49] The statutory definition of supervisor parallels that in LMRA and in many other state bargaining laws.[50] In determining supervisory status, the Pennsylvania Labor Relations Board (PLRB) has relied heavily on job descriptions. The PLRB has held that ". . . it is the existence of the power (to hire, discharge, etc.) and not past exercise of the power which constitutes supervisory status."[51]

The PLRB has also formulated a rigorous test of the "effectively recommend" portion of the definition of supervisor. The mere offering of "suggestions which may or may not be acted upon" without further investigation by superior officials does not act to designate an employee as a supervisor.[52] Finally, PLRB decisons have reflected the opinion that the Pennsylvania act requires that the requisite functions performed by a supervisory employee must be of a nonroutine nature and must involve the supervision of people, not of things.[53] Thus, it appears that many less than bona fide supervisors are not considered supervisors for purposes of the Pennsylvania act.

Pennsylvania, unlike others, falls in the category "Meet and Confer—Autonomous Units," by statutory language. However, it must be noted that the various tests used by the PLRB to determine bona fide supervisory status act to grant full bargaining rights to many employees who are supervisors in name only.

The Remaining States

Although sixteen states (again, by our count) have enacted comprehensive public employee bargaining legislation, we have focused on ten. The experience under these ten statutes provides the most comprehensive basis for thorough analysis in light of the length of their enactment and the volume of interpretive decisions handed down by the respective administrative agencies charged with their implementation. However, the six remaining statutes— those of Maine, New Hampshire, New Jersey, Alaska, Vermont, and Washington—do warrant mention; for one thing, none contains a specific definition of the term *supervisor* or *supervisory employee*.

Five statutes have been interpreted as allowing some form of supervisory collective bargaining. Maine and New Hampshire allow inclusion of supervisors in mixed units. The executive director of the Maine Public Employee Relations Board is authorized to exclude supervisors from bargaining, upon the public employer's request, if that position is characterized by certain "management control duties." New Jersey also permits mixed units where "established practice, prior agreement, or special circumstances" prevail; otherwise, New Jersey sanctions separate supervisor-only units. Under the regulations of the Alaska Department of Labor and the state personnel board, supervisors are placed in separate units. Section 908 of the Vermont Labor Relations Law, in language somewhat analogous to the Massachusetts and New York laws, allows "management level employees" below a major policymaking level to form autonomous units for the purposes of bargaining collectively. Finally, the Washington State Personnel Board has promulgated a rule (Section 366-42-010(2)) that excludes "supervisors" from any form of bargaining rights. Thus, under the Public Employees' Collective Bargaining Act of 1967, as amended in 1973, and Executive Order 71-04, supervisory employees in Washington are without representational status.[54]

Summary and Conclusions

The bargaining rights status of public sector supervisors is far from being settled. While it is clear that a federal employment experience has paralleled that of the private sector, several state legislatures and/or administrative agencies have chosen a more expansive approach, which has taken two principal forms.

The first approach is reflected by Wisconsin, Oregon, and Connecticut, which have chosen to exclude only bona fide supervisors from the coverage of their public employee collective bargaining laws. This has been accomplished by the application of a rigorous test of the statutory definition of *supervisor*. Thus, many individuals with supervisory titles are not held to be supervisors for statutory purposes. This policy is founded upon the often cited contention that many public employees in supervisory positions are not really managers.

As a rule, these "less than bona fide supervisors" are placed in the same bargaining units with rank-and-file employees.

The second view is exemplified by the actions of five states, Hawaii, Minnesota, New York, Massachusetts, and Michigan, which have elected to grant full bargaining rights protection to all supervisory employees. The policymakers in these states apparently do not see any conflict of interest (between the supervisors' role as a member of management and their participation in collective bargaining with management) when bona fide supervisors are allowed to bargain collectively. In these jurisdictions bona fide supervisors are placed in autonomous bargaining units, while less than bona fide supervisors are included in rank-and-file units. This approach is analogous to the final position adopted by the National Labor Relations Board prior to enactment of the Taft-Hartley amendments.[55]

Several factors have contributed to the divergent direction taken by the states vis-à-vis the private sector and the federal government. Perhaps foremost among them is the desires of the supervisors themselves. In several jurisdictions, public sector supervisors have demonstrated a strong desire to be included in the bargaining process. This desire is manifested in elections and unit determination petitions and also was no doubt felt through lobbying activities when much of the legislation was developed. This activity, coupled with the questionable managerial status of many supervisors in public employment, has undoubtedly weighed heavily upon the decisions of the various state legislatures and administrative agencies.

The early stage of development of public sector collective bargaining must also be considered a critical factor. In many public sector bargaining relationships, the major emphasis has yet to shift from contract negotiation to contract administration. In the private sector, the grievance procedure is well institutionalized, and the supervisor's key role in contract administration is widely recognized. Since successful contract administration has not yet become the focus of the labor relations programs in the majority of public sector jurisdictions, the role of the supervisor in those labor relations structures has not been clearly delineated. Therefore, the role ambivalence felt by public sector supervisors has not yet emerged as a major concern which their superiors have considered in depth.

The diversity that exists at present in the statutory treatment of supervisors is not likely to persist. The major reason for this observation is the strong possibility that some form of national public employee collective bargaining legislation will be enacted in the immediate future. It appears likely that such national legislation will incorporate the private sector approach to supervisory bargaining rights. This conclusion is based on three primary factors: the well-established policy position of the federal government, which essentially excludes all supervisors from any form of bargaining rights protection; the pervasive effect of the private sector treatment of supervisors; and the disruptive effect that a continuing expansion of supervisory bargaining rights in public employment will have on private sector labor relations.

If national public employee legislation is enacted, it is reasonable to assume that the influence of the executive branch of the federal government would be considerable. The position of the executive branch on the supervisory bargaining rights issue is clear from the discussion here. The language of EO 11838 gives no indication of a change in that policy.

A national public employee collective bargaining statute granting bargaining rights protection to supervisors would inevitably result in a demand by private sector supervisors for similar treatment. There is no evidence to suggest that Congress would be willing to amend the Taft-Hartley Act in such a manner. The disruptive effect of such an act on the relatively stable collective bargaining structure in the private sector would be of such a magnitude as to make it politically infeasible. The convergence of private and public sector collective bargaining is clear. Because of the factors discussed here, it seems highly probable that, if national public employee collective bargaining legislation is enacted, supervisory bargaining rights is one area in which the private sector treatment will prevail.

Notwithstanding the persuasive arguments that all but the top echelon of public employees should be allowed to bargain collectively, and the lack of negative reports from those jurisdictions pursuing such a policy, it is our feeling that an effective statutory structure must provide that true bona fide supervisors be excluded from statutory bargaining rights protection. The heart of a viable labor relations structure lies in effective contract administration. It is a widely accepted fact that in mature bargaining relationships, the key person in day-to-day contract administration is the front-line supervisor. The formidable problems inherent in weakening that first line of management–labor communication and cooperation by allowing such individuals to bargain collectively are apparent.[56]

Because there are many individuals in public employment with supervisory titles who do not have consequential management responsibilities or authority, the authors advocate a statutory and interpretive policy that requires substantial proof of bona fide supervisory status before an individual is excluded from bargaining rights protection. The policy and practice of the Wisconsin Employment Relations Commission best exemplify this approach.

The authors have advanced the view that only supervisors who possess consequential managerial responsibilities and authority should be excluded from bargaining rights protection. If such a policy is adopted by public employers, many factors that have prompted public sector supervisors to seek statutory bargaining rights protection will diminish in importance. The emergence of this type of labor relations structure should contribute greatly to the achievement of stability and maturity in public sector labor management relations.

Notes

1. Labor–Management Relations Act (Taft-Hartley Act), Section 2(3), 61 Stat. 156 (1947). The authors wish to express their appreciation to the following individuals who assisted in the preparation of this article: Robert E. Doherty, director, Institute of Public Employment, New York State School of Labor and Industrial Relations, Cornell University; Donald R. Crowell II, special assistant to the secretary of labor; and Thomas P. Gilroy and Richard E. Pegnetter of the University of Iowa.

2. The term *statutory* refers to EO 11491 and municipal ordinances, as well as to state public employee bargaining statutes.

3. For purposes of this study, *bona fide supervisors* are defined as employees with supervisory titles who possess consequential managerial responsibility and exercise consequential management authority. *Less than bona fide supervisors* are defined as employees with supervisory titles who neither possess consequential managerial responsibility nor exercise consequential management authority.

4. EO 11491, Section 6(1).

5. Regulations of the Federal Labor Relations Council, Section 2 411.12. Considerations governing review 37 F.R. 20668, October 3, 1972.

6. EO 10988, Section 6(a)(3).

7. *Study Committee Report and Recommendations, August, 1969, Which Led to the Issuance of Executive Order 11491* (Washington, D.C.: Federal Labor Relations Council, 1971), p. 6.

8. EO 11491, Sections 1(b), 2(b), 2(c), 2(e), 10(b), and 24.

9. The section 24 "Savings Clause" of EO 11491 does grant bargaining rights to a very limited group of supervisory personnel in occupations where supervisors have traditionally bargained collectively in the private sector. This grandfather clause has had the effect of permitting the recognition of a few supervisory units in the maritime trades.

10. *Department of the Navy, United States Naval Weapons Center, China Lake, California* (A/SLMR no. 128, FLCR no. 7aA-11, May 25, 1973).

11. Ibid.

12. *Ohio Power v. NLRB* (6th Cir., 1949), 24 LRRM 2350. See also *NLRB v. Edward G. Budd Manufacturing Company,* 332 U.S. 840 (December 1947), and *Corn Products Refining Company v. Plant and Grain Processors, AFL,* 87 NLRB 187 (1949).

13. *Department of the Navy, Mare Island Naval Shipyard* (A/SLMR no. 129, FLRC 72A-12, May 25, 1973). Thus, such qualifiers as *sufficient* authority, *formal* disciplining, or *permanent* transfers are not to be used in making determinations of supervisory status under the Executive Order.

14. *USDA—Northern Marketing and Nutrition Research Division, Peoria, Illinois.* A/SLMR no. 120, FLRC no. 72A-4 (April 17, 1973).

15. *McConnell Air Force Base, Kansas,* A/SLMR no. 134. FLRC no. 72A-15 (April 17, 1973).

16. *Department of the Navy, United States Naval Weapons Center, China Lake, California* (A/SLMR no. 128, FLRC no. 72A-11, May 25, 1973).

17. *Internal Revenue Service, Chicago,* A/SLMR no. 279 (June, 1973). This case dealt with an interpretation of Section 7(d)(1) of EO 11491, which states, "Recognition of a labor organization does not . . . preclude an employee, regardless of

whether he is in a unit of exclusive recognition, from exercising grievance of appellate rights established by law or regulations; or *from choosing his own representative in a grievance or appelate action,* except when presenting a grievance under a negotiated procedure as provided in Section 13" (emphasis added).

18. *Government Employee Relations Report* (Washington, D.C.: Bureau of National Affairs), no. 592, February 10, 1975, p. A-11.

19. Reference here is to statutes that, among other provisions, require collective bargaining by the public employer, establish an administrative agency to interpret and apply the statute, and provide criteria for unit determination.

20. The sixteen states are Alaska, Connecticut, Hawaii, Iowa, Maine, Massachusetts, Michigan, Minnesota, New Hampshire, New Jersey, New York, Oregon, Pennsylvania, Vermont, Washington, and Wisconsin.

21. Wisconsin *Statutes,* Chapter III, Sub. Chapter V; L. 1971, Chapter 270, effective April 30, 1972, Section 111.83(15).

22. Ibid., Section 111.81(19).

23. Ibid., Sub Chapter IV; L. 1959, Chapter 509, as amended; Law 1971, Chapter 124, Section 111.70(1)(b).

24. Ibid., Section 11.70(3)(d).

25. Wisconsin Employment Relations Commission, *AFSCME Local 2, District Council 48 and Greenfield School District no. 6,* Case XIII, no. 15041 MC-718, Decision no. 10788 (February 14, 1972).

26. Wisconsin Employment Relations Commission, *Stanley Boyd Area School, Joint District No. 4,* Case III, no. 16162 ME-854, Decision no. 11589-A (July 19, 1973).

27. Wisconsin Employment Relations Commission, *Washington County Sheriff's Association and Washington County,* Case X, no. 15386 ME-764, Division no. 10845-A (April 18, 1972).

28. Wisconsin Employment Relations Commission, *Stanley Boyd Area School....*

29. Oregon *Revised Statutes,* Sections 243.711-243.795, as last amended L. 1973, Chapter 536, effective October 5, 1973, Section 243.650(17).

30. Ibid., Section 243.650(14).

31. Connecticut State Board of Labor Relations, *Clifford W. Beers Guidance Clinic and AFSCME Local 1303,* Case no. E-2358, Decision no. 1104 (January 12, 1973).

32. *Governmental Employee Relations Report* (Washington, D.C.: Bureau of National Affairs), no. 526, October 22, 1973, p. B-20.

33. Connecticut State Board of Labor Relations, *Clifford W. Beers . . .,* and information in a letter to the authors from Donald R. Crowell II, special assistant to the secretary of labor, August 19, 1974. Connecticut has a separate statute regulating collective bargaining by public education personnel. Under that statute, supervisory personnel and intermediate administrators are explicitly granted bargaining rights with provision made for "administrators units."

34. Hawaii *Revised Statutes,* Chapter 89, Laws of 1970, c. 171 as amended, Section 89-6(a). This section also provides that supervisors may be included with nonsupervisory employees in units of registered nurses; nonprofessional hospital and institutional employees; firemen; policemen; and professional and scientific employees, if both supervisors and nonsupervisors mutually agree to such a unit.

35. Ibid., Section 89-2(18).

36. *Government Employee Relations Report* (Washington, D.C.: Bureau of National Affairs), no. 518, August 27, 1973, p. B-18.

37. Minnesota *Statutes,* Sections 179.61-179.76; L. 1971, Chapter 33; effective July 1, 1972, as amended, Section 179.65(6). Note that the "essential employee" reference in this section appears to be of little practical significance.

38. Minnesota Public Employment Relations Board, *Firefighters Local 1275 and Village of Edina,* Case no. 73-PR-390A (June 25, 1973).

39. Minnesota Public Employment Relations Board, *AFSCME Council 6 and Winona State College,* Case no. 72-PR-1099 (May 9, 1972).

40. Minnesota Public Employment Relations Board, *City of Rochester and Rochester Police Benevolent Association; City of Rochester and IAFF Local 520,* Cases no. 72-PR-228-A and no. 72-PR-187-A (June 15, 1973).

41. McKinney's Consolidated Laws of New York, Civil Service Law, Sections 200-214; L. 1967, Chapter 392 as amended, Section 201(7)(a); Annotated Laws of Massachusetts, L. 1973, Chapter 1078, Sections 2-2B, 4-8, effective July 1, 1974, Section 1.

42. Massachusetts Labor Relations Commission, *City of Chicopee, School Committee and Chicopee Federation of Teachers, Local 2416, AFT, AFL-CIO and Chicopee Teachers Association,* Case no. MCR-1228 (November 18, 1974).

43. Ibid.

44. New York State Public Employment Relations Board, *Matter of Board of Education of the City School District of New York,* PERB Case no. E-1044(B) (June 28, 1973).

45. New York State Public Employment Relations Board, *Matter of Copiague Public Schools,* PERB Case nos. E-0025, E-0026, and C-0709 (January 3, 1973), and information in a letter to the authors from Robert D. Doherty, director, Institute of Public Employment, New York State School of Labor and Industrial Relations, Cornell University, November 25, 1974.

46. New York State Public Employment Relations Board, *Matter of Board of Education . . .* and *Matter of Copiague Public Schools.*

47. *School District of the City of Dearborn v. Labor Mediation Board of the State of Michigan* (now MERC) and *Dearborn Schools Operating Engineers Association,* Michigan Court of Appeals, Division 1, no. 6550 (filed February 25, 1970), and Michigan Employment Relations Commission, *Wayne County Sheriff Department and Metropolitan Council 23, AFSCME and Service Employees Local 502-M,* MERC Case nos. R710-187 and R71F-246 (February 4, 1972).

48. Ibid.

49. Pennsylvania *Statutes, Annotated,* Chapter 19; L. 1970, no. 195, Section 604(5).

50. Ibid., Section 301(6).

51. Pennsylvania Labor Relations Board, *Bellefonte Area School District,* Case no. PERA-R-2372-C (March 1, 1973).

52. Pennsylvania Labor Relations Board, *Altoona Area School District,* Case no. PERA-U-2571-C (April 4, 1973).

53. Pennsylvania Labor Relations Board, *City of Jeannette,* Case no. PERA-U-2227-W (December 15, 1972).

54. Information in a letter to the authors from Donald R. Crowell II, special assistant to the secretary of labor, August 19, 1974.

55. *Packard Motor Car Company,* 61 NLRB 4 (1945). The NLRB held that supervisors were "employees" for purposes of the NLRA and that when organized in autonomous units they could constitute appropriate bargaining units.

56. It is often argued, and the authors agree, that the problems caused by supervisory collective bargaining are less severe when supervisors are in autonomous units. As discussed here, the five states that allow bona fide supervisors to bargain collectively place them in autonomous units.

Changing Structures of Bargaining Relationships

The previous material emphasized the role of employer preferences and union behavior in structuring public sector collective bargaining relationships. Later in this section, we will examine another dimension of union employee behavior as it bears on bargaining structure, but now we focus on the internal dynamics of management as a component of bargaining structure. Particular attention is given to the establishment of a collective bargaining function in government; the behavior of management representatives in negotiations; and the role of the management labor negotiator as a mediator of internal, conflicting interests.

When faced with the imperative of public employee unionism, public employers must decide how to organize themselves for collective bargaining— even if something less than full-blown bargaining is required of or desired by them. The dominant practice among American governments, especially large ones, has been to establish a formal labor relations staff function headed by a director of labor relations, who usually serves as management's chief negotiator. This was the dominant pattern of management organization found by Burton in his survey of forty American local governments.[1] More recently, Derber observed that "centralization of management responsibility in [governmental] collective bargaining was fostered by a mounting recognition that the bargaining process demands professional skills, specialized knowledge, quick access to relevant data, and quantities of time and energy."[2] Most writers on this subject, who base their views and recommendations heavily on private sector labor relations practices, strongly advocate such a pinpointing of management responsibility for labor negotiations.

It should not be assumed, however, that a labor relations staff function is easily formed or implemented in government. As Burton showed, in the process of establishing such a function there occurs a transfer of responsibility (that is, of power) from the legislative to the executive branch and, within the executive branch, from the chief administrative officer, budget director, civil service commission, department heads, and/or other management actors to the chief executive.[3] Such transfers of power are resisted, of course, both before and after the fact, so that end runs, lobbying, and other political tactics of public labor relations organizations, which typically precede the formalization of bargaining in government and are the principal outlet of such organizations' energies prior to bargaining, do not quickly dissipate upon management's creation of a labor relations function. In the long run, however, according to Burton, the need to coordinate management's bargaining position outweighs other considerations, thereby "resolving" these internal management conflicts. Indeed, Burton argues that, in the clash between collective bargaining and the civil service system in government, the latter "seems doomed."[4] This is consistent with his view that public employee unionism challenges governments to overcome their fractionalized management structures, and that the establishment of a formal labor relations function centralizes management's authority for and position in collective bargaining.

Others have expressed similar views. For example, Shaw and Clark cite the lack of labor relations expertise among public officials and managers as the major rationale for their belief that management's authority for bargaining should be centralized in a formal labor relations function, and for their judgment that the end run must be eliminated for collective bargaining to operate effectively in government.[5] They further contend that government officials must follow the lead of the private sector, not only in structuring their labor relations functions but also in motivating public managers. From this perspective, public managers, especially negotiators, must be convinced of the need to represent government agencies' interest in bargaining and to retain management's decision-making prerogatives; supervisors should be considered part of management and the management bargaining team; and governmental compensation schemes should be revised to reward outstanding—and punish poor—performance. Moreover, note Shaw and Clark, public management should view itself as the acting rather than the reacting party in collective bargaining specifically and in the employment relationship generally. A strong management rights clause in collective agreements presumably expresses this concept of management. Finally, these authors argue that public managers must reexamine their virtual total opposition to public employee strikes and should weigh the costs and benefits of work stoppages in relation to other bargaining outcomes. As Shaw and Clark put it, "a [public employee] strike may reduce . . . employee demands and . . . may well be a good investment in the future."[6]

Whether these policy prescriptions would, if followed by governments, fundamentally alter the nature of public sector collective bargaining is questionable. On the surface, they appear to move government closer to the dominant bargaining model and negotiating practices of the private sector. But they do not eradicate some of the special characteristics of government or some of the differences between the public and private sectors that Shaw and Clark, Wellington and Winter, and others have identified.[7] These include the lack of a profit motive in government, the political component of decision making in public entities, and the lack of clear distinctions between managerial and nonmanagerial employees of public organizations. In such circumstances, it may not be possible fully to centralize authority and overcome a fractionalized management structure, to eliminate a multiplicity of managerial interests, or to subsume diverse interests under and invest policy-making responsibility in a chief labor negotiator. In other words, efforts to centralize public management's authority for labor relations formally, in a manner analogous to that of the private sector, may have only limited impact in terms of altering the internal dynamics of governmental management as well as collective bargaining.

This conclusion is reinforced by Kochan's examination of the role and functions of the management negotiator in public sector collective bargaining.[8] This study was based on an analysis of survey data concerning fire department labor relations in 221 municipalities in the United States. Kochan found that power is broadly dispersed within the managements of city governments; that the broader the dispersion, the more internal conflicts that occur; and that conflicts revolve around differences in the goals and interests of various management officials, including city council members, labor negotiators, fire chiefs, mayors, city managers, and civil service commissioners. The more conflicts that occur among city officials, the more bargaining takes on a multilateral rather than a bilateral character; that is, negotiations involve more than two distinct parties and operate in such a way that no clear separation exists between the employee and management organizations.[9] In this context, it is not possible to confine bargaining to the formal negotiations process inasmuch as various city officials bargain informally with each other as well as with organized employees. Hence, management faces the problem of coordinating multiple interests before and during formal negotiations.

This is the principal task facing management's negotiator in public sector labor relations. To accomplish it, Kochan proposes a dual role for the negotiator—on the one hand as a mediator of internal management disputes, on the other hand as an external bargaining representative in negotiations. This is not the conventional concept of the governmental labor negotiator's role, especially among negotiators who tend to see themselves as policymakers and dominant management actors. The latter view, however, overlooks the distribution of power among municipal officials and the legitimate interests that such officials have within the political decision-making processes of government. Unless the management negotiator is prepared to deal openly with and coordinate these often conflicting internal interests, he or she is unlikely to represent the public employer effectively in external bargaining. Thus, Kochan's analysis of the manner in which internal management dynamics affect the negotiator's behavior clearly indicates that such dynamics cannot simply be done away with merely by formally centralizing management's authority for governmental labor relations in the executive branch of government.

Once a structure of bargaining is established in a particular government, will it remain in place or be altered? Although bargaining structures may be affected by changes in environmental variables—notably bargaining laws and the decisions of administrative agencies established to implement such laws—the dominant variable in this regard is the set of interests and preferences of the direct parties to bargaining.

Unfortunately, very little research on changes in public sector bargaining units and bargaining structures has been conducted. Concerning the management organization in the context of bargaining structure, Derber and Wagner demonstrated that growing fiscal stress during the 1970s tended to shift bargaining authority away from governmental labor negotiators and toward governmental budget-making officials in the twenty-seven Illinois public jurisdictions that were included in their study.[10] Relatedly, Lewin showed that authority for labor negotiations in Los Angeles's municipal government shifted away from the city council and department heads and to the city's mayor under conditions of employee work slowdowns and threatened work stoppages.[11] These studies, however, did not reveal any formal or lasting changes in management's organization for collection bargaining in response to changing environmental factors or changing employee preferences and behavior.

Fortunately, one study of the stability of bargaining units in the public sector has been conducted and is included as the single reading selection in this section. Angle and Perry focused their research on public transit (bus) systems in attempting to determine how union member attitudes towards their labor organizations *and* their employer organizations were related to bargaining unit stability. Of the twenty transit bargaining structures studied, sixteen featured union representation of employees and four featured the employee association form of representation. Subsequent to the authors' initial administration of a survey instrument to union members, four of the union organizations were decertified and two of the associations were supplanted by unions. Thus, most of the data were interpreted to contrast the six "unstable" with the fourteen "stable" bargaining units in these transit systems.

Angle and Perry report three major findings. First, public transit employees who decertified their labor organizations were dissatisfied with both their unions' performance and their own influence with management. Second, the members of employee associations who subsequently adopted a union form of organization displayed highly positive attitudes toward their original associations. Angle and Perry interpret this finding to support an "escalation of unionism" thesis. Third, members of the stable labor organizations perceived themselves as having significantly more influence with management than did members of either type of unstable labor organization. Hence, the authors suggest that the stable organizations were more effective in providing "voice" to their members than either the displaced or replaced labor organizations.[12]

Although some of these interpretations of the data may be questioned (and the reader should carefully scrutinize the evidence presented in this article), Angle and Perry also propose that public employees are capable of exercising dual loyalty—that is, to their union (or employee association) and to their employer. If this is so, it may mean that changes in public sector bargaining units and bargaining structure that flow from employee (as distinct from management) preferences reflect a certain satisfaction with, rather than a challenge to, management. Indeed, this point is underscored by the high incidence of decertifications in the transit organizations studied by Angle and Perry. Finally, the reader should also note that this study is one of the relatively few examples of behavioral research that has been conducted on the topic of bargaining structure.[13]

Notes

1. John F. Burton, Jr., "Local Government Bargaining and Management Structure," *Industrial Relations* 11 (May 1972), pp. 123–140.

2. Milton Derber, "Management Organization for Collective Bargaining in the Public Sector," in Benjamin Aaron, Joseph R. Grodin, and James L. Stern, eds., *Public-Sector Bargaining* (Washington, D.C.: Bureau of National Affairs, 1979), pp. 94–95.

3. Burton, "Local Government Bargaining," pp. 133–135.

4. Ibid., p. 137. For a contrary view, see David Lewin and Raymond D. Horton, "The Impact of Collective Bargaining on the Merit System in Government," *The Arbitration Journal* 30 (September 1975), pp. 199–211.

5. Lee C. Shaw and Theodore Clark, Jr., "The Practical Differences Between Public and Private Sector Collective Bargaining," *UCLA Law Review* 19 (August 1972), pp. 867–886.

6. Ibid., p. 883.

7. See Harry Wellington and Ralph K. Winter, Jr., *The Unions and the Cities* (Washington, D.C.: Brookings Institution, 1971), and David Lewin, Raymond D. Horton, and James W. Kuhn, *Collective Bargaining and Manpower Utilization in Big City Governments* (Montclair, N.J.: Allanheld Osmun, 1979).

8. Thomas A. Kochan, *Resolving Internal Management Conflicts for Labor Negotiations* (Chicago: International Personnel Management Association, 1973).

9. See the reading by Kochan in chapter 4 of this book for a fuller definition and an empirical test of the concept of multilateral bargaining.

10. Milton Derber and Martin Wagner, "Public Sector Bargaining and Budget-Making under Fiscal Adversity," *Industrial and Labor Relations Review* 33 (October 1979), pp. 18–23.

11. David Lewin, "Local Government Labor Relations in Transition: The Case of Los Angeles," *Labor History* 17 (Spring 1976), pp. 191–213.

12. These authors' use of the concept of *voice* is based on Albert O. Hirschman, *Exit, Voice, and Loyalty* (Cambridge, Mass.: Harvard University Press, 1970).

13. See David Lewin and Peter Feuille, "Behavioral Research in Industrial Relations," *Industrial and Labor Relations Review* 36 (April 1983), pp. 341–360. For a fuller development of the concept of dual allegiance in the context of union–management relationships, see Harold L. Angle and James L. Perry, "An Empirical Assessment of Organizational Commitment and Organizational Effectiveness," *Administrative Science Quarterly* 26 (March 1981), pp. 1–14.

Union Member Attitudes and Bargaining Unit Stability in Urban Transit

Harold L. Angle
*James L. Perry**

Increasing instability in the leadership and organization of transit labor unions has been reported in recent years. This instability mirrors turbulence elsewhere within the industry—reflected in changing ownership forms, subsidy levels, and legislative and regulatory reforms. Does the instability in transit labor organizations conform to any predictable pattern? In this reading we investigate a particular facet of this question: namely, the relationship between member attitudes and bargaining unit stability.

A shrinkage has occurred in the U.S. labor movement in recent years, for a number of reasons including labor's demographic shift toward the service sector and away from traditional blue-collar employment (long the mainstay of organized labor). Deauthorization and decertification elections have played no small part in what, from a union perspective, represents a disturbing trend (Anderson, O'Reilly, and Busman, 1980; Dworkin and Extejt, 1979).

Actually, union members are, simultaneously, members of two systems— the union as manifest in the local bargaining unit, and the employing organization. The quality of their relationship with their employer would appear to be conditioned by the efficacy of the union in representing their interests. Where members have a voice (or a vote), it would appear that the bargaining unit's continued existence would become jeopardized when attitudes fall

*University of Minnesota and University of California, Irvine, respectively. Reprinted from *Proceedings of the Thirty-sixth Annual Meeting*. Madison, Wisc.: Industrial Relations Research Association, 1984, pp. 284–290.

below some critical threshold level. In addition to this relatively straightforward relationship between members' attitudes toward their union and bargaining unit stability, we suggest that there could be similar relationships for certain attitudes toward the job and the organization—at least to the extent that members see their satisfaction as dependent on the union's advocacy on their behalf.

The Study

The present study investigated the relationships between bargaining unit stability and members' attitudes toward several aspects of their union (or employee association), as well as their work and employing organization. The study was conducted in twenty West Coast public transit organizations (fixed-route bus systems). Sixteen of the bargaining units were unionized, while the other four were local employee associations. Questionnaires were administered on site and were filled out anonymously by 1,244 members of the bus operators' bargaining units during the summer of 1977.

Measures of union attitudes were adapted from the University of Michigan Organizational Assessment Package (Institute for Social Research, 1975). Job satisfaction was measured with the short form of the Minnesota Satisfaction Questionnaire (MSQ) (Weiss, Dawis, England, and Lofquist, 1967). Commitment to the organization was measured by means of Porter's Organizational Commitment Questionnaire (OCQ) (Porter, Steers, Mowday, and Boulian, 1974). Attitude measures and their scale reliabilities are listed in tables 1 and 2. Response rate was 64 percent.

During a period that began 18 months after questionnaire administration and ended 21 months later (that is, 39 months after administration), four of the unionized bargaining units were decertified, while two of the employee associations were replaced by unions. This left a residue of fourteen participating bargaining units that remained stable. This study, then, investigates systematic attitude differences across members of the three types of bargaining units—those that subsequently moved toward unionization, those that moved away from unionization, and those that did not change.

Data Analysis and Results

One-way analysis of variance (ANOVA), including analyses of between-category differences, revealed a number of systematic relationships between preexisting member attitudes and subsequent bargaining unit changes. Tables 1 and 2 present the results of these ANOVAs. In comparison with the fourteen stable bargaining units, members of decertified bargaining units

Table 1

ANOVA Results: Union/Association Attitudes and Dual Loyalty with Bargaining Unit Stability as the Categorical Variable

Independent Variable[a]	Alpha[b]	Category (N =)[c]	Mean	F-Ratio	Cell	Contrasts
Satisfaction with union or association efforts on member behalf (15)	.94	1 (104) 2 (913) 3 (111)	4.54 4.16 3.52	16.6***	1–2**	2–3***
Commitment to the union or employee association (4)	.76	1 (94) 2 (867) 3 (95)	4.81 4.66 4.47	1.8(n)		
Union/association solidarity (7)	.78	1 (94) 2 (866) 3 (95)	4.30 4.53 4.24	3.8*	1–2(n)	2–3*
Satisfaction with union or association leadership (10)	.94	1 (95) 2 (871) 3 (97)	4.58 4.14 4.04	4.3*	1–2*	2–3(n)
Members' evaluation of union or association process (10)	.89	1 (93) 2 (870) 3 (94)	4.51 4.24 4.17	2.1(n)		
Union's or association's perceived influence with management (10)	.90	1 (96) 2 (891) 3 (104)	2.71 3.04 2.34	14.7***	1–2*	2–3***
Members' perceived influence in union/association decision making (12)	.92	1 (91) 2 (861) 3 (93)	3.71 3.34 2.92	7.2***	1–2*	2–3***
Dual allegiance to union/association and to management (5)	.71	1 (90) 2 (869) 3 (98)	4.91 4.38 3.95	15.2***	1–2***	2–3***

[a]Number in parentheses indicates number of items in scale.

[b]Cronbach's alpha was employed in assessing scale reliability.

[c]1 = association-to-union; 2 = no change; 3 = decertification.

 *$p < .05$.

 **$p < .01$.

 ***$p < .001$.

were less satisfied with union efforts on their behalf, with their jobs in general, and specifically with such extrinsic factors as pay and job security. They perceived less personal influence in bargaining unit decision making, and saw their unions as having less influence with management. This group also indicated less union solidarity, less tendency toward dual allegiance, and a lower level of commitment to the organization—particularly commitment to continued membership (cf. Angle and Perry, 1981).

By contrast, attitude differences for members of the two employee associations that were subsequently replaced by actual unions were generally in

Table 2
ANOVA Results: Attitudes Toward Organization and Job with Bargaining
Unit Stability as the Categorical Variable

Independent Variable[a]	Alpha[b]	Category (N =)[c]	Mean	F-Ratio	Cell	Contrasts
Organizational commitment (15)	.89	1 (110)	4.94	12.7***	1–2***	2–3*
		2 (974)	4.48			
		3 (121)	4.22			
Value commitment (9)	.89	1 (110)	4.98	8.3***	1–2***	2–3(n)
		2 (973)	4.55			
		3 (121)	4.31			
Commitment to membership (5)	.72	1 (110)	5.06	10.9***	1–2***	2–3**
		2 (973)	4.63			
		3 (121)	4.32			
Job satisfaction (20)	.91	1 (110)	5.23	11.9***	1–2***	2–3*
		2 (982)	4.80			
		3 (124)	4.56			
Satisfaction with treatment by the organization (5)	.86	1 (110)	4.63	15.1***	1–2***	2–3(n)
		2 (981)	3.84			
		3 (124)	3.59			
Satisfaction with personal influence on the job (4)	.78	1 (110)	4.79	5.3**	1–2**	2–3(n)
		2 (981)	4.39			
		3 (124)	4.20			
Satisfaction with sense of accomplishment (3)	.81	1 (110)	5.41	6.7**	1–2***	2–3(n)
		2 (981)	4.87			
		3 (124)	4.81			
Satisfaction with the work itself (2)	(r = .28)	1 (110)	6.05	3.6*	1–2*	2–3(n)
		2 (984)	5.83			
		3 (124)	5.70			
Satisfaction with pay job security (2)	(r = .32)	1 (110)	5.50	12.6***	1–2(n)	2–3***
		2 (983)	5.59			
		3 (123)	4.98			

[a]Number in parentheses indicates number of items in scale.
[b]Cronbach's alpha was employed in assessing scale reliability.
[c]1 = association-to-union; 2 = no change; 3 = decertification.
*$p < .05$.
**$p < .01$.
***$p < .001$.

the opposite direction. In comparison to members of the stable bargaining units, they expressed greater satisfaction with association efforts on their behalf, as well as with the effectiveness of their association leadership, and with their jobs—particularly with respect to the way they were treated by the organization, and such intrinsic aspects as the work itself, their level of influence, and their sense of accomplishment. They expressed greater personal influence in bargaining unit decisions and a stronger tendency toward dual allegiance. This group also disclosed a higher level of organizational commitment, including value commitment as well as commitment to membership (Angle and Perry, 1981).

Only one relationship ran counter to this pattern. Oddly, the association-to-union group indicated that their association had a lesser amount of influence with management than did members of the stable bargaining units. Although directional differences in means were as expected, the overall *F*-ratios were not statistically significant for either of the two remaining attitudinal variables: union commitment and members' evaluation of the union/association process.

Discussion

The study reported herein is something akin to a naturally occurring field experiment. It was fortuitous that six bargaining unit changes occurred in a relatively brief period of time after collection of survey data. The temporal ordering of these events allows at least a modicum of causal inference.

The overall pattern of findings provides a conpelling case that the attitudes of bargaining unit members are predictive of bargaining unit changes. In general, bargaining units whose members are disaffected appear strongly prone toward decertification. In contrast, there is the finding that members of employee associations that dissolve in favor of unionization actually have more positive attitudes toward their present bargaining units than do members of units that remain intact. We suggest that, rather than voting their distaste for collective bargaining (as appears to be the case with the decertified unions), what may be happening in such instances is a sort of escalation of unionism. Members of successful employee associations may become motivated to "go the rest of the way"; that is, members of such bargaining units become inclined toward an even deeper commitment to collective bargaining. Thus, a group of employees who have successfully "experimented with unionism" through participation in an in-house employee association would extend their involvement by voting in a bona fide union. This, too, is bargaining unit instability, but of a rather different sort from the decertification of an existing union.

There is one striking anomaly in the pattern of findings. Members of *both* types of unstable bargaining units saw their units as having less influence with management than did members of the stable units. While consonant with the overall pattern for the decertified units, this seems out of alignment with the overall attitudinal patterns for the association-to-union group. This anomaly, however, can be readily explained by Hirschman's (1970) concepts of exit, voice, and loyalty. Hirschman's central argument is that individuals confronted by *exit* (represented here by decertification) and *voice* (represented by the association-to-union change) options will usually choose to exit unless compelled otherwise by special attachment to an organization. This special attachment is what Hirschman terms *loyalty*. The likelihood of voice increases with the degree of loyalty.

A comparison of patterns between the decertification group and the association-to-union group indicates significant differences in attitudes related to Hirschman's loyalty concept. Among the attitudes expressed by members of the decertification group are low satisfaction with their organization's efforts, a perceived lack of influence with management, and a lack of influence within the union or association. These negative attitudes are compounded by low commitment to membership in the employing organization, reflecting low attachment to the labor organization as well.

In all respects, these loyalty factors are just the opposite in the association-to-union group. Members of this group express satisfaction with their association's efforts, as well as their influence within the association. Moreover, they exhibit high commitment to membership in their transit organization. Given this structure of positive attitudes, the "activation of voice," as Hirschman terms it, is an attempt to modify the association's perceived lack of influence with management, that is, the apparent anomaly in the data. This interpretation of our results is also consistent with the theory of cognitive dissonance on which Hirschman's loyalty concept is based.

Another interesting aspect of this study is the finding that attitudes toward the union or employee association and toward the employing organization tended to go hand in hand. Bargaining unit members whose attitudes were more positive toward one system tended also to have more positive attitudes toward the other. This touches upon an ancient issue in labor–management relations—that of dual allegiance (Martin, 1981; Purcell, 1960). Taken as a variable in its own right, dual loyalty was more pronounced in the association-to-union group, and less so in the decertified bargaining units. The overall pattern of results indicates that there is no inherent incompatibility between attitudes toward management and toward the union.

We would anticipate that these results could be replicated outside the urban transit industry. However, there are several facets of this study that may be of particular concern to the transit industry. First, there is the surprisingly large number of decertifications within our sample of organizations. While we have no readily comparable data on which we could base a more objective assessment, this may be symptomatic of serious problems at the local level. Second, maintenance of member loyalty is becoming increasingly difficult, with the emergence of federal subsidy cutbacks, quality of working life issues, and the "new breed" of transit employees whose attachments to work are reportedly quite different from their more senior counterparts.

Finally, the rules and regulations governing transit labor–management relations that have evolved in federal, state, and local governments in the past decade may have eroded some of labor's once-dominant legal position, making it more difficult to maintain member loyalty in the future.

As an overall conclusion from the research, it seems fair to state that employee attitudes are important precursors of significant changes in bargaining unit status. In particular, the study discloses some attitude–behavior relationships of major importance to unions. Indeed, we may be so bold as to suggest that these findings ought to contribute toward the reopening of a long-lost collaboration between the psychologist and the union (see Gordon and Burt, 1981; Rosen and Stagner, 1980).

References

Anderson, John C., Charles A. O'Reilly III, and Gloria Busman. "Union Decertification in the U.S.: 1947–1977." *Industrial Relations* 19 (Winter 1980), pp. 100–107.

Angle, Harold L., and James L. Perry. "An Empirical Assessment of Organizational Commitment and Organizational Effectiveness." *Administrative Science Quarterly* 26 (March 1981), pp. 1–14.

Dworkin, James, and Marian Extejt. "The Union Shop Deauthorization Poll: A New Look after 20 Years." *Monthly Labor Review* 102 (November 1979), pp. 36–39.

Gordon, Michael E., and Robert E. Burt. "A History of Industrial Psychology's Relationship with American Unions: Lessons from the Past and Directions for the Future." *International Review of Applied Psychology* 30 (April 1981), pp. 137–156.

Hirschman, Albert O. *Exit, Voice and Loyalty: Responses to Decline in Firms, Organizations and States.* Cambridge, Mass.: Harvard University Press, 1970.

Institute for Social Research. *Michigan Organizational Assessment Package: Progress Report II.* Ann Arbor, Mich.: Survey Research Center, ISR, 1975.

Martin, James E. "Dual Allegiance in Public Sector Unionism: A Case Study." *International Review of Applied Psychology* 30 (April 1981), pp. 245–259.

Porter, Lyman W., Richard M. Steers, Richard T. Mowday, and Paul V. Boulian. "Organizational Commitment, Job Satisfaction and Turnover among Psychiatric Technicians." *Journal of Applied Psychology* 59 (October 1974), pp. 603–609.

Purcell, Theodore V. *Blue Collar Man: Patterns of Dual Allegiance in Industry.* Cambridge, Mass.: Harvard University Press, 1960.

Rosen, Hjalmar, and Ross Stagner. "Industrial/Organizational Psychology and Unions: A Viable Relationship?" *Professional Psychology II* (June 1980), pp. 477–483.

Weiss, David J., Rene V. Dawis, George W. England, and Lloyd H. Lofquist. *Manual for the Minnesota Satisfaction Questionnaire: Minnesota Studies in Vocational Rehabilitation,* vol. 22. Minneapolis: Industrial Relations Center, University of Minnesota, 1967.

The Potential for Employer and Union Alliances

In examining the structure of public sector bargaining, the focus of the previous section was on internal management, intragovernmental dynamics, and intraunion dynamics. In contrast, this section focuses on the potential for intergovernmental and interunion alliances in the public sector—alliances that at present are extremely rare.

In recent years, considerable speculation has emerged concerning the prospects for multiemployer bargaining in government. Such speculation is most commonly focused on teacher–school board labor relations, with some observers and participants foreseeing the development of multiemployer arrangements. Despite the speculation, hardly any systematic empirical study of this issue has been reported in the literature.

This deficiency is partially remedied by the first reading included in this section, authored by Feuille, Juris, Jones, and Jedel. These authors first review the factors potentially supporting and mitigating the development of multiemployer bargaining in government. Perhaps the key considerations here are the product market monopoly (or near-monopoly) and independent political jurisdiction of each American local government, factors that do not provide strong incentives for intergovernmental cooperation, let alone multiemployer bargaining. It is instructive to note that the product market, specifically a highly competitive product market, seems to be the leading variable "explaining" the emergence of multiemployer bargaining in private industry.[1]

Next, Feuille and his associates report the empirical results of their own research which was designed to assess the extent of and climate for multiemployer bargaining in local government. The authors studied 225 governments located in four major metropolitan areas; concentrated on teacher, police, firefighter, and public works employees; and conducted 97 interviews of employers, union representatives, mediators, and fact-finders.

The research uncovered no instances of permanent multiemployer bargaining among these governments and few attempts to establish such bargaining. Instead, the parties seemed to prefer single-employer, single-union bargaining, with the procedural difficulties of coordinating negotiations across diverse jurisdictions and the potential reduction of individual employers' autonomy being the major factors accounting for the lack of formal multiemployer relationships.

Then the authors analyzed the incidence of labor relations information exchanges among these governments. Surprisingly, perhaps, these exchanges were broad, frequent, and widespread. They indicate that some local public employers in major metropolitan areas are well aware of local labor market conditions, the status of negotiations in other governments, and the range of wage and fringe benefit offers made or expected to be bargained over by their counterparts in other jurisdictions. Additionally, a few small governments used the same outside consultants to negotiate their labor agreements. As of yet, however, these information exchanges have not led to alterations of bargaining structure in local government, and certainly not to multi-employer bargaining. Public employers remain strongly wedded to the proprietary interest in their own bargaining activity, bargaining data, and decision-making authority. Feuille and his associates conclude, therefore, that although government employers are willing to devote resources to cooperative information sharing, their concern with autonomy translates into very little support for multiemployer negotiations in the public sector irrespective of what some observers presume to be the advantages of this type of bargaining structure.

Many have speculated about the potential for employer alliances in public sector bargaining, but few have done so with respect to bargaining alliances among public sector unions. Public sector labor organizations often form alliances to support specific labor legislation, certain broader public policies, and particular candidates for political office. But the formation of interunion alliances or coalitions to bargain with public employers has rarely been observed or proposed. This is no doubt due in part to the aforementioned emphasis on decentralized bargaining in the U.S. system of industrial relations, especially the integrity and autonomy of the individual bargaining unit. Yet, over the period from the late 1960s to the early 1980s, full-scale coalition bargaining developed in the nation's largest municipal government, New York City, and it is this development that is analyzed in the final reading in this chapter, by Lewin and McCormick.

These authors systematically examine the factors that contributed to the adoption of a coalition bargaining structure. These included the reduction of interunion rivalries, the growth of pattern bargaining, and the enactment in 1967 of New York City's Collective Bargaining Law. The reduction of interunion rivalries was due in large part to the evolution of several large labor organizations with relatively stable leadership, a process that dated to the mid-1950s, when, through mayoral directives, municipal employees were accorded (nonstatutory) unionism and bargaining rights. Pattern bargaining could be said to have developed out of necessity, as the intramunicipal wage comparisons made by the city's 250,000 employees, who at one point were represented by 85 separate unions and were distributed among more than 400 bargaining units, took on the status of wage-setting decision rules. This bargaining phenomenon was reinforced by the decisions of various impasse panels, which were often appointed to resolve negotiating impasses and which viewed pay parity relationships as contributing to labor peace. The city's Collective Bargaining Law created a citywide bargaining unit to negotiate certain terms of employment that were required by other statutes to be uniform for career personnel, and it also established a Municipal Labor

Committee that was charged with coordinating union participation in the administration of the local bargaining system by the tripartite Office of Collective Bargaining (OCB).

But the main factor that gave impetus to coalition bargaining in New York's municipal government was the fiscal crisis that struck the city in the mid-1970s. Lewin and McCormick show how the crisis spurred the formation of union coalitions and the use of these coalitions to bargain master agreements covering virtually all municipal workers in 1975, 1976, 1978, and 1980. In addition to these master agreements, subsidiary agreements covering noneconomic matters were permitted to be negotiated on a unit-by-unit basis; these helped to preserve the autonomy of individual union leaders, which the large coalition otherwise threatened (the authors refer to this as two-tier coalition bargaining). Of particular interest was the city management's support of coalition bargaining (or, perhaps more accurately, lack of opposition to it), which helped municipal *and* union officials not only to reach bargaining agreements with each other but also to "negotiate" the terms of the city's fiscal rescue with other governing bodies—the state of New York and the federal government—that, in the aftermath of the fiscal crisis, acquired greater control over New York's municipal affairs. Lewin and McCormick thus conclude that coalition bargaining served both union and management interests in New York City under conditions of fiscal adversity.

In the years following publication of the Lewin-McCormick article, New York City's financial conditions has improved markedly, although its strengths and weaknesses and its prospects for the future remain subject to considerable debate. More important for purposes of this section, the unified union coalition that developed in New York City government in the late 1970s has since come apart, with separate coalitions of uniformed and non-uniformed employees having been formed.[2] Whether or not this dual coalition structure will endure for the 1980s is uncertain, but the New York City experience in toto suggests at the very least that fiscal adversity is a necessary, though probably not a sufficient, condition for the development of a coalition bargaining structure in the public sector.

In any case, we remind the reader that in evaluating the conclusions reached by Lewin and McCormick and by the authors of the other papers included in this chapter, careful consideration should be given to the empirical bases of the findings, the diversity of public sector labor relations, and the relatively short history of collective bargaining in American governments. Future changes as well as those now underway in the environment of public sector labor relations may well cause significant alterations in the structure of collective bargaining. As with other aspects of public sector labor relations, the structure of collective bargaining needs to be reappraised periodically if its dynamic changes are to be documented and understood.

Notes

1. For a theoretical assessment of bargaining structure research, see Marianne Koch, David Lewin, and Donna Sockell, "The Determinants of Bargaining Structure: A Case Study of AT&T," in David Lewin, David B. Lipsky, and Donna Sockell, eds., *Advances in Industrial and Labor Relations,* vol. 4 (Greenwich, Conn.: JAI Press, 1987), pp. 223–251.

2. See Raymond D. Horton and David Lewin, "Human Resources Management," in Gerald Benjamin and Charles Brecher, eds., *The Two New Yorks: State–City Relations in the Changing Federal System* (New York: Russell Sage), forthcoming.

Multiemployer Bargaining among Local Governments

Peter Feuille
Hervey Juris
Ralph Jones
Michael Jay Jedel*

The emergence of collective bargaining in government has resulted in research into a variety of bargaining structure topics, including unit fragmentation, supervisory units, and management organization for bargaining. However, relatively little attention has been devoted to the general extent and shape of interemployer relationships and the conditions that foster or hinder their development. This reading is intended as one step to meet this need by presenting and discussing some findings from an exploratory study of interemployer bargaining relationships in four metropolitan areas.

Interemployer Bargaining Relationships

Very few interemployer bargaining arrangements have been reported among North American public employers.[1] The lion's share of this small literature has focused on the key success story of multiemployer bargaining in government: the negotiations between the Minnesota Twin City Metropolitan Area

*University of Illinois, Northwestern University, private consulting and Georgia State University, respectively. Reprinted from *Proceedings of the Twenty-ninth Annual Meeting*. Madison, Wisc.: Industrial Relations Research Association, 1977, pp. 123–131.

Managers Association, representing thirty separate jurisdictions, and Operating Engineers Local 49 for a succession of contracts covering public works employees. In addition, there have been reported instances of employer association bargaining in British Columbia[2] and instances of multiunit bargaining in various federal agencies.[3] There have also been two unsuccessful attempts to establish multiemployer bargaining with firefighter locals, one in California's Alameda County[4] and the other in some Minneapolis–St. Paul suburbs.[5] These reports of public sector experiences demonstrate that there has been some experimentation with expanded negotiating units, but they tell us very little about the extent to which the phenomenon is practiced generally or has been attempted elsewhere.

Further, it is not at all clear on an a priori basis that multiemployer bargaining should appear as a widespread practice in public sector bargaining. On the one hand there are some significant incentives for local government employers in a particular metropolitan area to establish such relationships: the employers in each area compete for the bulk of their labor in the same local labor markets: this labor market competition means that individual employers look to other employers in the same area for comparative data to use at the bargaining table and are affected by the terms of bargaining settlements in nearby jurisdictions; and the employers in an area frequently may deal with locals of the same union for any particular occupational group. On the other hand, however, the fact that each local government employer enjoys product market monopolies and is an independent political jurisdiction with its own elected and appointed officials dependent for support on separate citizen-voter-taxpayer constituencies suggests that there are minimal incentives for interemployer bargaining cooperation.

The private sector bargaining literature[6] presents a similarly bifurcated message. Some employers create and participate in interorganizational bargaining structures because they perceive that they can secure more advantageous terms acting in concert than individually, and these perceptions seem to be associated with several environmental conditions. First, the product market tends to be highly competitive, and the employers' products are relatively undifferentiated. Second, the employers tend to compete for labor in the same labor markets. Third, the employers tend to be in close geographical proximity with one another. Fourth, the employers tend to deal with the same union or set of unions, and each employer tends to be small relative to the union. To test the validity of these general conditions, consider that employer association bargaining is the norm in the construction, trucking, garment, coal, and many big city local service industries (such as hotels, restaurants, and laundry delivery), and in these industries most of the aforementioned conditions exist. However, employers in other industries (autos, electrical equipment, airlines, oil refining, chemical products) with different conditions have continued to bargain on a single-employer basis. Of all these private sector conditions just specified, the only one that does not apply to the local government bargaining situation is the competitive product market dimension. However, the absence of competitive product market pressures may be more important than the presence of all the other conditions that may give rise to multiemployer bargaining arrangements in government.[7]

As a separate consideration, it is possible that while the official structure of local government bargaining may adhere to a single employer–single union paradigm, the actual structure may reflect interemployer cooperation via the exchange and use of bargaining information. Employer negotiators may be able to achieve some kind of structural integration across separate bargaining units through formal and informal exchanges of information with their counterparts in other jurisdictions. As a result, we decided to examine the information collection and dissemination practices of employers to see what kinds of interemployer decision connections, if any, emerged from these information exchanges.

Research Design

To assess the extent to which conditions arguing for and against multiemployer bargaining might be operating in the current local government bargaining climate, we selected for study the interemployer relationships established by local public employers in four geographically diverse metropolitan areas (each with a population in excess of one million): Bay City (in the New England census region), Industrial City (in the Middle Atlantic region), Sun City (South Atlantic), and Lake City (East North Central). The majority of governmental employers in each metropolitan area have been engaged in collective bargaining at least since 1970 (and in one case since 1960), so there was a substantial (for the public sector) history of bargaining in each area. Because bargaining structures can differ by occupation and because different types of governmental jurisdictions are involved in teacher and nonteacher bargaining, we selected four occupations for examination: teachers, police officers, firefighters, and general public works employees. This geographical and occupational diversity should improve the generalizability of our results.

We collected data from a sample of employer and union bargaining representatives for each occupation in each metropolitan area and from selected neutrals (mediators and fact-finders). The employers in the sample were selected on the basis of size because the larger governmental employers generally have lengthier bargaining histories. A total of ninety-seven interviews were conducted during 1975 in the central city, the central city school district, the core county, and several of the larger suburban municipalities and school districts in the four areas. Each interview followed the same

Table 1
Sample Characteristics

Metropolitan Area (Census Region)	Number of Municipalities	Number of School Districts	Number of Continuing Interemployer Bargaining Relationships	Number of Continuing Interemployer Information Exchange Relationships
Bay City (New England)	31	48	0	4
Industrial City (Middle Atlantic)	35	30	0	2
Sun City (South Atlantic)	27	1	0	2
Lake City (East North Central)	21	31	0	3

format, with the interviewers asking each respondent a set of questions about the interorganizational bargaining and information exchange relationships in which the respondent participated. Table 1 shows, for each metropolitan area, the number of local governments included in the study for which interemployer cooperation was an option.

Results and Analysis

The interview responses showed two distinct patterns of interorganizational cooperative relationships: The first involves bargaining structure, and the second involves the exchange of bargaining information.

Bargaining Structure

Table 1 shows that we found *no* lasting interemployer bargaining alliances in these four areas. The employers in this sample maintain autonomous bargaining relationships, that is, each of them handles the collective bargaining process on an individual basis and does not engage in association, coordinated, or coalition bargaining with other employers. The few attempts to establish coordinated bargaining serve to emphasize the prevalence of these autonomous relationships.

We discovered two efforts each in the Industrial City and Lake City areas of employers attempting to establish coordinated bargaining. In Industrial City in 1972 several suburban school district negotiators agreed to coordinate their positions on salaries during bargaining with the respective teacher union locals. This effort consisted of two elements: a common upper limit (apparently 5 percent) and no salary settlement without group approval. This informal coalition failed to attain its objectives as individual districts settled for more than the guideline without seeking group approval. A second Industrial City effort was made in 1973 involving primarily the blue-collar or public works employees represented by American Federation of State, County, and Municipal Employees (AFSCME) locals of four area employers (the central city, central city school district, sewer authority, and housing authority). All the unions and employers negotiated together at the same bargaining table, and the ostensible goal was to bargain a uniform contract to cover the employees in the separate bargaining units. After a few meetings the effort dissolved, apparently because of a reluctance to make concessions for the sake of uniformity and because of interpersonal rivalries.

In the Lake City area there were also two coordination attempts. In 1973, at the central city's urging, the city, county, city school district, area vocational education district, sewage commission, and several of the suburban municipalities coordinated their bargaining efforts with various employee groups in that they agreed on common settlement limits and the timing of their offers. The key employer negotiator involved believed that this effort was successful; that is, the dollar cost of the settlements was smaller than it would have been in the absence of this coordination effort. However, in the next round of negotiations, in 1975, this informal bargaining coalition never really came together, as each of the jurisdictions bargained and settled on an individual basis.

In addition, in the Sun City area in 1974 employer negotiators from the central city, two large suburbs, and the county discussed the possibility of establishing an official bargaining coalition with their firefighter locals, but such a coalition was never established, apparently because of the difficulties involved in achieving bargaining uniformity across four different employment contexts.

A variety of reasons were offered by employer respondents for the prevalence of autonomous bargaining relationships, and these reasons can be grouped into two categories: the procedural difficulties of coordinating bargaining across numerous contexts, and a perception that interorganizational relationships would reduce the decision-making autonomy of the employers surveyed. Most of the respondents believed that securing and maintaining employer commitment to a united bargaining strategy across multiple employers with varying employment conditions would be a very complex and difficult task which would not necessarily result in an improvement in individual employer welfare. In addition, the respondents placed a large positive value on the political autonomy or decision-making descretion of their employing organization, and they perceived that an interorganizational bargaining relationship would reduce that autonomy in return for an uncertain outcome.

Consequently, we found very little interemployer bargaining cooperation in general and no continuing coodinative or coalitional relationships in particular. The history of the coordinative failures just described suggests that there are substantial centrifugal pressures in those interemployer interdependencies where member units retain their decision authority. In turn, these centrifugal pressures seem to be associated with differences in employment conditions across employers and with a concomitant unwillingness of both employers and unions to make changes for the sake of group uniformity in the absence of any compelling reason to do so. These results suggest that interemployer bargaining interdependencies, in spite of their potential benefits,[8] will not be adopted by local governments until the perceived benefits clearly outweigh the perceived costs of reduced autonomy.

Informational Exchange

In contrast to the autonomous nature of bargaining relationships, the employers surveyed had established a variety of interemployer connections for the purpose of acquiring and exchanging bargaining information. The most visible relationships are the eleven formal organizations (four in the Bay City area, three in the Lake City area, and two each in the Industrial City and Sun City areas) that exist in whole or in large part to facilitate the exchange of bargaining information (wage and fringe data, contract language, current negotiation developments, and the like) among member employers. While the existence of a few of these organizations antedates the emergence of collective bargaining, and while a few are statewide organizations, all of them devote all or a major portion of their resources to the exchange of information among employers in the four areas.

These organizations vary considerably in the amount and types of services they provide their members. Some organizations have substantial income (primarily dues and fees from members) and their own staff to perform or facilitate information collection and dissemination services, while other organizations have no staff, almost no income, and do little more than hold periodic meetings to facilitate informal, face-to-face information exchanges (primarily "war stories"). For example, in order to prevent whipsawing, the thirty-one school district employers in the Lake City area school district negotiators association regularly report to each other via the association on the results of each of their own negotiating sessions. Negotiators for the suburban Industrial City area school districts meet regularly, under the auspices of the county association of school boards, to exchange negotiation development and employment condition information. At least five of these organizations regularly conduct wage and fringe benefit surveys and disseminate the results to members. As the foregoing examples may indicate, the most structured of these information exchange relationships exist among the school district negotiators in three of the four areas surveyed (in the Sun City area there is only one countywide school district.)

In addition to these institutionalized information exchanges, the employers in each area engage in substantial ad hoc surveys of and discussions with other employers, usually via telephone, as the need arises. In these ad hoc exchanges the suburban employers appear to concentrate primarily on other suburban employers in the same metropolitan area and secondarily on other employers in the state; the central city employers appear to concentrate primarily on other large cities and secondarily on local metropolitan area employers. Also, most of the employers purchase substantial information via publications issued by trade associations, labor relations reporting services, and specialized government agencies. Finally, a special kind of information exchange process exists where consultant negotiators represent employers at the negotiating table. In each of the four areas, we encountered several people (usually lawyers) who perform negotiating services on a consulting basis, usually for suburban employers too small to support a full-time labor relations representative. These consultants establish de facto interorganizational information exchanges among the employers they represent.

The large number of continuing information exchange relationships stands in marked contrast to the absence of any continuing coordinated or coalition bargaining activities. These results suggest that the employers in this sample perceive some substantial benefits resulting from the exchange of bargaining information. However, these information exchange perceptions have not resulted in significant interemployer cooperation during the bargaining process; that is, they have not led to changes in the official or actual structure of bargaining. The employers in this sample, then, are willing to incur substantial costs (money, time) to collect and exchange information relevant to the discharge of their bargaining responsibilities; they are unwilling to relinquish their bargaining decision autonomy to an interorganizational system in which group interests may supersede individual interests.

Conclusions

Many worthwhile claims have been made on behalf of multiemployer bargaining in the public sector: It protects against whipsawing, it avoids the costly duplication involved in repeated negotiations for similar contracts among proximate employers, it may result in greater expertise at the bargaining table, and it is a flexible arrangement which can be changed by the participants as they mutually see fit.[9] However, the results of this study suggest that local government employers apparently perceive that these potential benefits are outweighed by the costs associated with a multiemployer arrangement. First, employer respondents anticipated considerable procedural difficulties in coordinating bargaining across several bargaining units with different employment conditions and abilities to pay and with different union leaders. These difficulties are compounded by different management structures and decision processes, even in contiguous jurisdictions.[10] Employer respondents were especially dubious of the willingness of the participants to make bargaining concessions for the sake of uniformity in the absence of any compelling reason to do so (that is, competitive product market pressures). Second, these respondents spoke of employer decision autonomy in strongly positive terms as a behavioral dimension worth preserving (or else perceived by their respective citizenries as worth preserving).

Finally, our interview responses produced some information which questions the value of multiemployer bargaining as a device to reduce costly duplication. It was readily apparent from the responses of both union and management representatives that many respondents had little or no desire to reduce such duplication because to do so would reduce their organizational stature or even eliminate their current livelihood. For instance, one consultant negotiator in the Industrial City area was strongly opposed to multiemployer bargaining because it would reduce the total number of negotiations and hence the market for his services. The reduction of costly, tax-supported, duplicated services may be a worthy goal, but at the same time it negatively affects the self-interest of large numbers of current and future union and management representatives, and this in turn encourages resistance to the concept.

In sum, multiemployer bargaining among local governments has been touted as a very worthwhile phenomenon. If our study is indicative of widespread bargaining realities, however, it suggests that it is a phenomenon whose time has not yet come.

Notes

1. Cyrus F. Smythe, Jr., "Public–Private Sector Multi-Employer Collective Bargaining—The Role of the Employer Representative," *Labor Law Journal* 22 (August 1971), pp. 498–508; David L. Norgaard and Karl Van Asselt, *Cities Join Together for Bargaining: The Experience in Minnesota and British Columbia,* Strengthening Local Government through Better Labor Relations, no. 10, Labor–Management Relations Service, September 1971; *California Public Employee Relations,* no. 19 (December 1973), pp. 25–28; and Richard Pegnetter, *Multiemployer Bargaining in the Public Sector: Purposes and Experiences,* Public Employee Relations Library, no. 52 (Chicago: International Personnel Management Association, 1975).

2. Norgaard and Van Asselt, *Cities Join Together.*

3. Pegnetter, *Multiemployer Bargaining,* pp. 11–13.

4. *California Public Employee Relations.*

5. Pegnetter, *Multiemployer Bargaining,* p. 14.

6. For example, see Arnold R. Weber, ed., *The Structure of Collective Bargaining* (New York: Free Press, 1961); Arnold R. Weber, "Stability and Change in the Structure of Collective Bargaining," in the American Assembly volume *Challenges to*

Collective Bargaining, ed. Lloyd Ulman (Englewood Cliffs, N.J.: Prentice-Hall, 1967), pp. 13–36; Jesse T. Carpenter, *Employers' Associations and Collective Bargaining in New York City* (Ithaca, N.Y.: Cornell University Press, 1950); and Edwin F. Beal, Edward D. Wickersham, and Philip Kienast, *The Practice of Collective Bargaining* (Homewood, Ill.: Richard D. Irwin, 1976).

7. For a discussion of the conditions that increase the possibility of multi-employer bargaining units, see Smythe, "Public–Private Sector Multi-Employer Collective Bargaining," pp. 507–508.

8. Pegnetter, *Multiemployer Bargaining,* pp. 21–26.

9. Ibid.

10. For a discussion of this phenomenon in Los Angeles city and county, see David Lewin, "Local Government Labor Relations in Transition: The Case of Los Angeles," *Labor History* 17 (Winter 1976), pp. 191–213.

Coalition Bargaining in Municipal Government: The New York City Experience

David Lewin
*Mary McCormick**

In both 1978 and 1980, the nation's largest municipal government and its public employee unions used a formal coalition bargaining structure to negotiate basic wage agreements that covered more than a quarter-million workers. These negotiations were preceded by others in the mid-1970s that featured informal coalition bargaining on a smaller scale. The emergence and development of coalition bargaining in New York City, particularly during a period of sustained fiscal crisis, raise several questions about the structure and future direction of public sector bargaining. It is clear that generalizations about coalition bargaining, or, more broadly, bargaining structure in the public sector, cannot rest on the experience of a single government or a group of labor organizations in a single city; yet New York City's experience should not be overlooked, especially since in many respects over the past two decades this city has been a trendsetter in the development of public sector labor relations in the United States.[1]

Why, in view of the aversion to coalition bargaining of most unions and managements in both the public and private sectors, has such a structural

*Columbia University and Rockefeller Brothers Fund, respectively. Reprinted from *Industrial and Labor Relations Review* 34, no. 2 (January 1981), pp. 175–190.

arrangement emerged in New York City's municipal government? What historical, environmental, and institutional factors have contributed to this development? Will municipal coalition bargaining stabilize, develop further, or decline in New York City during the 1980s? What are the prospects for coalition bargaining elsewhere in the public sector? These questions will be addressed in this reading.

Bargaining Structure

In recent years, some scholarly attention has been paid to the formation of union and management coalitions for bargaining purposes in the private sector. The basic purpose of such coalitions is to augment the bargaining power of one or the other parties to negotiations.[2] The development of private sector union coalitions has been sparked by the rapid growth of the conglomerate form of corporate organization in the 1960s and 1970s.[3] This is reflected in the efforts of the Industrial Union Department (IUD) of the AFL-CIO to coalesce for bargaining purposes differentially affiliated local unions in companies where single-plant, single-union bargaining has predominated.

But corporate conglomeration is not a necessary precondition to the formation of a union coalition. Recall, for example, General Electric, which was met in the late 1960s by a coalition of thirteen unions countering the company's final-offer-first approach to collective bargaining (known as Boulwarism). Rulings by the National Labor Relations Board and the courts that supported coordinated bargaining at General Electric helped focus attention on this case.[4]

Note that coordinated bargaining occurs when "two or more unions negotiate jointly for *individual* union contracts containing common terms," whereas coalition bargaining refers to situations in which "two or more unions bargain jointly for a *common* 'master agreement' covering all employees they . . . represent."[5] Thus, some union coalitions may be engaged in coordinated bargaining while others are engaged in coalition bargaining with a single employer or an employers' association. Furthermore, these two types of bargaining may be distinguished from pattern bargaining, which refers to the negotiation by one union and one employer of terms and conditions of employment that establish targets for other unions and employers.[6]

Considerably more research attention has been devoted to employer than to union coalitions in the private sector, perhaps because as many as 40 percent of all labor agreements in this sector are reached through multiemployer bargaining.[7] Most of the research is addressed to the question of why multiemployer bargaining develops in some industries—construction, garment manufacturing, trucking, coal mining, and local services, for example—but not others.[8] The evidence indicates that the tendency toward multiemployer bargaining in the private sector is strongest where product and labor markets are highly competitive, where employers are in close geographical proximity and negotiate with a common union or set of unions, and where firms are small in size relative to the union.

The structure of bargaining is much less diversified in the public than in the private sector. The dominant pattern in government is bargaining between a single employer and a single union, as both management and labor have opposed coalition structures. Public employers oppose multiemployer bargaining because of (1) procedural difficulties involved in coordinating negotiations across several bargaining units with differences in employment conditions, ability to pay, union leaders, management structures, and decision processes, and (2) the desire to preserve their decision-making autonomy.[9]

Most, if not all, public sector labor organizations also have opposed coalition bargaining, especially on a formal basis. Unions such as the American Federation of State, County, and Municipal Employees (AFSCME) and the Service Employees' International Union (SEIU) often have several locals in a particular city or state government. Bargaining involving these locals may proceed (formally or otherwise) on a coordinated basis. But when it comes to the joining of different unions, perhaps with different national affiliations or simply independent local organizations, for the purpose of bargaining a master agreement with a single governmental employer, leaders and members of public employee unions generally have displayed as strong an aversion to coalition bargaining as their management counterparts have shown to multiemployer bargaining.

In addition to employer and union opposition, aversion to coalition bargaining is supported by several other factors: regulatory policy that designates an exclusive bargaining representative for a particular group of employees; decentralized collective bargaining; a labor movement organized on the principles of union autonomy and exclusive jurisdiction; and, in the public sector until just recently, an expansionary fiscal climate.

Despite these and other barriers to coalition bargaining in the public sector, such bargaining is now practiced in the city of New York. The central question is why, given the general aversion to it, did formal coalition bargaining develop in New York City in the late 1970s? In the next three sections, we examine the historical, institutional, economic, and political factors that underlie this development.

Developments Prior to the Fiscal Crisis

Not only is the city of New York the largest municipal government in the United States, but for a quarter-century it has also been a leader in the development and institutionalization of collective bargaining in the public sector. A review of this labor relations history suggests that interunion relationships, negotiating practices, and regulatory procedures that evolved prior to the fiscal crisis of 1975 contributed in fundamental respects to the development of formal coalition bargaining.[10]

First, by 1975, interunion relationships had matured to the point of relative stability and were marked by a lack of jurisdictional rivalry. This maturity was related to New York City's long tradition of support for the union movement and to the fact that municipal unions had been formally recognized for almost twenty years. A majority of these municipal labor organizations represented single occupational groups, such as teachers, sanitationmen, police, fire and corrections officers, but by 1967, District Council 37 of AFSCME and its several locals had won the right to represent more than two-thirds of the city's nonuniformed, nonpedagogical employees. Thus, by the late 1960s, the municipal unions in New York City generally were secure with respect to their separate constituencies and faced few challenges from rival organizations.[11]

Second, pattern bargaining accompanied the development of collective bargaining in New York's municipal government and contributed to inter- and intraunion stability. In many ways, pattern bargaining was a precursor of the formal coalition bargaining that emerged in the late 1970s. Despite the fact that six major unions dominated the municipal labor relations process during the 1960s and 1970s, the city's 250,000 employees were represented by as many as 85 separate unions and 405 separate bargaining units and were employed in approximately 2,500 different job titles. Some unions had as many as 60 separate locals; in some cases, a single bargaining unit encompassed several local unions. This organizational format resulted in an intricate web of horizontal and vertical parity relationships among unions, bargaining units, and job titles. Pattern bargaining was also reinforced by the rulings of impasse panels, which were often appointed to resolve municipal labor disputes.[12] Although in earlier years no single bargained wage settlement consistently served as the relevant comparison for all others in the city, the 1974 agreement between the Transit Workers Union (TWU) and the Metropolitan Transit Authority (MTA) set the wage pattern for the entire municipal work force.[13]

A third factor that contributed to the emergence of coalition bargaining in New York City was the codification of the municipal labor relations process, which occurred in 1967 when the New York City Collective Bargaining Law took effect. The law institutionalized and extended many of the practices and relationships that developed in the previous decade, several of which fostered coalition-type activity among municipal employees.[14]

One provision of the law mandated, for example, the creation of a citywide bargaining unit to negotiate terms and conditions of employment, such as time and leave benefits and health insurance, that were required to be uniform for approximately 120,000 employees in the city's Career and Salary Plan.[15] Because its members constituted over 60 percent of the total, District Council 37 was designated the exclusive bargaining representative for this unit, but the unit also encompassed employee members of more than 30 separate municipal labor organizations.

Another provision of the law mandated the creation of the Municipal Labor Committee (MLC), an organization that was to be responsible for coordinating union participation in the tripartite Office of Collective Bargaining (OCB), which was charged with administering the statute. Subsequently, the MLC became the vehicle for developing common bargaining (and political) policies among city labor organizations, both before and during the period of fiscal crisis.

By the early 1970s, then, the municipal labor relations process in New York City was well established. More than 95 percent of all municipal employees were represented in collective bargaining; interunion relationships were relatively stable and peaceful; the turnover of union leadership was infrequent; and, under the auspices of OCB, the number of bargaining units declined from more than 400 in 1968 to approximately 100 in 1975.[16] This reduction of units permitted some municipal labor organizations—District Council 37, for example—to coordinate better their bargaining activity on behalf of constitutent locals, and it also facilitated the coordination of management's position in negotiations with municipal unions. Thus, prior to the emergence of the fiscal crisis in 1975, the structure of municipal collective bargaining in New York City had shifted considerably away from strict unit-by-unit and union-by-union negotiations.

The Fiscal Crisis and Bargaining

The fiscal crisis set the stage for further restructuring of the collective bargaining process in New York City's municipal government. The new economic climate provided direct impetus toward a more formal union coalition and also spurred changes in the city's management structure for collective bargaining.[17] The overriding characteristic of municipal labor relations during the 1975–1976 period was that the actions the direct participants in the bargaining process—city management and city unions—could take were severely constrained. Underlying all decision making in New York City municipal government during this period, including collective bargaining decisions, was the goal of fiscal solvency.

When the public credit markets closed to the city in the spring of 1975, the municipal government had an operating deficit of $2 billion and faced the task of refinancing $6 billion of outstanding short-term debt. From the perspective of the unions, bankruptcy would have reduced employee benefits, jeopardized pension contributions of member employees and pension benefits of retirees, further decreased the work force, and significantly diminished the role of municipal union leaders in the labor relations and political processes. For the city's management, bankruptcy implied a dramatic and perhaps permanent curtailment of the power of elected officials. Thus, the threat of bankruptcy and the financing requirements necessary to avoid it made even more salient the interdependent relationship between the city and its organized workers. Furthermore, the willingness of municipal union leaders and the city's officials to bargain on a coalition basis was strengthened by the shifting of responsibility for managing the fiscal crisis from the local to the state and federal governments as well as some private actors and institutions (such as several of the city's largest banks). These were the principal factors underlying centralization of the municipal bargaining structure during the mid-1970s.

Brought about by financing needs required to avoid insolvency, three specific developments served as key precedents for the formal coalition wage bargaining that was to occur in 1978 and 1980. These were the wage deferral agreement of 1975, the emergence of the municipal unions as the major financiers of the city, and the 1976 contract negotiations.

The 1975 Wage Deferral Agreement

In the spring of 1975, the city of New York's fiscal crisis was initially perceived as a local problem that, it was believed, could be managed at the local level. The mayor laid off municipal employees and reduced nonpayroll expenditures, while leaders of the municipal labor unions indicated their "willingness" to forgo certain negotiated benefits.[18] By June 1975, however, it was apparent that the city was able neither to manage the crisis by itself nor to meet the financing requirements necessary to avoid bankruptcy.

Joint pressures from the city and the state spurred New York's municipal labor organizations to engage in coalition bargaining. On July 1, 1975, a previously negotiated 6 percent wage increase was scheduled to go into effect for almost 200,000 of New York's municipal employees. At that juncture, however, the city was on the verge of default and lacked the funds to pay the approximately $300 million of prospective salary increases. In June, the state had created the Municipal Assistance Corporation (MAC), a public benefit corporation with limited oversight responsibilities that was empowered to help the city of New York restructure its debt, thereby, it was hoped, restoring the city's fiscal credibility. However, the task of financial resuscitation was more difficult than anticipated. To enhance the city's standing with investors, MAC sought proof that the budgetary reductions necessitated by the fiscal emergency were being made. Specifically, MAC called for a wage freeze on the slated 6 percent increase.

At this point, organized municipal employees faced a hostile political climate as well as an unfavorable economic environment. The public generally perceived the municipal unions as major contributors to the city's fiscal problems. Furthermore, as the crisis deepened, it appeared likely that the mayor would be sustained by the courts if he invoked his emergency power to invoke a unilateral wage freeze. Such a ruling would have established a precedent for unilateral managerial actions in the area of labor relations that could well have isolated the municipal labor union leaders from the decision-making process. As the complexity of the situation increased, it also became evident to most municipal union leaders that no one of them alone could count on managing the fiscal crisis to his own or his members' advantage. Thus, responding to these new economic pressures, the major municipal unions (with the exception of the teachers and police), acting in coalition, negotiated a wage deferral agreement with city, state, and MAC officials.[19]

This agreement accomplished several objectives for the labor organizations that made up the coalition: (1) the wage freeze became a wage deferral to be in effect for only one year and was tapered to protect the earnings of low-paid employees;[20] (2) a cost-of-living adjustment (COLA) that had been agreed to in 1974 and that was scheduled to go into effect in fiscal year 1976 was preserved; (3) individual unions within the coalition could negotiate separate agreements provided that these met the conditions of the wage deferral agreement; and (4) a claim was established by employees to receive the deferred wages at a future date. The provision for separate agreements assured each member union of the coalition a measure of autonomy while, more generally, the coalition structure assured each member union that no other labor organization would do better—or worse—concerning the wage deferral provisions.

Municipal Unions as Financiers

Soon after the wage deferral agreement, the fiscal crisis forced the municipal unions to assume the even more critical role of financier. By late summer of 1975, it was apparent to political officials that a stronger control mechanism with broader financial and managerial oversight responsibilities than MAC was required for the city of New York to avoid insolvency. In early September the state legislature passed the Financial Emergency Act and created the Emergency Financial Control Board (EFCB). The board was given the authority to exercise broad powers over municipal affairs, including labor relations. Although the hope was that through the EFCB's management of municipal budgetary affairs the city would be able to return to the public credit markets within a few months, its need to finance $5.7 billion of debt between November 1975 and June 1976 overwhelmed the attempts of the state to restore investor confidence in the city.[21]

During this period the city's five major employees' pension systems, with assets of more than $7 billion, emerged as major sources of loans to the city. Controlled by union officials, the pension funds had purchased city and MAC securities in the spring and summer of 1975 on an ad hoc, uncoordinated basis. By November, however, the unions became the city's major financiers on a systematic, integrated, long-term basis. Specifically, they agreed to invest $2.5 billion of pension funds in city paper and to roll over their earlier $1.2 billion investment as part of a complex $6.6 billion, three-year financing plan that also involved the city's major banks, the state government, and the federal government. As part of this financing arrangement, the federal government guaranteed $2.3 billion in seasonal loans to New York City.

The development of a coordinated policy to manage their pension fund investments in city and MAC securities contributed to the further development of a strong union coalition and formal coalition bargaining. The fact of this major financing role not only expanded the municipal unions' participation in the decision-making processes of the city government, but also placed them in a more collaborative relationship with city officials. This collaborative relationship and the strengthened sense of union solidarity were reinforced by the involvement of a new set of political actors in New York City's municipal government—namely, the federal government, particularly the Department of Treasury and Congress. Thus, the fiscal crisis contributed not only to the development of coalition bargaining in New York's municipal government, but to an alliance between the city government and the municipal unions for the purpose of negotiating terms of the city's fiscal rescue with New York State and the federal government.

The 1976 Bargaining Round

The economic and political conditions that prevailed in 1976 further stimulated coalition activity among the municipal unions. A critical factor in the 1976 bargaining round was the role played by the EFCB and the U.S. secretary of the treasury. The control board promulgated wage policy guidelines consistent with the wage freeze that had been mandated by the Financial Emergency Act and to which all participants in the municipal collective bargaining process were bound. Additionally, the board was required to approve all municipal collective bargaining contracts, thereby ensuring conformance with the city's three-year financial plan.

The wage policy guidelines were an important limitation on the scope of bargainable issues in the 1976 negotiations. They were intended to serve two purposes: first, to preserve the substance of the city's financial plan; second, to permit some salary adjustments in order to protect employees against inflation, but in a manner that would not increase total labor costs budgeted in the financial plan. A critical condition established by the Department of

Treasury was that the municipal labor contracts, scheduled to expire on June 30, had to be settled before the federal loans, expiring on July 2, would be renewed. This stipulation created substantial pressure on the city and the municipal labor organizations to reach a new agreement.

Given the large number of municipal unions and bargaining units, a coalition bargaining structure provided a means of ensuring that the deadline would be met, that all unions would adhere to the wage guidelines, and that no one union would outdo any other. Thus, leaders of the municipal unions, again acting in coalition, concluded a two-year agreement with the city on June 30, 1976.[22] This agreement, the Memorandum of Interim Understanding, satisfied federal and state requirements, met the deadline for renewal of federal loans, and incorporated the substance of the EFCB's wage policy guidelines, including a $48 million fringe benefit reduction. As with the 1975 wage deferral agreement, however, the 1976 agreement also provided a two-tier bargaining structure. After labor leaders signed the agreement, the representatives of each bargaining unit (of which there were approximately 100 in 1976) negotiated a separate contract with the city to determine other terms and conditions of employment for members of that unit—which had to be in conformity with the Memorandum of Interim Understanding. Among the major issues dealt with in individual unit bargaining were the manner in which each unit would satisfy the allocated reduction in fringe benefits for its members and the particulars for implementing a productivity program to which the COLA was tied.[23]

In summary, the 1975–1976 period of fiscal crisis featured two major instances of coalition bargaining, thereby expanding a bargaining structure that had first emerged several years earlier. Throughout this period, the paramount concern of the parties to negotiations was the financial solvency of the city. As the state and federal governments assumed increased responsibility for the city's fiscal and municipal affairs, specific bargaining guidelines and deadlines were set by them. Bargaining through a coalition structure facilitated compliance with these guidelines and deadlines, ensured that all the municipal labor organizations shared in the costs of retrenchment, and helped to avoid the bankruptcy of the nation's largest local government. Additionally, by ensuring that all municipal labor organizations shared in the costs of retrenchment and by permitting separate nonwage agreements, the two-tier bargaining format addressed some major concerns of municipal unionists—namely, autonomy and interunion competition for resources.

Coalition Bargaining in 1978

Although the city of New York did not face imminent default in 1978, complex state and federal legislation and many delicate financial negotiations were needed in order to secure the municipality's future. Both the state's Financial Emergency Act and the federal seasonal loans were scheduled to expire in mid-1978. The federal government would not consider new legislation to aid the city until the state passed a law containing financial safeguards similar to those provided in the 1975 financial emergency legislation and until municipal labor negotiations were concluded.

These pressures for coalition bargaining were partially offset by local economic and political developments. The city enjoyed greater financial stability in 1978 than at any time during the previous three years; the wage freeze, which was the cornerstone of the 1976 negotiations, did not apply to the 1978 contracts; and a new mayor, Edward I. Koch, assumed office on January 1, 1978. Koch ran for office on a platform that emphasized an adversarial relationship with the municipal unions, in contrast to the cooperative relationship that had been advocated during the previous administration of Abraham D. Beame.

Koch was initially reluctant to agree to coalition bargaining, believing that economic and political conditions would favor the city in separate union or unit negotiations. A few municipal union leaders also supported a return to a more conventional bargaining structure. But the difficulties of organizing both a new political administration and a revised (or a return to the traditional) format for labor relations, combined with the need for new federal loan guarantees and perhaps the realization that such guarantees had to be negotiated with other authorities, led the mayor to consent to formal coalition bargaining.

Unlike negotiations over the wage deferral agreement in 1975 and the Memorandum of Interim Understanding in 1976, in which the participants had agreed to basic financial parameters *before* formal bargaining commenced, the 1978 negotiations began without a union–management consensus on the dimensions of the settlement. The only point on which the parties agreed was that in order to ensure that the necessary federal aid would be forthcoming, it would be beneficial if an agreement could be reached simultaneously with the TWU-MTA contract deadline of March 31.

The Scope of Bargaining

The two prior negotiations had established a two-tier bargaining structure in city government; the question in 1978 was whether or not both "economic" and "noneconomic" issues should be settled within a single-tier coalition framework. The lack of consensus was especially pronounced within managerial ranks. Some city officials felt that all issues should have been included in coalition bargaining or, alternatively, that bargaining should have proceeded over economic issues only, with unit bargaining suspended and the noneconomic terms of existing contracts carried forward for two more years.

These officials believed that a two-tier bargaining format subjected the city to a second round of bargaining in which it could only lose ground. A few union leaders, believing that they could gain little from separate negotiations, also favored comprehensive (or one-tier) coalition bargaining.

In contrast, management supporters of two-tier bargaining argued that such bargaining would help achieve the overriding goal of securing new federal aid, even if this arrangement helped one or another union to do better than it would have otherwise. If the bargaining experiences of 1975 and 1976 held, the signing of a coalition agreement would satisfy federal authorities. The union leaders who favored a two-tier bargaining structure believed that the coalition arrangement would help reduce interunion rivalries, while unit bargaining would afford each of their organizations some measure of independence and autonomy, if not necessarily a "second bite of the apple."

That the unions were more united than management in their position on this issue was reflected in the twelve demands the union coalition submitted, all of which dealt with wage increases or cost-of-living allowances common to coalition members. By contrast, the city's opening bargaining position reflected the lack of managerial consensus; it included sixty-two demands or items, ranging from broad wage provisions that affected all employees to very detailed provisions that involved one or another small bargaining unit.

As each self-imposed negotiating deadline approached, the unions and management agreed that there was not sufficient time to bargain to agreement on both economic and noneconomic items. As the various deadlines passed and agreement was not achieved, the scope-of-bargaining issue surfaced again and again, but with less and less force as the ultimate deadline of June 30 drew nearer. No one can say with certainty that, had there been a management consensus one way or another on this issue, the scope of bargaining or the outcomes of the 1978 negotiations would have been different. What is certain is that in 1978, as in 1975 and 1976, the negotiations took place on a two-tier basis, with wages and some additional economic items subjected to coalition bargaining, and other issues, including most noneconomic ones, treated in separate unit negotiations. There is no evidence that, in any of these negotiations, some municipal unions did appreciably better or worse than others in reaching separate unit agreements, a fact that underscores the notion that such two-tier bargaining permits, and is in part motivated by the desire of, union leaders to maintain some measure of autonomy and independence.

Parties to the Coalition

The city did not require the unions to declare formally their membership in the coalition. Each union retained the right to autonomy even if it chose not to exercise that right. In fact, only those unions that did not wish to associate themselves with the coalition were explicit regarding their membership status. Nonetheless, all major city employee unions except those representing rank-and-file uniformed personnel (firefighters, police, and corrections officers) eventually participated in the bargaining coalition. The official leadership of the coalition rotated among five labor organizations: United Federation of Teachers, Uniformed Santiationmen's Association, District Council 37, Local 237 of International Brotherhood of Teamsters, and United Fire Officers Association. The presence of the 60,000 member teachers' union in the 1978 coalition was particularly notable, for it formally broadened the basis for the coalition beyond that which had existed previously.

The Negotiations

The union coalition and the city did not reach agreement simultaneously with the contract settlement on March 31 between the TWU and the MTA. Over the next two months, however, the pressures for a settlement were intense, particularly those from the federal government. Finally, on June 5, 1978, the city and the municipal unions reached a Coalition Economic Agreement (CEA). The cost of this two-year contract was estimated at $1.2 billion; it provided for a total wage increase of 8 percent, payment of the unpaid portion ($567 per employee) of the 1978 productivity-based COLA, and an annual cash bonus payment of $750 per employee in 1979 and 1980 in lieu of productivity COLAs. The provision of a general wage increase, the first in three years, contrasted sharply with the terms of the 1975 and 1976 coalition bargaining agreements.[24] Furthermore, the city abandoned its demand for contractual givebacks, and 48 million in fringe and pension reductions, which had been required by the Treasury Department and agreed to in the 1976 bargaining round, were canceled.

By fall 1978, the only major unions that had not signed the CEA—but which nevertheless incorporated its terms and provisions into their separate unit agreements—were the Patrolmen's Benevolent Association and the Uniformed Firefighters Association. In 1978, therefore, coalition bargaining in New York's municipal government directly and indirectly involved virtually all municipal labor organizations and covered most key economic items, while leaving some economic and noneconomic issues to be resolved in individual unit bargaining.

Coalition Bargaining in 1980

Given that New York City was not seeking federal loans in 1980 and that a balanced budget was forecast for fiscal 1981, there seemed to be fewer external pressures for coalition bargaining in 1980 than at any time since the onset of the fiscal crisis.[25] Nevertheless, the 1980 negotiations were conducted in a coalition framework. This may have occurred because, by that time, coalition bargaining had taken firm hold in New York City and was therefore less sensitive to external financial and political pressures. It also may have continued, however, because the parties anticipated serious financial problems resulting from a projected budgetary deficit of approximately $1.2 billion in fiscal 1982.

Many of the issues concerning coalition bargaining that were raised in 1978 surfaced again in the 1980 negotiations but were disposed of with greater dispatch than before. For example, the mayor repeated his reluctance to bargain within a coalition structure, but quickly acceded to this format. Some city officials preferred that economic and noneconomic issues be considered together in single-tier bargaining, but the negotiations were conducted within a two-tier framework.

The major difference between the 1978 and 1980 negotiations was the emergence in 1980 of a second union coalition made up principally of the labor organizations that did not formally join the coalition in 1978—unions of rank-and-file police, firefighters, and corrections officers. These unions formed the nucleus of this 43,000 member Uniformed Coalition. The coalition of 1978 (known as the Municipal Coalition in 1980) continued largely in place, representing about 200,000 city employees in coalition bargaining, including all but one group of uniformed superior officers. The only defections from the Municipal Coalition to the Uniformed Coalition were the Uniformed Fire Officers' Association (UFA) and the Uniformed Sanitationmen's Association (USA).

Negotiations with both coalitions proceeded smoothly, especially by historical standards. The Municipal Coalition reached overall agreement with the city in early June 1980, three weeks prior to the expiration of the master and individual unit agreements. The Uniformed Coalition and the city reached agreement simultaneously with the expiration of the uniformed forces contracts. Members of the Municipal Coalition received annual 8 percent wage increases and adjustments in other benefits for a total two-year settlement of about 17 percent. The uniformed employees received wage increases of 9 percent the first year and 8 percent the second year; the total settlement, including fringe benefit adjustments, was approximately 19 percent. The terms of these new coalition agreements reflected the pattern established by the TWU-MTA agreement, concluded in the spring of 1980, which provided for annual wage increases of 9 percent and adjustments to fringe benefits over the two-year period, 1980–1982. Unlike the 1978 negotiations, however, when individual bargaining unit (second-tier) agreements had to be signed before the wage increases were paid, this stipulation was removed in 1980. This meant that wage increases provided under the 1980 master

Table 1
Chronology of Key Events in New York City Municipal Labor Relations

Time Period	Events
1954–1965	Mayoral authorization of unionism and bargaining rights for employees; informal negotiation of labor agreements; growth of municipal employee unionism.
1966–1974	Ninety-five percent of municipal employees represented in collective bargaining; development of pattern bargaining and stabilization of interunion relations and union leadership; enactment of Collective Bargaining Law; creation of Citywide Bargaining Unit and Municipal Labor Committee; reduction of bargaining units.
1975–1977	Emergence of fiscal crisis; creation of MAC and EFCB; two-tier coalition bargaining of the Wage Deferral Agreement and Memorandum of Interim Understanding; coordinated investments of employee pension funds in NYC notes and MAC bonds; passage and renewal of federal seasonal loans.
1978–1980	Election of Mayor Koch; long-term extension of EFCB; new federal loan guarantees; two-tier bargaining of the Coalition Economic Agreement; formation of the Uniformed Coalition; two-tier bargaining of the Municipal Coalition and Uniformed Coalition agreements.

coalition agreements were payable subject only to union ratification of these agreements. Such an arrangement suggests a strengthening in 1980 of the commitment to coalition bargaining in the city of New York, even as a second union coalition appeared on the scene and negotiated a master agreement with city officials. Highlights of the evolution of coalition bargaining in New York City from 1954 through 1980 are shown in table 1.

Summary and Prognosis

New York City has a longer history of municipal collective bargaining than all but a few American cities. During the 1970s, this bargaining took place increasingly on a coalition basis. By 1980, union coalitions encompassed all the city's labor organizations and represented all 243,000 municipal employees covered by collective bargaining. The coalition bargaining agenda included wages, cost-of-living allowances, and some fringe and pension benefits.

Precedents for formal coalition bargaining were established by the reduction of interunion rivalries, the development of widespread pattern bargaining, and the enactment of the city's Collective Bargaining Law in 1967; it was the fiscal crisis of 1975, however, that gave special impetus to coalition bargaining. The goal of fiscal survival served to override the remaining barriers to coalition bargaining. The negotiation within a coalition structure of the

1975 wage deferral agreement and major economic provisions of the 1976 municipal labor contracts provided tangible evidence of union and management responses to the new economic and political climates and were important precursors to broader and more formal coalition bargaining in 1978 and 1980. The coalition structure strengthened the city's ability to carry out fiscal planning within the requirements imposed by other governments and provided the vehicle for municipal labor's "representation" in this critical planning process. Even more fundamentally, this bargaining structure was the mechanism for linking labor *and* management in a de facto coalition to negotiate with federal and state authorities over the terms and conditions of the fiscal rescue of the City of New York.

Is coalition bargaining likely to persist, expand, or decline in New York City's municipal government? In analyzing private sector labor relations, Weber comments that "bargaining structure will be strongly influenced by the market context within which negotiations take place."[26] The notion of markets is not easily applied to the public sector, but the emergence of severe fiscal constraints on a government, especially to the point of threatening bankruptcy, may be taken as a proxy for market forces. These, in turn, impinge upon bargaining structure. If coalition bargaining in New York City did develop primarily in response to the fiscal crisis and to the related realignment of financial and political relationships among the municipal, state, and federal governments, then the future of coalition bargaining must be linked to the future fiscal condition of the city. Whether economic conditions will worsen or moderate in the near future in New York City is uncertain, but at this point (early 1981) the city projects substantial budgetary deficits and, perhaps more important, probably will not soon regain access to the credit markets. Moreover, the city will remain subject to the powers of the Emergency Financial Control Board, which has been extended by state law (and renamed the Financial Control Board) to the year 2008. All this implies that coalition bargaining will remain the characteristic form of bargaining structure in New York City, at least for the near future.[27]

Even with severe external economic and political pressures, however, individual unit and union bargaining is unlikely to be entirely eliminated from New York's municipal government. With respect to bargaining structure in the private sector, Weber observes that

> the formation of a common front inevitably involves a partial relinquishing of individual group goals. Each group will press for, or acquiesce in, the expansion of the worker alliance as long as the rate of substitution between the gains derived from the increment to bargaining power are greater than the perceived losses associated with the denial of autonomy in decision making. At some point, this rate of substitution will become negative, and tensions will develop within . . . the associated bargaining structures for the accommodation of special group interests or the fragmentation of the alliance.[28]

The mechanism of two-tier bargaining in New York City permits leaders of individual unions to accommodate some of the special interests of their respective members while, at the same time, relinquishing others of their members' interests and some of their own autonomy to a larger coalition. These are difficult tasks for the leaders of otherwise independent and some-times competing organizations to accomplish successfully.

Thus, if the reduction of interunion rivalries and growth of relatively stable labor organizations were also conducive to the development of coalition bargaining in New York City municipal government during the 1970s, then it is to these characteristics as well as to fiscal conditions that the future of the coalition structure should be linked. On balance, both severe fiscal strain and relatively stable interunion relationships have been instrumental to the development of coalition bargaining in New York's municipal government. As long as these conditions continue, as is anticipated, it is possible to forecast continued adherence to a two-tier coalition bargaining structure that permits common as well as separate union interests to be addressed.

Generalizing from New York City

What are the prospects for coalition bargaining elsewhere in municipal government or in the public sector more broadly? The prospects appear limited. Coalition bargaining has emerged in parts of the public hospital sector, especially in large urban hospitals; in negotiations with publicly employed craft workers at local, state, and federal levels; in some public school districts, such as the city of Chicago; and in some governments that have only recently begun to engage in collective bargaining, such as the city of Los Angeles. However, some of these arrangements represent carryovers of bargaining structures from the private sector; others are limited to unions that enroll only members of similar skills or whose members are employed in but one service or one unit of a government; and still others represent a one-time rather than a sustained bargaining tactic.[29]

These developments point up the need for a more theoretical perspective on bargaining structure in the public sector. Labor relations in the public sector, as in the private, may be conceptualized as diverse rather than uniform.

> This diversity, which is rooted in historical, legal, functional and political features of government, contains several implications for public sector labor relations, but, in particular, it suggests that there is a no *a priori* reason to assume that the labor relations process in a (particular) state, county or municipality necessarily will closely resemble the labor relations process else-where in government.[30]

Proceeding from this conceptualization, two-tier coalition bargaining of the type that exists in New York's municipal government might be replicated in some other governments. Even if this occurs, however, single-tier coalition bargaining, coalitions limited to unions in single services or agencies, conventional union-by-union bargaining, or various combinations thereof will likely exist in the public sector. The analytical task thus becomes one of identifying the "historical, legal, functional and political features of government" that give rise to a particular form of bargaining structure.[31]

Taking particular account of the economic-political forces that have affected the development of coalition bargaining in New York City, it appears that this form of bargaining structure is not likely to spread throughout the public sector, though it may emerge in some governments. It appears from the New York experience that coalition bargaining is most likely to develop under conditions of intense budgetary and fiscal pressure, which not only heighten the common interests of union organizations but of labor and management vis-à-vis other fiscal and political authorities. Few governments in the United States at present face the degree of fiscal stringency found in New York City; few have had to cede governing powers and managerial control to other public authorities; and few have had to rely on the federal government to bail them out.

Nonetheless, market forces are dynamic, not static, and the rapid growth of state and local governments in the United States, which marked the third quarter of the twentieth century and stimulated the rapid expansion of public sector unionism and bargaining, has ended. Substantial evidence exists of a fundamental reappraisal by citizens and elected officials of the size, scope, and performance of public institutions. This appraisal implies that the trend toward slower growth, stabilization, and even decline of the revenues made available to governments, which first began to be noticed in the mid-1970s, will continue and perhaps quicken in the 1980s. A more stringent economic climate for government provides less political support for or even outright opposition to public employee unionism and bargaining as well as the reappraisal of management strategies for dealing with labor relations.[32] These developments suggest that, in some instances, the economic and political climates of the public sector may be such as to favor the development of coalition bargaining through which some union leaders and local public officials will seek greater protection of their interests and powers than is afforded them by conventional negotiating structures.

But for reasons identified in the analysis of coalition bargaining in New York City and suggested by bargaining structure and labor relations theory, this prognosis must not be carried too far. Both the labor movement and collective bargaining in the United States are characterized by decentralization and autonomy; public sector labor organizations are particularly heterogeneous. Like the employers with whom they negotiate, public sector union leaders share bargaining information with each other, but, also like public employers, they are chary of structural realignments that threaten their autonomy and livelihood.[33] Thus, to temper union rivalries is not to eliminate them, especially in much of the public sector where (unlike New York City) substantial proportions of employees are unorganized, and to coordinate bargaining is not to engage in coalition bargaining. Furthermore, the fact that a public employer rarely merges with another government means that, unlike their private sector counterparts, leaders of public sector labor organizations do not face the prospect of bargaining with a conglomerate and, consequently, are not pressed to form union coalitions for the purpose of countering that form of employer organization. Indeed, by bargaining as a single labor organization with one employer, individual public employee unions have been found to bring about a reallocation of budgetary resources toward the services in which their members are employed and away from other less well organized services.[34]

In conclusion, the New York City experience suggests more generally that the diminution of interunion rivalries, the spread of pattern bargaining, and the reduction-consolidation of bargaining units are necessary but not sufficient conditions for the development of coalition bargaining in the public sector. It is when fiscal crisis threatens the political viability of a government entity that public sector labor organizations will be motivated to pursue coalition bargaining and that a public employer will be willing to negotiate with a union coalition.[35] In such circumstances, an alliance is struck among the unions and between the unions and a government employer, not only as a way of containing internal rivalries but as a mechanism by which these normally risk-averse parties may negotiate with other political authorities in the hope of achieving a positive "rate of substitution between the gains derived from the increment to bargaining power and the losses associated with the denial of autonomy in decision-making."[36] If and when economic pressures on a particular government ease and local political control and autonomy are less threatened, the perceived rate of substitution may become negative and tensions may develop "for the fragmentation of the alliance"—especially if the public employer judges his interests to be harmed rather than served by continuance of the union coalition.[37] The validity of these observations as generalizations about the public sector awaits cross-sectional research into the determinants of public sector bargaining structures. At present, however, these observations suggest that while coalition bargaining in the city of New York during the 1970s is an important development worthy of close scrutiny, this structural arrangement is unlikely to be widely replicated in municipal government or in the public sector more broadly during the 1980s.

Notes

1. Specific examples include the rapid growth of public employee unionism, use of militant union tactics, negotiation of written labor agreements, and legal

sanctioning and third-party regulation of public employee bargaining. These developments spread widely throughout the public sector during the late 1960s and the 1970s, but occurred earlier in the city of New York.

2. See William Chernish, *Coalition Bargaining: A Study of Union Tactics and Public Policy* (Philadelphia: University of Pennsylvania Press, 1968), and Arnold R. Weber, *The Structure of Collective Bargaining* (New York: Free Press, 1961). The formation of union and management coalitions for bargaining purposes may be considered subsets of broader interorganizational relations. See Richard H. Hall et al., "Patterns of Interorganizational Relationships," *Admininstrative Science Quarterly* 22, no. 3 (September 1977), pp. 457–474.

3. See, for example, Wallace Hendricks, "Conglomerate Mergers and Collective Bargaining," *Industrial Relations* 15, no. 1 (Februrary 1976), pp. 75–87, and Kenneth O. Alexander, "Conglomerate Mergers and Collective Bargaining," *Industrial and Labor Relations Review* 24, no. 3 (April 1971), pp. 354–374.

4. As reported in *NLRB:* General Electric Company v. NLRB, 69 LRRM 1305, (1968); *Federal Court (Circuit Court):* General Electric Company v. NLRB, 71 LRRM 2418, (1969); and *Federal Court (Circuit Court):* National Labor Relations Board v. General Electric Company, 72 LRRM 2530, (1969). See also James W. Kuhn, "A View of Boulwarism: The Significance of the G.E. Strike," *Labor Law Journal* 21, no. 9 (September 1970), pp. 582–590.

5. The quotations are from Phillip J. Schwarz, *Coalition Bargaining*, Key Issues in Industrial Relations Series, no. 5 (Ithaca: New York State School of Industrial and Labor Relations, Cornell University, 1970), p. 3. See also Donald E. Cullen and Louis Feinberg, *The Bargaining Structure in Construction: Problems and Prospects* (Washington, D.C.: U.S. Department of Labor, 1980). The NLRB and court decisions discussed by Cullen and Feinberg as well as those listed in note 4 provide legal support for coordinated bargaining but not coalition bargaining in the private sector. The latter can occur where both parties voluntarily agree to merge bargaining units into a single coalition; but if one party objects to negotiating with more than one unit at a time, the other party may not legally force the issue—although it may pursue a coordinated strategy of seeking the same goals in different bargaining units. Consequently, some private sector employees have attempted to characterize the coordinated bargaining activity of unions as coalition bargaining and to make such bargaining the subject of unfair labor practice charges.

6. For a discussion of pattern bargaining in selected manufacturing industries, see Neil W. Chamberlain, Donald E. Cullen, and David Lewin, *The Labor Sector,* 3rd ed. (New York: McGraw-Hill, 1980), pp. 249–253.

7. The Bureau of Labor Statistics reports in *Characteristics of Major Collective Bargaining Agreements, July 1, 1975,* Bulletin 1957 (Washington, D.C.: U.S. Government Printing Office, 1977), that about 43 percent of workers covered under major collective bargaining agreements were in multiemployer units. The proportion of workers so covered in "minor" agreements is presumed to be somewhat smaller. Together these data produce the estimate that 40 percent of all organized workers in the private sector are covered by multiemployer bargaining agreements.

8. Representative works include Weber, *The Structure of Collective Bargaining;* Weber, "Stability and Change in the Structure of Collective Bargaining" in Lloyd Ulman, ed., *Challenges to Collective Bargaining* (Englewood Cliffs, N.J.: Prentice-

Hall, 1967), pp. 13–36; and David H. Greenberg, "The Structure of Collective Bargaining and Some of its Determinants," in Industrial Relations Research Association, *Proceedings of the Nineteenth Annual Winter Meeting, December 28–29, 1966, San Francisco* (Madison, Wisc.: IRRA, 1967), pp. 343–353.

9. See Peter Feuille, Hervey Juris, Ralph Jones, and Michael Jay Jedel, "Multiemployer Negotiations among Local Governments," in David Lewin, Peter Feuille, and Thomas A. Kochan, *Public Sector Labor Relations: Analysis and Readings* (reprinted in chapter 3 of this book) (Glen Ridge, N.J.: Thomas Horton and Daughters, 1977), pp. 113–120.

10. The history of municipal collective bargaining in New York City prior to the 1970s is well documented. See, for example, Raymond D. Horton, *Municipal Labor Relations in New York City: Lessons of the Lindsay–Wagner Years* (New York: Praeger, 1973), chaps. 2–4.

11. Note also that most municipal union leaders had long tenures in office. As an example, John Delury, who retired in 1978, headed the Uniformed Sanitationmen's Association for more than forty years and was a key figure in the negotiation of (informal) labor agreements during the three-term administration (1953–1965) of Mayor Robert F. Wagner.

12. See Mary McCormick, "A Functional Analysis of Interest Arbitration in New York City's Municipal Government, 1968–1975," in Industrial Relations Research Association, *Proceedings of the Twenty-ninth Annual Winter Meeting, September 16–18, 1976, Atlantic City* (Madison, Wisc.: IRRA, 1977) pp. 249–257.

13. TWU members are employed by the MTA, a state agency responsible for the subway and commuter rail lines in New York City and its surrounding counties. The city provides an annual operating subsidy to the MTA, but the mayor has no formal role in negotiations between the TWU and MTA. Municipal union leaders in New York City have sought to institutionalize the pattern-setting role of TWU-MTA agreements because (1) wages for TWU members are tied to the state's rather than the city's fiscal condition; (2) the TWU has greater bargaining leverage than most city labor organizations, given that there are very few substitutes for subway and rail service and that a subway strike in particular can impose substantial economic hardship on the city; and (3) the TWU (unlike most municipal unions) has a tradition of no contract, no work.

14. This law also created some institutional barriers among city labor organizations, though these tended to reflect a traditional division in city government between mayoral and nonmayoral agencies. In particular, employees of mayoral agencies— those under direct budgetary and management control of the mayor—came under the jurisdiction of the city's Collective Bargaining Law and its administrative agency, the Office of Collective Bargaining (OCB), while employees of virtually all nonmayoral agencies came under the aegis of the state's Public Employees' Fair Employment (Taylor) Act and its administrative agency, the Public Employment Relations Board (PERB). The latter group of employees, numbering over 100,000, work principally in the Board of Education, the Board of Higher Education, the Housing Authority, and the Off-Track Betting Corporation.

15. Career and Salary Plan employees are designated as such by a 1954 Civil Service classification. Major exclusions from this category are pedagogical and uniformed employees (police, fire, sanitation and corrections personnel) and prevailing wage

workers—certain blue-collar workers whose compensation is set according to the prevailing wage provisions under section 220 of New York State Labor Law.

16. We have neither sufficient information nor space to discuss more fully this remarkable reduction in bargaining units except to underscore the point made immediately below in the text that municipal labor, management, and OCB officials all judged the reduction to serve their particular interests.

17. For other perspectives on the effects of the fiscal crisis on New York's municipal labor relations, see Mary McCormick, "Management of Retrenchment: The City of New York in the 1970s" (Ph.D. dissertation, Columbia University, 1978), and Joan P. Weitzman, "The Effect of Economic Restraints on Public-Sector Collective Bargaining: The Lessons of New York City," *Employee Relations Law Journal* 2, no. 3 (Winter 1977), pp. 286–312.

18. According to the city's Office of Management and Budget, New York's municipal work force declined by about 38,000 full-time personnel during calendar year 1975, though it is not possible to distinguish precisely among layoffs, retirements, and quits. The benefits referred to here included the traditional shorter work week during summer months ("summer hours"), guaranteed overtime (for sanitationmen), and payment (to firefighters) for one day per year for donating blood. These benefits were not actually forgone in 1975, but they were eliminated in subsequent rounds.

19. The teachers were on a different bargaining cycle than other municipal labor groups in 1975 and their contract with the Board of Education was scheduled to expire on September 9th of that year. In addition, intraunion rivalries, which featured major challenges to the leadership of the Patrolmen's Benevolent Association (PBA) in particular, prevented this organization from becoming a party to the 1975 Wage Deferral Agreement.

20. Specifically, the entire 6 percent increase was deferred for municipal employees earning $15,000 or more annually; 4 percent was deferred and 2 percent was granted to employees earning between $10,000 and $15,000 annually; and 2 percent was deferred and 4 percent was granted to employees earning less than $10,000 annually.

21. In November 1975, the state declared a moratorium on the repayment of all outstanding New York City notes, an action that eliminated any short-term restoration of investor confidence in the municipal government.

22. The police were party to this agreement but the teachers were not. Shortly after the agreement was signed, however, the teachers accepted its terms and conditions and incorporated them into their contract. This required a one-year extension of the contract (to 1978) and meant that it would expire in the same year as most other municipal labor agreements. This arrangement facilitated the teacher union's membership in the 1978 coalition bargaining round, which will be discussed later in this reading.

23. For the 1976–1978 contractual period, increases in employee salaries were to be paid as cost-of-living adjustments, referred to as Productivity COLAs. Although it was intended that these payments were to be funded principally through monies raised by productivity improvements, the EFCB wage policy stipulated that COLAs could be funded through "gains in productivity, reduction of fringe benefits or through other savings or revenues." Each bargaining unit was required to develop a

program to fund Productivity COLAs. For more on this contractual arrangement, see Mary McCormick, "Productivity Issues," in Raymond D. Horton and Charles Brecher, eds., *Setting Municipal Priorities, 1980* (Montclair, N.J.: Allanheld Osmun, 1979), pp. 171–194.

24. The 1976 agreements, which were in effect for two years, provided for no direct wage increases. The increases scheduled for 1975 (based on 1974 labor agreements) were deferred in the manner described in note 20. As an incentive for union members to ratify the CEA, the agreement provided for immediate payment of the 1978 COLA ($567) and "timely" payment of the 1979 cash bonus ($750). Municipal employees could not be eligible for wage increases, however, until individual bargaining unit agreements were concluded.

25. It is too early now (early 1981) to provide a detailed analysis of the 1980 municipal labor negotiations, but the leading characteristics of these negotiations are discussed in this section.

26. Weber, "Stability and Change in the Structure of Collective Bargaining," p. 15.

27. As fiscal conditions become less severe, either labor or management may feel freer to move for a departure from coalition bargaining if it believes that such action will serve its particular interests. As noted earlier, a return to unit-by-unit bargaining for the 1980 municipal labor negotiations in New York City was initially advocated by the Koch administration. The fact of some managerial opposition to coalition bargaining serves as a reminder that coalition bargaining needs to be distinguished from a union coalition. New York's municipal labor organizations may be able to maintain their coalition(s), but coalition bargaining requires the acquiescence of the other party to negotiations. Both parties must judge coalition bargaining to serve their respective interests; if management reaches a different position and sustains that position, then coalition bargaining may recede in New York City even while one or more union coalitions remain on the scene.

28. Weber, "Stability and Change in the Structure of Collective Bargaining," p. 18.

29. Perhaps the clearest example other than New York City of sustained coalition bargaining in the public sector—bargaining that has not been transported from the private sector and that involves several unions whose members represent various skill levels, occupations, and service categories—is in the local government sector of British Columbia. See Shirley B. Goldenberg, "Public-Sector Labor Relations in Canada," in Benjamin Aaron, Joseph R. Grodin, and James L. Stern, eds., *Public-Sector Bargaining* (Washington, D.C.: Bureau of National Affairs, 1979), pp. 254–291, esp. pp. 272–274, and David Lewin and Shirley B. Goldenberg, "Public Sector Unionism in the United States and Canada," *Industrial Relations* 19, no. 3 (Fall 1980), pp. 239–256.

30. David Lewin, Raymond D. Horton, and James W. Kuhn, *Collective Bargaining and Manpower Utilization in Big City Governments* (Montclair, N.J.: Allanheld Osmun, 1979), p. 9.

31. This task was partially undertaken by Weber, "Stability and Change in the Structure of Collective Bargaining," pp. 15–22, who identified market forces, the nature of bargaining issues, representation factors, government policies, and power tactics in the bargaining process as determinants of bargaining structure in the private

sector, but who did not specify (or test) how the interaction of these variables leads to a particular structural form. See, more recently, D.R. Deaton and P.B. Beaumont, "The Determinants of Bargaining Structure: Some Large Scale Survey Evidence for Britain," *British Journal of Industrial Relations* 18, no. 2 (July 1980), pp. 199–216.

32. In San Francisco, for example, where organized labor in the public and private sectors is particularly strong, voters passed several referenda in the late 1970s revising generous city pay formulas and cutting the salaries of city workers by as much as $4,500 annually. See Harry C. Katz, "Municipal Pay Determination: The Case of San Francisco," *Industrial Relations* 18, no. 1 (Winter 1979), pp. 44–58, esp. pp. 55–57. Another example is the recent adoption of laws by some state and local governments that permit selected groups of public employees to strike following the exhaustion of one or another impasse procedure. See David Lewin, "Public Sector Collective Bargaining and the Right to Strike," in A. Lawrence Chickering, ed., *Public Employee Unions: A Study of the Crisis in Public Sector Labor Relations* (San Francisco: Institute for Contemporary Studies, 1976), pp. 145–163.

33. On information sharing for bargaining purposes among public employers, see Feuille et al., "Multiemployer Negotiations among Local Governments," pp. 113–120. On employer coalitions in the hospital sector, see Peter Feuille, Charles Maxey, Hervey Juris, and Margaret Levi, "Determinants of Multi-Employer Bargaining in Metropolitan Hospitals," *Employee Relations Law Journal* 4, no. 1 (Summer 1978), pp. 98–115.

34. See, for example, Stanley Benecki, "Municipal Expenditure Levels and Collective Bargaining," *Industrial Relations* 17, no. 2 (May 1978), pp. 216–230, and Harry C. Katz, "The Municipal Budgetary Response to Changing Labor Costs: The Case of San Francisco," *Industrial and Labor Relations Review* 32, no. 4 (July 1979), pp. 506–519.

35. That economic adversity in the *private* sector stimulates coalition bargaining is suggested by Alan M. Gustman and Martin Segal, "The Skilled–Unskilled Wage Differential in Construction," *Industrial and Labor Relations Review* 27, no. 2 (January 1974), pp. 261–275.

36. Weber, "Stability and Change in the Structure of Collective Bargaining," p. 18. The notion of risk aversion among public employers and public unionists is developed in Henry S. Farber and Harry C. Katz, "Interest Arbitration, Outcomes and the Incentive to Bargain," *Industrial and Labor Relations Review* 33, no. 1 (October 1979), pp. 55–63.

37. The quoted phrase is from Weber, "Stability and Change in the Structure of Collective Bargaining," p. 18.

4

Labor–Management Interactions

The text and readings of the first three chapters provided an overview of the economic, political, legal, organizational, and structural contexts in which public sector collective bargaining processes take place. With this background we can now turn to an examination of the interaction process itself. We begin by giving a brief overview of several important concepts that have been used to describe the process of bargaining in the private sector, and then suggest how these concepts need to be modified to fit the public sector context.

The Bargaining Process

One of the most widely read theories of collective bargaining has been developed by Walton and McKersie.[1] In describing the bargaining process, they argue that it is important to distinguish between the "distributive" and "integrative" aspects of bargaining. The term *distributive bargaining* is used to describe interactions between labor and management over which a clear conflict of interest exists. *Integrative bargaining,* in contrast, is used to describe interactions where the parties perceive a common interest. In distributive bargaining, the mode of behavior is adversarial and conflict oriented. The parties seek to manipulate information in order to mount the strongest arguments in favor of their case. Threats, bluffs, and other coercive tactics are considered a normal part of the process. In integrative bargaining the mode of interaction is one of mutual problem solving—openness of communication, joint search for solutions, and examination of alternatives.

The essential argument of the Walton-McKersie model is that all bargaining relationships contain a mix of distributive and potentially integrative issues. The integrative potential arises out of the interdependent nature of the employment relationship: the parties need each other for mutual survival and goal attainment. At the same time, there is an inherent conflict of interest in all employment relationships because of the different economic interests of employees and employers and the structure of the employment relationship.

How would this framework be applied to conceptualizing the bargaining process in the public sector? How does distributive bargaining work in the public sector, given the complexity of the legal, political, and organizational characteristics that have been discussed in the preceding chapters? Is there any potential for integrative bargaining in the public sector, or are the relationships too complex and too immature or unstable to allow joint problem-solving processes to work? The readings in this chapter are included in part to shed some light on these questions.

Since distributive bargaining involves a conflict of interest, the process is very directly affected by the relative bargaining power of the parties. Bargaining power has been described as the basic motivating force that provides the incentive for parties to compromise their positions in order to reach an agreement. Chamberlain and Kuhn offer one of the most widely accepted descriptions of how bargaining power induces parties to reach an agreement.[2] They argue that parties will agree when the "costs of disagreeing" with the other party's proposal are greater than the "costs of agreeing" to the proposal. In the private sector, the primary costs are the economic ones associated with a strike; therefore, the threat of a strike is viewed as the major motivating force behind the bargaining process.

Thus, at the heart of distributive bargaining is the assumption that two parties are engaged in bilateral negotiations in which they use their willingness and ability to engage in or take a strike to induce their opponent to settle the dispute. In the public sector, this view of distributive bargaining must be modified somewhat because the interests at stake are much more diffuse and, consequently, the bilateral paradigm is less accurate. Instead, bargaining in the public sector has been conceptualized as *multilateral* in nature—that is, involving the interplay of multiple interest groups. In short, the process of distributive bargaining in the public sector must accommodate the interest groups that share power in public sector bargaining. Therefore, in addition to the economic costs that could be imposed by a strike or a lockout, distributive bargaining in the public sector is affected by the political costs of agreement and disagreement.

The first reading presented in this section on the interaction process reflects the general premises outlined here regarding the nature of public sector bargaining. In it, Kochan develops the notion of multilateralism in the public sector and proposes some conditions under which this type of bargaining process emerges in local governments.[3]

Notes

1. Richard E. Walton and Robert B. McKersie, *A Behavioral Theory of Labor Negotiations* (New York: McGraw-Hill, 1965).

2. Neil W. Chamberlain and James W. Kuhn, *Collective Bargaining,* 3rd ed. (New York: McGraw-Hill, 1986), chap. 5.

3. For an insightful examination of the political strategies employed by public sector unions to affect the interaction process, see Paul F. Gerhart, *Political Activity by Public Employee Organizations at the Local Level: Threat or Promise* (Chicago: International Personnel Management Association, 1974), esp. chaps. 3 and 4.

A Theory of Multilateral Collective Bargaining in City Governments

*Thomas A. Kochan**

Although a vast descriptive and prescriptive literature concerning the nature of the collective bargaining process in the public sector has accumulated in recent years, little progress has been made toward developing theoretical models of these bargaining processes. This reading will address that issue by presenting a behavioral theory of the bargaining process in city governments.[1] In addition, the results of an empirical test of the theory based on data collected from 228 cities that bargain with locals of the International Association of Fire Fighters (IAFF) will also be presented.

The Institutional Context

Collective bargaining in city government can be viewed as a special type of decision-making process that has both inter- and intraorganizational aspects. Traditionally, collective bargaining has been conceptualized as a bilateral process involving the interaction of representatives of employees on one side and management on the other.[2] With the growth of bargaining in the public sector, this traditional view of bargaining has come under serious attack. Since the organizational structures found in city governments have been designed to conform to the principle of separation of powers,[3] a number of semiautonomous management officials often share decision-making power over issues traditionally raised by unions in collective bargaining. Because power is shared by both administrative and elected officials, it has been argued that what often begins as a "variant of private sector bargaining" ends up by becoming an extension of machine politics.[4]

*Reprinted from *Industrial and Labor Relations Review* 27, no. 4 (July, 1974), pp. 525–542.

The basic thesis of the model tested in this reading is that these political and organizational characteristics of city government lead to the development of a multilateral bargaining process. Although others have discussed this type of bargaining in the public sector,[5] this reading is believed to be the first to present a formal theory of multilateral bargaining in which the concept is operationally defined and to test empirically several hypotheses concerning the determinants of this form of bargaining.

The Concept of Multilateral Bargaining

Multilateral bargaining is defined as a process of negotiation in which more than two distinct parties are involved in such a way that a clear dichotomy between the employee and management organizations does not exist. In the language of game theory, the concepts of bilateral and multilateral bargaining correspond to two-party and n-party games, respectively. As Caplow has demonstrated, the difference between a two-party and a three-party game reflects a basic qualitative difference between the types of processes that take place within each game.[6] The involvement of any more than three parties, however, is seen as merely an extension of a three-party process.

In this model, it will be the degree of multilateral bargaining experienced in a city that will serve as the dependent variable. The complete model of the bargaining process that was developed and tested in this research project consists of two stages. The first stage addresses the development of internal management conflict. It proposes that internal conflict is a function of the diversity of goals and the dispersion of power within the city management structure. The second stage then relates internal management conflict and a number of other management and union characteristics to the occurrence of multilateral bargaining. It is the second stage of the model that will be discussed in this reading.[7]

A number of researchers have attempted to apply the general concept of multilateral bargaining to the context of local government labor relations and to refine its definition to fit this institutional context. The most basic problem in developing an operational measure of the concept is determining the identity of the parties to the process. McLennan and Moskow have defined a *party* in this context as any individual or collective body that is capable of imposing a cost on at least one of the other direct parties to the agreement.[8] Those authors were primarily concerned with the impact of interest groups in the community on the bargaining process, however, and thus they did not need to be concerned with identifying the "direct parties" to the process. Juris and Feuille point out that another type of multilateral bargaining is common in city governments—namely, the involvement of what they call "non–labor relations city officials" in the bargaining process.[9] Although these two descriptions suggest that the involvement of both community groups and certain city officials should be included in a definition and therefore a measure of multilateral bargaining, there is still the problem of distinguishing between labor relations and non–labor relations city officials. In order to resolve this problem, characteristics distinguishing bilateral from multilateral bargaining processes must be specified. Unfortunately, this in itself is a problem, since the collective bargaining literature does not provide a clearly defined set of behaviors that are consistent with a bilateral process. Consequently, some assumptions about bilateral bargaining need to be made in order to develop a measure of multilateral bargaining.

It is assumed that a bilateral bargaining process is one in which a formally designated negotiator or negotiating team represents the employer in direct negotiations with a corresponding negotiator or negotiating team representing the employee organization. The purpose of these two individuals or groups is to reach a tentative bargaining agreement. When an agreement is reached, the negotiating representatives take the package back to their respective principals for ratification. An extremely important assumption here is that all interactions between management officials and the employee organization are channeled through the formally designated negotiators. In addition, the negotiators are assumed to serve as the public spokesmen for the parties on bargaining issues.

This is obviously an oversimplification of the way collective bargaining works in any context, but this description is useful as a base line in testing any model that attempts to explain departures from the conventional bilateral pattern of behavior. Thus, the specific types of behavior used in this study to measure the extent of multilateral bargaining in a city are those that clearly violate this assumed pattern of bilateral behavior.[10] Because of the importance of this concept to the model and to bargaining theory in general, the specific types of behavior used to characterize it in this context are described in detail in a later section of the reading.

Determinants of Multilateral Bargaining

Now that the concept of multilateral bargaining has been delineated, its major determinants can be hypothesized. The major proposition in the model is that *the greater the extent of internal conflict among management officials, the more likely that multilateral bargaining will take place.*[11]

To understand why internal management conflict is proposed as the most important cause of multilateral bargaining, it is useful to think of the relationship among city management officials in terms of a coalition. In essence, for bargaining to be bilateral, the management officials who share decision-making authority must coalesce and act as a single unit vis-à-vis the union. If the management coalition does not form or breaks apart at some point during the internal decision-making process so that different officials openly favor different positions on bargaining-related issues, internal conflict occurs. When internal conflict occurs, management officials have two basic options: (1) to resolve their differences internally and then allow the designated management negotiators to represent their mutual interests in bargaining with the union, or (2) to attempt to represent their interests separately, by directly intervening in the bargaining process. If they choose the latter option and internal conflicts are carried over into the bargaining arena, either because of tactics of the employee organization or on the initiative of management officials, the necessary condition for multilateral bargaining—the involvement of more than two distinct parties—is fulfilled.[12] Typically, in this type of situation, factions can be identified within management that (1) advocate a position more favorable to the employee organization on an issue, or (2) support a bargaining position that is inconsistent with the positions of either the employee organization or the designated management negotiators.[13]

Although the model proposes that internal conflict is the basic determinant of multilateral bargaining, it also assigns a role of influence to several other variables. For example, it is plausible to assume that the degree of multilateral bargaining would be affected by the extent of management commitment to negotiations. Although most cities that have an established bargaining relationship with their employees have set up formal procedures that specify bilateral negotiations, not all city officials are likely to be equally committed to using these channels as a mechanism for decision making on employment relations matters.[14] Hildebrand suggests that a basic reason for this aversion is that elected officials experience role conflicts when faced with the task of representing the interests of their constituents and acting as a member of a management that is engaged in negotiations with a union.[15] Furthermore, the introduction of collective bargaining into an organization necessarily requires some shifting of the locus of decision making and is bound to be met with resistance from those who feel threatened by such shifts. This is especially true in city governments because of the strong role civil service commissions have traditionally played in making employment relations policy and the interest that those responsible for these functions have in maintaining their autonomy.[16]

Thus, city officials who are not committed to collective bargaining are likely to seek alternative mechanisms for policy making and, by doing so, to reduce the likelihood that bargaining will remain within the formal bilateral channels. It is therefore proposed that *the weaker the commitment of management decision makers to collective bargaining, the more likely that multilateral bargaining will occur.*

Another variable that would influence the level of multilateral bargaining is the conflict resolution policies of management. Some cities have recognized the problems inherent in coordinating the roles of the various management officials in bargaining and have developed policies for achieving the commitment of all relevant decision makers prior to the beginning of negotiations. Hildebrand labeled such policies as mechanisms for obtaining a "family understanding" concerning the procedural and substantive issues related to bargaining. For example, New York, Baltimore, and a few other large cities have set up labor policy committees composed of city officials from the various decision-making units within the management structure, and a growing number of cities have established specialized labor relations departments.[17] To the extent that such procedures are successful, a kind of coopted commitment of the management officials is achieved, and the ability of the parties to influence decisions outside of the formal negotiation process is constrained. Consequently, it is suggested that *the greater the number of internal conflict resolution procedures that exist, the less likely that multilateral bargaining will occur.*

Union Political Strength

Up to this point, only city management characteristics that lead to multilateral bargaining have been considered. A number of characteristics of the union involved, however, are also likely to have an important effect on the type of bargaining that occurs. Since multilateral bargaining is basically an outgrowth of the political relationships that exist among city officials, most of the union characteristics that are proposed as determinants of multilateral bargaining reflect some aspect of the union's political strength.

Political pressure tactics by unions, for instance, can produce situations of multilateral bargaining. Chamberlain and Kuhn have suggested that an alert union will be aware of differences among the decision preferences of management officials and will devise tactics to take advantage of these internal differences.[18] In the public sector, the high level of publicity given rivalries among city officials should increase this awareness of employee representatives. As an alternative to engaging in confrontation tactics such as a strike, union leaders might attempt to influence the outcome of bargaining by inducing officials with interests similar to their own to actively represent their position in the management policymaking process. The use of such tactics has been widely discussed in the public sector bargaining literature. Consequently, it is suggested that *the more frequently that employee organizations use political pressure tactics, the more likely that multilateral bargaining will occur.*

For a union to be successful in inducing city officials who are not part of the formal negotiation process to actively support its demands, it must possess sufficient political resources to influence these city officials, or it must feel that the constituency preferences of the officials are similar enough to the union's interests so that the officials will react favorably to the union demands. This type of relationship has been thoroughly discussed in the political science literature as the concept of *political access*.[19] Thus, it is suggested that *the more political access the union has to city officials, the more likely that multilateral bargaining will occur.*

Not all the political tactics that affect the nature of the bargaining process are employed during the actual period in which bargaining takes place. Employee groups realize that maintaining political access and being successful in the use of political pressure during negotiations requires taking an active role in electoral politics within the community.[20] Thus, it is proposed that *the more the local union is involved in city elections, the more likely that multilateral bargaining will occur.*

These three union variables are likely to be highly interrelated. A union is not likely to attempt to apply political pressure during negotiations if it does not have access to city officials, and if it has not been instrumental in putting and maintaining elected officials in office, it is not likely to enjoy access to them. Since these are three distinct sets of union activities or characteristics that help one understand the *process* by which elected officials are motivated to become involved in the bargaining process, however, it will be useful to measure their separate impact on multilateral bargaining before assessing their combined effects.

One final union tactic that needs to be incorporated into the model of multilateral bargaining concerns the effects of pressures applied by a union when an impasse is reached in negotiations. It has already been suggested that if the union chooses to apply political pressure during negotiations, multilateral bargaining is more likely to result. The effects of tactics designed to apply pressures similar to those of a strike—such as a work slowdown, a "sickout," or picketing—are more difficult to predict. For example, city officials may perceive strike pressure to be an external threat and respond to it by resolving their differences. This type of behavior would be consistent with the Walton and McKersie model of intraorganizational bargaining.[21] McLennan and Moskow, however, suggest that exactly the opposite is likely to result.[22] They argue that multilateral bargaining is likely to increase as negotiations move from the initial discussion to the hard bargaining and impasse stages, since the disagreements become more visible to the public during these stages and interest groups become activated.

Throughout this discussion of the nature of the bargaining process in city government, the importance of the "politics" of the relationships both among city officials and with the union has been stressed. Consequently, it is expected in this study that the pressure to assume their roles as political leaders motivates city officials to respond by becoming active participants in bargaining when a visible impasse is reached in negotiations. It is thus proposed that *the greater the number of visible impasse pressure tactics that a union uses in negotiations, the more likely that multilateral bargaining will occur.*

Sample and Methodology

The research design employed in this analysis might best be described as a cross-sectional comparative field study or, in more formal terms, as an ex post facto correlation design. Because of the cross-sectional nature of the design, the data are not capable of providing a strict test of the causal propositions presented in the model. This limitation is dealt with by clearly specifying the theory tested and then analyzing the data accordingly. Thus, these data can only provide a test of the plausibility of the relationships posited in the model and can only disconfirm rather than confirm the theory.

Data were collected by means of a series of mailed questionnaires sent to all 380 cities (in forty-two states) that had a formal bargaining relationship with the IAFF in 1971.[23] Questionnaires were sent to the following sets of management officials in each city: (1) management negotiators, (2) city managers or mayors, (3) fire chiefs, (4) a random sample of three city council members, and (5) members of the civil service commission with jurisdiction over the fire department. Data were solicited from all of these city officials in order to increase the reliability of the measures of the variables in the model for each city. The responses from officials in each city were then combined to obtain an overall city score for each variable. In addition, a questionnaire designed to measure union tactics and behavior was sent to a representative of the IAFF local in each city.

Usable questionnaires were returned by 65 percent of the management negotiators, 70 percent of the fire chiefs, 27 percent of the other city officials, and 59 percent of the union representatives. From these responses, enough data were obtained to include 228 cities in the analysis. (The criterion for including a city was responses from two or more management officials.) This provided an overall response rate of approximately 60 percent.[24] A comparison of the characteristics of respondent and nonrespondent cities showed that the cities that responded are slightly smaller and pay slightly higher wages and fringe benefits than those that did not respond. In addition, a comparison of wages and working conditions in 1972 in the 228 cities used in this study and in 667 cities covered by an IAFF wage survey showed that mean wages and fringe benefits were significantly higher in the study sample than in the larger sample.[25]

Table 1

Means and Standard Deviations of Measures of Multilateral Bargaining and Total Index
(N = 228)

Measure	Mean	Standard Deviation
City officials took actions outside negotiations that affected the bargaining leverage of city negotiators.	2.67	1.20
Employee representatives discussed bargaining demands with city officials who are not on the formal bargaining team.	3.85	1.29
Interest groups in the community became involved in bargaining.	2.20	1.00
City officials overturned or failed to apply agreements reached in negotiations.	2.33	0.96
Elected officials intervened in an attempt to mediate an impasse.	2.69	1.27
Total multilateral bargaining index	13.73	4.16

Note: Measures were constructed from ratings by city officials on a seven-point scale.

Measure of Multilateral Bargaining

Table 1 presents the results of applying an index composed of five items that is used as an overall measure of the relative amount of multilateral bargaining that occurs in city governments bargaining with IAFF locals. The city officials who were surveyed in each city were asked to rate on a seven-point scale the extent to which a number of activities had occurred in the past, in the course of bargaining with the Fire Fighters. An overall index was obtained by summing the city responses on the five items.

It has been argued that multilateral bargaining can result from either the involvement of city management officials who are not part of the formal city negotiating team or from the involvement of external community interest groups in bargaining. Only one item is included to assess the extent to which community interest groups become involved in the process, since firefighter bargaining issues usually have a less visible impact on the community than, for example, the issues discussed in bargaining with teachers or with police. City officials were asked to rate the extent to which "interest groups in the community become involved in bargaining." The mean response to this item was 2.20 on the seven-point scale.

The other four items used in the construction of the multilateral bargaining index attempt to measure the extent of multilateral bargaining that arises from the actions of some city officials. One of the assumptions underlying the definition of bilateral bargaining is that members of the two parties involved channel all communications to the opposing party through their official representatives and do not engage in actions that are not sanctioned by their spokesmen. One of the most frequent complaints made by city labor negotiators, however, is that the union is constantly making "end runs" around them to other city officials and obtaining concessions not granted in negotiations. For example, in Madison, Wisconsin, in 1969, the IAFF local was successful in obtaining a recommendation for a return to parity with police salaries from a Civil Service Board that it was not able to obtain through direct negotiations with the city negotiating team. In Janesville, Wisconsin, in 1970, a similar situation occurred in which the city negotiator and the IAFF local had reached an impasse and the union was successful in getting several members of the city council to call the city negotiator to a special meeting with the union in an effort to obtain the essential salary demands that the negotiator had been opposing. Thus, by doing so, the negotiator's bargaining leverage was considerably weakened.[26]

Still a third variant on this same pattern occurs when an elected official (usually the mayor) attempts to intervene when negotiations reach an impasse in an attempt to mediate the dispute. This normally turns the process into a multilateral one, since it involves a member of the management organization attempting to act as a neutral third party rather than as a supporter of the management position. This means that the city is no longer able to act as a single entity, since the city negotiator or negotiating team is forced to respond to the mediating party as a new interest. Consequently, both the union and the city negotiators respond to this added party in an attempt to form a coalition against their negotiating opponents.[27]

These activities represent multilateral bargaining through involvement of non–labor relations city officials during the course of negotiations. There are a number of instances, however, in which the city and the union agree to a settlement, but some other city official then overturns or fails to implement the agreement. An example of this occurred in the Madison study: the city agreed to an amnesty clause in a strike-settling agreement with the union, but the Police and Fire Commission later disregarded it by suspending the union president for his leadership role in the strike. In the Janesville study, the city negotiator agreed to a cost-of-living wage increment, but the city council later refused to include enough money in the budget to implement the agreement because of its opposition to this particular clause.[28]

In one of the cities in the current study, a similar situation occurred. The city and the union agreed in negotiations to a change in the job classification of a certain fire department position. When the Civil Service Commission was later asked to imlement this change, however, it refused to do so since it felt the change was unwarranted. Most of the examples of this type of multilateral bargaining involve situations in which either civil service commissions or the city department heads are unwilling to abide by what was agreed to and ratified by the city in bargaining. A few cases of this type also involve a rejection by the city council of clauses agreed to by the negotiators or a mayor's veto of agreements ratified by the council.

To measure the extent to which these types of activities occur in the course of bargaining, city officials were asked the extent (on a one- to seven-point scale) to which each of the following had occurred in firefighter bargaining in the past: "City officials took actions outside of negotiations that affected the bargaining leverage of city negotiators"; "Employee representatives discussed bargaining demands with city officials who are not on the formal bargaining team"; "City officials overturned or failed to apply agreements reached in negotiations"; and "Elected officials intervened in an attempt to mediate an impasse."

The data in table 1 show that the type of multilateral bargaining that occurs most frequently in firefighter bargaining in these cities is the end run variety. In addition, the involvement of elected officials at the time of impasse and actions by city officials that affect the bargaining leverage of management negotiators also seem to be relatively frequent phenomena. The failure to implement bargaining agreements and the involvement of community interest groups are less common.

In table 2, the intercorrelations among the items used to measure multilateral bargaining are presented along with the item-to-total score correlations. In order to form a reliable index, these items should be positively intercorrelated and highly correlated with the total score. The items clearly meet these criteria. Cronbach's alpha, a measure of index reliability,[29] is .79, clearly indicating that these items combine to form a highly reliable and internally consistent index of multilateral bargaining.

Table 2
Intercorrelations among Multilateral Bargaining Index Items
(N = 228)

Measure	1	2	3	4	5	6
1. Bargaining leverage jeopardized	1.00					
2. End runs occurred	.61	1.00				
3. Interest groups involved	.38	.37	1.00			
4. Contract not implemented	.31	.50	.27	1.00		
5. Elected officials intervened	.49	.36	.33	.41	1.00	
6. Total index	.78	.81	.60	.61	.78	1.00
Total index-item corrected correlation[a]	.66	.71	.46	.48	.57	

Note: All correlations in this table are significant at the .01 level. Cronbach's alpha = .79.

[a]This is the corrected item-to-total-index correlation. It corrects for the bias in the item-to-total-index correlation that occurs because the total score on the index is partially determined by the item. This corrected correlation was computed in the Itempack program for item analysis of the Data and Computations Center, University of Wisconsin.

Measurement of Independent Variables

Internal Management Conflict

Three measures of internal conflict were obtained. City officials were asked to rate on a seven-point scale (a) the amount of conflict they experienced with other city officials in general in making bargaining decisions; (b) the amount of conflict they experienced specifically with each set of other management officials (mayors or city managers, city council members, labor negotiators, fire chiefs, and civil service commissioners); and (c) the amount of conflict that they experienced over decision making on five sets of bargaining issues (wages and fringe benefits, departmental work rules, grievance procedures, management rights, and discipline and discharge issues). From the data on conflict among officials and across issues, indices were constructed by summing the aggregated city responses for each of the five items. Cronbach's alpha coefficient is .62 for conflict among officials and .68 for conflict across issues. Each of the three measures of conflict is treated separately in the analysis.

Management Commitment to Bargaining

City officials were asked to rate on a seven-point scale the extent to which they felt collective bargaining is the most appropriate way to make decisions on the five sets of issues described above (wages, work rules, and so on). A total score for management commitment was obtained by summing the city score for each item. Cronbach's alpha for this index is .68.

Internal Management Conflict Resolution

The chief management negotiator was asked to indicate whether the city had no policy, an informal policy, or a formal written policy for resolving intra-management conflicts on (a) who participates in negotiations, (b) how agreements are ratified by the city, and (c) jurisdictional conflicts between the bargaining process and the civil service commission and conflicts over the substantive bargaining issues. Again, a total score for each city was obtained by summing the ratings assigned to each item. Cronbach's alpha for this index is .64.

Union Political Pressure Tactics

City officials were asked to rate on a seven-point scale the extent to which the Fire Fighters (a) appealed directly to the mayor or city manager, (b) appealed directly to city council members, and (c) attempted to use publicity in the community in order to achieve their bargaining demands. An overall index of political pressure tactics was then obtained by summing the scores on these three items. Cronbach's alpha for this index is .32.

Union Election Involvement

The union respondent in each city was asked to check whether or not the union engaged in the following activities: (a) endorsing candidates for mayor, (b) endorsing candidates for city council, (c) contributing to the campaigns of city officials, and (d) contributing manpower to city election campaigns. For each item, a score of one was assigned if the union reported that it engaged in the activity; zero was assigned otherwise. An overall election involvement index was obtained by summing the scores on the four items. Cronbach's alpha for this index is .69.

Union Impasse Pressure Tactics

Similarly, the union representatives were asked to indicate which of the following tactics the local had employed: (a) work slowdowns, (b) "sickouts," and (c) picketing. A score of one was assigned for each of these pressure tactics if the union had used it, and zero was assigned otherwise. An overall index was obtained by summing these values. Cronbach's alpha for this index is .50.

Union Political Access

The city labor negotiator was asked to rate the degree to which the IAFF local possessed political influence with the mayor or city manager, the city council, the fire chief, and the civil service commission. These influence scores were to be summed for each official in order to arrive at an overall access measure. The items, however, did not meet the criterion of internal homogeneity, and thus the overall index was not used in the analysis. Instead, union influence with the city council alone was used as the measure of access.

Zero Order Correlations

Table 3 presents the zero order correlations of each of the independent variables with the multilateral bargaining index, and table 4 presents the results of a series of multiple regression equations computed to estimate the combined effect of all of the hypothesized determinants of multilateral bargaining. Both the correlations and the regression results are presented here in order to provide a complete assessment of both the relative magnitude of the associations of each independent variable and their net effects, holding constant the effects of intercorrelations among the independent variables.

Table 3
Intercorrelations among the Hypothesized Determinants of Multilateral Bargaining and Their Correlations with the Multilateral Bargaining Index
(N = 2 2 8)

Independent Variable	1a	1b	1c	2	3	4	5	6	7	8
1. Internal management conflict										
1a. Conflict among city officials in general	1.00									
1b. Conflict across issues	.39	1.00								
1c. Conflict with specific groups of city officials	.29	.41	1.00							
2. Management commitment	.12	.17	.12	1.00						
3. Management internal conflict resolution	−.06	.03	.05	−.05	1.00					
4. Union political pressure tactics	.25	.21	.18	.07	.05	1.00				
5. Union election involvement	.17	.03	.19	−.03	−.10	.21	1.00			
6. Union impasse pressure tactics	.21	.11	.02	.08	−.08	.19	.27	1.00		
7. Union political access	.15	.17	.13	.08	−.09	.20	.19	.19	1.00	
8. Multilateral bargaining index	.52	.44	.34	.17	−.06	.34	.21	.32	.19	1.00

Note: $r \geq .13$ is significant at the .05 level; $r \geq .18$ is significant at the .01 level.

Table 4

Standardized Regression Coefficients for the Hypothesized Determinants of Multilateral Bargaining

(t-values in parentheses, N = 228)

Independent Variable	Equations		
Conflict among city officials in general	.402 (7.03)***		
Conflict with specific groups of city officials		.264 (4.43)***	
Conflict across issues		(0.97)	.365 (6.37)***
Management commitment	.110 (2.02)**	.124 (2.17)**	.114 (2.07)
Management internal conflict resolution	−.022 (−0.40)	.056 (0.97)	−.085 (−1.52)
Union political pressure tactics	.189 (3.28)***	.232 (3.87)***	.208 (3.58)***
Union election involvement	.054 (0.94)	.042 (0.68)	.101 (1.75)*
Union impasse pressure tactics	.168 (.293)***	.239 (3.96)***	.197 (3.41)***
Union political access	.039 (0.70)	.040 (0.68)	.001 (0.20)
R^2	.37	.29	.35

*Significant at the .10 level.
**Significant at the .05 level.
***Significant at the .01 level.

More specifically, table 3 presents the correlation matrix showing both the intercorrelations among the hypothesized determinants of multilateral bargaining and (in line 8) their correlations with the multilateral bargaining index. The correlations of the three measures of internal management conflict with multilateral bargaining are: .52 for conflict among city officials in general, .44 for conflict across issues, and .34 for conflict with specific groups of city officials. These correlations are all significant well beyond the 1 percent level and thus provide very strong support for the major proposition in the bargaining model—that internal conflict is the key determinant of multilateral bargaining.

The hypothesis concerning the impact of management commitment is not supported by the data. The .17 ($p < .05$) correlation between management commitment and multilateral bargaining shows that more multilateral bargaining takes place in cities where the management officials are more highly committed to the use of collective bargaining for determining employment relations policies. This suggests that multilateral bargaining is clearly not a transitional phenomenon that disappears once city officials accept collective bargaining and gain some experience with the process. This "lack of experience" argument is often found in the prescriptive discussions of the bargaining process in the public sector.

The existence of procedures for resolving internal management conflicts does not appear to reduce the amount of multilateral bargaining. The correlation is in the hypothesized direction, but is very weak (– .06). Thus, the mere existence of procedural devices for coordination does not appear to be sufficient for reducing the general level of multilateral bargaining.

The strong positive correlations obtained for union political pressure tactics, impasse pressure tactics, and degree of access to the city council support the hypotheses concerning their effects on multilateral bargaining. In no case, however, do these correlations exceed the correlations between internal conflict and multilateral bargaining. They are all significant, however, at the .01 level or above.

The correlations between the use of political pressure in bargaining by the union and the occurrence of multilateral bargaining provide strong support for an underlying argument throughout this research—namely, that there is a strong relationship between the political process in cities and the bargaining process. These data clearly show that one cannot understand the nature of the bargaining process in city governments without first assessing the nature of the political relationships among the parties involved. The high positive correlation between the use of strike pressure tactics (slowdowns, "sickouts," and picketing) and multilateral bargaining provides strong evidence that when city officials are in a position of choosing between their roles as management officials involved in a bargaining situation and their roles as elected politicians responsive to their constituencies, their roles as politicians take precedence.

Regression Analysis

In order to assess the combined effects of these determinants of multilateral bargaining, three regression equations were computed; each equation included one of the three measures of internal management conflict along with the other management and union variables. Table 4 presents the results of these regressions.[30] The models presented were all linear regression models.[31]

The data in table 4 confirm the finding in table 3 that internal management conflict is probably the most important determinant of multilateral bargaining, since the regression coefficients for the internal conflict measures remain highly significant even when all the other management and union characteristics are entered into the equation. Thus, it appears that the strong zero order correlations in table 3, between internal management conflict and multilateral bargaining, are not a result of an intercorrelation with some other variable in the model.

The addition of the other two management characteristics, commitment to bargaining and internal conflict resolution procedures, increases the amount of variance explained by only between 1 and 2 percent in the three models.[32] By adding the union variables to the model, however, the amount of variance explained increases 13 percent for the model using general management conflict and conflict across issues and 15 percent for the model using conflict with specific groups of officials. Together, the union and management determinants of multilateral bargaining included in this model explained 37 percent of the variance using general conflict, 29 percent of the variance using conflict with specific officials, and 35 percent of the variance using conflict across issues.

Since there are high intercorrelations among the union variables included in the model, it is not surprising that some of the regression coefficients fail to remain significant when all these variables are entered. Those that do remain significant are political pressure and impasse pressure tactics. The results on the impasse pressure variable suggest that city officials are somewhat reluctant to become involved in bargaining—that is, behavior by city officials that leads to multilateral bargaining seems to be more a *response* to union pressures than an autonomous desire to become actively involved in bargaining. The positive association between visible impasse tactics and multilateral bargaining supports the McLennan and Moskow contention that multilateral bargaining tends to reach a peak after an impasse in negotiations occurs.

Control Variables

In any empirical study that uses a nonexperimental design to test its hypotheses, questions arise over whether some alternative variable can account for the correlations observed between the independent and dependent variables. To resolve this question, a number of control variables were included in this study. Since none of these variables showed a strong relationship with multilateral bargaining, they were not entered in the regression analyses presented in the previous section. The correlations between these control variables and the multilateral bargaining index are presented in table 5.

These control variables were chosen in order to test several aspects of the conventional wisdom that is presented in the literature on public sector bargaining. It should be noted that it has seldom, if ever, been explicitly argued that the factors discussed below are causes of multilateral bargaining.

Table 5
Correlations between Control Variables and the Multilateral Bargaining Index
(N = 228)

Control Variable	Correlation
Comprehensiveness of bargaining law	– .05
Fact-finding procedure in the law	– .02
Compulsory arbitration procedure in the law	.06
Age of the bargaining relationship	.13
Years of private sector experience of management negotiator	– .12
Years of public sector experience of management negotiator	.02
Professionalism of management negotiator	.01
City population	.11

Note: $r \geq .13$ is significant at the .05 level; $r \geq .18$ is significant at the .01 level.

Implicit in much of the prescriptive literature, however, is the argument that public sector bargaining is an abnormal deviation from the way collective bargaining "ought to" work and that as soon as the parties gain experience with the process, or public policies formalize and regulate the bargaining process, negotiations will conform more closely to the private sector (presumably bilateral) model.

To test the argument that comprehensive legislation promoting collective bargaining for public employees will encourage negotiations to become more formalized and therefore conform more closely to a bilateral model, an index was developed to measure the comprehensiveness of the law governing bargaining between city governments and fire fighters in each state.[33] Its correlation with multilateral bargaining in these cities is shown to be only – .05.

A few states have attempted to deal more directly with the problem of dispersion of power within management (on the assumption that dispersion of power is the key cause of multilateral bargaining) by spelling out in the state law who management is and further specifying how the bargaining process should operate. Specifically, New York and Connecticut have provisions in their laws identifying the executive as the management representative in bargaining. If these laws are having an effect on the bargaining process, there should be less multilateral bargaining in these states than in the country as a whole, and also the model should overpredict the extent of multilateral bargaining in these states because this provision in their laws is not accounted for in the regression equations. Neither of these results occurred. The average score on the multilateral bargaining index is 14.4 for all cities studied in New York state, 13.2 for all cities in Connecticut, and 13.7 for all 228 cities studied, indicating that neither of these states deviates significantly from the national average. Furthermore, an examination of the residuals of the regression equations showed no tendency to overpredict multilateral bargaining in the cities in these two states.[34]

It might also be argued that the existence of more formalized impasse resolution procedures in the state law should reduce the amount of multilateral bargaining. Again, however, this is not the case—the correlation between multilateral bargaining and the existence of fact-finding procedures is −.02, and between multilateral bargaining and the existence of compulsory arbitration procedures, it is .06. Consequently, the extent of multilateral bargaining is affected little by the nature of the laws governing public sector bargaining in each state.

Another argument often found in the literature is that one of the reasons for the lack of bilateralism in the public sector is the lack of "maturity" in the bargaining relationships. Those suggesting this argue that as soon as the parties learn how collective bargaining is "supposed to" work, public sector bargaining will conform to the bilateral pattern that characterizes private sector negotiations. To test this alternative explanation, a correlation was computed between the number of years the city and the union have been negotiating labor agreements and the city's score on the multilateral bargaining index. This correlation is .13 ($p < .05$), indicating that the more mature the bargaining relationship between the parties, the *more* multilateral bargaining occurs. This finding not only rejects the lack-of-maturity hypothesis, it also reinforces the view that multilateralism is not a transitional phenomenon growing out of the parties' lack of expertise and is instead a natural outgrowth of the institutional context of city government decision making.

The same type of reasoning concerning the lack of expertise or understanding of how collective bargaining "ought to" operate led to the examination of the relationship between multilateral bargaining and the extent to which management is represented by professionals with prior experience in labor relations. Again, negative correlations with experience and professionalism variables would be expected if this argument is valid. Yet, table 5 shows the correlations with the multilateral bargaining index to be .01 for a measure of professionalism (number of professional labor relations associations to which the negotiator belongs), .02 for the number of years of experience the management negotiator has in public sector labor relations, and −.12 for the number of years of private sector experience that the management negotiator has. Thus, the only professionalism variable that seems to have any negative relation with multilateral bargaining is the amount of private sector experience the management negotiator brings to city government bargaining, and this effect is slight.

Another control variable that was examined was city size. Since the bargaining process is generally thought to be more formalized in larger cities and since the larger cities have been bargaining longer than smaller cities, it was felt that size of city might be negatively correlated with multilateral bargaining—again based on the lack-of-maturity argument. The correlation between size of city and multilateral bargaining is .11, however, and so again the evidence does not support the alternative explanation.

In summary, none of the control variables show strong enough correlations with multilateral bargaining to provide an alternative explanation for the findings presented in tables 3 and 4.

Conclusions and Implications

This analysis has demonstrated that variations in the extent of multilateral bargaining within a large sample of cities are systematically related to a number of union and management characteristics. These findings show quite clearly that the nature of the collective bargaining process in city governments is a natural outgrowth of the political context in which it operates. The close relationship hypothesized in the bargaining model between the political conflicts that occur within city governments and the nature of the union–city bargaining process received strong support. The importance of the political relationship among the parties was further reinforced by the correlation found between the political strength of the unions and multilateral bargaining.

Perhaps the model and empirical evidence presented here will put to rest the belief that the type of bargaining often found in city governments is an abnormal deviation from "normal" collective bargaining that will be eliminated as the parties and the laws under which they operate become more sophisticated. Such an argument simply ignores the underlying forces that influence the bargaining process in the public sector. As the evidence presented here suggests, the process responds to the nature of the relationships that exist among the diverse interests that share power over bargaining issues.

Finally, it is hoped that this exercise has shown the applicability of the techniques of theory construction, behavioral measurement strategies, and quantitative analysis to an area of collective bargaining theory. The strategy employed was first to develop an empirically based understanding of the process by means of case study research. This provided the foundation and the general framework for developing the propositions of the model. Then, by formally developing a behavioral model of the process and employing a comparative research design, the model was put to an empirical test.

It is hoped that others will join in similar efforts to expand and improve the model presented here as well as to develop models of the collective bargaining process along other dimensions of interest. By doing so, the overly descriptive and prescriptive orientation of collective bargaining research can be changed to one in which a balance is struck among theoretical, empirical, and prescriptive orientations.

Notes

1. The central concepts and propositions included in the model were derived from two earlier case studies of collective bargaining in Madison and Janesville, Wisconsin. The present study, therefore, is an effort to expand on, formalize, and test the hypotheses suggested by the results of these case studies. See Thomas A. Kochan, *City Employee Bargaining with a Divided Management* (Madison, Wisc.: Industrial Relations Research Institute, 1971).

2. See, for example, F.Y. Edgeworth, *Mathematical Psychics* (London: Paul, 1881); Neil W. Chamberlain and James W. Kuhn, *Collective Bargaining,* 2nd ed. (New York: McGraw-Hill, 1965); Richard E. Walton and Robert B. McKersie, *A Behavioral Theory of Labor Negotiations* (New York: McGraw-Hill, 1965); or Myron Joseph, "Collective Bargaining and Industrial Relations Theory," in Gerald G. Somers, ed., *Essays in Industrial Relations Theory* (Ames: Iowa State University Press, 1969).

3. Edward C. Banfield and James Q. Wilson, *City Politics* (New York: Vintage Books, 1963).

4. George H. Hildebrand, "The Public Sector," in John T. Dunlop and Neil W. Chamberlain, eds., *Frontiers of Collective Bargaining* (New York: Harper and Row, 1967), pp. 125–154. Almost everyone who has written about management structure in public sector bargaining has discussed the dispersion-of-power issue. See, for example, David T. Stanley, *Managing Local Government under Union Pressure* (Washington, D.C.: Brookings Institution, 1972); John F. Burton, J.r, "Structure and Process of Public Employee Bargaining," *Industrial Relations* 11, no. 2 (May 1972), pp. 123–140; James A. Belasco, "Municipal Bargaining and Political Power," in J. Joseph Loewenberg and Michael H. Moskow, eds., *Collective Bargaining in Government: Readings and Cases* (Englewood Cliffs, N.J.: Prentice-Hall, 1972), pp. 235–248; Harry H. Wellington and Ralph K. Winter, *The Unions and the Cities* (Washington, D.C.: Brookings Institution, 1971); or Frederick O.R. Hayes, "Collective Bargaining and the Budget Director," in Sam Zagoria, ed., *Public Workers and Public Unions* (Englewood Cliffs, N.J.: Prentice-Hall, 1972), p. 91.

5. For one of the earliest theoretical statements on this issue, see Kenneth McLennan and Michael H. Moskow, "Multilateral Bargaining in the Public Sector," *Proceedings of the Twenty-first Annual Winter Meeting* (Madison, Wisc.: Industrial Relations Research Association, 1968), pp. 34–41. For a further discussion, see Michael H. Moskow, J. Joseph Loewenberg, and Edward J. Kozaria, *Collective Bargaining in Public Employment* (New York: Random House, 1970).

6. Theodore Caplow, *Two against One: Coalitions in Triads* (Englewood Cliffs, N.J.: Prentice-Hall, 1968).

7. A future paper will link the two stages of the model together. A test of the entire model is presented in Thomas A. Kochan, "Internal Conflict and Multilateral Bargaining in City Governments (Ph.D. dissertation, University of Wisconsin, Madison, 1973).

8. McLennan and Moskow, "Multilateral Bargaining in the Public Sector," p. 31.

9. Hervey A. Juris and Peter Feuille, *Police Unionism: Power and Impact in Public Sector Bargaining* (Lexington, Mass.: D.C. Heath, 1973).

10. Juris and Feuille used this definition of multilateral bargaining in their study of police bargaining in twenty-two cities. They found that the concept provided a valid description of the union–management interactions in these cities and thus provided further empirical evidence for the construct validity of this characterization of the bargaining process. See Juris and Feuille, *Police Unionism,* pp. 45–51.

11. Although other investigators have speculated about the causes of multilateral bargaining, none have explicitly focused on internal conflict as the most important determinant. Love and Sulzner, for example, use the term *shadow parties* to describe the involvement of third parties in the bargaining process and argue that the dispersion of power among management officials is the key determinant of multilateral bargaining; the model presented here includes internal conflict as an intervening variable in this linkage. Juris and Feuille make a similar argument concerning the importance of the structural fragmentation of decision-making power, but they also imply that conflicts among city officials are also important. See Thomas M. Love and George T. Sulzner, "Political Implications of Public Sector Bargaining," *Industrial Relations* 11, no. 1 (February 1972), pp. 18–34; and Juris and Feuille, *Police Unionism,* p. 50.

12. In other words, the occurrence of internal conflicts within a city management provides the motivation for the various city officials to directly pursue their interests in the interorganizational bargaining process. On the other hand, if little or no disagreement exists among the management officials, or if their disagreements are adequately resolved through the internal management decision-making process, there is no incentive for the various officials to intervene directly in the union–city negotiations process. As will be developed more fully later, one reason that this problem is far more prevalent in the public sector than in private industry is that there are multiple points of access to public officials that allow unions to apply pressures that further push the officials toward direct involvement. Also, because decision-making power is so often shared among public officials, they can usually intervene in the bargaining process (if they have the incentive to do so) far more easily and effectively than can management officials in a private company who are not designated negotiators.

13. One might argue that intraorganizational conflicts within the union could also lead to multilateral bargaining. If the present model were to be applied to other institutional contexts, there would be no theoretical reason for rejecting intraunion conflicts as a determinant of multilateral bargaining. Indeed, in another context one might even argue that intraunion conflict does serve as an important determinant of multilateral bargaining. For example, if black workers' organizations continue to grow in strength and number, they may be able to challenge the employee organizations that have exclusive bargaining rights and thereby create the likelihood of multilateral bargaining among the interests within the management, the black employees' organizations, and the white-dominated employees' organizations.

In the bargaining relationships studied in this research, however, there was neither theoretical nor prior empirical evidence to suggest that internal union differences would have any substantial effect on the bargaining process. Thus, no attempt was made to explore intraunion conflicts. Future researchers who attempt to apply this model, however, should be aware of the asymmetrical nature of the model in this respect and should perhaps investigate both intramanagement and intraunion conflicts as potential sources of multilateral bargaining.

14. For an empirical assessment of differences in commitment to the bargaining process by local government officials, see George Fredrickson, "Role Occupancy and Attitudes toward Labor Relations in Government," *Admininstrative Science Quarterly* 14, no. 4 (December 1969), pp. 595–606.

15. Hildebrand, "The Public Sector."

16. See, for example, Murial M. Morse, "Shall We Bargain Away the Merit System," *Public Personnel Review* 24, no. 4 (October 1963), pp. 239–243; Chester Newland, "Collective Bargaining Concepts: Applications in Government," *Public Administration Review* 28, no. 2 (March–April 1968), pp. 117–126; and Milton Derber, "Who Negotiates for the Public Employer?" in Public Employee Relations Library, Special Issue, *Perspectives in Public Employee Negotiations* (Chicago: Public Personnel Association, 1969), pp. 52–58.

17. The Labor Management Relations Service, *The City Prepares for Labor Relations* (Washington, D.C., 1970). This survey showed that 100 cities had specialized labor relations units at this time.

18. Chamberlain and Kuhn, *Collective Bargaining,* p. 218.

19. For discussion of the use of these strategies in other political decision-making processes, see Michael Lipsky, "Protest as a Political Resource," *American Political Science Review* 62, no. 4 (December 1968), pp. 1144–1158; and Ralph H. Turner, "The Public Perception of Protest," *American Sociological Review* 34, no. 6 (December 1969), pp. 815–831.

20. For examples of union election involvement, see James A. Craft, "Fire Fighter Strategy in Wage Negotiation," *Quarterly Review of Economics and Business* 11, no. 3 (Autumn 1971), pp. 65–75.

21. Walton and McKersie, *A Behavioral Theory of Labor Negotiations,* pp. 281–351.

22. McLennan and Moskow, "Multilateral Bargaining in the Public Sector," p. 34.

23. For a more complete description of the design and measurement techniques, see Kochan, "Internal Conflict and Multilateral Bargaining in City Governments," chap. 4. For further evidence concerning the reliability and validity of the measures, see appendix A of that dissertation.

24. Where responses were received from the management officials but not the union, mean values were inserted for the missing data on the union variables. The means were calculated from those unions that responded.

25. These are 667 locals out of a total of 1,300 IAFF locals that responded to an IAFF survey of wages and working conditions in 1972. These data are the best source available for a comparison of our sample to the universe of IAFF locals.

26. See Kochan, *City Employee Bargaining with a Divided Management,* pp. 31–56.

27. Ibid., pp. 39–41.

28. Ibid., pp. 34, 48.

29. See Jum Nunnally, *Psychometric Theory* (New York: McGraw-Hill, 1967), pp. 210–213. Cronbach's alpha is a measure of the internal consistency of the items

combined in an index. Basically, it correlates each item with the total score on the index and serves as a measure of the extent to which the items are similar enough to be combined and interpreted as measures of the same construct.

30. Three separate regression equations are calculated, rather than one equation in which all three measures of conflict are included, in order to test the stability of the regression coefficients for the alternative measures of internal conflict. If all three were included in the same equation, a problem of redundancy would exist; that is, measures of three aspects of the same concept would be in the same equation. This would bias the regression coefficients and would not test the theory as it has been stated here.

31. A regression model with interaction terms was also computed, but it failed to add anything to the proportion of the variance explained.

32. The equations were computed in a stepwise fashion by adding each variable one at a time. The equations for each step are not shown in table 4 but are available from the author on request.

33. A complete description of this index, along with an empirical analysis of its environmental correlates, can be found in Thomas A. Kochan, "Environmental Correlates of Public Sector Bargaining Laws," *Industrial Relations* 12, no. 3 (October 1973), pp. 322–335.

34. Residuals measure the difference between the predicted and observed values on the dependent variable.

Cooperation and Adversarialism

Although the literature on multilateral bargaining provides a picture of how distributive bargaining unfolds in the public sector, we have little research or understanding of the extent of integrative bargaining between public employers and public employee organizations. This paucity of research may reflect the reality of practice in government. Despite many calls for union–management cooperation in the public sector, especially regarding productivity, there seems to be much more talk than action in this area. Few careful and objective studies of the results of labor–management cooperative efforts in the public sector have been conducted.

We are fortunate, therefore, to have an intriguing description of an attempt at productivity bargaining in the public sector, written by Melvin Osterman, the former director of employee relations for the state of New York. Although it describes events of the early 1970s, we have chosen to retain the Osterman reading in the third edition of this book because he suggests a number of reasons that productivity bargaining, and perhaps union–management cooperation in general, is not widespread in the public sector. Osterman describes the causes of a failure in productivity bargaining between the state of New York and the Civil Service Employees Association. His interpretation of this effort illustrates the complexity of the problems in successfully structuring an experiment in union–management cooperation in an environment characterized by a broad diffusion of power across multiple interest groups. In a short afterword to the Osterman reading, Robert B. McKersie adds some additional insight into why the New York State experiment failed by comparing the experiment to the two forms of productivity bargaining that have been popularized in previous literature on the subject, namely, the buyout and the gain-sharing approaches. His comments offer clear guidelines for other practitioners who may venture down this dangerous but essential road in the future.

Indeed, we follow these comments with a brief summary of a productivity bargaining agreement achieved in New York City in the early 1980s to illustrate one of McKersie's points, namely, that a buyout strategy is more likely than a gain-sharing strategy to work in large, politically complex jurisdictions in cases involving the introduction of new technology. This case is also instructive for the creative role played by a neutral third party in bringing about the agreement. Moreover, in appraising McKersie's perspective on productivity bargaining in government as well as the New York State experience described by Osterman, the reader should recognize that, in the public sector as in the private sector, there exists controversy over the scope of bargaining and, concomitantly, the obligations of the employer and the union to bargain in good faith. Although state statutes regulating public sector bargaining are generally patterned on the private sector principle of good faith bargaining, state bargaining laws may vary considerably in terms of the scope of bargainable issues and in terms of what are considered mandatory versus permissive subjects of negotiations.[1]

It would be difficult to find a more graphic example of adversarial bargaining in the public sector than that between air traffic controllers and the federal government. This formal bargaining relationship ended in early 1981, when President Reagan fired striking air traffic controllers and the Federal Labor Relations Authority removed the status of the Professional Air Traffic Controllers Organization (PATCO) as a certified bargaining agent. These highly publicized events, as well as others that preceded them, are examined by Northrup in the third reading presented in this chapter.

Northrup begins by chronicling the record of militancy that characterized PATCO from 1968 to 1981. During that period, PATCO conducted several work stoppages and work slowdowns, which in turn brought about judicial restraining orders and contempt citations, financial penalties, and the suspension and discharge of some controllers. The Federal Aviation Administration (FAA) and the courts were able to implement these "countervailing" actions in part because PATCO was never able to organize the controller work force fully or to command the allegiance of its members when it came to strikes and picketing activity. In 1970 and 1976, for example, some controllers followed union directives to strike and to slow down the pace of work, but other controllers did not. This limited internal support of PATCO's militant action, together with the FAA's substitution of management personnel for striking controllers and the air carriers' rescheduling and consolidating of certain flights, gave the federal government the upper hand as employer in its dealings with unionized controllers.

Northrup goes on to detail PATCO's efforts in the late 1970s to build a strike fund (despite its officers' knowledge that federal employee strikes were illegal), marshal membership support for substantial pay and benefit increases in the 1981 negotiations, and obtain strike authorization to enforce those demands if that became necessary. Although Northrup argues that PATCO was basically seeking to gain the right to bargain under private sector rules, and although he soundly criticizes the actions of the union's leadership, the larger contribution of Northrup's article may well lie in its discussion of management's strategy and organization for bargaining with PATCO. In this regard, a detailed management plan for dealing with a controller's strike was developed in the final year (1980) of the Carter administration. Among other things, the plan outlined the methods to be used for operating air traffic facilities during a strike and the entreaties to be made to the courts to thwart a strike. The major elements of this plan were subsequently adopted and implemented by President Reagan and FAA officials. Interpreted in light of Kochan's analysis of multilateral bargaining in municipal government, the key management actors in the federal government appear to have overcome their internal conflicts to deal in a unified (almost bilateral) manner with the air traffic controllers' strike in 1981. This interpretation accords with other research (such as, for example, that by Katz) showing that under certain circumstances local government employers are able to counter union militancy effectively.[2]

That the interpretation of public sector collective bargaining processes (and outcomes) rests in part on the value judgments of the researcher is clearly shown in Hurd and Kriesky's critique of the Northrup article, which is reprinted here. In essence, Hurd and Kriesky contend that:

1. The secondary sources cited by Northrup and the actions of the federal Congress and of PATCO do not support the conclusion that the union was seeking a version of private sector wage bargaining.

2. Northrup did not adequately deal with FAA management's policies and practices that brought about the workplace conditions that, in turn, spurred militant action by organized controllers.

3. The internal dynamics of and leadership changes in PATCO were insufficiently analyzed.

4. Northrup was too quick to applaud the Reagan administration's actions in the PATCO situation and did not examine alternative actions that could have stimulated integrative as opposed to adversarial labor relations.

Whether or not these criticisms render Northrup's analysis fundamentally wanting is a judgment we will leave to the reader. For this purpose, we have also reprinted Northrup's reply to Hurd and Kriesky. From a larger perspective, however, several questions about the public sector bargaining process are raised by the controversy over the PATCO case. First, is collective bargaining a suitable vehicle for dealing with such fundamental contemporary workplace problems as job stress, substance abuse, career advancement blockages, and insufficient leisure time? Each of these problems has been alleged to characterize the air traffic controller work force, yet they persist despite the efforts of labor and management to negotiate satisfactory terms and conditions of employment and despite the demise of PATCO.[3] Put differently, decertification of the bargaining agent for federal air traffic controllers does not seem to have altered the conditions of work that Hurd and Kriesky, among others, contend accounted for the militancy of the controllers' union.

Second, did the Reagan administration's hard bargaining stance in dealing with the controllers provide an object lesson for other public (and private) employers? Although the popular answer to this question is apparently "yes," we believe the lesson is a limited one at best. The federal government is financed largely by income taxes, so the Reagan admininstration (and the Carter administration before it) was able to use tax revenues to fund the recruitment, selection, hiring, placement, and training of a new air traffic controller force numbering in the thousands. No other public or private employer is likely to be able to replicate such a monopoly position or the power that accrues to it. To the contrary, most private employers and, increasingly, public employers must compete for financial resources, customers, and employees, so that in these respects the federal government is sui generis.

Third, should the federal government be in the business of providing air traffic control services? With the growing deregulation of industry and the increased privatization of "public" services in the 1980s, it is not inconceivable that some or all air traffic control may come to be privately provided. Should that occur, it is also likely that few employers would summarily dismiss an entire controller work force, even in the event of a strike or an "outrageous" bargaining demand. The reader should note in this regard that Northrup cites some existing examples of the private employment of air traffic controllers.

Fourth and in light of the Angle-Perry reading discussed previously, is it possible that some employee-members of public sector labor organizations display little or no loyalty to their employers *or* to their labor organizations? In the industrial relations and organizational behavior literatures, the topic of dual loyalty has been broached in terms of the question, "Can an employee be loyal to *both* the employer and the union?" But if this is a permissible research question, then so too is the question, "Can an employee have little or no loyalty to *either* focal organization?" Instructively, the conceptual basis of the latter question is nested in the behavioral literature on collective bargaining, of which Walton and McKersie provide a leading example. They observe that integrative bargaining is analogous to a variable-sum game in which both parties (to a negotiation) may win *or* lose. Following this conceptualization, it is conceivable that some employees display high loyalty to their employer and to their union, other employees display high loyalty to their employer (union) and low (or no) loyalty to their union (employer), and still other employees display low (or no) loyalty to both. The case of PATCO, as examined by Northrup and by Hurd and Kriesky, seems to offer an example of low employee loyalty to the employer and to the union. Their analyses strongly suggest that the potential for integrative bargaining is very low in the arena of federal air traffic control.

Notes

1. For an analysis of this subject, see Harry T. Edwards, "The Impact of Private Sector Principles in the Public Sector: Bargaining Rights for Supervisors and the Duty to Bargain," in David B. Lipsky, ed., *Union Power and Public Policy* (Ithaca: N.Y.: New York State School of Industrial and Labor Relations, Cornell University, 1975), pp. 51–74.

2. See Harry C. Katz, "Municipal Pay Determination: The Case of San Francisco," *Industrial Relations* 18 (Winter 1979), pp. 45–58.

3. See, for example, Robert M. Rose, C. David Jenkins, and Michael W. Hurst, *Air Traffic Controller Health Change Study* (Washington, D.C.: U.S. Department of Transportation and U.S. Federal Aviation Administration, 1978); and Lawrence M. Jones, David G. Bowers, and Stephen H. Fuller, *Management and Employee Relationships within the Federal Aviation Administration* (Washington, D.C.: U.S. Federal Aviation Administration, 1982).

Productivity Bargaining in New York— What Went Wrong?

Melvin H. Osterman, Jr.,
with an afterword by *Robert B. McKersie* *

I am writing this paper as an advocate of productivity bargaining, with somewhat tarnished credentials. The subject of the impact of productivity on labor–management negotiations is a challenging and vital one. It is one that,

---

*Former Director of the Office of Employee Relations for the State of New York, now in the private practice of law, and Massachusetts Institute of Technology, respectively. Reprinted from a speech presented at the Tenth Annual Conference on Management Analysis in State and Local Government, October, 1973.

particularly in times of an inflationary economy and continuing fiscal stringency, must be given serious consideration by all who are engaged in collective bargaining in the public sector. In preparing these remarks, therefore, I
first turned to the excellent material published by the National Commission
on Productivity, to the study prepared for the Joint Economic Committee of
the Congress, and to the many scholarly texts that have been published on
this subject. Yet, as I continued preparing material on this topic, it became
clear to me that my remarks might be more valuable if I were to relate the
practical experience that my state—New York—has had in trying to make
productivity bargaining a reality—even though those efforts have not been
successful. There are, I think, valuable lessons that management, labor, and
the public in general may learn from the New York experience.

On June 20, 1972, I signed a collective agreement with the Civil Service
Employees Association, Inc., a union representing 135,000 employees in the
state of New York. That contract contained a clear commitment to productivity bargaining and looked toward the establishment of mechanisms to
make it a reality.

The state had gone into productivity bargaining with high hopes. In
1972, Dr. T. Norman Hurd, secretary to Governor Rockefeller, spoke before
the American Statistical Association Convention and commented:

> In jurisdictions, like New York, which have highly developed collective
> bargaining procedures, the desired changes may have to be negotiated and
> quid pro quos offered. We are fortunate that the CSEA, our largest union,
> seems to understand the need for increasing state productivity as evidenced
> by their willingness to take the first step with us.
>
> I am sure you know that there are great risks associated with this effort.
> Productivity measurement in the public service, at this time, is more an
> emerging notion than a well-charted program.
>
> Like all experimentation, however, whatever the initial result we will
> gain knowledge and insights not available in any other way. And success may
> well revolutionize the current pattern of public administration in New York
> and, perhaps, throughout the nation.

The revolution anticipated by Dr. Hurd did not occur.

On June 20, 1973, a year to the day after our first agreement, I signed
another agreement with the Civil Service Employees Association (CSEA); this
second agreement was wholly silent on the subject of productivity bargaining. In the year that had intervened, both the state and the union had concluded that their respective interests would be better served by avoiding direct
reference to productivity.

How we came to our first agreement on productivity bargaining and
what went wrong in the intervening year will provide the focus for my
remarks in this reading.

New York State, under the Taylor Law, has, since 1967, been committed to meaningful collective negotiations with organizations representing its employees. State employees' salaries, fringe benefits, and all other terms and conditions of employment are determined solely through the processes of collective negotiations. The Office of Employee Relations (OER) is charged under state law with the responsibility for representing the Governor and the Executive Branch in these negotiations. It is assisted in this effort by representatives of the state civil service commission and the Division of the Budget. Since it will become relevant for later remarks, it is worth noting that within the Division of the Budget there is a management unit that has been concerned for many years with assessing the efficiency of state government and devising methods for improving the productivity of state workers and the effectiveness with which state services are delivered.

The largest union with which the state deals, the CSEA, is an independent union with approximately 200,000 members. It represents 135,000 state workers, plus almost all the noninstructional employees in school districts throughout the state and a majority of the employees in various counties, towns, and villages. CSEA has engaged in an informal bargaining relationship with the state for the past two decades and in a formal negotiating relationship for the past eight years.

Each of CSEA's various collective agreements with the state run to approximately seventy-five pages. They are comprehensive contracts covering wages, health insurance, time and leave matters, and a whole host of working conditions. They all contain the same broad management-rights clause, including, specifically, a provision reserving to the state the right "to direct, deploy and utilize the work force." This clause, as we will see, had a very real impact on our efforts in the area of productivity bargaining.

The state entered negotiations with CSEA in the fall of 1971 with a real problem—it had no money. Managements traditionally commence each round of negotiations with a plea for mercy on the ground that the cupboard is bare. This time, however, our plea was more than a formality. The state was in a period of austerity. Over ten thousand state employees had been laid off the preceding year. We were facing the prospect of a seriously unbalanced budget and the need for even further layoffs in the work force. We were aware of the real need to review state services to assess whether we were doing the best job we could.

Yet, even with these concerns, we were not entirely unrealistic in approaching the negotiations. With all our problems, we were aware of advances in the cost of living and recognized that CSEA would not lightly accept our pleas of inability to pay as an excuse for deferring a pay increase. We came to the concept of productivity bargaining as a method of bridging our concerns with our budget and efficiency of operation and CSEA's need to protect the interests of its members.

We first broached the subject of productivity in February 1972, several months into the negotiations. We argued that CSEA should seriously consider whether there were methods of enhancing the "productivity" of the state's work force and argued that if there were demonstrable gains in productivity, perhaps they might be the bases for an accommodation of our mutual interests. At that stage of negotiations, we did not define what we meant by productivity. We simply talked in terms of a trade-off. Indeed, at this stage of the negotiations, we really did not know the parameters of the proposal we were launching. Our exploratory probe fell on deaf ears. CSEA indicated that it was not interested in trade-offs, and the issue was not raised again until the week preceding the expiration of our contract.

By that time, negotiations had proceeded to the point where the state's salary offer had reached 4 percent. The state's negotiators indicated that, to justify an increase in this amount, they would require CSEA to make a variety of trade-offs under which the state would receive something back in return for the salary increase.

On the Sunday preceding the expiration date, we advanced a number of specific proposals under the headline "productivity improvements." They included

- The exclusion of temporary employees from leave coverage, at a "savings" of $1.5 million
- A requirement that employees with less than 100 days of accumulated sick leave charge the first day of sick leave to personal leave credits, at a "savings" of $12 million
- A requirement that state employees remit fees paid to them for jury duty, at a "savings" of $150,000
- The establishment of a uniform forty-hour work week for state employees, at a savings of $24 million.

The fact that these items were characterized as productivity improvements perhaps speaks to the naiveté with which we approached the subject of productivity bargaining. It is remarkable, when going through the writings in the area, how rarely the term *productivity* is defined. It is easy to find an explanation of the concept, in which productivity is related to the ratio of in-inputs to outputs. Perhaps this is the only consistent attempt at a definition that is possible. For when one goes beyond that, one often sinks into an intellectual and verbal morass. Most of what we were talking about at this stage of the negotiations was not real productivity in any technical sense of the term. Certainly requiring employees to remit fees for jury duty or denying holidays and vacation to temporary workers can in no way be characterized as improvements in productivity. On the other hand, they are, in a sense related to the concept of productivity bargaining—that is, an attempt through the process of collective negotiations to obtain changes in work rules or practices that will permit the employer to reduce the cost or improve the quality or quantity of the services it provides.

We spent the next three days debating the merits of these trade-offs. On Wednesday, with only two days before the expiration of the contract, the union advised us that none of the trade-offs could even be considered acceptable, and discussion moved toward other methods of financing the salary increase.

The other methods of financing did not prove acceptable, and on Friday night 7,700 union members struck state facilities across New York. Fortunately, the strike occurred on a weekend, and the impact on most state services was minimal. In addition, we received a massive outpouring of volunteer support, which also tended to mitigate the effects of the strike. On the other hand, a strike at a hospital for the mentally retarded or a prison—facilities that are open on the weekend—is never pleasant to contemplate.

During the course of the strike, negotiations continued in Albany. Again, the subject of productivity and trade-offs was introduced. At this point, however, the state itself began to have some second thoughts. During the negotiations, the state's representatives were continuing to refine their perceptions of the concept they were pursuing. They were engaged in a process of considering alternative methods of approaching productivity and attempting to give flesh and blood to that concept. Meanwhile, we were aware that if we intended to pursue productivity bargaining, we should do so on a basis that would be meaningful and would provide real savings to the state. We were not interested in a "public relations" approach which would merely permit us to claim increases in productivity to justify salary increases to state employees.

It was a keystone of our efforts that we be able to demonstrate actual improvements in service and real savings, a portion of which we would propose to share with employees. We were aware of the difficulties in nailing down a satisfactory definition of productivity. We recognized that in government there might be reliable indicators of input, but indicators of output were substantially more ambiguous. For example, how does one measure the productivity of a personnel or budgeting unit? We were also faced with other problems involving evaluation. For example, does one regard a unit that is working at 50 percent of normal efficiency as productive when it brings itself up to 75 percent efficiency? In addition, we were concerned about some special governmental considerations. What would happen to the civil service merit system if employees were paid on the basis of performance as determined by supervisors? These were very real concerns that troubled us deeply. We felt, however, that if we could start in the direction of solving some of these problems, we could develop a program that would have long-run benefits to both the state and its employees.

Fortunately, several of the union leaders agreed with us. They recognized that there was substantial rank-and-file resistance to the concept of productivity (we ourselves heard employees speak of the specter of time and motion studies). These union leaders were willing, however, to take some initial steps toward the adoption of this approach, even if only on a limited and tentative basis.

To reinforce this receptiveness among some of the leaders, and to make headway in establishing productivity bargaining, the state offered to increase its salary proposal. On Sunday, thirty-six hours after the strike commenced, we reached agreement with CSEA on a total contract, which included a specific commitment to pursue productivity bargaining. Article 8.1 of that contract provided:

> 8.1. The State and CSEA agree on the need for cooperative efforts toward increasing productivity in State operations, thereby providing improved efficiencies and service to the public and job enrichment and economic benefits arising from such improvements to employees.

The agreement called for the establishment of a state-CSEA committee to commence negotiations immediately, with a deadline for reaching agreement of December 1, 1972. The committee's task was specifically delimited. Many of the trade-offs that had been debated during the previous week again appeared as subjects of study. The committee was to consider establishment of a standard work week of forty hours, amendment of the system by which the performance of state workers was evaluated, and amendment of time and leave rules so that tardiness would be chargeable against individual leave credits. There were, however, some new items to be considered, which reflected the increasing sophistication of the state's approach. The committee was to study application of a system of flexible hours in which employees would be permitted to select starting and closing times of their work. It was to consider increased flexibility in work assignments, a matter of critical importance to the state, since each of its 3,500 positions has a specific and limiting job description. The committee was to look into applications of the four-day work week and job security in relation to productivity improvement. The agreement provided a guarantee that productivity savings would be shared: 25 percent of any savings would be paid across the board to all employees; 25 percent would be paid to those units and employees who had contributed to the improvement; and the remaining 50 percent would be retained by the state.

In what was perhaps the most important provision, the committee was charged with the development of criteria and procedures for the measurement of productivity and for the allocation of savings resulting from the implementation of proposals in the specific areas assigned to the committee. The state took the position that, in order to be successful, productivity would have to be launched on a concrete and factually reliable basis. We regarded this commitment to study productivity measurement and methods of allocating savings as the most critical task assigned to the labor–management committee. To help assure the success of the committee's effort, the state promised that if agreements were reached on such criteria and procedures, a bonus of 1.5 percent would be paid to all state employees on April 1, 1973.

In retrospect, there were some real problems with our agreement. The mixing of trade-offs and true productivity improvement reflected an initial lack of preparation on both sides to deal with some of the technicalities in this area. A number of the items of study were red flags to particular groups of employees. The inclusion of a specific formula for the allocation of savings was a mistake. The allocation of such savings should have been left flexible so that we would have had greater ability to deal with varying forms of improvements. Finally, our worst miscalculation was our belief that we could motivate a union that was not wholeheartedly and independently committed to productivity bargaining.

Barely a month passed before reservations about the agreement began to surface from all parties concerned. Following the settlement of the strike, the state legislature appointed a select committee to investigate the strike and to evaluate the negotiated agreement. The legislative committee recognized that the productivity improvement program as initiated by the agreement might have far-reaching fiscal advantages for the state. It expressed concern, however, that the legislature was being asked to endorse in advance an agreement that might be used as a justification for the payment of substantial sums to state employees without effective controls. The committee recommended and the legislature enacted a specific legislative caveat that would guide the executive branch in pursuing the subject of productivity bargaining.

Specifically, the legislative committee stated:

> However, we want assurances that proper quality controls are maintained; that bonuses paid are a direct result of increased effort on the part of the employee and not paid where efficiencies are the result of outside factors such as improved equipment or prevailing economic conditions; that work standards be established to insure that bonuses are paid only for extra effort and not for what normally could be expected from an employee.
>
> We applaud the efforts to establish such a program which can benefit the State, the employees and the taxpayers. We are concerned lest inadequate controls work to the State's disadvantage.
>
> For these reasons, we are recommending that this session of the Legislature neither approve nor disapprove the secton of the CSEA contracts providing for a productivity improvement program.

Within weeks, further concerns were expressed. A number of the state's managers, who had never been enthusiastic supporters of the program, expressed their continuing disagreement with a program that might result in the allocation of funds to state employees without specific and tangible returns. They further expressed concern over the impact of productivity bargaining on the state's own efforts at management improvement, which had been going on without union participation. At meetings of the budget director's Management Advisory Council, state managers expressed reservations about the effect of productivity bargaining on what they regarded as their prerogative to seek unilateral changes on a continuing basis. The contractual right to "direct, deploy and utilize the work force" had been won in hard-fought battles in earlier negotiations. State managers were therefore concerned over the possible erosion of this right through concessions made in productivity bargaining.

The summer and early fall of 1972 were busy for the staff of OER. An effort was made to assemble and review a substantial portion of the literature in this field. Field trips were made to a number of firms that had attempted productivity improvements and whose operations were comparable to those of the state government. We met with a variety of consultants who gave us valuable insights into the way we should approach productivity negotiations. We met with the National Commission on Productivity and sought its counsel in determining the appropriate method of launching our program. We developed a strategy for the forthcoming negotiations that was designed to place productivity on a firm basis by developing reliable indicators of output; this would, we hoped, satisfy the concerns expressed by the legislature and some state administrators.

This period was an equally busy time for the CSEA negotiators. As reports on the implications of the settlement began to flow back from the field, they began to have increasing concerns about the direction they had taken. Many of these concerns were based on misconceptions of either the settlement or what was contemplated under the agreement. Other objections stemmed from actual experiences with productivity improvements. The state, for example, in its period of financial crisis, had established a program of vacancy control. As a result of that program, there were, after two years, approximately 2,000 fewer filled positions in the Department of Mental Hygiene. The employees in that department took the position that since they were doing "the same job" with 2,000 fewer employees, their productivity had increased and they should not be required to participate further in order to share in gains from productivity improvement. Moreover, clerical employees were particularly concerned about the clause in the committee's charge to study the establishment of a uniform 40-hour work week. These employees regarded their 37½-hour work week with almost religious fervor and were not prepared to participate in any program that even suggested the possibility of its loss. Substantial concern was created by a speech given by one of the legislative leaders at a CSEA conference in which he pointed to the desirability of working people out of title to enrich their jobs and enhance their performance. CSEA had for many years been a firm supporter of the merit system and became concerned that productivity improvement could be used to erode many of the gains it had achieved over the years. The cumulative effect of these pressures and the criticism directed at various of its manifestations dampened whatever enthusiasm many of the CSEA leaders had once had for the program.

When the state-CSEA committee first met in formal session in October 1972, the chairman of the union's regotiating committee reflected this loss of enthusiasm in a most forceful manner. The first words out of his mouth were, "I don't care about the 1½ percent for myself. You can take it and stuff it!" His concerns were quickly echoed by the union's first vice-president and the chief negotiator for its institutional employees.

With this ominous beginning, the next several negotiating sessions were spent in an effort to reconvince CSEA that the bargain it had struck in April was, in fact, a good bargain and that it would serve our mutual interests to continue pursuing productivity bargaining.

We proposed to CSEA to proceed initially by a deductive process. We recommended that the state and CSEA jointly sponsor a variety of specific projects, testing out various methods of improving productivity. We suggested proposals to test out incentive compensation, flexible work hours, the four-day work week, and a broadening of selected job definitions to permit the employees to take on wider ranges of responsibilities. We solicited the views of state agencies concerning projects they thought might be useful to explore in a collective negotiations context.

Two things quickly emerged. First, CSEA became extremely apprehensive about projects that did not involve all of the employees in the state. Their negotiators argued that if all state employees were to get the benefit of the 1½ percent productivity bonus, all should participate in producing whatever savings might accrue to the state from the program. They also expressed concern that any individual group might receive a benefit that was not shared by the others.

From the state's point of view, we discovered an equally surprising development. Representatives of individual state agencies, however supportive they were of the concept of productivity bargaining, seemed reluctant to put forth specific proposals for discussion with CSEA. In large part, this arose from the fear that if a particular proposal was laid on the table and rejected by CSEA, it would be impossible to put it into effect thereafter. In part, it resulted from an unwillingness to share with other agencies pet projects that individual managers were developing. Finally, and to a more limited extent, it reflected a resistance by certain of the state's managers to admit that a union had any role to play in the determination of the mechanics of productivity improvement.

Negotiations proceeded slowly with CSEA through the fall of 1972. In an effort to force the union team to grapple with some of the conceptual issues involved in productivity bargaining, we pursued the question of whether a layoff of employees necessarily meant added work load and hence greater productivity for those remaining. We discussed whether improved department performance, which was due to increased supervision, would constitute increased productivity. We discussed whether the substitution of capital for labor—for example, television cameras to replace prison guards—was a matter in which employees should share, and how capital costs should be set off against estimated savings. We considered methods by which productivity output could be reliably and factually measured. We noted the difficulty of measuring specific jobs and proposed alternate methods of measurement. Finally, we sought to pin down what both the state and the CSEA could reasonably expect from productivity bargaining.

While these theoretical discussions were proceeding, however, a series of events occurred which were to have a profound effect on the negotiations. First, a time and motion study was initiated by the state university in its power plant operation at the State University of New York (SUNY) campus at Oswego. This study had been planned for some time and was wholly unrelated to our negotiations. CSEA employees at Oswego argued, however, that this was what "productivity" was all about, and supporting protests were received from throughout the state. At almost the same time, the Department of Mental Hygiene announced the institution of a four-day work week in the food service operation at Pilgrim State Hospital. Again, waves of protest followed. Finally, Mental Hygiene announced the establishment of an overlapping fourth shift at Willowbrook State Hospital in an effort to provide increased coverage at mealtimes to improve the care provided to the institution's mentally retarded children. Although each of the individual employees had been consulted about the need for the change and most in fact had agreed, there were several who were concerned that the new shift would not mesh with local bus service to the institution.

The protests, which came from around the state, soon surfaced at the negotiating table. It soon became quite clear that CSEA was not going to agree to a program that would include specific productivity improvements as one of its elements. The adverse reactions that the various state-initiated projects had invoked had made the union negotiators chary of further exploration.

We were forced, therefore, to move away from individual projects and seek a more conceptual way of moving productivity bargaining forward. We concluded that it was unlikely that we would be able to reach agreement with CSEA at the table on specific standards and criteria. Instead, we proposed a jointly financed study by an outside consultant that would (1) provide research data to the state and the CSEA on procedures for measuring output data, (2) develop an inventory of state services and functions to determine which services and functions were measurable, and (3) provide guidance concerning methods of solving problems of job security related to productivity.

Based on the anticipated work of the consultant, we then proposed that we would proceed to develop work measurement data in those areas in which the inventory had indicated measurement was possible. We argued that we should allow the negotiators for each side to evaluate any changes in output-input data and to debate at the negotiating table the reasons for change and whether the employees were entitled to participate in any savings resulting from particular increases in productivity.

We also proposed that an attempt be made to work out some general guidelines for the respective roles of the state and CSEA in further productivity improvements. In this respect, we happened on a bit of good fortune. CSEA had been meeting with Professor Walter Balk of the state university and had sought his counsel regarding how to proceed in the negotiations. He was able to provide many of the technical skills that CSEA had heretofore been unable or unwilling to procure. We were doubly fortunate since Professor Balk's views did not substantially deviate from those of the state. The agreement that we were able to reach is in large part a tribute to the guidance he was able to provide to CSEA.

Our revised proposal, based on principles that we had been developing at the table, was presented to CSEA in December. We debated the language of the proposal throughout the month and on December 26 reached agreement on a method of proceeding.

The preamble to the agreement is perhaps its most important feature. In it, we attempted to analyze the respective roles of the state and CSEA and to lay down guideposts for our future relationship.

Let me review some of the important provisions of the preamble. With respect to productivity measurement, we concluded:

> One cannot measure productivity or determine savings without developing some factual data to determine relationships between output and input along with output and service standards. Therefore, knowledge of output is a central and critical factor in productivity measurement. Ease of measurement (or fact-gathering) is often a function of the degree of routineness of tasks. Extremely routine tasks require fewer output indicators and production data is reasonably valid and reliable. Less routine task output indicators must be more numerous and, by their nature, are not as valid and reliable.
>
> State operations differ widely in the amount of routine inherent in their operations. Therefore, predictably, output data "hardness" and the style of interpretation will vary according to the amount and type of task routine in each function. For example, the reliability and interpretation of output data from the Department of Motor Vehicles would be expected to be substantially more firm than that from the Department of Commerce.

With respect to productivity planning, we agreed:

> A major reason why administrators are distinguished from employees is that they are charged with responsibility for and should be trained to innovate and maintain systems to improve productivity. Administrators should have specialized administrative, technical and social knowledge; this leads to better planning, more rational risk-taking and, eventually, higher productivity. . . . [T]he preparation of new systems of control depends upon management's initiative and involvement.

Finally, with respect to motivating employees, we stated:

> One safe assumption is that people will be better motivated to do something when they perceive a gratifying personal result. In the case of employees another safe assumption is that often factors relating to pay and job conditions will be more gratifying motivationally than other factors. Experience indicates that it is important to involve employees in the process of implementation so that they understand what is being proposed and how it will affect their jobs and working conditions. In addition, to the extent that there are changes in the terms and conditions of employment, the Taylor Law requires the participation of employee organizations certified or recognized as representatives of employees in the implementation of the proposals.

With these principles as our basis and backed by a commitment of $100,000 from the state and CSEA, we thus engaged a research consultant. We attempted to provide some guidance to the consultant. We directed him first to study state functions in which an improvement would directly benefit the public, ones which were uniform over a period of time and not subject to cyclical or seasonal variations, and ones in which the components contributing to changes in productivity could easily be segregated. On receiving the consultant's report, the state and CSEA agreed to meet further to develop a procedure for the establishment of work measurement data. We also agreed to consider specific productivity projects primarily in the area of the four-day work week and flex time. We agreed to the establishment of a floating holiday in lieu of Lincoln's Birthday, the net effect of which was to keep state offices open for an additional day.

Our agreement was signed on December 6, 1972 and was ratified by the state legislature shortly thereafter.

Within two weeks of the signing of the productivity agreement, we went into full-scale negotiations with CSEA for a contract to replace the 1972–1973 agreement. We stated, as one of the state's initial goals, the continuation of the productivity agreement and, indeed, the expansion of the scope of study.

As the negotiations progressed, however, both the state and CSEA became increasingly concerned about the practical consequences of the course that they had selected. In proceedings under the contractual grievance procedure and before the state's Public Employment Relations Board, CSEA began to argue that the obligation to negotiate over productivity precluded unilateral action by the state to implement any such changes. CSEA acknowledged that the management rights clause of its contracts had, since 1969, authorized the state to "direct and deploy" the work force. They argued, however, that the new commitment to productivity bargaining prohibited unilateral action by the state to reschedule shifts of individuals, establish new shifts, or change the starting and closing times of shifts. They resisted, on technical grounds, a proposal to restructure the duties of state tax examiners, a proposal that the Division of the Budget estimated might result in savings of $100 million.

CSEA was thus in a difficult position. It was under increasing pressure from employees to resist changes in individual assignments and to utilize the productivity clause as the vehicle to prevent the implementation of myriad changes in terms and conditions of employment. Indeed, virtually every change in state work procedures seemed to be viewed as an application of "productivity bargaining" and to be resisted on that ground alone.

It soon became quite clear to the state negotiators that, having achieved a preliminary agreement and secured the payment of the 1.5 percent bonus, CSEA was not interested in a broadscale approach to productivity bargaining. An indication of the degree of CSEA's concern was the fact that it considered and agreed in the closing night of negotiations to trade off a career ladder article under which members of the negotiation units had received $13 million in the preceding two years for a discontinuance of the commitment to productivity improvement. In the state's view, CSEA's resistance to productivity bargaining was so complete that our continued insistence on the concept was becoming counterproductive. Accordingly, in the agreement that was reached in April 1973 and executed in June, the productivity bargaining article was deleted and preparations for the study that had been commissioned in December were discontinued.

The state is now working under a three-year contract that has no commitment to or provision for productivity bargaining. Only vestiges of the commitment remain. These are ongoing studies of out-of-title work and workday/workweek. Productivity bargaining itself, however, is not mentioned. Does this mean that productivity bargaining was a failure? Certainly, in the short run our attempts to initiate it on a broad scale failed. I think, however, something was learned from the experience, and, given a continuing commitment on the part of the state to the improvement of service and productivity, it may work in future years.

What lessons can be derived from this experience?

1. Our experience has reinforced the state's belief that productivity bargaining will be profitable only if both parties make meaningful efforts to produce real savings—and not merely use the process as a public relations tactic. It would have been easy, at any stage of the proceedings, to put together numbers that would indicate that the productivity of state workers had increased or that vast savings had been achieved through changes in particular working conditions. Although this might have provided a short-term justification for individual wage increases, it would have served neither the state nor CSEA well. This approach would have exacerbated the very real concerns of those who have apprehensions about the impact of collective bargaining on public service or the expenditure of public funds.

2. The principal lesson we learned is that it is impossible to make pro-ductivity bargaining work unless the union is fully committed to the concept and wants to make it work. We thought we could supply incentive with the productivity bonus and that the 1.5 percent carrot would move us far enough forward to generate momentum. That just did not work. This is a process that is so delicate and so new that it requires a genuine effort to move for-ward.

3. It is equally clear that productivity bargaining will not work unless there is a complete commitment to the concept from all levels of manage-ment. Those who would resist change or would resist the increasing incur-sions of collective bargaining must be brought into the process and convinced that they can benefit from trading some of their prerogatives for cooperation from the union. The mere fact that this is a change from the way things have been done in the past generates resistance. There must be a mutual desire to overcome that resistance.

4. There must be technical expertise on both sides of the bargaining table. On management's side, there is often a management improvement unit that can provide technical advice and counsel. All too often, however, that technical expertise is not shared on the other side of the table. I am reminded of a story that a corporate officer told us as we were preparing for negotia-tions. A clause in the collective bargaining contract *required* the union to retain a time and motion study expert. At the time I thought the story amus-ing, particularly when he went on to add that after two years of productivity bargaining, the union fired its own expert because he was agreeing too often with management. In retrospect, perhaps the story isn't funny. If one is going to expect his counterpart across the table to deal with the technical issues of savings and allocation of savings, it may be necessary to require that he obtain the technical support that is essential.

5. Our search for hard data as a precondition to specific improvements

probably was the wrong approach. This is an area of collective bargaining that cannot be handled on a theoretical or abstract level. Our experience confirms that there is no way to go about this, other than on a case-by-case basis. Management must search out specific terms and conditions that it wants to change, but cannot change—legally or practically—without the union's concurrence. It then must put those demands on the table. Similarly, unions cannot expect serious consideration of salary or other demands if these demands are based on amorphous gains in productivity. They too will have to demonstrate specific changes in productivity that are amenable to meaningful evaluation.

6. It was an error to insert in the agreement a specific formula for the allocation of savings. This created an inflexibility and raised expectations among employees, which could not be easily satisfied. Employees who were involved in specific improvements knew that the most they could gain from their improvements was 25 percent of the savings. In larger units in which those savings would have been allocated among many employees, this reward frequently provided no incentive at all. The techniques of productivity bargaining are manifold, and it is necessary to maintain great flexibility to make them succeed. In some cases, management may well be willing to give a greater share to employees in cases in which greater employee incentive is required. In other instances, changes in nonpecuniary terms and conditions of employment may be sufficient to achieve the necessary motivation.

7. Finally, the subject of job security was probably improperly committed as a subject of study to the committee. In this respect, the state is in a dilemma. It is critical for management to realize real savings, and real savings are frequently derived from having fewer people do the same amount of (or more) work. At the same time, it is unreasonable to expect a union to give support to a program that may reduce the size of its membership. Throughout our negotiations, we were concerned over what we were asking CSEA to do to itself. Having come through a period of austerity in which the union had lost substantial numbers of its members, it was perhaps unreasonable to expect it to participate fully in a program that *might* result in even further losses.

Our experience was such that I think it is essential that the contract contain an express guarantee that productivity improvements will not be implemented without a commitment to achieve any reductions in the work force through attrition or to guarantee to retrain those who might be adversely affected by productivity improvements.

As a final note, I might add that, although productivity bargaining was not established in the 1973 contract negotiations with CSEA, there is still hope that it can be initiated in future bargaining situations. To this end, the state should develop its productivity proposals early and formulate them in consultation with the union. I believe that productivity bargaining will work. The task of making it work will be a difficult one, but it will be worth the effort.

Afterword

This reading is a remarkably frank and informative treatment of an attempt by the state of New York to connect productivity improvement with labor–management relations. Although the experiment was not a "success," the experience provided many important lessons, as Osterman carefully documents.

Osterman outlines quite clearly why, despite the compelling circumstances for productivity bargaining, things went wrong. My comments will not dwell on the state's experience as much as they will compare that experience to productivity bargaining that has been practiced elsewhere, especially in New York City and Nassau County.

One way to explain the failure of productivity bargaining in New York State is that the strategy chosen fell betwixt and between the two main modes of productivity bargaining. It was neither pure buyout nor pure gain sharing. As a result, it experienced the disadvantages of both approaches.

The buyout approach has been practiced in New York City. Using this strategy, management conducts a thorough analysis of its operations and develops a plan of productivity improvement. Only after it has established its goals and considered the likelihood of their successful implementation does management go to the bargaining table to secure the cooperation of the union in the adoption of the plan.

The gain-sharing approach is open-ended and relies on labor–management cooperation as a means for improving productivity. Rewards are shared after the program of change has been implemented and productivity improvements can be evaluated through a measurement system. This approach has been practiced in Nassau County in negotiations between the county and CSEA and between three towns in the county and CSEA.

The following table compares the strategies of buyout and gain sharing with the approach followed in New York State. As the chart indicates, the New York State approach represented a mixture of the two established strategies. For example, money was paid in advance, as in the buyout approach, but achievement was not specified and was left to the process of labor–management collaboration, as in the gain-sharing approach.

If I were to recommend to New York State the strategy to follow, I would strongly recommend the buyout approach, for the following reasons:

Table 1
Comparison of Productivity Agreements

	New York State	*New York City*	*Nassau County*
Initiative for program	Management–labor	Management	Management–labor
Size of governmental unit	Very large	Very large	Large
Time frame for program	Presumably during the period of the contract	During the period of the contract	Open-ended
Nature of rewards	Downpayment with remainder paid 25% to department, 25% uniform, and 50% retained by government	Payment in advance and uniform for the union involved	Payment after results and uniform for all employees

1.   The buyout approach is required when the scope and complexity of operations is large. In a governmental jurisdiction as large as New York City or as large as the state of New York, considerable planning has to be done at the central level, usually by staff specialists. If responsibility for designing productivity improvement is decentralized, usually little will happen in a large organization.

The analysis of the operations and the development of general plans for productivity improvement usually are done much more effectively at the central level. For example, in the case of New York City, the central staff groups delineated the main approaches: technological change (such as the introduction of slippery water for the fire departments), the more rational deployment of the work force (the matching of available manpower to the demand for services in such areas as police and firefighting), better effort utilization (monitoring of start and stop times), and the development of output standards.

2.   The buyout approach is required in instances in which labor–management relations tend to be arm's length and the union takes a relatively militant approach to collective bargaining. Given the orientation of CSEA at the state level—one of examining every proposal very critically and insisting on quid pro quos—the only approach to productivity bargaining would be the buyout.

What are some of the principles that should be honored if the buyout approach is to be effective?

1.   Management must do the preparatory work and develop the rough cut for the productivity improvement program. In some cases, management

may need to do some belt tightening on its own before bringing the plan to the bargaining table for review and ratification. Since any kind of productivity improvement program puts front-line and middle management on the spot, considerable training and orientation of management itself will be required prior to and during implementation of any productivity agreement.

2. Certain key guarantees must be made so that the employees and the union are set free to engage in the program. Productivity bargaining, as it has been practiced in the private sector, has usually involved a guarantee from management that no employees will lose their jobs as a result of the program. If fewer employees are required, the excess will be absorbed through attrition. In the case of New York State, where extensive layoffs had occurred in the early 1970s, the atmosphere was negative and productivity bargaining could go forward only if and when management offered employment guarantees.

3. The buyout has to be used sparingly. The exchanging of money for productivity improvement is a high-risk process. It may need to be done as a way of removing some barriers, but, if practiced very long, it teaches people the lesson that looseness is worth money. It also leads to the sort of orientation that developed in New York State—that every time management made a change in operations, the union would demand that it be considered a part of the productivity improvement program. Such an orientation is clearly counterproductive, and consequently the buyout must be viewed as a particular process that moves in to eliminate specific problems in an organization. The measurement of savings is extremely important in any form of productivity bargaining. Typically, with the buyout approach, the financial rewards are paid up front as a way of inducing acceptance of the desired changes. Management has calculated the expected savings and is willing to share a portion of them through regular wage negotiations in return for assurance from the union that certain changes in work practices will be implemented. The function of measurement is to ascertain whether the savings have been achieved and whether the bargain has been a sound deal from management's point of view.

It is clear that the next several years will see considerable experimentation with productivity bargaining. Productivity in the public sector is an idea whose time has come. Given the presence of collective bargaining in an increasing number of government jurisdictions, it is likely that management's quest for productivity improvement will intersect, in some fashion, the institution of collective bargaining.

The experience of New York State and the intelligent analysis by Melvin Osterman should serve as an informative source to practitioners as they move into this new field of productivity bargaining.

1981 Update: The New York City
Sanitation Agreement, by the Editors

After (1) numerous start and stop efforts at productivity improvements via labor-management committees, (2) several bargains that made the payment of cost-of-living allowances during the life of the agreement contingent on productivity savings, and (3) at least one major negotiation that promised but failed to deliver significant productivity savings in the transit system, New York City finally appears to have achieved a tangible and real productivity improvement program via a recent arbitrated agreement. In December 1980, New York City and its Sanitation Workers' Union announced their acceptance of an arbitration award written by Matthew Kelly that provides the city with the right to introduce larger and more efficient two-man sanitation trucks (replacing three-man trucks) on selected routes. Each worker on a two-person crew in turn will receive an $11 per shift bonus.[1] The city also agreed to put off for two years its plan to experiment with contracting out sanitation services to private firms.

This agreement is important for several reasons. First, it is the most clear-cut and measurable productivity improvement program achieved to date in New York City—a city that has had a long history of trying various strategies to improve productivity in the face of continuous fiscal crises. Second, it demonstrates one of McKersie's main arguments—that is, in large, politically complex bargaining units, the buyout strategy is more likely to work than is an open-ended commitment to develop a gain-sharing plan via a joint labor–management committee. This is especially true when new technology is available and the (potential) cost savings can be carefully estimated before the fact.

Third, it demonstrates the innovative use of a neutral party in bringing about the change. Note that it required an arbitration award that the parties accepted to bring about the new agreement. One of the conventional wisdoms regarding arbitration is that it is an inherently conservative procedure—arbitrators tend not to break new ground or innovate, but rather to rely on comparable practice or past practice, or, when interpreting an agreement in grievance arbitration, on the wording and intent of the clause at issue. Thus, this use of arbitration clearly breaks with many of the traditions and conventional practices of the past. It represents a major innovation that was achieved with the help of a dispute resolution process that falls somewhere between the conventional labels we normally use to describe arbitration, fact-finding, and mediation. Clearly, on the one hand, the arbitrator could not have fashioned this type of award unless he sensed the parties were ready and able to accept it. The parties, on the other hand, could not easily agree to this plan on their own and needed the assistance of a knowledgeable and trusted third party.

It may be that this type of heavy-handed yet delicate third-party role is needed to confront many of the substantive problems currently found in the public sector. Whether it will be used in other jurisdictions depends on the willingness and ability of the parties to open themselves up to this type of direct attack on their problems and past practices.

Note

1. This case is reported in *Government Employee Relations Report* no. 893, December 22, 1980, pp. 26–27.

The Rise and Demise of PATCO

Herbert R. Northrup *

The strike by the Professional Air Traffic Controllers Organization (PATCO), which began in August 1981 and resulted in the dissolution of the union, was undoubtedly a watershed event in governmental labor relations. It is the thesis of this reading, however, that the strike was the inevitable result of PATCO's long-term drive to "privatize" its relations with the Federal Aviation Administration (FAA), its public sector employer; of the weak response thereto by the federal government until the later years of the Carter administration; and of the failure of PATCO's new leadership to understand the greatly altered political and economic environment of 1981. In order to understand the strike and its aftermath, it is therefore necessary to summarize the federal government's labor relations policy. PATCO's thirteen-year struggle with the FAA, and PATCO policies that were designed to develop a special framework for its bargaining.

The Bargaining Environment

As federal government employees, controllers have their salaries set by Congress, pursuant to the civil service system. FAA management does not control wages, benefits, the length of the workday or work week, or key personnel practices. The FAA does have a major voice in such matters as work schedules, hours, holiday and overtime pay, merit promotions, and personnel relations on the job.

*University of Pennsylvania. Reprinted from *Industrial and Labor Relations Review* 37, no. 2 (January 1984), pp. 167–184.

Controller–FAA relations take place within the federal employee relations system, which was set on its current course by Executive Order (EO) 10988, issued by President John F. Kennedy on January 17, 1962; modified on October 29, 1969, by EO 11491 issued by President Richard M. Nixon; and, since 1978, governed by the Civil Service Reform Act (CSRA),[1] Title VII of which superseded the executive orders but maintained their basic policies. A three-member Federal Labor Relations Authority (FLRA), modeled after the National Labor Relations Board (NLRB), administers regulations like those in the Taft-Hartley Act concerning unfair labor practices and union representation. Like the NLRB, the FLRA has an independent general counsel, and its orders are subject to judicial review. The CSRA forbids strikes, and it also outlaws compulsory unionism by protecting an individual's right to join or not to join a union.

Matters in the purview of Congress are excluded from the grievance procedure. Unsettled grievances must be submitted to arbitration. Either party may ask the FLRA to review an arbitration award. Impasses in negotiation are referred first to the Federal Mediation and Conciliation Service and, if not settled, to the Federal Service Impasses Panel (FSIP) created by EO 11491. The FSIP has wide latitude to effectuate a settlement, including the right to "take whatever action may be necessary," which includes binding arbitration. Strikes are an unfair labor practice, and penalties for a union that promotes or encourages a strike include decertification.[2]

Policy Development at the FAA

The FAA grew up with the aviation industry, and for many years it was a small, paternalistic organization operated with a tinge of military flavor.[3] Following the tragic two-plane collision over the Grand Canyon in the late 1950s, Congress authorized greater expenditures on air traffic control, which resulted in the purchase of new equipment and the rapid expansion of the air traffic controller labor force. At the same time, the FAA embarked on a program to upgrade controllers' status and pay. Its emphasis on the stress and responsibility of controllers was later adopted by PATCO as the rationale for its economic program of higher wages, shorter hours, and special considerations for controllers who claimed disability.

Initially, the FAA was ill prepared for collective bargaining as initiated under EO 10988 and was especially unprepared for the type of militancy that PATCO exhibited at an early date. Committees appointed as early as 1969 and as late as 1982 criticized the FAA's relations with its employees, although pointing out that PATCO leadership was heavily to blame.[4] The FAA has attempted to address these issues with varying success and has stationed labor relations personnel in each of its several regional offices. Policy determinations in personnel and labor relations matters, however, as in operations, are made at the national level.[5]

PATCO's Tumultuous Career, 1968–1980

The strike that ended PATCO's bargaining days was just one of many during its tumultuous career. Almost from its inception, its history was marked by confrontations, as its officials fought not only for improvements in salary and working conditions but actually for superior rewards in these areas—and did so both by political and by direct action. Moreover, the entire PATCO history featured a determination to escape from the constraints of civil service labor relations, so that wages could be bargained and strikes legalized.

PATCO's Pre-1981 Strikes

From its organization by a group of New York City controllers in January 1968 until its 1981 strike, PATCO was involved in no fewer than six serious disruptions of air transport services. In July 1968, under the leadership of F. Lee Bailey, its lawyer/executive director, PATCO sponsored a month-long slowdown that seriously disrupted key airports.[6] The FAA and the federal government were in a "state of shock" and did nothing.[7]

One year later, a three-day slowdown induced the then secretary of transportation to appoint a committee to look into FAA–PATCO relationships. The resultant Corson Report criticized both parties and recommended changes in FAA policies.[8] In addition, the FAA suspended eighty controllers for up to fifteen days for their participation in the job action.[9]

In March 1970, PATCO instituted a sick-out that lasted twenty days and was the most disruptive job action to that date, as 2,200 controllers at key major airports called in sick. This time, the Air Transport Association (ATA), the airlines association whose members had lost millions of dollars because of PATCO's tactics, was prepared for action. It won an order directing that the stoppage be ended and that individual defendant controllers return to work.[10] The FAA won similar orders in Minnesota[11] and Alaska.[12] When PATCO and striking controllers ignored those orders, the U.S. District Court, Eastern District of New York, found them in contempt of court and levied fines on a daily basis for each day lost. The district court in Alaska also issued fines for contempt. An additional complaint filed by the ATA in New York sought collective damages in excess of $50 million. Individual controllers, fearful that their homes and life savings could be lost, pressed for settlement. Negotiations between PATCO and ATA lawyers resulted in a September 9, 1970 stipulation of settlement, under which the ATA waived its damage claims and PATCO agreed to a permanent injunction, issued by the U.S. District Court, which stated:

> PATCO, its officers, agents, employees and members, it successors or
> assigns, and any other person acting in concert with it or them, is perma-

nently prohibited and enjoined from, in any manner, calling, causing, authorizing, encouraging, inducing, continuing or engaging in any strike (including any concerted stoppage, slowdown, or refusal to report to work) by air traffic controllers employed by an agency of the United States, or any other concerted, unlawful interference with or obstruction to the movement or operation of aircraft or the orderly operation of any air traffic control facilities by any agency of the United States.[13]

The stipulation-order also provided that if PATCO engaged in any action that violated its terms, then the union would be required to pay the ATA or its assignees $25,000 per day for each day during which the violation occurred and that this obligation was "in addition to and without prejudice to any other rights" of the plaintiffs, but that PATCO could ask the court to vacate or to revise this judgment if Congress made PATCO strikes lawful. The ATA thus had a weapon that it could, and would, bring to bear in the future.

The FAA also discharged 67 controllers for their participation in the 1970 sick-out. Twenty-seven of the controllers were later reinstated by civil service appeals, and then, in February 1972, Secretary of Transportation John Volpe ordered the rehiring of the remaining ones. His action was probably influenced by the facts that 1972 was an election year, the Nixon administration was then negotiating with the maritime unions over their threats to refuse to transport the Soviet Union's new grain purchases, and PATCO had recently affiliated with the Marine Engineers Beneficial Association (MEBA), a small but politically significant AFL-CIO maritime union.[14]

The 1970 strike also resulted in the end of Bailey's tenure as executive director of PATCO, the abolishment of his job, and the election of John F. Leyden as president, a position he held until his ouster ten years later. In addition, PATCO was disqualified as a bargaining agent for 126 days by Assistant Secretary of Labor W.J. Usery, pursuant to EO 11491. After the union was reinstated by Usery, it won an exclusive bargaining rights election in 1972 and its first agreement with the FAA in March 1973.[15]

Peace reigned until 1976. In July and August of that year, after the Civil Service Commission refused to reclassify controllers to higher salary grades, PATCO staged slowdowns for five days at the nation's busiest airports,[16] just before the Republican National Convention scheduled for Kansas City. PATCO rescinded slowdowns before the ATA could secure an injunction, but the action was successful. On January 13, 1977, the commission reversed itself and increased most controllers' wages after PATCO threatened another stoppage.

Two years later came another disruption. Controllers the world over have often claimed that they should be entitled to "familiarization flights" so that they can observe how flight controls work aboard airplanes.[17] When the U.S. international airlines abolished such free rides, PATCO called a "spontaneous" slowdown on May 25–26 and June 6–7, 1978 at major airports. This resulted in the second judicial rebuff of such tactics when the ATA asked for a contempt citation pursuant to the permanent injunction the parties had agreed to in September 1970.

PATCO claimed that the 1970 injunction did not apply because it applied to a sick-out and the understaffing of facilities, whereas the 1978 actions pertained to familiarization flights. The District Court, Eastern District of New York, found this argument specious, concluding that the "injunction is still in full force and . . . effect." Since, therefore, PATCO had disobeyed the injunction on four days, the court ordered "PATCO to pay the plaintiff Air Transport Association of America the sum of $100,000, i.e., $25,000 for each daily violation of the 1970 injunction, as provided for in that injunction." In his comments, Judge Thomas G. Platt also expressed dismay that the U.S. Department of Justice did not join the issue, declaring, "It is . . . the sworn duty of the attorney general to enforce . . . [the laws prohibiting strikes by federal employees] but for reasons not fathomable to this court, they have yet to initiate any investigative or enforcement proceedings."[18]

The final disruption before 1981 occurred at Chicago's O'Hare International airport on August 15, 1980. Following the FAA's refusal of a PATCO demand for an annual tax-free bonus of $7,500 to compensate for the alleged greater stress on the job at that busy airport, PATCO members there initiated a slowdown that caused 616 delays of 30 minutes or more and cost the airlines more than $1 million in wasted fuel. This time the FAA sought a court order from the District Court, Northern District of Illinois, but this action was dismissed on the ground that the enactment of the CSRA had deprived district courts of jurisdiction in such matters, and that relief could now be obtained only pursuant to the CSRA on application of the FLRA's general counsel after an FLRA complaint had been issued. Although this decision greatly emboldened the strike advocates in PATCO, it was later reversed and never concurred in by other district or appellate courts.[19]

The Strike Fund and Other PATCO Policies

In 1977 PATCO established a thinly disguised strike fund known as the National Controller Subsistence Fund, to which was allocated 15 percent of the membership dues received by the national organization. By August 1981 over $3 million was in this fund, and three controllers who had been discharged for strike activity were receiving payments from the fund equal to their full salaries.[20] The FAA filed a complaint with the FLRA charging that the fund violated the no-strike provisions of Title VII of the CSRA, and a second one when PATCO established regulations to administer the fund. The FLRA dismissed both, reasoning that preparing for a strike was a legal activity, provided that no strike ever occurred![21]

Under Leyden's leadership, PATCO had as an objective the establishment of a separate FAA corporation, modeled on the U.S. Postal Service, but providing for PATCO and other union participation on the board of directors and for the right to strike for its employees. PATCO hired a consultant to draw up this proposal, and a bill incorporating the idea was introduced in Congress. The objective, of course, was wage determination on a private sector model.[22]

Making good use of claims that controllers were subject to extraordinary stress, PATCO also won an extraordinarily liberal retirement and disability program.[23] In 1972, President Nixon signed the Air Traffic Controllers Career Program Act (Public Law 92-297),[24] which authorizes controllers to retire at age 50 if they have twenty years of active service. (In contrast, the normal age of voluntary retirement for federal employees, which in turn is more liberal than that under the social security system, is 55 after 30 years of service or age 60 after 20 years.) The Controllers Program Act also stipulates very liberal disability retirement provisions, plus a "second careers" program: up to two years training at government expense at full salary for controllers who have to leave traffic control work because of a medical or proficiency disqualification.

In 1974, Congress greatly liberalized the Federal Employees' Compensation Act, providing a means for generous retirement allowance to federal employees who suffer slight disabilities.[25] Thereafter, both disability claims by controllers and "system errors"[26] committed by them suddenly rose significantly. A careful academic study found a significant correlation between the increase in system errors and controller disability applications during this period.[27] An error could be used as proof that a controller's job performance was declining and would therefore aid his disability application. In addition, it could be claimed that the error resulted in such stress that it disabled the controller, and doctors' testimony could be used to support such claims. Indeed, one Atlanta psychiatrist "diagnosed as totally disabled 154 air traffic controllers."[28] In 1978, following a report of the U.S. comptroller general, Congress ended the funding of the "second careers" program authorized by Public Law 92–297, and controller disability claims dropped steadily, although they still remained numerous.[29] One of PATCO's demands in the 1981 negotiations was a reinstitution of this program.

A third endeavor of the Leyden administration was to bring PATCO within the mainstream of organized labor. The affiliation with MEBA aided this, as did Leyden's courting of the Air Line Pilots Association (ALPA) and his strong personal bond with John J. O'Donnell, then ALPA president.[30]

Leyden also sought international support for his union, initially from the International Federation of Air Traffic Controllers' Associations (IFATCA). Founded in 1961, IFATCA is a combination of an international trade union secretariat and a semiprofessional organization that affiliates national controllers' organizations throughout the world. PATCO had affiliated with it in 1971, and, by reason of the size of the U.S. air transport industry, PATCO was the largest IFATCA affiliate and the largest financial contributor; in fact, it was larger than all other affiliates combined. During this period, the IFATCA stressed its role as a professional, rather than union, organization. Since PATCO leaders were more interested in mutual support activities than in other aspects of IFATCA's activities and were unhappy about contributing so much more financial support than other IFATCA affiliates, PATCO disaffiliated in 1976.[31] Between 1974 and 1980, PATCO, through MEBA, was also affiliated with the International Transport Workers' Federation (ITWF), an international trade union secretariat that affiliates unions in all transportation industries.[32]

PATCO also became especially close to and admiring of the Canadian Air Traffic Controllers Association (CATCA), which has waged a number of successful strikes and which, as later events would demonstrate, controlled the key North Atlantic route through which most flights between Europe and North America pass. Regular visits of CATCA and PATCO officials began in 1968, and joint briefings were an obvious and a regular feature of those visits.[33]

A final objective of the PATCO program during these years was the unionization of noncontroller employees of the FAA under PATCO's aegis and control and then expansion to other "elite" groups of government employees. To that end, PATCO sponsored and financed the growth of three organizations: the Professional Airway Systems Specialists (PASS), which on December 31, 1981, defeated an incumbent union to win bargaining rights for 8,500 FAA electronics technicians; the National Association of Flight Standard Employees (NAFSE), which was certified to represent the 200 employees stationed in Oklahoma City who check airline performance in flight; and the Professional Aeronautical Center Employees (PACE), which represents instructors at the FAA's Oklahoma City instructional facility for controllers. All three had been expected to affiliate with PATCO just before its demise, and to pave the way for PATCO to recruit elsewhere in the federal service among technical and professional employees.[34] The final strike, however, came before this program could be completed.

The Coup and Strike Preparations

PATCO entered the 1980s in a seemingly very strong position. Its membership, as a group, was among the highest paid government employees, averaging $33,000 annually by mid-1981.[35] Controllers' fringe benefits, including the already noted disability and pension provision, were superior to those of other government employees, which in turn are generally superior to those in private industry.[36] Although controllers in several busy metropolitan airports certainly worked under stressful conditions, others in the less-traveled areas could claim no such pressure. Moreover, as was later made clear by the 1981 strike, there was considerable evidence of overstaffing in the system.

In the political arena, PATCO had won the support of many U.S. congressmen and senators, both conservative and liberal. The union distributed political funds carefully but generously and, as described earlier, was able to gain support for laws that met many of PATCO's aspirations. Moreover, the FLRA's decisions were often supportive of the union. With a checkoff dues income of approximately $5.5 million per year, cash balances in excess of $3.5 million, and almost an equal amount in its thinly disguised strike or "subsistence" fund, PATCO in 1981 was clearly an economically sound and effective organization of approximately 15,000 members.

There were, however, some elements of disquiet. The strikes involving familiarization flights and the O'Hare bonus convinced Langhorne M. Bond, the FAA administrator appointed by President Carter, of the need to devise an effective antistrike mechanism. Deciding that the FLRA had "an antimanagement record" and that it was "almost impossible for management to achieve a fair result under the FLRA," Bond was determined to develop a program to deal with strikes in collaboration with the Department of Justice and to use the courts for relief. He also developed a detailed strike plan, which called for operation of air traffic facilities during a strike and for the federal courts to enjoin and to punish strikers.[37] To emphasize his determination, in 1980 Bond published his strike contingency plan in the Federal Register.[38]

The Coup

The most serious problem facing PATCO, however, was dissension at the top. In January 1980, before the expiration of Leyden's term of office, the PATCO executive board forced his resignation and replaced him with Robert Poli, the executive vice-president who had quietly won control of the board. The coup was legitimized in June 1980, when Poli was elected president after Leyden did not contest the election.[39] Poli then placed his own supporters in key positions and employed new staff and attorneys.

The coup, however, caused PATCO to lose significant support. Discharged employees in the national office filed charges of unfair labor practices—charges that the National Labor Relations Board sustained.[40] Officials of other unions rallied to Leyden's defense, and the ALPA temporarily put him on its payroll. Then, the AFL-CIO Public Employee Department, with which Leyden had worked as PATCO's delegate, appointed him its executive director, a position he still holds today. Poli had been PATCO's "inside man" during his ten years as executive vice-president, and he was relatively unknown among the labor establishment, except among the public employee unions; apparently, he did not court his fellow union officials or seek their advice. As a key union official told the author in confidence, "Few of us knew him and he did not consult us." Rather, Poli concentrated his efforts on preparing for what he described as "our most difficult challenge . . . which will test our union as it has never been tested,"[41] namely, the "definitive strike" aimed at achieving PATCO's basic aims of inducing Congress to establish an independent FAA, permitting wage bargaining, and legitimizing strikes.[42]

Poli and his associates did solidify one union relationship that Leyden had neglected, namely, the international one. Robert E. Meyer, long a vice-president for PATCO's Great Lakes region, was appointed executive vice-president after the coup. He was a close friend of H. Harri Henschler, formerly vice-president of the Canadian Air Traffic Control Association, who had become president of IFATCA. Meyer had been a vice-president of IFATCA, and soon after the coup, PATCO reaffiliated and Meyer again become one of IFATCA's officers. By then, IFATCA had assumed a much more militant union stance, as is described next.[43]

Strike Preparations

After winning election to office in June 1980, the Poli administration moved rapidly in its strike preparations. The message carried to the field was direct: 1981 was to be the year in which the definitive strike would win PATCO its goals. Since FAA negotiators had no authority to grant wage or other key demands and since Congress might be reluctant to do so, PATCO's reasoning was that Congress would act only if a strike paralyzed air traffic. The Poli administration assumed that both Congress and the Reagan administration would then support legislation granting PATCO both substantially improved economic conditions and its basic objective, bargaining freedom under an independent FAA.

The union's plan called for very high initial demands, such as $10,000 per year salary increases, a thirty-two-hour workweek, increased pension and disability benefits, and a liberal number of familiarization flights. If, as expected, no agreement were reached by the contract expiration date in June, and if membership support for a strike were less than overwhelming (less than 80 percent), the plan was to have the union negotiating committee agree to a tentative contract and Poli to persuade the media that membership ratification was likely—but then to have the tentative agreement overwhelmingly repudiated by the executive board and, it was hoped, by the membership as a result of an "education campaign." This action, in turn, would provide the necessary strike rationale: the members were presumably too militant to be controlled by the reasonable union negotiators. To gain support for this plan, controllers were assured that any members disciplined for striking would receive their salary and benefits from PATCO until reinstatement was obtained through political pressures.

Poli and other union officers were extraordinarily explicit in communicating this plan. It was described in call-in telephone recordings and at "cluster" meetings (geographic groups of local union representatives brought together to hear the plan explained by national officers), and it was clearly hinted at in public comments.[44] A group called the "choir boys" was recruited to insure that tight dicipline from the top was maintained,[45] and detailed financial plans to cover legal costs were made.[46] On the political front, PATCO leaders, sharply critical of FAA Administrator Bond in the Carter administration, endorsed Ronald Reagan for president in October 1980—receiving in return a letter endorsing an efficient control system and fairly compensated controllers, but making no mention of strike support.[47]

The PATCO leadership seemed to ignore in its staging of the strike one key group: the federal managers. Former Secretary of Transportation Drew Lewis and former FAA Administrator Lynn Helms, both of whom came to their positions with experience in labor matters, had Bond's strike contingency plan updated and strengthened and, as will be discussed, established good relationships with their foreign counterparts. Most important, they gave their subordinates full support, kept the White House fully informed, and in turn received the President's full backing in their negotiations and policies.[48]

Negotiations and Strike Votes

Upon its ascendency in January 1981, the Reagan administration faced the possibility of not one, but two strikes affecting the airline industry. In addition to PATCO, the ALPA had threatened to strike on March 1, 1981, unless new two-engine planes were operated with three-member cockpit crews. But the ALPA leadership persuaded the president to appoint a study commission, which recommended against its demand, and ALPA acquiesced and defused the issue among its members.[49]

Whereas the ALPA leadership had concentrated on overcoming strike sentiment, the opposite occurred within PATCO. On many occasions, Poli told the media that a strike would occur, and he continued such belligerent talk down to the June 22, 1981, deadline.[50] But when that day arrived, he agreed to a generous contract offer that provided that the Reagan administration would seek congressional approval to grant all controllers an immediate pay raise in excess of $2,000; pay at overtime rates after 36 hours per week instead of after 40; an increase in the night shift differential from 10 to 15 percent; 14 weeks' severance pay to experienced controllers who left work for medical reasons; and a greater voice to PATCO in establishing operation and safety policies. These pay and benefit increases, which averaged 6.6 percent, were to be in addition to a salary increase of 4.8 percent due in October 1981 for all federal employees. Thus, if Congress had approved this final offer, controllers would have gained pay increases in excess of 11 percent, or more than twice that gained by other federal employees,[51] and PATCO would, in effect, have negotiated wages and major working conditions—subjects presumably reserved to Congress.

If PATCO had stopped here, accepted the contract, and joined the administration in seeking congressional approval for its effectuation, the union would not only be alive and well today, but it would also have made considerable progress in its drive to negotiate wages—a subject Congress had retained as its prerogative. The administration, anxious to avoid a strike, apparently convinced that controllers deserved an increase higher than the general one for other government employees, and conscious that if a strike came the administration's position would be strengthened by an offer that was clearly discerned as "fair,"[52] came as close to wage negotiations on the private model as it is possible for an administration to do with civil service employees. Previous administrations had reacted similarly to the demands of the controllers, as in the 1974 negotiations preceding the controllers' retirement and disability legislation, but the negotiations in 1981 came closer than any other to the private sector model. If the union had accepted the administration's offer, it could have established a precedent that might have altered all labor relations in the federal service, contrary to the desire of the administration and probably to that of Congress as well.

In spite of this opportunity, Poli's apparent acceptance of the government's final offer merely followed the script that already had been laid out in the cluster meetings. A strike authorization vote taken before the June 22, 1981, deadline was claimed to have won support from 70 percent of the membership who voted. PATCO maintained that its "longstanding policy" was to order a strike only after an 80 percent endorsement vote.[53]

Although Poli told reporters just after the June 22 settlement that he "felt good" about the contract, the PATCO executive board met on July 2 and recommended unanimous rejection of the contract negotiated by their president and the several other board members who sat on the executive committee. The membership then voted by mail to reject the contract, 13,495 (95.3 percent) to 616 (4.7 percent), on ballots that carried their names. Poli immediately set a new strike deadline for 7 A.M. August 3, 1981, and raised PATCO's demands to an amount that the FAA claimed would add $38,914 to the airlines' costs per controller. Secretary Lewis told Poli that his "union proposals are excessive and an affront to the American public. . . . We cannot yield to, or even entertain, such demands."[54] Meanwhile, strike sentiment was whipped up by Poli and his central staff with press conferences, publicity statements, and other propaganda by his adherents in the field.[55]

Negotiations with the government resumed but were fruitless, as Poli remained uncompromising. As the new strike deadline drew near, he refused to extend it despite requests by Lewis, the speaker of the House of Representatives, and the director of the Federal Mediation and Conciliation Service. Poli also ignored a very explicit warning drafted by a majority of the Senate and several members of Congress that PATCO would receive no strike support from them.[56] The PATCO strike plan moved inexorably toward its goal, despite yet other warnings from the president and several cabinet members that there would be no amnesty for strikers and no talks with PATCO during a strike and despite clear indications that the FAA would institute its plan to keep the air transport system moving at whatever capacity was possible.[57]

There is no evidence that PATCO officials conducted a secret-ballot strike vote. Although Executive Vice-President Meyer later claimed that 82 percent of the membership favored a strike, he could give no details under questioning regarding how or when that figure was computed.[58]

The Strike and the Demise

PATCO's long-planned strike began on schedule at 7 A.M. on August 3, 1981. The FAA was ready with its strike plan. All flights were controlled by the central flow operation, so that none was cleared locally until a signal was given at the national level; this served to prevent overcrowding any locations by not permitting flights until the receiving airport control staff could accept them. At first, about 50 percent of all flights were cleared; then, the number was raised to 70 percent about ten days later; and gradually, the number was increased as new controllers were trained. The towers and stations were staffed by controllers who refused to strike, military personnel lent by the U.S. Department of Defense, retirees called back, and supervisors. Some smaller airports were denied controllers who were needed elsewhere, and it was readily apparent—as is often the case when a company operates during a strike[59]—that the system had been overstaffed. It was also soon obvious that PATCO had failed to shut down the air traffic system as its officials had believed it would and that airline executives and the general public were neither panic-stricken by nor sympathetic to PATCO's action. Gradually, the system had moved toward full capacity while employing about one-fifth fewer personnel (13,000 in place of 16,395). The last military controllers who were assisting the FAA returned to the armed services in June 1983.[60]

Of course, the strike was damaging. Many potential customers undoubtedly hesitated to fly until they were assured about their safety. On that point, Secretary Lewis, FAA personnel, the ALPA, and individual pilots all reassured the public.[61] No accident occurred that could have been attributed directly to operations during the strike, although one crash has raised questions.[62] The public was soon satisfied that the airways were safe, despite the continued unsupported claims to the contrary by PATCO spokesmen and, as noted later, by its international allies. Nevertheless, the airlines were badly hurt by the strike. Already staggering from recession, they were forced to cut back key flights, and they lost much-needed revenues while spending millions on costly delays.[63]

The Administration's Counterattack

Besides its carefully executed plan to maintain operations, the Reagan administration moved swiftly to punish PATCO, its officials, and striking members for their illegal action. A flood of injunctions, criminal actions, and contempt actions poured forth, brought by both the government and the ATA. PATCO's strike fund was sequestered to pay for fines of several million dollars per day assessed by courts against the union.[64]

Four hours after the strike began, President Reagan personally announced that any striker who was not back on the job within forty-eight hours would be discharged and could not be reemployed by any federal agency. This policy was effectuated. About one-fourth of the controllers—4,199—had not heeded the strike call and continued to work. Another 875 returned to work before the president's deadline expired, leaving 11,301 who remained on strike and were discharged.[65] For replacements, the FAA expanded its Air Traffic Service Academy training program, and by late 1983 the air traffic control system was fully staffed.

The FAA promptly moved before the FLRA to decertify PATCO, according to the requirements of the Civil Service Reform Act. After some rather extraordinary administrative behavior, for which the Court of Appeals, District of Columbia, sharply criticized the FLRA, PATCO was decertified, and this action was later affirmed by the same court.[66]

The Union Response in the United States

As noted, Poli had made little effort to seek support from other unions before the strike, nor had he realistically assessed the extent to which organized labor could render direct assistance without undergoing severe legal penalties.[67] Once the strike began, the president's resolve became obvious, the airlines achieved a 70 percent capability to schedule flights, and it became clear to experienced labor officials that, barring an unexpected development or an emotionally charged accident attributable to controller error, PATCO had embarked on a doomed course. Finally, PATCO's exorbitant demands in light of the already high salaries of its members aroused little sympathy among organized labor's largely blue-collar rank and file.

As a consequence and with few exceptions, the union establishment's support of PATCO was largely confined to issuing statements, a symbolic court case which was quickly dismissed,[68] equally symbolic walking on picket lines, contributions to a relief fund for the discharged strikers, a limited boycott of the airlines, and pressure on Congress and the president to lift the prohibition against rehiring PATCO strikers.[69] The president in part defused the last effort by issuing an order providing that controllers not convicted of wrongdoing during the strike could be employed by the federal government in jobs other than controller or related ones.[70] This order neither satisfied organized labor nor provided jobs for many strikers. Attempts by some members of the House of Representatives to pressure the Reagan administration to rehire the strikers were both rebuffed by the administration and set back by a poll, conducted by members of Congress who favored reinstating the strikers, which demonstrated that most controllers who stayed on the job were opposed to permitting strikers to return or to working with them.[71]

A fundamental failure of PATCO's approach was its total lack of success in gaining any support whatsoever from the ALPA, the leaders of which had been completely estranged by Poli's coup and who were also completely opposed to a strike that was believed to endanger pilot jobs. ALPA President O'Donnell and individual pilots repeatedly countered claims by PATCO spokespersons that the airways were not safe after the strike commenced, and they cited the excellent cooperation that they were receiving from working controllers. These statements did much to reassure the public and to lighten the task of the administration and the FAA. At the same time, however, the ALPA did join organized labor in urging amnesty for the strikers.[72]

Despite their serious reservations about PATCO's course and tactics, the leaders of other unions were certainly concerned about the effect of PATCO's crushing loss. In particular, officials of public employee unions feared that the administration's actions would become a precedent for other governmental bodies. Moreover, the president's hard line, and the support it won from the public, could encourage a similar employer reaction to strikes in private industry.[73]

International Union Response

Since unions in one country seldom support strikes by those in another,[74] it is rather astonishing that PATCO's strongest support came from the Canadian Air Traffic Controllers Association (CATCA) and other affiliates of IFATCA, which by this time was determined to assume a more active role in industrial disputes. A few days after PATCO struck, the IFATCA executive board invoked its Resolution A5, which reads in part:

> (a) . . . Member Associations will not clear aircraft into airspace under the jurisdiction of substituted services [i.e., those taking the place of striking controllers], and in addition . . .

(b) . . . [they should] consider refusing [air traffic control] service to U.S. Registered Aircraft.[75]

The overt rationale for such action was, of course, that the airways were not safe when a dispute involving IFATCA affiliates existed. Even before the IFATCA communication was sent out, controllers in New Zealand,[76] Norway,[77] France,[78] and later those in Portugal,[79] began delaying or refusing clearance to U.S.-flag or U.S.-bound aircraft. It was the Canadians, however, who inflicted the most damage. For two days, August 10 and 11, 1981, CATCA refused to clear any planes to or from the United States. The result was a virtual shutdown of traffic on the busy North Atlantic route, causing massive inconvenience during the height of the summer travel and costing the airlines millions of dollars. CATCA officials claimed that this action was necessary because of innumerable near-accidents, a list of which they had furnished to Canadian flight control authorities.[80]

This action by Canadian controllers proved to be the high watermark of PATCO and IFATCA efforts to shut down the U.S. air system. They failed because the U.S. authorities had prepared their foreign counterparts with information about the dispute and the likelihood of IFATCA-sponsored action. Both Dutch and Danish authorities visited U.S. facilities and pronounced them safely and expertly handled.[81] The Director of Air Traffic Services, Transport Canada, investigated each of twenty-two alleged hazardous incidents reported by CATCA and found them either nonexistent or routine. In a telegram to CATCA on August 11, he gave the facts on each occurrence and commented:

> More accurate information in your report of alleged incidents would be appreciated. . . . We have not found any occurrence that required "evasive action" or "action to avoid collision." . . . The irregularities were minor in nature and have occurred in the past when the U.S. air traffic control system was manned in a normal manner. I hope . . . that you will publicly correct some erroneous statements that you have made in recent days.[82]

According to J. Lynn Helms, then FAA administrator, a "vital element" in ending the CATCA boycott was the commitment of the United States to open up and, if necessary, maintain air traffic control over transoceanic routes. Helms reported:

> When the Canadian controllers started their initial efforts to exclude U.S. traffic across the North Atlantic, I went to ICAO [International Civil Aviation Organization] and obtained agreement that under the Chicago Accords if Canada was not able to fulfill its obligations to handle international air traffic then the airspace control should be assigned to the U.S. Obviously, this was clearly coordinated with my Canadian counterpart, Mr. Walt

McLeish. During his negotiations with the Canadian controllers, they rejected the possibility.

In the key conversation with Mr. McLeish, I outlined my plan and intent to use AWACS airplanes and missile cruisers, all with FAA controllers aboard, and that we definitely *would* open up the North Atlantic, the Azores, and the North Pacific routes. Based on this, he returned to the negotiators, advised them he now knew how we planned to do it, and agreed it could be done. Therefore, they would permanently forfeit their jobs. They returned to work, and this broke the back of the foreign support so the French and Portuguese accepted the finality of it within 24 hours. At no subsequent time did I face major concerns from foreign controllers and the American labor movement accepted that position as final.[83]

Threatened by dismissals and other sanctions, the Canadians called off their boycott on August 13.[84] IFATCA held three emergency meetings to seek support for PATCO, but found that a majority of affiliates were unwilling to risk penalties at home in order to support a strike abroad.[85] Moreover, the claims of safety violations in the United States were becoming more obviously hollow as the system continued to function, as air traffic directors from various countries reported otherwise, and as pilots affirmed their satisfaction.[86]

PATCO's Demise

Decertified and overwhelmed by debts, PATCO first tried reorganization. Poli, Meyer, and Trick all resigned.[87] That did not alter anything. Bankruptcy and finally dissolution followed.[88] A new organization, the United States Air Traffic Controllers' Organization (USATCO), rose from the ashes, headed by Garry Eads, a former PATCO vice-president and Poli's successor as PATCO president, but it has had little success in enrolling working controllers.[89] Meanwhile, many of the striking controllers have risked more of their life savings for legal fees on thus far quite unsuccessful efforts through civil service procedures to win reinstatement. It now appears that fewer than 5 percent are likely to succeed in this endeavor.[90]

Concluding Observations

The PATCO strike did more than inconvenience air travelers, inflict great economic damage on airlines, cost 11,000 controllers their jobs, and destroy a union. The strike also raised serious questions about employee relations in the public service and about whether the whole matter could have been handled differently. It both affected and reflected labor relations in this era.

Federal Employee Bargaining

Unions in the federal service have always found their main role to be political lobbying. The fact that wages and basic conditions of work are set by Congress makes this inevitable. Formerly under the Kennedy and Nixon orders, and now pursuant to the CSRA, unions have a greater bargaining role than they did before the 1960s, but it is still quite limited. The result is often two-fold: union officials' frustration over their inability to negotiate basic wages and benefits, and their search for issues that will enhance their standing with the rank and file. This, in the words of a careful student of the problem, "causes relatively unimportant and even frivolous issues to clutter negotiations, and [to] tend to linger on the table because not much is accomplished by disposing of them."[91] Moreover, because strikes are illegal, the pressure to settle on the part of unions and management is considerably lessened, and preparation for bargaining by both parties is frequently poor.[92]

From its inception, PATCO strove to operate outside these constraints by using the strike weapon. To be sure, PATCO followed the model of the federal civil service union by effective lobbying and by support of its congressional friends. Nonetheless, until Langhorne Bond, FAA administrator under President Carter, initiated a turnabout in FAA philosophy and approach and the Reagan administration, unlike all its predecessors, had the will when tested to meet the challenge. PATCO had also been very successful in operating an aggressive private sector bargaining policy in a public setting. The willingness of the Reagan administration to bargain over wages, and to recommend substantial wage increases, not only brought PATCO close to its goal but could well have altered the whole course of federal labor relations, if PATCO's leadership had not risked everything by its 1981 strike.

Unquestionably, if PATCO had succeeded in that strike, the right to bargain for wages and to strike in the public sector would, in effect, have been granted. It is important to note that to prevent this from occurring once PATCO had struck, the Reagan administration needed not only the will but the political muscle to accomplish its objective. Even in the face of the strong public support of the president's actions, PATCO's congressional supporters, in a vain effort to obtain a deal for reinstatement of the strikers, were able to prevent the payment of salary increases to working controllers until late 1982.[93]

In the past, the government's reaction to illegal strikes by controllers was equivocal at best, and more strikes occurred despite the sweeping injunction won by the ATA in 1970. These government policies encouraged Poli and his supporters to believe that such a procedure would be repeated, and thus contributed to the 1981 strike. If the 1981 strikers were to be reinstated, the federal government would again signal indecision about its belief in the traditional strike proscription in the federal service.[94] Yet such reinstatement has been advocated in 1983 by one congressional committee, although opposed by another.[95] The cost of reinstatement, in terms of possible future service disruption and wage escalation, would be high, and also the investment in defeating PATCO's challenge to the rules could be lost. On the other hand, if the present stance is maintained, then it should be clear that federal sector labor relations are considerably different from those in the private sector.

Another Approach?

The success of the Reagan-Lewis approach of discharging the strikers and of maintaining the federal service bans on strikes has been criticized by some as a case of overkill. For example, Ronald W. Haughton, former chairman and now a member of the FLRA, suggested in 1982 that the case could have been referred to the Federal Services Impasses Panel (FSIP), a public hearing held, pressure put on PATCO to conform to legal procedures, and, if necessary, arbitration required of the issues in dispute.[96] Haughton even proposed that instead of decertifying the union, the government should levy no penalty against PATCO if the strikers returned to work.[97]

This suggestion clearly represents a far different approach to federal sector strike prohibition than that of the Reagan administration; it follows the soft line of the FLRA, which refused to see the creation of a strike fund by a union forbidden to strike as an unfair labor practice. It is always possible that the Haughton proposals could have ended the strike. Yet, given PATCO's record and the government's historically ambivalent approach to the previous strikes, it seems likely that if the strike had ended without severe penalties, including discharges, fines, and decertification, the PATCO leadership, having come so close to achieving unrestrained wage bargaining and the de facto right to strike, would again have created a crisis to gain their goals.

PATCO and the Current Scene

It is difficult to assess the general effect of the PATCO strike, except to note its undoubted effect on other unions' propensity to initiate a strike in the federal sector. The strike occurred during a period of economic recession, while a conservative administration was attempting to curtail excessive government spending, to restrain the upward march of federal transfer payments, and to reduce government regulation of enterprise. In such a period, union power is certain to be diminished, and this trend has been exacerbated by the problems of key industries in which union strength has been concentrated, such as automobiles, steel, trucking, air transport, and farm equipment. Furthermore, the PATCO strike was a decided setback for organized labor in government employment—unionism's major, if not only, growing sector. It also marks a defeat in organized labor's long-term and still basically unsuccessful attempt to organize the salaried and service sectors. Finally, the Reagan administration's handling of the dispute probably stiffened government bargaining at the municipal and state levels, but to what extent cannot be quantified.

Whatever the broader implications of the strike, one thing is certain: the PATCO leaders committed about every strategic blunder in the bargaining book. They overestimated their ability to shut down the airline system; they underestimated their ability to hold their members in line; they overestimated their support from their political friends, the public, and other unions; they had a great victory and a giant step toward their goal of private sector wage bargaining but threw it away; and worst of all, they ignored management's preparations to resist the strike and President Reagan's determination to break with the past and to enforce the law. Rarely has such an amateurish performance by a union been displayed so publicly or dealt with so decisively.

Notes

1. P.L. 95-454, 92 Stat. 1111, effective January 11, 1979.

2. Under Title VII of the CSRA, the FLRA can issue cease-and-desist orders, require negotiations, or in case of strike decertify the striking union and "take any other appropriate disciplinary action." Strikes are also forbidden by other laws, such as 5 U.S.C. 73, which states that "an individual may not accept or hold a position in the Government of the United States or the Government of the District of Columbia if he participates in a strike . . . against the Government of the United States or the Government of the District of Columbia." The definition of *strike* as set forth in the National Labor Relations (Taft-Hartley) Act includes a slowdown or "other concerted interruption of operations by employees." Stating that "at common law, no employee, whether public or private, had a constitutional right to strike in concert with his fellow workers," the U.S. Supreme Court upheld the constitutionality of this provision. See *U.S. Federation of Postal Clerks v. Blount,* 404 U.S. 802 (1971).

3. This comment is based on the recollection of longtime FAA employees interviewed in Washington, D.C., in February 1982.

4. For the early Corson Committee report, see *The Career of the Air Traffic Controller—A Cause of Action* (Washington, D.C.: U.S. Department of Transportation, 1970); for the recent Jones report, see *Management and Employee Relationships within the Federal Aviation Administration,* Contract no. DTG A01-82-C-30006 (Washington, D.C.: FAA, 1982), 2 vols.

5. M.J. Fox, Jr., and E.G. Lambert, "Air Traffic Controllers: Struggle for Recognition and Second Careers," *Public Personnel Management* 3, no. 2 (May–June 1974), pp. 199–200. The author has confirmed that central control of labor relations still exists and, given the nature of the operations and bargaining arrangements, seems to be required.

6. Widespread publicity on this stoppage appeared in all the general and industry newspapers and labor relations services. See, for example, *Aviation Daily,* throughout the month-long period.

7. As characterized by an FAA employee, personal interview, February 1982.

8. See note 4.

9. See, for example, *Government Employee Relations Report,* no. 306 (July 21, 1969), p. A-5; and *Aviation Daily,* October 24, 1969, p. 353.

10. The material on this slowdown is taken from the extensive litigation and various briefs pertaining thereto. See, in particular, *Air Transport Ass'n v. Professional Air Traffic Controllers Organization,* 313 F. Supp. 181 (E.D.N.Y. 1970), *rev'd in part sub nom. United States v. PATCO,* 438 F. 2d 79 (1971), *cert. denied,* 402 U.S. 915 (1971).

11. *United States v. Professional Air Traffic Controllers Organization,* 312 F. Supp. 189 (D. Minn. 1970).

12. This order was affirmed in *United States v. Robinson,* 449 F. 2d 925 (9th Cir. 1971).

13. The terms of the agreed-upon order were upheld in *Air Transport Ass'n v. Professional Air Traffic Controllers Organization,* 453 F. Supp. 1287 (E.D.N.Y. 1978), *aff'd,* 594 F. 2d 851 (1978), *cert. denied,* 441 U.S. 944 (1979).

14. See *Aviation Daily,* February 9, 1972, p. 221, for strike details.

15. See Fox and Lambert, "Air Traffic Controllers," pp. 201–203; *PATCO Newsletter,* July 23, 1972, p. 1, and May 3, 1973, pp. 1–5. Prior to this time, PATCO bargained only for its members; Executive Order 11491 was the first to provide for exclusive representation.

16. The press noted that the slowdown had varying effects but was most noticeable in New York, Chicago, and Washington, D.C.

17. *The Controller,* the official publication of the International Federation of Air Traffic Controllers Association (IFATCA), makes frequent reference to the "need" for such flights, as does the *PATCO Newsletter.*

18. The case is cited in note 13.

19. See *United States v. PATCO,* 504 F. Supp. 432 (N.D.Ill. 1980); *rev'd,* 653 F. 2d 1134, 107 LRRM 3057, no. 80-2854 (7th Cir., 1981); *cert. denied,* 454 U.S. 1083 (1981).

20. Deposition of Robert E. Poli, then president of PATCO, August 12, 1981, vol. 1., pp. 34–80, and of Robert E. Meyer, then executive vice-president, August 13, 1981, vol. 1, pp. 34–68—both in *In the Matter of Air Transport Association v. Professional Air Traffic Controllers Association,* Civil Docket no. 70, Cir. 400 (U.S.D.C., E.D. N.Y.).

21. Re: *Professional Air Traffic Controllers Organization,* Case no. 22-09583 (CO). Decision letter to Edward V. Curran, director of labor relations, FAA, from Alexander T. Graham, regional director, Washington Regional Office, FLRA, April 30, 1979; and Re: *Professional Air Traffic Controllers Organization,* Case 3-CO-50. Decision letter to Edward V. Curran, director of labor relations, FAA, from Bruce D. Rosenstein, acting regional director, FLRA, November 30, 1980.

22. The report of the consultant is summarized in the *PATCO Journal,* November–December 1975, pp. 21–24. See also a reprint of the article, "Controllers Seek Divorce from Federal Government," *PATCO Newsletter,* August 1979, pp.

11–12; a story by United Press International based on interviews with PATCO officials, released July 13, 1981; a statement by Leyden, *PATCO Newsletter,* June 1979, p. 2; and Robert E. Poli, "Maybe It's Time to Dismiss the FAA," *New York Times,* August 16, 1981, p. E-19. This last article appeared two weeks after the "definitive strike" began. Representative William Clay reintroduced the idea in 1981 in a bill (H.R. 1576) that would also have given PATCO all of its economic demands. Ironically, some smaller airports hired controllers from the private sector after the strike began; those airports had lost their FAA controllers, who were reassigned to larger flight centers at least until the impact of the strike lessened. See Brenton R. Schlender, "Some Small Airports Hiring Firms to Provide Air Traffic Controllers," *Wall Street Journal,* March 14, 1982, p. 29.

23. See Fox and Lambert, "Air Traffic Controllers," for a good summary of the developments of P.L. 92-297.

24. 86 Stat. 141 (1972).

25. For criticisms of the loose construction of this law and its equally loose administration by the U.S. Department of Labor, see several reports of the U.S. Comptroller General and a popular version, Fern Schumer, "I'm *Not* All Right, Jack," *Forbes,* June 25, 1979, p. 78. See also *Daily Labor Report,* no. 140 (July 22, 1981), E pages, and no. 62 (March 31, 1982), E pages.

26. *Systems errors* are defined as situations in which planes being monitored by a controller violate separation standards.

27. Michael E. Staten and John Umbeck, "Information Costs and Incentives to Shirk: Disability Compensation of Air Traffic Controllers," *American Economic Review* 72, no. 5 (December 1982), pp. 1023–1037.

28. Sam Hopkins, "Psychiatrist Facing Trial in Controller Stress Suit," *Atlanta Constitution,* August 29, 1981, pp. 1-A, 6-A. The *PATCO Newsletter,* April 9, 1976, pp. 7, 14–15, contained excerpts from an article by this doctor stating that air traffic controllers had "a very special type of personality structure," and that because of inadequate equipment, controllers could not "follow any type of medical regimen aimed at alleviating their medical conditions," which he ascribed to them. This doctor has been the subject of litigation brought by insurance companies.

29. Data are from the source cited in note 27.

30. See, for example *PATCO Journal,* November–December 1975, pp. 29–35, for one of the frequent stories on O'Donnell and favorable mention of the ALPA.

31. See *PATCO Newsletter,* October 24, 1973, p. 15; Christmas 1973, p. 17; April 1, 1974, p. 11; July 5, 1974, p. 8; Christmas 1974, p. 4; and June 1980, p. 3; *PATCO Journal,* May 1975, p. 43; and the *Controller,* December 1971; no. 2 (no month), 1978, pp. 3–5; and no. 4, 1980, p. 17.

32. Reference to the ITF affiliation is found in *PATCO Newsletter,* November 11, 1974, p. 2; and August 5, 1972, p. 16. For a discussion of ITF policies in ocean and air transport, see Herbert R. Northrup and Richard L. Rowan, *Multinational Collective Bargaining Attempts,* Multinational Industrial Relations Series, no. 6 (Philadelphia: Industrial Research Unit, Wharton School, University of Pennsylvania, 1979), pp. 473–520.

33. The depositions of Poli and Meyer contain numerous references to CATCA meetings, and correspondence and telegrams in the author's possession confirm this. Such meetings on earlier occasions occurred frequently and are repeatedly mentioned in the *PATCO Newsletter.*

34. Poli deposition, pp. 229–241; and *PATCO Newsletter,* January 30, 1978, p. 3, and November 1978, p. 10. PASS affiliated with MEBA in June 1983.

35. The data are from the FAA.

36. See Gordon F. Bloom and Herbert R. Northrup, *Economics of Labor Relations,* 9th ed. (Homewood, Ill.: Richard D. Irwin, 1981), chap. 22, for a comparison of fringe benefits in government and in private industry.

37. Don Francke, "The FAA's Finest Hour . . . An Interview with Langhorne M. Bond," *Journal of Air Traffic Control* 24 (January–March 1982), pp. 6–11.

38. See 45 Fed. Reg. 221, November 13, 1980, DOT/FAA, 14 CFR, Part 91; 46 Fed. Reg. 43, March 5, 1981; and 46 Fed. Reg. 149, August 4, 1981, 14 CFR Part 91, for what was originally termed the FAA "Job Action Contingency Plan," and later the "National Air Traffic Control Contingency Plan."

39. There was some opposition to Poli at the 1980 convention of PATCO, but the failure of Leyden to go to the membership and the care of Poli and his group to avoid overt action before the convention both demoralized and softened the opposition. Confidential discussions with several sources suggest that Leyden was wholly surprised by the coup and had expected the January 1980 executive board meeting to be a routine one. Instead, it lasted all night. Both Leyden and Poli resigned, but the executive board, probably as planned, accepted Leyden's resignation, which it had demanded, but refused to accept Poli's and then designated him president.

40. Professional Air Traffic Controllers and PATCO Employees' Union, 261 NLRB no. 132 (May 14, 1982); *White Collar Report,* no. 1304 (January 21, 1982), pp. A-3–A-4. A group of those discharged by Poli sent a letter to the membership on August 4, 1980, detailing the discharges and resignations and explaining why the employees of PATCO had formed a union (a copy is in the author's possession).

41. See Poli's letter in the *PATCO Newsletter,* January 1981, p. 3.

42. The term *definitive strike* shows up in various places, but was most widely used in the PATCO call-in telephone recordings described below.

43. See *PATCO Newsletter,* June 1980, p. 3; and the *Controller,* no. 1, 1980, p. 17.

44. Several of the telephone recordings are in the author's possession, as are the minutes of the Sacramento, California, cluster meeting, April 30, 1981, in which the PATCO strategy is very explicitly set forth and it is noted that the same message was being given all around the industry at similar union meetings. (Copies of these documents, and of others cited in this article that are not publicly available, will be provided, within reason, by the author, provided anyone requesting copies pays the full cost of reproduction and mailing.)

Poli's strike threats were widely reported in the press prior to the June 22 deadline. Repeatedly he declared, "The only illegal strike is one that fails." See, for example, William M. Carley, "Rough Flying: Air Traffic Controllers Put Reagan on Spot with Threat to Strike," *Wall Street Journal,* June 17, 1981, p. 1.

45. David Trick, director of organization under Poli and third man in the PATCO hierarchy, termed choir boys "educators and organizers" in his deposition, p. 45, in the New York district court case (see footnote 20 for citation). It was quite probable, however, that choir boys (and one "choir girl") were selected for their physical size, aggressiveness, and loyalty to Poli and his policies. I believe that they were, in fact, enforcers, having been described in the minutes of the Sacramento cluster meeting as "responsible for building a strike force which is ready to go when

necessary." (See note 44.) This belief is also based on my discussion with several sources whose identity must remain confidential. As pointed out later, the government's extensive preparation for and sharp reaction to the strike kept violence to a minimum, and the role of the choir boys apparently did not develop as planned.

46. Additional monies were transferred to the strike ("subsistence") fund; bank loans of $650,000 were obtained; $100,000 cash was given to PATCO's lawyers, prior to the strike; and $300,000 in cash was withdrawn from a safe deposit box. See depositions of Poli, pp. 38–98, and of Meyer, vol. 1, pp. 36–77 and vol.2, pp. 161–177. At the Sacramento cluster meeting, reference was also made to a large fund in a California bank that was never explained in the depositions or elsewhere that I have found.

47. A copy of the Reagan letter of October 20, 1980, was reproduced in a *New York Times* advertisement, August 16, 1981, p. 69.

48. This was attested throughout my FAA interviews and is clearly reflected in subsequent events, as described later.

49. For this and other ALPA policies, see my article, "The New Employee Relations Climate in the Airline Industry," *Industrial and Labor Relations Review* 36, no. 2 (January 1983), pp. 167–181.

50. See note 44.

51. A copy of the contract offer is in my possession.

52. This point was made clearly by Secretary Lewis in several press conferences immediately after the strike.

53. According to David Trick, director of organization, PATCO called off the strike set for June 22 because it "lacked the 80% membership support required for a strike." Joann S. Lublin, "Air Traffic Union Lacked 80% Vote It Needed to Strike," *Wall Street Journal,* June 24, 1981, p. 12. This author has found no record of a strike vote prior to the first six PATCO strikes, but he does have a copy of a PATCO policy statement, released by a member of the O'Hare cluster, that contains the 80 percent "policy".

54. "Statement of Secretary of Transportation Drew Lewis," news release, U.S. Department of Transportation, August 1, 1981. The FAA calculated the total costs of these demands at $681 million in 1982, exclusive of the costs of a thirty-two-hour week.

55. A clipping file collected for this article shows this whipping up of strike sentiment throughout the country.

56. The July 28, 1981, letter from 55 senators and 19 members of Congress advised Poli that "any illegal action by PATCO and its members will be viewed with extreme disfavor in the Congress." A copy is in the author's possession.

57. See, for example, Richard Witkin, "Air Control Union is Warned by U.S. As a Strike Looms," *New York Times,* August 3, 1981, pp. A-1, A-12, in which Secretary Lewis is quoted as saying that if PATCO struck, there would be "no amnesty" and "no negotiations while a strike persisted." He further stated that these warnings "come directly from President Reagan." The same article quoted the Secretary of Defense as willing to provide 600 to 700 controllers if there were a strike, and the attorney general as stating that anyone who violated the ban on strikes by federal employees would be prosecuted "to the fullest extent permitted by law."

58. Meyer deposition, vol 1, pp. 182–204.

59. For general experience, see Charles R. Perry, Andrew M. Kramer, and Thomas J. Schneider, *Operating During Strikes,* Labor Relations and Public Policy Series no. 23 (Philadelphia: Industrial Research Unit, Wharton School, University of Pennsylvania, 1982).

60. The data are from the FAA.

61. Secretary Lewis was the chief spokesman for the Reagan administration, and he repeatedly gave interviews, spoke on television, and generally communicated the concern for safety. Then-president of ALPA J.J.O'Donn.ll and numerous individual pilots countered claims of danger and disregard of safety made by Poli and other PATCO spokesmen on many occasions. See, for example, the *New York Times* and *Wall Street Journal* throughout August and September 1981, especially August 3–15.

62. Three major crashes occurred during the 1981–1982 strike period. In the first, involving World Airways at Boston, a plane skidded into the harbor, killing two persons. The National Transportation Board ruled that the primary cause of the crash was the failure of the FAA to provide adequate information on runway ice conditions—as had happened in several pre-strike accidents. Controller failure was not considered a factor. New computer equipment, now authorized, should greatly remedy this lack of information. See National Transportation Safety Board, *Aircraft Accident Report, World Airways, Inc., Flight 30H . . . Boston Logan International Airport, January 23, 1982,* Report no. NTSB/AAR-82-15 (Washington, D.C.: NTSB, December 15, 1982).

The second crash was that of an Air Florida plane into a Potomac River bridge in January 1982, killing 78 people. The principal cause appears to have been ice on the wings. In turn, this was the result of inadequate deicing; poor communications between American Airlines maintenance personnel who did the deicing and Air Florida pilots; the relative inexperience of Air Florida pilots in such weather; or increased separation of flights mandated by the shortage of experienced controllers, which caused ice to form on wings of planes while they awaited take-off; or some combination of the above. Since no other plane taking off just before the ill-fated one had the same problem, the fourth possible cause—increased separation of flights—does not seem likely. See National Transportation Safety Board, *Aircraft Accident Report, Air Florida, Inc. . . . Near Washington National Airport, January 13, 1982,* Report no NTSB/AAR-82-8 (Washington, D.C.: NTSB, August 10, 1982).

The final crash, that of a Pan American plane at New Orleans after take-off, killing 153 persons, was attributed to a wind shift, which the weather experts acknowledge they know too little about. A new drive is now underway to accumulate knowledge about this problem. No controller error was apparently involved. See National Transportation Safety Board, *Aircraft Accident Report, Pan American World Airways, Inc. . . . New Orleans International Airport, July 9, 1982,* Report no. NTSB/AAR-83-102 (Washington, D.C.: NTSB, March 21, 1983).

63. See the citation in note 49, for many details of the airlines' problems during this period.

64. Data on legal actions are from FAA files. See also various issues of *Daily Labor Report,* from August 5 through September 30, 1981.

65. Data provided by the FAA's labor relations office.

66. *Professional Air Traffic Controllers Organization v. Federal Aviation Administration,* FLRA Case no. 3, CO-105, October 22, 1981; *aff'd* 685 F. 2d 547

D.C. Cir. 1982); *Daily Labor Report* no. 104 (October 22, 1981), pp. E-1–E-9. The decision process of the FLRA included negotiations among members, discussions with interested labor officials, public criticism of one board member by another, and other actions indicating that the FLRA may well require a thorough restructuring and new administrative and operating rules.

67. Since the private sector airline unions are within the jurisdiction of the Railway Labor Act, and since strikes in violation of contracts thereunder are clearly enjoinable and striking unions are subject to damage suits, airline unions could not easily support the strike. See *Brotherhood of Railroad Trainmen v. Chicago River and Indiana Railroad Co.*, 353 U.S. 30 (1957); and *Flight Engineers Int'l Assoc. v. American Airlines, Inc.*, 303 F. 2d 5 (5th Cir. 1962).

68. A group of union officials, Ralph Nader, and others filed suit to force the government to rehire the strikers. The suit was dismissed for failure to exhaust administrative remedies and no appeal was taken. *Douglas Fraser v. Lewis* (D. D.C., Cir. no. 81-2729, December 21, 1981). The union officials also filed a request with the FAA and with other agencies to change rules and rehire the strikers. This was denied as was a request for reconsideration.

69. For a good summary of the situation, see "Unions Wary of Legal Risks in Honoring PATCO Picket Lines," *Daily Labor Report,* no. 152 (August 7, 1981), pp. A-10–A-11. See also "AFL-CIO Sets Up Fund to Aid Air Controllers," *Daily Labor Report,* no. 162 (August 21, 1981), p. A-1. The airlines boycott was largely ignored by the time of the November 1981 AFL-CIO convention, and it also did not ground the executive fleet of the Teamsters, the IAM, and other unions that own such appurtenances. See "Many Union Officials Traveled by Plane," *New York Times,* November 20, 1981, p. A-21, which reported on the diminishing air travel boycott.

70. The president's statement and memorandum are found in *Daily Labor Report,* no. 236 (December 9, 1981), p. E-1. See also Jeff Sommer, "Despite Amnesty, No Ex-Controllers Get Federal Jobs," *Philadelphia Inquirer,* March 20, 1982, p. 4-A.

71. The Roper Organization was retained by the Subcommittee on Investigations and Oversight of the Committee on Public Works and Transportation, U.S. House of Representatives, after the FAA and PATCO differed on whether nonstrikers objected to strikers returning. In February 1982 Roper sent carefully constructed questions to a randomly selected 20 percent of the working controllers at their home addresses. "An almost unprecedented response for a mail survey that employed no follow-up mailing and . . . no . . . incentive for responding" resulted in an 82 percent return. Fifty-eight percent were against the return of the strikers under any condition, 31 percent would permit them back under certain conditions, and only 10 percent felt that they should be hired unconditionally. See *Aviation Safety, Air Traffic Control (PATCO Walkout), Hearings before the Subcommittee on Investigations and Oversight of the Committee on Public Works and Transportation,* House of Representatives, 97th Cong., 1st and 2d sess. (Washington, D.C.: U.S. Government Printing Office, 1982), pp. 741–788.

72. Initially, O'Donnell suggested that the former director of the Federal Mediation and Conciliation Service (FMCS), W.J. Usery, be hired as a special mediator; he and other ALPA officials also joined in approving a resolution at the AFL-CIO convention asking that the controllers be rehired. See Richard Witkin, "Judge Orders Fine: Head of Air Pilots' Union Suggests Mediator as Deadlock Persists," *New York Times,* August 5, 1981, pp. A-1, A-14; and Warren Brown, "AFL-CIO's Executive

Council Votes to Raise Dues $14.6 Million by '83," *Washington Post,* November 15, 1981, p. A12. O'Donnell's most important act, however, was to call a press conference on August 19, 1981, in order to declare that the airways were safe and specifically to refute Poli's claims to the contrary. See "Pilot Union Chief Calls Airways 'Safe', Says Near-Misses Are Below a Year Ago," *Wall Street Journal,* August 20, 1981, p. 8.

73. See, for example, William Serrin, "Unionists Anxious over PATCO Strike," *New York Times,* October 21, 1981, p. A24.

74. Northrup and Rowan, *Multinational Collective Bargaining Attempts,* reviews the claims of transnational support of strikes and finds little evidence to support any such claims.

75. IFATCA, "The Federation: Past-Present-Future," IFATCA conference document, 21st Annual Conference, Amsterdam, the Netherlands, May 3–8, 1982, Agenda Item A.1.6., pp. 1–2.

76. New Zealand controllers first denied clearance to U.S.-bound aircraft, then delayed them. Effectiveness was limited by lack of cooperation from Australian controllers who were not affiliated with IFATCA. (IFATCA, "Annual Report of the Regional Vice President, Pacific Region," IFATCA conference document, 21st Annual Conference, Amsterdam, the Netherlands, May 3–8, 1982.) A strong message from Secretary Lewis to the New Zealand transportation minister aided in ending the disruption. (A copy of this message is in the author's possession.)

77. The head of the Norwegian controllers was a leader of the proboycott faction in IFATCA, but obstructions in Norway were few and short lived.

78. French controllers issued many statements supporting PATCO, but after a few days of intermittent boycotts and slow clearance tactics, they yielded to pressure from their government and ceased interference.

79. After several postponed announcements of boycott, the Portuguese controllers at the key Azores station began a forty-eight-hour boycott on August 16. Transatlantic carriers rerouted their flights with only very minor problems. See Robert D. McFadden, "Controllers in Azores Set Boycott but Atlantic Flights Are Rerouted," *New York Times,* August 16, 1981, pp. 1, 37.

80. "Some Air Routes to Europe Shut for Hours as Strikers Get Canadian Group's Help," *New York Times,* August 11, 1981, pp. A-1, B-7–B-9; "European Flights Slashed amid Big Delays as Canada Fails to Halt Union Backers," *New York Times,* August 12, 1981, pp. A-1, A-22. Similar stories can be found in many Canadian and U.S. newspapers published during this period.

81. Reports of the Dutch and Danish inspectors are in the author's possession.

82. The communication was sent to PATCO Executive Vice-President Meyer by W.J. Robertson, president of CATCA, who had received it on August 11, the second day of the Canadian boycott.

83. Letter from J. Lynn Helms, FAA administrator, to the author, July 26, 1983. The ultimatum from the ICAO to Canada's air traffic control authorities was confirmed in my interviews with officials of Transport Canada in August 1983.

The Chicago Accords to which Helms refers are the international agreements that allocate international air space to the air traffic control organizations of various countries. The accords require each country to provide the control services agreed on; failure to do so permits the ICAO to delegate a country's control authority to others.

84. See Joann S. Lublin and Frederick Rose, "Atlantic Flights Begin Resuming

Normal Service," *Wall Street Journal,* August 13, 1981, p. 3. The Canadian authorities suspended 154 controllers for their refusal to handle planes from the United States, but an attempt to charge controllers with contempt of court in the matter was dismissed ("Canada to Suspend 154 Air Controllers," *Financial Times,* October 7, 1981, p. 3; and "Canadian Order Dismissed," *New York Times,* September 17, 1982, p. A-19).

85. See Richard L. Hudson, "Foreign Air Controllers Postpone Plans for Boycott, but Industry Remains Wary," *Wall Street Journal,* August 14, 1981, p. 3; John Tagliabul, "World Controllers Say They Back Strike but Avoid Immediate Move," *New York Times,* August 24, 1981, p. A-1; and a confidential report to the FAA on the IFATCA meeting, Rome, November 13–14, 1981, in the author's possession.

86. In the *Monthly News Bulletin* of the International Federation of Air Line Pilots' Association (IFALPA), September 1981, p. 2, appeared this statement:

> No reports of incidents in USA airspace had been received by IFALPA, the first six weeks of the strike. . . . A number of individual pilots, including Principal Officers and Regional Vice-Presidents [of the IFALPA] had reported that they were satisfied that their own flights in USA airspace had been as safe as flights were before the USA Air Traffic Controllers dispute began.

87. "Poli Resigns Post with Controllers," *New York Times,* January 1, 1982, p. 7.

88. "'The Union is Gone' PATCO Says; Organization Files for Bankruptcy," *White Collar Report,* no. 131 (July 9, 1982), pp. A-9–A-10. PATCO had requested Chapter 11 status on November 26, 1981; this permitted it to operate with court protection against creditor lawsuits while it attempted to work out a plan for paying the enormous debts assessed against it for contempt on numerous counts. On July 2, 1982, PATCO bankruptcy was converted to a Chapter 7 proceeding, which involves no possibility of a viable reorganizing action.

89. James Crawford, "New Organization Hopes to Unionize Controllers," *Federal Times,* April 4, 1983, pp. 4, 15; and "New Air Traffic Controllers' Union Being Built by Veterans from PATCO," *Daily Labor Report,* no. 90 (May 9, 1983), pp. A-2–A-5.

90. See Gregory Jaynes, "Lawyers at Odds on Tactics to Aid Striking Controllers," *New York Times,* February 21, 1982, p. 26; and Sara Schwaider, "Air Controllers: Paying the Price," *Philadelphia Inquirer,* February 8, 1982, p. 1. The success rate for reinstatement has been very low, whether the striker is represented by counsel or not. Thus, as of May 18, 1983, of 12, 015 appeals filed, only 351 were initially granted a reversal of their discharges by the initial hearing officer, and some of these could be reversed on appeal (data from the FAA). Precedent-setting legal action has gone decisively against the attempts of controllers to gain reinstatement. See *United States v. Gary Greene et al.*—F. 2d (5th Cir., January 31, 1983); *Ketcham v. Department of Transportation,* FAA, Merit Systems Protection Board, no. DAO 75281 F0713, March 16, 1982; *Brown v. Federal Aviation Administration,* Merit Systems Protection Board, no. NVO 75281 F457, May 19, 1983; and *Schapansky v. Department of Transportation,* FAA, Merit Systems Protection Board, no. DAO 75282 F1130, October 28, 1982.

91. Douglas M. McCabe, "Problems in Federal Sector Labor–Management

Relations under Title VII of the Civil Service Reform Act of 1978," Industrial Relations Research Association, Proceedings of the 1982 Spring Meeting, *Labor Law Journal* 33, no. 8 (August 1982), p. 560.

92. Ibid.

93. Democratic Representative William D. Ford of Michigan, a strong supporter of PATCO and chairman of the U.S. House of Representative, Post Office and Civil Service Committee, bottled up the increase for this period, but his proposed bill providing amnesty for the discharged controllers lost on the House floor in 1982.

94. In 1978, for example, Representative Ford successfully pressured the postal service to grant reemployment rights to postal employees who had struck two major facilities in New Jersey. "Settlement of Postal Strike Suit Gives Strikers Chance for Rehire," *Daily Labor Report,* no. 116 (June 16, 1982), pp. A-1–A-2.

95. The report of the U.S. House of Representatives, Committee on Appropriations, *Department of Transportation and Related Appropriation Bill, 1984,* Report no. 98-246, 98th Cong., 1st sess. (Washington, D.C.: U.S. Government Printing Office, 1983), p. A-27, states: ". . . the Committee urges the FAA to consider certain previously dismissed air traffic controllers eligible for reinstatement . . . and placed on the 'reinstatement eligibles' lists . . . ." On the other hand, the Committee on Appropriations of the U.S. Senate opposed this recommendation as "a serious mistake that could result in grave consequences . . . inconsistent . . . extremely disruptive to the air traffic system [and] . . . a severe blow to the morale of controllers who stayed on the job and worked diligently and efficiently during the rebuilding period." U.S. Senate, *Department of Transportation and Related Agencies Appropriation Bill, 1984,* Report no. 98-000 (draft), 98th Cong., 1st sess. (Washington, D.C.: U.S. Government Printing Office, 1983), pp. 30–31.

96. See the testimony of Mr. Haughton before the U.S. House of Representatives, Subcommittee on Investigations, Committee on Post Office and Civil Service, February 24, 1981, 97th Cong., 2nd sess. (mimeo).

97. Haughton at first dissented to the FLRA decertification order, but when PATCO did not return to work, he later concurred.

Communications: "The Rise and Demise of PATCO" Reconstructed

Richard W. Hurd
*Jill K. Kriesky**

In "The Rise and Demise of PATCO" (Northrup, 1984), Herbert Northrup presents a narrow and misleading explanation of the ill-fated air traffic controllers' strike of 1981. Northrup's thesis is that the goal of the Professional

*Reprinted from *Industrial and Labor Relations Review* 40, no. 1 (October 1986), pp. 115–127.

Air Traffic Controllers Organization (PATCO) strike was to establish the right to bargain over wages within a private sector framework. He attributes the failure of the strike to the union's inept leadership and praises the Reagan administration for its firm response to the challenge presented by PATCO.

Although most of the facts he reports are accurate, Northrup omits crucial information regarding the management style of the Federal Aviation Administration (FAA) and the internal dynamics of PATCO. Based on this additional information, we will argue that PATCO's primary goal was to address the work-related problems of the rank and file specifically by reducing the workweek and improving the retirement system; that the primary cause of the strike was rank-and-file frustration with autocratic management; and that the Reagan administration joined forces with career FAA managers to destroy PATCO without giving sufficient consideration to less drastic alternatives.

The PATCO Bargaining Objectives

The weakest link in Northrup's analysis is his assertion that the basic objective of the 1981 PATCO strike was "wage determination on a private sector model" (Northrup, 1984, p. 171). This theme is subject to two possible interpretations. In its weaker version the goal of PATCO could have been to stretch federal labor relations law to the limit by bargaining over wages subject to congressional approval. In its stronger version the goal of PATCO could have been to break away from the constraining civil service system by forcing the privatization of the FAA. PATCO could have attained the weaker form of private sector wage determination by ratifying the tentative contract signed on June 22, 1981. As Northrup interprets the situation, the union stubbornly refused to be satisfied with this precedent-setting agreement and instead staged "the 'definitive strike' aimed at achieving PATCO's basic aims of inducing Congress to establish an independent FAA, permitting wage bargaining, and legitimizing strikes" (Northrup, 1984, p. 174).

To support his thesis that this stronger version of private sector wage bargaining was the objective, Northrup refers to five PATCO sources (Northrup, 1984, p. 171n). Three of the five are not directly relevant to the 1981 negotiations because they predate Robert Poli's ascendancy to the presidency of the union. The remaining two sources are fatally flawed. The article "Maybe It's Time to Dismiss the FAA," which appeared in the *New York Times* on August 16, 1981, is credited to Robert Poli by Northrup when in fact it was written by Robert Poole, who has no association with PATCO. Poole is a long-time advocate or privatization of public services, and is clearly identified in an insert to the article as president of the Reason Foundation (Poole, 1981). The July 13, 1981, UPI article referenced by Northrup in support of his position in fact contradicts him quite clearly. When asked to comment on a proposal to establish a private company to provide air traffic control services, PATCO officials disavowed any association with the plan. In fact, PATCO's eastern regional vice-president specifically disassociated the privatization proposal from the pending strike: "I'm sure we'll devote all our efforts to obtaining a new contract and realistically . . . we cannot rule out the possibility of a strike. So this [privatization] plan doesn't fit in at all under the present circumstances" (UPI, 1981, p. 16).

In addition to the five PATCO sources, Northrup refers to a bill, H.R. 1576, introduced by Representative William Clay on PATCO's behalf in 1981. The Clay bill would have established a separate salary schedule for air traffic controllers, required the FAA to bargain over wages with the collective bargaining agent of the controllers, and provided for adjustment of the salary schedule to reflect any future collective bargaining agreement. The bill also included language that would have allowed the air traffic controllers to strike (U.S., House of Representatives, 1981a).

Certainly H.R. 1576 would have enabled PATCO to negotiate under private sector rules, as argued by Northrup. What Northrup fails to report is that on July 30, 1981, Clay introduced a revised version of the legislation, H.R. 4332. *The revised bill deleted the provision for automatic adjustment of the salary schedule subject to collective bargaining, and omitted the right to strike* (U.S., House of Representatives, 1981b). PATCO officials had agreed to these changes because they recognized that the bill stood no chance of serious consideration in its original form (Shostak and Skocik, 1986, chap. 5). The PATCO leaders most certainly would not have accepted such revisions four days before the strike if bargaining under private sector rules had been their primary objective.

Even when chastising the union for not accepting the weaker version of private sector bargaining, Northrup focuses on *wages:* "The willingness of the Reagan administration to bargain over wages . . . brought PATCO close to its goal" (Northrup, 1984, p. 183). This claim still misses the point. The publicly stated negotiating demands of PATCO indeed included a substantial wage increase. Besides inflicting considerable damage on the union's public image, the wage demands masked the key issues in the conflict. In five surveys conducted for the union by Drexel University sociology professor Arthur Shostak during 1979, 1980, and 1981, PATCO members consistently reported that their primary concerns were (1) wage gains, (2) a shorter work-week, and (3) an improved retirement plan (Shostak and Skocik, 1986, chap. 5). Although the wage package offered by the Reagan administration was not as large as PATCO had hoped, both President Poli and Chief Negotiator Dennis Reardon are firm in their position that the wage improvement would have been acceptable had the contract also addressed the other two key issues (Poli, 1985; Reardon, 1985). In terms of narrow bargaining objectives, the priorities at the time of the strike were to shorten the workweek and improve the retirement system (Leyden, 1982; Maher, 1985; Poli, 1985; Reardon, 1985; Taylor, 1985).

In fact, the July 1981 UPI article referenced by Northrup, although it did *not* support his thesis that PATCO's goal was to privatize its relations with the FAA, clearly reflected the true objectives of the union. The article reported that the contract faced likely rejection "by an overwhelming margin on the grounds that it does not address . . . [controllers'] main concerns—a shorter workweek and better retirement benefits" (UPI, 1981, p. 16). By some accounts, the shorter workweek became the more important objective as the strike deadline approached. As *Business Week* summarized the situation, "Federal Aviation Association and union officials alike are now saying that the membership is homing in on the reduced work week issue" (*Business Week,* 1981, p. 26).

The Role of FAA Management

A second flaw in Northrup's analysis is his omission of any careful evaluation of management's role in the conflict. The reports of three groups of neutral outside experts, appointed by the Department of Transportation to assess the personnel difficulties of the FAA and to recommend solutions, contain a wealth of information on management's contribution to the recurrent hostilities. Northrup briefly mentions these studies, concluding that the reports "criticized the FAA's relations with its employees, although pointing out that PATCO leadership was heavily to blame" (Northrup, 1984, p. 168). As we read them, the reports document in detail the failings of FAA management and make only secondary references to PATCO's role.

The Corson Committee was appointed after the PATCO job actions of 1968 and 1969. Its report, issued in January 1970, documents a series of problems with working conditions and recommends numerous changes in management policies. It includes stinging criticisms of management, such as the following:

> [The] FAA cannot now command the full support of many members of the work force in its terminals and centers. Indeed, members of this committee have never previously observed a situation in which there is as much mutual resentment and antagonism between management and its employees. (Corson 1970, p. 97).

It is true that the report also condemns PATCO's tactics, but it places substantial blame for the poor relations on management, decrying "the failure of FAA's management at all levels to truly understand the role of the employee organizations" (Corson, 1970, p. 108).

In 1973 the FAA commissioned a five-year study of the effect of the occupation on the health of employees under the direction of Boston University psychiatrist Robert Rose. The 1978 Rose Report concludes that air traffic controllers have an unusually high prevalence of hypertension and that job stress contributes to the psychiatric problems experienced by nearly half of the controllers. It also confirms the existence of a burnout phenomenon, concluding that "the period of maximum productivity as a controller is a limited one, perhaps 10, 15, but not more than 20 years" (Rose, 1978, p. 16). The report ties the problems of hypertension, job stress, and burnout directly to the management practices of the FAA. In its conclusion, the report notes "dissatisfaction among a large enough group to warrant a review of management policies and practices" (Rose, 1978, p. 628).

Following the PATCO strike, yet another task force was appointed. The Jones Report, issued in March 1982 and endorsed by all three members of the task force, provides direct evidence that the "para-military, heavy handed style" of FAA management contributed to the PATCO strike (Jones, Bowers, and Fuller, 1982, p. 10; Witkin, 1982). The report describes the "rigid and insensitive system of people management within the FAA" (Jones, Bowers, and Fuller, 1982, p. 1). It concludes that "the strike by air traffic controllers [is] consistent with what might have been expected—negative organizational conditions, treatment, and experiences, not peer pressure, caused most individuals to decide to strike" (Jones, Bowers, and Fuller, 1982, p. 68).

It is our impression that Northrup fails to recognize the provocative role played by management because of his reliance on interviews with FAA officials as the basis for much of his analysis. The explanation of the strike offered by top FAA managers is reviewed in an article by David Bowers, a member of the Jones Task Force and a research scientist at the University of Michigan Institute for Social Research. The management assessment parallels Northrup's closely. FAA managers believed that the key concerns of PATCO were much higher pay and benefits, and Northrup argues that the key objective was wage bargaining on a private sector model. FAA managers believed that PATCO had unrealistic expectations because of past FAA "indulgence" of the union's demands, and Northrup traces PATCO's behavior to the "equivocal" response of the federal government to past job actions. FAA managers believed that most controllers struck because of peer pressure, and Northrup identifies Poli's "adherents in the field" as instigators "whipping up" strike support (Bowers, 1983, p. 6; Northrup, 1984, pp. 167, 177, 184).

Bowers emphatically rejects the FAA top management version of what transpired, noting that "the findings [of the Jones task force] stand in almost polar opposition to the views obtained in interviews and conversations with a wide array of key managers" (Bowers, 1983, p. 17). We also reject Northrup's version. Because he ignores the rigidity of FAA management, Northrup misses the catalyst role it played in the strike. The frustration of working controllers with their supervisors created a potentially explosive situation.

For its part, the FAA took a familiar management position. It blamed morale problems on PATCO and chose to ignore the evidence offered in the Corson and Rose reports. Rather than correcting management inadequacies, the FAA prepared for what Raymond Van Vuren, Director of Air Traffic, described in 1980 as an "inevitable" strike (BNA, 1980, p. 11). If the agency could weather the strike, PATCO would be destroyed and the problems would disappear.[1]

Based on the information in the three consulting reports and the Bowers article, we conclude that FAA management never accepted PATCO as a legitimate representative of the air traffic controllers, and the union predictably responded with an aggressive, confrontational approach. The controllers' support for PATCO and its strategies is best viewed as a reflection of management's failures (Hurd, 1981).

Internal Dynamics of PATCO

A third weakness in Northrup's article is its lack of clarity regarding changes within PATCO that contributed to the events of 1981.[2] The unsavory work environment revealed in the task force reports enhanced PATCO's standing with air traffic controllers. Membership increased steadily in the years preceding the strike, peaking at nearly 94 percent of those eligible in the summer of 1981 (Spector and Beer, 1982, p. 13). The union actually began internal strike preparations in the fall of 1978. In response to rank and file discontent with a three-year contract signed earlier that year, President John Leyden established a committee to begin planning for the next round of negotiations. Each of the seven regional vice-presidents selected a rank-and-file leader (the seven original "choir boys") to be a member of the "'81 Committee," with Executive Vice-President Robert Poli representing the national office. Leyden asked the committee to plan a legislative agenda, conduct a public relations campaign, and (as a last resort) prepare for a strike. To assure membership support in the event that a strike became necessary, a new policy was adopted requiring that 80 percent of all air traffic controllers (or roughly 90 percent of PATCO members) vote in favor of any such action (Leyden, 1982).

After he ousted Leyden from the presidency in January 1980 as described by Northrup, Poli allowed the '81 Committee to focus its attention more single-mindedly on the mechanics of strike preparation (Maher, 1985). Once a strike plan was developed, it was explained at regional PATCO meetings and in an April 1980 memo from Poli (Poli, 1980). Additional choir boys were selected by the '81 Committee to implement the plan locally. Eventually, there was one choir boy at each facility, or over 400 nationally. The choir boys were typically activists chosen for their ability to articulate positions and for their influence with the rank and file. Although a commitment to strike if necessary was required of each choir boy, PATCO officials insist that "non-violence was at all times primary and mandatory" (Maher, 1984; Reardon, 1985; Taylor, 1985).

Each choir boy was instructed by the '81 Committee to organize seven local committees, with assignments ranging from picketing to family support. Most members of the union were assigned to a committee, ensuring the broadest possible participation in strike preparation (Maher, 1985; Poli, 1980; Vacca, 1982). The weakness in this system was the exclusive focus of the committee on *strike* preparation. The tight internal cohesiveness became so powerful that it developed a momentum of its own, increasing the likelihood of a strike. It also increased the confidence of PATCO's leadership that the controller work force would strike if necessary (Reardon, 1985; Taylor, 1985), contrary to Northrup's conclusion that the leaders "underestimated their ability to hold their members in line" (Northrup, 1984, p. 184).

As the contract expiration date approached, the influence of the '81 Committee and the choir boy system increased. Because of the unusually high degree of membership involvement, PATCO essentially became captive to the controllers' frustration with management. As Bowers has noted, the bargaining process was ill equipped to address the employee dissatisfaction with managerial behavior, and the demands were "projected onto 'harder' economic issues" (Bowers, 1983, p. 8). When bargaining with the FAA broke down, and the support from President Reagan that Poli had anticipated failed to materialize, the '81 Committee's strike plan became the only viable option. The high degree of internal organization assured PATCO's leaders of widespread member support for a strike. In fact, the momentum was so strong that aborting the strike would have been difficult. As former PATCO president Leyden cynically put it, "Disproportionate democracy led to a runaway ship" (Leyden, 1982).

According to Northrup, the PATCO "script" called for Poli to accept the final offer of the Reagan administration in June, then have the executive board repudiate the offer and use it to whip up support for a strike. The supporting evidence provided is exceedingly thin, consisting of "call-in telephone recordings" and minutes from a local union meeting in Sacramento (Northrup, 1984, p. 175n). Northrup could provide us only with the meeting notes and a tape of a series of conversations between two controllers in Memphis and Indianapolis. The Sacramento meeting notes do not mention how PATCO intended to build strike support. They do, however, quote the choir boys conducting the meeting as stating, "If we get into the strike hall and come up short, . . . Mr. Poli will 'con' the media and will probably call an 11th hour settlement to try to 'save face.'" We can find no evidence that this was national policy. Efforts to contact the choir boys who presided at this meeting to determine where they got this idea were unsuccessful. Dominic Torchia, the vice-president of the western region in which the meeting occurred, suggests, however, that an enthusiastic attempt to prepare the membership for a strike may have produced this speculative scenario (Torchia, 1985).

On the tape, controllers from two locations discuss how they intend to build support in their workplaces for a future strike vote and which locals need to increase strike commitment. Although their conversation takes place in July 1981, it contains only vague allusions to using the June 22 contract to build strike support.

In short, based on the information that Northrup provided us, it appears that he has linked together two isolated local sources, one referring to what would happen if the June 21 strike vote fell short of the required 80 percent, the other referring to building support for the August 3 strike vote. But no logical connection exists. Interviews with national union officials, including Poli and several other negotiating committee members, suggest that the following very different series of events took place. After negotiations with the FAA broke down in late April, a June 22 strike deadline was announced. PATCO leaders believed that there was sufficient support for a strike. But when a strike vote conducted under the auspices of the '81 Committee on the day before the deadline fell slightly short of the necessary 80 percent, the PATCO negotiating team was backed into a corner. Even though the final offer of Secretary Lewis did not address the key issues of a reduced work week and improved retirement system, it was accepted on June 22 by the negotiating team essentially because the team felt that it had no other option (Poli, 1985; Maher, 1985; Trick, 1985; Reardon, 1981, 1985; Taylor, 1985).

Torchia, the western regional vice-president and a member of the executive board, recalls, however, that by the time the full executive board met in Chicago in early July, widespread rank and file opposition to the contract had surfaced. Any executive board member who had voted to support the contract might well have been forced by the members to resign (Torchia, 1985), which contributed to the board's recommendation that the contract be rejected by the members. Poli specifically denies the script described by Northrup, claiming that there was no contingency plan in the event the strike vote came up short ("We weren't that smart"; Poli, 1985).

The Reagan Administration Strategy

Northrup applauds the Reagan administration which "unlike all its predecessors . . . had the will when tested to meet the challenge" presented by PATCO (Northrup, 1984, p. 183). We do not believe that the resolve is worthy of such unrestrained praise. Instead, we are convinced that the administration's actions actually contributed to the difficulty of reaching a negotiated settlement.

Although space limitations preclude a detailed review of the Reagan administration's negotiating tactics, even a brief summary reveals the underlying theme. Three particular actions exacerbated an already hostile collective bargaining environment. First, in February 1981 the Department of Transportation contracted with the law firm Morgan, Lewis, and Brockius to handle bargaining with PATCO (at an eventual cost of $376,000) (Hershow, 1982). This firm advocates a noncompromising approach to labor negotiations, and is known in labor circles as a "union buster" (AFL-CIO, 1981, 1983). Second, in March 1981 Reagan appointed J. Lynn Helms to head the FAA. While president of Piper Aircraft, Helms had developed a firm anti-union reputation (Reinhold, 1981, p. B9; Carley, 1981, p. 22).

Finally, the six-week hiatus between the tentative contract agreement and the strike was used by the FAA to secretly revise and strengthen a strike contingency plan originally prepared and published under the Carter administration. Had the strike occurred on June 23, the Carter plan (with minor changes published early in the Reagan administration) would have been used. The revised plan implemented on August 3 was considerably less restrictive than the original. It permitted the airlines, in the event of a strike, to schedule more than twice as many flights as the Carter plan would have permitted. It also allowed the airlines to decide which flights should be canceled (FAA, 1981; Meadows, 1981; Richardson, 1981). The revised plan was endorsed in advance of the strike by the major airlines and the Air Transport Association (Richardson, 1980), but it was not divulged to PATCO officials (Young, 1981). PATCO struck without knowing that the strike plan had been greatly changed. In an interview after the strike, PATCO's chief negotiator stated that prior knowledge of the revised plan would have given union negotiators pause and forced them to reevaluate their belief that a strike would virtually paralyze the system (Reardon, 1981).

The ultimate step in Reagan's hard-line strategy was his decision to fire all striking air traffic controllers who did not return to their jobs within forty-eight hours of his back-to-work ultimatum. Given the hostility felt by the striking controllers, and the union's lack of knowledge of the revisions in the FAA's strike contingency plan, it is not surprising that most PATCO members ignored the back-to-work ultimatum. Although Northrup's praise of this "determination to break with the past and to enforce the law" (Northrup, 1984, p. 184) may seem reasonable to some observers, we side with the labor relations experts who argue that less severe alternatives should have been pursued. John Dunlop accurately summarized this position in the week following the walkout: "The administration has decided . . . to leave no avenue of escape for the union. You just don't do that . . . [Such an approach] is quite unusual, even going back to the turn of the century" (Taylor, 1981, p. A1).

The Reagan administration's tactics were clearly legal and perfectly acceptable if the goal was to severely weaken or eliminate PATCO. Our disagreement with Northrup on this point is essentially a difference of opinion. As an alternative to firing the controllers, Dunlop suggested that some type of mediation could have been pursued beyond the prestrike mediation by the FMCS. "What is absolutely without precedent, at least in modern times, is that [the Reagan administration] has brought in no outside, dispassionate group to look at the problem. That ain't right" (Taylor, 1981, p. A1).

Dunlop's position is similar to that taken by W.J. Usery, Jr., a former secretary of labor. Two weeks after the strike began, Usery publicly suggested that a panel of three former labor secretaries be assembled to mediate a settlement (Eaton and Cimons, 1981, pp. 1, 14; *Los Angeles Times,* 1981). The Reagan administration, however, rejected all recommendations to seek mediation and remained firm in its firing decision. We believe that the collective bargaining environment in the United States was harmed by this hard-line attitude, which encouraged antiunion managers in the public and private sectors to follow the president's example.

Conclusion

A complex set of circumstances contributed to PATCO's ultimate decision to strike. Despite advice from independent task forces to revise management practices, the FAA persisted in its autocratic treatment of controllers. In response, PATCO became increasingly militant, and by 1981 the internal activities of the union were narrowly focused on strike preparation. The hard line taken by the Reagan administration legitimized the stubbornness of FAA management and presented the challenge PATCO militants had been anticipating. With this combination of factors, the strike was virtually inevitable.

A different conclusion could have been reached. Had FAA management been more responsive to the concerns of its employees, the situation would not have deteriorated as it did and PATCO would not have been able to adopt so militant a posture. The strike could also have been averted had the Reagan administration addressed the concerns of the controllers by seriously negotiating over the issues of retirement and hours of work. On the other hand, PATCO might have emerged from the negotiations victorious, or at least survived the strike, with a better strategy. Although the union's internal organizing efforts were extensive and effective, its external relations were largely ignored: coordination with other unions was not pursued, public relations were poor, and political activities were misguided.

Northrup's analysis closely resembles the myopic assessment of the strike offered by career FAA managers. As such, it misses the flaws in management and the internal dynamics of PATCO. We believe that the information we have presented fills in the gaps in his analysis and completes the picture of this complex, precedent-setting confrontation.

Notes

1. Predictably, however, the problems did not go away. The Jones task force conducted a follow-up study in 1984, and concluded that the FAA had not heeded the commission's earlier advice to institute humane labor management techniques. Instead, the FAA has developed a human relations program "viewed [by the controllers] as inconsequential, as largely slogans and superficial window dressing" (Feaver, 1984).

2. Given his reliance on anonymous FAA sources for much of his information, it is not clear how Northrup developed his version of the internal dynamics of PATCO. We base most of this section and our prior discussion of the PATCO bargaining objectives on interviews with PATCO officials, some conducted in 1981 and 1982 as part of a prior research project and the remainder conducted in 1985 as we prepared this piece.

References

American Federation of Labor–Congress of Industrial Organizations. 1981. "Red Cross—Union Buster (?)." *Report on Union Busters,* no. 28 (September), pp. 1–2.

———. 1983 "Strike 'Security'—Goon Squads Are Busting out All Over." *Report on Union Busters,* no. 39 (August), p. 5.

Bowers, David G. 1983. "What Would Make 11,500 People Quit Their Jobs?" *Organizational Dynamics* 11, no. 3 (Winter), pp. 5–19.

Bureau of National Affairs. 1980. *Government Employee Relations Report,* October 6, no. 882, p. 11. Washington, D.C.: BNA.

Business Week. 1981. "Air-Traffic Controllers Set a Walkout Date." August 3, pp. 25–26.

Carley, William M. 1981. "Rough Flying—Air Traffic Controllers Put Reagan on the Spot with Threat to Strike." *Wall Street Journal,* June 17, pp. 1, 22.

Corson, John J. (chairman, Air Traffic Controller Career Committee). 1970. *The Career of the Air Traffic Controller—A Course of Action.* Washington, D.C.: Department of Transportation, Federal Aviation Administration.

Eaton, William J., and Marlene Cimons. 1981. "Controller Mediation Proposed." *Los Angeles Times,* August 19, pp. 1, 14.

Feaver, Douglas B. 1984. "Controllers Report Overwork." *Washington Post,* December 15, p. A1.

Federal Aviation Administration. 1981. *National Air Traffic Control Contingency Plan.* Washington, D.C.: Federal Aviation Administration, February 27.

Hershow, Sheila. 1982. "Law Firm Helped DOT Control Air Strikers," *Federal Times,* August 30, p. 5.

Hurd, Richard W. 1981. "How PATCO Was Led into a Trap." *Nation,* December, 26, pp. 696–698.

Jones, Lawrence M., David G. Bowers, and Stephen H. Fuller. 1982. *Management and Employee Relationships Within the Federal Aviation Administration.* Washington, D.C.: Federal Aviation Administration.

Leyden, John. 1982. Personal interview, Washington, D.C., June 24.

Los Angeles Times. 1981. "Usery Denies Mediation Report, Was Speaking 'Hypothetically,'" *Los Angeles Times,* August 20, p. 14.

Maher, Jack (PATCO '81 Committee member). 1984. Personal letter, October 27.

———. 1985. Telephone interviews, June 12, 14.

Meadows, Edward. 1981. "The FAA Keeps Them Flying." *Fortune,* December 28, pp. 48–52.

Northrup, Herbert R. 1984. "The Rise and Demise of PATCO." *Industrial and Labor Relations Review* 37, no. 2 (January), pp. 167–184.

Poli, Robert E. 1980. *PATCO Educational Package.* Washington, D.C.: Professional Air Traffic Controllers Organization, April 15.

———. 1985. Telephone interview, November 19.

Poole, Robert. 1981. "Maybe It's Time to Dismiss the FAA." *New York Times,* August 16, p. E19.

Reardon, Dennis (1981 PATCO bargaining committee chairman). 1981. Telephone interview, September 28.

———. 1985. Telephone interview, November 18.

Reinhold, Robert. 1981. "Enigmatic FAA Chief." *New York Times,* August 11, p. B9.

Richardson, John (1981 data control officer, FAA). 1981. Telephone interview, September 18.

Rose, Robert M., C. David Jenkins, and Michael W. Hurst. 1978. *Air Traffic Controller Health Change Study.* Washington, D.C.: Department of Transportation, Federal Aviation Administration.

Shostak, Arthur, and David Skocik. 1986. *The Air Controllers Controversy: Lessons from the PATCO Strike.* New York: Human Sciences Press.

Spector, Bert A., and Michael Beer. 1982. "Air Traffic Controllers." Harvard Business School, case study 9-482-056. Boston: President and Fellows of Harvard College.

Taylor, Benjamin. 1981. "Labor Meets a Tough Presidential Foe." *Boston Globe,* August 9.

Taylor, Bill (Former PATCO choir boy; current director, PATCO Lives). 1985. Telephone interviews, April 3, June 6, 7, 10.

Torchia, Dominic (PATCO western regional vice-president). 1985. Telephone interviews, October 18, 31.

Trick, Dave (1981 PATCO Bargaining Committee member). 1985. Telephone interview, June 13.

United Press International. 1981. "Controllers Seek to Form Private Company." *Manchester Union Leader,* July 13, pp. 1, 16.

U.S., House of Representatives. 1981a. *House Bill 1576.* 97th Cong., 1st sess., February 3.

———. 1981b. *House Bill 4332.* 97th Cong., 1st sess., July 30.

Vacca, James (1981 Boston Center choir boy). 1982. Telephone interview, March 20.

Witkin, Richard. 1982. "U.S. Agency's Handling of Controllers Criticized." *New York Times,* March 18, p. A18.

Young, Ted (FAA, Air Traffic Control Operations Division). 1981. Telephone interview, September 15.

Reply

Herbert R. Northrup

The thesis of my article, "The Rise and Demise of PATCO,"[1] was clearly stated in the first paragraph:

> The strike was the inevitable result of PATCO's long-term drive to "privatize" its relations with the Federal Aviation Administration (FAA), its public sector employer; of the weak response thereto by the federal government until the later years of the Carter administration; and of the failure of PATCO's new leadership to understand the greatly altered political and economic environment of 1981.[2]

As a basis for this thesis, the article recounted not only the strike's development, action, and results, but also the PATCO–FAA bargaining history and "PATCO policies that were designed to develop a special framework for its bargaining."[3]

Two criticisms have been raised about my history and analysis, mostly by PATCO partisans, particularly the former organization's consultant, Arthur Shostak,[4] but also by David Bowers and others involved in the so-called Jones Report.[5] Basically, the first group questions my sources, denies that PATCO was really in the wrong, and even claims that the strike was actually won by PATCO because it led to some "reform" of FAA policy. The second emphasizes the alleged "hard line" of FAA managers and blames the strike on the failure of FAA staff to handle people properly.

Hurd and Kriesky (H-K) attempt to merge the two points of view to attack my article. Unfortunately, a combination of failure to research adequately, partisan information, and what appears to be naiveté about the dynamics of labor relations nullifies their efforts. For readers' convenience, I shall analyze their arguments in the order in which they presented them.

Bargaining Objectives

H-K attempt to refute my contention that the Poli leadership of PATCO induced the strike as a means of gaining their objective of negotiating wages and benefits and of eventually winning the right to strike. To make this attempt, H-K attack my sources by misrepresenting them. In fact, as I pointed out, the PATCO leadership followed a prearranged script to the letter, which provided for pushing hard, accepting a contract, repudiating it, and striking, with the aim of shutting down the commercial air transport system and inducing Congress to grant PATCO what it desired—the right to bargain on wages outside the civil service system and even the right to strike. Indeed, Poli and his group showed a basic weakness by being inflexible at a time when conditions had changed and they had already won many of their demands.

The prearranged script, the existence of which H-K attempt to refute, was widely distributed to the membership in various forms, and thoroughly via the "cluster organizations" (regional union groupings). I cited the Sacramento cluster minutes as illustrative, certainly not as the sole source. (The O'Hare version of the script is cited in my note 53.) I also used a number of recordings in which PATCO adherents were taped utilizing (illegally) FAA facilities to propagandize their plans. I provided H-K with a copy of one, also as an example, and suggested that they contact the FAA for the several others that I had borrowed and returned, but I find no evidence that they did so.

H-K also give no indication that they examined the myriad of court decisions and briefs I cited, or the depositions of Poli, Meyer, and Trick, the three top PATCO officials, taken a few days after the strike began, which I also cited. And, of course, they largely ignore the implications of the several pre-1981 illegal strikes, all described in the article, in which PATCO often won concessions and in which the federal government failed to enforce the law, thus emboldening the PATCO leadership and assuring its rank and file that strikes would bring rewards; nor do they emphasize sufficiently the implications of the numerous workshops, seminars, and other meetings held around the country by PATCO officials and staff that were designed to prepare the membership for "the definitive strike."

H-K cite a survey in which Shostak, acting as PATCO consultant, found that the rank-and-file controllers had some real issues and grievances. It would be surprising if they did not have any real issues and grievances; the question is whether those they had were strike issues. The claim that the real issues and the rationale for a strike were demands in particular for a shorter workweek and an improved retirement system falls flat given the fact, clearly stated in my article, that the government proposals substantially met the workweek demand and also included an 11 percent salary increase, as compared with 4.4 percent for other federal employees, and many other generous terms. As I noted, if this offer had been accepted, "PATCO would, in effect, have negotiated wages and major working conditions—subjects presumably reserved to Congress."[6]

H-K attempt to refute this interpretation by interviews with former PATCO officials whose reported statements are at variance with their pre-strike ones and with their published plans. Nor can H-K justify Poli's substantial increase of PATCO's wage demands after the agreement that he

negotiated was rejected unanimously by the executive board that he dominated and then by the membership via a tainted ballot that each controller
voting was required to sign.[7] The fact that PATCO agreed that Representative Clay change his proposed law, which would have given PATCO its
goals but which had little chance of passage, does not in any way weaken my
analysis. The objectives were to be won by an illegal strike, and the bill could
then have been altered accordingly to ratify the event. The typographical
error that substituted "Poli" for "Poole" as the author of a *New York Times*
comment was a last-minute insertion that is, of course, regrettable, but insignificant. It is the only actual error H-K found in the article, and was an
unnecessary addition to an otherwise more than adequate series of citations.

My analysis of PATCO's bargaining objectives is emphatically seconded
by Kenneth E. Moffett, who in 1981 was Director of the Federal Mediation
and Conciliation Service (FMCS). I asked Moffett to read my article and the
Hurd-Kriesky comment and to give me his reaction. In reply, he first noted
that he mediated the original PATCO dispute in 1980, and then stated:

> From that time on, I was intimately involved with PATCO, attended
> most of their annual conventions as a speaker, whether it was in Honolulu,
> San Diego or wherever. From 1970 to PATCO's decertification, I partici-
> pated in all of their subsequent negotiations with the FAA (DOT).
>
> After having lived and worked through the entire PATCO debacle, I
> have to agree with you that the ultimate plan of PATCO was to become
> separated out from under the Civil Service Reform Act, similar to the U.S.
> Postal workers, but their nirvana would have been to become a private sector
> organization with all airport facilities and their employees falling under the
> Taft-Hartley Act, as amended.
>
> I base these conclusions on the many conversations and dealings I have
> had through the years with both PATCO members, their officers, FAA
> management, DOT management and attorneys employed by both parties.
>
> No matter what anyone is quoted as having said regarding PATCO's
> goals, or what has been printed, there has never been any doubt in my mind
> that PATCO's ultimate desire was to get out from under the system that they
> all detested. Namely, the present Civil Service Reform Act.[8]

Role of FAA Management

H-K cite various reports, all referred to in my article, in an attempt to show
that FAA hard-line management and job stress were basic causes of the strike.
Controller job stress was emphasized for many years and led to a special
program that resulted in substantial abuse and was eliminated by Congress
before the Reagan presidency. Purported stress was also, as I noted, utilized
by PATCO as an effective bargaining tool.[9]

The hard-line FAA management charge was noted in my article, but was hardly a reason for the strike. One looks in vain for evidence that it was a matter of discussion during the negotiations. Moffett, who participated directly in the negotiations, has advised me that no such issue surfaced.[10]

Actually, there was a great deal of frustration on both sides, and I believe that Bowers and his colleagues of the Jones Report did not adequately comprehend its nature. I pointed out that the PATCO leadership's frustration over the limitations of bargaining in the federal service was of major importance.[11] It is frustrating, indeed, for a union leader to have to find trivialities to talk about in order to serve the membership because he has no control over wages, fringes, and many basic conditions that are pertinent to the employment relationship. The lack of advancement opportunities for most controllers is also understandably frustrating, even if their work is well paid. By the same token, however, administrators who have to try both to handle people and to uphold the law must suffer considerable frustration when their efforts are completely undercut by politicians—which is precisely what occurred all during the Nixon and Ford administrations and at least halfway through the Carter administration. H-K studiously ignore a basic problem that I stressed—namely, that PATCO had been rewarded in the past for transgressing the law, making it natural for many members as well as leaders to think that illegal means were the way to get things done also under the Reagan admininstration, despite other evidence to the contrary.

Internal Dynamics of PATCO

H-K also rewrite history in discussing PATCO's strike preparation and the relationship between the leadership and the rank and file. In fact, the rank-and-file members were promised payments equal to their salaries for an indefinite period if they struck and were disciplined. Large sums were taken from banks and given to their lawyers, and the rank and file were not only briefed but "educated" on the strike plans.[12] Speaking to his National Executive Council on December 11, 1980, Kenneth T. Blaylock, president of the American Federation of Government Employees, stated:

> The Public Employee Department just had their planning conference for next year and I got a chance to talk to Bob Poley [sic] who is president of PATCO. They presently have a team of, I think, three of their people in their headquarters office, and they are using organizers in the field. They are now conducting a series of these types of seminars and workshops around the country; a very detailed planned program, because they are looking very much for the possibility of a strike around their negotiations that are coming up sometime in the summer.
>
> In order to prepare their locals and their organizations to make sure what they did was effective, they developed a very planned program. I have

asked Bob if he would be willing to sit down with a couple of our people and give us the benefit of what they're doing and he indicated he would be glad to.[13]

Despite the strike preparations of the leadership, H-K see the strike as a determined rank and file running away from their leaders. If this strike was, as they allege, a "runaway ship" resulting from "disproportionate democracy," why did the PATCO leadership have to send out a ballot to which employees were required to sign their names? And why were they unable to produce in depositions of the district court any evidence that a reasonably accurate strike ballot had occurred before the final walkout, or even what were the results of the vote, if any, for the final strike?[14] And most important, if the rank and file were so anxious for a showdown, why did 30 percent brave the torment and the choir boy enforcers to cross the picket line?[15]

The Reagan Response

All the materials H-K used to criticize my article are very weak, but weakest of all is their support of the view that the Reagan administration was out to destroy PATCO. In fact, PATCO was offered the most generous contract in the public service, and one that could really have made it very difficult to hold the wage line in that service. PATCO was also offered bargaining beyond which no government agency had ever gone, and a deal that, had it been accepted, could have put the union close to its long-term goals.

The claim that the FAA secretly planned its strategy to operate during the strike is complete nonsense. The contingency plan was written and published in the *Federal Register* in early 1980 during the Carter administration. It was revised under the Reagan administration, and the revisions appeared in the *Federal Register* in March 1981. Final revisions were made before the strike and published in August 1981 the day after the strike began, but both revisions in 1981 were primarily concerned with the mechanics of operating during a strike, and the last made no change in the philosophy that an attempt would be made to operate during any strike.[16] In addition to the obvious fact that management is not obligated to advise unions about its strategy in the event of a strike, or vice versa, PATCO officials were told publicly and privately by the president and several cabinet members that, as I wrote, "there would be no amnesty for strikers and no talks with PATCO during a strike";[17] the secretary of defense stated prior to the strike that he was willing to provide 600–700 Army controllers if a strike occurred; and 55 senators and 19 members of Congress signed a letter warning PATCO that "any illegal action by PATCO and its members will be viewed with extreme disfavor in the Congress."[18] H-K quote with apparent belief an ex-PATCO official's statement that PATCO might have not called a strike if they had been warned about the government's "secret plan"! What surprised the PATCO leadership was not the government's response, but how swiftly it worked, and how ineffective the strike was.

The Reagan administration's response was dictated not only by PATCO's intransigence, but also by some basic economic and policy considerations. After the carefully rehearsed rejection of the generous agreement negotiated in good faith by Drew Lewis, Poli immediately raised the PATCO demands to an amount that the FAA calculated would add $38,914 per controller per annum. It was obvious to the Reagan administration that it could not accede to such demands if inflation was to be brought under control. PATCO wage increases might be justified up to a point as a special case, but the increases demanded would have seriously hurt the government's effort to rein in employee wage increases as part of the anti-inflation campaign. Moreover, lurking in the background were the postal unions, which were talking strike under a new, aggressive leadership who, as local officials, had precipitated walkouts during the Nixon administration without serious governmental penalty. If PATCO had succeeded in its aims, strikes probably would have been de facto tolerated in the federal service, just as public sector strikes are both illegal and common in many states.

H-K cite John Dunlop and W.J. Usery to the effect that the dispute could have been settled through mediation. My article noted that Ronald Haughton, then chairman of the Federal Labor Relations Authority, who initially opposed sanctions against PATCO for its illegal strike, suggested that mediation and, if necessary, compulsory arbitration should be invoked pursuant to the Federal Services Impasses Panel.[19] Such an approach, however, ignores the inflexibility of the PATCO leadership and their determination to stay with their planned illegal strike. They rejected Haughton's "no sanctions if you abandon the strike" proposal. Moffett noted that PATCO had refused to postpone the strike deadline in order to continue negotiations and mediation, first as requested by Drew Lewis, then by himself, and finally by Tip O'Neill, speaker of the House of Representatives. Given this intransigence, Moffett believed that mediation was not a practical alternative.[20] Moreover, as I concluded, "if the strike had ended without severe penalties, including discharges, fines, and decertification, the PATCO leadership, having come so close to achieving unrestrained wage bargaining and the de facto right to strike, would again have created a crisis to gain their goals."[21]

Conclusion

The record, as described in my article, remains fully accurate. Attempts to rewrite history by telephone interviews with the ex-PATCO leadership, or by claiming that a carefully planned strike in which 30 percent broke ranks was a rank and file uprising, or by claiming that, somehow, I followed the line of career FAA managers, whoever they may be, are certain to lack credence. The record of the PATCO strike is available in a myriad of court decisions, briefs, depositions, and other legal records, and in hundreds of newspaper and magazine articles, union and FAA publications, and interviews with interested and pertinent parties. It requires much time and effort to put together. It is, however, a case of great significance and worth the effort. I would enjoy discussing it with anyone who researches it as deeply as it deserves, regardless of the conclusions reached.

Notes

1. *Industrial and Labor Relations Review* 37, no. 2 (January 1984), pp. 167–184 (hereafter cited as "PATCO article").

2. Ibid., p. 167.

3. Ibid.

4. See Arthur Shostak and Dave Skocik, *The Air Controllers' Controversy: Lessons from the 1981 PATCO Strike* (New York: Human Sciences Press, 1986); and Shostak, "Second Thoughts on the PATCO Strike," *Social Policy* 16, no. 3 (Winter 1986), pp. 22–28.

5. Bowers was a member of the so-called Jones Group, which issued a report in 1982 criticizing the handling of people by FAA administrators (cited in PATCO article, p. 168, note 4). Bowers summarized his views in "What Would Make 11,500 People Quit Their Jobs?" *Organizational Dynamics* 11 (Winter 1983), pp. 5–19. This early article represents the basis for this line of criticism as cited by H-K.

6. PATCO article, p. 176.

7. Ibid., p. 177.

8. Letter to author, May 16, 1986. Mr. Moffett is currently assistant to the president, National Association of Broadcast Employees and Technicians.

9. PATCO article, pp. 171–172, and the Staten-Umbeck article in the December 1982 *American Economic Review,* cited in note 27, p. 172. In a letter to me dated May 15, 1986, Barton Pakull, M.D., Chief of Psychiatry, Office of Aviation Medicine, states:

> In dealing with the air traffic controller "stress problem" over the past 16 years, I have personally experienced what you allude to (and is not well known to the general public) as an important factor in the emerging strategy of the air traffic controllers. That is, the spurious "stress issue." Stress was used as a justification for increased pay and benefits for air traffic controllers. For this reason, individual medical stress claims which were quite unjustified were aggressively supported by the union. All of this led to chaotic management interactions and staffing problems. We have never encountered any true stress problem in the Federal Aviation Administration and yet most lay and semi-professional articles about the matter point to the air traffic controllers as an example of the existence of stress in the workforce. Although there never was a medical stress problem, this entity has (for other political reasons) escaped into industry and public service sectors in general, and now festers as a drag on productivity.

10. Mr. Moffett and I discussed the situation in some detail in Bryn Mawr, Pennsylvania, April 3, 1986, where we both were attending a meeting.

11. PATCO article, pp. 182–183.

12. Poli, Meyer, and Trick admitted all these matters in the depositions frequently cited in the article.

13. Original Transcript of Proceedings, American Federation of Government Employees, Meeting of the National Executive Council, December 11, 1980, pp. 574–575.

14. PATCO article, p. 177.

15. Of the 16,395 controllers then on the FAA payroll, 11,301 remained away from their jobs, but about 20 were on sick or vacation leave and later returned; 4,199 stayed on the job from the inception of the strike; and 875 returned to work before the president's forty-eight-hour deadline expired. The fact that so many returned would seem to refute Meyer's claim that 82 percent voted for the strike. I have observed that when an employer attempts to operate during a strike and 25–30 percent of the bargaining unit crosses the picket line at the strike's inception, the union will lose the strike unless some dramatic counterevent occurs.

16. See PATCO article, p. 174, including note 39.

17. PATCO article, p. 177, including note 57, which references the very informative Witkin article in the *New York Times,* August 3, 1981.

18. PATCO article, p. 177.

19. Ibid.

20. Moffett interview, supra, note 10.

21. PATCO article, p. 184.

Dualism in Public Sector Bargaining Relationships

Perhaps the best test of the potential for integrative bargaining in the public sector is offered by an analysis of a single public service that examines labor and management responses to changes in a fundamental environmental variable. Such a test can be said to be provided by Lewin in the final reading included in this chapter.

Lewin analyzes the effects of technological change in municipal sanitation service during the late 1970s and early 1980s. His empirical work shows that technological change was instrumental to the reconfiguration of sanitation work forces. In a nutshell, sanitation *technology* came to be substituted for sanitation *labor*. Given the high incidence of unionization in public sanitation service, however, many of the consequences of technological change had to be negotiated between public employers and public union officials.

Lewin's research indicates that two fundamental patterns of union–management response to technological change in public sanitation service have prevailed in recent years. In one set of negotiations, the parties dealt adversarily with technological change, so that strikes, work slowdowns, picketing, boycotts, employee discharges, disciplinary actions, and subcontracting occurred. In contrast, another set of sanitation labor negotiations resulted in the formation of joint labor–management committees to deal with job redesign, payment methods, and monitoring of responses to technological change; the establishment of formal training and development programs for employees and managers of public sanitation service; and new initiatives to enhance the productivity of sanitation service.

Lewin's research is less successful in isolating the variables that determine whether parties to public sector labor relations follow an integrative as opposed to a distributive bargaining approach.[1] Yet, the same can be said of research into contemporary private sector labor relations. That is, industrial relations researchers have not been particularly adept at explaining why cooperative labor relations occur in some settings and adversarial labor relations occur in other settings. Lacking an overriding explanatory framework or schema in this regard, we may nevertheless conclude that public sector labor relations in the 1980s are characterized by a pronounced dualism, featuring cooperation on the one hand and conflict on the other. Which, if either, of these predominant modes of labor relations will prevail in the future is probably a judgment that the reader is as well equipped to reach as the authors of this book.

Note

1. For a subsequent attempt to identify such determinants, see David Lewin, "Cooperative and Adversarial Bargaining Responses to Technological Change in the Public Sector: An Analysis of Determinants," Working Paper, Graduate School of Business, Columbia University, 1987.

Technological Change in the Public Sector: The Case of Sanitation Service
*David Lewin**

How does technological change affect the social organization of the workplace and, in particular, labor–management relations? This question is now being widely addressed by researchers, who are studying a variety of workplace contexts.[1] Most of this research deals with the private sector of the U.S.

*Reprinted from Daniel B. Cornfield, ed., *Workers, Managers, and Technological Change*. New York: Plenum, 1987, pp. 281–309.

economy; however, the same question may be posed about the public sector generally and specific services within it.

This reading examines recent technological changes in local sanitation service and their effects on the process and outcomes of labor–management relations. The reading begins with a description of the organizational, employment, and labor relations characteristics of local sanitation departments in U.S. cities. Then a conceptual model of the public sector labor relations process is presented together with a discussion of technological change as one of the variables operating within this model. Next, several quantitative assessments of the effects of technological change on sanitation employment and unionization are offered. This is followed by a combined quantitative and qualitative examination of the effects of technological change on labor relations in municipal sanitation departments. Finally, the analysis and findings about sanitation service are assessed in terms of their larger significance for technological change and labor relations in the public and private sectors.

Characteristics of Sanitation Service

Sanitation service is popularly thought to be provided to service recipients by municipal governments, but most cities have two or more types of service providers. Moreover, the mix and proportional distribution of service providers vary by category of service recipients.[2] Municipal governments provide the bulk of sanitation service for streets and other open or public spaces, while private firms provide the largest share of sanitation service to institutional, commercial, and industrial recipients. In the case of residential recipients, the distribution of service providers varies by detailed category of recipient, but clearly municipalities, private firms, and self-service all have important places in this "market." Note that the use of special districts or authorities to provide sanitation service is substantial in the cases of streets, parks, and litter baskets and, to a lesser extent, for institutional recipients.

On average, there were 46 full-time paid personnel per municipal sanitation department in the United States in 1983, or 0.70 per 1,000 population.[3] More notable, however, are recent changes in municipal sanitation employment.[4] Between 1975 and 1983, proportional sanitation employment in U.S. cities declined by fully half, from 1.41 to 0.70 full-time paid employees per 1,000 population. This way, by far, the sharpest proportional decline among the three major categories of uniformed service personnel— police, firefighters and sanitation workers—employed by municipal governments.

Data concerning the unionization of publicly-employed sanitation personnel are given in table 1. In 1980, approximately 40 percent of all full-time

Table 1
Sanitation Employment, Unionization, Bargaining Units, and Representation, 1980

	Local Governments				
Labor Relations Characteristics	*Total*	*County*	*Municipal*	*Township*	*Special District*
Total full-time employment	119,274	10,802	102,746	5,322	404
Full-time employees who belong to a labor organization	47,981	1,612	43,003	3,271	95
Percentage of full-time employees who belong to a labor organization	40.2	14.9	41.9	61.5	23.5
Number of bargaining units	475	NAª	NA	NA	NA
Number of employees represented	31,492	NA	NA	NA	NA
Number represented as a proportion of employees belonging to labor organizations (%)	65.5	NA	NA	NA	NA

Source: U.S. Bureau of the Census, *Labor–Management Relations in State and Local Governments: 1980,* State and Local Government Special Studies No. 102. Washington, D.C.: U.S. Government Printing Office, 1981, pp. 7 and 155.

sanitation employees of local governments belonged to labor organizations (unions and associations). However, less than two-thirds of all organized sanitation employees are actually represented by their labor organizations for purposes of collective bargaining. The difference between organization and representation reflects (1) the failure of certain labor organizations to attain the status of certified bargaining agents in local governments, (2) the prevalence of public sector bargaining laws in certain states that do not require or otherwise provide for the certification of bargaining agents, and (3) the failure of some labor organizations to negotiate first or successor contracts with local government employers. Despite these factors, the difference between sanitation employee membership in labor organizations and employee representation in collective bargaining declined by more than nine percentage points between 1972 and 1980.[5]

How has sanitation employee membership in labor organization changed over time, and how does it compare with the incidence of labor organization in local government generally? Figure 1 contains data relevant to these questions. In essence, unionization among full-time sanitation employees declined by 10 percent between 1972 and 1980, compared to a 1.5 percent decline

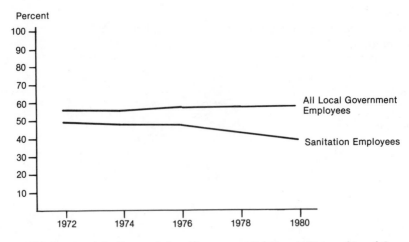

Source: U.S. Bureau of the Census, *Labor–Management Relations in State and Local Govern-ments: 1974, 1976, 1978 and 1980,* State and Local Government Special Studies, nos. 75, 88, 95 and 102 (Washington, D.C.: U.S. Government Printing Office, 1976, 1978, 1980, and 1981), various pages.
Note: Data are for paid full-time personnel.

Figure 1. Local Government and Sanitation Employee Unionization Rates, 1972–1980

among full-time local government employees as a whole. For both sanitation employees and local government employees, almost all of the decline in the incidence of unionism took place between 1976 and 1980. Moreover, compared with other specific local government services, the incidence of unionism among sanitation employees is relatively low, as the following data (percentage of full-time employees who belong to a labor organization) indicate:[6]

Education	61.3%
Instructional staff	67.9
Other	44.4
Highways	37.6
Public welfare	42.4
Hospitals	29.4
Police protection	52.8
Local fire protection	70.6
Sanitation (other than sewage)	40.2
All other	38.3

Particularly notable is the considerably higher incidence of unionism among police and firefighters than among sanitation personnel; these three employee groups are often lumped under the heading of "uniformed services." Additionally, the (proportional) decline in the unionization of sanitation employees between 1972 and 1980 was larger, by far, than for any other functional employee group listed above.

Conceptualizing Technological Change and Public Sector Labor Relations

What factors can explain the recent decline of employment *and* unionism in public sanitation service in the United States? In particular, what role does technological change play in these respects? In considering these questions, we must first recognize the significant advances that have been made in the modeling and empirical study of public sector labor relations. Drawing on this research, figure 2 presents a model of the public sector labor relations process. While, as shown, the model assumes that public employees are organized (into unions and associations) and negotiate written agreements with public employers concerning terms and conditions of employment, it can easily be generalized to include unorganized employees and management-determined terms and conditions of employment.

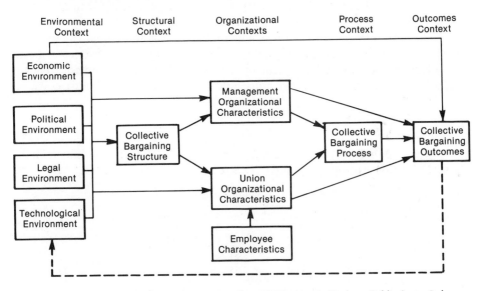

Source: Adapted from David Lewin, Peter Feuille, and Thomas A. Kochan, *Public Sector Labor Relations: Analysis and Readings,* 2nd ed. (Sun Lakes, Ariz.: Thomas Horton and Daughters, 1981), p. 3.

Figure 2. A Model of the Public Sector Labor Relations Process

The "economic context" is especially important to the analysis of public sector sanitation service employment and unionism. First, the mid-1970s marked the end of a quarter-century in which local government was the fastest growing "industry" in the United States. Public and managerial attention began to focus heavily on the costs of government services and the potential for improving governmental efficiency and productivity.[7] Previously, attention had been directed primarily toward expanding the role of government services in the economy, and local (as well as state and some federal) taxes were raised to finance these services. By the late 1970s and early 1980s, citizen tax revolts became prominent, if not commonplace.[8]

Second, and specific to sanitation service, evidence began to be produced in the mid-1970s that showed publicly provided sanitation service to be significantly more costly than privately provided sanitation service. For example, a 1975 study of 315 municipalities found that "the average city with a population of more than 50,000 [which was] served by a municipal [sanitation] agency had costs which are [sic] from 29 to 35 percent more than the costs of an average city of the same size served by a private [sanitation] firm with an exclusive territory."[9] In the same study, similar, if smaller, cost differentials between privately and publicly provided sanitation service were found to exist in smaller cities.

Third, and in light of the two aforementioned points, government officials and managers undertook initiatives to reduce the cost and improve the productivity of sanitation service. One initiative was to expand the use of private sanitation service, typically on an exclusive franchise (contract) basis.[10] The data in table 2 provide one rationale for this behavior. They show that the average cost per household for weekly curbside refuse collec-

Table 2

Average Annual Cost per Household for Once-a-Week Curbside Collection, by Collection Arrangement and City Size

	When Population Held Constant at				
Collection Arrangement	*3,000*	*15,000*	*30,000*	*60,000*	*90,000*
Contract	$23.25	$17.77	$17.30	$18.40[a]	18.26[a]
Municipal	25.51	19.51	19.95	23.77[b]	23.59[b]
Private	29.49[b]	22.55[b]	25.10[b]	24.10[b]	23.92[b]

Source: Barbara J. Stevens and E.S. Savas, "The Cost of Residential Refuse Collection and the Effect on Service Arrangement," in *The Municipal Yearbook—1977.* Washington, D.C.: International City Management Association, 1977, p. 204.

Note: Annual cost was estimated holding wage rate, refuse per household, density, service level, and temperature variation constant.

[a]Significantly different from the cost of municipal collection at $p = < .05$.
[b]Significantly different from the cost of contract collection at $p = < .05$.

Table 3

Management Practices in Sanitation Service, by Collection Arrangement and City Size

Management Practice	Population				Cities Having Backyard Collection Location	
	50,000 and Under		Over 50,000			
	Municipal	Contract	Municipal	Contract	Municipal	Contract
Mean crew size	3.08	2.06	3.26	2.15	3.04	1.98
Mean truck capacity (cubic yards)	19.04	22.21	20.63	27.14	19.90	23.50
Mean absentee rate	12%	6%	12%	6.5%	12%	4%
Mean percentage of vehicles loading at front and side	26%[a]	23%[a]	13%	44%	16%	30%
Mean percentage of cities with incentive system	57%	80%	80%[a]	86%	73%	87%[a]

Source: Barbara J. Stevens and E.S. Savas, "The Cost of Residential Refuse Collection and the Effect on Service Arrangement," in *The Municipal Yearbook—1977.* Washington, D.C.: International City Management Association, 1977, p. 204.

[a]No significant difference at $p = < .05$.

tion is consistently, and in some cases statistically significantly, lower under a contract arrangement than under municipal and private (competitive bidding) arrangements.

What accounts for these cost differences? Table 3, which compares municipal and contract collection arrangements, provides some clues. Private contractors use larger trucks and proportionately fewer rear-loading vehicles than municipal sanitation agencies. However, the most significant differences have to do with labor utilization. Private contractors employ smaller crews, have less absenteeism, and operate under incentive systems more frequently than municipal sanitation agencies, and the differences are statistically significant in most cases. Hence, operating costs appear to be significantly lower and productivity significantly higher in contract than in municipal sanitation collection arrangements.[11] This provides a clear incentive for financially strapped municipalities to adopt contracting arrangements, which is consistent with the observed proportional growth of private contracting and decline of municipality-provided sanitation service since the mid-1970s.

Another recent initiative undertaken by local government officials and managers has been to alter the technology of sanitation collection (and disposal). What are these changes? Probably the most important has been the introduction and expanded use of semiautomated and automated collection systems.[12] Whereas conventional refuse collection featured a rear-loading vehicle with a three-person crew, modern refuse collection features semiautomated and fully automated vehicles that load from the side or front and that operate with two- and sometimes one-person crews. Put differently, municipal refuse collection increasingly favors continuous process–type technology over batch-type technology. This means, in essence, that refuse is loaded onto a truck's waste bin by the truck's automated equipment rather than by manual labor. Recall that private sanitation collection differs from public sanitation collection primarily in terms of the types of vehicles used and in crew size. Within the public sector, municipal sanitation agencies appear to be adopting "privatelike" sanitation collection policies and practices.

Accompanying the use of semiautomated and fully automated refuse collection systems in some cities is the use of standardized carts, typically of 82–90 gallon capacity, which are issued to residents by the municipality. The carts provide a uniform size container that permits the use (and purchase by the municipality) of a single type of automated vehicle designed specifically to lift and unload the standardized container. A preceding—and, in some cases, accompanying—"technological" change was the conversion from metal cans to plastic bags for the containment of refuse. Such bags are lighter than cans, more easily (and economically) lifted, are disposable (whereas cans must be reused), and, most important, are relatively more consistent with automated technology. Note, further, that conversion from metal cans to plastic bags for residential *and* commercial refuse collection is associated with a significant reduction in sanitation worker injuries irrespective of whether a municipality adopts an automated refuse collection system.[13]

Just as a municipal refuse collection system incorporates managerial and worker behavior, it also encompasses consumer-resident behavior, and the introduction of automated equipment significantly affects consumer behavior. Specifically, automated refuse collection systems operate on the principle of curbside collection rather than backyard collection. Thus, in altering its refuse collection system to emphasize automated collection, a municipality must convince its residents to agree to curbside collection. Put differently, a municipality must get its citizens to agree to use their own labor, rather than municipal employees' labor, to haul refuse to the curb (and not leave it in the backyard).

While most municipalities that have adopted curbside collection have been able to convince residents of the net advantages of such an arrangement, the "convincing" comes at a cost (of advertising, promotion, trial periods, noncompliance, and so on) and reflects a new social organization with respect to a particular public service.[14] The extensive literature on resistance to change in the workplace[15] can be generalized to the consumption context, and this literature helps us understand why community residents do not necessarily or immediately give a favorable response to a major alteration in the arrangements for providing a traditional public service. Consumer behavior may arguably be considered a component of "technological" change in the provision of sanitation service, but it is unarguable that such behavior must be carefully considered in adopting—and can significantly affect the success of—new refuse collection arrangements.

In the same vein, many cities that have adopted automated refuse collection and curbside pickups have also altered—which is to say reduced—their collection schedules. Specifically, residential refuse collection has been reduced from twice a week to once a week in perhaps 30 percent of U.S. cities that feature automated refuse collection and curbside pickup.[16] As with curbside pickup itself, alteration of refuse collection schedules affects the social organization of the local community, requires an investment by the municipality to obtain customer-resident acceptance of the change, and must be taken into account in planning and implementing change if the putative net benefits of the change are, in fact, to be realized.

Numerous other changes in the technology of sanitation service have occurred in recent years and can be mentioned here only briefly. These include the use of trucks with longer life diesel-type engines, longer life radial tires for sanitation vehicles, and roll-off and tilt-type truck frame beds; more efficient and longer life trash compactors; computer-controlled refuse collection and compaction equipment; two-way truck radio systems for crew assignment and response to refuse collection "problem" situations; three-wheel scooters for certain types of lighter trash collection; and supercarts for high-density refuse generation and collection locations.

How have these and other changes in the technology of local government refuse collection affected sanitation employment and sanitation employee unionization? This question is addressed quantitatively in the next section.

Quantitative Analysis of Technological Change, Sanitation Employment, and Unionization

To examine the effects of technological change on employment and unionism in municipal sanitation service, we must first consider the determinants of technological change itself. The reason for this is that as with employment, unionism, pay, and bargaining outcomes, technological change may be endogenously determined, that is, determined within the system represented by local government. Previous research has shown that measures of unionism and union effects on wages and other terms and conditions of employment vary substantially when such phenomena are treated as endogenously rather than exogenously determined.[17]

To conduct this analysis, data were obtained on technological change in the municipal sanitation services of 147 cities. This "convenience sample" was drawn from published accounts of technological change that occurred in these cities between 1975 and 1983.[18] Hence, cities for which no technological changes were reported and cities that had no public sanitation service (between 1975 and 1983) are not included in the data base. Further, data on the independent variables included in the analysis, which are discussed below, are cross-sectional data where the point of observation is any single year between 1975 and 1983. The data tend to cluster around 1980, but the reader should be aware of the different points (years) of observation included in the analysis and of the need to pool the cross-sectional data over several years.

In order to subject the data to quantitative examination, a rating scale reflecting the extent and type of technological change was developed. The scale ranges between zero and 100 points, and weights a "major" technological change, such as adoption of fully automated equipment, more heavily than a "minor" technological change, such as conversion from cans to bags for refuse storage and pickup. Further, changes in consumer-resident behavior, such as acceptance of curbside rather than backyard collection and the instigation of reduced collection schedules, were included in the index of technological change.[19]

What factors determine technological change in municipal sanitation service? The following variables are included in the analysis.[20]

Es = The ratio of municipal sanitation employment to municipal population

Ps = The ratio of privately provided sanitation service to publicly provided sanitation service, measured by tons of refuse collected

Fs = The fiscal stress experienced by a municipality, measured by the difference between the actual and the legal maximum tax rate per $100 of assessed property value

A = Age of the municipal government, measured in years

R = Ratio of payroll costs to total costs of municipal sanitation service

U = Extent of unionization of municipal sanitation employees, measured by percentage organized

S = The log of the size of city, measured by population per square mile

L = Location of city, represented by a discrete variable where Northeast = 3, Midwest = 2, South = 1, and West = 0

G = Form of government, where council-manager = 1, all other forms = 0.

The estimating equation thus takes the following functional form:

$$TC_r = TC(Es, Ps, Fs, A, R, U, S, L, G, \text{ and } e) \qquad (1)$$

where TC_r = rate of technological change in local government sanitation service, measured by an index of technological change; e = an error term; and all other variables are as previously defined.[21]

Of the continuous variables included in the analysis, Es and R are expected to be positively related to TC_r. The rationale for these hypotheses is that the more labor intensive the sanitation service provided by the municipality, the greater the incentive to make technological changes in sanitation collection. The other continuous variables, $Ps, Fs, A, U,$ and S, appear at first glance to be indeterminate, a priori. For example, a city with a relatively high Ps might have less incentive to change the technology of municipal sanitation collection than a city with a relatively low Ps on the ground that, in the former, a substantial portion of the community receives relatively efficient (or relatively cheap) sanitation service. Alternatively, the presence of a relatively large (and more efficient) private sanitation sector may spur a city to adopt technological changes in order to improve municipally provided sanitation service and, hopefully, reduce the private sector–public sector efficiency (or cost) differential.

Fiscal stress (Fs) may, on the one hand, negatively affect technological change because financial resources are not available to fund such change. On the other hand, Fs may motivate city officials to improve service efficiency and/or reduce service cost, and thus lead to a positive effect on TC_r. The age of a municipality (A) may have negative or positive effects on TC_r, depending on whether it generates a preference for or dissatisfaction with the provision of public services in traditional, well-known ways.

Employee unionization (U) may have a negative effect on TC_r if, out of concern for possible threats to their livelihood, union members and officials oppose new technology and structure their bargaining agreements with local government employers accordingly. Alternatively and given that unionization brings about higher pay and benefits for public employees,[22] such higher costs may provide an incentive for government employers to invest in technological change. Moreover, most unions, whether in the public or the private sector, have sought to bargain over the effects of technological change, notably in the area of job security, rather than to oppose technological change per se.[23] City size (S) may be negatively related to TC_r if city officials judge the scope and diversity of residential housing and sanitation arrangements to mitigate effective implementation of technological change. However, S may be positively related to TC_r if it is perceived by city officials to provide returns to scale from investment in new technology. On balance and taking account of plausible arguments to the contrary, we expect $Ps, Fs, U,$ and S to be positively related to TC_r, and A to be negatively related to TC_r.

With respect to the discrete variables, L and G, we expect to find that location in the South and West and a council-manager form of government are positively related to TC_r. The former hypothesis stems from the fact of relatively rapid population growth in the southern and western regions of the United States in recent years, and an associated belief that such growth generates relatively high demand for more efficient public service delivery, including sanitation service. The latter hypothesis rests on conceptual arguments in the public administration and management literature that city manager–operated governments are relatively more efficient than other types of governments because the city manager form of government affords relatively greater centralization and control of management decision-making.[24]

Ordinary least squares (*OLS*) estimates of the coefficients on the variables in equation (1) are shown in table 4. As predicted, *Es, Fs, U,* and *S* were significantly positively associated with technological change in the sanitation services of local governments over the 1975–1983 period. These findings mean that a city is more likely to make technological changes in refuse collection the more labor intensive its sanitation service, the more it experiences

Table 4
OLS Estimates of Coefficients on Variables from the Technological Change Equation
(*t-values in parentheses*)

Independent Variable	Dependent Variable
	Index of Technological Change (TR_c)
Es	+4.22** (2.62)
Ps	−2.88 (−1.54)
Fs	+5.61** (3.04)
A	+1.72 (1.04)
R	+2.67 (1.38)
U	+3.74* (2.09)
S	+3.47* (2.03)
L	−1.62 (−1.02)
G	+1.04 (0.64)
N	147
R^2	.43

*Significant at the .05 level in a two-tailed test.
**Significant at the .01 level in a two-tailed test.

fiscal stress, the more unionized its sanitation work force, and the greater its population density. The signs of the coefficients on variables Ps, A, and L were opposite of those predicted, but the coefficients were not statistically significant. Nevertheless, the results suggest that older cities and those located in the Northeast and Midwest are *more* likely to make technological changes in sanitation service than are younger cities and cities located in the South and West, respectively.

Having identified some of the determinants of technological change in local government sanitation service, we proceed next to specify a sanitation employment equation that includes the following variables:

$$Ps, Fs, A, U, S, L, G, TC_r$$

$$Ma = \text{the proportion of 18–35-year-old}$$
$$\text{males in a city's population}$$

The estimating equation thus takes on the following functional form:

$$Es = Es(Ps, Fs, A, U, S, L, G, TC_r, Ma, \text{and } e) \qquad (2)$$

where Es = as previously defined, e = an error term, and all other variables are as previously defined.

The variables Ps, Fs, and U are predicted to be negatively related to Es, whereas positive relationships are expected between A and Es and S and Es. Cities located in the Northeast and Midwest are expected to have higher ratios of municipal sanitation employment to municipal population than cities located elsewhere.[25] Because it is often thought to be a less efficient or more patronage-conscious form of government than other types of governments, a mayor-council form of government is expected to be positively related to sanitation employment (for this purpose, the variable G was coded as mayor-council = 1, all other forms = 0). The variable Ma, which represents the potential labor supply available to municipal sanitation departments, is also expected to be positively related to Es.

Table 5 presents the results of *OLS* tests of equation (2). As expected, Ps and Fs are significantly negatively associated with Es, thereby demonstrating that the extent of private sanitation service and fiscal stress reduce municipal sanitation employment, other things being equal. As predicted, the size (S) of a municipality is positively related to municipal sanitation employment, and such employment is significantly higher in northeastern and midwestern cities than in southern and western cities. Perhaps most important for the present analysis, technological change has a significant negative effect on municipal sanitation employment. Specifically, the results for this variable suggest that a 1 percent increase in (the rate of) technological change in municipal sanitation service is associated with an 0.4 percent reduction in municipal

Table 5

OLS Estimates of Coefficients on Variables from the Employment Equation

(t-values in parentheses)

Independent Variable	Dependent Variable Sanitation Employment Ratio (Es)
Ps	-4.27** (-2.43)
Fs	-3.31 (-2.17)*
A	+1.04 (0.62)
U	-1.37 (-0.82)
S	+3.14 (2.09)*
L	+2.97 (2.01)*
G	+1.25 (0.77)
TC_r	-4.14** (-2.39)
Ma	+1.19 (0.73)
N	147
R^2	.59

*Significant at the .05 level in a two-tailed test.

**Significant at the .01 level in a two-tailed test.

sanitation employment. Note that the variables U, A, G, and M are not significantly associated with Es.

To this point, the empirical results indicate that both technological change and employment in municipal sanitation departments are systematically determined (by exogenous variables). However, decisions about technological change and employment are made by local officials within the context of municipal government. Thus, these variables appear to be endogenous to the system of municipal government and should be modeled accordingly. Indeed, if this is not done, then there is a substantial probability that the *OLS* estimates previously derived are biased. To deal with this problem, we specify and subsequently test a simultaneous equation system in which TC_r and Es serve as the dependent variables, respectively, and in which the equations take the following functional forms:

$$TC_r = TC_r(Es, Ps, Fs, A, R, U, S, L, G, \text{and } e) \qquad (3)$$

$$Es = Es(Ps, Fs, A, U, S, L, G, TC_{r^*}, Ma, \text{and } e) \qquad (4)$$

Table 6

TSLS Estimates of Coefficients on Variables from the Employment Equation Simultaneously Determined with the Technological Change Equation

(t-values in parentheses)

Independent Variable	Dependent Variable Sanitation Employment Ratio (Es)
Ps	-4.65^{**} (-2.61)
Fs	-3.47^{*} (-2.30)
A	$+1.41$ (0.75)
U	-2.90^{*} (-1.95)
S	$+2.99^{*}$ (2.02)
L	$+2.81$ (1.89)
G	$+1.31$ (0.79)
TC_{r^*}	-5.06^{**} (-2.71)
Ma	$+1.10$ (0.66)
N	147

*Significant at the .05 level in a two-tailed test.
**Significant at the .01 level in a two-tailed test.

Note that the value of TC_{r^*} is that estimated from the TC_r equation.[26] Table 6 presents the results of two-stage least squares ($TSLS$) estimates of the Es equation within this simultaneous system. The coefficients (and associated *t*-values) indicated that TC_{r^*} and Ps are significantly negatively associated with municipal sanitation employment ($p = <.01$). Further, U and Fs are also significantly negatively associated with Es, while S is significantly positively associated with Es. To summarize, the level of municipal sanitation employment in U.S. cities declines with the size of the private sanitation market, the extent of fiscal stress, the degree of employee unionization, and the rate (index) of technological change, and increases with city size. Moreover, there is a tendency (though not a statistically significant one) for northeastern and midwestern cities to have reduced municipal sanitation employment more than southern and western cities over the 1975–1983 period. These findings are believed to be the first to be produced via systematic empirical testing using a large cross-sectional and longitudinal data base.

If technological change and employment are endogenous to the system of local government, cannot the same be said about unionization? Although scholars disagree over the proper treatment of unionization in this regard, there is no denying that quantitative estimates of the effects of unions, especially public sector unions and specifically unions of sanitation workers,[27] change substantially when unionism is treated as an endogenous variable and modeled within a simultaneous equation system.[28] Further, we also wish to know what role, if any, technological change has played in the recent decline of public sector sanitation unionism.

In light of these considerations, a sanitation unionization equation can be formed which includes the following variables:

$$Ps, Fs, A, R, S, L, G, TC_r$$

Ps_u = the rate of unionization of private sector employees for the state in which a city is located.[29]

The estimating equation is

$$U = U(Ps, Fs, A, R, S, L, G, TC_r, PS_u \text{ and } e) \tag{5}$$

where U = as previously defined, e = an error term, and all other variables are as previously defined.

The variables A, R, S, and PS_u are expected to be positively related to U, whereas Ps and Fs are predicted to be negatively related to U. Cities located in the Northeast and Midwest are expected to have higher levels of sanitation employee unionism than are cities located in the South and Midwest, and such unionism is also expected to be relatively higher in municipalities with a mayor-council form of government (compared to other forms of municipal government). These predicted relationships are based on recent theoretical and empirical research which emphasizes the determinants of the demand for and supply of union services.[30] The main independent variable of interest, TC_r, cannot be predicted, a priori, in terms of its effects on U. While as noted (and as found) previously, TC_r can be expected to be negatively related to Es, there is no theoretical or empirical justification for predicting such a relationship or, alternatively, a positive relationship between TC_r and U. Because of the aforementioned concern about simultaneity bias, we estimate the U equation simultaneously with the TC_r equation (equation 3) and limit the discussion to the results of the $TSLS$ estimates. As before, the value of TC_{r*} is that estimated from the TC_r equation.

Table 7 shows that, in all cases, the signs of the coefficients on the independent variables are in the predicted directions. However, significant coefficients were attained only for the variables $Ps(-)$, $R(+)$, $S(+)$, $L(+)$, and $PS_u(+)$. Fiscal stress (Fs) is negatively but not significantly associated with

Table 7

TSLS Estimates of Coefficients on Variables from the Unionization Equation Simultaneously Determined with the Technological Change Equation

(t-values in parentheses)

Independent Variable	Dependent Variable
	Percentage of Sanitation Employees Unionized (U)
P_s	-3.64^*
	(-2.17)
F_s	-2.43
	(-1.58)
A	2.73
	(1.68)
R	3.11^*
	(2.02)
S	3.69^*
	(2.20)
L	3.42^*
	(2.06)
G	1.09
	(0.37)
TC_{r^*}	-1.82
	(-1.03)
PS_u	3.21^{**}
	(2.09)
N	147

*Significant at the .05 level in a two-tailed test.
**Significant at the .01 level in a two-tailed test.

sanitation employee unionism (U), whereas age of a city (A) is positively but not significantly associated with U. The incidence of sanitation unionization does not vary significantly by form of government (G). Most important, technological change is not significantly associated with U (although TC_{r^*} is negatively related to U).

To test further for the effects of technological change on sanitation unionization, equation (3) was rerun using the rate of change in sanitation unionism (Ur) over the 1975–1983 period as the dependent variable. The results of this test (not reproduced in detail here) show the following for the TC_{r^*} variable with respect to U:

$$-3.34^*$$
$$(2.12)$$

*Significant at the .05 level in a two-tailed test.

Hence, in this specification, the rate of technological change in sanitation departments of U.S. cities during the latter 1970s and early 1980s is shown to be significantly negatively associated with the unionization of sanitation employees during roughly the same period.[31]

In toto, the empirical findings of this section indicate that certain factors systematically determine the rate of technological change in public sanitation service in U.S. cities. Such change, in turn, is significantly negatively associated with levels of sanitation employment and sanitation unionization, especially in older cities located in the northeastern and midwestern regions of the country.

These conclusions have been reached through quantitative analyses, and perhaps because of this, pertain to the most "obvious" (or the most quantifiable) aspects of labor relations, namely employment and the incidence of unionism. But how has technological change affected the labor relations process in public sanitation departments, particularly the responses of labor and management officials to such change? This question is taken up and explored for the most part qualitatively in the next section.

Technological Change and the Sanitation Labor Relations Process

In the U.S. system of industrial relations, adversarial relationships predominate, and this is no less true of the public than the private sector.[32] How have recent technological changes in sanitation service affected sanitation labor relations? Basically, there have been two contrasting effects.

On the one hand, technological change seems to have exacerbated adversarial labor relations in certain sanitation departments, contributing to labor–management conflict and in some cases producing work stoppages. On the other hand, technological change appears to have spurred labor –management cooperation in some sanitation departments, producing or contributing to integrative bargaining and bringing about creative efforts to deal with such change.

To gain perspective on and understanding of this issue, consider the data in table 8. They show the proportion of all organized local government employees, by function, who engaged in work stoppages in 1974 and 1980. Clearly, by this measure, sanitation is the most strike-prone public service. This fact is consistent with the related fact that the demand for public sanitation service is relatively inelastic compared to the demand for other public services,[33] and with the further related fact that unions representing organized sanitation employees—for example, the Teamsters, the Communications Workers of America (CWA), the International Laborers' Union (ILU), the Service Employees International Union (SEIU), and the American

Table 8

Proportion of Full-Time Organized Local Government Employees Involved in Strike Activity by Functional Service Category, 1974 and 1980

Functional Service Category	Proportion (%)	
	1974	1980
All functions	3.8	5.6
Education	3.4	5.0
Instructional staff	3.2	5.0
Others	4.2	5.0
Highways	4.8	2.9
Public welfare	0.7	3.9
Hospitals	1.2	4.5
Police protection	0.5	1.7
Fire protection	1.4	3.6
Sanitation other than sewerage	10.4	8.3
All other	7.9	10.5

Source: Derived from U.S. Bureau of the Census, *Labor–Management Relations in State and Local Governments: 1974 and 1980.* State and Local Government Special Studies, nos. 75 and 102 (Washington, D.C.: U.S. Government Printing Office, 1976 and 1981), pp. 9 and 87 (1976) and 7 and 112 (1981).

Federation of State, County, and Municipal Employees (AFSCME)—are well-established organizations that have used the strike, albeit selectively, to achieve bargaining ends.[34]

The introduction of technological change into an adversarial labor relationship with a relatively high "militancy content" could plausibly be expected to make the relationship even more adversarial, especially if the change portends employment (and union membership) reductions. This is, in fact, what has occurred in some cities that have initiated technological change in sanitation service. For example, between 1978 and 1982, the city of Tampa, Florida, instituted equipment changes, route adjustments, and reduced crew sizes for residential refuse collection, with the principal technological change being the (gradual) replacement of rear-loading with side-loading vehicles.[35] These actions precipitated a one-day employee walkout in mid-1979 and a four-day wildcat strike in early 1980, despite the presence of a no-strike clause in the union's labor agreement with the city. Striking employees were suspended and those who did not return to work within forty-eight hours were discharged. Subsequently, the city's mayor contracted out one-quarter of the refuse collection service to a private hauler.

Similar events occurred in Salt Lake City, Utah, in 1980.[36] The city's replacement of rear-loading with side-loading vehicles for refuse collection and the planned reduction of three-person to one-person crews, with the intermediate use of two-person crews, was met by an employee walkout that resulted in a reversion to the use of three-person crews. Subsequently, and as in the Tampa case, management officials of the Salt Lake City government contracted out one-quarter of the municipality's refuse collection and, one year later, successfully instituted the one-person crew arrangement.

These examples of militant sanitation employee responses to technological change are paralleled by other examples of responses to the contracting out of sanitation service. In Camden, New Jersey, where the city adopted a plan in 1979 to contract out sanitation service, a fledgling union instigated a short work stoppage, which was followed by a two-week work slowdown, demonstrations before the City Council, and the initiation of a lawsuit to prevent the city from implementing its plan.[37] The lawsuit was withdrawn when the city agreed to a no-layoff provision for sanitation employees.

At about the same time, the city of Berwyn, Illinois, whose governing council had voted to contract out sanitation service, was confronted with sustained employee picketing of council offices and a union-initiated lawsuit to countermand the vote.[38] Further, refuse collection trucks were damaged and a fire bomb was hurled at an alderman's house. A judicial order ended the picketing and resulted in employees returning to work, but contract collection was eventually implemented in Berwyn. In Covington, Kentucky, and Middletown, Ohio, unionized sanitation employees conducted "sick-outs," filed grievances, and undertook lawsuits to prevent contracting-out plans from being implemented in 1980 (and, in Covington specifically, to prevent the city from selling its refuse vehicles).[39] These actions delayed the contracting arrangements but, as in Berwyn, did not prevent their eventual implementation.

But if technological change has contributed to the adversarial nature of certain municipal sanitation labor relationships, in other cases it has provided opportunities for instituting or enhancing labor–management cooperation. For example, in Rochester, New York, where in 1980 new refuse collection vehicles with high-speed trash compaction capability were adopted, crew size was reduced, and the method of financing refuse collection was changed from general taxation to user fees, an agreement was reached with the sanitationmen's union that provided for reductions in force via attrition and monetary incentives for remaining employees.[40] The city further agreed not to contract out sanitation service to private haulers. City officials and union representatives jointly conducted communication and training sessions with employees to explain the new refuse collection arrangements and to ensure the smooth implementation of these arrangements.

In Clinton, Oklahoma, in 1982, the conversion from rear-loading to fully automated side-loading refuse collection vehicles and the replacement of trash cans with standardized carts were achieved with the full cooperation of the sanitation workers' union.[41] Work force reductions were achieved via attrition, jobs were redesigned to raise skills and pay, and sanitation employees—who became drivers and equipment operators where they had once been laborers—experienced statistically significant increases in morale and job satisfaction (as determined through the analysis of responses to mail questionnaires). A similar experience took place in Kingsville, Texas, in 1982, where technological changes of the type undertaken in Clinton were coupled with skill upgrading for sanitation employees, who were converted from truck drivers to route managers responsible for the physical condition of alleyways and the relay of street maintenance orders to the city's Street Department.[42]

In Atlanta, Tulsa, Detroit, Washington, D.C., Erie, St. Louis, Fort Lauderdale, Phoenix, Chicago, and several other cities, technological changes in municipal sanitation service—changes of the type noted here— were instituted in the late 1970s and early 1980s with the explicit cooperation of sanitation employee unions.[43] In some cases, displaced employees were transferred to jobs in other city agencies and departments, but more common were plans for phased attrition, skill upgrading, and periodic communications to employees informing them of the details of and schedules for implementing the changes in technology. A few of these cities developed videotapes showing the reduced physical effort and work injuries as well as the productivity improvements associated with the new technology of refuse collection. Perhaps most important under the new refuse collection arrangements, employees who remained in sanitation service typically received a 5 to 15 percent pay increment due to the combination of skill upgrading and productivity improvement.

Indeed, what may (because of its size) be the most notable example of union–management cooperation in municipal sanitation service under the impetus of technological change occurred in New York City during the early 1980s.[44] There, city officials and the Sanitation Workers' Union (a Teamsters affiliate) engaged in productivity bargaining and, under the aegis of an arbitration award, agreed to replace smaller, less efficient refuse collection vehicles operated by three-person crews with larger, more efficient semiautomated vehicles using two-person crews. The 1981 agreement, which covered selected rather than all routes, contained a no-layoff provision, and work force reductions were to be achieved (and, in fact, were achieved) through attrition. Additionally, each employee member of a two-person crew received an $11.00 per shift bonus, and an experiment in contracting out was postponed for two years. In light of the city's frustrating and ineffectual record of productivity bargaining with municipal unions during the 1970s and the frequency of sanitation employee strikes and work slowdowns during the same period,[45] the parties were probably correct in describing their agreement as "historic." From an analytical perspective, this agreement, along with other sanitation labor agreements that have been reached in certain U.S. cities, demonstrate that technological change can bring about union–management cooperation even where adversarial labor relations have predominated.

Referring once again to the model of public sector labor relations presented in figure 2, this section has emphasized the effects of technological change on the labor relations (or collective bargaining) process in municipal sanitation departments. As shown in the model, other variables besides technological change affect the bargaining process, and in certain instances the direction and magnitude of the effects of such other variables may run counter to or override the effects of technological change. Lacking a comprehensive data base, we were not able to conduct multivariate analyses that would permit us to separate the effects of technological change from the effects of other variables on the bargaining process in municipal sanitation departments. Nevertheless, the qualitative analysis undertaken here illustrates that the parties to labor–management relations in municipal sanitation departments respond to technological change in one of two fundamental ways.

One type of response to technological change in public sanitation service is characterized by distributive bargaining in which each party, labor and management, attempts to minimize its own and maximize its "opponent's" losses.[46] The issues that arise in conjunction with technological change are perceived as areas or arenas of conflict, and each party seeks to gain an advantage over or impose a cost on the other. In sanitation labor relations characterized by this type of response to technological change, opposition to the change prevails, as does an authoritarian mode of implementing the change; strikes and work slowdowns occur, and workers are suspended and discharged; management threatens or proceeds to carry out subcontracting, and minimal investments are made in communicating and explaining the changes to employees; militant employee actions often delay and sometimes prevent the changes from taking place; and, occasionally, violence accompanies opposition to the change.

In a second and far different type of response to technological change in public sanitation service, labor and management perceive such change as an opportunity, and the parties engage (or continue to engage) in integrative bargaining.[47] Issues associated with technological change are treated as problems to be solved, and the parties seek to obtain net benefits for both sides; the change is accepted and provisions are made for skill upgrading and work force reductions (where they occur) through attrition; management invests in programs to communicate and explain the changes to employees, and union officials cooperate with and often join management in carrying out such programs; emphasis is placed on the reduced physical effort and work injuries associated with the new technology; joint labor–management productivity improvement and technological change monitoring committees are sometimes established; and revisions in the implementation of technological change are made periodically, with the intent of improving the change process.

Recognizing the limitations on the analysis of sanitation labor relations presented herein, it may nevertheless be suggested that integrative bargaining seems to have become more prominent, and distributive bargaining less prominent, in public sanitation service. The reduced incidence of municipal sanitation strikes, the case examples of sanitation bargaining in certain municipalities described earlier, and especially the changing patterns of labor relations in other sectors of the U.S. economy that have experienced severe competitive stress, shrinking unionization, and major bargaining concessions, support this observation.[48] Such a conversion from predominantly distributive to predominantly integrative bargaining is perhaps particularly characteristic of U.S. labor relations, in which the parties to bargaining apparently come to recognize opportunities for joint or mutual gain only under extremely threatening environmental conditions—including rapid technological change.

Note, however, that whether integrative or distributive bargaining and labor–management relations prevail in response to technological change in municipal sanitation service, certain outcomes are common or similar. Typically, indeed almost without exception, employment is reduced; pay is increased; subcontracting is undertaken, contemplated, or discussed; work injuries decline; productivity improves (though with considerable variation); and bargaining agreements are in fact reached. But the emphasis in this section is on process, specifically the labor relations and bargaining process, not outcomes, and the recent experience of U.S. cities in responding to technological change in sanitation service shows that such change produces a diversity rather than a uniformity of reactions on the part of labor and management. The intriguing question—one that remains unanswered and therefore provides an opportunity for further research—is, "What factors determine how the parties to a particular labor–management relationship respond to technological change in public sanitation service?"

The Sanitation Labor Relations Experience in Larger Context

Placed in larger context, the record of labor–management responses to technological change in public sanitation service during the 1970s and early 1980s accords closely with the broader public and private sector industrial relations experience of the United States. The major elements of this accordance are as follows.

First, changes in one or more environmental contexts cause the parties to rethink service (or goods) "production," technology, and labor relations. In public sanitation service, the major recent environmental changes have been financial and economic. The reduced rate of growth of the U.S. public sector, which emerged in the mid-1970s following a sustained twenty-five-year expansion of that sector, and the development and increased recognition of private markets for sanitation service, combined to stimulate discussion, debate, and analysis of local government arrangements for sanitation service. Mayors, city councils, city managers, town commissions, and, more basically, citizens of local communities became more aware of the relatively greater efficiencies and lower costs of privately provided compared to publicly provided sanitation service. In some communities, this recognition was translated into specific decisions to contract with private firms for some or all sanitation service, either on a single franchise or competitive basis.

Second, with growth of and changes in the demand for sanitation service, expansion of the supply of privately provided sanitation service, and increased competition between the private and public sectors for sanitation service, strong incentives emerged for the development of new refuse collection (and disposal) technology. The advent of new equipment, indeed of whole new systems, for refuse collection provided local government officials with an alternative to private contracting, namely, the retention and modernization of publicly provided sanitation service via the adoption of new technology. And, as we have seen, many governments availed themselves of this option during the 1970s and early 1980s.

Third, the new sanitation technology is fundamentally labor-saving (rather than labor-neutral) technology, and its adoption by local governments translated into major sanitation work force reductions. In fact, virtually every recent change in the technology of publicly provided sanitation service (for which documentation exists) has been accompanied by a permanent work force reduction and a decline in the rate of sanitation unionization.[49]

Fourth, and in light of this, it is hardly surprising that sanitation union officials and members have evidenced great concern about the consequences of technological change. But concern does not necessarily translate into opposition, and what is probably most notable about sanitation labor relations in an era of rapid technological change is that the dominant response of managers and organized workers to such changes has been to pursue more integrative and less distributive bargaining. Unionists have basically sought to bargain over technological change and to cushion the workers they represent from the effects of technological change, though even then the cushioning rarely takes the form of outright job or income guarantees. To the contrary, sanitation unions have in the main focused on improving the terms and conditions of employment for those who remain employed in public sanitation service following the implementation of technological change. Typically the improvements are in the form of skill upgrading, higher pay and benefits, and productivity improvement incentives and rewards.

If this predominant union response to technological change has come as a surprise to local government officials and sanitation department managers, it should not be surprising to students of industrial relations. From longshoring and maritime to automobile and steel manufacturing, from printing and publishing to pulp and paper manufacturing, from railroads and airlines to oil and chemical manufacturing, unions, when faced with technological change, have attempted to mitigate its effects on their members rather than to oppose or prevent it.[50] This is not to deny that some unions—and some unorganized workers—have on occasion successfully warded off technological change through distributive bargaining and related tactics; that militant action, including violence, has accompanied certain instances of technological change; or that unions generally raise the cost to management of adopting and implementing technological change.[51] Rather, it is to support the premise that the dominant response of private sector unionists to technological change—and also of public sector unionists in education, social welfare, health care, police and fire protection, and other services—is to bargain or seek to bargain integratively over the effects of change on union members. The recent experience in public sanitation service is fully in keeping with this historical tradition.

Fifth, managerial approaches to labor relations in public sanitation service in the context of rapid technological change also appear to accord closely with history and experience in the private sector as well as in other public services. Recall that, in recent years, management officials in numerous cities decided to contract out sanitation services to the private sector, and that such action was motivated in large part by a desire to reduce labor costs and avoid work stoppages. Precisely the same rationale has motivated private managers to subcontract work previously performed by union members, and subcontracting has mushroomed in the private sector since about 1970.[52]

In undertaking technological change in sanitation service, public managers have focused the bulk of their attention on the decision to adopt such change, and only later have they addressed the implementation of change. In other words, public managers have rarely permitted or invited organized (and, for that matter, unorganized) sanitation employees to exercise joint authority in decisions to adopt technological change—and unions have rarely pressed for such joint authority. Similarly, it is the rare private company management that seeks or is willing to share decision-making authority with unionized workers over planned technological change. In general, private and public managers regard decision making about technological change as the exclusive prerogative of management.[53] Consequently, integrative bargaining (whether in sanitation service or elsewhere) may emerge during an early stage of technological change, but may develop more fully only if such change persists or, indeed, quickens.

The doctrine of reserved management rights perforce limits employee involvement and participation to matters of implementing management-initiated changes, and it is in the implementation process that one observes major variation in management approaches to labor relations. We have seen that, in some sanitation departments, management has involved organized employees closely in the implementation of technological change, and has undertaken policies and programs to make union and worker participation a reality in this regard. In other sanitation departments, however, management has implemented technological change more or less unilaterally, and has kept union and worker participation to a minimum. In still other sanitation departments, management has encouraged limited union and worker participation in implementing technological change, often focusing such participation on a single dimension of change, for example, training in the use of new sanitation equipment and collection procedures.

In the private sector and in other public services, the recent emphasis on concession bargaining and two-tier labor agreements and the enhanced use of worker participation schemes, such as joint productivity and quality-of-work-life committees, plans for profit sharing and employee stock ownership (in the private sector), and even occasionally membership on boards of directors (in the private sector),[54] may seem to imply that labor relations in the United States have become more cooperative and less adversarial. But it has yet to be shown that these are more than short-term or cyclical changes—there is some truth to the assertion that when it can't give money to workers, management gives participation—and during this same recent period other private managements have filed for bankruptcy to overturn labor agreements, used consultants to ward off unionization, and refined various techniques, such as shifting production to offshore locations, to limit union participation in the enterprise.[55]

Whether managers of local government sanitation departments are, on average, more or less inclined than their private or other public sector counterparts to encourage union participation in implementing technological change is uncertain, and the "average" managerial posture toward this matter may not be relevant in any case. Rather, and as has been shown here, sanitation labor relations tend toward distinctive patterns, with cooperative, integrative relations on the one hand and adversarial, distributive relations on the other hand being the dominant types.

The irony in all of this—and it is an irony characteristic of labor relations more broadly—is that technological change improves the position and conditions (that is, the "outcomes") of workers *who remain employed*. In public service, and irrespective of whether a particular labor relationship is predominantly cooperative or adversarial, recent technological changes have raised employee pay and benefits, generated skill upgrading, reduced work injuries, and enhanced employee autonomy and control over the work process. These beneficial effects of the new economic and social organization of the public sanitation workplace must be given considerable weight in any assessment of technological change in sanitation service. However, the costs attending such change cannot be overlooked, and these costs primarily take the form of worker displacement, which, as earlier analysis showed, was substantial during the 1970s and early 1980s.

In the U.S. system of decentralized industrial relations, management and union officials who are party to a specific labor relationship are not well equipped or positioned to deal with the specific worker displacement effects of technological change. This is perhaps especially true for the union which, as Dunlop has shown, must choose between maximizing membership and maximizing "benefits" per member.[56] In public sanitation service, union leaders have given more emphasis to the latter objective, though not entirely ignoring the former. In this, they mirror the "objective function" of the public managers with whom they deal, and reflect the dominant, if not singular, behavior of union leaders in the private sector and in other public services in the United States.

Acknowledgment

The research assistance of Nancy Lewis in the preparation of this reading is gratefully acknowledged.

Notes

1. See, for example, Daniel B. Cornfield, "Workers, Managers and Techno-logical Change," in Cornfield, ed., *Workers, Managers, and Technological Change: Emerging Patterns of Labor Relations* (New York: Plenum, 1987), pp. 3–24.

2. See E.S. Savas and Christopher Niemczewski, "Who Collects Solid Waste?," in *The Municipal Yearbook—1976* (Washington, D.C.: International City Management Association, 1976), p. 18.

3. See Gerard J. Hoetmer, "Police, Fire, and Refuse Collection and Disposal Departments: Personnel, Compensation, and Expenditures," in *The Municipal Yearbook—1984* (Washington, D.C.: International City Management Association, 1984), p. 146.

4. Ibid., p. 145.

5. For further analysis of the differences between union membership and union representation in the public sector generally, see John F. Burton, Jr., "The Extent of Collective Bargaining in the Public Sector," in Benjamin Aaron, Joseph R. Grodin, and James L. Stern, eds., *Public-Sector Bargaining* (Washington, D.C.: Bureau of National Affairs, 1979), pp. 1–43.

6. U.S. Bureau of the Census, *Labor–Management Relations in State and Local Governments: 1980,* Special Study no. 102 (Washington, D.C.: 1981), p. 7.

7. See David Lewin, "Collective Bargaining and the Right to Strike in the Public Sector," in A. Lawrence Chickering, ed., *Public Employee Unions: A Study of the Crisis in Public Sector Labor Relations* (San Francisco: Institute for Contemporary Studies, 1976), pp. 145–163.

8. David Lewin, Peter Feuille, and Thomas A. Kochan, *Public Sector Labor Relations: Analysis and Readings,* 2nd ed. (Sun Lakes, Ariz.: Thomas Horton and Daughters, 1981), pp. 17–24. Note that during the 1960s and early 1970s the major environmental influence on public sector labor relations was the "legal context," as numerous states enacted legislation supporting unionization and collective bargaining rights for public employees in state and local governments.

9. Barbara J. Stevens, "How Management Decisions Explain Cost Differences between City Pickup Systems," *Solid Wastes Management* 20 (September 1977), p. 32.

10. See Eileen Brettler Berenyi, "Union Opposition Could Not Overcome Movement toward Contract Collection," *Solid Wastes Management* 23 (October 1980), pp. 14–16, 105–106, and Savas and Niemczewski, "Who Collects Solid Waste?" pp. 167–172.

11. Barbara J. Stevens and E.S. Savas, "The Cost of Residential Refuse Collection and the Effect on Service Arrangement," in *The Municipal Yearbook—1977,* (Washington, D.C.: International City Management Association, 1977), pp. 200–205. Here and in the remainder of this reading, the emphasis is on residential refuse collection rather than on commercial and industrial refuse collection, street and park maintenance, or litter basket collection.

12. See Stevens, "How Management Decisions Explain Cost Differences," pp. 32, 36, 72, 98, 100, 102–105, and Berenyi, "Union Opposition," pp. 14–16, 105–106. Other examples of technological change in sanitation service discussed in this section were drawn from accounts contained in various issues of *American City and County, Public Works, Solid Wastes Management, Waste Age,* and *World Wastes* published between 1971 and 1984.

13. See "Refuse Pickup Personnel Injuries Are Nine Times National Industry Average," *Solid Wastes Management* 19 (January 1975), pp. 10–11, 44, 48; Ralph Stone, "Survey Reveals Trends in the Use of Disposable Refuse Bags," *Public Works* 101 (September 1970), pp. 86–87; and Don Campbell, "One City's Analysis of Accidents," *Waste Age* 15 (May 1984), pp. 75–77.

14. See, for example, "Atlanta: The Biggest Municipal Collection System to Adopt Cart Service," *Solid Wastes Management* 19 (February 1976), pp. 24–25, 28, 52.

15. As examples, see Lester Coch and John R.P. French, Jr., "Overcoming Resistance to Change," *Human Relations* 1 (July 1948), pp. 512–532, and R.M. Steers, "Antecedents and Outcomes of Organizational Commitment," *Administrative Science Quarterly* 22 (March 1977), pp. 46–56.

16. Robert J. Bartollatta, "Several Strategies to Improve Collection Systems," *Solid Wastes Management* 19 (September 1976), pp. 54, 74, 78, 84, and Jim Talebreza, "Overhaul of Collection System Produces Dramatic Results," *Public Works* 114 (April 1983), pp. 44–45.

17. See, for example, Ann Bartel and David Lewin, "Wages and Unionism in the Public Sector: The Case of Police," *The Review of Economics and Statistics* 63 (Feb-

ruary 1981), pp. 53–59. For a specific application to sanitation service, see Linda N. Edwards and Franklin R. Edwards, "The Effects of Unionism on the Money and Fringe Compensation of Public Employees: The Case of Municipal Sanitation Workers," Working Paper, Queens College, City University of New York, 1979.

18. Specifically, these sources include those given in note 9, articles and data contained in *The Municipal Yearbook* annual volumes published between 1975 and 1983, and data supplied by E.S. Savas from his study, *The Organization and Efficiency of Solid Waste Collection* (Lexington, Mass.: Lexington Books, 1977 (see appendices A, B, and C of this work for a detailed description of the data collection methods used in the study of 315 municipalities).

19. For guidance in constructing this index, we relied on J. Guilford, *Psychometric Methods,* 2nd ed. (New York: McGraw-Hill, 1954); Fred N. Kerlinger, *Foundations of Behavioral Research,* 2nd ed. (New York: Holt, Rinehart and Winston, 1973); and Lawrence R. James, Stanley A. Mulaik, and Jeanne M. Brett, *Causal Analysis: Assumptions Models, and Data* (Beverly Hills, Calif.: Sage Publications, 1982). The index was also discussed with two managers of municipal sanitation departments, who made several recommendations for revision, and with three academics who were asked to rate technological change in a subset of thirty cities, using the index. The resultant interrater reliability of .74 (significant at $p = <.05$) provided additional support for use of the index in the present analysis.

20. The model year of the data for the variables listed here was 1980 in five cases and 1976 in two cases, with one case each in 1977, 1979, and 1982.

21. The variables included in equation 1 and in other equations to follow were drawn from careful reviews of the relevant literature and considerations of the particular characteristics of sanitation service. Equation 1 is, in essence, a reduced form of a larger set of equations specifying determinants of the demand for and supply of public sanitation service. Recall that annual data for 1975–1983 are pooled to derive cross-section estimates of the independent variables.

22. See David Lewin, "Public Sector Labor Relations: A Review Essay," *Labor History* 18 (Winter 1978), pp. 133–144.

23. See, for example, Jack Barbash, "The Impact of Technological Change on Labor–Management Relations," in Gerald G. Somers, Edward L. Cushman, and Nat Weinberg, eds., *Adjusting to Technological Change* (New York: Harper and Row, 1963), pp. 44–60, and Harold Levinson, Charles R. Rehmus, Joseph P. Goldberg, and Mark L. Kahn, *Collective Bargaining and Technological Change in American Transportation* (Evanston, Ill.: The Transportation Center, Northwestern University, 1971).

24. See, for example, O. Glenn Stahl, *Public Personnel Administration,* 8th ed. (New York: Harper and Row, 1983), and Thomas P. Murphy and Charles R. Warren, *Organizing Public Services in Metropolitan America* (Lexington, Mass.: Lexington Books, 1974).

25. Recognize that, in most northeastern and midwestern cities, sanitation personnel also perform snow removal service. This larger set of job duties is expected to translate into higher sanitation employment/municipal population ratios in the colder regions of the United States.

26. The rationale and specific techniques for estimating simultaneous equation systems are more fully discussed in Peter Schmidt, "Estimation of a Simultaneous

Equations Model with Jointly Determined Continuous and Qualitative Variables: The Union-Earnings Equation Revisited," *International Economic Review* 19 (June 1978), pp. 453–465. Note that to satisfy the estimating conditions of simultaneous equation testing, at least one independent variable must be exclusive to each equation.

27. See, for example, Daniel J.B. Mitchell, *Unions, Wages, and Inflation* (Washington, D.C.: Brookings Institution, 1980), pp. 104–111, and Linda N. Edwards and Franklin R. Edwards, "Wellington-Winter Revisited: The Case of Municipal Sanitation Collection," *Industrial and Labor Relations Review* 35 (April 1982), p. 313.

28. Bartel and Lewin, "Wages and Unionism in the Public Sector," pp. 57–58, and David Lewin and Harry C. Katz, "Payment Determination in Municipal Building Departments under Unionism and Civil Service," in Werner Z. Hirsch, ed., *The Economics of Municipal Labor Markets* (Los Angeles: Institute of Industrial Relations, University of California, 1983), pp. 90–121.

29. This variable is commonly used in modeling the determinants of public employee unionism. See, for example, David Lewin, "The Effects of Civil Service Systems and Unionism on Pay Outcomes in the Public Sector," in David B. Lipsky, ed., *Advances in Industrial and Labor Relations,* vol. 1 (Greenwich, Conn.: JAI Press, 1983), pp. 150–151. Inclusion of the PSu variable in equation 5 also allows us to satisfy the aforementioned condition of one exclusive variable per each equation in a simultaneous system.

30. See, for example, Lewin, Feuille, and Kochan, *Public Sector Labor Relations,* chap. 1; David Lewin, "The Effects of Regulation on Public Sector Labor Relations: Theory and Evidence," *Journal of Labor Research* 6 (Winter 1985), pp. 77–95; Richard B. Freeman and James L. Medoff, *What Do Unions Do?* (New York: Basic Books, 1984), chaps. 1, 3; and William T. Dickens and Jonathan S. Leonard, "Accounting for the Decline in Union Membership, 1950–1980," *Industrial and Labor Relations Review* 38 (April 1985), pp. 323–334.

31. Other TSLS analyses were conducted in which equations 3, 4, and 5 were simultaneously estimated. The results of these analyses were not significantly different from those presented in the text. Note that we also chose not to include an employment variable in the unionization equation because there is no theoretical or empirical justification for such inclusion—that is, employment, per se, is not conceived to be a determinant of unionism.

32. See, for example, Lewin, Feuille, and Kochan, *Public Sector Labor Relations,* chap. 4, and Gordon F. Bloom and Herbert R. Northrup, *Economics of Labor Relations,* 8th ed. (Homewood, Ill.: Irwin, 1981), chaps, 1, 4, 6.

33. Orley Ashenfelter and Ronald G. Ehrenberg, "The Demand for Labor in the Public Sector," in Lewin, Feuille, and Kochan, *Public Sector Labor Relations,* pp. 33–39.

34. See Leo Troy and Neil Sheflin, *Union Sourcebook: Membership, Structure, Finance, Directory,* 1984, ed. (West Orange, N.J.: Industrial Relations Data and Information Service, 1985).

35. Pamela K. Day and Robert D. Fiero, "When Should Refuse Collection Change?" *American City and County* 97 (April 1982), pp. 51–55.

36. "Cities Contract Out Collection to Save Money and Avoid Headaches," *Solid Wastes Management* 23 (August 1980), pp. 40–45.

37. Berenyi, "Union Opposition," p. 15.

38. "Cities Contract Out . . .," pp. 42–43.

39. Berenyi, "Union Opposition," p. 105.

40. "We Cut Collection Cost, Not Service," *American City and County* 96 (March 1981), pp. 39–43.

41. Carl Sidney, "System Solves Labor Cost Problem," *Solid Wastes Management* 25 (August 1982), pp. 38–40.

42. "News and Views," *American City and County* 97 (March 1982), p. 12.

43. See, for example, John O'Connor, "Refuse Collection Practices 1980: An Exclusive National Survey," *American City and County* 95 (April 1980), pp. 34–38; "Atlanta: The Biggest Municipal Collection System to Adopt Cart Service," *Solid Wastes Management* 19 (February 1976), pp. 24–25, 28, 52; "Team of City Officials Modernizes Collection System," *Solid Wastes Management* 20 (February 1977), pp. 36–37; Paul Baker and John Albert, "Automated Refuse Collection Stresses Cycle Time," *World Wastes* 26 (July 1983), pp. 41–43; Larry Roth, "Chicago—Home of the World's Largest Cart System," *World Wastes,* 27 (May 1984), pp. 66–70; and "Mechanized Collections for Big City Neighborhoods," *Waste Age* 14 (September 1983), pp. 47–50.

44. This account draws liberally from Lewin, Feuille, and Kochan, *Public Sector Labor Relations,* pp. 177–178. For additional background, see Mary McCormick, "Labor Relations," and James M. Hartman assisted by Linda Mitchell, "Sanitation," in Charles Brecher and Raymond D. Horton, eds., *Setting Municipal Priorities, 1982* (New York: Russell Sage, 1981), chaps. 7 and 10, respectively.

45. See, for example, "Strike Chokes New York City," *Solid Wastes Management* 18 (July 1975), p. 76; "Rear Loaders Preferred in New York City," *Solid Wastes Management* 20 (October 1977), pp. 14–15; McCormick, "Labor Relations," pp. 199–214, and David Lewin and Mary McCormick, "Coalition Bargaining in Municipal Government: New York City in the 1970s," *Industrial and Labor Relations Review* 34 (January 1981), pp. 175–190.

46. The term *distributive bargaining* was coined by Richard E. Walton and Robert B. McKersie, *A Behavioral Theory of Labor Negotiations* (New York: McGraw-Hill, 1965), chap. 1.

47. Ibid. It should be recognized that "cooperative" labor–management efforts to deal with technological changes are more likely to be reported in the type of industry and trade publications cited above than are adversarial or "uncooperative" efforts. Thus, in the account presented in this section, we may have underrepresented the incidence of adversarial bargaining over technological change in public sanitation service.

48. See, for example, David Lewin, "Public Sector Concession Bargaining: Lessons for the Private Sector," *Proceedings of the Thirty-fifth Annual Meeting of the Industrial Relations Research Association.* (Madison, Wisc.: IRRA, 1983), pp. 383–393, and David Lewin, *Opening the Books: Corporate Information-Sharing with Employees.* (New York: The Conference Board, 1984). Unfortunately, the present study does not allow us to test for the effects of intercity variation in political party affiliation or variation in local union structure, centralization, and affiliation (with a regional or national union) on variation in integrative bargaining among municipal sanitation departments.

49. As determined by the author's assessment of written accounts of techno-

logical change in public sanitation service published between 1971 and 1984 in *American City and County, Public Works, Solid Wastes Management, Waste Age,* and *World Wastes.* Some 161 accounts of technological change in municipal sanitation departments were published in these journals between 1971 and 1984, of which 135 reported employment data. In 127 cases, sanitation department employment declined after the technological change, and in 8 cases no employment change occurred. Not a single case of employment expansion following technological change in sanitation departments was reported during these years. Note also that for cities reporting precise posttechnological change employment data, the average decline in sanitation employment during the first two years following technological change was 21 percent.

50. See, for example, Barbash, "The Impact of Technological Change," chap. 1; Levinson, Rehmus, Goldberg, and Kahn, *Collective Bargaining,* chap. 11; Neil W. Chamberlain and James W. Kuhn, *Collective Bargaining,* 3rd ed. (New York: McGraw-Hill, 1986), chaps. 9–11; Sumner H. Slichter, James J. Healy, and E. Robert Livernash, *The Impact of Collective Bargaining on Management* (Washington, D.C.: Brookings Institution, 1960), chaps. 24–27; James J. Healy, *Creative Collective Bargaining* (Englewood Cliffs, N.J.: Prentice-Hall, 1965); Paul T. Hartman, *Collective Bargaining and Productivity: The Longshore Mechanization Agreement* (Berkeley: University of California Press, 1969); Robert B. McKersie and L.C. Hunter, *Pay, Productivity and Collective Bargaining* (New York: St. Martin's, 1973); and Gerald Somers, Arvid Anderson, Malcolm Denise, and Leonard Sayles, *Collective Bargaining and Productivity* (Madison, Wisc.: Industrial Relations Research Association, 1975). On the public sector, see Chester A. Newland, ed., *MBO and Productivity Bargaining in the Public Sector* (Chicago: International Personnel Management Association, 1974), and Melvin H. Osterman, "Productivity Bargaining in New York—What Went Wrong?," in Lewin, Feuille, and Kochan, *Public Sector Labor Relations,* pp. 162–174.

51. Albert Rees, *The Economics of Trade Unions,* rev. ed. (Chicago: University of Chicago Press, 1977), chaps. 7–9, and Paul A. Weinstein, ed., *Featherbedding and Technological Change* (Lexington, Mass.: Heath, 1965).

52. U.S. Bureau of Labor Statistics, *Subcontracting,* Bulletin no. 1425-8 (Washington, D.C.: U.S. Government Printing Office, 1969), and U.S. Bureau of Labor Statistics, *Characteristics of Major Collective Bargaining Agreements—January 1, 1980,* Bulletin no. 2095 (Washington, D.C.: U.S. Government Printing Office, 1981).

53. See, for example, Chamberlain and Kuhn, *Collective Bargaining,* chap. 5, and Paul Prasow and Edward Peters, "New Perspectives on Management's Reserved Rights," *Labor Law Journal* 18 (January 1967), pp. 3–14.

54. See D. Quinn Mills, "When Employees Make Concessions," *Harvard Business Review* 61 (May–June 1983), pp. 103–113; Peter Cappelli, "Concession Bargaining and the National Economy," *Proceedings of the Thirty-fifth Annual Meeting of the Industrial Relations Research Association* (Madison, Wisc.: IRRA, 1983), pp. 362–371; Allen M. Ponak and C.R.P. Frasor, "Union Members Support for Joint Programs," *Industrial Relations* 18 (May 1979), pp. 197–209; and Michael Beer, Bert Spector, Paul R. Lawrence, D. Quinn Mills, and Richard E. Walton, eds., *Human Resource Management: Text and Cases* (New York: Free Press, 1985), chap. 5.

55. See for example, John J. Lawler and Robin West, "Attorneys, Consultants, and Union-Avoidance Strategies in Representation Elections," Paper presented to the Berkeley Conference on Industrial Relations, February 1985, and Robert J. Flanagan, "Compliance and Enforcement Decisions Under the National Labor Relations Act," Paper presented to the Berkeley Conference on Industrial Relations, February 1985.

56. John T. Dunlop, *Wage Determination under Trade Unions,* rev. ed. (New York: Macmillan, 1950). While Dunlop offers an economic analysis of this trade-off, others emphasize the political dynamics of unions in deciding the tradeoff. See, for example, Arthur Ross, *Trade Union Wage Policy* (Berkeley: University of California Press, 1948). Whether viewed from an economic or a political perspective, union behavior and the effects of technological change on unions can be distinguished from individual employee behavior and the effects of technological change on employees. In the context of public sanitation service, some unions that have seen their membership reduced by private contracting and technological change have organized private sanitation workers. Thus, on balance, sanitation union membership may be reconstituted rather than reduced by technological change in public sanitation service. Note, further, that if integrative bargaining is sustained or spreads more widely through municipal sanitation service, it may permit the parties to achieve new and different "membership-wage" combinations than are obtainable via distributive bargaining.

5
Dispute Resolution

T he resolution of negotiating disputes is the most visible aspect of public sector labor relations. This visibility stems from the use of strikes, and of procedural substitutes for strikes, as methods for resolving union–management differences at the bargaining table. In this chapter we will look closely at strikes and at dispute resolution procedures, with a special focus on interest arbitration.

The Private Sector Background

Because the institutionalization of collective bargaining in the private sector preceded the large-scale emergence of bargaining in government, and because private sector practices had a substantial impact on the development of governmental bargaining, we begin our analysis with a brief sketch of dispute resolution policies and practices in private industry.

Negotiating disputes in the private sector historically have been resolved by the threat or use of "concerned activities." Unions in the United States have relied primarily on collective bargaining (or private action) rather than government legislation (or public action) to secure direct benefits for their members. The unions long ago recognized that employers would be unwilling to accede to union demands if the unions could not make the employers pay for their recalcitrance. As a result, U.S. unions have developed an imaginative repertoire of concerted activities, such as strikes, slowdowns, picketing, and boycotts, aimed at interfering with the employers' normal operations and thereby increasing the costs of disagreeing with the unions' terms.[1] In most union–management relationships, the key source of union power is the strike threat underlying contract negotiations, followed by the actual strike that will occur if the results of the negotiations do not satisfy the union's minimum demands.[2]

From a public policy perspective, most strikes existed in something of a no-man's land until 1935. Prior to that time, most U.S workers had no statutorily protected right to bargain collectively or to conduct work stoppages, but neither were they legislatively prohibited from bargaining or striking.[3] In this legislative vacuum, the legality of strikes was controlled primarily by judges, who until the early 1930s frequently issued antistrike injunctions (and were also willing to apply the Sherman Antitrust Act's penalties to union boycott activities). A long period of judicial hostility toward strikes ended with the passage of the Norris-LaGuardia Act in 1932. With this statute Congress forbade federal judges to issue injunctions in labor disputes. Then, in the historic 1935 National Labor Relations (Wagner) Act, Congress took a giant step beyond Norris-LaGuardia by legislatively guaranteeing to most private workers the right to join unions, bargain collectively, and engage in concerted activities. As a result, after 1935 the official labor relations policy of the federal government encouraged the practice of collective bargaining and protected the right to strike.[4]

This right to engage in concerted activities has been steadily abridged since the unions' heady organizing days of the late 1930s, most notably in the 1947 and 1959 amendments to the Wagner Act, and also in the continuing line of National Labor Relations Board and federal court decisions dealing with these activities. Such abridgment does not mean that U.S. workers' strike rights have been emasculated; instead, the federal government has established a body of rules designed to limit when, where, how, and why strikes or other activities may occur. The three major thrusts of these rules have been to replace the use of economic muscle with peaceful procedures to resolve particular kinds of disputes (union recognition, jurisdiction over work assignments, and the like); to achieve an approximate balance of power between the contending parties; and to limit the arenas of conflict to the primary combatants and hence protect noninvolved third parties. Subject to a variety of specific constraints, however, the general right to strike is still legally protected.[5]

The federal government also has a statutory, albeit rather limited, right to intervene in peacetime labor disputes to assist the parties in reaching agreement. In the 1947 Labor Management Relations (Taft-Hartley) Act, Congress created the Federal Mediation and Conciliation Service (FMCS), an agency designed to monitor contract negotiations (especially the more important ones) and offer its mediation services to help the disputing parties reach agreement.[6] The FMCS, however, can only mediate; it has no power to impose a settlement on anyone. In addition, in disputes that could or have become "emergencies," the president has the statutory authority under the Railway Labor Act (covering railroads and airlines) and the Taft-Hartley Act (covering most private industries) to inject the federal government more forcefully into the disputes. Under Taft-Hartley, for instance, the government can secure an injunction that for eighty days will prevent a strike from starting or end a strike that has begun. The primary purposes of these intervention procedures are to protect against strikes that have harmful public or political ramifications and to prod the parties into reaching an agreement. It is important to note, however, that the government's statutory intervention authority expires after a fixed term, leaving the parties legally free to resume their concerted activities.[7]

At present there is no general legislative or executive authority for the federal or state government to mandate or impose terms of settlement on unions and employers.[8] On four separate occasions Congress has ordered the arbitration (or its equivalent) of particular railroad industry disputes, but these arbitration authorizations have not been applicable beyond the specific dispute in question.[9] At the state level, several states in the early post–World War II period statutorily provided for the compulsory arbitration of public utility labor disputes, but a 1951 U.S. Supreme Court decision declaring one of these laws unconstitutional effectively made all the statutes inoperable.[10] Finally, there has been some experimentation with voluntarily negotiated arbitration procedures (most notably in the basic steel industry), but these experiments involve only a tiny fraction of all private sector negotiations. The lack of arbitral authority over private sector negotiations is the result of a long-standing and deeply held belief on both sides of the negotiating table that the substantive terms of employment relationships are best established through the direct negotiations of unions and managements and should not be imposed by a third party.

We can conclude this oversimplified sweep of private sector dispute resolution policy and practice by noting four highlights:

1. From both a functional and a public policy perspective, the strike is a fundamental—some would say inescapable—part of the collective bargaining process in the United States. The operational implication of this conclusion is that collective bargaining is almost meaningless without the right to strike.

2. Public policy has placed some very definite limits on when, where, why, and how strikes may occur, so this right to strike is not absolute or unqualified.

3. The federal government, in its role as government-as-regulator, has some authority to intervene in labor disputes, but this authority is limited and clearly is secondary to the parties' own efforts to reach agreement.

4. As a corollary of this third point, compulsory arbitration is rarely used to settle negotiating disputes.

Public Policy in the Public Sector

The large-scale emergence of collective bargaining in government has occurred largely in the wake of state legislation granting bargaining rights to various groups of public employees. In this section we consider the various kinds of dispute resolution options available to policymakers and some of the arguments for and against their use.

Procedures Instead of Strikes

Our society has long taken for granted that governmental workers do not (and should not) have the right to strike (although this view is changing, as we will see later). As Lewin notes, this conventional wisdom is based on several arguments, the most prominent being governmental sovereignty (that is, as the sovereign power, government cannot engage in coercive contests with private groups), the essentiality of government services to the public welfare, and the unduly strong power position that government unions presumably would enjoy because of the employer's position as a monopolist.[11] For decades, these and other arguments were used to deny public employees the right to strike and also the right to bargain collectively—in part because strikes were seen as an inextricable component of the collective bargaining process.

During the past twenty-five years this conventional wisdom has been modified considerably by changing events. In 1962 President Kennedy authorized a limited form of collective bargaining for federal employees, and these federal employee bargaining rights were expanded under presidents Nixon and Carter. Throughout the 1960s and 1970s public employee organizations mounted scores of lobbying campaigns in various state capitols seeking bargaining legislation. These lobbying efforts, though not uniformly successful, did result in the passage of some form of bargaining legislation in more than thirty states. These laws usually established the right to bargain collectively, but prohibited strikes. During these two decades the amount of collective bargaining activity increased substantially, and it is hardly surprising that this increase in bargaining activity has been matched by an increase in strike activity (see table 5–1).

A variety of policy options is available to regulate the strike question. Some states, such as Louisiana and Colorado, have not passed any bargaining statutes, but strikes in these states are usually illegal as a result of court decisions or attorney generals' opinions. A second option is to prohibit strikes statutorily (either as part of a collective bargaining statute or in a separate piece of legislation). Sometimes such statutory prohibitions are supported by strike penalties (for example, public employees in New York are fined a day's pay—in addition to the day's pay lost by not working—for each day they are on strike), and a large majority of public sector bargaining statutes contain some kind of strike prohibition.

It is necessary to keep in mind, however, that this statutory strike prohibition option masks an important difference between official public policy in the state capitol (what the statute says) and operational public policy in bargaining units (what the parties actually do). As the figures in table 5–1 indicate, the number of public employee strikes—most of them illegal—rose dramatically in the late 1960s, continued at a high level through 1980, and declined substantially in 1981 (there are no comprehensive strike figures after 1981 as a result of Reagan administration budget cuts at the Department of Labor, but the overall number of public sector strikes in the early 1980s was below the level of the late 1970s).[12] This continuing stream of (mostly illegal) strikes suggests that operational or de facto public policy is not as condemnatory of strikes as the official or de jure policy appears to be on the basis of its statutory strike prohibitions. For instance, strikers, with some exceptions, are infrequently fired, fined, jailed, or otherwise penalized beyond the pay they lose by not working. The usual response by struck employers is to negotiate a settlement that will end the strike. Similarly, some state courts in states with statutory strike prohibitions have ruled that strikes may not be enjoined unless they clearly endanger the public welfare.[13] We may conclude that in many jurisdictions, an unspoken public policy recognizes that strikes will occur and tolerates them (at least up to a point) in spite of statutory strike prohibitions.

A third policy response is to implement procedural substitutes for the strike, and in those states with bargaining legislation this is the route that lawmakers have normally taken (usually in tandem with strike prohibitions). Operationally, this option involves the legislative implementation of mediation, fact-finding, arbitration, or some combination of these procedures (which we will describe later). This option is popular for two key reasons:

1. These procedures strengthen the unions' bargaining position over what it would be with no procedures, and can be justified on the equity grounds that without the strike the unions need some mechanisms to manipulate management's costs of disagreement.

2. These procedures have as their common theme the intervention of a third party to help the contending parties reach a settlement, and thus can be justified as protecting the public's interest in continuously receiving governmental services.

Mediation is the most widely available and frequently used procedure, and fact-finding is also available to many employee groups. Compulsory arbitration procedures have been mandated in twenty-one states, although

Table 5–1
Public Employee Work Stoppages by Level of Government, United States,
1958–1981

	Total[a]			Federal Government		
	Number of Stoppages	Workers Involved (thousands)	Days Idle During Year (thousands)	Number of Stoppages	Workers Involved (thousands)	Days Idle During Year (thousands)
1958	15	1.7	7.5	—	—	—
1959	25	2.0	10.5	—	—	—
1960	36	28.6	58.4	—	—	—
1961	28	6.6	15.3	—	—	—
1962	28	31.1	79.1	5	4.2	33.8
1963	29	4.8	15.4	—	—	—
1964	41	22.7	70.8	—	—	—
1965	42	1.9	146.0	—	—	—
1966	142	105.0	455.0	—	—	—
1967	181	132.0	1,250.0	—	—	—
1968	254	201.8	2,545.2	3	1.7	9.6
1969	411	160.0	745.7	2	0.6	1.1
1970	412	333.5	2,023.2	3	155.8	648.3
1971	329	152.6	901.4	2	1.0	8.1
1972	375	142.1	1,257.3	—	—	—
1973	387	196.4	2,303.9	1	0.5	4.6
1974	384	160.7	1,404.2	2	0.5	1.4
1975	478	318.5	2,204.4	—	—	—
1976	378	180.7	1,690.7	1	—	—
1977	413	170.2	1,765.7	2	0.4	0.5
1978	481	193.7	1,706.7	1	4.8	27.8
1979	593	254.1	2,982.5	—	—	—
1980	536	223.6	2,347.8	1	0.9	7.2
1981	219	131.5	2,604.8	1	11.4	650.5

Sources: U.S. Department of Labor, Bureau of Labor Statistics, Work Stoppages in Government, 1980, Bulletin 2110 (Washington, D.C.: U.S. Government Printing Office, 1981), p. 4; U.S. Department of Labor, Bureau of Labor Statistics, Handbook of Labor Statistics, Bulletin 2175 (December 1983), p. 404.

Note: Because of rounding, sums of individual items may not equal totals.

[a]The Bureau of Labor Statistics has published data on strikes in government in its annual reports since 1942. Before that year, they had been included in a miscellaneous category—"other nonmanufacturing industries." From 1942 through 1957, data refer only to strikes in administrative, protective, and

they are often limited to police and firefighter negotiating disputes. Many statutes specify a combination of procedures; for example, in Iowa, negotiating impasses must proceed through mediation and fact-finding before they arrive at the terminal step of arbitration. Finally, there is a great deal of diversity in impasse procedures across these state statutes.

Procedures and Strikes

A fourth policy option is the statutory legalization of the right to strike. As noted in table 5–2, strike rights have been legislatively granted in ten states

State Government			Local Government		
Number of Stoppages	Workers Involved (thousands)	Days Idle During Year (thousands)	Number of Stoppages	Workers Involved (thousands)	Days Idle During Year (thousands)
1			14	1.7	7.4
4	0.4	1.6	21	1.6	57.2
3	1.0	1.2	33	27.6	67.7
—	—	—	28	6.6	15.3
2	1.7	2.3	21	25.3	43.1
2	0.3	2.2	27	4.6	67.7
4	0.3	3.2	37	22.5	57.7
—	—	1.3	42	11.9	145.0
9	3.1	6.0	133	102.0	449.0
12	4.7	16.3	169	127.0	1,203.0
16	9.3	42.8	235	190.9	2,492.8
37	20.5	152.4	372	139.0	592.2
23	8.8	44.6	386	168.9	1,330.5
23	14.5	81.8	304	137.1	811.6
40	27.4	273.7	335	114.7	983.5
29	12.3	133.0	357	186.7	2,166.3
34	24.7	86.4	348	135.4	1,316.3
32	66.6	300.5	446	252.0	1,903.9
25	33.8	148.2	352	146.8	1,542.6
44	33.7	181.9	367	136.2	1,583.3
45	17.9	180.2	435	171.0	1,498.8
57	48.6	515.5	536	205.5	2,467.1
45	10.0	99.7	493	212.7	2,240.9
20	33.0	348.7	270	87.1	1,596.6

sanitary services of government. Stoppages in establishments owned by government were classified in their appropriate industry; for example, public schools and libraries were included in education services, not in government. Beginning in 1958, stoppages in such establishments were included under the "government" classification. Stoppages in publicly owned utilities, transportation, and schools were reclassified back to 1947, but a complete reclassification was not attempted. After 1957, dashes denote zeros.

since 1970 (and state courts in California and Idaho also have judicially extended the right to strike to some groups). This slow but steady trend represents the most visible evidence of the erosion of the conventional wisdom that governmental sovereignty, essentiality of services, and union bargaining power render the strike inappropriate for government employees.[14] This development is consistent with the emergence of a second generation of public sector bargaining, for the many strikes of recent years have resulted in an increasing awareness that such stoppages do not necessarily impugn governmental sovereignty, that many public services are temporarily dispensable, and that union power is often more imagined than real. As a result, policymakers in these states seem to have concluded that "labor

Table 5–2
Summary of State Bargaining Laws That Permit Public Employee Strikes

State	Strike Policy
Alaska	Strike prohibited for essential employees; permitted for semiessential employees (utilities, snow removal, sanitation) but may be enjoined if there is threat to public health, safety, or welfare; strike permitted for nonessential employees if approved by majority of unit in secret ballot election; no direct provision governing teachers.
Hawaii	Pertains to state and local government employees, police, firefighters, and teachers; strike prohibited for 60 days after fact-finding report; 10-day notice required; strike not permitted where public health or safety is endangered; can be enjoined by circuit court.
Illinois	Pertains to all state and local government employees except police, fire, and security employees; strike permitted provided the employees are unionized, the contract has expired, the employer and the union have not agreed to arbitrate the dispute, mediation has been used or requested, and the union has given notice of intent to strike.
Minnesota	Nonessential employees may legally strike if (1) an agreement has expired or, if there is no agreement, an impasse has occurred; (2) the employer and the union have participated in mediation sessions for at least 45 days; and (3) written notification of intent to strike has been served. Also, if a request for binding arbitration has been rejected or an employer fails to comply with a valid arbitration award, the strike right is available. The strike right is also available for teachers under the same conditions except that they must have participated in mediation for at least 60 days, 30 days of which have occurred after the expiration date of the collective bargaining agreement. State nonessential employees may strike if the legislature fails to ratify a negotiated agreement or arbitration award, or if the legislative commission on employee relations does not approve a negotiated agreement of arbitration award within 30 days during a legislative interim.
Montana	Pertains to state and local government employees, transit workers, police and firefighters; strike permitted; also pertains to nurses, but stoppage prohibited if simultaneous strike occurs within 150 miles; labor organization must give written notice and specify strike date.
Ohio	Pertains to state and local government employees except police, fire, and security employees; strike permitted provided that mediation and fact-finding have occurred and the union has given notice of intent to strike.
Oregon	Pertains to state and local government employees, and teachers; limited right to strike for employees included in appropriate bargaining unit certified by PERB for which final and binding arbitration is not provided; mediation and fact-finding and other statutory procedures must have been exhausted; injunctive relief can be granted if the strike is a threat to public health, safety, and welfare; strike is prohibited for police and firefighters, but the dispute must be submitted to binding arbitration if unresolved after mediation and fact-finding.
Pennsylvania	Pertains to state and local government employees, and to teachers (police, fire, and court employees excluded); limited right to strike after exhaustion of impasse procedures unless strike creates clear and present danger to public health, safety, and welfare; injunction may not be issued prior to strike.
Vermont	Pertains to local government employees, police, firefighters, and teachers; limited right to strike; stoppage is prohibited and enjoinable if it occurs 30 days after a fact-finder's report, after parties have submitted dispute to

Table 5–2 (continued)

State	Strike Policy
	arbitration, or if it is shown that the strike will endanger public health and safety; for teachers, a strike may be disallowed if it is ruled a clear and present danger to a sound program of education by a court of competent jurisdiction.
Wisconsin	Pertains to local government employees and teachers (but excluding police and firefighters); mandates mediation and final offer arbitration, except that if both parties withdraw their final offers prior to arbitration, the labor organization may strike after giving 10 days written advance notice.

Sources: David Lewin, "Collective Bargaining and the Right to Strike," in A. Lawrence Chickering, ed., *Public Employee Unions* (San Francisco: Institute for Contemporary Studies, 1976), pp. 155–56; Bureau of National Affairs, *Government Employee Relations Report,* Reference File-171 and 176. Washington, D.C.: BNA, December 4, 1978, pp. 21:1001–21; 1059, and December 8, 1983, pp. 27:1212–47; U.S. Bureau of the Census, 1982 Census of Governments, Volume 3, Public Employment, Number 2, Compendium of Public Employment, Washington, D.C.: Government Printing Office, pp. 21–52.

peace"—avoidance of strikes—should not necessarily be the top priority of public sector labor relations policy.

The information in table 5–2 suggests that public employee strike rights are considerably more constrained than strike rights in private industry. For example, public employee strike rights can be abridged if such strikes threaten the public health or safety; moreover, such rights often become operational only upon completion of dispute resolution procedures (usually mediation and/or fact-finding), and the employer can sometimes prevent such strikes altogether by agreeing to arbitration.

Consequently, we must conclude that the trend toward legal public employee strikes is a slow and cautious one of rather modest proportions. However, this trend does indicate a much wider acceptance of public employee strikes than existed twenty years ago.

The Practice of Dispute Resolution

It is much easier to describe how various dispute procedures are designed to operate than to assess their impacts on bargaining processes and outcomes. Much of the difficulty in doing the latter can be traced to two methodological problems: the problem of obtaining the relevant operational data, and the problem of controlling the multitude of other variables that influence bargaining processes and outcomes. As a result, it is fashionable for writers in this area to proclaim how little is known about these subjects and, consequently, how necessary further research is. Although we do not disagree with these proclamations, in this chapter we emphasize the dispute resolution information that *is* available in order to reach some conclusions, however tentative, about how settlements are achieved in governmental bargaining.

Strikes

The vast majority of negotiations produce agreements without strikes, but many of these agreements are created as a result of strike threats, and each year many of these threats become reality. The experiences with public employee strikes suggest several conclusions.

First, the data in tables 5–1 and 5–3 show that these strikes occur primarily between local government employers and employees, principally over money issues. In almost any given year, 90 percent or so of all government strikes occur among the municipalities, counties, school districts, and special districts that compose local government. Teacher strikes are more numerous than walkouts by other occupational groups, and several states account for a disproportionate share of strikes. This array of strike facts is hardly surprising when one considers that local governments employ more than half of all public employees, that these workers are more solidly organized and usually more militant than state and federal employees, that local governments tend to face greater financial scarcities than do state and federal governments, and that a lot more bargaining goes on in some states than in others.

Second, the data in table 5–4 show that public employee strikes have somewhat different characteristics than work stoppages in private industry. Public employee strikes are much shorter than strikes in private industry, and as a result the number of days of idleness per striker is much lower in government. In addition, the comparatively small number and short duration of government strikes means that the proportion of all work time lost because of strikes is lower in the public sector than in private industry (although proportions for both groups are very small).

Third, some recent research shows that strike penalties may reduce the number of strikes. In a study of the "propensity to strike" among teachers, police, firefighters, and other municipal employees in several states during the mid-1970s, Olson found that strong and consistently enforced strike penalties reduce strikes compared to situations where strikes are legal or where strikes are illegal but strikers and their unions are not penalized. For instance, in New York the Taylor Law's strike penalties—strikers lose two days pay for each day on strike, and unions of striking employees lose their dues checkoff privileges for a period of time, with these penalties consistently enforced by the state—led to a significant reduction in the number of strikes. In addition, Olson found that compulsory arbitration was another effective method for reducing the probability of a strike. As a result, his research (which is much more informative than earlier studies of public strike policies) indicates that policymakers have two effective policies—strong and consistently enforced strike penalties, and compulsory arbitration—that they can implement to prevent many strikes that otherwise might occur.[15]

This same propensity-to-strike research also revealed that strikes are

Table 5–3
Work Stoppages by Major Issue, Occupation, and State, 1980

Major Issue			
All issues	536	Idaho	3
General wage changes	399	Illinois	51
Supplementary benefits	10	Indiana	14
Wage adjustments	3	Iowa	—
Hours of work	1	Kansas	—
Other contractual matters	27	Kentucky	2
Union organization and security	17	Louisiana	2
Job security	28	Maine	1
Plant administration	44	Maryland	3
Other working conditions	4	Massachusetts	20
Interunion or intraunion matters	3	Michigan	75
Occupation		Minnesota	7
		Mississippi	1
All occupations	536	Missouri	7
Teachers	232	Montana	3
Nurses	8	Nebraska	2
Other professional and technical	17	Nevada	—
Clerical	10	New Hampshire	2
Blue-collar and manual	138	New Jersey	50
Police	37	New Mexico	—
Firefighters	9	New York	21
Police and firefighters	6	North Carolina	1
Other protective	8	North Dakota	—
Other	71	Ohio	60
		Oklahoma	1
State		Oregon	2
All States	536	Pennsylvania	82
Alabama	1	Rhode Island	8
Alaska	2	South Carolina	—
Arizona	2	South Dakota	—
Arkansas	2	Tennessee	10
California	51	Texas	5
Colorado	4	Utah	—
Connecticut	3	Vermont	—
Delaware	1	Virginia	1
District of Columbia	2	Washington	14
Florida	6	West Virginia	5
Georgia	4	Wisconsin	5
Hawaii	—	Wyoming	—

Source: U.S. Department of Labor, Bureau of Labor Statistics, *Work Stoppages in Government 1980,* Bulletin 2110 (Washington, D.C.: U.S. Government Printing Office, 1981), pp. 7, 8, 9.

influenced by other factors (in addition to strike penalties). For instance, Olson examined teacher and municipal employee strikes in six states and found that the probability of a strike was much higher in larger school districts (those with more than 5,000 students) and cities (those with more than 25,000 residents) than in smaller jurisdictions.[16] In addition, Olson also examined teacher strikes in Pennsylvania (a state where teacher strikes are

Table 5–4

Selected Work Stoppage Measures, All Industries and Government, 1980

Measure	All Industries	Government Stoppages		
		Total	State	Local
Days of idleness as a percentage of working time	0.14	0.06	0.01	0.09
Workers involved as a percentage of total employment	1.5	1.4	0.3	2.2
Average number of workers involved per stoppage	352	417	222	431
Average days of idleness per worker	24.4	10.5	10.0	10.5

Source: U.S. Department of Labor, Bureau of Labor Statistics, *Work Stoppages in Government, 1980,* Bulletin 2110 (Washington, D.C.: U.S. Government Printing Office, 1981, p. 5.

legal) and found that the probability of a strike was higher in school districts that had rescheduled school days lost in an earlier strike.[17] In other words, teachers who had not lost income during an earlier strike (because of the rescheduled days) were more willing to go on strike again (presumably because of the expectation that they would not lose any income by striking again). In related research, Stern and Olson found that strike rates varied across occupational groups. In a national sample of negotiations during 1975–1977, they found that about 4 percent of teacher negotiations resulted in a strike, while about 2.3 percent of firefighter negotiations and about 1.6 percent of police negotiations involved a walkout.[18] These strike rates varied substantially from state to state, however, and the decline in public sector strikes after 1980 suggests that these percentages might be lower today. Taken together, the research by Olson and his colleagues usefully explains many of the factors that influence strike occurrences in government.

Fourth, there is some research that explores the relationship between strikes and bargaining outcomes. Logical reasoning suggests that strike-induced settlements may be more favorable to employees than nonstrike settlements on the grounds that the struck employers are willing to pay a premium to have the withheld services restored. The available evidence, however, suggests that this scenario may be followed only some of the time. For instance, Delaney found that teacher strikes in Illinois resulted in larger salary settlements and, eventually, in more favorable contract terms compared to bargaining districts that experienced no strikes.[19] Gerhart correlated an index of favorable union bargaining outcomes with a state strike activity index and found a positive but weak association.[20] Kochan and Wheeler correlated firefighter strikes with favorable union outcomes and found no discernible relationship, but they did find favorable outcomes correlated with union pressure tactics such as picketing and slowdowns.[21] Anderson found that over the long run Canadian federal employees have not been able to use strikes or strike threats to obtain higher wages or better contractual benefits than their peers who bargained under a compulsory arbitration system, but that in particular years actually going on strike seemed to yield large payoffs for some groups.[22] Further, since the late 1970s public management has shown an increasing willingness to "hang tough" in strike situations, and many strikes have ended on less than victorious terms for the unions involved (including, in a few cases, the permanent discharges of striking employees).[23] As a result of this mixed bag of information, it is very difficult to offer any unequivocal conclusions about the impact of strikes on bargaining outcomes. The most accurate answer to the question of "Who wins?" in strike situations is "It depends."

Fifth, the relationship between government strikes and the maintenance of the public welfare is similarly ambiguous. As a general conclusion, we believe that the danger most public employee strikes pose to the citizenry's health, safety, or welfare is more rhetorical than real; the public appears to survive the vast majority of these strikes with a minimum of apprehension and inconvenience. To take one prominent example, the citizens of Chicago survived a twenty-three-day strike by most of the Windy City's firefighters in early 1980 with about the same amount of fire-related death and destruction that occurred in comparable (nonstrike) periods in previous years.[24] More generally, Feuille argues in his selection in this chapter that it is very difficult to demonstrate systematically that the public needs to be protected from strikes of its own employees. Further, the large number of strikes that have occurred since the late 1960s indicates that these activities are occurring more and more as "normal" events, which increasingly are built into the parties' expectations. This admittedly subjective assessment is supported by the increasing legalization of strikes and the increasing willingness of management to withstand strikes in order to implement its demands for "less" relative to union demands for "more." Just as this society has learned to cope with private sector strikes, so we see the same process occurring in the public sector.

The PATCO Strike. The most visible public strike since 1919 (the year the Boston police walked out and fueled a decades-long antipathy toward public employee unions) occurred in 1981 when about 12,000 federal air traffic controllers walked off the job in a quest for higher wages and fringes and a shorter work week. This strike occurred after their union, the Professional Air Traffic Controllers Organization (PATCO), had forced the federal government to bargain over monetary items and had negotiated gains that were not available to other federal employees. When these negotiating table successes were rejected by the membership, the union demanded more, the government refused, and the controllers struck. This strike was a watershed event, pitting a very militant union against the strongly determined Reagan administration over the employment terms of a large and highly visible group of federal employees whose services were essential to the functioning of the air traffic system.

The PATCO strike turned into the most disastrous walkout in memory for public workers and public unions. The striking controllers were fired, and almost all their appeals for reinstatement have been denied. Some of the strike leaders were temporarily jailed. The union was decertified, was fined heavily, went bankrupt, and has ceased to exist. The government, the airlines, and airline passengers weathered the strike much better than expected, despite considerable short-term disruption of airline schedules and balance sheets. The strikers were replaced, and a new controller work force now staffs the nation's control towers. Ironically, the new controllers complain about many of the same working conditions as did their fired predecessors and, as a result, have selected a new union (NATCA, the National Air Traffic Controllers Association) as their bargaining representative.

During and immediately after the PATCO strike, there was considerable speculation that this debacle for organized labor would create a union-busting ripple effect throughout government as managers everywhere would try to emulate President Reagan's toughness in dealing with PATCO. Six years later, however, it is difficult to detect any such phenomenon. Because there have been very few strikes in the federal government over the years, the general absence of federal employee strikes since 1981 should not be attributed to the fallout from the PATCO affair. The number of state and local employee strikes, especially by teachers, declined in 1981 and 1982 compared with 1980, but this result is probably attributable more to the fiscal scarcity and reduced rate of inflation engendered by the nation's severe economic recession during those years than to fear of a PATCO-style execution. Similarly, there have been no reports of state and local managerial attempts to decertify unions as a result of PATCO.

The reasons for PATCO's demise have been analyzed elsewhere and do not need to be repeated here.[25] The PATCO strike, however, stands as a stark and sobering exception to the usual public employee strike scenario of short strikes, negotiated settlements, returning employees, and the resumption of business as usual. For about 11,300 former air traffic controllers, business as usual has not resumed.

Mediation

Of the three third-party intervention procedures we will examine (mediation, fact-finding, and arbitration), mediation is the most difficult to describe. This is because the mediation process is relatively informal and unstructured, reflecting the personal style of the mediator, the preferences of the union and employer representatives, and the intensity of the dispute. Mediation is invoked when the parties declare that an impasse exists; a mediator is then assigned to the case by the state's public sector labor relations administrative agency. The mediator's job is to help the union and the employer reach agreement, but the form of this assistance may vary widely across different disputes. Typically, the mediator begins by sitting down in a joint session with the union and employer negotiating teams and reviewing the unresolved issues and the parties' positions on those issues. Then the mediator usually moves the two teams into separate rooms and deals with them sequentially. In these back-and-forth meetings, the mediator focuses the parties' attention on the issues and conveys offers, counteroffers, and other messages to each negotiating team in a manner designed to produce agreement. Sometimes a settlement is reached quickly, but at other times a settlement may be reached only after a long and arduous effort, and at still other times a settlement cannot be achieved. As this description implies, the mediation process does not involve a formal hearing or a written award; instead, it involves a series of discussions, with the mediator controlling the flow of information between union and employer representatives. As this description also implies, the mediator has no power to require the parties to agree to anything. The mediator can ask, persuade, cajole, or even beg the parties to settle, but he or she cannot force them to settle. Consequently, the use of mediation is no guarantee that a settlement will occur.

Mediation is probably the most used and least studied dispute resolution procedure. It is widely used because many public sector bargaining laws require that mediation be used as the first step toward resolving negotiating disputes. In addition, unions and employers have generally positive attitudes toward mediation because they retain joint control over the outcome, so that there is essentially no risk that mediation will result in an unacceptable settlement. The modest amount of careful study of mediation is due to the fact that mediation's unstructured and behind-the-scenes nature, plus the absence of any written award, makes it very difficult for researchers to obtain pertinent information. Further, most mediators appear convinced that their craft is more art than science and hence is not especially amenable to systematic inquiry and generalization. One of the few studies that has probed into the dynamics of mediation is the Kressel reading, which we believe represents a fascinating account of how a sample of mediators work to bring the parties together.[26]

How effective is mediation? The most widely used measure of effectiveness is the proportion of impasses settled at mediation. Using this yardstick, Hoh's analysis in this chapter shows that more than three-quarters of all Iowa impasses are settled at the mediation step of that state's three-step statutory impasse procedure (although the declaration of impasses in Iowa is artificially inflated by a statutory filing requirement). Also, Hoh's analysis shows that mediation resolved significant proportions of disputes in other states, a result confirmed by Stern for the mediation experience in Wisconsin.[27] In addition, in many states a large number of disputes are mediated into agreement at the fact-finding or arbitration steps. The conventional wisdom in dispute resolution circles is that mediation is the most preferred (or least undesirable) form of third-party intervention because it is much less coercive than fact-finding or arbitration; hence, any mediated settlements primarily reflect the desires of the parties. The large proportion of all impasses settled through mediation tends to support this conventional wisdom.

The increasing availability of fact-finding and arbitration has posed an important question for the continued effectiveness of mediation: How does the availability of these more structured and coercive procedures affect mediation's effectiveness? There are no conclusive answers to this question, in part because of a scarcity of information. For instance, one study reported that a sample of mediators perceived that mediation is more effective in reaching agreement when followed by arbitration rather than by fact-finding, and that mediation is more effective under final offer than under conventional arbitration.[28] These perceptions, however, were not supported by any statistical evidence. A careful investigation of this question has been made by Kochan and his associates in their study of New York police and firefighter impasse resolution before and after the introduction of conventional arbitration. They found that mediation appeared to be equally effective—as measured by the proportion of mediated agreements and by the perceptions of union and management negotiators—when fact-finding was the final impasse step as when conventional arbitration was the final step.[29]

The nature of the negotiating impasse probably has more impact on mediation's usefulness than postmediation procedures. It has been hypothesized that mediation works well in those disputes where the parties are inexperienced in bargaining and hence unsure of themselves, lack knowledge of contract language, and are especially susceptible to personality conflicts. In these situations mediators can play a useful role in helping the parties develop an improved appreciation of the negotiating process. Mediation may work less well in situations where there are strong constituent pressures, scarce resources, and sophisticated negotiators who know how to manipulate dispute procedures to their advantage. In cases where these factors are present and where mediation is followed by fact-finding or arbitration, the proportion of impasse settled via mediation is likely to be relatively small.

Another important factor influencing mediator success is the style or philosophy of the mediator or mediation agency, usually expressed on an aggressive–passive or degree-of-intensity continuum. For instance, Kochan and Jick found that aggressive mediators were more successful in obtaining mediated settlements than were passive mediators.[30] Going a step further, Gerhart and Drotning found that high-intensity mediators were more effective than low-intensity mediators in facilitating settlements in tough bargaining cases.[31] These differences in mediator styles are not only a function of the preferences and personalities of individual mediators, but also may reflect different mediator philosophies across mediation agencies. Kolb compared mediator activities in a regional office of the Federal Mediation and Conciliation Service and in a state mediation agency and found that the state mediators (the "dealmakers") were uniformly aggressive in trying to achieve settlements, whereas the federal mediators (the "orchestrators") were comparatively more passive.[32] However, Kolb's assessment has been criticized as an "interesting, bad theory of mediation" on the grounds that the intensity of the dispute rather than the mediator's agency affiliation is the primary determinant of mediator tactics.[33] More generally, Carnevale and Pegnetter examined the use of mediation tactics by public sector mediators in Iowa and found that mediators tailored their tactics to the particular circumstances of the dispute. For example, mediators who encountered negotiators with unrealistic expectations worked to reduce these expectations, mediators who encountered too many issues worked to simplify the agenda, and mediators who dealt with inexperienced negotiators tried to educate them about the impasse process.[34] We still need a great deal more research to discover which specific mediator activities are best suited to various bargaining circumstances, but it is readily apparent that the term *mediation* encompasses a very wide variety of dispute resolution behaviors.

As the preceding discussion suggests, mediation and the other impasse procedures should not be regarded as techniques to be used only after the parties have thoroughly explored every settlement possibility in direct negotiations and have bargained to exhaustion. Although some impasses are accurately described in such a manner, it is more likely that negotiators manipulate impasse procedures to gain tactical negotiating advantages, and the first step in such manipulation usually is to trigger the mediation process (see the Kressel reading for an elaboration of this phenomenon). Further, the unions are more likely than management to be the party initiating these impasse steps. Bargaining purists may decry this procedural manipulation, but the fact that the parties have incorporated such manipulation into their negotiating strategies should not be surprising given, first, the absence of the right to strike in most states and, second, the requirement in some states that these procedures be used prior to conducting a legal strike.

Fact-finding

Fact-finding is a misnamed process—rarely does it produce "facts" not already found—that combines elements of mediation and arbitration (sometimes it is called *advisory arbitration*). It has much of the structure and ritual of arbitration, including a hearing, testimony from each side, and a written report; but, as in mediation, the third party's settlement recommendations are not binding upon the parties. Further, in that the ostensible purpose of the procedure is to use a third party to create a settlement range that the two contending parties will find acceptable, the fact-finder's function is conceptually similar to that of a mediator. In addition, mediation and fact-finding often overlap, and in some disputes it is difficult to tell where one stops and the other begins. In part, this blurred distinction results from the mediation efforts of many fact-finders as well as from the mediation efforts that sometimes occur after a fact-finding report has been issued (indeed, fact-finding can be thought of as "mediation in writing").

During the 1970s, fact-finding acquired an increasingly poor reputation. Its bad name, largely undeserved, resulted primarily from a deadly mixture of high expectations and low performance. Expectations are high because the procedure appears quasi-adjudicative, but performance often is low because either party can—and often does—reject the fact-finder's report. The strongest condemnations of fact-finding have occurred in states where fact-finding was (or still is) the terminal step in the official impasse procedure. The evidence from these jurisdictions suggests that fact-finding's lack of finality limits its usefulness as a substitute for strikes, that some parties may incorporate fact-finding into their negotiating strategies and may not begin to bargain seriously until after receipt of the fact-finder's report, and that public pressure on the parties to accept the fact-finder's recommendations—one of the key reasons for fact-finding's existence—almost never occurs (usually because the public either doesn't know or doesn't care that the process is being used).[35] In addition, fact-finding may be ineffective in bringing the parties together when it is followed by conventional arbitration, as occurred in New York police and fire impasses during 1974–1977.[36] Finally, fact-finding may be least useful in situations involving financial scarcity, for there is often a wide gap between employers' and employees' expectations that cannot be bridged simply with the well-meaning suggestions of a third party.

During the 1970s compulsory arbitration and the right to strike became more common as the terminal step in statutory dispute procedures, in part because of employee and union dissatisfaction with fact-finding. This dissatisfaction indicates that when fact-finding is the terminal step in a dispute procedure, it may be doomed to a fairly short effective life once the parties have become experienced at manipulating the impasse process to their own advantage. Fact-finding can, however, play a very useful role in helping unions and managements resolve their difference, as Gallagher indicates in his research on fact-finding and arbitration in Iowa.[37] The key to fact-finding's success in Iowa—more than half of the fact-finding cases are settled at fact-finding and do not go on to arbitration, and arbitrators tend to confirm fact-finder recommendations in those cases where an arbitration award is necessary—is the great likelihood that an arbitrator will impose the fact-finder's judgment on the parties. Knowing this, the parties can—and do—use this information to fashion their own settlements.

Gallagher's research suggests that fact-finding may be effective in those states where the fact-finding has a direct impact on arbitration. In addition, the substantial number of mediated and negotiated settlements at the fact-finding step in several states indicates that many parties are willing to use the fact-finder's help in resolving their disputes. Finally, the lack of a binding award may be fact-finding's greatest virtue, for the procedure's open end leaves room for the parties to fashion their own agreement—which is the purpose of collective bargaining.

Compulsory Arbitration

Of the three impasse resolution procedures examined here, compulsory and binding interest arbitration has captured the lion's share of attention.[38] As of 1986, there were twenty-one states with some type of compulsory arbitration statute,[39] and most of these laws were passed by state legislatures as a result of union lobbying efforts (usually over the opposition of management lobbying against such statutes). Most of these laws cover police and fire employees and employers, but some cover a wider range of occupations (for example, the Iowa arbitration law covers all state and local government employees in that state). Some of these laws provide for *conventional* arbitration, which allows the arbitrator to fashion the award he or she deems appropriate on the disputed issues. Some of these laws specify *final offer* arbitration (sometimes called last offer, best offer, last best offer, one-or-the-other, or either-or arbitration), which requires the arbitrator to choose either the union's final offer or the employer's final offer, with no room for compromise. Further, there are two kinds of final offer arbitration: final offer by package, where the arbitrator must select one side's final offer on all the disputed issues, and final offer by issue, which allows the arbitrator to select either side's final offer on an issue-by-issue basis (which means that in a multi-issue dispute the arbitrator can select some union final offers and some employer final offers). Some statutes specify different types of arbitration for different types of issues (such as, in Illinois and Michigan, which require final offer by issue arbitration for economic issues and conventional arbitration for noneconomic issues). Some laws provided for a tripartite arbitration panel (composed of a union-appointed arbitrator, an employer-appointed arbitrator, and an impartial chairperson) to make decisions. Still other laws call for a single arbitrator format (*single* refers to number of arbitrators rather than marital status). Because no two state arbitration statutes are the same, there is a great deal of procedural diversity across the twenty-one arbitration states. In most states, unions and employers are allowed to take any bargainable issue to arbitration, but the Delaney and Feuille reading in this chapter indicates that in a large sample of police arbitration cases, most of the arbitrated issues were economic rather than noneconomic.

The key feature of arbitration that sets it apart from mediation and fact-finding is that the third party—the arbitrator—issues an award that is binding on the union and the employer. In other words, it is the arbitrator who decides on the substantive terms of the disputed issues rather than leaving these terms to be resolved by the parties at the bargaining table. Arbitration has had numerous impacts on governmental labor relations, and most of these impacts can be traced to the binding nature of the procedure.

Strikes. The most widely used rationale supporting arbitration laws is that arbitration reduces strikes. Arbitration has this effect because its binding award eliminates almost any opportunity for one side to provoke or conduct a work stoppage for terms more favorable than those provided by the arbitrator.[40] Most of these statutes apply to police and firefighters, who arguably provide state and local government's most essential services; thus, these laws try to ensure that the citizenry will receive vital public safety protection on an uninterrupted basis.

The usual test for how well or poorly arbitration has performed its strike prevention function is to compare strike occurrences among covered employees in states with and without arbitration. Although the available evidence indicates that arbitration is not a perfect form of no-strike insurance (a few strikes *have* occurred under these statutes), the evidence shows that far fewer strikes occur where arbitration is mandated than where it is not.[41] Consequently, arbitration appears to have done an effective job of preventing strikes by covered employees.

However, arbitration should not be viewed as the quid pro quo for the right to strike, for the employee groups covered by arbitration have not given up any right they previously enjoyed.[42] A more accurate interpretation of arbitration statutes is that they represent political quid pro quos. In return for the unions giving up their ability to conduct (illegal) strikes, the politicians pass arbitration statutes and presumably collect political IOUs in return.

Bargaining Outcomes. Unions perceive arbitration as a low-cost power equalizer that increases their strength at the bargaining table. Without arbitration, public employee unions may need to resort to strikes or political alliances to achieve their desired bargaining terms. If a union faces an unreceptive bargaining or political environment, however, these tactics may be ineffective, and the employer may be able to insist on its own terms. In contrast, when arbitration is available, a union may respond to the employer's insistence on its own terms by invoking the arbitration procedure and presenting its case to the arbitrator (under compulsory arbitration, either side may invoke arbitration; thus, it is not necessary for the union and the employer voluntarily to agree to arbitrate). Assuming that the arbitrator wants to continue working as an arbitrator, his or her need to preserve a reputation for impartiality in order to remain acceptable to unions and employers, combined with the ability of unions and employers to veto the selection of specific arbitrators, mean that the arbitrator will strive to fashion a "fair" award that is responsive to the concerns expressed by both sides. In practice, this reasoning suggests that the arbitrator may award a set of outcomes that is more favorable (to the union) than the union could have negotiated if the arbitration procedure did not exist. Expressed another way, in the absence of arbitration the employer is usually more able to impose its version of a fair settlement than is the union. Consequently, arbitration should enable a union to come closer to its version of a fair settlement than is otherwise possible.[43]

Even when arbitration is not actually used, it may have an impact on bargaining outcomes. Both parties can examine the arbitration experiences in their state to anticipate what an arbitrator is likely to award; because neither side will prefer a negotiated settlement that is less favorable than the expected award, they can use this knowledge to negotiate a settlement. In fact, in arbitration states unions and employers usually negotiate their own agreements even though they could have received arbitration awards.

In recent years there has been considerable investigation of arbitration's influence on bargaining outcomes. This research indicates that the existence of an arbitration statute is associated with union-favorable bargaining outcomes. Specifically, the wages and contract provisions of police and firefighters tend to be more favorable to the union in arbitration states than where these groups are not covered by such a law.[44] These differences exist after controlling for other influences on bargaining outcomes, such as city size, location, and socioeconomic characteristics. For instance, one study found that police wage levels were 1 to 9 percent higher in arbitration states than in nonarbitration states after controlling for these other influences, but that the size of this wage effect varied across states, across years, and across the different statistical techniques used.[45] Similarly, another study found that police contracts in arbitration states contained nonwage provisions that were about 20 percent more favorable to the unions (as measured by a complex contract scoring index) than provisions of contracts in nonarbitration states.[46]

In addition, this research indicates that it is the *availability* of arbitration, rather than the actual *use* of the procedure, that is associated with union-favorable outcomes. This finding implies that over time the existence of an arbitration statute may shift both arbitrated and negotiated outcomes in the direction desired by the unions. This research also shows, however, that negotiated and arbitrated outcomes in the same arbitration state in any given year tend to be very similar. This is not surprising when we consider the important role played in the arbitration process by "comparability" (comparisons of the employment terms of the group at arbitration with those of similarly situated employees elsewhere).[47] The parties rely heavily on comparability evidence when they formulate their offers, and arbitrators rely heavily on comparability evidence in formulating awards; thus, it is difficult for arbitration awards as a group to diverge substantially from the negotiated settlements in the same state.[48]

The research evidence permits us to say with considerable confidence that arbitration is associated with union-favorable outcomes. We are less certain, however, that arbitration is the direct cause of these outcomes. For instance, some of this research shows that employers in arbitration states paid high wages and benefits even before arbitration laws were passed.[49] In addition, this research also shows that bargaining outcomes are strongly influenced by factors (such as city size and location) that have nothing directly to do with the presence or absence of an arbitration law. As a result, the strength of the association between arbitration and union-favorable outcomes may or may not be an accurate indicator of the extent to which arbitration is the direct cause of these outcomes. In any case, however, arbitration's coexistence with union-favorable employment terms has generated and will continue to generate a pattern of union support for arbitration and employer opposition to it.

Bargaining Process. Arbitration is sometimes criticized as a procedure that is harmful to the collective bargaining process. In particular, conventional arbitration is often alleged to have a chilling effect on the parties' incentives to reach their own agreement. The reasoning behind this allegation is that if either one of the parties perceives—for whatever reasons—that it may get a better deal from an arbitrator than from a negotiated agreement, it will have an incentive to cling to excessive demands in the hope of tilting the arbitration award in its favor. If one side acts this way, the other side has no realistic choice but to respond in like manner, and the result is surface bargaining on top of a wide gap between the parties' positions. This lack of hard bargaining will occur because of the very small costs attached to remaining in disagreement: there will be no strike by the union and no unilateral changes by the employer, and the compromise nature of the typical award will give the employees less than the union has asked for but more than the employer has offered. This compromise award is made possible by the discretion the arbitrator possesses to fashion the award he or she deems appropriate on the disputed issues. In addition, there is the fear that over time a "narcotic effect" may emerge as the parties become addicted to having arbitrators resolve their disagreements. In other words, the criticism is that the parties will become dependent on outside arbitrators rather than on their own negotiating efforts to resolve bargaining disputes.

Policymakers in several jurisdictions, including Illinois, Iowa, Michigan, New Jersey, and Wisconsin, have responded to this criticism by implement-

is response

ing *final offer arbitration,* a procedure that attempts to preserve the strike prevention and impasse finality features of conventional arbitration while simultaneously increasing the parties' incentives to reach their own agreement. This kind of arbitration attempts to increase the parties' costs of not reaching agreement by eliminating arbitral discretion and thus forcing the arbitrator to select one or the other party's final offer—with no room for compromise. The final offer theory predicts that each side will develop ever more reasonable negotiating positions in the hope of winning the award, and that these convergent movements will result because of the fear that the arbitrator will select the other side's offer.

The considerable research devoted to arbitration's impact on the bargaining process indicates that the availability of arbitration does influence the parties' negotiating incentives. For instance, researchers who have compared arbitration and strike usage rates in particular jurisdictions have found that far more parties are willing to arbitrate than to strike.[50] These findings indicate that the parties view arbitration as a significantly lower cost procedure than the strike, and thus are willing to use arbitration more frequently (in other words, some of the time there is a chilling effect). In addition, and consistent with the final offer theory, final offer arbitration seems to encourage more negotiating behavior than does conventional arbitration, and final offer by package arbitration appears to do an effective job of reducing the number of issues that are taken for arbitration. More generally, the characteristics of the arbitration procedure may affect how often the procedure is used. Further, the Chelius and Extejt reading in this chapter suggests that in some states there may be a short-term narcotic effect in the first few years after an arbitration statute is passed (that is, some unions and employers may use arbitration repeatedly), but that in the long run no such effect is apparent—parties who had been using arbitration are able to break their dependence on it. We also know that triggering the arbitration procedure does not inevitably lead to an award, for many parties use the process as a forum for additional negotiations. Moreover, in practically all arbitration states there are many more negotiated agreements than arbitrated awards.[51] Taken together, these research findings suggest that bargaining and arbitration are generally compatible, although the degree of this compatibility varies substantially from city to city.

Arbitration and Democratic Government. Another criticism is aimed at arbitration's alleged constitutional and political incompatibility with our democratic system of representative government. In this system the citizens elect government officials who are responsible for the allocation of scarce public resources—both dollar and nondollar. If a majority of the citizenry is dissatisfied with these allocation decisions, the relevant officials may be voted out of office. In addition, the government's financial resources are coerced from the citizenry in the form of taxes, and government officials should be accountable for the use of these funds. Arbitration critics point out that under the typical arbitration procedure the arbitrator often is appointed by an outside agency, enters an impasse on an ad hoc basis, issues an award, and leaves the scene. He or she is not elected to this position and is not accountable to those groups—employees, employer, citizens—who must live with and bear the impact of the award. Further, the arbitration process itself rarely, if ever, provides an opportunity for the direct involvement of citizen interest groups. Consequently, arbitration is said to be an unwarranted delegation of governmental authority to a private party that is inconsistent with our system of government.

If this argument was compelling, we would expect to find the courts striking down compulsory interest arbitration statutes as unconstitutional. Similarly, we would expect to find that either considerably fewer state legislatures would have passed arbitration laws or else that considerably more of the legislatures that had passed such laws would have rescinded their earlier actions. The record shows that twenty-four state legislatures have passed arbitration statutes, that no legislature that passed such a law has reversed itself on the arbitration question (although, as noted earlier, three such laws were struck down by other means), and that state arbitration statutes have been constitutionally approved in fourteen of the eighteen states where this question has been litigated (as of 1983).[52] Accordingly, the factual record just cited removes much of the forcefulness from this line of criticism. In other words, the constitutional and political defects of compulsory arbitration have appeared more rhetorical than real in many state legislatures and appellate courts.

Benefits and Costs. Compulsory arbitration is a form of labor market regulation, for it specifies a procedure that constrains or prevents behavior that otherwise might occur.[53] Like most forms of regulation, arbitration provides some benefits and imposes some costs. For instance, to the extent that arbitration results in higher wages and benefits, it benefits employees and imposes costs on taxpayers. Similarly, to the extent that arbitration results in fewer strikes, it benefits employees, managers, and citizens by eliminating the inconvenience and anxiety associated with work stoppages; but arbitration's availability may reduce the parties' incentives to strive diligently for a negotiated settlement. As these two examples indicate, the beneficiaries of arbitration may differ from those who bear the costs. The Feuille selection in this chapter explores more fully some of the benefits and costs of arbitration. The author's main points are that (1) arbitration statutes are implemented and renewed to serve partisan interests rather than the "public interest," (2) arbitration does much more than prevent strikes, and (3) most conclusions about arbitration tend to result more from preexisting normative positions for or against the process rather than from objective examinations of available evidence.

Conclusion. The available evidence indicates that arbitration is an acceptable and effective method for absorbing various employee and employer pressures that might emerge as overt labor–management conflict. Arbitration is associated with a reduction in strikes; it has been given a constitutional stamp of approval in most states where it exists; the collective bargaining process usually functions effectively in the presence of arbitration; and union and management compliance with the arbitration process and its awards is widespread, though not equally enthusiastic. But arbitration also generates conflict as well: most public managements are as opposed to arbitration as most public unions are in favor of it, with the result that there often is sharp labor–management disagreement over whether arbitration should be legally mandated. Although arbitration statutes have existed in some states since the 1960s, conflict over this form of dispute resolution seems to be in no danger of disappearing.

Finally, the arbitration experiences in many U.S. and Canadian jurisdictions strongly suggest that in order to fully understand how these procedures influence negotiating behaviors and outcomes, we must pay careful attention to the procedural fine points of the various statutory schemes. Expressed another way, once you have seen one arbitration procedure, you have *not* seen them all.[54]

Third-Party Dependency

As long as public sector labor relations policy prohibits strikes, impasse resolution procedures will be implemented and used. Much of our analysis has focused on how often governmental unions and managements rely on third parties to help them reach agreement (via mediation or fact-finding) or to impose a settlement (via arbitration). One of our concerns is that unions and managements will rely too much on third parties to the detriment of the effective functioning of the collective bargaining process, and we have seen that in selected jurisdictions the availability of various procedures—especially conventional arbitration—has substantially reduced the parties' efforts to negotiate their own agreements.

We should qualify our perceptions, however, by repeating an earlier point: there is no formula to determine how much third-party intervention is "too much." For example, some observers will conclude that a 25 percent arbitration award rate is evidence of too much dependency, whereas others will emphasize that three-quarters of the negotiations ended in agreement. In addition, if policymakers place greatest weight on protecting the public from strikes, then the extent of third-party intervention is of secondary importance. Further, any settlement achieved via mediation or fact-finding can occur only with the combined approval of the two contending parties, so there is an inherent limit to the role played by third parties in nonbinding procedures. In sum, it seems fair to say that public sector experiences with third-party impasse resolution procedures have demonstrated that most of the time collective bargaining can function effectively without the right to strike.

Concluding Comments

We close this introductory portion of chapter 5 by reemphasizing our earlier point about the tremendous diversity that exists in the impasse procedures and practices across the federal government, the fifty state governments, and countless local governments. This diversity is well illustrated by the numerous dimensions along which these procedures can and do vary (in addition to those already mentioned): the employee groups covered, who initiates the process, who provides the impasse services, the procedural timetable, the requirements for moving from mediation to fact-finding to arbitration (if available), the criteria to be used by the third parties in reaching their decisions, who pays the costs, and so on. Adding to this diversity is the changing nature of the impasse resolution scene over time, especially the growth of arbitration statutes and of the right to strike, and the increasing aggressiveness of management. We believe this diversity is healthy, for it means that there is more impasse experimentation than would be the case otherwise. In turn, this experimentation means that the public sector can offer some valuable impasse resolution suggestions to the private sector.

Earlier in this chapter we briefly examined private sector dispute practices, emphasizing the reliance on the strike—subject to the government's rules regulating its use—and the relative unimportance of third-party intervention. We have discussed two public sector trends, one that converged with private sector practice and another that diverges from it. We believe that the growth of the right to strike and management's apparent increasing tolerance of strikes indicate that, on the one hand, public sector practices may be moving—however slowly—toward private sector norms. On the other hand, the public sector continues to increase its reliance on third-party procedures—witness the growth of arbitration statutes—and this phenomenon contrasts sharply with private industry practice. On balance, then, we believe the public and private sectors will be distinguished for some time to come by their respective reliance on procedures and on strikes to resolve negotiating disputes.

Notes

1. See Neil W. Chamberlain and James W. Kuhn, *Collective Bargaining,* 3rd ed. (New York: McGraw-Hill, (1986), chap. 6, for a perceptive analysis of bargaining power as the manipulation of the adversary's costs of agreement and disagreement.

2. See Albert Rees, *The Economics of Trade Unions* (Chicago: University of Chicago Press, 1962), chap. 2, for an insightful treatment of the sources of union power.

3. The basic source for most of this paragraph is Charles O. Gregory, *Labor and the Law,* 2nd rev. ed. with 1961 supplement (New York: Norton, 1961).

4. For an analysis of why these fundamental changes in U.S. labor relations law emerged, see Sanford Cohen, "An Analytical Framework for Labor Relations Law," *Industrial and Labor Relations Review* 14 (April 1961), pp. 350–362.

5. Section 13 of the amended National Labor Relations Act reads in its entirety: "Nothing in this Act, except as specifically provided for herein, shall be construed so as either to interfere with or impede or diminish in any way the right to strike, or to affect the limitations or qualifications on that right."

6. Many states have their own mediation agencies, which provide the same kind of dispute settlement services.

7. For a very readable and insightful analysis of emergency strikes, see Donald E. Cullen, *National Emergency Strikes,* ILR Paperback no. 7 (Ithaca, N.Y.: New York State School of Industrial and Labor Relations, Cornell University, 1968).

8. The 1971–1974 wage and price controls were an exception to this statement, but these controls established financial ceilings that settlements could not exceed and did not attempt to write contract language.

9. See Benjamin J. Taylor and Fred Witney, *Labor Relations Law,* 5th ed. (Englewood Cliffs, N.J.: Prentice-Hall, 1987), pp. 572–573.

10. Maurice S. Trotta, *Arbitration of Labor-Management Disputes* (New York: AMACOM, 1974), chap. 11.

11. David Lewin, "Collective Bargaining and the Right to Strike," in A. Lawrence Chickering, ed., *Public Employee Unions* (Lexington, Mass.: D.C. Heath, 1976), pp. 145–163.

12. Bureau of National Affairs, *Government Employee Relations Report* 21 (January 3, 1983), pp. 14–16; U.S. Department of Labor, Bureau of Labor Statistics, *Handbook of Labor Statistics,* Bulletin 2175 (December 1983), p. 404.

13. Two such states are Michigan and Rhode Island; see U.S. Department of Labor, Labor–Management Services Administration, *Summary of Public Sector Labor Relations Policies* (1981).

14. This erosion has not reached police and firefighters, for these two groups are almost always specifically excluded from strike rights.

15. Craig A. Olson, "Strikes, Strike Penalties, and Arbitration in Six States," *Industrial and Labor Relations Review* 39 (July 1986), pp. 539–551.

16. Ibid.

17. Craig A. Olson, "The Role of Rescheduled School Days in Teacher Strikes," *Industrial and Labor Relations Review* 37 (July 1984), pp. 515–528.

18. James L. Stern and Craig Olson, "The Propensity to Strike of Local Government Employees," *Journal of Collective Negotiations in the Public Sector* 11 (1982), pp. 201–214.

19. John Thomas Delaney, "Strikes, Arbitration, and Teacher Salaries: A Behavioral Analysis," *Industrial and Labor Relations Review* 36 (April 1983), pp. 431–446; and "Impasses and Teacher Contract Outcomes," *Industrial Relations* 25 (Winter 1986), pp. 45–55.

20. Paul F. Gerhart, "Determinants of Bargaining Outcomes in Local Government Labor Negotiations," *Industrial and Labor Relations Review* 29 (April 1976), pp. 347–349.

21. Thomas A. Kochan and Hoyt N. Wheeler, "Municipal Collective Bargaining: A Model and Analysis of Bargaining Outcomes," *Industrial and Labor Relations Review* 29 (October 1975), pp. 55–56.

22. John C. Anderson, "Arbitration in the Canadian Federal Public Service," in David Lewin, Peter Feuille, Thomas A. Kochan, eds., *Public Sector Labor Relations: Analysis and Readings,* 2nd ed. (Sun Lakes, Ariz.: Thomas Horton and Daughters, 1981), pp. 326–344.

23. Thomas A. Kochan, "Dynamics of Dispute Resolution," in Benjamin Aaron, Joseph R. Grodin, and James L. Stern, eds., *Public-Sector Bargaining* (Madison, WI: Industrial Relations Research Association, 1979), pp. 150–190.

24. Bureau of National Affairs, *Government Employee Relations Report,* no. 853 (March 17, 1980), pp. 27–28.

25. Herbert R. Northrup, "The Rise and Demise of PATCO," *Industrial and Labor Relations Review* 37 (January 1984), pp. 167–184; Richard W. Hurd and Jill K. Kriesky, " 'The Rise and Demise of Patco' Reconstructed," and Herbert R. Northrup, "Reply," *Industrial and Labor Relations Review* 40 (October 1986), pp. 115–122 and 122–127, respectively. Reprinted in chapter 4 of this book.

26. Another useful account of mediation in operation, written by an experienced mediator, is Arnold M. Zack, *Public Sector Mediation* (Washington, D.C.: Bureau of National Affairs, 1985).

27. James L. Stern, "The Mediation of Interest Disputes by Arbitrators under the Wisconsin Med-Arb Law for Local Government Employees," *The Arbitration Journal* 39 (June 1984), pp. 41–46.

28. James L. Stern, Charles M. Rehmus, J. Joseph Loewenberg, Hirschel Kasper, and Barbara D. Dennis, *Final-Offer Arbitration* (Lexington, Mass.: D.C. Heath, 1975), pp. 126, 175.

29. Thomas A. Kochan, Mordechai Mironi, Ronald G. Ehrenberg, Jean Baderschneider, and Todd Jick, *Dispute Resolution under Factfinding and Arbitration: An Empirical Evaluation* (New York: American Arbitration Association, 1979), chap. 5.

30. Thomas A. Kochan and Todd Jick, "The Public Sector Mediation Process: A Theory and Empirical Evaluation," *Journal of Conflict Resolution* 22 (June 1978), pp. 209–238.

31. Paul F. Gerhart and John E. Drotning, "Dispute Settlement and the Intensity of Mediation," *Industrial Relations* 19 (Fall 1980), pp. 352–359.

32. Deborah M. Kolb, "Roles Mediators Play," *Industrial Relations* 20 (Winter 1981), pp. 1–17.

33. Robert C. Rodgers, "An Interesting, Bad Theory of Mediation," *Public Administration Review* 46 (January–February 1986), pp. 67–74.

34. Peter J.D. Carnevale and Richard Pegnetter, "The Selection of Mediation Tactics in Public Sector Disputes: A Contingency Analysis," *Journal of Social Issues* 41 (1985), pp. 65–81.

35. For instance, see William R. Word, "Factfinding in Public Employee Negotiations," *Monthly Labor Review* 95 (February (1972), pp. 60–64; William R. Word, "Implications for Factfinding: The New Jersey Experience," *Journal of Collective Negotiations in the Public Sector* 3 (Fall 1974), pp. 339–343; and Lucian G. Gatewood, "Factfinding in Teacher Disputes: The Wisconsin Experience," *Monthly Labor Review* 97 (October 1974), pp. 47–51.

36. Kochan et al., *Dispute Resolution under Factfinding and Arbitration,* chap. 7.

37. Daniel G. Gallagher, "Factfinding and Final Offer Arbitration in Iowa," in David Lewin, Peter Feuille, and Thomas A. Kochan, eds., *Public Sector Labor Relations: Analysis and Readings,* 2nd ed. (Sun Lakes, Ariz.: Thomas Horton and Daughters, 1981), pp. 345–357.

38. As used in this section, *arbitration* refers to compulsory and binding interest arbitration, both conventional and final offer, unless specifically noted otherwise. As a result, this analysis does not deal with grievance arbitration, voluntary interest arbitration, or advisory interest arbitration.

39. These states include Alaska, Connecticut, Hawaii, Illinois, Iowa, Maine, Michigan, Minnesota, Montana, Nebraska, Nevada, New Jersey, New York, Ohio, Oregon, Pennsylvania, Rhode Island, Vermont, Washington, Wisconsin, and Wyoming. Massachusetts had an arbitration statute during 1974–1980, which was eliminated by a referendum vote, and the South Dakota and Utah legislatures passed arbitration laws that were struck down by state courts as unconstitutional.

40. Arbitration statutes typically require that the arbitrator's award must be adopted by the parties, and these statutes also prohibit strikes. In addition, court review of arbitration awards is extremely limited (that is, trying to persuade a judge to overturn an arbitration award rarely succeeds).

41. Casey Ichniowski, "Arbitration and Police Bargaining: Prescription for the Blue Flu," *Industrial Relations* 21 (Spring 1982), pp. 149–166; Craig A. Olson, "Strikes, Strike Penalties, and Arbitration in Six States"; Richard A. Lester, *Labor Arbitration in State and Local Government* (Princeton, N.J.: Industrial Relations Section, Princeton University, 1984); and Hoyt N. Wheeler, "An Analysis of Fire Fighter Strikes," *Labor Law Journal* 26 (January 1975), pp. 17–20.

42. This quid pro quo reasoning does apply, for instance, to private sector grievance arbitration, for in that context unions have surrendered their right to strike over contract interpretation disputes in return for the employer's promise to arbitrate such disputes.

43. A fuller explanation of this reasoning can be found in Peter Feuille, John Thomas Delaney, and Wallace Hendricks, "The Impact of Interest Arbitration on Police Contracts," *Industrial Relations* 24 (Spring 1985), pp. 161–181.

44. See Feuille, Delaney, and Hendricks, "The Impact of Interest Arbitration on Police Contracts"; Peter Feuille, John Thomas Delaney, and Wallace Hendricks,

"Police Bargaining, Arbitration and Fringe Benefits," *Journal of Labor Research* 6 (Winter 1985), pp. 1–20; Peter Feuille and John Thomas Delaney, "Collective Bargaining, Interest Arbitration, and Police Salaries," *Industrial and Labor Relations Review* 39 (January 1986), pp. 228–240; Thomas A. Kochan and Hoyt N. Wheeler, "Municipal Collective Bargaining: A Model and Analysis of Bargaining Outcomes," *Industrial and Labor Relations Review* 29 (October 1975), pp. 46–66; Craig A. Olson, "The Impact of Arbitration on the Wages of Firefighters," *Industrial Relations* 19 (Fall 1980), pp. 325–339.

45. See Feuille and Delaney, "Collective Bargaining."

46. Feuille, Delaney, and Hendricks, "The Impact of Interest Arbitration on Police Contracts."

47. See Max H. Bazerman, "Norms of Distributive Justice in Interest Arbitration," *Industrial and Labor Relations Review* 38 (July 1985); pp. 558–570; Max H. Bazerman and Henry S. Farber, "Arbitrator Decision Making: When Are Final Offers Important?" *Industrial and Labor Relations Review* 39 (October 1985); pp. 76–89.

48. Susan Schwochau and Peter Feuille, "Interest Arbitrators and Their Decision Behavior," *Industrial Relations,* forthcoming. However, the experience with strikes and arbitration in the Canadian federal government presents a different picture. In that system, each union can choose (before negotiations begin) to negotiate either under an arbitration procedure or under a strike procedure. Wage data indicate that during the early 1970s the unions were able to obtain larger wage increases under the strike route than under the arbitration route. The difference is partly attributable to a centralized and "conservative" arbitration process, which apparently need not give as much weight to negotiated settlements as occurs under decentralized interest arbitration procedures in the United States. See George Saunders, "Impact of Interest Arbitration on Canadian Federal Employees' Wages," *Industrial Relations* 25 (Fall 1986), pp. 320–327.

49. See Feuille and Delaney, "Collective Bargaining," and Feuille, Delaney, and Hendricks, "Police Bargaining."

50. Anderson, "Arbitration in the Canadian Federal Public Service," in Lewin, Feuille, and Kochan, *Public Sector Labor Relations;* Allen Ponak and Hoyt N. Wheeler, "Choice of Procedures in Canada and the United States," *Industrial Relations* 19 (Fall 1980), pp. 292–308.

51. Lester, *Labor Arbitration.*

52. John Delaney, Peter Feuille, and Wallace Hendricks, "The Regulation of Negotiating Disputes: Interest Arbitration in Government," in David Lewin and David Lipsky, eds., *Advances in Labor and Industrial Relations,* vol. 3 (Greenwich, Conn.: JAI Press, 1986), pp. 83–118.

53. This labor market regulation perspective is more fully developed in Delaney, Feuille, and Hendricks, "The Regulation of Negotiating Disputes."

54. These procedural variations are more fully explored in Lester, *Labor Arbitration.*

Labor Mediation: An Exploratory Survey

*Kenneth Kressel**

The Study and Its Setting

Labor mediation, one of the most highly institutionalized methods of resolving social conflict, has infrequently been the subject of systematic inquiry. . . . The present investigation was undertaken as an exploratory study of the attitudes of labor mediators towards various aspects of their craft. . . .

The Interview

The interview schedule was designed to obtain information on a wide range of topics. Because of the exploratory nature of the inquiry, respondents were given considerable latitude in framing their answers, and prepared questions were modified or abandoned when it seemed desirable to pursue topics that had not been anticipated originally.

Interviews lasted, on the average, about an hour and a quarter. They were conducted at each respondent's office, and tape-recorded for later transcription. All respondents were assured of anonymity.

The Respondents

Thirteen labor mediators served as respondents. By any standards they constituted an elite group. Four held top administrative posts in public mediation agencies and two others had previously held such positions. Respondents included seven with law degrees and three Ph.D.'s. Three were university professors, one was a university dean, and two had private labor arbitration practices. Eight of the group had written one or more articles for professional journals, and, during the three-month course of the study, at least four of the respondents were involved, either as mediators or as members of impasse panels, in disputes of sufficient importance to be prominently reported in the public press. The average age of the group was fifty-three.

---

*Columbia University. Reprinted from Kenneth Kressel, *Labor Mediation: An Exploratory Survey,* Association of Labor Mediation Agencies, 1972.

The Plan of the Report

The report is divided into two parts. In the first section, respondents' views on the *process of mediation* are discussed. The material in this section deals with the respondents' accounts of their behavior as mediators and their reasons for behaving as they do.

In the second section, the repondents' perceptions of *mediation as a profession* are documented. The primary theme is that of mediation as art rather than science, and aspects of the professional life of the mediator that appear related to this view are examined. . . .

Given the small number of respondents and the unique character of the sample, several caveats seem in order. First, it is clear that the views documented cannot be interpreted as representing the attitudes of the profession at large. Second, when an attempt is made to explain certain expressed attitudes on the basis of other information provided by the respondents, the admittedly speculative nature of the effort should be borne in mind. Finally, it should be noted that although explicit disagreement among those interviewed is often pointed out, for certain purposes it seemed desirable to develop a composite account of how the mediator conceives of his work. This composite should not be taken as indicating consensus among the respondents in every respect.

The Process of Labor Mediation

The Framework

It may be helpful to begin with a brief sketch of the institutional context in which mediated collective bargaining occurs.

There are two broad types of mediation to be distinguished: that which is conducted under the auspices of some public mediation agency and that which is arranged for privately by the parties. By far the larger volume of labor mediation is conducted by public agencies, and can, in turn, be divided into mediation in private enterprise (the private sector) and that involving government employees on either federal, state, or local levels (the public sector).

Among the mediation agencies, the Federal Mediation and Conciliation Service (FMCS) has jurisdiction in disputes in the private sector as well as in those involving federal employees. Nearly every state has its own state board of mediation which operates in private industry within the state. In those states that have granted public employees the right to bargain collectively, a separate state agency may exist to handle public sector disputes. Mediators may be full-time employees of an agency, or they may be affiliated with it on a per diem basis, being called on only when the existence of a dispute requires their services.

Among the present group, four respondents were full-time members of public sector agencies, and eight were, or had been, full-time members of state mediation boards, operating in the private sector. Most of those interviewed had had some experience in both sectors at some point in their careers. Unfortunately, it was not possible to interview members of the Federal Mediation and Conciliation Service.

Entering a Dispute

Three major issues related to entering a dispute may be identified from the respondent's remarks: (1) The *acceptability* of the mediator, (2) the *strategic implications* of a request for mediation, (3) the *timing* of entry.

Acceptability of the Mediator. On the matter of acceptability, respondents were in universal agreement. Since a mediator's success depends in large measure on the willingness of both parties to confide in him and accept his suggestions, the more eager both are to have him mediate their dispute the easier his job will be.

> It's the individual and his acceptability that is more important than anything else. Jones, they will take him. "We like him. We trust him." Smith, who has the same credentials, may be totally unacceptable. And, I might say, possibly for irrational reasons. I know some mediators—very fine mediators—who are unacceptable to one side or the other for reasons that don't make any sense. You say, "Why don't you, why can't you, use so and so?"
>
> Well it's hard for us to explain," they say. "But we don't feel comfortable with him." That's all you have to hear. You don't really probe much deeper. One side or the other says to you, "We just don't feel comfortable with that fellow," that's enough to rule him out. Unless, of course, there's nobody else and he's the least objectionable.

However desirable mutual acceptability of the mediator may be in theory, in practice—as the last sentence hints—it may be compromised in a variety of ways. In particular, the method by which the mediator makes contact with the dispute, and the public statutes that govern his intervention, may place constraints on the enthusiasm with which the parties receive him.

The respondents discussed three principal ways that a mediator may make contact with a dispute:

1. Both parties may make a joint request for mediation to the agency with jurisdiction.
2. One of the parties may request mediation.
3. The agency itself may take the initiative in contacting the parties.

From the point of view of acceptability, a joint request is clearly preferable. It is even better if, in making their request, the parties indicate a desire for a particular mediator.

Unfortunately, joint requests for mediation are in the minority. (In a recent year one of the agencies represented handled approximately 200 joint requests for mediation, as opposed to 400 unilateral requests.) Moreover, when joint requests are made, they do not always include a request for a specific mediator. In that case, agencies handle the matter somewhat differently. One provides the parties with a list of potential mediators from which the parties then choose. The process of choosing argues for a degree of investment in the individual selected. This same agency also requires that both parties share the cost of paying for the mediator's services, on the grounds that this too increases their commitment to him. (This is in distinction to the traditional practice of providing mediation gratis.)

Another agency prefers to assign the parties a mediator of its own choosing. Since its clients are primarily inexperienced public sector disputants, this method had the advantage of permitting the director of mediation to select a person who may be particularly qualified for the dispute in question. Whatever their merits, however, both methods involve the probability of a somewhat lower level of commitment to the mediator than is theoretically desirable.

Acceptability can also be compromised by the inability of the disputants legally to refuse mediation. This, at least, can be inferred from the respondent's descriptions of impasse procedures in the public sector. Historically, mediation has been a voluntary process, and this is entirely consistent with the notion that to be effective the mediator must be more or less welcomed into the dispute. In recent years, however, what may be termed *compulsory mediation* has developed in public sector bargaining. The parties are required by law to accept mediation as the first step in an impasse procedure. Only after they have "exhausted" mediation may the parties proceed to the next stage, which may be some form of arbitration or fact-finding and, if necessary, a legislative hearing. Since the parties have no choice, and since they are also aware that mediation is only the first stage in what may be a long and complex process, its seems entirely possible that, in such a context, the mediator's efforts may be met with only pro forma compliance.

Acceptability was often linked with another concept, that of impartiality. The majority of those interviewed felt that a prerequisite for the mediator's acceptability was the belief of both sides that he was genuinely neutral. Any behavior that could be taken as evidence that the mediator was more favorably disposed to one side or the other was to be scrupulously avoided. As one may put it, "A mediator, like Ceasar's wife, must be beyond reproach."

A minority of the respondents expressed a different opinion about the relationship between acceptability and impartiality. In their view, the major component of acceptability was the belief of both sides that the mediator can *effectively* represent their best interests. The belief that the mediator is also impartial is of decidedly secondary importance. Indeed, "impartiality"—in the sense of equal personal distance from each side—is likely to be a handicap, since, according to these respondents, in the collective bargaining situation it is the union, not the employer, that experiences the greatest control over the outcome; that being the case, it is to the mediator's advantage—and ultimately to that of the employer—for the mediator to establish a close relationship with the union leaders. To do this, it may be necessary to transcend the bounds of what, in legalistic terms, would be regarded as "scrupulous neutrality." Thus, for several of the respondents it is apparently common practice to socialize with union leaders, speak at union affairs, and in other ways familiarize themselves with the attitudes and feelings of union members. Having established their credentials with the union, they are then in a position to oppose firmly some of the more injudicious union demands in the interests of a settlement that will be mutually acceptable.

The ambiguous relationship between acceptability and impartiality was perhaps best illustrated by a respondent, himself an advocate of strict neutrality, who cited the remark of a well-known union leader during a major strike. The leader, after listening patiently to all the distinguished individuals who were available to mediate the dispute—a list, however, that omitted the name of a mediator particularly dear to his own heart—demanded to know why Mr. X had not been mentioned. Where, he wanted to know was *his* "impartial"?

Strategic Implications of a Request for Mediation. Respondents had no illusions that a call for mediation was divorced from the strategy of bargaining. Since they conceived of a request for mediation as a tacit admission of a willingness to compromise, if only one of the parties feels the need for mediation (and several respondents noted that such a feeling might be a sign of a sophisticated understanding of the uses of mediation rather than of a difficult bargaining position), the problem of introducing the mediator can be a delicate one: how to do so without seeming weak.

Respondents also noted that requests for mediation are not always made out of an honest desire to resolve a dispute. It has already been noted that in some states disputants in the public sector are required to accept a mediator. Respondents also observed that mediators were sometimes called in when one or both disputants merely desire the facade of mediation without its substance. It may be politically inexpedient, for example, for either side to refuse mediation and be publicly branded recalcitrant, even though neither has any real intention of bargaining in good faith, and both may be convinced of the need for a strike (to prove their mettle, to encourage group solidarity, and so forth). In some instances collusion may be involved. The leadership on both sides, having worked out an agreement between themselves, may wish to create the impression in the minds of the public, the rank and file, or a regulatory agency that the dispute has been honestly fought. The presence of the mediator may seem to provide such evidence. Blatant abuses of the latter kind were characterized as chronic but relatively infrequent, and all who discussed the problem were agreed that a mediator who becomes aware that he is being used in such a fashion has an obligation to withdraw immediately.

Timing of Entry. There were two views on the most favorable time to enter a dispute. A sizable majority of those interviewed favored coming in "late."

The majority preference for late entry was founded on the belief that mediation is most effective when the parties' motivation to bargain is at its highest. Motivation is highest when the pressure to settle is highest—that is, when there is a clear and impending deadline.

Aside from the level of the parties' motivation to bargain, there were several other factors cited as justifying late entry. One interviewee felt that the major contribution of the mediator is his ability to suggest novel solutions—to be a "new voice," as he put it.

Perhaps the most important concept of their role that respondents held was the notion that they should be instrumental in bringing about a settlement that the parties could "live with." In a later section the matter of "livability" will be explored at greater length. It is sufficient to note here that the ability of the parties to live with a settlement is enhanced if they feel that it is largely of their own devising. Consequently, an additional argument for late entry is that it gives the parties maximum opportunity to resolve by themselves all but a few of the most intractable issues.

The Goals of the Mediator

Once a mediator enters a dispute, his behavior is likely to be varied and complex. As a context for viewing this behavior it will be useful to examine first some of the concepts of mediation and collective bargaining that respondents bring with them to a dispute.

Respondents were asked about their overall objectives in entering a dispute. The most frequent response was to disavow any goal other than settlement, and it was stressed that this settlement was to be an expression of the parties' needs and desires, not those of the mediator. Respondents included in their disclaimers a concern for equity and, in particular, the "public interest."

> I do not take the view, I've never taken the view, that the mediator is the third party at the bargaining table to protect the public. I think it's an erroneous view that the mediator is a public official in there to reach a general accord within the guidelines, or within the prescribed goals, or within the

economic requirements of the community. . . . I think the management official, in the case of the public employer, is there to protect the taxpayer; that's his role and if he doesn't protect them properly he ought to be thrown out of office. In private industry the company negotiator is there to report to the board of directors and if he doesn't properly protect them he ought to be thrown out. The marketplace should seek its own level.

In addition to this laissez-faire interpretation of collective bargaining, two additional reasons were given for declining the role of public protector. The difficulty of defining the public interest was one. Perhaps more fundamental was the explanation that a mediator who attempts to protect the public interest runs the considerable risk of alienating the disputants and, hence, of losing his usefulness altogether.

There is some evidence, however, that the recent emergence of the public sector as a critical bargaining area has raised the salience of the public interest in the minds of many of the respondents, even if they end up by disavowing such responsibility—and not all of them do. Three interviewees accepted some explicit responsibility for protecting the public welfare. Interestingly, all of them worked primarily in the public sector—where pressures to protect the public interest might be expected to be greater—and all appeared somewhat conflicted about their admission.

Although the majority of respondents were most comfortable with the view that their obligation was to get a settlement and not to defend some abstract notion of public well-being or equity, nearly all of them were willing to sketch a variety of criteria by which to distinguish "good" settlements from the less good and the downright poor.

By far the most common response to a request to define a good settlement was the phrase, "something the parties can *live with*." A settlement that can be "lived with" may refer to:

1. A settlement that the negotiators feel is their own, and not one into which they have been manipulated or finessed by the mediator—whether or not the mediator's role has, in fact, been a large one.

2. A settlement that the parties like.

3. A settlement that is ratified by the respective constituencies. (Several respondents did observe that since (a) the vast majority of agreements are ratified anyway and (b) there are times when the constituents are going to reject an agreement no matter what its terms, ratification per se is a poor criterion by which to judge the quality of an agreement.)

4. A settlement in which neither side feels that it has been forced to accept terms imposed by the other. While there was little willingness to endorse overt efforts to prevent such settlements from being reached, there

appear to be things that mediators can do to try to avoid creating a feeling of victory for one side and defeat for the other. Several respondents expressed an enthusiasm for "complex" settlements for this reason.

5. A settlement that does not have adverse political consequences for the leadership—particularly the union leadership. This criterion is related to the previous one, in the sense that "defeat" is of the sturdiest platform from which to hold elected office.

6. A settlement in which the terms of agreement are unambiguous, all major issues are resolved, and little, if anything, is left for later determination. In essence, this is the idea that a good settlement is one which produces stability in the relationship.

Apart from the umbrella term of livability, several other criteria of a good mediated settlement were mentioned. These included:

7. Settlements that succeed in averting physical violence.

8. Settlements that give the parties an understanding of "what the collective bargaining process is all about, what mediation is all about, the art of compromise." Public sector bargaining was singled out as an area in which such an achievement was especially desirable.

9. Settlements that violate no law.

10. Settlements in which the parties have bargained in good faith, as opposed to those in which the mediator has been called in to give the appearance of honest bargaining.

11. Settlements that fall within the range established in comparable plants or industries.

When the respondents' criteria for good settlements have been enumerated, however, the question of whether they attempt to promote such settlements receives no clear answer. As in the case of protecting the public interest, there appear to be honest differences of opinion as well as some genuine, albeit implicit, conflict.

To the observer, the surest source of such conflict is the exceedingly large and impressive list of activities that the respondents deemed appropriate for the mediator. The range of these activities will soon become clear. It is sufficient to note that a modest, retiring conception of the mediator's role was by no means a popular one.

Even those who indicated that a more passive demeanor was sometimes desirable—particularly when the parties were resolving issues on their own—stressed that mediation is an active process, whatever the outward appearance may be. "I think the mediator has to recognize when he is supposed to be passive, and that is an active determination in and of itself."

But if the mediator's role is to be an active one, what is it that guides his activity? Since the needs and desires of the parties are not unalterable, nor clearly visible at the outset, and since, in fact, by many of their actions mediators may be instrumental in forming and modifying those needs and desires, it appears somewhat disingenuous to say that the mediator has no goal other than settlement, that he does not propound his own views, and that everything that is decided is decided voluntarily.

The Strategies and Tactics of Mediation

At first glance, the respondents' remarks about their behavior as mediators appear so varied and so dependent on the particular dispute being discussed, that any attempt at a general summary seems apt to prove an unfruitful exercise. This, in fact, was the explicit opinion of several of those interviewed. Nonetheless, it is possible to discern three broad types of strategies and some of the tactics which cluster around them. I shall refer to *reflexive, nondirective,* and *directive* strategies of mediation.

By *reflexive* strategies is meant those behaviors by which the mediator attempts to orient himself to the dispute and to establish the groundwork on which his later activities will be built. As the term implies, reflexive strategies are designed primarily to affect the mediator, rather than the parties: to make the mediator the most effective instrument for the resolution of conflict possible under the circumstances. *Nondirective* and *directive* strategies, on the other hand, are aimed specifically at the conflict and the parties to it. In a concrete sense, they are what the mediator *does* to resolve a dispute.

Nondirective interventions refer to attempts at increasing the probability that the parties themselves, with a minimum of manipulation or suggestion from the mediator, will hit upon a mutually acceptable solution to the dispute. If one thinks of the mediator as an instrument for assisting at the "birth" of a settlement, then one might describe nondirective strategies as a "midwifery" kind of mediation.

In contrast, directive interventions refer to those strategies by which the mediator actively promotes a specific solution or attempts to pressure or manipulate the parties directly into ending the dispute. Pursuing the obstetric analogy, one might think of directive interventions as the "caesarean" approach to mediation.

Reflexive Strategies

Gaining the Trust and Confidence of the Parties. The respondents were in general agreement that this was the first and most important task of the mediator. Tactics designed to achieve the necessary rapport include:

1. *Explicitly stating the mediator's role.* The mediator's introductory remarks to the parties will generally include a statement to the effect that under no conditions will he reveal a confidence unless given permission to do so, and that he is the servant of the parties and of nobody else. This, of course, is nothing more than a statement of purpose; by itself it will not elicit confidence or trust. Nonetheless, it puts the mediator's conception of his role on record. With naive parties such a preamble may avoid unnecessary confusions, i.e., the suspicion that the mediator is an agent of the governor's office with instructions to get a settlement in the "public interest"; that he is the personal choice of the union, there to do its bidding, etc.

2. *Explicitly stating concern with the dispute.* This is another tactic that does not, by itself, inspire confidence. It is, however, additional evidence to the parties, that they are no longer alone in their difficulties.

> I open with a general discussion which means nothing; that I'm very concerned that a high public interest is involved; ten, twelve thousand employees are out of work, and a large business is not operating, and money is being lost, and the public is being hurt. Now this is not to tell them how to settle, but just as a general statement which they know beforehand, but they listen; I'm saying something.

3. *Speaking the language of the parties.* Respondents observed that it is important to convey to the disputants that the mediator is the type of person who is capable of understanding their problems. Respondents warned, for example, about the dangers of appearing patronizing. Several interviewees also referred to the fact that mediation, unlike arbitration, tends to be an informal process. A highly judicial hearing and an insistence on protocol are not generally desirable. It is the mediator's task to set the tone of informality in his own manner and speech (unless, of course, the parties clearly expect a more formal proceeding).

Once past the initial joint meeting the mediator's ability to inspire confidence depends on a wide range of skills.

4. *Demonstrating competence.* It is important for the mediator to be able to handle substantive matters expertly.

> Part of the ability of the mediator's acquiring confidence has to do with his ability to have some mathematical soundness; to sit there while the parties are talking, while somebody throws out a number, to say: "Well, that's 1.2% and that would represent 18 million, or if you did it this way, it would be 13 and let me show you how." And after you do this a few times, the parties get to the point where they will trust anything you say.

The mediator must also demonstrate that he understands the bargaining process and the occasional necessity for the parties to strike poses.

5. Using humor effectively.

I think a lot of it is the ability to have a good story, to have a repertoire of good jokes. I can go into a union committee of thirty guys who look at you like a Stone Age man. You know, they're glaring at you; they each got a hammer. And you tell a joke and they laugh. And then you tell another joke and you leave them there. And when you go out they invariably say to each other, "Jesus, that was a great story he told." And then when you go down the hall, the guy will say, "Hey, that was a great story." Now he's talking to you.

6. Demonstrating an empathic understanding of each side's position. It is essential for the mediator to convey to both sides that he understands their respective positions fully, and does so without passing judgement.

Discovering the Real Issues

It will hardly do to walk into a dispute at the first meeting and say to an employer: "You really ought to give them another 25 cents an hour to satisfy their demands." That's the best way I know to become an ex-mediator very quickly. There must be a reason why the situation is polarized; there are reasons why it can be unpolarized. The difference in the two situations lies in the needs and feelings of the people and you've got to find out what they are.

One of the first tasks of the mediator, as a newcomer to a dispute, is to educate himself to the important issues in the conflict. This task is made more complicated by the fact, noted earlier, that the genuine issues may not have been clearly formulated by the time of his arrival.

"Just listening" was frequently cited as a tactic for uncovering the salient issues. The mediator must be alert not only to what is being said, but to what is *not* being said. If, for example, wages are being completely omitted from the discussion, the mediator might wonder if this is an issue touching such deep-seated feelings that neither side is willing to discuss it openly for fear that the entire negotiations may be jeopardized. On the other hand, does it seem likely that matters receiving all the initial attention are going to be of ultimate importance? Here the mediator must use whatever knowledge he has of the industry and the disputants, as well as healthy amounts of common sense.

While listening with the "third ear" remains characteristic of the mediator's behavior throughout the dispute, in the effort to uncover the central issues, it gradually gives way to a more active probing of each side's position. Probing usually occurs when the mediator has separated the parties. (Although most of the respondents felt that separate meetings were the most effective means for clarifying issues, one interviewee preferred to continue joint sessions for as long as possible. He felt that the mediator can all too easily lose his perspective when confronted with the arguments of only one side, whereas direct and even heated exchanges permit him to keep constantly in view all the forces and interests at play.)

On one point all respondents agreed: the worst possible tactic for eliciting the parties' genuine feelings about the issues is to ask for them directly. Since, for reasons of strategy, honest answers to direct questions will generally not be given, such questions can put a premature end to any useful dialogue between mediator and negotiators.

> I, at all times, avoid asking the parties what their final position is. That's a dirty question, because you are seeking to penetrate the bargaining facade the parties have put up; you imply, by that, that you don't believe what they're saying, whereas it's important to give the impression that you believe a bargaining position is a sincere position. It's also a futile question because it's not going to be answered and, therefore, you're encouraging a form of dishonesty with someone with whom you are trying to establish an open relationship.

Identifying the Real Leaders. Just as the real issues may be masked at the outset of the mediator's entry into the dispute, so too for the real leaders — the persons with the power to make or break a proposed settlement. The mediator's problem here appears to be on two levels.

First, there is a problem of identifying those few individuals, *physically present* at the bargaining table, who are most able to determine the direction which their side will take in the bargaining. The second problem of identification facing the mediator is establishing the *effective,* as opposed to the theoretical, constituencies of both sides — that is, the parties (individuals or groups) who are most able to make the negotiator's experience produce consequences — either favorable or unfavorable. Unfortunately, effective constituencies are sometimes difficult to locate. It is a well-known fact that not every membership effectively holds their leaders to account. In public sector disputes it is particularly difficult to separate the theoretical from the effective constituency. "The public" is always the constituency of record for the public employer. Effectively, however, it is more likely to be a mayor, a city council, or a school board that is in a position to strike down a proposed settlement or, at the least, make the negotiator wish he had gotten into another line of business. The lines of responsibility may be difficult to trace.

Understanding the Relationship between the Disputants. Several respondents noted that negotiations frequently have a past and that this past can affect the present in a very decided fashion. Parties can become accustomed to having agreements written down and meticulously spelled out. In other disputes, expectations about the physical form a contract ought to take may be considerably more flexible. In still other instances, the parties may expect formal reports to the membership at a specific time during the talks, or it may be understood that the company attorneys are to report back periodically to the employer for further instructions. It may even be the case that, as a matter of tradition, the parties have gotten used to doing without mediators altogether. One respondent cited an entire industry where just such a tradition had developed. The more familiar the mediator is with these historical matters, the easier it will be for him to avoid pitfalls and understand resistance to his interventions.

More contemporaneous aspects of the parties' relationship were stressed by many respondents. Interviewees referred repeatedly to the need for the mediator to understand the "nature of the power relationship" between the parties, or the importance of "getting an assessment of the people and their relationships with one another" or of getting to know the "problems" that exist in a particular relationship. The mediator becomes aware of the present state of the parties' negotiating relationship in the same way that he identifies the real issues: by keen observation of the parties' interactions in joint meetings and by observing the responses to his questions when he meets with the parties separately.

Nondirective Strategies

Nondirective strategies may be subdivided into two categories: (1) those designated to make *the context* in which bargaining occurs more favorable to settlement, and (2) those designed to help *the parties* become more adept bargainers.

Of the strategies designed to affect the context of bargaining, the following may be noted.

Producing a Favorable Climate for Negotiations. The first tactic under this heading has already been encountered: patient listening. The psychological benefits of such attention can be considerable. Another, more active, technique for improving the bargaining atmosphere consists of creating positive expectations by obtaining agreement on small, relatively easy to resolve issues early in the negotiations. Later, when the going gets rougher and the negotiators begin getting discouraged, the mediator may point to these earlier achievements as evidence that agreements are possible.

The mediator also has a role to play in controlling the expression of hostility, or what one writer has referred to as "ludic" outburst, in general. Several respondents noted that the open expression of anger was sometimes to be encouraged. The cathartic effects of an occasional mediator-arranged confrontation was noted by one man, who remarked:

There are some times when I know some steam will be blown off and the best way to do it is to call a joint session. For example, if I hear one side say something particularly vindictive about the position of the other and I can see the anger and hostility is just at the breaking point, I'll say: "I'm not going to tell that to the other side. Nah, you feel that way about it, you're going to tell them yourself. Now, you tell them yourself what you think of them when they ask for that."

"All right, we'll tell 'em," and off he goes. And there's a wild explosion and that's done with. You have to be careful about it because you can't bring them together to the point where the explosion is so extreme as to break off talks.

There are two things to note in these comments. In the first instance, it is the mediator's responsibility to *control* the expression of anger. How exactly he does this is not entirely clear. The simplest answer is that he "knows" when things are going too far (by using his "antennae" or intuition) and will then intervene and suggest separate meetings.

Second, and perhaps implied in the notion of intuition, the mediator permits the expression of hostility that is *issue* oriented—not personally oriented. To be sure, attacking the bargaining stance of the opponent may involve disturbing reflections on his or her personal character or antecedents. Nonetheless, it is the mediator's job to distinguish in a relative fashion between the two types of anger. (The respondent spoke, for example, of hearing one side "say something indicative about the bargaining *position* of the other side.")

Handling Administrative Details. It is clear from the remarks of several respondents that the administrative role of the mediator, while at first glance constituting the most mundane of his activities, has important implications for the atmosphere under which negotiations will be conducted. Perhaps the simplest of these administrative activities is alerting the parties to logistical problems involved in collective bargaining—housing, meeting space, transportation to and from meeting, and the like—and advising them on the objectives to be served in solving such problems.

Perhaps the central administrative function of the mediator is establishing an agenda for the bargainers: What issues will be considered first? Can issues be broken down and farmed out to subcommittees for more efficient use of time and personnel? The technique of *bulking* issues—identifying those problems that can be handled more or less as a unit—all those matters related to fringe benefits, all the "economic" issues, and so on—was mentioned by three respondents as being of special importance.

Bulking issues is useful for three reasons. First, disputes with a great number of issues have a tendency to overwhelm the parties: there appears to be so much disagreement on so many separate questions that a strike seems all but inevitable. By grouping the issues, the mediator brings a sense of order and manageability to the proceedings. There really aren't fifty separate issues, but only three or four major areas of disagreement.

Second, by classifying issues under larger headings, the mediator makes it easier for the parties to see where trade-offs and swaps may be arranged. Previously it may have seemed that all fifty issues were on more or less the same footing.

Pacing the Negotiations. It is the mediator's job to ensure that movement towards settlement proceeds at an orderly pace; too slow, as well as too rapid, movement is to be avoided.

Too slow movement is bad because it produces discouragement, fatigue, and frustration. Personal attacks are likely to become more frequent, and the goal of settlement lost sight of. One respondent noted that too slow a pace may also provide a little too much time for reflection.

> When I have a sense of momentum, when I feel a sense of momentum is there, I don't want to break for supper, I don't want to break for sleep, I don't want to break for anything. You have to exploit that, because once there is time for reflection and then for figuring out the political consequences and trying to find everything that's wrong with a settlement, you can tear any settlement apart—so you don't leave that time for reflection available.

Too rapid achievement of a settlement may be inadvisable for another reason: the political nature of the bargaining process requires that the negotiators give evidence to their constituents that the battle has been hard fought.

> The committees that represent both the employer and the union will have to go back, and since they settled at three o'clock in the afternoon when people know that people settle different situations at three in the morning, somebody is going to get up in the back of the room and say, "What was your big rush? If you would have held out another two hours we would have gotten another seven cents." And politically, you see, the committees know this, and they're not there to settle quickly unless they *have* to.

Unfortunately, it is very difficult to capture precisely what pacing involves. How does the mediator *know* when the pace is too fast or too slow? As in so many other areas of mediator behavior, the only answer is to be found in such words as intuition or instinct.

Maintaining the Privacy of the Negotiations. Respondents generally agreed that a goldfish bowl atmosphere is inimical to dispute settlement. The dangers of public mediation, as the respondents saw them, were twofold. First, public statements tend to fix bargaining positions prematurely. A negotiator who, in the heat of the moment, has declared before the radio microphones or TV cameras that he will *never* agree to a thirty-cent-an-hour wage increase, will find the inevitability of such a settlement much more difficult to face than one who has kept his opinions restricted to the bargaining table. (Of course, it is precisely for such reasons that the parties may find opportunities to unburden themselves publicly so alluring. It is the mediator's job to prevent this kind of maneuver by pledging the parties to a ban on public statements.)

Second, public statements about the substance of bargaining can lead to the growth of internal resentments that can eventually force a negotiator to rescind an offer, or to the failure of the constituency to ratify the settlement.

The second category of nondirective strategies are those aimed, not at affecting the context in which bargaining occurs but, rather, at helping the parties become more adept bargainers. The most frequently discussed strategies of this kind included the following.

Helping the Parties Establish Which Issues Are Significant to Them. Just as the mediator is concerned with educating himself to the real issues, he may also wish to give each side a clearer understanding of where its own true interests appear to lie. As a nondirective strategy, the emphasis here is not on attempts to convince one side or the other that a specific proposal should be accepted or rejected but, rather, on getting each to see the broad requirements of a satisfactory settlement.

The mediator, in focusing discussions in this manner, may also make some effort to give each party a certain amount of insight into the reasons behind the stand taken by the opposition. The purpose is to defuse feelings of anger and resentment by pointing out that the other side is attempting to satisfy pressing practical needs of its own (to run for reelection, to compete successfully in the marketplace, and so on).

Educating the Parties about the Nature of the Bargaining Process. This function is particularly important with naive parties. In addition to an explicit statement that he is the confidante of both sides and is acting exclusively in their interests, the mediator may also use the initial joint meeting to make explicit some other aspects of mediated collective bargaining. He may stress to the parties that they must be willing to compromise, and that his job is to mediate, not to do their bargaining for them. The educating process will continue by example, of course, as the negotiations proceed. (Respondents who dealt with public sector disputes were more prone to stress this educative function than were mediators in the private sector, where the parties are usually sophisticated.)

Directive Strategies

Discovering Areas of Compromise. This function of the mediator is closely related to reflexive attempts to discover the underlying issues in a dispute. It is included under directive strategies primarily because it was most often mentioned as an important preliminary to the formulation, in the mediator's mind, of the type of settlement that will ultimately be acceptable to both sides, and consequently, as the first clear step on the road to the mediator's direct efforts to bring about an agreement.

Most of the mediator's attempts at discovering areas of compromise occur in private caucuses. By careful probing the mediator begins to get a notion of just how far apart the disputants are, and what compromises it will take from each side to get a settlement. One respondent referred to this process as discovering the "ambit of expectancy" of the parties. The mediator is aided in these efforts by the trust he has established with each side. Respondents were aware, however, that no amount of high regard for the mediator will suffice to get feuding parties instantly to abandon strategically adopted positions.

Making the Parties Face Reality. The mediator may force the parties to confront facts that, swept up in the conflict, they are unable or unwilling to face. In other cases, reality testing may be required for quite the opposite reason — because one of the parties is unmotivated to bargain out of the mistaken belief that its position is so invulnerable that there is nothing to lose by *not* bargaining. It may be the mediator's job to correct such impressions. Some of the realities that the mediator may discuss with the parties include:

1. *The financial costs of a strike.* Several respondents alluded to the occasional necessity of making one or both parties face squarely the potential costs involved in not coming to terms until after a strike has occurred.

2. *The range of settlements in similar industries or situations.* One of the important guidelines in helping the parties develop an overlapping ambit of expectancy is a knowledge of what others in similar situations have agreed to. Part of the mediator's expertise consists of having a broad acquaintance with patterns of settlement.

3. *The needs of the constituencies.* Earlier it was observed that the mediator may aid each party in clarifying its own objectives by getting it to review the needs of its total membership. This tactic may also be used to blunt a demand that threatens to stall negotiations. The mediator wants the demand retracted or modified without antagonizing the party making it.

4. *The high-priority issues.* The mediator may not only help the parties discover which issues are salient for them, but may also assist each party to see where each issue fits into the total scheme of settlement.

5. *The position of the opponent.* Earlier this tactic was described as functioning to reduce anger by making the opponent's position more understandable. It may also facilitate the intelligent formulation of compromise proposals which have some realistic chance of being accepted.

As a directive strategy it may involve more than a logical explanation of the other side's point of view. Rather, the mediator becomes a forceful advocate of each side's position. Of course, the mediator runs a risk in becoming an advocate for the opposition and, indeed, in all his efforts at pressing home unpleasant facts of life. He may so alienate and antagonize the parties that his usefulness is all but over. Something of the art of dealing with "resistances" is conveyed in the following remarks.

> Now you say, "Well, why don't they throw you out of the room?" Maybe sometimes they do. They never have to me. I've gone as far as I can sometimes without antagonizing people all the way. I've had committees say to me, "Look, we don't have to take this from you." And I say to them, "We're just talking. We're friends. I have a record: I have a track record; I have an experienced record. Check with anybody. Most of you guys know me. I'm not taking you over the coals, but I'm just telling you my view. Now don't get offended by it. You don't have to accept it, but at least let me tell it to you. I think you're crazy." And you say it long enough, you'll find that out of a committee of twenty guys, two or three of them say, "He's right, we are crazy." You tell them, "Look, maybe you'll get a $1,000 a week raise if you're out on strike for five years, you know, I mean, you want to take a five-year strike or you want to start talking sense?"

In this small illustration it is possible to identify at least five different tactics aimed at bringing disputants bluntly but not disruptively into touch with reality: (1) reassurance of the mediator's fundamental empathy ("We're friends," "Most of you guys know me"); (2) reiteration of the mediator's competence ("I have a track record"); (3) emphasis on the voluntary nature of the relationship with the mediator ("You don't have to accept it"); (4) disarming use of colloquial language ("You're crazy"); (5) the entire presentation leavened with a touch of humor, which, not incidentally, also introduces a needed perspective ("Look, maybe you'll get a $1,000 a week raise if you're out on strike for five years"). It is performances like these that mediators have in mind when they pronounce mediation an art rather than a science.

Making Suggestions for Settlement. This aspect of the mediator's role may range from tentative speculations aloud (fishing expeditions) through the formal issuance of public recommendations. At its most imperceptible it may not involve suggestions at all but, rather, rediscussions of the issues in a fashion calculated to stimulate the parties to novel reformulations of their own.

From the respondents' remarks three types of suggestions for settlement may be identified.

1. *Suggestions for modifying proposals already made by the parties.* This is the art of restructuring or rephrasing, and one of its major objectives is to make things more palatable. It is also the most active type of proposal making with which the respondents, as a group, felt comfortable. The making of such proposals follows familiar guidelines: they must be tactfully put ("Does it make any sense to . . . ?") and well-timed (when confidence and trust have been established and the "crisis" point close enough to make acceptance probable).

2. *Formal mediator recommendations for settlement (made to the parties only).* This was a tactic mentioned by only a few respondents, and then with distaste. The problem with explicit, detailed, and formal recommendations for settlement, is that once they have been made, the mediator must thenceforth operate under at least one and possibly two disadvantages. First, he can no longer make a claim to the status of true neutral. He now, like the parties themselves, has a "position," and the presumption is that he will attempt to promote this position. Second, and perhaps more damaging, if one or both sides have been displeased by his recommendations — as they almost certainly are if the proposal has not ended the dispute — any further discourse becomes compromised by an atmosphere of hostility and suspicions of betrayal.

3. *Public recommendations.* This is the extreme form of mediator proposal making and in general respondents expressed aversion to it. It belongs conceptually with pressure tactics, discussed later.

Applying Pressure for Settlement. This was not a function for which the respondents expressed a great deal of enthusiasm. However, they did feel, as has already been seen, that crises — usually in the form of a strike threat — are a necessary motivating force in collective bargaining. In some cases, particularly in the public sector where strikes are generally illegal, it may be necessary for the mediator to "create" a crisis. The most commonly cited tactic was to inform the parties that after a certain date the mediator would no longer be available because of personal or professional commitments that could not be deferred. Other pressure tactics mentioned were the controlled and strategic expression of anger and dissatisfaction with the way the parties are negotiating; the use of the press, either to express hope that negotiations will soon reach a successful conclusion or, more bluntly, to brand one side or the other as intransigent; the making of public recommendations. . . .

"Selling" the Proposed Settlement to the Bargaining Committees. Much of the actual work of collective bargaining is carried out either by small subcommittees or by two or three key people on each side. The proposal that is arrived at in this manner must be ratified by the entire union bargaining committee before it can be submitted to the union membership for a final vote. One respondent indicated that this function included motivating the principal negotiators to "sell" the proposal to the rest of the bargaining committee. In the event that they have difficulty in this regard, he is available to help them argue their case.

By way of summarizing the respondents' views on strategies and tactics of mediation, it can be observed that reflexive, nondirective, and directive strategies appear to correspond in a rough way to three distinct stages of the bargaining process.

In the *early* stage, issues are of subsidiary importance. There is, instead, a staking out of bargaining positions for later compromise, accompanied, perhaps, by ritual displays of anger and indignation. The parties are feeling out each other as well as the mediator. This early stage is dominated, from the mediator's point of view, by *reflexive* strategies. What are the most pressing issues? How can he establish his credentials and get the disputants to rely on his judgment and abilities?

In the *middle* stage of negotiations, more active but still tentative bargaining has begun. The parties may now be meeting in separate caucuses at the mediator's request, and through him are beginning to exchange offers and counteroffers. Small subcommittees may have been formed to work out particularly difficult issues. Here the mediator's role may be primarily *nondirective*. If possible, he would like the parties to hit on a settlement with minimal intrusiveness on his part. He may confine himself primarily to working on the atmosphere surrounding the negotiations: establishing a workable agenda; dealing with disruptive, angry outbursts or permitting hostility to be vented when this appears fruitful; educating naive parties about the nature of the bargaining process. He may also be probing gently to discover areas of potential compromise that he will exploit later on, when the parties seem to have reached an impasse.

The *final* stage may be characterized by feverish exchanges of proposals or by an apparent total lack of movement. In retrospect, however, it will be clear that the parties were very close to a solution. In this last stage, *directive* strategies predominate. The mediator may attempt to bridge the gap with more frequent suggestions at compromise. He may put these forward with less of his earlier hesitancy and, sometimes, with veiled or not so veiled attempts at pressuring the parties to accept.

The Profession of Labor Mediation

Mediation: Art versus Science

Perhaps the best place to begin an examination of the professional situation of the mediator, as it is reflected in these interviews, is with a more thorough investigation of the respondents' distrust of generalizations about their work. They preferred to view mediation as art rather than science. In nearly every case, warnings were given to the interviewer that nothing being said about the mediator's behavior should be taken as having very wide applicability. The most common explanation for this presumed state of affairs was the idiosyncratic and ever-changing nature of the work. Respondents also took a dim view of the desirability of establishing professional schools to train mediators. Some, in fact, did not accept the premise on which this idea was based, namely that mediation is a professional discipline. Interviewees did consider a knowledge of industrial relations, economics, labor law, and the process of collective bargaining important adjuncts to the mediator's personal skills. These subjects, however, are already incorporated into various professional and graduate curricula, and respondents saw no reason to tailor a program specifically to the needs of mediators.

To the relative unimportance of formal academic preparation, respondents contrasted the salience of personal qualifications:

> It is more a field of men than it is law. There's no law on mediation; there's no statute that tells you how to mediate—what the parties have to do and what the mediator should do.

> The key to the whole thing is: Do the parties trust you? Do they have confidence not only in your integrity but in your ability? Have you demonstrated to them that you are sensitive to their needs? That you will work hard on the part of both of them in the interest of a common solution? That you maintain confidences and never breach them? That they feel comfortable with you? So it's the individual and his acceptability that is more important than anything else.

When asked for personal traits desirable in a mediator, respondents mentioned intelligence, tenacity, physical stamina, a sense of humor, the ability to persuade, subtlety, the ability to emphasize with and understand positions not one's own, self-effacement, and ingenuity in proposing novel solutions. However desirable such qualities may be, they are not the stuff of which professional curricula are made. As one man put it, "How do you teach a course in 'I'll think of something'?"

Aspects of Professional Development

The view that mediation depends primarily on idiosyncratic combinations of elusive personal qualities, rather than on general principles capable of being inculcated by formal training, undoubtedly reflects a fundamental truth: labor mediation, like any intervention that attempts to affect complex human relationships, must in some fundamental sense, remain a mystery, even to its most successful practitioners. Nonetheless, the insistence with which this view was reiterated appears related to aspects of the mediator's professional life that extend beyond the complex, demanding nature of the work. Four such aspects can be identified: (1) the absence of clear criteria for success, (2) professional isolation, (3) unstructured methods of recruitment and training, and (4) the changing social environment for mediation with the advent of public sector bargaining.

The Absence of Clear Criteria for Success. The respondents balked at the notion that straightforward criteria of success are available to the mediator. Settlement, the most obvious criterion of success, was rejected as unsatisfactory on at least two grounds: first, the great majority of all contracts are settled without mediators and work successfully; second, since the parties are mutually dependent on one another, they will settle regardless of what the mediator does and, indeed, whether or not he makes an appearance at all.

It is conceivable, of course, that criteria of success could be developed. It would appear, however, that for the same reason that they are reluctant to admit attempting to produce "good" settlements, so the respondents are unwilling to promulgate notions of "successful" mediation. The process is a voluntary one, which rests largely on the disputants' belief that the mediator's goals are parallel to their own. A mediator whose explicit idea of "success" in any fashion gave cause for doubt on this score might soon find himself persona non grata.

Whatever the explanation, the lack of criteria of success poses a dilemma for professionalization: without criteria of success, techniques that lead to success cannot be identified; without identifying techniques that lead to success, training must remain confined mainly to the hope that, by whatever lights are given him, each new recruit will become a skilled "artist" in his own right.

Professional Isolation. The theme of professional isolation was a strong one. The commonest explanation for this conclusion was the fact that mediation requires privacy and confidentiality. It is not hard to see how such professional autonomy and isolation could produce, in an almost Darwinian fashion, a diversity of approaches genuine enough to establish the notion that mediation is an irreducibly "artistic" enterprise. Moreover, a high level of pluralistic ignorance could further magnify the differences that exist, with each man imagining that, like him, everybody has struggled through to his own unique solution to the problems that mediation presents.

The Informal Process of Recruitment and Training. The multiplicity of styles that is often taken as evidence that mediation is art rather than science may reflect the recruitment of candidates with a wide range of prior experience and the absence of concerted efforts to establish uniform criteria of selection, as much as the ethereal demands of the job. The best description of how an individual becomes a mediator was given by one respondent who characterized the process thus:

> I don't know anybody who starts out with the determination that he is going to school and become a mediator who becomes a mediator. I don't think anybody anticipated becoming a mediator. He slides into it laterally somewhere along the line, unintentionally, by force of circumstances, by opportunities that arise, but not because he does it intentionally.

The growth of the mediation services seems to have produced more formalization than is reflected in the preceding two accounts. There are now civil service examinations that must be passed before a candidate is eligible for training. Even so, requirements tend to be broad, usually specifying only general experience in industrial relations and some knowledge of collective bargaining, economics, and labor law. Oral examinations, where they exist, are, according to one respondent, more or less improvised on the spot by the examiners. Criteria for evaluating candidates' responses appear equally spontaneous.

Once a person is deemed an acceptable candidate, there is far less chance in mediation, as compared to many other professions, that major differences in orientation between him and his more experienced colleagues will be eliminated in the course of training.

Overall, however, there was little indication that respondents were much concerned about improving training in any systematic fashion. Most appeared satisfied that the best way to learn to mediate is to start mediating.

The Effectiveness of Mediation in Public Sector Arbitration Systems: The Iowa Experience

Ronald Hoh *

The advent and dramatic expansion of collective bargaining among public employees has hastened the enactment of numerous state public sector collective bargaining statutes during the past fifteen years. Such statutes have gen-

*Iowa Public Employment Relations Board. Reprinted from *The Arbitration Journal* 39, no. 2 (June 1984), pp. 30–40.

erated a myriad of approaches for the resolution of the inevitable impasses that arise in public sector negotiations — approaches that may include mediation, fact-finding, arbitration, the right to strike, or some combination thereof. The effectiveness of these dispute settlement procedures and the experience under them have been the target of intense examination.

Such analyses have generally focused on the use of the final arbitration step of the impasse procedure and the effect of arbitration on the willingness of the parties to resolve their impasses voluntarily prior to its implementation. Little, however, has been written about either the experience under the Iowa public sector collective bargaining law or the effectiveness of "intermediate impasse steps" in the presence of further impasse steps — that is, the effectiveness of mediation when the final impasse step is arbitration.

Available Literature

Mediation is probably the most widely practiced dispute resolution procedure in collective bargaining. It is also the least researched. Even less research has been done on mediation in the public sector and less yet on its effectiveness.

In contrast, there are numerous studies on the effectiveness of dispute resolution procedures providing for arbitration and the effect of arbitration on the bargaining process itself. As a result, any information concerning the effectiveness of intermediate impasse steps such as mediation is generally to be found in conjunction with, or as an afterthought to, assessments of the effectiveness of arbitration.

Much of the conventional theoretical wisdom on the effectiveness of intermediate impasse steps relates to the perceived impact of arbitration on the bargaining process. Critics have argued that the availability of arbitration as the final impasse step adversely affects or even destroys collective bargaining (and bargaining's extension, mediation) because (1) it shifts the parties' attention away from good faith bargaining and toward impasse procedures;[1] (2) the parties become more concerned about posturing for arbitration than with exhausting avenues of voluntary agreement,[2] and (3) the parties tend to shift responsibility for settlement to the arbitrator.[3]

These arguments postulate that the more complex and structured the impasse mechanism, the less attention is paid to the bargaining process and its various avenues of voluntary agreement.[4] According to Arnold Zack, the effectiveness of the public sector mediator operating within the context of possible fact finding and/or binding arbitration is diluted by these potential impasse steps:

It is evident that the parties increasingly seek to utilize all the available steps of the procedures to get their "little bit more." The very availability of fact-finding tends to assure its invocation and consequently diminishes the likelihood of settlement in mediation. Mediation, with fact-finding waiting in the wings, sometimes takes on the appearance of a rite which must be gone through before the parties get to real crisis bargaining.[5]

Walter Maggiolo echoes a similar concern in his work on mediation techniques. He notes that mediators themselves have recognized a tendency of parties to hold back when they know other impasse steps are to follow. Thus, the existence of an impasse step beyond mediation tends to lessen the mediator's chance of effectuating a settlement.[6]

The empirical data on the subject, however, though limited, suggest a substantially different conclusion from that advanced by the theoreticians. Thomas Kochan's New York study in 1979 focused on the bargaining process as affected by a legislative change of the final impasse step from fact finding to arbitration. This two-year study of police and fire disputes found a 13–18 percent increase in the effectiveness of mediation when binding arbitration was the final impasse step, rather than fact finding. Also significant was Kochan's finding that in 70 percent of all cases resolved by an arbitration award, the arbitration panel adopted the fact finder's award on wages.[7]

Lawrence Holden's report on the Massachusetts experience in 1976 described the intermediate fact-finding step as "the cornerstone of the entire procedures." During the first year of the public sector law in Massachusetts, 143 cases went to mediation, of which 102 also went to fact-finding. Only 25 continued to arbitration and only 11 of those cases required an arbitration award.[8] Peter Feuille's 1975 general overview of those jurisdictions having arbitration as a final impasse step postulated a substantial decrease in the proportion of impasses culminating in an arbitration award when mediation and fact-finding were part of the bargaining process. He also found that the absence of these nonbinding intermediate steps contributed to an increased use of the binding arbitration step.[9]

James Stern's 1975 study compared the impasse procedures culminating in arbitration in three states—Michigan, Pennsylvania, and Wisconsin. He found reliance on arbitration to be much greater in Pennsylvania than in Michigan or Wisconsin, and, like Feuille, attributed much of the difference to the absence of an effective mediation effort in Pennsylvania. The Pennsylvania statute does not require prior mediation intervention.

Stern also found a stronger settlement incentive effect associated with mediation under final offer than under conventional arbitration. The more distant the mediation process was from the arbitration step of the procedure, however, the more the effect of mediation was diminished.[30]

In a study of the Iowa impasse system in 1979, Daniel Gallagher and Richard Pegnetter found an increasing pressure to settle as the parties progressed to each successive step of the impasse procedure. This "imminence pressure" to reach agreement exists immediately prior to each adjudicative step.[11]

Paul Gerhart and John Drotning's 1980 study of the impasse procedures in six states, including Iowa, focused on the characteristics of an effective mediator in the public sector, rather than on the effectiveness of mediation when arbitration is the final impasse step. Each of the impasse procedures studied ended in some form of binding arbitration or in the right to strike; nevertheless, the mediation stage, according to these authors, "stands out as the critical period in the achievement of policy objectives."[12]

Thus, while many would minimize the effectiveness of intermediate impasse steps when the final step is arbitration, the limited data available seem to indicate that such steps have a salutary effect on voluntary settlement and serve to limit the need for usage of the final arbitration step.

The Iowa Statutory Framework

The Iowa Public Employment Relations Act, enacted in 1974, is an all-inclusive collective bargaining statute that essentially covers all nonfederal public employees in the state. It mandates an employer's duty to bargain with the employees' chosen representative, although the negotiable areas are more limited in scope than the "wages, hours and other terms and conditions of employment" found in most other collective bargaining statutes. The act protects both employer and employee rights by proscribing certain conduct in a contextual format similar to that of the National Labor Relations Act's unfair labor practice provisions. It sets forth procedures for determining representation matters, including bargaining unit issues. It establishes an agency, the Public Employment Relations Board (PERB), to administer and enforce the provisions of the statute. Finally, and most germane to this analysis, it sets forth a complex process for the resolution of bargaining impasses, which includes mediation, fact-finding, and binding arbitration.

The Iowa statute is distinctive for a number of reasons. It provides for final offer, issue-by-issue arbitration as the last step in the impasse procedure, but with a unique twist: the fact-finder's recommendation on each issue offers the arbitrator a third choice on each impasse item. The statute also covers all categories of nonsupervisory public employees, making Iowa the only state to extend arbitration legislation to all public employees rather than limiting that right to specific categories of public employees, such as police and firefighters.[13]

The act also sets forth a sequence of impasse procedures, progressing from negotiation to mediation, fact-finding, and finally to binding arbitration, absent any voluntary agreement earlier in the process. Since the act instructs the parties, as a first step in their duty to bargain, to "endeavor to agree upon their own procedure for resolving any subsequent bargaining impasse," it clearly advocates an impasse procedure of the parties own making, although the statutory procedure applies in the absence of such agreement.

Finally, the statutory procedure is clearly related to the employer's budget-making process. The employer's duty to bargain arises upon board certification of the employee organization as the bargaining representative, with bargaining required to commence "reasonably in advance of the public employer's budget making process." Although the elements of such a requirement are unclear, the statute clearly creates a time relationship between the various stages of the impasse procedures and the budget certification date.

Upon a single-party request 120 days prior to the budget certification date, the board must appoint a mediator and a fact-finder 10 days after the mediator first meets with the parties, if the impasse persists. The fact-finder holds a hearing and issues his or her award within 15 days of the hearing, and the parties have only 10 days to consider it. In the absence of agreement, either party can request the next impasse stage of arbitration, but within 4 days after such request, the parties much exchange final offers on each impasse item in dispute. They are not allowed to amend their final offers before the arbitrator at any time thereafter.

The arbitrator or arbitration panel, selected from a list provided by the board, may then conduct a hearing (although a hearing is not required), administer oaths, issue subpoenas, and take testimony. Within 15 days of the hearing, the arbitrator or panel, following certain statutory criteria, must select "the most reasonable offers on each impasse item submitted by the parties, or the recommendation of the fact-finder on each impasse item." Any mediation efforts by the arbitrator are statutorily proscribed. The award is final and binding, although the statute allows for judicial review of the reward, "if its implementation would be inconsistent with any statutory limitation on the public employer's funds, spending, or budget, or would substantially impair or limit the performance of any statutory duty by the public employer."

Experience under the Statute

Although the statute was enacted with an effective date of July 1, 1974, the duty to bargain did not become effective until July 1, 1975. Because the statutory bargaining scheme and the impasse procedures were designed to activate bargaining in advance of the budget-making process, negotiations did not begin until late 1975 for contracts that would be effective in July of 1976.

The available data begin with this first year and cover eight bargaining years identified by the year in which the contracts took effect.

Table 1 sets forth the sequence of cases moving through the impasse process each year and the number and percentage resolved at each stage of the procedure. Because the Iowa statute does not permit voluntary recognition and requires board certification of the bargaining representative before the employer's duty to bargain arises, the precise number of potential negotiations (and thus potential impasse cases) at any particular time is known. The "Total Number of Units" column represents the number of certifications as of January 1 of each year. Units certified after that date are not entitled to all steps of the impasse procedure for that year, because of the impasse cutoff caused by the March 15 budget submission date for governmental bodies.

The table first reveals an interesting consistency: the increased numbers in each category correspond with the increased number of certified units; the relative percentages in each category, however, remain quite stable. The table

Table 1
Settlement Stage Statistics for the First Eight Years of Experience under the Act

Year	Total Number of Units	Mediation Petitions for Impasse Service	Cases Mediated	Cases Settled	Settlement Rate[a]
1976	421	305	195	145	74.0
1977	571	342	261	185	70.9
1978	638	397	315	248	78.7
1979	672	438	320	240	75.0
1980	724	475	396	323	81.6
1981	765	511	433	332	76.7
1982	785	568	448	399	89.1
1983	826	596	486	351	72.2

Year	Appt.	Fact-Finding Award	Percentage[b]	Arbitration Petitions	Arbitration Award	Percentage[b]
1976	44	44	10.4	25	25	5.9
1977	103	60	10.5	61	41	7.1
1978	110	36	5.6	48	27	4.7
1979	114	57	7.8	43	33	4.9
1980	131	43	5.9	50	31	4.3
1981	167	74	9.6	72	46	6.0
1982	176	44	5.6	73	44	5.6
1983	173	94	11.4	88	49	5.9

[a]Computed as percentage of cases mediated that were settled with the assistance of the mediator.
[b]Computed as a percentage of the total number of bargaining units negotiating contracts.

further shows that in any given year, about one-third of the universe either settles without a request for impasse services or does not engage in negotiations because of a multiyear contract. Thus, approximately two-thirds of the bargaining units request impasse services each year. Although this figure is somewhat larger than in other jurisdictions, it should be noted that mediation, because of the time rigidity of the impasse procedures, is often requested when it may not be necessary. Statutory impasse procedures must be implemented 120 days prior to the March 15 budget certification date (November 15), but many sets of negotiations (particularly in school districts) do not begin until mid-October. Such requests for mediation, however, do not prevent the parties from negotiating and frequently reaching agreement by themselves.

As the table shows, 20 percent of those requesting mediation settle without formal mediation assistance.[14] In the last four years, that figure has been further reduced to approximately 18 percent. Such a reduction may be a sign that the parties are improving their bargaining relationship and either have their disputes settled by November 15 or have a real (rather than a deadline-induced) need for mediation services. In any event, despite the large number of mediation requests received each year, slightly less than half of all potential impasses are settled without third-party assistance.

But the measure of the effectiveness of any impasse step is the number of bargaining disputes that are settled at that stage, and this analysis is primarily concerned with those cases where mediation actually occurred. As the Iowa figures for the first eight years of experience show, the percentage of settlements at mediation, measured against cases mediated, has remained both relatively consistent and remarkably high. Slightly less than 78 percent of actual cases mediated have been settled by mediation. Such a settlement rate at mediation is substantially higher than what is reported from other jurisdictions where, like Iowa, the final step of the impasse procedure is arbitration.

Stern's study of arbitration laws covering police and firefighters in Wisconsin, Michigan, and Pennsylvania shows a somewhat comparable record of mediation success only for Wisconsin. In that state, nearly 70 percent of those cases that went through mediation were settled at that step during the first two years (1973–1974) of the statute, which provided for final offer package arbitration as the next step.[15] That percentage, however, fell to between 50 and 60 percent of cases mediated in the first two years' experience under the med-arb amendments of 1978.[16]

In Michigan, which also has mediation as a prerequisite to arbitration for police and firefighters, about 58 percent of all cases submitted to mediation were settled at that stage, according to figures provided over a two-year period by the Michigan Employment Relations Commission.[17] Despite these Michigan figures, it is interesting to note that the parties view mediation as "largely a waste of time" since the 1973 final offer amendment.[18] Pennsylvania, which does not require mediation before arbitration, reveals 30.6 percent of police disputes and 48.7 percent of fire disputes settled by *arbitration* over the first six years of the law's existence.[19] Similarly, in Minnesota about 30 percent of all negotiations requesting mediation for essential service employees disputes resulted in *arbitrated* settlements for the eight-year period of 1973–1980.[20]

In Massachusetts, where a final offer by package arbitration procedure was superimposed in 1974 for police and fire employees on an impasse procedure that previously ended at fact-finding, the percentage of cases that were mediated successfully prior to fact-finding fell from the period 1972–1974 (police 62.1 percent; fire 59.3 percent) to the period 1975–1977 (police 37.1 percent; fire 30.4 percent).[21]

In New Jersey, which provides for final offer arbitration on a package basis on economic items and on an issue-by-issue basis for noneconomic items for police and firefighters, and allows either party to request mediation prior to implementation of arbitration, the parties requested implementation of the formal mediation step in only 12 percent of the cases that ultimately resulted in a petition for arbitration during the first two years of the act's existence.[22]

Statistics in Kochan's study show that mediation was successful in resolving only 30 percent of the police and fire disputes in New York over a three-year period.[23] The mediation success rate for all types of disputes over the first five years of the New York Public Employment Relations Board's operations ranged between 42 percent and 57 percent. (It should be noted, however, that the final step of the impasse procedure in New York during this time period was fact finding.[24])

Considering Iowa's success with mediation as set forth in the table, when compared to those cases requiring either a fact-finding report or arbitration award, there appears to be little support for *any* of the criticisms previously mentioned concerning the effectiveness of mediation when the final impasse step is arbitration. Iowa evidences no wholesale move by the parties to shift responsibility for settlement to the arbitrator, to utilize all available steps of the impasse procedure to get "a little bit more," or to shift emphasis away from exhausting all avenues of voluntary agreement. Rather than being "a rite which must be gone through before the parties get to real crisis bargaining," mediation in fact provides the essential element in the success of the impasse mechanism in the Iowa public sector.

Reasons for Success

As indicated, the mediation step of the impasse procedure has been extremely successful in resolving bargaining impasses in the Iowa public sector. Several reasons for that success can be identified by examining the statutory framework, the methods of implementation of the statute, and other extrinsic variables. These factors are not ranked in any particular order of importance.

One of the extrinsic variables has been the relatively stable economic climate in Iowa and the fact that the overall budget picture generally is known during the bargaining. This is particularly true in education disputes, where financing is based on a foundation system that draws funds largely from state aid and provides for a relatively fixed amount of local tax support. Because of such predictable financing, school budgets offer realistic parameters for possible economic settlements.

The stability of the economic system and its concomitant effect on the utility of the impasse system, however, may be wavering during the current period of economic difficulty. For example, in the middle of the 1981 negotiations season, the Iowa legislature cut approximately $40 million from the amount promised for school operations affected by those negotiations. Such a midstream cut was probably responsible for the lower settlement rate at mediation in 1981, compared to the settlement rate of both the year before and the year after. Similarly, during the current recession, the Iowa legislature, faced with a potential budget deficit, appropriated the smallest increase in funding for schools in the history of the bargaining statute for the 1983 negotiations. The decrease in the success rate for mediation for that year is probably largely attributable to that lower appropriation. Nevertheless, the relatively favorable economic climate thus far in Iowa has had a positive effect on voluntary settlement in this state when compared with the experience in many other states.

Other factors contributing to the Iowa statute's success at mediation relate to the statutory structure of the impasse process as a whole. First, the fact-finding and arbitration provisions of the statute have had an affirmative effect upon the success of the mediation step. The statute not only requires the exchange of final offers before arbitration, but also allows only one final offer and prohibits mediation by the arbitrator. Although the parties may continue bargaining, such a system prevents arbitration from becoming an extension of the bargaining process, because the parties have nothing to gain by withholding their best offer until they reach the arbitration stage. The inability to modify final offers coupled with the uncertainty regarding the arbitrator's award create distinctive pressure on the parties to settle. This clearly increases the effectiveness of the mediation steps.[25]

Certain PERB case decisions regarding fact finding and arbitration have further directed parties' attentions away from adjudication and toward voluntary settlement. The board has narrowly interpreted the term *impasse item,* which restricts the arbitrator's discretion and limits the areas of potential disagreement to impasse subject categories, rather than all areas within such a category.[26] In addition, the board has required that a party may not offer a proposal to the fact-finder or the arbitrator that has not previously been offered to the other party during the course of negotiations.[27] By more clearly defining and delineating what can and cannot be done for the purpose of enhancing one's position at fact-finding or arbitration, the board has enhanced the effectiveness of the voluntary settlement procedures.[28]

The aggregate effect of the impasse steps also creates a variety of pressures on the parties to move toward voluntary agreement. The first form of such pressure relates to the statutory time deadlines. Impasses under the statutory procedure must be completed within a 120-day time frame. Once the process is begun, the parties are very quickly forced to assess whether they should settle the dispute or whether they are able to put together a case allowing them to do better at a future impasse step, since the time period between the start of the mediation and any subsequent fact-finding hearing date generally encompasses a mere three to four weeks. An extension of this time pressure is what Gallagher and Pegnetter call an "imminence pressure." As their study showed, the approach of actual participation in an impasse step often generated increased pressure to negotiate a settlement immediately prior to that step. Since the board appoints a fact-finder (or sends a list of fact-finders) and establishes a hearing date shortly after the expiration of the ten-day mediation period, the effectiveness of mediation, even if it occurs after the allotted ten-day mediation period, is enhanced by the imminence of the fact-finding hearing.[29]

A third pressure-creating feature relates to the impact of final offer selection and the role of the fact-finder's recommendation as a third alternative choice for the arbitrator. The last best offer system is based on the assumption that the arbitrator will tend to select the more reasonable of the alternative choices and that the parties will tend to move toward a middle position in attempting to fashion a reasonable, and hence attractive, final offer. The parties' judgments regarding their ability to prevail at arbitration, however, are clearly affected by the third choice—the fact-finder's recommendation—which quite often lies somewhere between the final offers of the parties.

The marked tendency of arbitrators to select the fact-finder's recommendation rather than the final offer of either party creates additional pressure. A cursory review of arbitration awards by PERB officials has revealed that the arbitrator selects the fact-finder's report rather than either party's final offer in more than 80 percent of the cases.[30] This unique combination of impasse structures is undoubtedly a factor contributing to the low use of arbitration in this jurisdiction and clearly has a positive effect upon voluntary settlement. These factors, however, probably have more effect on voluntary settlements occurring after fact-finding and before arbitration than on the success of mediation.

One other section of the statute has also had a positive effect on the percentage of voluntary settlements and may be more directly related to mediation success. Section 9 of the act limits the scope of bargaining to a relatively clearly defined "laundry list" of bargainable areas and is to be contrasted with most other public sector statutes covering a full gamut of wages, hours, and terms and conditions of employment. The board's rules and regulations enforce this section of the statute by requiring that topics outside its scope be barred from the fact-finding or arbitration stages of the impasse procedures, unless their inclusion has been agreed to by the parties. And, as previously indicated, the board has interpreted the term *impasse item* narrowly. Because the scope of bargaining is narrower than that found in most other jurisdictions, the potential areas of disagreement are also fewer. More than likely this limited scope of bargaining has a salutary effect on voluntary settlement, if only because the parties have fewer areas on which they may disagree. The effectiveness of mediation is enhanced because the mediation stage generally provides a last chance to include areas outside of the mandatorily bargainable laundry list in the contract, since the parties are precluded, absent agreement, from taking such subjects to further impasse steps.

The board's methodology in administering the statute must also contribute to the success of mediation in this jurisdiction. It is the board's policy to place extra emphasis on mediation and less emphasis on the more adjudicatory steps, despite the statute's apparent opposite emphasis.[31] Although the statutory period for mediation is a meager ten days, the board does not assume mediation to be complete until the parties have either reached agreement or received the arbitration award. As a result, mediation assistance is available to the parties (and is aggressively offered by the agency) at any time during the course of the impasse procedures.

A large number of settlements therefore occur between completion of the ten-day mediation period and the fact-finding hearing or between issuance of the fact finding report and arbitration. In such cases, the board has attempted to focus the parties' attention away from the pending adjudicatory impasse steps and toward voluntary settlement. The statistics indicate that the board emphasis on mediation has produced the desired effect—high voluntary settlements and low use of fact-finding and arbitration.

A final factor relates to the board's emphasis on activist mediation style. Both the author and other PERB personnel believe that the public sector mediator must be especially assertive in creating pressure on the parties to settle rather than proceed to the next step. In a sense, he or she must construct that pressure, since the strike threat is not present to automatically provide it. This philosophy has been reflected in the board's training of its ad hoc mediators. Two studies of public sector mediation have found that intensive, activist mediators are more likely to be successful in public sector disputes than mediators who do not possess such qualities.[32] The board's emphasis on activist mediation style, and the success of mediation in this jurisdiction, are consistent with those findings.

Conclusion

At this writing, the Iowa Public Employment Relations Act has been in effect for eight complete bargaining seasons. Its impasse procedure provides for a complex three-tiered system of mediation, fact-finding, and arbitration, with the steps becoming progressively less voluntary and more judicial as movement through the procedure occurs.

The conventional theoretical wisdom generally holds that if arbitration is the final impasse step, the success of intermediate impasse steps such as mediation will be adversely affected, because the parties shift their emphasis away from exhausting avenues of voluntary agreement and toward the final arbitration step. The data available for the eight years of experience in the Iowa public sector, however, show support for *none* of the usual criticisms on mediation effectiveness when arbitration is the final impasse step. The average rate of settlement at the mediation stage of the procedure is nearly 78 percent of cases mediated—higher than that of all other states with similar statutes. In addition, the settlement rate at mediation has remained remarkably consistent over the eight-year period—a period long enough to indicate that the success of mediation may be relatively firmly ensconced, despite the presence of arbitration as the final impasse step.

Potential reasons for the success of the mediation step of the impasse procedure relate to the statutory framework, the Public Employment Relations Board's methods of implementation of the statute and case decisions interpreting it, and other extrinsic variables. These combined factors probably largely account for the success of the mediation step of the procedure. But whatever the definitive reason for the success of mediation, it is clear that mediation is the essential element in the success of the Iowa public sector impasse resolution process.

Notes

1. Robert Howlett, "Contract Arbitration in the Public Sector," *University of Cincinnati Law Review* 42 (1973), p. 65.

2. Phillip Garber, "Compulsory Arbitration in the Public Sector—A Proposed Alternative," *The Arbitration Journal* 26 (1971), p. 226.

3. Arvid Anderson, *Proceedings from the Secretary of Labor's Conference on State and Local Government Labor Relations* (Washington, D.C.: U.S. Department of Labor, Labor Management Services Administration, 1972), p. 35.

4. Victor Gotbaum, "Collective Bargaining and the Union Leader," in Sam Zagoria, ed., *Public Workers and Public Unions* (Englewood Cliffs, N.J.: Prentice-Hall, 1972), p. 82.

5. Arnold Zack, "Impasses, Strikes and Resolutions," in Sam Zagoria, ed., *Public Workers and Public Unions* (Englewood Cliffs, N.J.: Prentice-Hall, 1972), p. 109.

6. Walter Maggiolo, *Techniques in Mediation of Labor Disputes* (Dobbs Ferry, N.Y.: Oceana Publications, 1976), p. 111.

7. Thomas Kochan, Mordehai Mironi, Ronald Ehrenberg, Jean Baderschneider, and Todd Jick, *Dispute Resolution under Fact-finding and Arbitration: An Empirical Analysis* (New York: American Arbitration Association, 1979), p. 60.

8. Lawrence Holden, "Final Offer Arbitration in Massachusetts," *The Arbitration Journal* 31 (1976), p. 26.

9. Peter Feuille, *Final Offer Arbitration* (Chicago: International Personnel Management Association, 1975), pp. 36–37.

10. James Stern, Charles Rehmus, J. Joseph Loewenberg, Hirschel Kasper, and Barbara Dennis, *Final Offer Arbitration* (Lexington, Mass.: Lexington Books, 1975), p. 32.

11. Daniel Gallagher and Richard Pegnetter, "Impasse Resolution under the Iowa Multistep System," *Industrial and Labor Relations Review* 32 (1979), p. 338.

12. Paul Gerhart and John Drotning, *A Six State Study of Impasse Procedures in the Public Sector* (Washington, D.C.: U.S. Department of Labor, Labor Management Services Administration, 1980), p. 185.

13. Wisconsin's med-arb statute, enacted in 1978, provides the right to arbitration for all municipal public employees, but does not afford that right to state employees.

14. "Formal mediation assistance" refers to those disputes where the mediator actually conducted a meeting between the parties. It does not include cases where the mediator may also have telephonically assisted the parties in the settlement of their dispute prior to any formal involvement.

15. Stern et al., *Final Offer Arbitration,* p. 90.

16. Wisconsin Center for Public Policy, *The Effect of Senate Bill 15 Amendments to the Municipal Employment Relations Act,* Report submitted to the Wisconsin Legislative Council, 1980, pp. 23–24.

17. Stern et al., *Final Offer Arbitration,* p. 62.

18. *Ibid.*

19. *Ibid.,* p. 13.

20. Mario Bognanno and Fredrick Champlin, University of Minnesota, *A Quantitative Description and Evaluation of Public Sector Collective Bargaining in Minnesota: 1973–80,* Report submitted to the Minnesota Legislative Committee on Employee Relations, 1981.

21. David Lipsky and Thomas Barocci, "Final Offer Arbitration and Public Safety Employees: The Case of Massachusetts," *Proceedings of the 30th Annual Meeting, Industrial Relations Research Association* (Madison, Wisc.: IRRA, 1978).

22. Joan Weitzman and John M. Stochaj, "Attitudes of Arbitrators toward Final Offer Arbitration in New Jersey," *The Arbitration Journal* 35 (1981), p. 25.

23. Kochan et al., *Dispute Resolution under Fact-Finding and Arbitration,* p. 60.

24. New York State Public Employment Relations Board, *Annual Report* (1975): pp. 1–8.

25. John Loihl, "Final Offer Plus: Interest Arbitration in Iowa," in Barbara Dennis and Gerald Somers, eds., *Truth, Lie Detectors and Other Problems in Labor Arbitration, Proceedings of the Thirty-first Meeting of the National Academy of Arbitrators* (Washington, D.C.: Bureau of National Affairs, 1979), pp. 317–341.

26. West Des Moines Education Association, PERB Case no. 805 (1976), aff'd, 266 N.W.2d 118 (Iowa 1978).

27. Eastern Iowa Community College, PERB Case no. 973 (1977) [fact finding]; Everly Community School District, PERB Case no. 2444 (1983) [arbitration].

28. Loihl, "Final Offer Plus," p. 326.

29. Gallagher and Pegnetter, "Impasse Resolution," p. 335.

30. This figure was obtained through interviews with PERB officials and the author's personal review of arbitration awards. A definitive report on the actual percentage, while an extremely worthwhile subject for research, is beyond the scope of this article.

31. The statute consists of one paragraph regarding mediation, but thirteen paragraphs, two of which contain four subsections, regarding arbitration.

32. Gerhart and Drotning, *Six State Study of Impasse Procedures,* p. 185; Thomas Kochan and Todd Jick, "The Public Sector Mediation Process," *Journal of Conflict Resolution* 22 (1978), p. 209.

Police Interest Arbitration: Awards and Issues

John Delaney
*Peter Feuille**

Public sector interest arbitration became widely institutionalized during the past fifteen years and, as a result, the process has received considerable research attention. Most of this attention has focused on the compatibility of collective bargaining and interest arbitration[1] and, more recently, researchers have studied the effect that interest arbitration has had on employment terms.[2] In conducting a nationwide examination of collective bargaining and interest arbitration in the police service, a large number of interest arbitration awards were collected from around the country. This collection serves as the basis of a detailed analysis of the typical police interest arbitration case, with particular emphasis on issues taken to arbitration.

Awards Sample

In 1982–1983 the status of police collective bargaining and interest arbitration in 1,015 U.S. cities with populations of over 25,000 was examined. As part of this research, 343 usable arbitration awards (plus 903 contracts from

*Reprinted from *The Arbitration Journal* 39, no. 2 (June 1984), pp. 14–24.

arbitration states) applying to police patrol officers' bargaining units were collected. The sample contained a large number of multiyear awards, covering 525 award years (that is, an award with a duration of two years covered two award years). These 343 awards were in effect at various times during 1970–1983, with the vast majority (90 percent) effective some time during 1975–1982.

Awards were collected from cities and unions in sixteen states, although ten of these states accounted for almost all the awards. It was not possible to calculate precisely how many police awards were issued during 1975–1982 and thus there is no way of knowing what percentage of the total was obtained. This multistate sample of awards, however, is the largest such sample ever collected, in part because more police bargaining units are covered by arbitration laws than are the bargaining units of other occupational groups. If it is assumed that these 343 awards are reasonably representative, it is possible, based on the findings, to offer some conclusions about various characteristics of the public sector interest arbitration process.

Type of Arbitration Procedure

One widely used standard to differentiate among arbitration procedures is the amount of discretion arbitrators are allowed when fashioning their rulings. *Conventional* arbitration allows arbitrators the widest discretion, for such a procedure places no official limits on how an arbitrator rules, and the practical limits are established only by the parties' positions at arbitration. *Final offer* arbitration with *package* selection gives arbitrators the least discretion, for such a procedure requires that the arbitrator select—as a single package—either the employer's or the union's offer, without alteration, on all the disputed issues (that is, the arbitrator will make only one selection decision to settle the dispute, no matter how many issues are on the agenda).

In between is *final offer* arbitration with *issue* selection. Such a procedure requires the arbitrator to select either the union's or the employer's final offer, but these selection decisions are to be made separately on each disputed issue. In addition, a few states have hybrid or mixed procedures. Michigan, for example, requires final offer by issue arbitration on economic issues and conventional arbitration on noneconomic issues, while New Jersey specifies final offer by package arbitration on economic issues and final offer by issue arbitration on noneconomic issues—except that the parties may agree to use conventional arbitration. Further, Iowa specifies final offer by issue arbitration and also specifies that arbitrators may select the fact finder's recommendation on each issue rather than the employer's or union's final offer.

Table 1 shows that most of the awards in the sample were issued under conventional arbitration procedures: 60 percent of the awards involved con-

Table 1
Types of Arbitration Procedures

	Procedure[a]		
	Conventional	Final Offer by Issue	Final Offer by Package
Used on all issues in award	207	52	37
Used on some issues in award	15	45	27

Type of Panel	
Single Arbitrator	Tripartite
136	207

[a]These numbers do not total 343 becuse of the double counting involved in hybrid awards.

ventional arbitration, 15 percent were final offer by issue awards, and 11 percent were final offer by package awards. The remaining 14 percent involved a mixture of decision mechanisms. These data indicate that interest arbitrators in police disputes have considerable discretion in shaping their awards to fit the circumstances of each case. Expressed another way, even with all the attention given to final offer arbitration during the past dozen years, relatively few police unions and municipal employers actually negotiate with the truly all-or-nothing sword of final offer by package arbitration hanging over their heads.[3]

Another standard for differentiating among arbitration procedures is whether the award is issued by a single neutral arbitrator or a tripartite panel (union representative, employer representative, and neutral chairperson). As table 1 shows, 60 percent of the awards were issued by tripartite panels. It was not possible to tell from examining these awards how many of these panels existed because the law required them and how many of these panels were used (instead of the single arbitrator format) because the parties preferred the tripartite arrangement. In any case, the tripartite format is much more common in interest arbitration than in grievance arbitration.

Number of Arbitrators

For years, the conventional wisdom in the labor relations community has been that a relatively small number of "mainline" arbitrators have dominated the grievance arbitration process.[4] The accuracy of this view was not tested, but awards in this sample were checked to determine if this same phenomenon was occurring in interest disputes. With vary few exceptions, it was found that it was not.

The 343 awards were issued by 208 different individuals: 143 persons wrote one award, 32 people wrote two awards, and 15 individuals wrote three awards. In other words, the typical arbitrator in this sample wrote a single award. At the other extreme, one arbitrator issued 15 awards, another issued 13, a third person issued 9, a fourth issued 7, and two arbitrators each issued 6 awards. Nobody else issued more than 5 awards. This distribution of arbitration cases across a large number of persons has occurred for many reasons, including the preferences of some unions, employers, and state arbitration administrative agencies to use arbitrators who are residents of the same state in which the arbitration case is located. Whatever the reasons, the data show that, with a few exceptions, police interest arbitration does not appear to be dominated by a small number of mainline arbitrators.[5]

Number of Issues

The data show that interest arbitration cases involve large numbers of disputed issues. As seen in the top part of table 2, the number of issues handled in each of the 343 awards ranged from 1 to 57, with a *median* of 10 issues and a *mean* of 13 issues per award. As noted before, the vast majority of the awards were either conventional or final offer by issue awards, and thus the arbitrators in these cases were asked to make numerous decisions. (They did so in awards that ranged in length from one to 159 pages, with a *median* length of 13 pages and a *mean* length of 18 pages.)

The large number of issues per award, and in particular the fact that more than one-fifth of the awards involved more than 20 issues, strongly suggest that some of the unions and employers in this sample have used arbitration as much more than a dispute settlement procedure of last resort. Instead, it appears that some of the parties are practicing a "let's take these issues to arbitration and see what happens" approach to the process.

In addition, a rough test was conducted to evaluate the conventional wisdom that final offer arbitration, with the risks it poses for those parties who fail to agree at the bargaining table, will induce the parties to settle more issues during negotiations than will conventional arbitration.[6] If this notion is valid, there should be fewer issues per award in final offer arbitration states than in conventional arbitration states, and, further, there should be fewer issues per award under final offer arbitration with package selection than under issue selection.

In the bottom half of table 2, the arbitration awards have been grouped on a state-by-state basis, and the mean or average number of issues per award have been calculated. These data provide moderate support for the idea that final offer arbitration *with package selection* will encourage the parties to settle more issues in negotiations and thereby bring fewer issues to the arbitral hearing room than will the other two kinds of arbitration. In particular, Wis-

Table 2
Number of Issues per Award

Number of Issues	All Awards Number of Awards (%)	Other Characteristics
1–5 issues	86 (25.1)	Range: 1–57 issues
6–10	98 (28.5)	Median: 9.7 issues
11–15	51 (14.9)	Mean: 13.0 issues
16–20	31 (9.1)	Mode: 6 issues (26 awards)
21 or more	77 (22.4)	

State and Type of Arbitration Procedure[a]	State-by-State Distribution Mean Number of Issues per Award	Standards Deviation	Number of Awards[b]
Rhode Island (CON)	21.5	12.8	21
Minnesota (FOAI)	17.2	9.0	44
Connecticut (FOAI)	15.9	8.0	12
Pennsylvania (CON)	15.2	8.7	44
New York (CON)	13.7	13.4	47
Michigan (FOAI + CON)	11.8	7.9	33
Massachusetts (FOAP)	10.9	11.2	19
New Jersey (FOAP + FOAI)	10.5	8.5	66
Iowa (FOAI)	8.9	6.9	20
Washington (CON)	8.2	4.8	6
Oregon (CON)	3.5	3.0	4
Wisconsin (FOAP)[c]	2.5	1.6	19

[a]CON = conventional arbitration; FOAI = final offer arbitration with issue selection; FOAP = final offer arbitration with package selection. These are the types of arbitral decision mechanisms specified in the state statutes, but many statutes allow the parties to mutually agree to use another type of procedure.

[b]The state-by-state distribution excludes four awards, one each from Alaska, California, Nebraska, and Montana.

[c]The Wisconsin results exclude four Milwaukee police awards issued under a separate conventional arbitration statute for that city, and these four Milwaukee awards averaged 28 issues per award.

consin appears to be the most visible final offer success story to date, for the average number of issues per award in that state is well below the average in other states. These results, however, provide little support for the notion that final offer arbitration *with issue selection* will encourage the parties to hold down the number of issues they place before the arbitrator. In addition, the very wide variation in the state averages, and the rather large standard deviations within each state, suggest that other factors are more important than the type of arbitration procedure as determinants of the number of arbitrated issues.

Types of Issues

In the research, a contract/award scoring index was developed to evaluate or score the contracts and awards collected on the basis of how favorable they were to the union.[7] The index was constructed specifically for the police service and, as a result, contains 130 separate items (exclusive of salaries) that our previous research showed could exist in police contracts and awards. In addition, all of these 130 items were grouped into one of six subindex categories: (1) *working conditions* (such as scheduling and equipment issues); (2) *individual security* (examples include promotion, transfer, and layoff provisions); (3) *union security* (this includes membership requirements, dues checkoff, time for union business, and so on); (4) *equity* (all grievance procedure and displinary provisions belong here); (5) *fringe benefits* (all insurances, leaves, vacations, etc., belong here); and (6) *pay supplements* (this category includes all pay items, such as overtime pay and clothing allowances, over and above basic salaries). In addition, as many as eight different annual salary issues (patrol officer minimum, patrol officer maximum, corporal, sergeant, lieutenant, captain, dispatcher, and parking enforcers) were recorded (in dollars).

In these 343 awards, arbitrators decided 4,444 separate issues (covering a total of 6,833 issue years). It was possible to evaluate 3,587 (or 81 percent) of these issues with the scoring index. (The remaining 19 percent of the disputed issues were not included in the index.)

Table 3 indicates the frequency with which various issues occurred in these awards. Using the 3,587 issues evaluated with the scoring index, the first half of the table shows how frequently the various types of issues were placed on the arbitral agenda, and the second half of the table lists the ten most frequently arbitrated specific issues. Taken together, these data indicate that economic issues are much more frequent in police awards than are noneconomic issues. If it is assumed that fringe benefits, pay supplements, and salaries are economic issues and the rest are noneconomic, table 3 shows that more than three-fourths of the arbitral rulings that were scored involved economic issues. Further, all of the ten most arbitrated specific issues are economic in nature: three are salary issues, three involve pay supplements, and the other four involve various fringe benefits. In addition, table 3 also shows that these ten most arbitrated issues frequently appear in police contracts in arbitration states.

Many of the 130 items in the scoring index have direct law enforcement connections or implications: court appearance pay and false arrest insurance can affect officers' incentives to make arrests, residency requirements reflect political judgments about the relationships between officers and the citizens

Table 3
Types of Issues in Dispute

Type of Issue	Percentage of Awards with at Least One Issue in Category	Number of Arbitrated Issues in Categoty
Economic:		2,823
Salaries	91.0	716
Pay supplements	75.5	978
Fringe benefits	72.6	1,129
Noneconomic:		763
Union security	46.1	248
Working conditions	34.4	165
Individual security	33.2	179
Equity	22.7	171

Ten Most Arbitrated Specific Issues	Number of Awards (%)	Number of Contracts with This Issue (%)[a]
Police officer maximum salary	311 (90.7)	819 (90.7)
Patrol officer minimum salary	151 (44.0)	800 (88.6)
Longevity pay	129 (37.5)	761 (84.3)
Annual clothing allowance	127 (37.0)	795 (88.0)
Maximum amount of vacation	98 (28.7)	801 (88.7)
Additional insurance protection	92 (26.8)	415 (46.0)
Number of holidays	91 (26.6)	874 (96.8)
Shift differential pay	90 (26.2)	365 (40.4)
Sergeant salary	88 (25.7)	510 (56.5)
Dental insurance (employee)	81 (23.6)	326 (36.1)

[a]Calculated from the 903 contracts collected from arbitration states.

with whom they interact and also reflect operational judgments about the speed with which officers can respond to emergency calls to report for work, and so on.

In the top half of table 4, 15 specific law enforcement issues contained in the scoring index are listed. All of these are unique (or almost unique) to the police service, and thus they would rarely be found in the contracts of other occupational groups. Table 4 specifies the number of times that arbitrators ruled on these issues. These data confirm the findings just discussed by showing that law enforcement issues are rarely placed before arbitrators. In addition, the three most frequently listed law enforcement issues in the table are economic ones that can have a direct impact on the financial well-being of police officers. In other words, these results show that arbitrators very rarely have a direct impact on such things as a police department's weapons policy or internal investigation policy.

Management's ability to assign or deploy officers to particular shifts, activities, or beats, however, also may have a direct impact on a police department's effectiveness in delivering law enforcement services. It was not possible to establish a direct link between arbitration awards and law enforcement

Table 4
Issues at Arbitration

	Number of Awards Containing Issue (%)	Number of Contract Containing Issue (%)[a]
Law enforcement issues:		
Court appearance pay	42 (12.2)	696 (77.1)
False arrest insurance	33 (9.7)	370 (41.0)
Court appearance pay rate	27 (7.8)	728 (80.6)
Special equipment	24 (7.0)	279 (30.9)
Residency requirement	20 (5.8)	170 (18.8)
Officer bill of rights	15 (4.4)	353 (39.1)
Officer rights in citizen complaints	9 (2.6)	396 (43.9)
Off duty armament	9 (2.6)	51 (5.6)
Firearm qualification	4 (1.2)	125 (13.8)
Armament in squad cars	2 (0.6)	27 (3.0)
Type of ammunition used	2 (0.6)	84 (9.3)
Type of sidearm carried	1 (0.3)	102 (11.3)
Firearm review board	0	7 (0.8)
Use of arms/deadly force	0	9 (1.0)
Use of less than deadly force	0	9 (1.0)
Personnel allocation issues:		
Special assignment pay	50 (14.6)	380 (42.1)
Pay for out-of-title work	44 (12.8)	480 (53.2)
Vacancies/promotion procedure	30 (8.7)	467 (51.7)
Overtime pay	29 (8.5)	851 (94.2)
Staffing provision	24 (7.0)	150 (16.6)
Standby pay	22 (6.4)	222 (24.6)
Call-in pay	21 (6.1)	740 (81.9)
Shift assignment	18 (5.2)	472 (52.3)
Voluntary transfer	15 (4.4)	319 (35.3)
Choice of overtime pay or time off	14 (4.1)	171 (18.9)
Involuntary transfer	13 (3.8)	267 (29.6)
Shift exchange	11 (3.2)	278 (30.8)
Subcontracting	7 (2.1)	327 (36.2)
Job posting and bidding	3 (0.9)	224 (24.8)

[a]Calculated from the 903 contracts collected from arbitration states.

effectiveness, but it was possible to examine how often arbitrators rule on personnel allocation issues. As the figures in the bottom half of table 4 indicate, these kinds of issues also are infrequently taken to arbitration. Further, 180 of the 301 arbitral rulings on these 14 issues involved requests for extra pay for particular assignments rather than direct restrictions on assignment practices.[8] In other words, the results indicate that, just as management has almost no reason to fear that arbitrators will attempt to write law enforcement policies for police departments, so management has little reason to worry that arbitrators will tell them how to deploy their officers (though arbitrators may tell management how much particular deployment practices will cost).

In sum, the information in tables 3 and 4 indicates that disputes over money rather than those over management's ability to manage are the primary grist for the police interest arbitration mill.

Who Proposes Changes?

Except in rare cases, interest arbitration involves disputes over the renegotiation of existing contracts. The conventional arbitral wisdom suggests that in these disputes, it is the unions who propose most of the changes in the contracts and it is the employers who propose to continue the *status quo*. This notion was examined by recording which party proposed a change from the *status quo* on each arbitrated issue.

Table 5 indicates that this view is applicable to nonsalary issues but not to salaries. The figures in the table show that unions propose most of the changes in the nonsalary portions of the contract but that both parties propose changes in salary issues. These results are not particularly surprising, for management has little incentive to place nonsalary items in the contract, while the unions see such items as protection for their members. In contrast, both sides have a strong incentive to influence the size of salary increases, for the standard question in this era of the annual pay raise is not "if" but "how much?" Further, these change-proposing techniques would be even more pronounced if it were possible to classify accurately the issues in the "unable to determine" category. It was not possible to determine from the language in some awards, however, precisely who proposed changes in the contract.

Arbitrator Responses

How do arbitrators respond to these proposals? In particular, how do arbitrators respond to proposals for improvements in existing contractual items and the insertion of new items into the contract? Again, the conventional wisdom has portrayed interest arbitration as a conservative rather than innovative process, with arbitrators being generally reluctant to rewrite substantial portions of the parties' contracts.

This research provides an excellent opportunity to test the accuracy of

Table 5
Parties Proposing Changes in Issues at Arbitration

Party	Number of Nonsalary Issues (%)	Number of Salary Issues (%)
Union only	1,725 (60.1)	94 (13.1)
Management only	271 (9.4)	1 (0.1)
Both parties	229 (8.0)	455 (63.5)
Unable to determine[a]	646 (22.5)	166 (23.2)
Total	2,871	716

[a]For these 812 issues, information in the awards did not identify who proposed changes.

this assessment. Several years worth of police awards and contracts from numerous cities were collected; by examining these documents and the language in the awards, it was possible to determine how often arbitrators placed new nonsalary issues in the parties' contracts (for those issues in the scoring index). In addition, it could be determined how often arbitrators ordered improvements in existing contractual items. In the scoring index, *improvement* means changing an item so that it is noticeably more favorable to the union than formerly. For example, a change from a 40-hour work week to a 38-hour work week qualifies as an improvement in the "length of work week" item in the scoring index. Rewriting the existing work week language, however — even in a manner sought by the union — would not qualify as an improvement as long as the work week remained at 40 hours. In other words, the scoring index is purposefully constructing in such a way that it records only clear and unambiguous changes and excludes minor rewriting of existing language.

Table 6 indicates that interest arbitration does appear to be a conservative rather than innovative process. For instance, arbitrators do not seem eager to add new items to the contract, as only 400 of their 2,871 rulings on nonsalary issues (or 13.9 percent) resulted in the addition of new issues. (It would be informative to know how many new issue requests arbitrators received, but we were unable to collect this information.) Similarly, arbitrators do not appear eager to award improvements in nonsalary items to

Table 6
Changes in Nonsalary Issues Ordered by Arbitrators

New Issues Added by Arbitrators		Improvements (Including New Issues) Ordered by Arbitrators	
Number of New Issues per Award	Number of Awards (%)	Number of Improvements per Award	Number of Awards (%)
0	179 (52.2)	0	131 (38.2)
1	80 (23.3)	1	78 (22.7)
2	30 (8.7)	2	40 (11.7)
3	27 (7.9)	3	43 (12.5)
4	9 (2.6)	4	19 (5.5)
5	5 (1.5)	5	11 (3.2)
6 or more	13 (3.8)	6	21 (4.7)
Total	343		343

Range:	0–23 new issues	Range:	0–23 improvements
Median:	0.5 new issues	Median:	1.0 improvements
Mean:	1.2 new issues	Mean:	1.8 improvements
Mode:	0 new issues	Mode:	0 improvements
Total:	400 new issues	Total:	603 improvements

the unions, at least as that term is defined here. A total of 603 improvements out of 2,871 rulings (21.0 percent) were counted, and that figure *includes* the new items just discussed. These results suggest that unions should not look to arbitrators for major revisions in the nonsalary portions of their contracts.

This conclusion is subject to several caveats. First, 19 percent of the arbitrated nonsalary issues were not scored on the index, and many of these issues may have involved new items or improvements in existing items. Second, the stringent definition of *improvements* undoubtedly has omitted some changes sought and obtained by the unions—changes that the employers and unions would say have been to the unions' advantage. Third, the data presented here do not permit us to say anything about the *availability effect* that arbitration may have had (that is, the union might seek and the employer might agree to new items during negotiations simply because both sides are aware of arbitration's availability). Finally, the data in table 6 do not address how arbitrators have resolved salary issues.

Even with these caveats, however, the table 6 results indicate that interest arbitrators are generally reluctant to order wholesale changes in the nonsalary sections of police contracts. Less than one-seventh of their nonsalary rulings inserted new issues into these contracts, and about four-fifths of these rulings resulted in no significant improvements in these nonsalary items. With a few exceptions, then, the data imply that interest arbitrators define their role in a conservative rather than innovative manner.

Summary and Conclusions

The data in this article tell several things about the "typical" police interest arbitration case and resulting award. As long as observers realize that there are many, many exceptions to the "typical" case, this information provides an improved understanding of how the police interest arbitration process functions.

First, these results show that interest arbitrators usually have considerable discretion to fashion the awards they deem appropriate. More than four-fifths of these awards were issued under conventional or final offer by issue arbitration procedures, and thus the all-or-nothing feature of final offer by package arbitration seems to be less attractive to labor relations policymakers and practitioners than to dispute settlement theoreticians. The results also suggest that the exercise of this discretion may not lead to recurring work as an interest arbitrator, for more than two-thirds of the neutral arbitrators in this sample produced only a single award. Of course, these same persons may have rendered other interest arbitration awards that were not collected, and a few individuals in this sample were selected over and over again. The data strongly imply, however, that nobody relies on interest arbitration work as the mainstay of his or her dispute settlement practice.

Second, the number of issues decided in these awards indicates that some unions and employers are burdening the interest arbitration process with more issues than the process was designed to handle. Half of these awards involved fewer than ten issues, but half involved more, and some awards involved many more. Above all else, compulsory interest arbitration is a process designed to settle negotiating disputes without strikes.[9] This purpose clearly implies that the issues taken to arbitration should be those which—if not settled—would lead to a union decision to call a strike or an employer decision to take a strike.

Observers, however, properly may be skeptical that 20, 30, 40, or 57 strike issues actually existed in some of the arbitration cases examined here. Expressed another way, the results imply that some police unions and employers view interest arbitration as a very low risk method for seeking favorable contract terms, and thus the procedure plays host to a larger number of issues than would a high-risk procedure. Further, this conclusion is supported by the Wisconsin results. The average number of issues per award in that state is well below the national average, and final offer by package arbitration as practiced there is a truly high-risk, all-or-nothing procedure (final offers, once certified, cannot be individually modified; and there are no fact-finder recommendations in which to seek refuge). In other words, the results suggest that conventional arbitration and final offer by issue arbitration may be susceptible to a sort of "issue inflation" by some users of these procedures.[10]

Third, most of the issues taken to arbitration involve money. Specifically, 78 percent of the issues evaluated with the scoring index were economic issues involving salaries, pay supplements, or fringe benefits. Further, all of the ten most arbitrated specific issues in these 343 awards involved either salaries, pay supplements, or fringe benefits. In contrast, the law enforcement issues that are unique to the police service are rarely placed in front of arbitrators. Similarly, arbitrators are infrequently asked to rule on personnel allocation provisions—though they may be asked to put price tags on particular assignment/deployment practices. Not surprisingly, police unions proposed most of the changes in the nonsalary provisions taken to arbitration, but both unions and employers proposed changes in the salary items.

Finally, arbitrators appear reluctant to engage in the wholesale rewriting of police contracts. About 14 percent of the arbitral rulings on the nonsalary issues evaluated with the scoring index resulted in the insertion of new items into the parties' contracts. Further, only about one-fifth of these arbitral rulings resulted in substantial improvements for the police unions who participated in these cases (though the definition of *improvements* is a stringent one that undoubtedly understates what unions and employers consider to be contractual improvements). As a result, the data imply that interest arbitrators view themselves as conservative adjusters of police contract terms rather than as innovative molders of police union–management relationships.

Notes

1. For a review of this literature, see John C. Anderson, "The Impact of Arbitration: A Methodological Assessment," *Industrial Relations* 20 (Spring 1981), pp. 129–148.

2. For an example of this research, see John Delaney and Peter Feuille, "Bargaining, Arbitration, and Police Wages," *Proceedings: Thirty-fifth Annual Meeting of the Industrial Relations Research Association* (Madison, Wisc.: IRRA, 1983), pp. 207–215.

3. Apparently, most of the state legislatures that have enacted police arbitration laws have agreed with Charles Rehmus's view that final offer by package arbitration can be a "draconian procedure." Charles Rehmus, "Varieties of Final Offer Arbitration," *The Arbitration Journal* 37 (December 1982), pp. 4–6.

4. Anthony V. Sinicropi, "Arbitrator Development: Programs and Models," *The Arbitration Journal* 37 (September 1982), pp. 24–32.

5. This dispersion of interest arbitration cases across a large number of arbitrators stands in marked contrast to the arbitration system used in the Canadian federal government. Under that tripartite procedure, neutral and advocate arbitrators are appointed from a permanent pool of arbitrators, with the result that, over time, the same arbitrators are used again and again. See John C. Anderson, "Arbitration in the Canadian Federal Public Service," in David Lewin, Peter Feuille, and Thomas A. Kochan, eds., *Public Sector Labor Relations,* 2nd ed. (Sun Lakes, Ariz.: Thomas Horton and Daughters), pp. 326–344.

6. Peter Feuille, "Final Offer Arbitration and the Chilling Effect," *Industrial Relations* 14 (October 1975), pp. 302–310.

7. This instrument is an example of the Kochan-type scoring indexes that have been widely used to evaluate the provisions of union contracts. The index here was used to evaluate the contracts and awards collected by searching through each contract and award and assigning point values to the various items based on the values listed in the index, with larger point values assigned for items as they become increasingly favorable to the union. The index and a description of its use can be found in Peter Feuille, Wallace Hendricks, and John Delaney, "The Impact of Collective Bargaining and Interest Arbitration on Policing," Final Report to the U.S. Department of Justice, University of Illinois, 1983. A similar index used to evaluate firefighter contracts can be seen in Thomas A. Kochan and Hoyt N. Wheeler, "Municipal Collective Bargaining: A Model and Analysis of Bargaining Outcomes," *Industrial and Labor Relations Review* 29 (October 1975), pp. 46–66.

8. The data in tables 3, 4, and 5 confirm the observation offered years ago that police unions have pressed for price tags to be placed on assignment practices that formerly had been costless to management; see Hervey A. Juris and Peter Feuille, *Police Unionism* (Lexington, Mass.: D.C. Heath, 1973), chap. 7.

9. See Orme W. Phelps, "Compulsory Arbitration: Some Perspectives," *Industrial and Labor Relations Review* 18 (October 1964), pp. 81–91.

10. Awards issued in Washington and Oregon, conventional arbitration states, also had comparatively few issues. The small numbers of awards in those two states, however, make us reluctant to draw conclusions from those results.

The Narcotic Effect of
Impasse Resolution Procedures

James R. Chelius
*Marian M. Extejt**

Does any use of impasse resolution procedures increase the tendency of negotiators to use such procedures in the future? The empirical evidence on this
important issue is quite unclear.[1] A recent issue of the *Industrial and Labor
Relations Review* presented an exchange of opinions on appropriate methods
for estimating this "narcotic effect." Butler and Ehrenberg (B & E) questioned the earlier work of Kochan and Baderschneider (K & B) on whether
certain impasse resolution procedures in New York's Taylor Act had proved
habit forming. K & B responded to this criticism with agreement on some
methodological issues and empirical results, but this disagreed with B & E's
key finding of a negative narcotic effect during later bargaining.[2]

It is the purpose of this reading to clarify briefly the current evidence of
the narcotic effect and to extend this knowledge by applying a test for direction to the New York State data previously analyzed by K & B and B & E.
We will then apply this test to new data on public sector collective bargaining
from Indiana, Iowa, and Pennsylvania.

Background

The narcotic effect in public sector impasse resolution has been scrutinized
and controversial because it has serious implications for the trade-off
between two important goals of public policy. The first is to prevent serious
labor conflict in the public sector. Many observers believe that labor strife is
unusually costly in the public sector because of the monopolistic and essential
nature of most government services. In general, production lost during a
strike cannot be replaced by the inventory or purchase of services from non-
struck competitors, as can often be done in the private sector. Another
important policy goal is that the parties settle their dispute on their own.
Independent settlements are valued because it is believed only the parties can
accurately assess and weigh the disputed issues and thereby achieve the best
compromise. Self-determination is also considered crucial in achieving the

*Rutgers University and John Carroll University, respectively. Reprinted from *Industrial and
Labor Relations Review*, Vol. 38, No. 4 (July 1985), pp. 629–637.

level of participation necessary for free and stable collective bargaining in the long run.[3]

In an effort to achieve the first goal, many states have passed statutes that provide for neutral agencies to assist labor and management in their pursuit of agreement. The issue raised in discussions of the narcotic effect is whether such intervention causes the parties to avoid settling on their own. Impasse resolution procedures may impair settlement in several ways. In addition to the narcotic effect, there may be a *chilling effect,* such that the parties are reluctant to compromise because they anticipate the neutral will split the difference between the last positions of union and management, and the *half-life effect,* such that the effectiveness of a procedure will decrease over time if it is not acceptable to the parties.[4] Failure to differentiate precisely among these impediments to bilateral settlement is central to the ambiguity about the impact of impasse resolution procedures on bargaining. Unfortunately, the narcotic effect has often been used as a catch-all phrase describing the extensive use of an impasse-resolution procedure. We follow B & E and K & B in defining the narcotic effect as a decrease or increase in the subsequent use of an impasse procedure as a result of the parties' having previously used the procedure. A positive narcotic effect, such that the use of the procedure increases subsequent use (that is, reduces the chances of bilateral settlement), is the type of narcotic effect considered troublesome. The narcotic effect is thus only one criterion by which an impasse procedure's effect on bargaining should be evaluated. Nevertheless, if we are to understand the overall impact of impasse resolution procedures, we must begin by careful analysis of each way in which they might influence the parties. The analysis presented here is designed to determine whether the narcotic effect is a significant characteristic of these procedures.

The Exchange of Views

As part of their original study of the determinants of impasses, K & B estimated the conditional probability of going to impasse given the impasse experience of previous bargaining rounds. They concluded that there is a "definite pattern of reusage (a [positive] narcotic effect)."[5] B & E criticize this method because "such conditional probability calculations do not allow one to differentiate between the narcotic effect explanation and an explanation based on a simple heterogeneity in the . . . bargaining units."[6] Both B & E and, in their response, K & B agree that a Bernoulli runs test is superior to a conditional probability test for estimating the dependence of subsequent impasses on previous impasse when there is a possibility that the bargaining units have different predispositions toward bilateral settlement. Both sets of authors also agree that during the first three bargaining rounds under New York's Taylor

Law, police and firefighter units exhibited a positive and significant narcotic effect. That is, the probability of a bargaining unit using the impasse resolution procedure was positively related to previously having done so.[7]

Although the two studies agree on the appropriateness of the runs test method and the presence of a positive narcotic effect during the first three rounds, they reach different conclusions for the last three rounds studied. B & E conclude that there was actually a *negative* narcotic effect during the last three rounds, that is, prior use of the impasse resolution procedure was then associated with reduced future use. K & B, also using the runs test, find no evidence of either a positive or a negative narcotic effect in the later rounds. The reason for this difference in results using the same analytical technique is a difference in decision rules for including units in the sample, with B & E choosing more limited criteria than K & B.[8] We examine the impact of these different decision rules later in our reanalysis of the New York data.

One problem with the method used by K & B and B & E is that there is no objective criterion for judging the direction of the impasse patterns. Fortunately, a nonparametric test for the directionality of such relationships is available. The following section describes this statistical procedure, which is then used to reexamine the New York data as well as data from other states.

The Appropriate Statistical Test

The Bernoulli runs test, which both B & E and K & B deem appropriate, is based on the concept that the pattern of observed impasses will be random if there is no dependency between prior and subsequent use of an impasse resolution procedure. Thus, for a sample of bargaining units with two impasses over three bargaining rounds, the pattern will be random (a Bernoulli process) if there is an equal incidence of impasses in rounds 1 and 2 (110), 2 and 3 (011), and 1 and 3 (101). The χ^2 test used by B & E compares the observed frequencies to the frequencies expected under a Bernoulli process. If the test indicates a nonrandom pattern, the observed frequencies are ranked and the resulting ranks are then examined to determine whether they connote a positive or negative narcotic effect.[9]

Unfortunately, a χ^2 test detects any deviation from a predicted distribution. In this case, the null hypothesis is for equal proportions (p) of each pattern $(p^1 = p^2 = p^3)$. When examining the addictive properties of prior experience, one is not interested in just any deviation, but, rather, in a specific deviation. The narcotic effect implies a particular ordering to the proportions. When the degrees of freedom are greater than one (such as with three bargaining rounds), the χ^2 test is insensitive to the presence of order.[10] Categorizing the observed frequencies into ranks causes problems in a test for direction, since many subtleties of cardinal frequency measures are lost if they are collapsed into ordinal rank measures. Just as there may be many differences between a close and a distant second-place finish in any contest, information can be lost if one considers the rankings rather than the frequencies of the observed patterns.[11]

A much more satisfactory procedure is available: the Armitage test for the trend in observed frequencies. This test is used primarily in the medical field for determining the addictive properties of drugs.[12] The precise details of the Armitage test are relegated to the appendix, but it can be simply defined as a nonparametric test that uses the available cardinal data to test for the presence of a trend among a set of observed frequencies. The narcotic effect implies a hypothesis about the trend of frequencies. Among those units with one impasse within three bargaining rounds, for example, a positive narcotic effect is evident if the proportion (p) of units having a 100 pattern is less than the proportion of those having a 010 pattern, which in turn is less than the proportion having a 001 pattern. Similarly, for those with two impasses in three rounds, a positive narcotic effect is implied if $p(100) < p(101) < p(011)$.

If appropriate data and theory are available, the regression methods developed by B & E are preferable to the runs test. The necessary data for these statistical procedures include at least two cross-sections on the independent variables. Even a large data-gathering project like the one carried out by K & B had to use participant recall in order to obtain observations for different points in time one some independent variables. This is particularly troublesome when measuring perceptions such as "internal pressure on union officials going into negotiations."[13] The use of these regression models also implies a theory of one-way causation between the independent and dependent variables. It is not clear that the understanding of impasse procedure usage is developed enough to assert such a unilateral causation. One might well contend, for example, that "hostility between the parties,"[14] in addition to simply being a determinant of impasses as in the K & B and B & E model, is also a consequence of previous impasses. Such a relationship necessitates a simultaneous-equation system, which requires more data than are available even in the K & B data base. Since the very existence of the narcotic effect is controversial (even when heterogeneity is not controlled), simply determining its existence is an important finding. This can be achieved through the use of relatively simply techniques, without a complete theory or comprehensive set of independent variables. The use of several states, employee groups, and time periods serves as a partial control; if similar results occur across these different environments, one can be less concerned about heterogeneity problems.[15]

In the following section, we apply the Armitage test for trend to the New York data used by K & B and B & E, as well as to new data from Iowa, Indiana, and Pennsylvania. We also investigate the sensitivity of the results to the definition of impasse.

The Empirical Test

New York, Early Bargaining

The use of the Armitage test for trend confirms the conclusion of B & E and K & B that for the first three rounds of bargaining under the New York State impasse procedure, the combined samples of police and firefighter units exhibited a pattern of impasse consistent with a positive narcotic effect. Analysis of each occupational group separately yields the same positive narcotic effect.[16]

K & B chose to analyze the first three rounds because those rounds approximated the period during which fact-finding was the final stage of the impasse procedure. Because of differences among units in the beginning date of bargaining and the use of multiyear contracts, however, the first three rounds of bargaining took place in differing years across units. Thus, the use of the first three rounds is not an exact representation of the factfinding period. To determine whether this choice of number of rounds is crucial, we also examine the narcotic effect over the first four rounds. The data in table 1 indicate there was no narcotic effect over the first four rounds for police, firefighters, or the combined group.

It is also useful to consider whether these results are sensitive to the definition of impasse. While mediation is part of the government's impasse resolution procedure, if that step is the extent of intervention, it can hardly be said that the parties are unable to settle their own differences. The results in table 1 indicate that when units using only mediation are counted as bilateral settlements, there is still a positive narcotic effect for the first three rounds for firefighters and police, as well as for the combined groups; but for the first four rounds, there are no narcotic effects. Thus, the positive narcotic effect observed during early bargaining in New York is limited to the first three rounds of bargaining. The results are not sensitive to sample selection criteria, as can be seen from the fact that both the B & E and K & B samples suggest a positive narcotic effect for the first three rounds and no effect for the first four rounds.

New York, Later Bargaining

Table 2 shows that when the Armitage test is applied to the last three rounds of bargaining in New York State on which data are available, there is no narcotic effect for police, firefighters, or the combined groups.[17] As was the case

Table 1
The Narcotic Effect in Early Bargaining under the New York State Impasse Procedure

		First 3 Rounds		First 4 Rounds	
Sample	Sample Size	Mediation = Impasse	Mediation ≠ Impasse	Mediation = Impasse	Mediation ≠ Impasse
Police	72	+	+	No	No
Firefighters	65	+	+	No	No
Combined	141[a]	+	+	No	No
Combined (K & B)	121	+	+	No	No
Combined (B & E)[b]		+	+	No	No

Source: Date are from the original K & B (1978) analysis and were supplied by Richard Butler, with the permission of Thomas Kochan.

Legend: + = positive and significant effect ($p = .01$); No = no significant trend.

[a]The combined total is greater than the sum of the separate police and firefighter units because a few units that bargained jointly were used only in the combined test. K & B and B & E treated these joint units as a part of the firefighter group.

[b]This sample excludes those units from the K & B sample in which the parties were in the midst of a multiyear contract at the end of the sample period or had not settled their contract by the end of the data collection period; or no contract was negotiated during the first two sample years; or the contract duration was three or more years during the sample period; or a contract reopener rather than a full successor agreement was negotiated.

Table 2
The Narcotic Effect in Later Bargaining under the New York State Impasse Procedure

		Last Three Rounds[a]	
Sample	Sample Size	Mediation = Impasse	Mediation ≠ Impasse
Police	39	No	No
Firefighters	35	No	No
Combined	77	No	No
Combined (K & B)	79	No	No
Combined (E & B)[b]	81	−	No

Source: Data are from the original K & B (1978) analysis and were supplied by Richard Butler, with the permission of Thomas Kochan.

Legend: + = positive and significant narcotic effect ($p = .01$); − = negative and significant narcotic effect ($p = .01$); No = no significant trend.

[a]There were no significant trends over the last four rounds.

[b]See not *b* in table 1.

with the results on early bargaining, this finding does not change when "mediation only" is counted as a bilateral settlement. The results are sensitive to the sample-selection criteria. Although K & B's sample also implies no narcotic effect, the B & E sample yielded a negative effect. The important conclusion, however, is the absence of addictive properties in the New York impasse-resolution procedures during later bargaining.

The Experience in Other States

In their conclusion, B & E emphasize the tentative nature of their findings by pointing out "that it is imperative that researchers extend our analysis to other data bases, states, and time periods before drawing any policy inferences about the need to redesign public sector impasse procedures."[18] In this spirit, we obtained data on impasse patterns for three other states: Iowa, Indiana, and Pennsylvania. Iowa's public sector bargaining law provides for mediation, fact-finding, and mandatory arbitration if the parties are unable to settle. Data are available for police, firefighters, public school teachers, and all other state, county and municipal employees.[19] Indiana law covers only public school teachers and provides for mediation and fact-finding.[20] In both states, it is illegal to strike, although some strikes did occur during the sample period in Indiana. In Pennsylvania, it is legal for public employees other than police, firefighters, guards, and court employees to strike, but only after having pursued all the steps in the impasse resolution procedure.[21] In any jurisdiction without mandatory arbitration, each settlement is ultimately bilateral—even if it comes after the use of an impasse resolution procedure. Since the critical issue in determining the existence of a narcotive effect is the addiction to an impasse procedure, we will consider bilateral only those settlements reached without intervention.

Iowa

The analysis of impasse data for the years 1976–1982, shown in table 3, indicates that police, firefighters, and teachers all exhibited no narcotic effect in early bargaining. This result is not sensitive to whether mediation constitutes an impasse or whether three or four rounds are considered. The pattern of impasses for the group of all other public employees in Iowa exhibits no narcotic effect for the first three bargaining rounds but a positive narcotic effect for the first four rounds. These results are the same whether or not mediation is defined as an impasse. During later bargaining, defined as either the last three or the last four rounds and including or excluding mediation, there was no narcotic effect.

Indiana

Table 3 also outlines the analysis of the six years (1974–1979) of data on Indiana teacher bargaining that were available. The Indiana data suggest no narcotic effect in early bargaining. The results are not sensitive to the defini-

Table 3
The Narcotic Effect in Three Other States

Sample	Sample Size	First 3 (4) Rounds		Last 3 (4) Rounds	
		Mediation = Impasse	Mediation ≠ Impasse	Mediation = Impasse	Mediation ≠ Impasse
Iowa					
Teachers	391	No (No)	No (No)	No (No)	No (No)
Police	69	No (No)	No (No)	No (No)	No (No)
Firefighter	29	No (No)	No (No)	No (No)	No (No)
Other[a]	336	No (+)	No (+)	No (No)	No (No)
Indiana					
Teachers	231	No (No)	No (No)	No (No)	No (No)
Pennsylvania					
Teachers	504	— (No)	No (No)	—[b] (No)	—[b] (No)

Source: Data are from the unpublished files of the Iowa Public Employment Relations Board, the Indiana Education Employment Relations Board, and the Bureau of Mediation of the Pennsylvania Department of Labor.

Legend: + = positive and significant narcotic effect ($p = .01$); – = negative and significant narcotic effect ($p = .01$); No = no significant trend.

[a]"Other" includes employee groups other than teachers, police, and firefighters.

[b]In Pennsylvania, both the second three rounds and the last three rounds exhibited the significant narcotic effect.

tion of an impasse or whether three or four bargaining rounds are considered. There is no narcotic effect for the last three rounds, regardless of whether or not mediation is considered an impasse. For the last four rounds, there is no narcotic effect when mediation is considered an impasse and a negative narcotic effect when mediation is not considered an impasse.

Pennsylvania

Ten years of experience with Pennysylvania teacher bargaining were available for the period 1971–1980. The Pennsylvania data, also shown in table 3, indicate a negative narcotic effect during early bargaining if "mediation only" is defined as an impasse. When mediation is not counted as an impasse, there is no narcotic effect during early bargaining. For the first four rounds there is no narcotic effect under either definition of an impasse. The larger number of bargaining rounds within Pennsylvania allows "later bargaining" to be defined in a variety of ways. During the second three rounds or the last three rounds, there is a negative narcotic effect under either treatment of mediation. For the last four or even five rounds there was no narcotic effect under either definition of impasse. The key finding is the absence of a positive narcotic effect under either definition or time period.[22]

Overall Trends in the Impasse Rate

One of the points of disagreement between B & E and K & B was the usefulness of data from bargaining units that had either always gone to impasse or always settled bilaterally. With a precisely and narrowly defined narcotic effect, such units cannot be used to discern the addictive properties of using an impasse procedure. Data on those units are useful, however, when examining the broader issue of trends in the rate of bilateral settlement. For example, K & B reported an increase in impasse procedure usage over the first five rounds of bargaining under New York law.[23] In table 4, the Armitage test confirms the statistical significance of the upward trend they observed. This result does not hold true, however, when mediation is defined as a bilateral settlement.

There is also a positive trend in impasse-procedure usage for the group of "other" government employees in Iowa, but not when mediation is considered a bilateral settlement. For all other employee groups and in all states, there is no positive trend; in fact, there is a downward trend in usage among Indiana and Pennsylvania teachers, as well as Iowa teachers, when mediation is not considered as an impasse. Thus, even by the somewhat ambiguous standard of overall impasse procedure usage, there is not a widespread problem of increasing reliance on third-party intervention.

Table 4
Trend in the Proportion of Bargaining Units Going to Impasse in Each Bargaining Round

Sample	Number of Rounds	Mediation = Impasse	Mediation ≠ Impasse
New York			
Police	5	+	No
Firefighters	5	+	No
Iowa			
Teachers	7	No	−
Police	7	No	No
Firefighters	7	No	No
Other[a]	7	+	No
Indiana			
Teachers	6	−	−
Pennsylvania			
Teachers	8	−	−

Sources: New York data from the original K & B (1978) analysis and were supplied by Richard Butler, with the permission of Thomas Kochan. Other data are from the unpublished files of the Iowa Public Employment Relations Board, the Indiana Education Employment Relations Board, and the Bureau of Mediation of the Pennsylvania Department of Labor.

Note. In general, the results are not sensitive to whether constant users or nonusers are excluded from the samples. The exceptions are the following: Iowa police becomes positive when mediation equals an impasse; Iowa "other" becomes no trend when mediation equals an impasse; and Iowa teachers becomes no trend when mediation is not considered an impasse.

Legend: + = positive and significant narcotic effect ($p = .01$); − = negative and significant narcotic effect ($p = .01$); No = no significant trend.

[a]"Other" includes employee groups other than teachers, police, and firefighters.

Conclusion

The K & B and B & E exchange taught the importance of both a precise definition of the narcotic effect and an appropriate statistical technique for investigating it. This study has sharpened and expanded the use of the runs test of that effect by introducing a method for better inferring the direction of the effect and by extending the analysis to data from states other than New York. Although this method suffers from not directly addressing the question of heterogeneity among observations, its relative simplicity allowed testing data on a variety of states, employee groups, and time periods. The consistency of the results observed across these various settings serves as an indirect control of the differences that could not be measured in bargaining units and their environments.

The results show that after an initial period of adjustment, there were no positive narcotic effects, under any of the bargaining laws or for any of the employee groups analyzed. The concern frequently expressed over the positive narcotic effect[24] therefore appears to be exaggerated, if not groundless. To the extent it exists at all, a positive narcotic effect is apparently a phenomenon only of early experience under a public sector bargaining law.

Notes

1. In his recent review of studies on arbitration, Anderson began his conclusion with "[h]ow effective is compulsory arbitration? [W]e really don't know." The same generalization is valid for the impact of all forms of public sector impasse procedures. His conclusion is based on the lack of internal and external validity in the existing research. See John C. Anderson, "The Impact of Arbitration: A Methodological Assessment," *Industrial Relations* 20, no. 2 (Spring 1981), p. 144.

2. Richard J. Butler and Ronald G. Ehrenberg, "Estimating the Narcotic Effect of Public Sector Impasse Procedures," *Industrial and Labor Relations Review* 35, no. 1 (October 1981), pp. 3–20 (hereinafter cited as B & E, 1981); Thomas A. Kochan and Jean Baderschneider, "Estimating the Narcotic Effect: Choosing Techniques That Fit the Problem," *Industrial and Labor Relations Review* 35, no. 1 (October 1981), pp. 21–28 (hereinafter cited as K & B, 1981); Thomas A. Kochan and Jean Baderschneider, "Dependence on Impasse Procedures: Police and Firefighters in New York State," *Industrial and Labor Relations Review* 31, no. 4 (July 1978), pp. 431–449 (hereinafter cited as K & B, 1978).

3. An early statement on the importance of bilateral settlements was one by Commons. Although his comment was referring to all varieties of outside experts, not just government-appointed neutrals, the implications are the same. The outsider "becomes the expert because he is a specialist, and that signifies that he knows only the details of a small part of all the facts that must be weighed in reaching a decision. If the principals abdicate, and government [of the shop] by experts takes their place, the result is no less arbitrary and coercive than other forms of autocracy. . . . For no one person and no class of persons, however expert, can truly represent in due proportion all of the interests that clash and must be reconciled in reaching a final decision. Only the interests themselves, that is, the principals, must decide." John R. Commons, *Industrial Goodwill* (New York: McGraw-Hill, 1919), p. 177.

4. Additional details concerning these two effects may be found in John C. Anderson and Thomas A. Kochan, "Impasse Procedures in the Canadian Federal Service: Effects on the Bargaining Process," *Industrial and Labor Relations Review* 30, no. 3 (April 1977), pp. 285–286.

5. K & B (1978), p. 447.

6. B & E (1981), p. 5.

7. K & B (1981), p. 24, and B & E (1981), p. 8.

8. B & E chose to exclude those units in which (1) the parties were in the midst of a multiyear contract at the end of the sample period or had not settled their last contract by the end of the data collection period, or (2) no contract was negotiated during the first two sample years, or (3) the contract duration was three or more years during the sample period, or (4) a contract reopener rather than a full-successor agreement was negotiated.

9. Following notation used by B & E and K & B, a 001 pattern represents a three-period observation in which there was bilateral settlement in periods one and two, and an impasse in period three. The runs test method described in detail by

B & E implies that with a positive narcotic effect, the set of observations with one impasse in three periods will have the greatest proportion of units with impasse in the third period (001). The next greatest proportion will have impasses in the second period (010), and the smallest proportion will have the impasse in the first period (100). In other words, if use of the impasse procedure is addictive, a 100 pattern is unlikely to occur, since the observed subsequent periods did not give rise to an impasse and therefore provided contrary evidence. Similarly, a 001 pattern is most consistent with a positive narcotic effect (given one impasse in three periods) since there is no contrary evidence in subsequent periods. Two impasses in a three-year period follow the same logic; for a positive narcotic effect $p(110) < p(101) < p(011)$.

If we use the precise definition of the narcotic effect—that is, a change in the probability of going to impasse "because a unit went to impasse in the past, net of other factors (such as heterogeneity) that influence the probability of impasse" (K & B, 1981, p. 23)—frequencies of units with different numbers of impasses cannot be combined. This is because there is no way to tell whether the number (as opposed to the pattern) of impasses is the result of a narcotic effect or some other characteristic of the units. After testing for the trend with patterns from units with a given number of impasses, the statistics can be aggregated into an overall summary test. The appendix describes this aggregation procedure.

10. Sidney Siegel, *Nonparametric Statistics* (New York: McGraw-Hill, 1956), p. 59.

11. The loss of information caused by using ranks can be observed by the following example, in which a 1 in the "Pattern" column equals an impasse and a 0 equals a bilateral settlement over a three-year period:

Observed Frequencies

Pattern	Case 1	Case 2	Rank in Cases 1 and 2
100	25	47	1
010	24	2	2
001	1	1	3
Total	50	50	

One can readily observe that more information is contained in the "Observed frequencies" columns than in the "Rank" column.

12. The test is attributed to P. Armitage, "Tests for Linear Trends in Proportions and Frequencies," *Biometrics* 11 (1955), pp. 375–386. A clear description of the test appears in Byron W. Brown and Myles Hollander, *Statistics: A Biomedical Introduction* (New York: Wiley, 1977), pp. 211–215. Our thanks to professors Gregory Campbell of Purdue University and W.J. Conover of Texas A&M University for their generous help in sorting out the statistical issues.

13. K & B (1978), p. 441.

14. Ibid.

15. An interesting statement about the importance of examining crucial issues without complete information is contained in John W. Tukey, "Methodology and the Statistician's Responsibility for *Both* Accuracy and Relevance," *Journal of the American Statistical Association* 74, no. 368 (December 1979), pp. 786–793.

16. We used the K & B sample selecting criteria, since the presence of the narcotic effect may well manifest itself in the less typical bargaining situations excluded by

B & E. Our sample size is slightly larger than K & B's, however, because they used only units for which independent variables were available as required for their regression analysis. Our sample comprises 72 police bargaining units and 65 firefighter units under the definition that includes mediation as an impasse. When mediation is not defined as an impasse, there are 66 police units and 63 firefighter units. The difference in sample size across definitions results from the fact that when mediation is not counted as an impasse, some units become categorized as constant bilateral settlements, or constant intervention—groups that yield no information about the narcotic effect (see B & E, 1981, pp. 5–6).

17. This analysis of later bargaining experience was limited to units with five or more rounds of data, thus excluding units that would have counted the same two or more rounds in both the early and late periods.

18. B & E (1981), p. 18.

19. Iowa government employees are covered by the Iowa Public Employment Relations Act (1974). The statute requires mediation, followed by fact-finding with recommendations, followed by issue-by-issue, final offer arbitration. The statutory procedure is mandatory unless the parties mutually agree on an alternative. For a more detailed description of the Iowa statute, see Daniel G. Gallagher and Richard Pegnetter, "Impasse Resolution under the Iowa Multistep Procedure," *Industrial and Labor Relations Review* 32, no. 3 (April 1979), pp. 327–338. The data employed here were collected from the unpublished files of the Iowa Public Employment Relations Board. All public sector bargaining units are included.

20. Collective bargaining for public school teachers is provided for in Indiana by Public Law 217, enacted in 1973. Mediation, fact-finding, and mutually agreed on (voluntary) binding arbitration are the three impasse resolution procedures provided for by the statute. It is unlawful for any Indiana school employee, school employee organization, or any of their affiliates to take part in, or assist in, a strike. The data employed here are from the unpublished files of the Indiana Education Employment Relations Board and include all teacher bargaining units.

21. Collective bargaining for public sector employees, other than certain classes of public safety officials, in Pennsylvania is provided for by Act 195, the Public Employee Relations Act, approved in 1970. Mediation is mandatory in case of impasse, but appointment of a fact-finding panel is up to the discretion of the Employee Relations Board. Voluntary interest arbitration is allowed. Once the impasse resolution procedures are followed and exhausted, employees covered by this statute may strike. Police and firefighter units in Pennsylvania are covered by Act 111, which outlaws strikes by these employees but provides compulsary arbitration as a strike substitute. Complete data on the impasse history are not available for these bargaining units, and they therefore were not included in this analysis. The data were collected from the unpublished files of the Bureau of Mediation of the Pennsylvania Department of Labor. All teacher bargaining units are included.

22. An interesting variation on this analysis of the Pennsylvania data is to determine the narcotic effect of a strike when only strikes are considered impasses. Strikes do not exhibit a measurable narcotic effect.

23. K & B (1981), p. 23.

24. See, for example, K & B (1978), pp. 447–448.

Selected Benefits and Costs of Compulsory Arbitration

Peter Feuille *

In 1965 Wyoming became the first state to adopt compulsory arbitration[1] to resolve public employee bargaining disputes; by 1979 twenty states had implemented arbitration statutes covering various public employee groups.[2] Our understanding of the potential impact of such arbitration, however, may not have kept pace with this rapid growth in coverage. Labor relations scholars, for instance, who have done the lion's share of the writing on the subject, have focused on the labor relations functions and effects of arbitration while generally ignoring its political functions. Similarly, the analyses of these various functions have been shaped by some easily identifiable normative premises, but these premises have received little explicit attention. Furthermore, arbitration is most often viewed as an independent variable that affects such outcome variables as wages, strikes, or bargaining incentives; rarely is it seen as a dependent variable that might indicate the degree of interest group conflict or the distribution of political influence in a jurisdiction.

Accordingly, the following analysis considers three sets of benefits arbitration may provide and two sets of costs the process may impose. It does so by examining the normative premise and operational mechanisms associated with each of these five attributes and by discussing some tests (and accompanying research) that can be used to measure how well or poorly arbitration performs the various functions ascribed to it.

Part of this analysis focuses on arbitration as a negotiating dispute settlement process, and thus it deals primarily with the role of *government-as-employer* representing managerial interests in a unionized workplace. Another part of the analysis focuses on arbitration as a political process, and thus it deals primarily with the role of *government-as-regulator* of the entire polity. The first role is based on the relatively narrow efficiency and budgetary interests historically associated with management in employer–employee relations; the second is based on the broader regulatory and service-providing functions of government: managing conflict in matters of public importance and providing the services that policymakers have decided should not be provided through private markets.[3] Although the employer and regulator roles are analytically different, they overlap considerably at the operational level.

*Reprinted from *Industrial and Labor Relations Review*, Vol. 33, No. 1 (October 1979), pp. 64–76.

Therefore, it should be profitable to examine how public dispute resolution policies directed toward government-as-employer might also affect government-as-regulator.[4]

Guardian of the Public Interest

Arbitration's most visible attribute is the ability of its binding award to guarantee (almost) the absence of strikes among covered employees and hence to prevent the interruption of covered public services. Arbitration proponents have used this strike prevention function more than any other to explain why arbitration is desirable, arguing that the prevention of such strikes protects the public's interest in continuously receiving such services. After all, few political slogans are as attractive (and vague) as "the public interest."[5] Because strike prohibitions and arbitration tend to coexist, arbitration may at first seem superfluous as a device to prevent interruptions of public services. Yet policymakers have long recognized that prohibiting strikes merely makes illegal the strikes that do occur. Arbitration serves, therefore, as a no-strike insurance policy. This strike prevention function ostensibly explains why public safety services—presumably the most "essential" of local government services—are most likely to be covered by arbitration statutes. Of the twenty arbitration states, twelve require arbitration only for public safety personnel,[6] and the remaining eight cover public safety as well as other groups.

The usual test for whether arbitration has protected the public is comparing strike occurrences in jurisdictions with and without arbitration. The available evidence shows that far fewer strikes occur where arbitration is mandated.[7] Although arbitration substantially reduces the probability of strikes compared to other impasse resolution procedures, it is not a perfect form of no-strike insurance. It does not protect against wildcats or against stoppages over issues outside the scope of bargaining, and, as the Montreal police demonstrated in 1969, it may not always prevent an unusually militant union from striking in defiance of an unsatisfactory award (in other words, there may be strikes authorized by the union leadership over issues within the scope of bargaining).

The connections among the public's interests, strikes, and arbitration are more complex, however, than the extent to which strikes and arbitration are negatively correlated. Arbitration's public interest protection function assumes, first, that some or all public employee strikes are inappropriate and, second, that the public's overriding interest in governmental labor relations is "labor peace." In turn, the strength of this first assumption rests upon the reasons why some or all public employees should not have the right to strike, and the second assumption requires a demonstration of a clear public preference for labor peace over all other labor relations alternatives. These two assumptions need to be carefully examined, for if they wilt under critical scrutiny so does much of the support for the public interest protection function of arbitration.

The justification for denying public employees the right to strike is generally argued on the following bases: government is sovereign, elected and selected to reflect the collective desires of the citizenry, and hence it should not be subject to adversarial pressure tactics on behalf of the few at the expense of the many; because most governmental services are offered on a monopolistic basis, unions enjoy tremendous (and unfair) bargaining power when they threaten to strike; and some or all public employee strikes actually harm the public (or will after a certain duration).[8]

In response to the first argument, an appeal to popular sovereignty is an article of faith, not capable of being empirically tested; however, such an appeal ignores the pluralist and selfish nature of the group interests and pressures that pervade the U.S. political system and that form the basis for many (perhaps most) governmental actions.[9] Second, if the unfair bargaining power argument had merit, we should see public employee unions negotiating very favorable contracts. Yet, while there is a substantial body of evidence that public unions have a positive impact on wages,[10] the magnitude of this impact is not large. In fact, it appears to be smaller than in the private sector[11] — where the unions presumably do not enjoy such monopolistic protection. Furthermore, Kochan and Wheeler found that the presence of compulsory arbitration laws contributed much more to firefighter unions' ability to bargain favorable contracts than did the unions' use of militant tactics, such as slowdowns, sickouts, and picketing.[12] In addition, there is no evidence that the public unions in the seven right-to-strike states[13] have fared noticeably better at the bargaining table than their more constrained counterparts in other states. Thus, there is no systematic support for the belief that arbitration should or will serve as a check on public union monopoly power, nor is there any systematic evidence that supports the proposition that the unions possess such tremendous bargaining power in the first place.

In considering the third argument — that public employee strikes harm the public or will cause such harm after a certain duration — the observer wonders why this assertion never has been systematically documented. There certainly have been enough public employee strikes on which to perform strike impact research.[14] Even police and fire strike impacts, which are supposed to be horrendous, have received rather cursory attention. In fact, the industrial relations research community so far has seemed content to rely primarily on the commercial news media for "data" about the service deprivation effects of government strikes. Furthermore, it is possible to interpret the public employee strike experience in this country as demonstrating that this strikes-will-cause-harm assertion contains more rhetoric than substance. The hundreds of public employee strikes since 1965 (including 338 protective service strikes during 1965–1975[15]), the relatively minor (or even nonexistent) strike penalties, and the slow growth of the legal right to strike strongly suggest that such strikes, including those by police officers and firefighters, are rather minor threats to the public interest (in other words, the public can tolerate such strikes better than conventional wisdom suggests).[16] This de facto tolerance of strikes may have occurred because government services are less "essential" to the short-run public welfare than is commonly believed and because government managers are better at providing short-run substitutes for struck services than the conventional wisdom has suggested.[17]

The second assumption inherent in the notion of arbitration as the guardian of the public interest is that the public's only interest, or at least its primary interest, in public labor relations is labor peace, and that any other interests are relatively unimportant.[18] Expressed another way, this assumption ignores the possibility that the "public" may actually consist of numerous "publics" with multiple interests in public labor relations processes and outcomes that go beyond a desire not to be inconvenienced by strikes.[19] To take an obvious example, parents of school-age children and nonparents alike may prefer no teacher strikes; but the nonparents may be much more willing than the parents to have school district managements use strikes as a tool to support managerial demands for "less" relative to union demands for "more." Furthermore, there are public opinion poll data that suggest that the public may be more accepting of strike rights for some public employee groups than is commonly believed.[20] In addition, the conventional wisdom suggests that public management represents the interests of the public at the bargaining table and in the hearing room. If this suggestion has any merit, recent managerial behavior may also indicate changing public attitudes toward the strike (and certainly changing managerial attitudes). It still may be politically risky for candidates for public office to advocate public employee strike rights, but increasing numbers of public administrators seem to be more accepting of the right to strike, at least when the alternative is compulsory arbitration.[21] Instead of assuming a unitary public with an overriding interest in labor peace, research might profitably focus on the extent to which different groups hold convergent or divergent views about the costs and benefits of various labor relations impasse arrangements.

The apparent normative premise underlying the public interest protection function of arbitration is that the public is a monolithic entity that is rather helpless in the face of a collective withdrawal of important public services and hence needs and wants to be protected from such withdrawals. The assertions that flow from the premise are either normative expressions of faith or empirically undocumented, and thus it is difficult to demonstrate systematically that the public needs to be protected from such strikes—even those involving "essential" services. Arbitration may substantially reduce the probability of public employee strikes, but the case supporting the need for such a strike prevention device rests on empirically shaky ground.

Guardian of Employee Interests

Arbitration advocates argue that public employee strike prohibitions may make collective bargaining a one-sided process because employees have no readily available mechanism to manipulate management's costs of disagreeing with employee demands. Management can continue the status quo, ignore mediator or fact-finder recommendations, or implement unilateral changes (at least after impasse), but the employees have no countervailing weapons; thus, there is a serious imbalance of negotiating power in management's favor. Arbitration should correct this imbalance, for it eliminates management's ability to prolong the status quo indefinitely, ignore third-party recommendations, or impose its own terms (it also eliminates union abilities to do these same things, but it is rare that unions want or are able to do them). Arbitration, then, should increase the employees' negotiating strength until it is approximately equal with management's.

Some relevant tests of arbitration's effectiveness in fulfilling this function are the extent to which it promotes good faith negotiations and the extent to which arbitrated and negotiated outcomes are distributed in a manner that balances union and management interests. There are reports from some jurisdictions that the introduction of arbitration promotes more genuine negotiating behavior by management,[22] but there is also evidence that in many instances arbitration inhibits the parties' ability or willingness to negotiate their own agreements.[23]

The distribution of outcomes could be measured by comparing the parties' bargaining goals with actual outcomes, by comparing bargained agreements with arbitrated awards, by comparing award winners and losers under final offer arbitration, or by examining the parties' satisfaction (or lack of it) with the distributional nature of negotiation-arbitration processes. Some labor relations observers have concluded that arbitration outcomes are distributed in a balanced manner,[24] but many municipal managers object to arbitration, in large part because they perceive the process as more supportive of employee than employer interests.[25] Furthermore, the recurring line-up in state legislatures of union support for arbitration and managerial opposition to it[26] means that the unions perceive that arbitration is to their advantage in bargaining and managements perceive it is to their disadvantage. Some evidence suggests that these perceptions are accurate,[27] and so parties seem to be acting rationally. This line-up of support and opposition plus more rigorous research evidence suggest strongly that arbitration has worked effectively to enhance public employee negotiating interests.

Arbitration also may protect employee interests by acting as a labor market leveling mechanism. To the extent that Ross's "orbits of coercive comparisons" paradigm accurately specifies the process by which employee wage demands are formulated,[28] and to the extent that arbitration decisions are made primarily on labor market comparability criteria,[29] arbitration becomes "the visible hand" by which members of similar bargaining units seek to be treated similarly (at least within the same state). There is some evidence that on wages such an impact does occur, especially on behalf of covered employees in small bargaining units at the low end of the wage distribution.[30] This leveling or "regression to the mean" impact may cause some observers to conclude that arbitration is an efficient and effective method for ensuring equity and hence protecting employee interests, while others may question the need for such a mechanism in the absence of any persuasive reason that the covered employees should have such a protective device and other employees should not.

The normative premise on which this arbitration function is based is that public employees with no right to strike should be protected against managerial domination of the bargaining process. The logical implication of this premise is that arbitration should be most prevalent in those situations in which the employees are on the short end of the largest power imbalances. As discussed earlier, however, arbitration laws apply disproportionately to those groups with the greatest withholding power and who typically have acquired considerable political influence—police officers and firefighters.[31] Thus, the two occupational groups who would be expected to negotiate most effectively without arbitration are the two groups with the highest incidence of arbitration coverage. This fact suggests that there are distinct limits to the policymakers' acceptance of the employee interest–protection function as a rationale for why arbitration statutes should be enacted: such a rationale applies only to those employees represented by unions who happen to have the ability to manipulate skillfully the legislative process to their own advantage. In short, the incidence of arbitration coverage seems to reflect less concern among policymakers for the general welfare and more concern for accommodating the requests of influential interest groups.

Regulator of Interest Group Conflict

From a broad political perspective (in contrast to the narrower labor relations perspectives just examined), arbitration may perform a useful conflict regulation function. The unionization of public employees brought out into the open a set of group interests (those of the various employees and their representatives) that represent claims on public resources that were potentially rather costly. Although such unionization did not create these claims, it certainly made them more visible and helped make overt the potential conflicts between public employees and the public. The widespread use of collective bargaining, with its militant posturing and strident rhetoric, and the increasingly frequent use of the strike became the visible manifestations of these interest group conflicts.[32] One policy response to this situation has been to provide third-party impasse resolution procedures to regulate and contain the interorganizational and intraorganizational pressures that contribute to such overt conflict.[33]

These impasse procedures, including arbitration, regulate public–public employee conflict by institutionalizing trilateral decision mechanisms for the formation of public employment conditions and by absorbing the advocates' demands for particular outcomes. Arbitration performs this regulatory function primarily through the finality, impartiality, compromising, and face-saving features of the process. Supposedly, all the parties affected by an award will accept it because of legal requirements to do so and because of its issuance by a neutral third party who has attempted to balance employee and employer interests. Furthermore, managerial and union leaders can protect themselves from intraorganizational retaliation from their constituents by blaming the arbitrator for any unfavorable outcomes. As a result of these attributes, arbitration is said to absorb the interest group pressures that might cause strikes or other disruptions and, by absorbing them, to contribute to political and social stability. The normative premise underlying this arbitration function is that society needs such conflict absorption mechanisms to contribute to societal stability.

Arbitration's effectiveness in performing this regulatory function can be measured by examining the legality of the process and the extent to which affected unions and managements comply with or accept the process and awards, strikes are prevented, arbitration reduces bargaining hostility, and the affected parties believe their legitimate interests have been adequately considered in the process. A review of relevant court decisions suggest that most of the time arbitration is constitutionally acceptable and hence its awards are legally enforceable.[34] The evidence also suggests that union and management compliance with the process is widespread, if not always enthusiastic, at least in those states with substantial bargaining and arbitration histories.[35] In addition, as noted previously, arbitration is associated with a general absence of strikes.

There is little systematic evidence about the extent to which arbitration has reduced bargaining hostility or fostered impasse resolution legitimacy perceptions among the parties. To the extent that arbitration prevents strikes and strike threats it may reduce bargaining hostility, but these nonevents are very difficult to measure. There is a substantial body of evidence that union representatives believe arbitration legitimately considers employee interests, but this is not so for management representatives. And there simply are insufficient data to determine if citizens' views about arbitration are supportive, hostile, or apathetic.

The available evidence suggests, then, that arbitration effectively absorbs selected employer and employee pressures that might emerge as overt conflict and, in so doing, contributes to the institutionalized resolution of workplace conflict already begun by collective bargaining. However, the sharp divergence in enthusiasm for arbitration displayed by union and management representatives suggests that there are very different perceptions about the costs and benefits attached to arbitration's conflict-regulation function, and it appears unlikely that these perceptions will be reconciled. Furthermore, because empirical testing of this arbitration function may be difficult given its process (rather than outcome) focus, this function will win support primarily through a value judgment by those who place great importance on political pluralism and political stability.

Inhibitor of Representative Government

The conclusion that arbitration performs a useful political function is contrary to the conclusion that arbitration is a decision process inimical to the tenets and operation of our system of representative democratic government. This latter conclusion is based on the normative premise that our political system should be structured to reflect the will of the governed, as expressed through a pluralistic diffusion of interests, by allowing for active and legitimate groups to make themselves heard during public decision processes.[36] However, compulsory arbitration contains two related elements that detract from this desired governmental system: a lack of accountability for public decisions and an intensification of the bureaucratic forces that insulate public decision processes from public influence.

Arbitration allows for authoritative public allocation decisions to be made in a relatively private manner by a nonelected third party who is not directly accountable for his or her decisions.[37] Regardless of whether this delegation of authority is constitutionally permissible, it is deemed politically undesirable because it reduces management's accountability for these allocations of scarce public resources and allows public officials (and union leaders) to evade their responsibilities for these allocations by using arbitrators as mechanisms to absorb any constituent dissatisfactions with these decisions. In other words, arbitration is a classic example of the delegation of public authority to private actors that has pervaded our post–New Deal political system.[38]

Similarly, arbitration represents an undesirable intensification of the bureaucratic-professional control over governmental employer–employee relations begun by civil service and carried forward by collective bargaining.[39] As civil service and collective bargaining have come to be administered by professionals in numerous state and local bureaucracies, so arbitration is administered in a similar manner by labor relations professionals. One of the procedural costs of such professionalization, however, may be to increase the proportion of allocative decisions that are made by labor relations professionals whose primary allegiances are to the arbitration process itself and to their immediate union and management clients and who are much less concerned with the interests of the larger groups (such as taxpayers and other employees) affected by arbitration awards.[40] A second cost may be the development of arbitration constituencies among these professionals that act to ensure the continuation of arbitration legislation because of the tangible benefits (such as budget appropriations, income, and prestige) that arbitration provides to them.[41]

The major weakness of this critical view is that it tends to overlook the extent to which arbitration procedures can be "structured and limited in such a way as to preserve both the appearance and reality of the democratic process. . . ."[42] For instance, legislative bodies may restrict the scope of arbitrable subjects, limit the coverage of the arbitration legislation, specify exceedingly tight decision criteria, require that decisions be made by tripartite panels instead of single arbitrators, and mandate final-offer selection rather than conventional decision making. These and other procedural attempts to limit arbitral discretion may help make arbitration and the "democratic process" more compatible, though it is likely that arbitration critics would argue that the search for these procedural characteristics is an explicit admission that arbitration is inimical to democratic government.

This critical view of arbitration is difficult to test empirically, for it is not addressed to substantive differences between arbitrated and negotiated outcomes but to the processes used to produce those outcomes. Similarly, it is difficult to demonstrate empirically that arbitration is or may be inimical to democratic government without first formulating an explicit and normative definition of democracy. Furthermore, even with such a formulation, it may not be possible to give operational and hence measurable meaning to such key phrases as "accountability" and "professionalization." Instead, it is likely that this arbitration function will attract adherents and critics on the basis of its appeal to personal preference.[43]

Inhibitor of Genuine Bargaining

The belief that arbitration has a costly impact on bargaining incentives is often used to criticize the arbitral process. This conclusion is based on the normative premise that collective bargaining is a valuable and desirable decision-making process that should be protected from inimical forces. Arbitration is cast as a villain because it does not have the voluntary and joint decision-making properties of bargaining and because it may lure unions and managements away from the bargaining process.

More precisely, arbitration may be a too easily used escape route from the difficult trade-off choices that must usually be made in order to negotiate an agreement. Arbitration will be invoked because one or both sides believe that an arbitration award may be more favorable than a negotiated agreement *and* because one or both believe the costs of using arbitration are comparatively low (none of the trauma and costs of a work stoppage and none of the uncertainty of using other forms of political influence). As a result of this cost–benefit calculus, the availability of arbitration may have a "chilling effect" on the parties' efforts to negotiate an agreement, and over time there may be a "narcotic effect" as the parties become arbitration addicts who habitually rely on arbitrators to write their labor contracts. The logical conclusion of this reasoning is that arbitration will destroy and replace collective bargaining.

Researchers and practitioners have searched diligently for techniques to make arbitration and bargaining compatible, and this search has produced such proposals as final offer arbitration (in all its permutations), closed offer arbitration, and labor–management arbitration screening committees. In addition, there has been considerable research to measure this compatibility (or lack of it). The most widely used method seems to be the cross-sectional or longitudinal comparison of arbitration awards, as a proportion of all settlements, with other settlement techniques within or across one or more jurisdictions.[44] A second method measures the number of issues taken to arbitration under different procedures.[45] A third method tracks the amount of movement, usually on wages, exhibited during negotiations under arbitration, compared with no arbitration, to see if the availability of a binding award affects compromising activity.[46] While most of this research gathers data from actual negotiations, recently some researchers have used laboratory simulations to test more carefully arbitration's impacts on negotiating behaviors.[47] Another method examines negotiator and arbitrator attitudes about various arbitral features.[48] In short, we probably have a larger body of research results on arbitration's impact on bargaining than on any other aspect of the process.

Generalizations are hazardous, but this research seems to support the following conclusions:

1. The availability of arbitration has not destroyed bargaining, for in practically all arbitration jurisdictions a majority of agreements are negotiated.

2. In many cases the parties use the arbitration process as a forum for additional negotiations (or perhaps as a forum for their truly serious bargaining).

3. However, there are many union–management pairs who seem to have become quite dependent on arbitration, with such dependency influenced by employer size, degree of fiscal scarcity, prior use of impasse procedures, bargaining hostility, and so forth.

4. The shape of the impasse arbitration procedure may affect the parties' use of such procedures, for negotiating behaviors seem to vary with the nature and extent of arbitral discretion (the presence of a final offer selection requirement or the availability of fact-finding recommendations, for example).

In short, collective bargaining generally functions as a viable process in the presence of arbitration, but there is no doubt that arbitration has also increased union and management dependency on third parties to resolve their disputes and, in so doing, has frequently sapped the vitality of the bargaining process.

Perhaps more important, there are no precise formulas with which to evaluate the research results. This means that a given body of data can be used to support differing and even opposing conclusions,[49] and that personal preferences can play a strong role in the conclusions reached. Given that both collective bargaining and compulsory arbitration represent strongly held labor relations value judgments, the influence of personal preferences on these conclusions should not surprise anyone.

Discussion

The major components of each of these arbitration functions are summarized in the following table. The components include the impact that the procedure has (or is designed to have), the normative premise on which each function is based, the operational mechanisms by which each impact occurs, and some of the measures that might be used to evaluate how well or poorly arbitration performs these various functions. As table 1 suggests, arbitration advocates can point to three major benefits that arbitration might provide, while the skeptics can emphasize two sets of costs that these procedures may impose. The connecting thread among all these positive and negative functions is the set of premises on which they are constructed, for each premise assumes that there is some group, process, or political condition that needs to be protected or enhanced. Much of the debate among students of arbitration seems to result from the different normative premises they hold; and since there is no formula for determining the relative importance of these premises, there is no reason to expect that there will emerge a single arbitration paradigm on which everybody can, will, or should agree. These same students, however, should agree that since arbitration has multiple impacts, it should be evaluated along several dimensions rather than simply looking at how well it prevents strikes.

Table 1
Selected Components of Arbitration Functions

Arbitration's Purpose or Impact	Normative Premise	Operational Mechanisms	Measurement Tests
Protector of the public interest	The public needs and wants to be protected from strikes.	A binding award prevents strikes	Absence of strikes.
Protector of employee interests	Employees should bargain from position of equal strength with management.	Union can invoke arbitration over employer's objection and employer must accept award.	Comparison of awards with negotiated outcomes where arbitration is not available.
Regulator of interest group conflict	There is a need for social and political stability.	Third-party decision making absorbs and accommodates conflicting group pressures.	Comparison of the degree of overt labor relations conflict and hostility with and without arbitration.
Inhibitor of representative government	Public decision processes should be accessible and accountable.	Public authority is delegated to nonaccountable third parties.	Comparison of accessibility and accountability of labor relations decisions processes with and without arbitration.
Inhibitor of genuine collective bargaining	Bargaining incentives should be protected and strengthened.	There exists a high probability of satisfactory award and low usage costs.	Comparison of bargaining behaviors with and without arbitration.

This diversity of impact leads to a second point—that although arbitration is directed at government acting in its role as (unionized) employer, arbitration's more important long-run effects may be on government as regulator of the polity. For instance, arbitration's most valuable long-run function may be the manner in which it quietly absorbs and accommodates conflicting interest group claims over scarce public resources. The price for this accommodation, however, may be the insulation of these allocative decisions from the direct influence of many individuals or groups with strong interests in these decisions. In addition, such insulation may be particularly unwelcome because it occurs primarily at the local level, which is the level of government supposedly most responsive to citizen influence.

Whatever arbitration's political impacts may be, they need to be discussed in tentative terms, for there seems to be a sort of Gresham's law of arbitration research in which researchers' attention is drawn toward arbitration's labor relations impacts.[50] With all its labor relations labels, though, public sector interest arbitration is established through the political rule-making process (primarily at the state level) and then operates as a surrogate for the political resource allocation process (primarily at the local level).[51] Even though these political roles and impacts may be somewhat messy to study, they deserve more research attention than they have received to date.

In particular, there needs to be a careful examination of the balance struck between the public interest and private interest impacts of arbitration.

As noted earlier, the most visible rationale for arbitration has been the perceived need to protect the public from the withdrawal of supposedly vital public services (though such perceptions seem to be based on little or no empirical foundation). However, the public interest appears to refer only to this strike prevention objective, for once an arbitration system is implemented and working there seems to be little or no room for formal public participation in the arbitration proceedings. Furthermore, arbitration's availability reduces outcome uncertainty by eliminating the need for unions (or managements) to assume the risks of work stoppages or other forms of political-influence manipulation to press their demands.[52] Even if arbitration is not used, its availability tends to ensure that over time the level of negotiated benefits in a jurisdiction will not diverge substantially from the level of benefits obtainable via arbitration.[53] In short, the passage of arbitration legislation is consistent with Downs's theory that producers will influence government action more than consumers "because most men earn their incomes in one area but spend them in many. . . ."[54]

The adoption of the view that arbitration is primarily a response to interest group pressures should have a salutary effect on public labor relations research and policy making. Such a view seems far more consistent with how arbitration legislation actually is passed and renewed than the suggestion that such legislation results from the policymakers' concern for the general welfare. Similarly, this view might provide a useful framework for investigating and explaining why different jurisdictions have adopted so many different arbitration procedures. Further, this view would explicitly allow for the use of arbitration as a dependent variable that measures the distribution of political influence necessary to shape public labor relations systems in a desired direction. In addition, the interest group concept should focus more attention than has occurred to date on the political roles and effects of arbitration. Finally, thinking of arbitration as a response to interest-group pressures suggests the replacement of the unverified assumption that public employee strikes are inappropriate with empirical investigations of the comparative costs and benefits of strikes and arbitration. These investigations should produce much more informed debate about the desired shape of public dispute resolution arrangements than has occurred so far.

Notes

1. In pursuit of brevity and clarity, *arbitration* shall henceforth be used in this analysis to refer only to compulsory and binding interest arbitration, except when specifically noted otherwise.

2. Alaska, Connecticut, Hawaii, Iowa, Maine, Massachusetts, Michigan, Minnesota, Montana, Nebraska, Nevada, New Jersey, New York, Oregon, Pennsylvania, Rhode Island, Vermont, Washington, Wisconsin, and Wyoming. (In addition, the supreme courts in South Dakota and Utah declared unconstitutional compulsory arbitration statutes in those two states.) These statutes vary considerably in age, coverage, scope, and procedural requirements, but they all mandate the binding resolution of bargaining impasses between covered employees and employers.

3. Edward C. Banfield and James Q. Wilson, *City Politics* (New York: Vintage Books, 1963), p. 18.

4. Some caveats: no claim is made that the arbitration functions examined here exhaust the total possible list; relatively little attention is given to arbitration's procedural variations; and this analysis deals with bargaining and arbitration primarily among local governments in the United States.

5. For a complex definition of *the public interest* (in the context of public sector labor relations), see Richard P. Schick and Jean J. Couturier, *The Public Interest in Government Labor Relations* (Cambridge, Mass.: Ballinger, 1977), chap. 1. For a much shorter definition (in the same context), see Raymond D. Horton, "Arbitration, Arbitrators, and the Public Interest," *Industrial and Labor Relations Review* 28, no. 4 (July 1975), p. 503. For an insightful general discussion of the use of the phrase, see Murray Edelman, *The Symbolic Uses of Politics* (Urbana: University of Illinois Press, 1967), pp. 134–138.

6. Hawaii, Massachusetts, Michigan, Minnesota, Montana, Nevada, New Jersey, New York, Oregon, Pennsylvania, Washington, Wyoming.

7. Hoyt N. Wheeler, "An Analysis of Fire Fighter Strikes," *Labor Law Journal* 26, no. 1 (January 1975), pp. 17–20; J. Joseph Loewenberg, Walter J. Gershenfeld, H.J. Glasbeck, B.A. Hepple, and Kenneth F. Walker, *Compulsory Arbitration* (Lexington, Mass.: D.C. Heath, 1976), p. 165; James L. Stern, Charles M. Rehmus, J. Joseph Loewenberg, Hirschel Kasper, Barbara D. Dennis, *Final-Offer Arbitration* (Lexington, Mass.: D.C. Heath, 1975), p. 189; and Peter Feuille, *Final Offer Arbitration,* Public Employee Relations Library Series no. 50 (Chicago: International Personnel Management Association, 1975), pp. 10–11.

8. This list borrows heavily from David Lewin, "Collective Bargaining and the Right to Strike," in A. Lawrence Chickering, ed., *Public Employee Unions* (San Francisco: Institute for Contemporary Studies, 1976), pp. 145–163.

9. For instance, see David B. Truman, *The Governmental Process* (New York: Knopf, 1951); Edward C. Banfield, *Political Influence* (New York: Free Press, 1961); Banfield and Wilson, *City Politics.*

10. For a review of these studies through 1976, see David Lewin, "Public Sector Labor Relations: A Review Essay," *Labor History* 18, no. 1 (Winter 1977), pp. 133–144.

11. Sharon P. Smith, *Equal Pay in the Public Sector: Fact or Fantasy?* (Princeton: Industrial Relations Section, Princeton University, 1977), pp. 120–129.

12. Thomas A. Kochan and Hoyt N. Wheeler, "Municipal Collective Bargaining: A Model and Analysis of Bargaining Outcomes," *Industrial and Labor Relations Review* 29, no. 1 (October 1975), pp. 46–66. Gerhart found a positive relationship between favorable union contract provisions and a strike activity index among local government employees, but this relationship was not statistically significant in the pre-

sence of other explanatory variables. See Paul F. Gerhart, "Determinants of Bargaining Outcomes in Local Government Labor Negotiations," *Industrial and Labor Relations Review* 29, no. 3 (April 1976), pp. 331–351.

13. Alaska, Hawaii, Oregon, Montana, Minnesota, Pennsylvania, and Vermont. In 1978 Wisconsin started allowing municipal employees to strike if both the union and the employer refused to use final offer arbitration to resolve their dispute.

14. Contrast the apparent scarcity of current public sector strike impact research with the fairly substantial amount of research on "emergency" strike impacts in the private sector performed mostly in the 1950s, which is nicely reviewed in Donald E. Cullen, *National Emergency Strikes,* ILR Paperback no. 7 (Ithaca: Cornell University, New York State School of Labor and Industrial Relations, 1968), chap. 2.

15. This number is the sum of figures extracted from a variety of U.S. Bureau of Labor Statistics publications on government work stoppages: *Work Stoppages in Government, 1958–68.* Report 348 (1970); *Government Work Stoppages, 1960, 1969, and 1970,* summary report (November 1971); *Work Stoppages in Government, 1972, 1973, 1974, 1975,* Reports 434 (1974), 437 (1975), 453 (1976), and 483 (1976), respectively. The 1965–1970 strikes are for employees providing "administration and protection services"; the 1971–1975 figures are for employees in "protective occupations." Thus, the two categories are not strictly comparable, and they include more than just police and fire strikes.

16. There is no doubt that many public employee strikes can and do cause considerable apprehension, annoyance, and inconvenience, but they rarely seem actually to hurt the public health and safety. Such assessments, however, inevitably reflect the assessor's definitions (which usually are implicit rather than explicit) of such terms as *inconvenience, hurt,* and *health and safety.* See John C. Meyer, Jr., "Discontinuity in the Delivery of Public Service: Analyzing the Police Strike," *Human Relations* 29, no. 6 (June 1976), pp. 545–557. In addition, it is quite likely that the views espoused here will differ sharply from those of public managers (and union leaders) who have worked eighteen-hour days struggling with the many apprehensions, annoyances, and inconveniences created by such strikes.

17. The belief that public employee strikes will harm the public is based in large part on a very negative view of the ability of public managers to cope with such strikes. While there is little or no systematic research addressed specifically to this topic, several case studies suggest that public managers have learned to cope rather effectively with strike situations. For reports on a variety of police strikes, see Hervey A. Juris and Peter Feuille, *Police Unionism* (Lexington, Mass.: D.C. Heath, 1973), pp. 85–89; Richard M. Ayres, "Case Studies of Police Strikes in Two Cities—Albuquerque and Oklahoma City," and William J. Bopp, Paul Chignell, and Charles Maddox, "The San Francisco Police Strike of 1975; A Case Study," *Journal of Police Science and Administration* 5, no. 1 (1977), pp. 19–31 and 32–42, respectively.

18. See Lewin, "Collective Bargaining and the Right to Strike," pp. 152–157.

19. The assertion that the public's paramount labor relations objective is to avoid or minimize the inconvenience of strikes (which is said to be a prime source of union power) has never been specifically tested, but it has received considerable publicity. See Harry H. Wellington and Ralph K. Winter, Jr., *The Unions and the Cities* (Washington, D.C.: Brookings Institution, 1971), chap. 1. Similarly untested is the corollary of this assertion, that the public, when inconvenienced, will always pressure

management to settle the strike and terminate the inconvenience. For a well-publicized example of contrary behavior, see "Strike of San Francisco City Craft Unions Fails to Win the Support of Public or Labor," *Wall Street Journal,* April 15, 1976, p. 30.

20. See Schick and Couturier, *The Public Interest in Government Labor Relations,* pp. 244–245; and Victor E. Flango and Robert Dudley, "Who Supports Public Employee Strikes?" *Journal of Collective Negotiations in the Public Sector* 7, no. 1 (1978), pp. 1–10.

21. For example, the Missouri Municipal League recently approved a campaign to lobby for right-to-strike legislation in that state—for the express purpose of preventing compulsory arbitration legislation. See Bureau of National Affairs, *Government Employee Relations Report,* no. 779 (October 2, 1978), p. 17. For reports of statements by various managerial representatives or commentators that managements prefer strikes to compulsory arbitration, see Bureau of National Affairs, *Government Employee Relations Report,* No. 696 (February 21, 1977), pp. 15–17; no. 702 (April 4, 1977), pp. 12–13; no. 725 (September 12, 1977), pp. 21–22; and no. 754 (April 10, 1978), p. 19.

22. See the reports on arbitration in Michigan, Pennsylvania, and Wisconsin in Stern et al., *Final-Offer Arbitration.*

23. See Hoyt N. Wheeler, "How Compulsory Arbitration Affects Compromise Activity," *Industrial Relations* 17, no. 1 (February 1978), pp. 80–84; John C. Anderson and Thomas A. Kochan, "Impasse Procedures in the Canadian Federal Service," *Industrial and Labor Relations Review* 30, no. 3 (April 1977), pp. 283–301; and Peter Feuille, "Final Offer Arbitration and the Chilling Effect," *Industrial Relations* 14, no. 3 (October 1975), pp. 302–310. As would be expected, this (and other) research also suggests that negotiating incentives may vary with the shape of arbitration procedures and the nature of dispute resolution alternatives available.

24. Stern et al., *Final-Offer Arbitration.*

25. Thomas A. Kochan, Ronald G. Ehrenberg, Jean Baderschneider, Todd Jick, and Mordehai Mironi, *An Evaluation of Impasse Procedures for Police and Firefighters in New York State* (Ithaca: Cornell University, New York State School of Industrial and Labor Relations, 1977), chap. 10; and Hoyt N. Wheeler and Frank Owen, "Impasse Resolution Preferences of Fire Fighters and Municipal Negotiators," *Journal of Collective Negotiations in the Public Sector* 5, no. 3 (1978), pp. 215–224.

26. Stern et al., *Final-Offer Arbitration;* Thomas A. Kochan, "The Politics of Interest Arbitration," *The Arbitration Journal* 33, no. 1 (March 1978), pp. 5–9; Bureau of National Affairs, *Government Employee Relations Report,* no. 717 (July 11, 1977), pp. 13–14.

27. Kochan and Wheeler, "Municipal Collective Bargaining"; Stern et al., *Final-Offer Arbitration,* chap. 6; Kochan et al., *An Evaluation of Impasse Procedures,* chap. 6; Paul C. Somers, "An Evaluation of Final-Offer Arbitration in Massachusetts," *Journal of Collective Negotiations in the Public Sector* 6, no. 3 (1977), pp. 193–228.

28. Arthur M. Ross, *Trade Union Wage Policy* (Berkeley: University of California Press, 1948).

29. Charles J. Morris, "The Role of Interest Arbitration in a Collective Bargaining System," *Industrial Relations Law Journal* 1, no. 3 (Fall 1976), pp. 470, 477; Irving Bernstein, *The Arbitration of Wages* (Berkeley: University of California Press, 1954), pp. 26–33; and David B. Ross, "The Arbitration of Public Employee Wage

Disputes," *Industrial and Labor Relations Review* 23, no. 1 (October 1969), pp. 3–14.

30. Stern et al., *Final-Offer Arbitration,* pp. 144–145; Kochan et al., *An Evaluation . . . ,* pp. 216–217.

31. Political influence is difficult to measure, but there are some sources that attest to the reputation for political expertise police and fire unions have acquired: Juris and Feuille, *Police Unionism;* Don Berney, "Law and Order Politics: A History and Role Analysis of Police Officer Organizations," Ph.D. dissertation, University of Washington, 1971; Philip Kienast, "Police and Fire Fighter Organizations," Ph.D. dissertation, Michigan State University, 1972; Jack Steiber, *Public Employee Unionism* (Washington, D.C.: Brookings Institution, 1973), pp. 204–207.

32. For two contrasting paradigms about the role of collective bargaining in the conflict between public employees and the public, compare Wellington and Winter, *The Unions and the Cities,* chap. 1, and Clyde W. Summers, "Public Employee Bargaining: A Political Perspective," *Yale Law Journal* 83, no. 6 (May 1974), pp. 1156–1200.

33. Perhaps the best exposition of this regulatory function is in George T. Sulzner, "The Political Functions of Impasse Procedures," *Industrial Relations* 16, no. 3 (October 1977), pp. 290–297. Much of the material in this section is based on Sulzner's analysis.

34. For such a review, see Morris, "The Role of Interest Arbitration in a Collective Bargaining System," pp. 487–491. As Morris notes, a few state supreme courts have struck down arbitration statutes as unconstitutional, usually on the grounds that such statutes unlawfully delegate legislative authority. For reports on two such state supreme court decisions (in Colorado and Utah), see Bureau of National Affairs, *Government Employee Relations Report,* no. 708 (May 16, 1977), pp. 10–11, and no. 726 (September 19, 1977), pp. 12–13.

35. Stern et al., *Final-Offer Arbitration.*

36. This premise is contained in Wellington and Winter, *The Unions and the Cities,* chap. 1, and appears to be based on Robert A. Dahl, *A Preface to Democratic Theory* (Chicago: University of Chicago Press, 1956).

37. For a more complete statement of this characterization of arbitration, see Raymond D. Horton, "Arbitration, Arbitrators, and the Public Interest," *Industrial and Labor Relations Review* 28, no. 4 (July 1975), pp. 497–507.

38. Lowi refers to this phenomenon as "interest-groupo liberalism"; see Theodore J. Lowi, *The End of Liberalism* (New York: Norton, 1969), chap. 3.

39. For a brief discussion of the professionalization of governmental collective bargaining, see Thomas M. Love and George T. Sulzner, "Political Implications of Public Employee Bargaining," *Industrial Relations* 11, no. 1 (February 1972), pp. 23–25.

40. For instance, there is some evidence that advocate representatives, mediators, and fact-finders pay little if any attention to the "public interest" during contract negotiations or impasse resolution. See Thomas A. Kochan, George P. Huber, and L.L. Cummings, "Determinants of Intraorganizational Conflict in Collective Bargaining in the Public Sector," *Administrative Science Quarterly* 20, no. 1 (March 1975), pp. 10–23, esp. table 1; Kenneth Kressel, *Labor Mediation: An Exploratory Survey* (Albany, N.Y.: Association of Labor Mediation Agencies, 1972); and Jack Steiber and

Benjamin W. Wolkinson, "Fact-Finding Viewed by Fact-Finders: The Michigan Experience," *Labor Law Journal* 28, no. 2 (February 1977), pp. 89–101.

41. An interesting research effort would be to examine the actions or positions of state arbitration administration agencies and arbitrators in those situations in which the renewal of an arbitration statute is being considered by the legislature. For a report on the position of the New York State Public Employment Relations Board during the 1977 arbitration renewal debate in that state, see Thomas A. Kochan, "The Politics of Interest Arbitration," *The Arbitration Journal* 33, no. 1 (March 1978), pp. 5–9.

42. Joseph Grodin, "Political Aspects of Public Sector Interest Arbitration," *Industrial Relations Law Journal* 1, no. 1 (Spring 1976), p. 24. In this article Grodin explores how arbitration procedures can be made more comparable with the democratic process.

43. For an example, see Horton, "Arbitration, Arbitrators, and the Public Interest," and then see Joseph Krislov's "Comment" and Horton's "Reply" in *Industrial and Labor Relations Review* 31, no. 1 (October 1977), pp. 71–77.

44. In addition to the sources cited in note 23, see Stern et al., *Final-Offer Arbitration;* Peter Feuille, "Final-Offer Arbitration and Negotiating Incentives," *The Arbitration Journal* 32, no. 3 (September 1977), pp. 203–220; Thomas A. Kochan and Jean Baderschneider, "Dependence upon Impasse Procedures: Police and Firefighters in New York State," *Industrial and Labor Relations Review* 31, no. 4 (July 1978), pp. 431 • 449; Hoyt N. Wheeler, "Compulsory Arbitration: A 'Narcotic Effect'?" *Industrial Relations* 14, no. 1 (February 1975), pp. 117–120; Daniel G. Gallagher, "Interest Arbitration under the Iowa Public Employment Relations Act," *The Arbitration Journal* 33, no. 3 (September 1978), pp. 30–36; and David B. Lipsky and Thomas A. Barocci, "Final-Offer Arbitration and Public-Safety Employees: The Massachusetts Experience," Industrial Relations Association, *Proceedings of the Thirtieth Annual Winter Meeting* (Madison: IRRA, 1978), pp. 65–76.

45. Mollie H. Bowers, "A Study of Legislated Interest Arbitration and Collective Bargaining in the Public Safety Services in Michigan and Pennsylvania," Ph.D. dissertation, Cornell University, 1974; and Stern et al., *Final-Offer Arbitration.*

46. Wheeler, "How Compulsory Arbitration Affects Compromise Activity"; Kochan et al., *An Evaluation of Impasse Procedures.*

47. William W. Notz and Frederick A. Starke, "Final Offer versus Conventional Arbitration as Means of Conflict Management," *Administrative Science Quarterly* 23, no. 2 (June 1978), pp. 189 • 203; A.V. Subbarao, "The Impact of Binding Interest Arbitration on Negotiation and Process Outcome: An Experimental Study," *The Journal of Conflict Resolution* 22, no. 1 (March 1978), pp. 79–104.

48. Stern et al., *Final-Offer Arbitration:* Kochan et al., *An Evaluation of Impasse Procedures.*

49. For instance, see Mark Thompson and James Cairnie, "Compulsory Arbitration: The Case of British Columbia Teachers," *Industrial and Labor Relations Review* 27, no. 1 (October 1973), pp. 3–17; Peter Feuille, "Analyzing Compulsory Arbitration Experiences: The Role of Personal Preferences—Comment," and Thompson and Cairnie, "Reply," *Industrial and Labor Relations Review* 28, no. 3 (April 1975), pp. 432–438.

50. A recent review of political science and industrial relations journals revealed that almost all the scholarly writing on arbitration, including the few examinations of

its political role and impacts, has appeared in industrial relations outlets. Quite naturally, most of this writing focuses on how well or poorly arbitration and collective bargaining fit together. Given the labor relations training and interests of these authors, and the availability of relatively precise (or quantifiable) data about the labor relations impacts of arbitration, this concentration of research efforts is not surprising.

51. A particularly useful research topic is whether arbitration alters the proportionate shares of government resources allocated to covered and uncovered employee groups.

52. Arbitration may be particularly important to the unions as a risk-avoidance mechanism when they are faced with hostile environmental forces, such as "taxpayer revolts." During such periods, arbitration may be less important to the unions as a mechanism to get "more" and more important as a mechanism to protect against "less."

53. One recent analysis demonstrated that within a single jurisdiction negotiated and arbitrated outcomes are quite interdependent. Henry S. Farber and Harry C. Katz, "Interest Arbitration, Outcomes, and the Incentive to Bargain: The Role of Risk Preference," *Industrial and Labor Relations Review* 33, no. 1 (October 1979), pp. 55 • 63. See Stern et al., *Final-Offer Arbitration,* and Kochan et al., *An Evaluation of Impasse Procedures,* for empirical results showing the difference between negotiated and arbitrated wage increases are rather modest.

54. Anthony Downs, *An Economic Theory of Democracy* (New York: Harper and Row, 1957), p. 254.

Part II
Collective Bargaining
Impacts

6
Wage Impacts of Unionism

I n previous chapters, we examined the public sector collective bargaining process as a dependent variable shaped by external economic, political, and legal contexts as well as by the characteristics of union and management organizations. In this chapter and the next, bargaining is conceptualized as an independent variable, and the focus is on the outcomes or impacts of the collective bargaining process. The wage impacts of public employee unionism are explored in chapter 6, nonwage impacts in chapter 7.

For several reasons, it would be difficult to understate the importance of such impact research. First, despite the voluminous literature on public sector labor relations, it is only recently that systematic study of collective bargaining impacts has actually been undertaken. Second, some perceptions about the impacts of unionism on the consequences of bargaining in government are based on conventional wisdom, assertion, unsupported generalization, and limited case study. Third, the conceptual frameworks, research methodologies, and analytical techniques employed to study public sector bargaining impacts vary widely, often are not well articulated, and continue to have notable limitations. Finally, public policies regarding unionism and collective bargaining in government frequently are made or revised in the absence of data obtained from systematic research.

Measurement Problems

Essentially, impact research on public sector labor relations is concerned with the question, "What substantive difference does the existence of unionism and collective bargaining make?" Though simple to pose, the question is difficult to answer. By *substantive difference,* one may mean the depth or extent of bargaining's impact on a specific employment characteristic, such as the hourly wage rate, amount of overtime worked, pension benefits, or disciplinary practice. Alternatively, one may regard the range of breadth of issues negotiated as a measure of bargaining impact. Moreover, the latter focus may extend beyond formal bargaining over, say, wages, working conditions, and management policy issues to the impacts of public employee unionism on government structure and informal politics. Ideally, both depth and breadth criteria would be considered in any attempts to measure public sector bargaining impacts, but the practical limitations confronting researchers in this field generally mitigate such comprehensive assessments. Nevertheless, this discussion points up one of the key problems of impact research on public sector collective bargaining—namely, isolating the union's impact on a specific issue from its impact on all other issues.

A second, and in some ways more vexing, problem confronting students of this subject is that of isolating the impacts of unionism from those of other factors that affect the subject matter of bargaining. To gain perspective on this problem, recall the conceptual framework used to organize this book, as illustrated in figure 1–1 of the introductory chapter. There, bargaining was conceived as a variable intervening between environmental contexts and organizational characteristics on the one hand, and outcomes or impacts on the other. What at first glance may appear to be outcomes of bargaining in the public sector may, in fact, be due to other, more fundamental forces. In other words, bargaining is a conduit for environmental and organizational variables that affect wages, working conditions, and other issues that are negotiated at the bargaining table. These forces, in addition to unionism itself, are determinants of bargaining outcomes in government, and the researcher must attempt to separate them out in order to obtain accurate measures and identify the impacts of unionism.

This problem, a familiar one in the field of industrial relations, is further complicated by the tendency of bargaining participants and observers to attribute the terms of a contract settlement solely to the formal negotiations process. Thus, upon the conclusion of a labor agreement in the private sector, a manager typically assigns to the union responsibility for wage and other labor cost increases, and may then use this "explanation" to rationalize subsequent price increases for the firm's products. Similarly, union leaders take credit for the totality of wage, benefit, and working condition improvements they have negotiated. Union members generally accept this claim and, when they do not, usually turn to new leadership that promises to extract even more from management in subsequent negotiations. The public readily seems to believe the contentions of labor and management about the terms and conditions they have negotiated, even if sometimes holding them in opprobrium for having done so.

The same phenomenon, perhaps to an even greater degree, has emerged in the public sector. Popular opinion tends to overestimate the impacts of unionism and to be insufficiently appreciative of other variables—economic, political, legal, organizational—that affect the terms and conditions of public employment and the costs of government services. In such a context, it is incumbent on researchers to design their studies of public sector collective bargaining carefully so that the union impact may be isolated from all other sources of impact. When unable to do so completely, they should be cautious in interpreting their findings and in drawing conclusions about collective bargaining outcomes. Readers may judge for themselves the extent to which these caveats are heeded by the authors of readings presented in this chapter.

Another problem encountered in public sector collective bargaining research might, for lack of better terminology, be labeled an aggregation problem. It becomes salient as one inquires into the data base on which generalizations about public sector bargaining impacts rest. For example, available evidence indicates that the relative wage impact of public employee unions in the United States is, on average, between 5 and 15 percent.[1] Yet the empirical basis for this conclusion consists primarily of studies of teacher and protective service worker bargaining in local government. Most other groups of public employees—sanitation workers, clerical employees, hospital attendants, social workers, nurses—have received little or no attention in wage impact research. Therefore, the generalization about the wage outcomes of public sector bargaining noted earlier must be regarded as a narrow one and its limitations recognized.

That the impacts—wage and nonwage—of government employee unions may vary across occupational groups seems especially plausible in light of the diversity thesis of public sector collective bargaining that has been forwarded in the literature and is affirmed in this book.[2] This diversity may manifest itself among public jurisdictions and within each of them. Thus, Lewin has identified the multiple patterns of labor relations that prevail among the large local governments of Los Angeles, California, and the four major types of public employee labor organizations that exist in that city.[3] In another article, Kleingartner highlighted the different job-related concerns and, hence, potential bargaining impacts of professional and nonprofessional public employees.[4] Similarly, Derber has detailed the heterogenity of organizational arrangements that public sector managers have adopted to deal with unionism and collective bargaining.[5] Such diversity limits the generalizability of conclusions about public sector bargaining impacts that are based on disaggregated single-union, single-occupation, or single–work group studies, including those that encompass more (even many more) than one public employer.

The case study approach to public sector bargaining impact research has somewhat different limitations. Although it permits the investigator to explore in depth and usually over time multifaceted dimensions of public sector labor relations, including those that may best be examined qualitatively (as reflected in the Lewin-McCormick reading in chapter 3 and the Osterman reading in chapter 4), it simply does not permit generalization to other governments at the same level. Put differently, the more disaggregated the approach to public sector bargaining research (and the case study is the ultimate in disaggregation), the more limited is the potential for linking the findings to a larger setting and for building broad-based generalizations about the impacts of public employee unionism.

This limitation is partially overcome by the cross-sectional methodology that has been used by several researchers to study one or another aspect of public sector labor relations. For example, Anderson employed such an approach to study numerous outcomes of local government bargaining in Canada (see his reading selection in chapter 7). In the narrower area of wage impact research, Bartel and Lewin similarly used the cross-sectional methodology, as reported later in this chapter. The conclusions of these researchers provide a broader and more systematic basis for generalizing about the outcomes of public sector bargaining than was available heretofore.

These types of cross-sectional research also permit the application of quantitative techniques to public sector collective bargaining processes and outcomes, yielding a thoroughness of testing and level of validity usually not obtainable through other methodologies. Because of their exclusive focus on municipal government, however, these studies do not provide the basis for generalizing about all local governments or, of course, the public sector more broadly. Indeed, labor relations in the federal and state governments, especially the area of bargaining impacts, remain relatively unexplored by researchers.

The cross-sectional methodology has one other limitation (perhaps inherent less in the technique than in its application), namely, an inability to measure changes over time in public sector bargaining impacts. The bulk of both the wage and nonwage impact studies reported in this and the next chapter, most of which employ some type of cross-sectional research design, yield findings at particular points in time—typically points during the 1960s and 1970s. Thus, they provide static or snapshop views which may not endure over time.

To illustrate this point further, consider the data presented in tables 6–1 and 6–2 for the 1982–1986 period. Table 6–1 shows that annual changes in compensation were greater for public than for private sector workers throughout this period, although the rates of increase for both groups declined from the beginning to the end of the period. Both white-collar and blue-collar employees of state and local government experienced more rapidly rising compensation rates than their respective counterparts in industry. This contrasts markedly with the experience of the mid-1970s to the early 1980s, when rates of public employee pay increases in the United States were well and consistently below the rates of pay increase for private workers.[6]

Table 6–2 focuses more narrowly on unionized (or, more accurately, represented) workers in the public and private sectors. Clearly, unionized public employees fared much better than unionized private employees during

Table 6–1
Changes in the Employment Cost Index (ECI), by Sector, 1982–1986
(in percentages)

	Year				
	1982	1983	1984	1985	1986
State and local government workers					
Total	7.2	6.0	6.6	5.7	5.2
White collar	7.4	5.9	6.9	5.7	5.3
Blue collar	6.7	5.5	5.6	5.4	5.1
Schools	7.3	5.9	7.7	6.3	5.8
Private industry workers					
Total	6.4	5.7	4.9	3.9	3.2
White collar	6.5	6.4	5.1	4.8	3.5
Blue collar	6.1	4.9	4.2	3.2	2.7
Manufacturing	6.2	5.1	4.6[a]	3.4	3.1
Nonmanufacturing	6.6	6.0	5.1[b]	4.4	3.2

Source: U.S. Bureau of Labor Statistics.

Note: The Employment Cost Index (ECI) measures changes in compensation costs, which include wages, salaries, and employer costs for employee benefits.

[a]Category changed to "Goods Producing."

[b]Category changed to "Service Producing."

the 1982–1986 period, whether measured by changes in wages or by changes in total compensation. Indeed, by the end of the period, negotiated wage and benefit increases were more than three times larger in state and local government than in private industry. Again, this picture is very different from that of the 1970s and early 1980s, when rates of pay and benefit change were larger, often far larger, in industry than in government. Further, and although they are not shown here, the available data indicate that federal employee compensation increases, for both unionized and nonunion employees, surpassed the increases for private sector workers between 1982 and 1986.[7]

Although they are hardly conclusive, these data reveal that in the 1980s to date public employee pay and benefit increases substantially exceeded the increases received by privately employed workers (and also exceeded average annual changes in consumer prices).[8] Moreover, this was true for both unionized and nonunion workers, but especially for the former. All this suggests that the pay advantage that some public employees enjoyed over comparable private sector workers in the 1960s but which was reversed in the 1970s has to some extent been restored in the 1980s. While available data only permit speculation in this respect, it does appear that the second generation of public sector bargaining in the United States, which featured environmental charac-

Table 6-2
Major Collective Bargaining Settlements, by Sector, 1982–1986
(*in percentages*)

	1982		1983		1984		1985		1986	
	First Year	Over Life of Contract (OLC)	First Year	OLC	First Year	OLC	First Year	OLC	First Year	OLC
State and local government workers										
Wages[a]	7.2	7.2	4.4	5.1	4.8	5.1	4.6	5.4	5.7	5.7
Total compensation[a]	7.4	7.4	4.6	5.2	5.2	5.4	4.2	5.1	6.2	6.0
Private industry workers										
Wages[a]	3.8	3.6	2.6	2.8	2.4	2.4	2.3	2.7	1.2	1.8
Total compensation[a]	3.2	2.8	3.4	3.0	3.6	2.8	2.6	2.7	1.1	1.6

Source: U.S. Bureau of Labor Statistics.

[a]Wage adjustments cover settlements of 1,000 workers or more; total compensation covers settlements of 5,000 workers or more. In 1982 and 1983, state and local government wage adjustments covered settlements of 5,000 workers or more.

teristics that produced a declining relative and real wage position of the public work force, has ended. Certainly the relative and real wage position of public employees has improved in the 1980s. What is less clear about the emerging third generation of public sector bargaining, however, is whether and to what extent the improving pay position of public employees is due to increased productivity. Although there is some evidence to suggest that such enhancement has occurred in certain services and certain governments,[9] there has not yet been a comprehensive study of this key issue.

Beyond this, but also from an empirical standpoint, we believe that researchers will want to examine and compare the impacts of public employee unionism at various stages in the business cycle, rather than simply (and in disaggregated fashion) in an expansionary or a contracting economic period. To do so will require the application of longitudinal methodologies to the study of public sector bargaining effects. This type of analysis should permit the establishment of broader based generalizations about bargaining impacts in the U.S. public sector than are currently justified.

Some Normative Concerns

We concluded the introductory chapter of this book by discussing explicitly the personal preferences of public sector labor relations researchers and the ways in which those preferences may influence the choice of research topics and interpretation of findings. Specific examples of this phenomenon were shown in some of the readings included in chapters 4 and 5. Before presenting the major readings on wage and nonwage impacts of public employee unions in this chapter, we want to share with the reader some of our views of and concerns about such impact research.

First, in our considered judgment, wage impact research is overemphasized and nonwage impact research is underemphasized, not only in the study of public sector labor relations but in the field of industrial relations generally. This is not to denigrate the value of wage impact research—indeed, at the present time, we believe it to be, on balance, of higher quality than nonwage impact research—but, rather, to underscore its limitations, especially if we wish to answer the questions posed earlier in this chapter about the substantive consequences that derive from the existence of unionism and collective bargaining in government.

The strong emphasis placed on union wage impacts in industrial relations research is understandable. Because a major rationale for the existence of labor organizations is to take wages out of competition, it is natural to inquire into and perhaps focus centrally on union wage impacts. In such research in the private sector and, with some modifications, in the public sector as well, investigators use neoclassical price theory and its underlying analytic framework to examine systematically the wages of unionized workers compared to those of their nonunion counterparts. No other area of impact research has at its disposal a comparably well-developed theory or analytical framework; consequently, such research must proceed in relatively looser fashion. Furthermore, wage impact research deals in the finiteness and tangibility of numbers, and permits the application of quantitative techniques that are particularly appealing to social science researchers generally and economists in particular.

Yet to draw conclusions about the consequences of unionism and to evaluate the institution of collective bargaining solely on the basis of wage impact research is shortsighted, comparable perhaps to judging the whole by one of its parts. Consider, for example, the comments of Albert Rees concerning private sector union wage impact research:

> My own best guess is that the average effects of all American unions on the wages of their members in recent years would lie somewhere between 15 and 20 percent. . . . Unions, insofar as they have the power to raise relative wages, reduce employment in the union sector and increase it in the non-union sector. This is a worse allocation of labor than would exist without unions. . . .[10]

He goes on to add, however:

> The view that unions make for a worse allocation of labor does not necessarily imply an unfavorable judgment of the total effect of unions. There are many other aspects of union activity yet to be considered, and an economy has other and perhaps even more important goals than most efficient allocation of resources.[11]

Thus does Rees cogently state the case for avoiding judgments about the impacts of unionism that are based on partial (even if soundly derived) evidence. The caveat applies as readily to public as to private sector unionism and collective bargaining.

Second, important aspects of the public sector employment relationship have escaped the scrutiny of collective bargaining researchers. Most students of public sector union wage impacts, for example, have failed to deal adequately with fringe benefits, most notably pension benefits, in their analyses (see, however, the Bartel-Lewin reading in this chapter). Broadening the focus of such studies beyond wages to total compensation would provide a more complete basis for judging the monetary impacts of public employee unionism.

Similarly, such nonwage issues as productivity and job security in the public sector have been subjected to little systematic research. The former is commonly alleged to be low, the latter high, in relation to the private sector, but very few comparative studies across the sectors or even just among governments have been undertaken, particularly in terms of the impact of collective bargaining on these aspects of public employment. This probably says less about the orientation of researchers than about the limited availability of data concerning productivity and job security in government. It may have also been true, especially early on, that public sector labor and management officials were not especially interested in these issues. It appears, however, that they became more interested in productivity and job security matters during the economically restrictive second generation of public sector bargaining. If so, then during the third generation of bargaining, public managers may move more aggressively to tie wage and benefit increases to productivity improvements (rather than simply dealing in the cosmetics of productivity bargaining), and public employees may make stronger claims on broadened job security or, more basically, property rights in work. Collective bargaining researchers may then have access to more substantial data bases in attempting to assess the nonwage impacts of public employee unionism.

Finally, the methodologies employed to study public sector labor relations, specifically the nonwage impacts of unionism, will have to be refined and improved. It is unlikely that such studies can match the methodological sophistication of the wage impact research reported later in this chapter. Nevertheless, Anderson's analysis of bargaining outcomes in municipal government and the analytical frameworks and methods used by the authors of other readings contained in chapter 7 of this book provide tangible evidence of the potential for methodological improvement in studying the nonwage impacts of public employee unionism. We should add, however, that the lack of advanced analytical frameworks and methodologies to examine such bargaining impacts is due partly to the complexity of these nonwage issues. It would be unfortunate, in our view, if the absence of precise measures of nonwage bargaining impacts should lead readers—and researchers—to ignore the available evidence about these impacts (some of this evidence is also presented in chapter 7), or especially to base their judgments about the consequences of collective bargaining solely on the wage impacts of public employee unions. In essence, we prefer a broad over a narrow assessment of public employee unionism, even if this means accepting the methodological and measurement limitations of existing research.

Governmental Wage-Setting and Budget-Making Processes

Before considering empirical evidence about the wage impacts of public employee unions, it is necessary to understand some of the characteristics of wage setting and, more generally, cost determination in government. Referring again to the model presented in chapter 1, these processes may be regarded as organizational characteristics—independent variables—with which collective bargaining, where it develops, subsequently interacts. If the effects of public employee unions are to be properly gauged, then the outcomes of bargaining must be compared to outcomes that occur in governments without formal collective negotiations or to outcomes that resulted in the preunion period within specific public jurisdictions. Bargaining outcomes should not be compared with an ideal model of wage or cost determination in the public sector.[12]

In the first reading in this section, Fogel and Lewin identify and analyze some of the characteristics and consequences of governmental wage-setting processes. Underlying these processes in many governments is the prevailing wage principle, which, as the authors note, apparently makes good sense on both economic and political—that is, efficiency and equity—grounds.[13] Yet, in applying this principle, one that is pervasive in the U.S. public sector and that presumably commits governments to base their wages on prevailing community (especially private industry) rates, public employers systematically overpay their blue-collar and lower level white-collar workers while underpaying their professional and managerial personnel, relative to the private sector. These egalitarian wage structures may perhaps satisfy some equity objective or presage a restructuring of wage relationships in the broader society, but they have negative efficiency consequences and, in any case, are made without the explicit judgment of the voting—and taxpaying—public.

The Fogel-Lewin reading not only demonstrates that public employers depart from their own expressed ideals in the determination of wages, but also supports the view that bargaining wage impacts should be measured against empirical reality. By distinguishing the narrower wage-related concerns of government employees from the broader issues of interest to the general (voting) public, and by identifying the ways in which the former can influence the political processes that govern wage determination, this reading implies that government workers can affect their wages prior to or in the absence of unionization and formal collective bargaining. To the extent that such effects occur, they are extremely difficult if not impossible to detect, even by the sophisticated analytical methods employed in the wage impact studies reviewed later in this chapter. Consequently, those studies may misstate the impacts of collective bargaining on public sector wages.

Several studies of public–private sector wage (and benefit) relationships and wage structures have appeared since the Fogel-Lewin research was published, and some of these strongly suggest that the public–private wage differential is largest for women and blacks.[14] A substantial amount of this work focuses on the U.S. Postal Service, much of it is cross-sectional, and most of it ignores pay differentials in the professional and especially the managerial ranks. What this work does confirm, though perhaps unintentionally, is that the question of appropriate comparisons in determining public sector pay remains controversial and subject to widely varying interpretations. This is a key point of the Fogel-Lewin reading, which demonstrates that the introduction of collective bargaining in government and the subsequent measurement of union pay impacts should not result in comparisons of union-determined pay with a single-minded or a single comparability criterion model of management-determined pay.

Further, by ignoring public–private pay differentials in the upper portions of the occupational pay structure, current research provides little empirical or policy guidance on the question of whether and to what extent public sector *occupational pay structures* should be altered. Fogel and Lewin's research clearly implies that by "underpaying" professional and managerial employees, public employers can be expected to attract relatively low quality personnel to these jobs and to suffer relatively high turnover of personnel from these jobs (by "relative" we mean in relation to private employers). This issue has persisted at all major levels of government in the United States and was recently taken up by the Reagan administration, which encountered considerable controversy over its proposal (and subsequent actions) to raise judicial, cabinet, and senior executive service officials' salaries by substantial amounts.[15] Put in larger perspective, this is neither a Republican nor a Democratic issue; rather, it is a question of whether the public is prepared to pay (more or less) market-level wages and benefits for the relatively small group of professional and managerial personnel who are expected to direct the work of the relatively large group of clerical, skilled, and semiskilled workers who provide the vast bulk of government services to the citizenry. We urge the reader to assess this issue carefully when reading Fogel-Lewin.

Another key issue in the area of public sector pay determination concerns the integration—or lack thereof—between formal collective bargaining and the public budget-making process. An important study of this subject was conducted by Derber and Wagner, who examined labor negotiations during the late 1970s in twenty-seven Illinois public units (which, at the time, were not covered by a statewide public sector bargaining law).[16] The researchers found a close relationship between the bargaining and budget-making processes in those units where a tight—that is, severely constrained—economic environment existed, but a much looser connection between those two processes where a favorable economic climate prevailed. In the former governmental units, bargaining over new agreements typically was completed before or at about the same time as the submission of the budget to a legislative body for approval, whereas in the latter units bargaining proceeded well beyond budget completion deadlines. Furthermore, retroactivity of terms and conditions of employment characterized most of the negotiations that occurred in a favorable economic environment, but occurred in only one of the negotiations that took place in a tight fiscal climate. Where bargaining and budget making in public institutions are not closely integrated, public officials charged with budget-making responsibilities do not know the true costs of providing government services at the beginning of the relevant fiscal period. Hence, they often must pursue ad hoc revenue-generating measures, such as special tax assessments, to meet actual expenditures during the fiscal year — even where putatively formal prohibitions on such actions exist.

The Derber-Wagner study is also of interest because it replicates research conducted by these authors and their colleagues in the early 1970s in the same governmental units.[17] At that time, most of the units faced reasonably favorable economic environments, and the researchers found a very loose relationship, at best, between the bargaining and budget-making processes. Following the recession of 1974–1976 and the more general slowdown in the growth of the public sector (including in Illinois) during the 1970s, a more restrictive economic climate existed, particularly in some governmental units. As Derber and Wagner demonstrate, that climate generated pressures for a much closer link between bargaining and budget making in those Illinois governments.

We believe that the taxpayer revolts of the late 1970s and early 1980s, the widespread calls for improved public service productivity, and the mounting concern over federal budget deficits mean that even stronger pressures will operate on public managers and union officials during the third generation of public sector bargaining to integrate the bargaining and budget-making processes more closely. Such integration should facilitate the more realistic appraisal, and perhaps even containment, of the costs of government services, and should also enable the citizenry to hold elected officials more closely accountable for their managerial performance. To determine whether or not such consequences actually materialize, however, will require longitudinal research, including the type of research undertaken by Derber and Wagner in their examination of the relationship between bargaining and budget making in selected units of Illinois governments.

It should also be noted that Derber and Wagner reported a bimodal distribution of union responses to public employer claims (for bargaining purposes) of fiscal stringency. Roughly half of the union negotiators accepted these claims and adjusted their negotiating behavior accordingly. The other half either rejected such employer claims or contended that it was management's responsibility to obtain the funds necessary to finance the pay increases sought by the union negotiators. Derber and Wagner conclude, therefore, that the level of trust between the parties is an important determinant of the degree of integration between bargaining and budget making during periods of fiscal strain. The reader should consider this conclusion in light of the discussion in chapter 4 of integrative and distributive bargaining.

The second reading in this section, by Horton, provides one of the very few extant longitudinal studies of the interaction of the economic environment, budget making, and collective bargaining in government. Although it is a case study, it focuses on the nation's largest municipal government, namely, New York City, and also covers three distinct time periods—1970—1975, 1975–1983, 1983–1985—that constituted three distinct phases, if not generations, of collective bargaining in that municipality.

One of Horton's contributions is to show that the dominant wage allocation rule in New York City government, known as "uniform preference," prevailed in the first of the periods studied, was abandoned during the second period under conditions of major economic retrenchment, and reemerged during the third period. Also noteworthy is that relatively low paid workers in the city government improved their pay position relative to better paid workers during the period of retrenchment. Finally, Horton argues that labor (which, in New York City municipal government, means organized labor) actually increased its power over wage–employment trade-off decisions during the retrenchment period. This finding should be considered in light of private sector research showing that unions have tended to make their largest relative wage impacts during periods of economic recession.[18]

The reader should carefully appraise the analytical bases for these conclusions as well as for the unexpected finding that labor's share of total municipal government expenditure in New York City fell continually during the 1970s. Further, although this largely qualitative case study contrasts sharply with the quantitative studies of public sector union wage impacts that are summarized later in this chapter, it also contrasts with those studies in attempting to place the resource allocation decisions that flow from public sector bargaining in the larger context of political power and the budget-making process. We hope that other researchers not only will agree with Horton that "A logical next step would be a comparative study that examined how the labor-related resource allocation patterns of other governments have changed over time," but will also be motivated to conduct such studies.

Notes

1. By *relative* wages, we mean the wages of organized public employees compared to those of their unorganized counterparts. For evidence supporting this conclusion, see David Lewin, "Public Sector Labor Relations: A Review Essay," *Labor History* 18 (Winter 1977), pp. 133–144, and Richard B. Freeman, "Unionism Comes to the Public Sector," *Journal of Economic Literature* 24 (March 1986), pp. 41–86.

2. Raymond D. Horton, David Lewin, and James W. Kuhn, "Some Impacts of Collective Bargaining in Local Government: A Diversity Thesis," *Administration and*

Society 7 (February 1976), pp. 497–516, and David Lewin, Raymond D. Horton, and James W. Kuhn, *Collective Bargaining and Manpower Utilization in Big City Governments* (Montclair, N.J.: Allanheld Osmun, 1979), esp. chaps. 1 and 6.

3. David Lewin, "Local Government Labor Relations in Transition: The Case of Los Angeles," *Labor History* 17 (Spring 1976), pp. 191–213.

4. Archie Kleingartner, "Collective Bargaining between Salaried Professionals and Public Sector Management," *Public Administration Review* 33 (March–April 1973), pp. 165–172.

5. Milton Derber, "Management Organization for Collective Bargaining in the Public Sector," in Benjamin Aaron, Joseph R. Grodin, and James L. Stern, eds., *P ublic-Sector Bargaining*(Washington, D.C.: Bureau of National Affairs, 1979), pp. 80–117.

6. David Lewin, Peter Feuille, and Thomas A. Kochan, *Public Sector Labor Relations: Analysis and Readings,* 2nd ed. (Sun Lakes, Ariz.: Thomas Horton and Daughters, 1981), pp. 362–364.

7. Based on data supplied to the authors by the Office of Work Force Information, U.S. Office of Personnel Management, February 19, 1987. Between 1982 and 1986, federal employee salary increases averaged about 5.0 percent annually.

8. The Consumer Price Index for Urban Wage Earners and Clerical Workers in the United States rose as follows between 1982 and 1986: 1982–6.0%. 1983–3.0%, 1984–3.4%, 1985–3.6%, 1986–0.7%. See U.S. Bureau of Labor Statistics, *Monthly Labor Review* 109 (December 1986), p. 76.

9. See, for example, Freeman, "Unionism Comes to the Public Sector," pp. 62–66, and the sources cited in chapter 7.

10. Albert Rees, *The Economics of Trade Unions,* (Chicago: University of Chicago Press, 1977), pp. 74, 87–88.

11. Ibid., pp. 88–89.

12. This is comparable to the caveat issued by Rees, *The Economics of Trade Unions,* "In judging the consequences of union wage effects, we shall seek to compare the operation of organized labor markets with the operation of unorganized labor markets as they exist in the United States, for it would be unfair to compare the organized market with some theoretical model of a perfect market that never existed." Also see Richard B. Freeman and James L. Medoff, "The Two Faces of Unionism," *The Public Interest* 57 (Fall 1979), pp. 69–93.

13. See also Harry C. Katz and David Lewin, "Efficiency and Equity Considerations in State and Local Government Wage Determination," *Proceedings of the Thirty-third Annual Meeting of the Industrial Relations Research Association, 1980* (Madison, Wisc.: IRRA, 1981), pp. 90–98.

14. See, for example, Sharon P. Smith, *Equal Pay in the Public Sector: Fact or Fantasy?* (Princeton, N.J.: Princeton University Press, 1977); Joseph F. Quinn, "Are Postal Workers Over- or Underpaid?" *Industrial Relations* 18 (Winter 1979), pp. 124–155; Martin Asher and Joel Popkin, "The Effect of Gender and Race Differentials on Public–Private Wage Comparisons: A Study of Postal Workers," *Industrial and Labor Relations Review* 38 (October 1984), pp. 16–25; and Jeffrey M. Perloff and Michael L. Wachter, "Wage Comparability in the U.S. Postal Service," *Industrial and Labor Relations Review* 38 (October 1984), pp. 26–35.

15. "Congress Enacts Federal Salary Legislation," *The New York Times,* January 11, 1987, p. 1.

16. Milton Derber and Martin Wagner, "Public Sector Bargaining and Budget Making under Fiscal Adversity," *Industrial and Labor Relations Review* 33 (October 1979), pp. 18–23.

17. Milton Derber, Ken Jennings, Ian McAndrew, and Martin Wagner, "Bargaining and Budget Making in Illinois Public Institutions," *Industrial and Labor Relations Review* 27 (October 1973), pp. 49–62. Three of the thirty governmental units included in the initial study were not included in the follow-up study. For other research on this topic, see Stanley M. Benecki, "Municipal Expenditure Levels and Collective Bargaining," *Industrial Relations* 17 (May 1978), pp. 216–230; Daniel G. Gallagher, "Teacher Bargaining and School District Expenditures," *Industrial Relations* 17 (May 1978), pp. 231–237; and Peter Feuille, Wallace Hendricks, and John Delaney, *The Impact of Collective Bargaining and Interest Arbitration on Policing,* Final Report of the National Institute of Justice, U.S. Department of Justice, December, 1983.

18. Rees, *The Economics of Trade Unions,* chap. 3.

Wage Determination in the Public Sector

Walter Fogel
*David Lewin**

There is a growing body of evidence that government employment is attractive in terms of both wages and job security. A recent U.S. Bureau of Labor Statistics survey found that clerical, data-processing, and manual workers employed by municipalities in eleven large urban areas were substantially better paid than their counterparts in private industry.[1] In most cases, federal employees in the same cities were also paid more than comparable private sector workers. Fringe benefits in the public sector are also as good or better than those in the private sector, according to a national survey of U.S. municipalities.[2] Furthermore, job hiring and tenure practices provide considerable security to public workers: in 1971, 57 percent of nonfarm private employees worked a full year, whereas in the public sector, the proportion was 77 percent.[3] Attractive wages and salaries, steady demand for public services, and tenure practices all combine to produce low rates of employee turnover—19

---

*University of California, Los Angeles and Columbia University, respectively. Reprinted from *Industrial and Labor Relations Review* 27, no. 3 (April 1974), pp. 410–431.

percent in state and local government and 22 percent in the federal service in 1970, compared to 58 percent in private manufacturing.[4]

Because these rather surprising findings conflict with popular notions about government pay, it is appropriate to examine the process of wage determination in the public sector and the outcomes of this process for different occupational groups in government employment. Governmental wages and salaries affect the respective government budget and, therefore, the citizens' tax burden; they influence the relative attractiveness of employment in the public and private sectors; and they are an important factor in the continuing debate over the size and role of government in U.S. society.

The Prevailing Wage Principle

Almost all levels and agencies of government in this country, at the city level or higher, are required to pay wages comparable to those received by private employees performing similar work. This rule is commonly called the *prevailing wage principle*. For example, the Federal Salary Reform Act of 1962 requires that "federal pay rates be comparable with private enterprise pay rates for the same levels of work." The city of Los Angeles, one of the largest local government employers in the United States, is required by its charter to "provide a salary or wage at least equal to the prevailing salary or wage for the same quality of service rendered to private employers."[5]

These prevailing wage requirements are sensible in terms of both equity and efficiency. The output of government does not pass through the marketplace where its relative worth can be assessed by customers. In the absence of a product market discipline imposed on pay practices (a discipline that, incidentally, is not present in all parts of the private sector), what could be more fair than to pay government employees what their private industry counterparts are getting? Furthermore, to attract employees of at least average quality to the government, the pay offered must be comparable to that available in the private sector. For the government to pay more than the private sector, however, would be unnecessary and would waste government revenues. Therefore, the prevailing wage rule is efficient as well as equitable.

On the surface, the procedure seems quite simple and fair for all concerned. As one examines the applications of this rule closely, however, things appear less simple and certainly not fair for everyone. Aside from the administrative problems of applying the prevailing wage rule to an occupational structure that may include hundreds or even thousands of job classifications, this rule is dependent on the existence of smoothly functioning private labor markets. If these markets all operated like the textbook model of perfect competition, the prevailing wage rule would always provide efficient and equitable wages—and, in fact, such laws would probably not be needed at all. Private markets, however, are influenced by noncompetitive forces and also contain jobs that differ widely with respect to their nonwage attractiveness. The latter phenomenon produces a range of wage rates, rather than a single rate; the noncompetitive forces often produce a wage (or range of wages) above or below that which would prevail in a truly competitive market.

The existence of a range of wages for most occupations presents difficult administrative problems for government wage-fixing authorities. What rules should be applied to the range in order to come up with a prevailing wage? Should the average of the entire range be used, or the first quartile, or the mean, or the median? The decision could be made simpler by precisely defining the labor markets in which the government employer must compete for a work force. Rarely is this done, however. Instead, it will be shown that the more common practice is to seek wage information over the geographical area included within the governmental jurisdiction and then only from medium- and large-sized employers. Although this practice holds down the cost of wage surveys—surveying small firms or firms outside the local market is costly relative to the information obtained—it also imparts an upward bias to prevailing wage determinations, since only the core economy is surveyed. The periphery economy, which pays low wages, is excluded.[6]

Other Problems

The existence of a private sector market that pays wages that are either above or below the competitive wage presents a more difficult policy problem for governmental wage setters. Suppose a private sector wage is depressed because the market is monopsonistic or, more likely, because discrimination or other factors that impede mobility confine some workers to a small part of the total labor market. In such cases, is it appropriate for government to pay a wage that has resulted from the market power of the employer or from employee inability to compete? We will show that many government wage-setting authorities apparently think not, and in these cases they will often establish rates above those prevailing in such private markets.

This assumption is the basis for some of the support currently voiced for public employment programs. Advocates of these programs assume that governments will provide low-skilled workers with better compensation than they now receive in private "secondary" markets and hope that the scope of public employment efforts will be large enough to raise wages and improve working conditions in the secondary markets.[7] The latter objective is almost certain to be frustrated, however, since labor supply to most secondary markets is highly elastic at prevailing wages over the range relevant to feasible public employment programs.

On the other hand, suppose that a union, professional association, or licensing agency has achieved a wage above that which would otherwise prevail. For example, Lewis has estimated that, on average, U.S. unions have a 7 to 15 percent impact on the wages of those for whom they bargain,[8] and, because of their ability to influence labor supply, some unions, especially craft unions, have an even larger impact on wages. Should governments match wage rates that have been achieved through the exercise of private market power and, in effect, support and expand such power? For reasons to be stated later, we assume that, in their wage-setting actions, governments will indeed tend to match private market rates that have been raised through market power, even in instances in which lower rates would clearly attract an adequate supply of labor.

Another potential bias in government wage-setting practices occurs because of the narrow view of employment compensation contained in most prevailing wage statutes. Any reasonably sophisticated view of the labor market recognizes that the wage is merely the most variable part of employment compensation, the part that firms most easily adjust to offset other aspects of compensation (fringe benefits, working conditions, location, etc.) that are discernibly advantageous or disadvantageous. A private firm can experiment with its wage rates, relative to those of other firms, in order to discover the rates that, along with other characteristics of the firm, will attract an adequate work force. In contrast, government employers required to pay prevailing wages almost always interpret that requirement as precluding any attempt to take into account the attractiveness of nonwage aspects of government employment. As previously noted, one such nonwage aspect — job security — appears to be very attractive in government compared to the private sector. Failure to consider this difference in job security on the part of government wage setters would seem, *a priori,* to produce public wage rates that are higher than necessary to attract a work force.

Finally, for some public sector jobs (e.g., policemen, firemen, social workers), there is either no private market or, because of government's dominant employment position in these occupations, wage rates in the private market that does exist are pegged to the public sector rather than the reverse. Government employers probably overestimate the number of occupations of this type, but some do exist. How should the pay for such jobs be established?

To summarize, four aspects of labor markets create serious policy problems whenever public employers attempt to translate prevailing wage statutes into wage rates for their employees: the wide range of wages paid for most private sector jobs; the existence of wage rates established through the exercise of market power; the multifaceted nature of employment compensation; and the absence of a private market for some government occupations.[9] Because of these factors, much discretion must be exercised by public authorities in implementing prevailing wage statutes and fixing public sector wages.

It will be argued here that this discretion in decision making, plus the political processes involved in wage setting, produce upwardly biased wage rates for most government jobs.

The Politics of Wage Setting

Recently, several analysts have summarized the shortcomings of traditional wage theory in explaining public sector wage determination.[10] Major weaknesses include the absence of a motive for profit maximization in government and the related lack of a conventional demand curve for labor. Public employers' demand curves are inferred indirectly through "voter expressed demands for government services and directly through political bargaining between governments and employee groups," rather than through a marginal revenue product curve.[11] Thus, construction of a relevant public sector wage model apparently requires more explicit consideration of the motivations of public managers and public workers, as well as the political processes through which these motivations are filtered.

In his seminal work on democratic theory, Anthony Downs notes that "the main goal of every party (defined as a team of individuals) is the winning of elections. . . . Thus, all its actions are aimed at maximizing votes."[12] In pursuit of that goal, parties view the electorate as a number of interest groups, and they seek to determine and respond to the relative importance of such groups.

Thus, in their wage-setting decisions, political bodies are sensitive to two constituencies. First, there are the government employees directly affected by public wage decisions. In general, the larger the group whose wages will be affected by a legislative decision, the more responsive elected decision makers will be to the preferences of this group. The second constituency is the general public. The public is, of course, interested in keeping down its tax burden, but beyond this general constraint, it is usually uninformed and not especially interested in the specifics of government wage setting.

> In order to influence government policymaking in any area of decision, a citizen must be continuously well-informed about events therein. . . . The expense of such awareness is so great that no citizen can afford to bear it in every policy area. . . . If he is going to exercise any influence at all, he must limit his awareness to areas where intervention pays off most and costs least.[13]

Consequently,

many voters do not bother to discover their true views before voting, and most citizens are not well enough informed to influence directly the formulation of those policies that affect them.[14]

These considerations suggest that lawmakers are relatively more responsive to the first group—those directly affected by wage decisions—than to the second. Government employees will watch lawmakers' reactions to their proposed wage increases, and these reactions, especially negative reactions, can be the major determinants of employee voting behavior in subsequent elections. The general public, however, will probably not recall the lawmakers' votes on government wage questions and, furthermore, will be concerned with a variety of other issues in its voting decisions. In general, then, the combination of the direct interest of government employees in their wages and the diffusion of issues (including public sector pay issues) among the general constituency create the potential for an upward bias in public sector wage rates. Obviously, the potential bias increases with the size of the government sector in question.

Particular circumstances, of course, can operate to restrain this bias or even reverse it. At times, the public strongly opposes (further) tax increases; at these times, lawmakers are quite cautious in their wage decisions. Indeed, in these instances, lawmakers may be able to profit from negative decisions on the wages of some kinds of public employees, either because the group in question is in public disfavor or because it lacks political clout. College and university faculties are good illustrations of this phenomenon. Policemen may currently illustrate the opposite phenomenon—that is, a situation in which lawmakers gain from making positive wage decisions for a group riding the crest of public favor.

An organization of public employees will attempt to exploit this political condition. First, it will try to bring about solidarity among employees who are to be directly affected by wage decisions. Second, it will attempt to convey the force of this solidarity to the appropriate political body. Finally, it may attempt to gain broad support for its wage objectives by appealing directly to the public. At least part of the relative increase in public sector wage rates over the last ten to fifteen years is due to the effectiveness with which some public employee organizations have carried out these activities.[15]

In summary, because of the nature of the political process involved, there is a tendency for lawmakers and other elected officials to support the wage preferences of government employees. Indeed, "the position of public employees as voters and opinion-makers who partially determine whether or not the employer retains his job" has been cited as the major factor underlying motivational differences between public employers and private, profit-maximizing employers.[16] The tendency toward "high" public wages varies with the size of the group in question, its public "image," and its cohesiveness. Finally, this tendency has been increasing as government services have expanded and as employee organizations continue to develop in the public sector.

Major Patterns

In the balance of this reading, we shall present evidence showing that wage determination in the public sector tends to be characterized by the following practices:

1. Government employers deal with the range of private sector wages for any given occupation, in part, by excluding small firms from their wage surveys. This has the effect of giving an upward bias to the results of such surveys.

2. The public sector pays rates that are higher than existing private rates for jobs for which the private sector wage is relatively low because of monopsony or highly elastic supplies of unskilled laborers who are relatively immobile.

3. The public sector pays wages that are at least equal to those that exist in private markets where wage levels have been increased by supply-side institutional power.

4. Public agencies do not take into account favorable nonwage aspects of public sector employment or unfavorable aspects of private sector employment that have affected the private market wage.

5. Administrative procedures used to fix wages for "unique" public sector jobs bias the results upward.

These practices result from the effect of the political process underlying public sector wage setting on the discretionary areas inherent in the prevailing wage concept as it is applied to imperfect labor markets. The general result of these practices is that public sector wages tend to exceed those of the private sector for all occupations except high level managers and professionals. These relationships flow directly from the politicization of public sector wage determination. There are many more votes in the low-skill and middle-skill occupations than in managerial-professional jobs. Furthermore, public employees in the latter jobs tend to be more visible to a public that is skeptical, at best, of the contributions of "highly paid" government employees.

The Evidence

Government employers deal with the range of private sector wages for any given occupation, in part, by excluding small firms from their wage surveys. The Bureau of Labor Statistics (BLS) annually conducts wage surveys of (1) office clerical, (2) professional and technical, (3) maintenance and power plant, and (4) custodial and material movement occupations in more than ninety major metropolitan areas of the United States. In reporting the results of these surveys, BLS states explicitly that "establishments having fewer than a prescribed number of workers are omitted because they tend to furnish insufficient employment in the occupations to warrant inclusion."[17] Therefore, to be included in the survey in most areas, an establishment must employ at least fifty workers in manufacturing; transportation, communication, and other public utilities; wholesale trade; retail trade; finance, insurance, and real estate; or services. In twelve of the largest areas, the minimum establishment size is one hundred workers in manufacturing, transportation, communication and other public utilities, and retail trade.[18] Because wages vary directly with firm size,[19] these procedures have the effect of biasing survey results upward. Public wages set on the basis of survey rates will be similarly biased.

Since 1959 the BLS has also conducted the *National Survey of Professional, Administrative, Technical and Clerical Pay* (PATC), the results of which are used in the determination of wages for white-collar (General Schedule) civil service workers as well as employees in the postal field service and those covered by a few other statutory pay systems. Minimum establishment size requirements in this survey range from 100 employees in most industry divisions to 250 employees in manufacturing and retail trade. As in the area wage surveys, exclusion of relatively small, low-wage establishments results in upwardly biased wages in the PATC survey.

State and local government employers, especially those with large labor forces, sometimes undertake their own wage surveys. For example, in Los Angeles, four local public jurisdictions jointly conduct an annual survey of wages and salaries in Los Angeles County. To be included in this survey, an establishment, regardless of its industry classification, must employ more than 250 persons. Industry coverage parallels that of the BLS survey.

The exclusion of small establishments from public wage surveys produces both a direct and indirect upward bias in the survey results. The direct bias occurs, of course, because of the positive relationship that exists between size of firm and wage levels. The indirect bias occurs from the overrepresentation of high-wage industries and underrepresentation of low-wage industries produced by the exclusion of small establishments. For example, wholesale and retail trade accounted for only 9 percent of surveyed employment in Los Angeles County in 1970, when actually 26 percent of all workers in that county were employed in those industries. On the other hand, employment in the manufacturing and utilities-transportation sectors is over-represented in this survey.[20]

The magnitude of the bias produced by the exclusion of small firms from wage surveys is probably large. Approximately 60 percent of all nonfarm private sector employees work in establishments employing fewer than 250 employees.[21] Such workers are likely to be paid 15 to 20 percent less than employees of establishments with 1,000 or more employees.[22]

Low-Wage Jobs

The public sector pays more than existing private rates for jobs for which the private sector wage is relatively low because of monopsony or highly elastic supplies of unskilled laborers who are relatively immobile. Rather than ferret out the existence of monopsony and labor supply characteristics of private labor markets, we will present evidence on the simpler proposition that, for *most low-wage occupations, government pays more than the private sector.*

Table 1 shows that there is proportionately more low-wage employment in the private sector of the American economy than in the governmental sector. For example, among full-time, year-round, privately employed workers, about 12 percent earned less than $4,000 and 42 percent earned less than $7,000 in 1971, when the comparable proportions in the public sector were only 6 and 30 percent. Note that the proportion of low-wage employment is particularly small in the federal government, in which the median annual salary was $11,809 in 1971.[23] The relative advantage of the public sector would be increased by inclusion of private self-employed workers in the comparisons and, of course, by inclusion of part-time and part-year workers.

These public-private differences in earnings distributions could reflect differences in occupational composition rather than rates of compensation. Table 2, therefore, presents salary comparisons for low-wage occupations common to municipal, federal, and private employment in eleven large cities, including five of the six U.S. cities with populations over one million. In nine of these cities, municipal governments consistently paid higher salaries than private employers in 1970. Only in New Orleans and Kansas City did private sector pay exceed municipal pay for the occupations listed. The size of the municipal–private differential is often substantial. Of the 56 observations in table 2, 27 show a municipal wage advantage of 10 percent or more, and 19 show a municipal advantage of at least 20 percent.[24] It should be remembered as well that the private sector wages that are used to make the comparisons in table 2 contain some upward bias, since they do not encompass the rates paid by small establishments.

The superiority of municipal over private pay in major U.S. cities is fur-

Table 1

Earnings Distribution for Full-Time, Year-Round Wage and Salary Workers in the United States, by Sex and Employment Sector for 1971
(in percentages)

Employment Sector and Sex	Earnings below				
	$3,000	$4,000	$5,000	$6,000	$7,000
Private sector					
Male	3.4	6.5	11.3	18.2	26.3
Female	11.4	25.7	45.0	64.3	77.9
Average	5.8	12.3	21.5	32.1	41.8
Public Sector State and local government					
Male	1.5	3.6	7.2	12.5	19.8
Female	4.4	10.8	20.3	32.3	45.8
Average	2.6	6.4	12.4	20.3	30.1
Federal government (both sexes)	0	1.6	2.7	6.6	16.2

Source: U.S. Bureau of the Census, "Money Income in 1971 of Families and Persons in the U.S.," *Current Population Reports,* Series P-60, no. 85 (Washington, D.C.: Government Printing Office, 1972), tables 52 and 58, pp. 135–138; and U.S. Civil Service Commission, *Pay Structure of the Federal Civil Service* (Washington, D.C.: Government Printing Office, June 30, 1971), tables 11–14, pp. 29–32.

ther accentuated when hours of work are considered. In Los Angeles, Houston, Kansas City, and Atlanta, municipal white-collar employees worked a "standard" 40-hour week in 1970, but in Philadelphia the work week for these employees was 37.5 hours; in Chicago, Boston, New Orleans, and Buffalo, it was 35 hours; in Newark it was only 30 hours; and in New York City, municipal employees worked a 35-hour week for nine months and a 30-hour week during the remainder of the year.[25] Although these differences in work schedules partially reflect differences in area practices generally, the municipal work week is typically shorter than the work week in private employment. For example, in New York City in 1970, "96 percent of the white-collar workers in local government worked 35 hours or less per week as compared with 58 percent of private office workers."[26] Thus, pay differentials between municipal and private employment are even greater when considered on an hourly rather than a monthly basis.

The pattern of relatively high government pay for low-skill occupations may be even more pronounced in suburban areas than in central cities. This very tentative conclusion emerges from analysis of recently published data, presented in table 3, on the salaries of local government workers in New York City area. For the individual occupations shown in that table, average salaries in the two types of suburban governments ranged from 18 percent

Table 1
A Comparison of Monthly Salaries in Municipal Government and Private Industry in Seven Low-Wage Occupations and Eleven Cities for 1970
(private industry salary = 100)

Occupation	Equivalent Federal Salary (GS) Grade	New York	Chicago	Los Angeles	Phila-delphia	Houston	Newark	Boston	New Orleans	Kansas City	Atlanta	Buffalo
Messenger	1	114	98	107	136	123	125	107	86	–	–	–
Keypunch op.–B	2	102	101	120	114	111	120	103	91	95	104	115
Switchboard op.–B	2	105	112	134	–	142	107	–	105	–	119	135
Typist–B	2	102	105	123	142	–	107	102	89	101	102	122
Tab. mach. op.–C	2	109	107	–	140	–	–	–	–	–	–	–
Tab. mach. op.–B	3	–	103	–	131	–	–	114	83	–	112	–
Janitors, porters, and cleaners	–	98	137	122	131	124	109	127	88	95	100	111

Source: Stephen H. Perloff, "Comparing Municipal Salaries with Industry and Federal Pay," Monthly Labor Review 94, no. 10 (October 1971), tables 1–3, pp. 47–50.

Table 3
Average Weekly Earnings for Janitors and Office Clerical Occupations in New York Area Local Government for April 1970

Occupation	New York City Municipal Government Earnings (dollars)	New York Area Earnings at a Percentage of New York City	
		Counties	Suburban Cities and Towns
Typist—B	102.50	102	100
Messenger	103.00	102	112
Keypunch operator—B	106.00	108	116
General stenographer	107.50	102	107
Accounting clerk—B	108.00	116	113
Transcribing machine operator—B	111.00	101	94
Janitors, porters, cleaners	111.20	112	113
Bookkeeping machine operator—B	113.50	118	100
Switchboard operator—B	114.00	97	106
Senior stenographer	125.00	113	111

Source: U.S. Department of Labor, Bureau of Labor Statistics, Wages and Benefits of Local Government Workers in the New York Area, Regional Reports, no. 26, December 1971 (Washington, D.C.: Government Printing Office, 1972), tables 2, 4, and 6; and pp. 16, 21, and 25.

Note: Includes New York City municipal government and the governments of five counties and fifty-three cities and towns located in the New York standard metropolitan statistical area.

above to 6 percent below those in New York City. In only two cases, however, did suburban pay fall below central city pay in the New York area. Pay differentials between New York counties and the city exceeded 10 percent in four occupations; differentials between suburban municipalities and New York City exceeded 10 percent in five occupations. It is possible, of course, that this differential is neutralized by similar differentials in private industry salaries between the suburbs and the central city.

Relatively high minimum wages in government employment are sometimes explicitly mandated by legislative statute. In 1970, for example, the salary ordinance governing the largest local government employer in Southern California, the county of Los Angeles, required that, "notwithstanding any other provisions of this ordinance, the minimum salary for all positions . . . shall be $417 per month . . . or $2.40 per hour, as the case may be."[27] Similarly, the city of Los Angeles required that

the salary rate of any person . . . employed in any class, the salary schedule of which is fixed at Schedule 23 or lower, and who is receiving salary at a lower rate than the third step of the schedule for such class . . . shall be increased to the third step of the schedule prescribed for his class of position.[28]

The city's statute resulted in a minimum wage of $2.54 per hour in 1969. Minimum wages in the county and city of Los Angeles were thus 50 percent and 59 percent higher respectively than the minimum hourly wage of $1.60 then mandated for private employment under the Fair Labor Standards Act. These ordinances account for at least some of the public-private differentials that exist in the Los Angeles area, as shown in table 2 and also, using different sources and data, in table 4.

There is at least one important occupation, however, in which government wage levels have often accurately mirrored monopsony (low-wage) conditions in the private market. This is the case of hospital nurses as described by Devine.[29] Private labor markets for hospital nurses are frequently characterized by monopsony, with the local hospital association serving as the cartelizing agency. Devine's survey of hospital associations in major metropolitan areas found each one maintaining in the mid-1960s a "wage stabilization" program for nurses. These collusive agreements were predicated on the view that it is "undesirable for council members to enter into a competitive race among themselves to see which can offer the most favorable conditions of employment."[30]

Table 4
Median Monthly Salaries in Low-Skill Occupations in the Private and Public Sectors for the County and City of Los Angeles, Fiscal Year 1969–1970

| | Median Monthly Salary (dollars) | | | Differences between Public and Private Sectors (percentages) | |
| | | Public Sector | | | |
Occupation	Private Sector	County Government	City Government	County	City
Laundry worker	287	428	—	49.1	—
Institutional food service worker	358	447	—	24.9	—
Hospital attendant	385	453	—	17.7	—
Clerk	385	428	464	11.1	20.5
Clerk typist	418	447	489	6.9	17.0
Custodian	447	489	491	9.4	9.8
Gardener	495	—	591	—	19.4
Transcriber typist	480	518	—	7.9	—
Bookkeeping machine operator	475	489	516	2.9	8.6
Telephone operator	474	489	505	3.1	6.5
Vocational nurse	494	577	—	16.8	—

Sources: Derived from City of Los Angeles *et al.*, *Wage and Salary Survey in Los Angeles County*, March 1, 1969 (Los Angeles: City of Los Angeles, Printing Division, 1969); County of Los Angeles, *Salary Ordinance of Los Angeles County*, Ordinance no. 6222, as amended to July 1, 1969; and City of Los Angeles, City Administrative Officer, *Salary Recommendations* (processed, April 1969).

Although local government hospitals are typically not enrolled in the hospital associations, their wage policies (and rates) do reflect institutional wage determinations in the private sector. Municipal hospitals have continually incurred shortages of nurses (vacancy rates have sometimes exceeded 20 percent in recent years; this is about three times larger than the average overall vacancy rate in local government employment).[31] In the late 1960s, for example, the county of Los Angeles experienced a 27 percent vacancy rate in its hospital nursing positions, and vacancy rates for nurses in New York City municipal hospitals were about 60 percent![32] Salaries for nurses in each of these cities were based on rates set by the respective local hospital associations. Not surprisingly, both of these cities invested heavily in recruitment activities, frequently extending their search for nurses nationwide. The federal government, on the other hand, experienced less severe shortages of nurses than local governments (and some private hospitals), apparently because, under administrative provisions of the Federal Salary Reform Act of 1962, federal hospitals raised their nurses' salaries well above those offered by other hospitals.

In recent years, the loosening of cartel arrangements among private hospitals, along with a more aggressive collective bargaining stance among nurses' unions, have contributed to a substantial improvement in the relative wage position of hospital nurses, including those employed by government.

Craft Wages

The public sector pays wages at least equal to those that exist in private markets where wage levels have been increased by supply-side institutional power. Among U.S. unions, market power is perhaps most strongly exercised by construction unions. Moreover, governmental pay policies have broadened the wage impact of construction unions in the private sector and have extended it to public employment.

For example, at the federal level, the Davis-Bacon Act requires private contractors engaged in construction work valued at $2,000 or more and paid for by federal funds to compensate employees on the basis of prevailing wages. Secretaries of labor have generally considered the union rate to be the prevailing rate even in nonunion areas. Consequently, "unions need only secure a wage increase in a few locations where their control of the labor supply is firm . . . and under the law the government extends the wage gain far and wide."[33] It is little wonder that this act has been labeled a "superminimum wage law."[34]

At the state and local level, especially in very large cities, this approach has been carried one step further: through explicit policy or administrative practice, government craft employees are often paid construction industry rates and frequently only the union rates within construction. In these cases, public employers ignore the lower wages paid by nonconstruction employers for the same jobs. This practice undoubtedly accounts, at least in part, for the relatively high salaries for public craft workers in five of the eleven major cities for which data are presented in table 5.

Public employers are not unaware of the substantial public–private differentials for craft workers. In Los Angeles, for example, local government employers annually obtain data on craft wages in all sectors of the private market. Yet, when setting wages for municipal craft workers, these employers discard all market rates obtained through their survey and adopt, instead, construction industry-negotiated wage levels. This occurs despite important differences (to be discussed later) in the characteristics of craft employment between the public and private sectors. Consequently, an analysis of the 1969 local agency survey (not the BLS data reported in table 5) showed that Los Angeles government agencies paid craft workers salaries that were between 10 and 46 percent higher than those paid by private employers, and those differences would have been even larger if small (low-wage) employers had been included in the government's wage survey.[35]

Nonwage Factors

Public agencies do not take into account favorable nonwage aspects of public sector employment or unfavorable aspects of private sector employment that have affected the private market wage. As previously noted, government employment generally offers more favorable fringe benefits, employment stability, and job security than private employment. Yet government employers fail to take this into account when establishing their own wage rates.

In addition to the evidence previously cited of the favorable nonwage aspects of much government employment,[36] it is useful to examine comparative turnover data in more detail. Among thirty-three federal agencies reporting separation data, only three—Interior, Agriculture, and the Tennessee Valley Authority—experienced rates higher than those experienced by manufacturing industries in 1972, and the layoff rate along was 75 percent lower in the federal service than in manufacturing.[37] Although state governments experienced about the same separation rate as the federal sector (22 percent) in 1970, county and city governments experienced rates only three-quarters and two-thirds as large respectively as the federal government's.[38] These rates are especially significant in light of the fact that local governments employ more than two and one-half times as many workers as state governments in the United States.

The failure of public employers to consider the nonwage aspects of employment is most generally shown by the methods commonly used to

Table 5
Municipal Salaries as a Proportion of Private Industry Pay in Selected Crafts, 1970
(private industry salary = 100)

Occupation	New York	Chicago	Los Angeles	Phila-delphia	Houston	Boston	New Orleans	Kansas City	Atlanta	Buffalo	Newark
Carpenter, maintenance	162	125	118	106	91	91	76	80	98	88	141
Electrician, maintenance	162	148	121	107	113	–	87	87	91	82	141
Helper, maintenance trades	–	–	–	113	–	99	–	–	–	83	171
Painters, maintenance	136	108	107	114	95	101	75	81	100	93	139
Plumbers, maintenance	160	111	121	113	–	–	–	–	–	–	144

Source: Stephen H. Perloff, "Comparing Municipal Salaries with Industry and Federal Pay," *Monthly Labor Review* 94, no. 10 (October 1971), p. 49.
Note: Comparisons are of monthly salaries.

implement the prevailing wage rule. When they are undertaken, governmental wage surveys generally solicit only wage and salary information. Recently, the Department of Labor expanded some (but not all) of its area wage surveys to include selected fringe benefits, such as work scheduling, paid vacations and holidays, and health and welfare plans.[39] Most state and local public employers, however, have not similarly intensified their survey efforts, and the government has not yet sought unemployment or turnover data from private employers as part of its wage-setting process. Thus, public employers focus too narrowly on wages to the exclusion of other factors determining comparative net advantage in the labor market.

Inconsistent treatment of nonwage differences in employment is shown by pay determination procedures for public craft occupations. On the one hand, the higher public fringe benefits are often recognized by setting public wages for these jobs at the level of unionized industry rates minus some percentage reduction for the superior fringe benefits paid by the public jurisdiction. On the other hand, use of the negotiated construction rates ignores the fact that most public sector craft employees are more fully employed and apparently perform much more nonconstruction work (for which private sector wages are lower) than private sector construction workers. These procedures help to bring about heavy civil service filing and waiting lists for most craft occupations in many cities.[40]

Unique Jobs

Administrative procedures used to fix wages for "unique" public sector jobs bias the results upward. Various methods are used to set pay for jobs unique to the public sector.[41] Although these procedures do not uniformly result in upwardly biased wage rates, on balance, they have probably escalated rates beyond efficient levels.[42]

Because private market wage data are unavailable for jobs exclusive to government, public administrators often set pay for these positions on the basis of interagency or intergovernmental comparisons. For example, in Los Angeles, the Department of Water and Power, a city agency with independent salary-setting authority, has historically been a high-wage employer, compensating some uniquely public occupations at rates more than 20 percent above those of other departments. Because of this, city agencies in similar positions face continual upward pressures on wages, even in cases in which substantial civil service eligibility and waiting lists are maintained.

The county of Los Angeles determines pay for social work, probation, property appraisal, sanitation, and inspection positions by comparing its rates with those of the ten other largest counties in California and then making any pay adjustments required to maintain at least a third-place ranking among these governments.[43] Because the county is the principal employer of public service personnel in southern California, its wage decisions set the pattern for other governmental bodies in the area. To the extent that the other large California counties (and local governments) make similar pay comparisons, this practice creates the potential for circular wage escalation in positions exclusive to the public sector.

A procedure that establishes wage rates for many "unique" public employees is the "parity" arrangement. Wage parity between policemen and firemen is especially widespread; this arrangement was adhered to by more than 60 percent of all U.S. municipalities in 1969. Because of dissimilarities between the labor markets for police and firefighters, the parity rule probably results in the underpayment of police and certainly the overpayment of firefighters, judged by market criteria.[44]

Shortages of police and excess supplies of firefighters are well known and widespread. In Los Angeles, the police vacancy rate in 1970 was about twice that for all other occupations, a situation that mirrors the national pattern. New York City, which has the country's largest police and fire departments, reports substantial queues for fire positions and, like Los Angeles, administers entrance examinations for the fire service only once every two to three years. In contrast, New York has experienced shortages in the police ranks and has counteracted this by investing heavily in the recruitment of police applicants and offering police entrance examinations several times each year.[45] The attractiveness of a firefighter's job, compared to a police officer's at the same salary, is further reflected in a recent study that found that among a cohort of 1,915 men appointed to the New York City Police Department in 1957, 38 percent of those who left over the next eleven years obtained jobs with the city's fire department![46] No firemen transferred to the city's police force during the same period.

In some cities, sanitation workers are treated as a component (with police and firefighters) of the uniformed services. Where this occurs, there exists pressure for a more expanded form of wage parity—tripartite parity. Although sanitation workers have not yet achieved outright parity with police, and are generally paid about one-quarter less than police, the differential in 1970 was only about 15 percent in the largest cities (those with populations of more than one million) and about 13 percent in northeastern cities.[47] In New York, sanitation workers now earn 90 percent of police base pay, up from 60 percent in 1940, and the differential is even smaller when interdepartmental variation in overtime scheduling is considered. Because of this wage level, New York City experiences substantial queuing for positions in the sanitation service.

It has been suggested that pay for uniquely public jobs should be based on private sector wages for "occupations . . . to which individuals of comparable training and interests might be attracted."[48] Thus, in some cities, police and fire salaries are based on rates paid to skilled trades occupations in the local labor market, on the assumption that the two occupational groups attract persons of similar characteristics.[49] Aside from its dependence on a market sector that is strongly influenced by union power, this is not an unreasonable procedure, provided that its results are periodically checked against job turnover and vacancy experience.

A widely practiced procedure for dealing with exclusively public jobs is to establish their wage *levels* at a point in time by some system of internal job evaluation or salary comparisons and to base subsequent wage *increases* on the average rate of wage change occurring in the local private labor market. This is a generally commendable technique and is practically the only means of setting wages for some public jobs. All job evaluation systems, however, incorporate a large element of subjectivity and, consequently, are subject to the politicization process described earlier.

Two important occupations almost exclusive to the governmental sector—teachers and social workers—appear not to conform to our generalization about the upward bias in wage determination for unique jobs. Until recently, wage levels for these occupations were not high enough to equate supply with demand.[50] If the salaries of teachers and social workers had been based on salaries paid in alternative occupations, such as the salaries of college graduates with business administration degrees, the result would have been considerably higher wages for these public occupations. So far as is known, however, this inferential method was never employed for teachers and social workers. One possible explanation for the teacher–social worker experience is that most employees in those occupations are women, and public wage fixing for them may have reflected general discrimination against women.

The Total Wage Structure

Public sector wages tend to exceed those of the private sector for all occupations except high-level managers and professionals. Evidence demonstrating a tendency for public wages to exceed private levels for low-skilled and craft occupations has already been presented. There is ample information showing the reverse relationship for high-level occupations.

The National Manpower Council noted in 1964 that

> government employers have been handicapped by the salaries they offer . . . scientific, professional and managerial and executive personnel. . . . The discrepancy between public and private compensation for these categories of personnel . . . are larger on the upper rungs of the salary ladder.[51]

Table 6
Relationship of Federal Salaries to Private Industry Salaries for Selected Occupations, 1972

Occupation and Job Grade	Average Annual Salary for Private Industry (dollars)	Annual Federal Salaries as a Percentage of Private Industry Salaries
File clerk I (GS 1)	4,602	109
File clerk II (GS 2)	5,027	113
Messenger (GS 1)	5,087	99
Typist I (GS 2)	5,229	109
Keypunch operator I (GS 2)	5,756	99
Accounting clerk I (GS 3)	5,870	109
Typist II (GS 3)	6,093	105
General stenographer (GS 3)	6,181	104
File clerk III (GS 3)	6,214	103
Draftsmen–Tracer (GS 3)	6,288	102
Engineer VI (GS 13)	21,402	96
Attorney IV (GS 13)	23,443	88
Engineer VII (GS 14)	24,367	99
Director of personnel IV (GS 14)	24,738	98
Chemist VII (GS 14)	25,888	93
Chief accountant IV (GS 14)	26,521	91
Attorney V (GS 14)	27,528	88
Engineer VIII (GS 15)	27,885	101
Chemist VIII (GS 15)	30,827	91
Attorney VI (GS 15)	34,828	81

Source: Derived from U.S. Department of Labor, Bureau of Labor Statistics, *National Survey of Professional, Administrative, Technical and Clerical Pay, March, 1972,* Bulletin 1764 (Washington, D.C.: Government Printing Office, 1973), app. D, pp. 68–69.

Table 6 presents federal government–private industry salary comparisons for the ten lowest and ten highest ranking positions included in the most recent *National Survey of Professional, Administrative, Technical and Clerical Pay.* These data show that in 1972, for jobs with GS 1 through GS 3 classifications, the federal government paid between 1 percent less and 13 percent more than private industry, whereas for jobs with GS 13 through GS 15 grades, federal salaries ranged between 1 percent above and 19 percent below private salaries. In the same year, the highest pay schedule in government, that for the federal executive branch, contained salaries ranging from $36,000 to $60,000—well below the $144,000 median salary then paid to the chief executive officers of the United States' 774 highest paying corporations.[52] Although progress has been made, the conclusion reached ten years ago by the Advisory Panel on Federal Salary Systems still holds: "Federal agencies . . . lag far behind private employers in the monetary rewards they can offer executive and managerial . . . personnel even though they have duties and responsibilities equal to or greater than any to be found in private enterprise.[53]

Similar relationships between public and private occupational pay exist in state and local government. An analysis of wage data for one hundred governmental job classifications in Los Angeles produced public-private wage ratios ranging between 153.3 for the lowest ranked position (Laundry Worker) to 76.5 for top-ranking executive jobs (Health Officer, M.D., and County Counsel). Moreover, eight of the twelve lowest ranked positions in these governments had ratios exceeding 100 percent, whereas all sixteen highest ranked occupations had ratios below 90 percent.[54] The low salaries of city managers and chief executive officers in major cities, as displayed in table 7, provide additional support, when compared to the average salary of $144,000 of top executives in industry, of the fact that the occupational pay structure is more compressed in the public sector than in private industry.

Some observers believe, however, that the U.S. Bureau of Labor Statistics exaggerates the content of federal jobs when it conducts wage surveys of "comparable" private sector jobs. This charge has never been publicly documented, to the best of our knowledge, but it is clear that if such a bias in public–private job comparisons does exist, then a public-over-private wage differential extends farther up the occupational hierarchy than is shown by the available wage data. Unless the bias is greater for high- than low-level jobs, however, the finding of a more compressed wage structure for the public sectory is still valid.

Table 7

Average Salaries for Chief Administrative Officers or City Managers of Selected Major U.S. Cities, 1971

(in dollars)

City	Mean Salary
Atlanta	29,068
Boston	27,500
Chicago	31,000
Dallas	40,452
Los Angeles	42,888
New York	45,000
Philadelphia	34,000
Phoenix	37,500
Seattle	25,188
Washington, D.C.	36,000

Source: International City Management Association, *The Municipal Yearbook—1971* (Washington, D.C., 1972), p. 244.

Conclusion

The available data indicate that public — private pay relationships in the United States can be explained, at least in part, by a combination of two factors: the discretion that public employers must exercise in implementing the prevailing wage rule adopted by most cities and larger government units and the nature of the political forces that affect governmental wage decisions. The result is an occupational pay structure that is more "equalitarian" in the public sector than that in private industry, in the sense that public employers tend to pay more than private employers for low-skill and craft jobs and to pay less for top executive jobs.[55]

It is not appropriate for us to render a judgment about the equity of the public sector wage structure. The collective judgment of the American people may be that government wage structures should be more equalitarian than those existing in private industry. This is doubtful, however, since the relevant political pressures work toward producing that kind of public wage structure without benefit of any implicit or explicit public judgment about the equity question.

We can, however, draw a conclusion about the market efficiency of the public sector wage structure, and that conclusion is negative. Government employers frequently pay more than necessary to attract a work force at the low- and middle-skill ranges and generally pay less than necessary to attract employees of average quality at the upper managerial and professional levels. It is doubtful that high worker productivity offsets the high public wages, although research on this question is needed.[56]

Given the great increase in the number of college graduates expected during this decade, the public wage structure may well be a precursor of a general restructuring of wage relationships in society as the wages of highly educated workers suffer a relative decline. Such restructuring, however, is far from certain,[57] and until it occurs there is need for a dialogue on whether the equity benefits of the public sector wage structure are worth their costs in efficiency.

Finally, Ehrenberg has recently presented evidence confirming a widely held view that employment elasticities in state and local government are very low. Thus, "market forces do not appear to be sufficiently strong to limit the size of real wage increases which state and local government employees may seek in the future."[58] Consequently, he suggests, and we agree, that careful attention should be given to the evolving structure of collective bargaining in the public sector.

Notes

1. Stephen H. Perloff, "Comparing Municipal Salaries with Industry and Federal Pay," *Monthly Labor Review* 94, no. 10 (October 1971), pp. 46–50.

2. Edward H. Friend, *First National Survey of Employee Benefits for Full-Time Personnel of U.S. Municipalities* (Washington, D.C.: Labor Management Relations Service, October 1972). As an example, municipal workers in New York City receive four weeks' paid vacation after just one year of service. In New York's private industries, less than one-fourth of plant and one-third of office workers are eligible for four weeks' vacation, *even after fifteen years' service.* See U.S. Department of Labor, Bureau of Labor Statistics, *Wages and Benefits of Local Government Workers in the New York Area,* Regional Reports, no. 26 (Washington, D.C.: U.S. Government Printing Office, 1971), pp. 40–42.

3. U.S. President, *Manpower Report of the President—March, 1973* (Washington, D.C.: U.S. Government Printing Office, 1972), table B-16, p. 185. Also see Bennett Harrison, "Public Employment and the Theory of the Dual Economy," in Harold L. Sheppard, Bennett Harrison, and William J. Spring, eds., *The Political Economy of Public Service Employment* (Lexington, Mass.: D.C. Heath and Company, 1972), pp. 66–67.

4. Jacob J. Rutstein, "Survey of Current Personnel Systems in State and Local Governments," *Good Government* 87 (Spring 1971), p. 6; and U.S. Civil Service Commission, Bureau of Manpower Information Systems, *Federal Civilian Manpower Statistics* (Washington, D.C., May 1971), table 6, p. 14. See also, Robert E. Hall, "Turnover in the Labor Force," *Brookings Papers on Economic Activity,* no. 3 (Washington, D.C.: Brookings Institution, 1972), p. 715. The data cited in the text are separation rates.

5. Charter of the City of Los Angeles, Section 425. Also see *Pay Policies for Public Personnel: A Report of the Municipal and County Government Section of Town Hall,* (Los Angeles, 1961), p. 15.

6. These concepts underlie developing theories of labor market behavior. See Harrison, "Public Employment and the Theory of the Duel Economy," especially pp. 45–55; and Barry Bluestone, "The Tripartite Economy: Labor Markets and the Working Poor," *Poverty and Human Resources* 6 (July–August 1970), pp. 15–35.

7. See Sheppard, Harrison, and Spring, *The Political Economy of Public Service Employment,* pp. 13–82.

8. H. Gregg Lewis, *Unionism and Relative Wages in the United States* (Chicago: University of Chicago Press, 1963), p. 193.

9. We have purposely avoided some additional largely administrative problems of governmental wage determination, for example, deciding which public jobs should be directly compared with their private sector counterparts. These problems are reviewed in David Lewin, "The Prevailing Wage Principle and Public Wage Decisions," *Public Personnel Management* 3 (November–December, 1974), forthcoming.

10. Robert J. Carlsson and James W. Robinson, "Toward a Public Employment Wage Theory," *Industrial and Labor Relations Review* 22, no. 2 (January 1969) pp. 243–248; Donald Gerwin, "Compensation Decisions in Public Organizations," *Industrial Relations* 9, no. 2 (February 1969), pp. 175–184; Robert J. Carlsson and James W. Robinson, "Criticism and Comment: Compensation Decisions in Public Organizations," *Industrial Relations* 9, no. 1 (October 1969), pp. 111–113; and James A. Craft, "Toward a Public Employee Wage Theory: Comment," *Industrial and Labor Relations Review* 23, no. 1 (October 1969), pp. 89–95.

11. Mark V. Pauley, "Discussion Comments: Manpower Shortages in Local Government Employment," *American Economic Review* 59, no. 2 (May 1969), p. 565.

12. Anthony Downs, *An Economic Theory of Democracy* (New York: Harper and Row, 1957), p. 35.

13. Downs, *An Economic Theory of Democracy,* p. 258.

14. Ibid., p. 259.

15. The other major influence over this period has been the growth in the number of public employees, as this number (votes) has been brought to bear on the wage-setting process.

Some authors casually assign a large wage impact to public employee unions. Cf. Harry H. Wellington and Ralph K. Winter, Jr., *The Unions and the Cities* (Washington, D.C.: Brookings Institution, 1971), especially pp. 7–32. Yet, as Lewin suggests, the extent to which government wage increases are due to unionization as distinct from the increasing politicization of public wage-setting processes is not clear. See David Lewin, "Public Employment Relations: Confronting the Issues," *Industrial Relations* 12, no. 3 (October 1973), pp. 309–321.

16. Bernard Lentz, *Public Sector Wage Determination: A Democratic Theory of Economics* (Ph.D. dissertation, Yale University, 1976). Stanley notes further that "employees in the public sector exert influence not only as employees, as do private workers, but also as pressure groups and voting citizens." See David Stanley, *Managing Local Government Under Union Pressure* (Washington, D.C.: Brookings Institution, 1972), p. 20.

17. See, for example, U.S. Department of Labor, Bureau of Labor Statistics, *Area Wage Survey, The Los Angeles–Long Beach and Anaheim–Santa Ana–Garden Grove, California, Metropolitan Area, March 1972,* Bulletin no. 1725-76 (Washington, D.C.: U.S. Government Printing Office, 1972), p. 1.

18. U.S. Department of Labor, Bureau of Labor Statistics, *Wage Differences Among Metropolitan Areas, 1970–71* (Washington, D.C., July 1972), p. 1. Major exclusions from BLS wage surveys are construction, the extractive industries, and government.

19. See Richard A. Lester, "Pay Differentials by Size of Establishment," *Industrial Relations* 7, no. 1 (October 1967), pp. 57–67.

20. David Lewin, "Wage Determination in Local Government Employment" (Ph.D. dissertation, University of California, Los Angeles, 1971), pp. 77–110. The Los Angeles survey does not weight its sample results to reflect the actual industry composition of the county.

21. U.S. Bureau of the Census, *County Business Patterns: 1970* (Washington, D.C.: U.S. Government Printing Office, 1971), p. 29.

22. Lester, "Pay Differentials by Size of Establishment," p. 59.

23. U.S. Civil Service Commission, Bureau of Manpower Information Systems, *Pay Structure of the Federal Civil Service, June 30, 1971* (Washington, D.C., 1971), table 2, p. 18. The data are for domestically employed general schedule employees.

24. As a proportion of private pay, municipal salaries for the entire group of 16 office clerical positions surveyed by the BLS were as follows: New York—101; Chicago—108; Los Angeles—118; Philadelphia—133; Boston—109; New Orleans—93; Kansas City—97; Atlanta—108; Buffalo—122; and Newark—106. Perloff, "Comparing Municipal Salaries with Industry and Federal Pay," table 2, p. 49.

25. Ibid., table 1, pp. 47–48.

26. U.S. Department of Labor, Bureau of Labor Statistics, Middle Atlantic Regional Office, *Wages and Benefits of Local Government Workers in the New York Area,* Regional Report no. 26 (Washington, D.C.: Government Printing Office, December 1971), p. 53.

27. County of Los Angeles, *Salary Ordinance of Los Angeles County,* Ordinance no. 6222, as amended to July 1, 1969, p. 30.

28. City of Los Angeles, *Salary Standardization Ordinance,* Ordinance no. 89, 100, revised to September 20, 1966, amended to July 1, 1969, p. 25.

29. Eugene J. Devine, *Analysis of Manpower Shortages in Local Government* (New York Praeger, 1970), pp. 49–62. For econometric support of the monopsony thesis, see R.W. Hurd, "Equilibrium Vanacies in a Labor-Market Dominated by Non-Profit Firms: The 'Shortage' of Nurses," *Review of Economics and Statistics* 50 (May 1973), pp. 234–240.

30. Devine, *Analysis of Manpower Shortages in Local Government,* p. 56.

31. During 1970, vacancy rates of 6.6 and 6.7 percent were reported for counties and cities respectively. See Rutstein, "Survey of Current Personnel System in State and Local Governments," p. 6.

32. Devine, *Analysis of Manpower Shortages in Local Government,* pp. 51, 57.

33. James W. Kuhn, "The Riddle of Inflation: A New Answer," *The Public Interest* 27 (Spring 1972), p. 73.

34. Gordon F. Bloom and Herbert R. Northrup, *Economics of Labor Relations,* 7th ed. (Homewood, Ill.: Richard D. Irwin 1973), p. 493.

35. Derived from Lewin, "Wage Determination in Local Government," pp. 187–190.

Because construction unions have recently shown increased willingness to exercise market power, the differences between public and private sector craft wages are probably even larger than suggested here. By 1972, the hourly earnings of construction workers were about 60 percent more than those of manufacturing workers; in 1947, the differential was little more than 25 percent. See U.S. President, *Manpower Report of the President—March 1973* (Washington, D.C., 1972), table C-3, pp. 190–191.

36. See the first paragraph of this reading and the sources cited in notes 2, 3, 4.

37. Derived from U.S. Civil Service Commission, Bureau of Manpower Information Systems, *Federal Civilian Manpower Statistics* (Washington, D.C., March 1973), tables 7 and 8, pp. 17–18.

38. Rutstein, "Survey of Current Personnel Systems in State and Local Governments," p. 6. In this survey, counties reported a separation rate of 16.6 percent, cities 14.5 percent.

39. See U.S. Department of Labor, Bureau of Labor Statistics, *Area Wage Survey, The Newark and Jersey City, New Jersey, Metropolitan Areas, January 1972,* Bulletin 1925–52 (Washington, D.C., 1972), pp. 28–35.

40. Lewin, "Wage Determination in Local Government," pp. 165, 196–198; and Devine, Analysis of Manpower Shortages in Local Government, table 5 and 6, pp. 42–43.

41. Some jobs commonly regarded as unique to government, such as teaching and protective service positions, are also found in private markets. In this section,

we discuss occupations for which government is an exclusive or dominant employer.

42. The method of salary setting for . . . classes peculiar to the public service . . . may have raised the cost of government without a demonstrated need to increase these salaries as high as they have gone." See Louis J. Kroeger *et al., Pricing Jobs Unique to the Government* (Chicago: Public Personnel Association, n.d.), p. 5.

43. Lewin, "Wage Determination in Local Government Employment," pp. 260–275.

44. For further analysis of this issue, see David Lewin, "Wage Parity and the Supply of Police and Firemen," *Industrial Relations* 12, no. 1 (February 1973), pp. 77–85.

45. David Lewin and John H. Keith, Jr., "Managerial Responses to Perceived Labor Shortages: The Case of Police," processed (New York: Columbia University, 1974).

46. Bernard Cohen and Jan M. Chaiken, *Police Background Characteristics and Performance* (New York: New York City Rand Institute, August 1972), p. 45.

47. See Urban Data Service, Stanley M. Wolfson, *Salary Trends for Police Patrolmen, Firefighters and Refuse Collectors* (Washington, D.C.: International City Management Association) vol. 4, no. 10 (October 1972), pp. 5–6. These data are for cities with populations in excess of 100,000.

48. Kroeger *et al., Pricing Jobs Unique to Government,* p. 4.

49. See the Jacobs Company, *Report on Police and Fire Classification and Pay Studies,* City of Los Angeles (Chicago: Jacobs Company, 1970), p. 31.

50. Devine, *Analysis of Manpower Shortages in Local Government,* pp. 39 – 44, 103–120.

51. National Manpower Council, *Government and Manpower* (New York: Columbia University Press, 1964), pp. 34–35.

52. Derived from "Who Gets the Most Pay," *Forbes,* May 15 , 1972, pp. 205–236. The cited federal salaries exclude those of the president and vice-president.

53. National Manpower Council, *Government and Manpower,* pp. 159–161.

54. David Lewin, "Aspects of Wage Determination in Local Government Employment," *Public Administration Review* 34, no. 2 (March–April 1974), pp. 149–155.

55. Obviously, we do not purport to explain all elements of public wage structures. For example, we suspect that in some regions and in relatively nonurban areas, public sector wages are comparatively low. If, indeed, this is correct, our hunch wouldbe that the politica forces described in this article, particularly public worker organization, have not developed very far in these areas.

56. A strong believer in the efficiency of markets might argue that high government wages attract highly qualified workers but that productivity is unaffected because government agencies are unable or unwilling to identify and hire these workers or are unable to use them efficiently when they are employed.

57. See Lester Thurow, "Education and Economic Equality," *The Public Interest* 28 (Summer 1972), pp. 66–81.

58. Ronald G. Ehrenberg, "The Demand for State and Local Government Employees," *American Economic Review* 53, no. 3 (June 1973), p. 378.

Fiscal Stress and Labor Power
Raymond D. Horton*

Labor power in government has challenged theorists since collective bargaining was introduced to the public sector some two decades ago. Its early conceptualization drew on the axiom that public and private organizations are "essentially different," most notably because governments, unlike firms, are not subject to competition. Thus, public employees were viewed as holding substantial latent power that could be manifested if somehow they were able to capitalize on government's "inherent" monopoly power. Unionism and collective bargaining were seen as changes in the formal "rules of the game" that would facilitate the transfer of power (for some, "sovereignty") from elected officials to organized bureaucrats, thereby making them more powerful in labor–management relations than either their industrial counterparts or unorganized colleagues (Wellington and Winter 1971). And since collective bargaining would help insulate organized employees from whatever countervailing demands were operative in the "normal" political process, they also would enjoy a "structural" edge in the competition for community power with nongovernmental groups (Horton, 1973; Summers, 1974).

Gradually, however, labor power in government has come to be seen as conditional despite collective bargaining rather than inherent because of it. An early formulation of this perspective grew out of a comparative study of labor relations decisions in several big-city governments, including governments with collective bargaining and governments without collective bargaining in which the authors suggested that environmental factors, including local politics and economics in particular, might be more important determinants of labor power than the presence of collective bargaining (Lewin, Horton, and Kuhn, 1979). This "diversity" theory of labor power, so called because it stressed variance in the settings of American public administration and predicted diverse patterns of labor power therein, was supported by subsequent research conducted on the mid-1970s slowdown – and reversal in some celebrated cases like New York City – of growth trends in the state and local sectors.

Collective bargaining continued during the period of "fiscal stress," but changes in the bargaining process and in bargaining outcomes suggested that

*Columbia University. Reprinted from *Proceedings of the Thirty-Eighth Annual Meeting.* Madison, Wisc.: Industrial Relations Research Association, 1986, pp. 304–315.

collective bargaining did not, ratchetlike, protect labor power when employer finances deteriorated (Derber and Wagner, 1979; Lewin and McCormick, 1981). Aggregate trends in public employee compensation suggesting decreased labor power after the mid-1970s recently have been reconciled with earlier trends by a "good times, bad times" theory that draws on the earlier work of Rees (1977): during good times, when the public sector expands, labor power increases; during bad times, when the public sector stops growing or retrenches, labor power decreases (Lewin, 1986). The view that collective bargaining in government provides organized employees an inherent structural advantage that translates into increased power, at least relative to unorganized public workers, still has its adherents (Lieberman, 1983; Zax, 1985), but increasingly labor power in government is conceived of as being dependent on the variable of employer finances.

This reading studies labor power in New York City municipal government between 1970 and 1985 (union power in this case because nearly all of the city's employees are represented by a union for the purpose of collective bargaining). During this period municipal expenditures rose, fell, and rose again. By examining the allocation of public expenditure to labor, the allocation of public expenditure between compensation and employment, and the allocation of public expenditure for compensation among competing employee groups during these successive periods of growth, retrenchment, and growth, it is possible to gain some understanding of how changes in employer finances affected important dimensions of labor power. The reading's methodology rests on the premise that power in an organization is best measured by examining decisional outcomes, a positivist approach that reflects the utterance of an early-twentieth-century social scientist: "The budget is the skeleton of the state stripped of all misleading ideologies" (Goldscheid, 1964, p. 204).

Fiscal Stress and Allocation of Financial Resources

Table 1 establishes that the city of New York experienced the successive periods of growth, retrenchment, and growth noted before.[1] In the 1970–1975 period, operating expenditures rose sharply, 23 percent in constant or inflation-adjusted terms. In 1975, however, the city's creditors stopped financing its operating deficits and precipitated a cash-flow crisis that threatened bankruptcy. To avoid bankruptcy, new loans were made contingent on the city taking steps to eliminate its deficit—primarily by reducing expenditures rather than raising revenues. Municipal employee pension funds, along with local businesses, the state of New York, and the federal government, loaned the city the capital required to avoid bankruptcy (Boast and Keilin, 1979). While the budget was restored to balance in 1981,

Table 1
Trends in New York City Government Operating Expenditures, Labor Costs, Employment, Compensation, and Salaries: Fiscal Years 1970–1975, 1975–1983, and 1983–1985

(expenditures and labor costs in millions of 1970 dollars; compensation per employee and selected salaries in 1970 dollars)

Item	1970	1975	1983[a]	1985	Percentage Change		
					1970–1975[a]	1975–1983[a]	1983–1985[a]
Expenditures[b]	$6,154	$7,587	$6,351	$7,024	23.3%	−16.3%	10.6%
Labor costs[b]							
Total	$3,661	$3,981	$3,133	$3,635	8.7	−21.3	16.0
Share of expenditures	59.5%	52.5%	49.3%	57.8%	—	—	—
Employment							
Total	275,211	285,856	236,057	251,720	3.8	−17.4	6.6
Share of labor cost change	—	—	—	—	44.8	81.7	41.2
Compensation per employee							
Total	$13,302	$13,927	$13,272	$14,508	4.7	−4.7	9.3
Share of labor cost change	—	—	—	—	54.0	22.1	58.1
Selected salaries[c]							
Uniformed employee	$10,425	$11,689	$10,616	$11,210	12.1	−9.2	5.6
Civilian employee (low paid)	$6,667	$6,697	$6,217	$6,502	0.4	−7.2	4.6
Civilian employee (high paid)	$13,334	$13,394	$11,859	$12,404	0.4	−11.5	4.6

Sources: Expenditure and labor cost data from *Comprehensive Annual Report of the Comptroller*, 1970, 1975, 1983, and 1985 editions; the expenditure data were adjusted to account for reporting practices beginning in 1978 that removed Medicaid expenditures of the state of New York and federal government from the city's operating budget. Employment data from New York State Financial Control Board and the New York City of Management and Budget Salary data from New York City Office of Municipal Labor Relations', and data are the annual salary rates on the first day of the fiscal year. Adjustments to 1970 dollars were made on the basis of the Bureau of Labor Statistics' Consumer Price Index for All Urban Consumers (CPI-U) for the New York–northeastern New Jersey area.

Note: Column totals may not add due to rounding.

[a]The salary data in these columns are for 1984 rather than 1985 in order to recognize a change in wage relationships resulting from collective bargaining effective in 1984.

[b]The City of New York's accounting system was changed during the 1976–1978 period, thus the expenditure and labor cost data shown for 1970 and 1975 may not be fully consistent with the 1983 and 1985 data.

[c]Uniformed employee salary data are for Police Officer First Class, but the percentage changes are representative of all uniformed employees due to pay parity rules. The civilian employees' base salary data are hypothetical, but the salary changes throughout the period are actual.

retrenchment continued through 1983. During the 1975–1983 period, expenditures fell 16 percent. Growth resumed in 1984 and continued through 1985, totaling 11 percent in that two-year period alone.

Labor economists divide between those who measure labor (or typically, union) power by examining total labor expenditure and those who focus more narrowly on wages or total compensation per employee (Dertouzos and Pencavel, 1981). The rates of change in these conventional, albeit different, measures of labor power varied somewhat, but the trends were consistent with the "good times, bad times" hypothesis in each case: table 1 shows that labor spending, compensation, and wages all rose in the 1970–1975 growth period, fell in the 1975–1983 retrenchment period, and rose again in the 1983–1985 growth period.

Labor power, however, can be conceived of in a larger setting in which public employees compete with other groups for public expenditure. From this perspective, the best evidence of labor power is not absolute changes either in wages or total labor spending but, rather, changes in labor's share of total public expenditure. Was labor's "community power," as well as its power over wages and total labor spending, affected by fiscal stress? True to the hypothesis that labor power is affected by employer finances, labor's share of expenditure fell from 53 percent at the beginning of retrenchment to 49 percent at the end of retrenchment. Thus, labor suffered disproportionate cuts compared to nonlabor beneficiaries of public expenditure. During the growth period following retrenchment, moreover, labor's share of expenditure rose from 49 percent to 52 percent, indicating that labor enjoyed disproportionate gains during the most recent growth period. This also is consistent with the "good times, bad times" hypothesis. However, during the 1970–1975 growth period the share of labor spending fell from 60 percent to 53 percent (and at a sharper rate than during retrenchment). What accounts for this decline in labor's community power during a period of spending growth, and what are its implications for theories of labor power in government?

Labor's declining share of public expenditure in the 1970–1975 growth period resulted because during that period the local political system placed a higher value on the expenditure of its marginal dollars for other groups than labor, a triad that includes creditors who loan money to the city and seek to have it repaid with interest; suppliers who provide other factors of production (such as space and materials) as well as contractual services; and the dependent poor who are direct recipients of public expenditure through transfer payments. Notwithstanding the fact that public employees were able to realize absolute gains in both wages per employee and total labor spending prior to retrenchment, their power relative to nonlabor competitors fell. During retrenchment, when the allocation issue involved distributing a smaller supply of financial resources, New York City's government continued its preference for nonlabor expenditures by reducing them less than labor's allotment. It was not until the resumption of growth in 1984 that the municipal government placed a higher priority on labor expenditures than nonlabor expenditures. By decomposing spending for all claimants of public expenditure it is possible to identify more specifically which groups were "winners" and which were "losers" in the competition for public expenditure in the 1970–1985 period (Brecher and Horton, forthcoming). For the purposes of this reading, however, the significant point is that labor power, at least from the perspective of community power, declined prior to and thus independently of retrenchment or fiscal stress.

Thus the New York City experience supports the "good times, bad times" theory of labor power if labor power is conceived of as the ability to increase either the absolute level of wages per employee or total labor spending, the conventional means of measuring power employed by labor economists; however, if power is conceived of more broadly as the ability to compete successfully with other competitors, then the hypothesis is not supported—at least in the 1970–1975 period. The implications of this deviant period for the study and theory of labor power in government are discussed more fully in the concluding section.

Fiscal Stress and the Compensation–Employment Trade-off

Just as an organization must decide how much of its financial resources to allocate to labor, it also must decide how to divide those financial resources between spending for compensation and spending for employment. Does fiscal stress also affect resolution of the compensation–employment trade-off? Generally speaking, employees are thought to prefer resolution of the trade-off in favor of compensation; hence, one might hypothesize that fiscal stress would reduce labor's influence over the trade-off.

The decomposition of spending for labor into the components of employment and compensation per employee shown in table 1 indicates that employment increases accounted for nearly 45 percent of the increase in spending for labor in the 1970–1975 growth period and 41 percent of the increase in the 1983–1985 growth period. During retrenchment, however, when both employment and compensation fell, work force cuts accounted for 82 percent of the decline in labor costs. Why were municipal employees better able to assert their presumably desired resolution of the employment–compensation trade-off during retrenchment? And why, after retrenchment ended and labor's power over the budget increased, was labor less able to resolve the trade-off to its presumed advantage?

The answer to this seeming paradox appears to lie in the concept of "interest intensity" (Emerson, 1982; Bacharach and Lawler, 1981). According to this concept, the ability of a group to secure its interests in a competitive environment partly reflects the intensity with which it pursues its interests or goals and, conversely, the intensity with which other groups pursue conflicting goals. Was labor interested in protecting compensation at the expense of employment during the retrenchment period? One might reason that public employees, facing what seems a Hobson's choice between their jobs and their compensation, would have preferred to trade compensation for employment, particularly since labor market opportunities elsewhere in New York City were limited by the local economy's loss of 600,000 jobs—one-sixth of the total—in the 1969–1977 period.[2] Such an interpretation assumes, however, a degree of uncertainty about which employees would bear the costs of workforce reduction. It was municipal policy to make work force cuts by attrition when possible, and when layoffs were made they were determined by nonrandom seniority rules (Horton, 1985). Thus, only a small share of the city's employees faced a Hobson's choice given the rules governing work force reduction; most could prefer protecting their compensation with a high degree of certainty that others would bear the consequences.[3]

But what of union leaders, who sometimes have preferences that conflict with those of their members (Ashenfelter and Johnson, 1969)? Their Hobson's choice seemingly was between the size of union memberships and treasuries, on the one hand, and, on the other, "their own personal political survival" (Ehrenberg and Smith, 1985, p. 385). To the extent union leaders were interested in their own tenure, they apparently were more secure leading organizations with fewer but better paid voter/members than organizations with more but lesser paid voter/members.

That employees and their union leaders seem to have had strong preferences for trading employment for compensation under circumstances of fiscal stress does not, in and of itself, provide a complete explanation for their ability to do so. Did not municipal managers prefer the opposite trade with as much intensity as municipal employees, and did they not have increased leverage under conditions of fiscal stress to realize their preferences? In theory, yes; in fact, no. No "countervailing" managerial assertion to protect employment at the expense of compensation was made. Why? Because throughout most of the retrenchment period management was preoccupied with avoiding bankruptcy and, later, with balancing the budget. Remember, too, that municipal employee pension funds provided capital needed to avoid bankruptcy. Under the circumstances, management goals for resolution of the trade-off were more consistent than conflictual with labor's goals. Later, when budgetary balance was realized and the capital markets were reopened to the City, municipal priorities shifted to service improvements that were to be realized primarily by expanding the work force (Horton, 1985); under these circumstances, management's stake in resolution of the employment—

compensation trade-off was clearer, and labor power over the compensation-employment trade-off declined.

Fiscal Stress and Power Relationships among Employees

To this point, the analysis has focused on municipal employees as a group seeking to maximize its control over the city's financial resources and the allocation of those resources between spending for employment and spending for compensation. However, competition also exists among various employee groups over the allocation of spending for compensation. Did fiscal stress affect power relationships among municipal employee groups? By tracing changes in salary relationships it is possible to answer the question, if not explain it.

Historically, the dominant wage allocation rule in New York City government has been a "uniformed preference" rule whereby line employees who work in police, fire, sanitation, and corrections services receive larger percentage salary increases than civilian employees. The selected salary data in table 1 show that this rule was operative in the 1970–1975 period. During retrenchment real salaries of all employees fell, but wage compression occurred. Salaries of lower paid civilian workers fell the least, 7.2 percent; salaries of higher paid civilians fell the most, 11.5 percent; and uniformed salaries fell 9.2 percent. However, in the first round of bargaining after the retrenchment phase (covering the 1984–1987 period), contracts provided successive 6 percent annual increases for uniformed workers but only 5 percent, 5 percent, and 6 percent increases for civilian employees. What accounted for the hiatus during retrenchment of the wage allocation policy favoring uniformed employees over civilians?

The abatement of the uniformed preference rule appears to have been related to the development of coalition bargaining during retrenchment, an adaptation stemming in part from the fear of union leaders that the institution of bargaining was threatened and in part from their belief that they would have more influence over bargaining outcomes if they negotiated collectively rather than singly (Lewin and McCormick, 1981). The solidarity achieved by having virtually all of the city's civil service unions sitting together on one side of the bargaining table, as was the case during negotiations for labor contracts covering the 1976–1980 period, presumably made it more difficult for uniformed unions to "beggar their neighbors" by demanding the preferential treatment they had enjoyed historically. Why, though, were uniformed employees unable to bargain even as successfully as low-paid civilians during retrenchment? A review of the bargaining rounds during the retrenchment period suggests an answer.[4]

In the 1976–1978 period wages were frozen through collective bargaining between the city and a grand coalition of municipal employee unions; however, the first hint of a new wage allocation rule appeared when the previously negotiated 6 percent increase for all workers in 1976 was deferred in whole or in part depending on how much employees earned. In the 1978–1980 round of negotiations, one in which the grand coalition included all of the major unions except those of police officers and firefighters, all employees received successive 4 percent increases; however, what might be called an "equity" rule of wage allocation was introduced when all employees in 1980 had $441 folded into their salary base for the purpose of computing their negotiated 4 percent increase. This had the effect of raising the salaries of lower paid workers relative to higher paid workers. In negotiations for the 1980–1982 contracts the grand coalition divided into separate coalitions of civilian and uniformed workers; uniformed workers, no longer negotiating in solidarity with civilian workers, received a 9 percent increase in 1981 and an 8 percent increase in 1982 compared to successive 8 percent salary increases for civilians. In the 1982–1984 round, the uniformed coalition splintered, but the civilian coalition endured. On the face of things, uniformed groups again appeared to negotiate better contracts, receiving successive 8 percent settlements compared to 8 percent and 7 percent increases for civilians; however, a flat amount, $750, once again was added to the base pay of all workers for the purpose of computing their 1983 increases, a reassertion of the equity rule. As table 1 shows, the net effect of these serial bargaining outcomes during retrenchment was to raise low-paid civilian wages relative to salaries of higher paid workers. In the 1984–1987 round, however, the civilian coalition fragmented, and uniformed employees once again received a larger salary increase.

The analysis suggests that fiscal crisis promoted coalition bargaining, and that this, in turn, differentially affected the bargaining power of employee groups. During the depths of the fiscal crisis, when the coalition of unions was most inclusive, the uniformed preference rule was replaced with a wage policy that treated all employees the same. As the city's finances began to improve later in the retrenchment period, the grand coalition divided into separate coalitions of uniformed and civilian employees. During this period wage policy vacillated between the traditional uniformed preference rule and an equity rule, depending apparently on the cohesiveness of the respective civilian and uniformed coalitions. In the most recent round, with the fiscal crisis a thing of the past and with no bargaining coalitions operative, the uniformed preference rule of allocating wages was restored.

Conclusion

Retrenchment caused many changes, behavioral adaptations, in the management of New York City government, enough to suggest that public organizations are not necessarily the unmanageable leviathans caricatured by many theorists (Brecher and Horton, 1985). Of special interest to labor, behavioral changes occurred in the way the city of New York allocated its financial resources, resolved the compensation-employment trade-off, and divided wages among competing groups of employees. These behavioral changes reflected changes in power relationships, unless one assumes that the decisions by which public resources are allocated are determined on some other basis. The ability of public employees to maintain wages, to maintain total labor spending, and to maintain their share of public expenditure was reduced during the period of retrenchment; however, labor's influence over the tradeoff between compensation and employment increased; and finally, lower paid civilian workers were able to raise their wages relative to higher paid workers, including uniformed employees, during retrenchment.

Of course, the experience of a single government provides little basis for generalizing about the effect of fiscal stress on labor power or for evaluating the broader "good times, bad times" hypothesis. A logical next step would be a comparative study that examined how the labor-related resource allocation patterns of other governments have changed over time. (By including both bargaining and nonbargaining governments in such a study it also would be possible to investigate the two dominant but hitherto unintegrated theories of labor power in government in a single study utilizing the same data base.)

What insights from this case study of New York City might be worth considering in a broader and more systematic study of labor power in government? Perhaps the most important is that while fiscal stress may diminish labor power, it is not the only condition under which labor power may decline. Remember the "deviant" years between 1970 and 1975, when overall expenditures were growing but labor's share of those expenditures was declining. That experience illustrates that political preferences—and political power—over the allocation of resources may change independently of changes in the supply of resources. Labor may be unable to retain its share of the budget or, more conventionally, to maintain wage levels or total labor spending when overall spending is stable (or even rising) if political preferences change and accord other groups higher priority. Such conditions, from labor's perspective at least, represent "political stress" and are not necessarily dependent on the existence of fiscal stress. To the extent further analysis incorporates changing political preferences, or politics, into the theory of labor power, its predictive capacity will be enhanced.

A second point relevant to further study of labor power in government suggested by this study is the difficulty of building behavioral theory on the basis of static concepts of "interest." The interests or goals of organizational actors change. The presumption that labor's declining power over the budget during retrenchment would spill over to declining power over resolution of the compensation–employment trade-off was wrong, at least in New York City, because of the underlying assumption that managerial goals would conflict with labor goals. In fact, during retrenchment the dominant goals of the city's managers were to stay out of bankruptcy and to balance the budget—both goals that were easier to realize with labor's capital. Managers in other governments that experience fiscal stress but without the immediate threat of bankruptcy may have acted more in keeping with traditional behavioral assumptions and with different consequences for labor power.

The New York City experience also suggests that fiscal stress may alter the distribution of power among competing groups of employees. A comprehensive theory of labor power in government should take into account such effects. The experience in New York City, where low-paid workers were able to increase their wages relative to high-paid workers as a result of the emergence and subsequent splintering of bargaining coalitions, may not be typical; like the other specific findings of this paper, this one awaits validation or rejection from broader scrutiny.

Notes

1. Fiscal stress in this reading is equated with retrenchment or an absolute decline in public expenditure (adjusted for price changes). Since the demand for organizational expenditure almost always outstrips the supply of organizational resources, organizations experience some degree of stress in allocating their financial resources whether they are shrinking, stable, or growing. Analytically, then, fiscal stress is a difficult concept to operationalize unless it refers to an absolute decline in financial resources. While resource allocation is no less redistributive under retrenchment than growth, its redistribution character is believed to be more visible when "the pot gets smaller." This, according to the fiscal stress hypothesis, induces behavioral adaptations that weaken labor's power and increase the influence of at least some other competitors for public expenditure.

2. U.S. Department of Labor, Bureau of Labor Statistics, *Employment and Earnings, States and Areas, 1939–1978.*

3. While some municipal employees were laid off during the fiscal crisis, most of those who were prejudiced by the decision to trade employment for compensation were New Yorkers who would have become municipal employees but for imposition of attrition. In a sense, the political system "privatized" some of the costs of resolving the employment–compensation trade-off as it did. Had work force reduction been accomplished entirely by layoffs, and if layoffs had been determined randomly, as in a lottery, it is likely that labor's "interest" would have been to trade compensation for employment.

4. For a more detailed description of the individual rounds of bargaining during the retrenchment period, see Citizens Budget Commission, "Toward a More Responsible Wage Policy" (July 1984), pp. 7–10.

References

Ashenfelter, Orley, and George Johnson. "Bargaining Theory, Trade Unions, and Industrial Strike Activity." *American Economic Review* 59 (March 1969), pp. 35–49.

Bacharach, Samuel B., and Edward J. Lawler. *Bargaining.* San Francisco: Jossey-Bass, 1981.

Boast, Thomas, and Eugene Keilin. "Debt and Capital Management." In *Setting Municipal Priorities, 1980,* eds. Raymond D. Horton and Charles Brecher. Montclair, N.J.: Allenheld, Osmun, 1979. Pp. 79–111.

Brecher, Charles, and Raymond D. Horton. "Retrenchment and Recovery: American Cities and the New York Experience." *Public Administration Review* 45 (March–April 1985), pp. 267–274.

———. *Governing New York City: Politics in the Post-Industrial Metropolis.* New York: Oxford University Press, forthcoming.

Derber, Milton, and Martin Wagner. "Public Sector Bargaining Under Fiscal Adversity." *Industrial and Labor Relations Review* 33 (October 1979), pp. 18–23.

Dertouzos, James N., and John N. Pencavel. "Wage and Employment Determination Under Trade Unionism: The International Typographical Union." *Journal of Political Economy* 89 (December 1981), pp. 1162–1181.

Ehrenberg, Ronald G., and Robert Stewart Smith. *Modern Labor Economics.* New York: Scott, Foresman, 1985.

Emerson, R.M. "Power-Dependence Relations." *American Sociological Review* 27 (1982), pp. 31–40.

Goldscheid, Rudolph. "A Sociological Approach to Public Finance." In *Classics in the Theory of Public Finance,* eds. Richard A. Musgrave and Alan T. Peacock. New York: S. Martin's Press, 1964.

Horton, Raymond D. *Municipal Labor Relations in New York City: Lessons of the Lindsay-Wagner Years.* New York: Praeger, 1973.

———. "Human Resources." In *Setting Municipal Priorities, 1986,* eds. Charles Brecher and Raymond D. Horton. New York: New York University Press, 1985, pp. 170–203.

Lewin, David. "Public Employee Unionism and Labor Relations in the 1980s: An Analysis of Transformation." In *Unions in Transition,* ed. Seymour Martin Lipset. San Franciscod: Institute for Contemporary Studies, 1986, pp. 241–264.

Lewin, David, Raymond D. Horton, and James Kuhn. *Collective Bargaining and Manpower Utilization in Big City Governments.* Montclair, N.J.: Allenheld, Osmun, 1979.

Lewin, David, and Mary McCormick. "Collective Bargaining in Municipal Government: New York City in the 1970s." *Industrial and Labor Relations Review* 34 (January 1981), pp. 175–190.

Lieberman, Myron. "Educational Reform and Teacher Bargaining." *Government Union Bulletin* 4 (Summer 1983), pp. 59–71.

Rees, Albert. *The Economics of Trade Unions,* 2d ed. Chicago: University of Chicago Press, 1977.

Summers, Clyde W. "Public Employee Bargaining: A Political Perspective." *Yale Law Journal* 83 (1974), pp. 1156–1200.
Wellington, Harry, and Ralph K. Winter, Jr. *The Unions and the Cities*. Washington, D.C.: Brookings Institution, 1971.
Zax, Jeffrey S. "Municipal Employment, Municipal Unions, and Demand for Municipal Services." National Bureau of Economic Research. Working Paper no. 1728, October 1985.

The Impact of Unions on Public Sector Wages

The reading by Bartel and Lewin in this section and the others that will be summarized herein generally follow the approach developed by H. Gregg Lewis for estimating the impact of unions on wages in the private sector.[1] The measure of the effect of unions used in that study is the extent to which a union raises the wage of its members above the wages of comparable unorganized workers. Usually this is presented as a ratio of the union to nonunion wage, expressed in percentage terms. Numerous studies of this type have been carried out on samples of private sector employees and have provided a wide range of estimates of the average effect of unions on wages. In general, it has been shown that the relative impact of unions tends to be strongest during recessionary periods, since unions make it difficult for employers to reduce the wage or drastically moderate the rate of wage increase. Both union and nonunion employers have incentives to increase wages during periods of relatively full employment irrespective of their workers' union status.

Overall, as Rees notes, the relative wage impact of unions has varied over time and across occupational groups.[2] He concludes that unions had their peak wage impact during the Great Depression of the 1930s. At that time, according to his analysis of the evidence, the relative union effect was 25 percent or more. By the end of the decade, however, as inflation occurred and employment expanded, the union impact decreased to between 10 and 20 percent. The decline continued through World War II and beyond, so that by 1947 the relative union wage impact was only between 0 and 5 percent. Since the late 1940s and up to the mid-1970s, Rees estimates the union impact to have been between 15 and 20 percent, but cautions that some of the stronger unions, such as those in the construction trades, may have had considerably larger relative wage impacts.

A more recent summary of the evidence by Johnson essentially reinforces Rees's findings.[3] Johnson, however, adds further estimates of the union impact on an individual worker's wage; these range up to a maximum of 33 percent in some cases. Furthermore, the impact of unionism on an individual's wage varies across age, education, and racial groups. In summary, Johnson concludes that unions in the private sector have had their strongest effects on the wages of blacks, very young and very old workers, and those with lower levels of education.

An even more recent comprehensive review of the private sector union wage impact research has been provided by Freeman and Medoff.[4] Taking account of such important econometric issues as omitted, mismeasured, and unobserved variable bias, simultaneous equations bias, and sample selection bias, Freeman and Medoff conclude that the findings about union wage effects are important, real, and not artifacts of the analytical and methodological frameworks used to study them. In other words, there is considerable evidence from research conducted through the early 1980s to support the conclusion, stemming from Rees, that the average union relative wage impact in the private sector of the United States is in the 15 to 20 percent range.

Note also that Freeman and Medoff concluded that "the union fringe [benefit] effect . . . [is] . . . considerably greater in percentage terms than the union wage effect."[5] Beyond the obvious importance of this conclusion in and of itself, the evidence to support it comes from more than just an occasional study. Thus, in the 1980s, it can fairly be said that private sector researchers are redressing the historical imbalance between union wage impact studies, which have been voluminous, and union fringe benefit impact studies, which have heretofore been sparse.

There are essentially three ways to apply this type of analysis to the wage impacts of public sector unions. The first is to examine wages of union and nonunion employees at a single point in time, that is, cross-sectionally. The second, only rarely applied to public workers, is a longitudinal or time series analysis comparing the wages of employees during the period prior to unionization (and collective bargaining) with the wages established through collective bargaining after employees have unionized. The third, also only rarely applied to public workers, is to compare the wages of individual unionized and nonunion workers over time—a methodology that may become more widely used now that longitudinal data on samples of workers are more readily available.[6] In all three types of analysis, the researcher must develop a model which effectively controls for the impacts of economic, political, and institutional factors other than unionization and bargaining on wage levels or wage changes. Thus the accuracy of any estimate of union wage impacts depends partly, indeed largely, on the ability of the researcher to specify adequately other causal variables affecting the dependent variables.

Most of the studies produced so far have done a relatively good job of isolating economic forces other than unionism that affect public employee wages. Some progress is also being made in capturing political and institutional characteristics affecting bargained wage outcomes. For example, the impacts of government structure and the political climate of the community on public employee wages have been examined in several studies.[7] Some researchers have attempted to include in their analyses variables measuring the nature of the law governing bargaining in the public sector, the nature of impasse procedures, and the rate of strike activity among public employees.[8] In our judgment, these all represent steps in the proper direction. Further progress is needed, however, before most practitioners would be confident that the critical institutional factors affecting wage and fringe benefit settlements in the public sector have been adequately captured within existing analytical frameworks. The reader need only recall the characteristics of public sector wage determination and budget making that were discussed earlier to appreciate this point.

A further problem that confronts those attempting to assess the average effects of unions on wages within the models and methodologies outlined here concerns the spillover effects of union wage settlements. This problem arises because nonunion employers sometimes look at settlements negotiated by unionized employers and then adjust their own wage structures accordingly, either in order to continue to attract workers of equal quality or to avoid creating an incentive for their own employees to unionize. To the extent that this type of spillover occurs, the ratio of union to nonunion wages declines, and, therefore, estimates of the impact of unions on public sector wages are biased downward. Although this problem has long plagued industrial relations researchers, recent public sector studies have made important progress in attempting to resolve it. Several investigators have used a variety of ingenious adjustments to measure the geographic and occupational spillovers of union wage settlements.[9] As expected, to the extent that they have been able to account for the effects of these spillovers, the researchers' estimates of public sector union wage impacts are increased.

Two other problems are encountered in seeking to isolate the impact of unions on public sector wages. Both are treated in the single reading included in this section, by Bartel and Lewin. The first of these problems concerns fringe benefits. It is well recognized that fringe benefits are an important and growing portion of compensation in both the public and private sectors, and also that unions negotiate with employers over such benefits. Consequently, studies that are limited to the pay outcomes of public sector bargaining may be missing a key area of union impact. The absence of suitable data has prevented most researchers from investigating this issue, but Bartel and Lewin were able to analyze fringe benefit data from municipal police departments, and they report that the impact of police unions on such fringes exceeded the impact on direct pay.[10] (The reader should pay particular attention to the limitations of this portion of the Bartel-Lewin reading, limitations that the authors themselves point out.)

The second problem is more complex, concerning as it does the determinants of wages *and* unionism in the public sector. Consider that although many factors, including unionism, may determine the level of wages (or wage changes) for a certain type or group of employees, many factors, *including perhaps the level of wages,* may determine whether or not workers are organized. Most studies of union wage impacts, whether in the private or public sector, have examined only the determinants of wages and, thus, have treated unionism as an independent or exogenous variable. But if the level of wages is one of the factors (variables) determining unionism, then it may be erroneous to treat unionism as exogenous; instead, it should be treated as endogenous. This is what Bartel and Lewin do as they formulate separate wage and union equations in a simultaneous determination model.

Testing this model with wage and unionism data from 215 municipal police departments, Bartel and Lewin report two key results:

1. The measured impact of unionism on police wages (in 1973) doubled to around 14 percent when the simultaneous determination of wages and unionism (rather than only the determination of wages) was considered.

2. The demand for unionization among police—the probability of a police union existing in a municipal police department—was greater in low wage cities.

Thus, American police apparently are most likely to unionize for the purpose of raising their relatively low salaries and seem to have been reasonably effective in actually raising those salaries. The reader is advised to consider carefully the quantitative techniques, the distinction between unionism and collective bargaining (that is, the CONTRACT variable), and the treatment of public sector bargaining laws in the Bartel-Lewin reading. Those who are especially interested in this subject may care to peruse some recent studies of private sector union wage impacts—studies that also employ simultaneous equation models but that reach conclusions somewhat different from those offered by Bartel and Lewin.[11]

Furthermore, the Bartel-Lewin study is only one among many that deal with public sector union wage impacts. To place this study in perspective, we provide in table 6–3 a summary of many studies reported in the literature through the mid-1980s.[12] Viewed as a whole these studies suggest that, on average, the relative wage impact of public employee unions is in the 10 to 15 percent range. This relatively larger estimate than was made in the first and second editions of this book stems largely from more recent research that has controlled for (or measured) the spillover effects of public sector bargaining. Recognize, however, that these estimates are still lower than those produced for the private sector. Note also from the studies in table 6–3 that the wage impacts of teacher and hospital employee unions are generally smaller than the impacts of unions of protective service workers, particularly firefighters, and that the studies that employ data for samples of individual workers (instead of occupations, departments, or services) report comparatively large union wage effects. On balance, we interpret these findings to provide sup-

Table 6–3
A Summary of Public Sector Union Wage Impact Studies

Author(s)	Employee Group and Year(s) of Data	Major Finding(s)
Kasper (1970)	Teachers, 1967–1968*	Insignificant; adds 0%–4% to average salary.
Ashenfelter (1971)	Firefighters, 1961–1966	Significant; adds 6%–16% to hourly wage.
Thornton (1971)	Teachers, 1969–1970*	Significant; adds 23% to highest step, 1%–4% to all other steps.
Baird and Landon (1972)	Teachers, 1966–1967*	Significant; adds 4.9% to beginning salary.
Hall and Carroll (1973)	Teachers, 1968–1969*	Significant; adds 1.8% to average salary.
Schmenner (1973)	Teachers, police-fire, other municipal employees	Mixed results, some significant, some not. Adds 0%–15% to beginning salaries and/or average earnings.
Ehrenberg (1973)	Firefighters, 1969	Significant; adds 2%–18% to hourly wage.
Ehrenberg and Goldstein (1975)	Ten categories of non-educational municipal employees, 1967	Significant; adds 2%–16% to average monthly earnings.
Lipsky and Drotning (1973)	Teachers, 1967–1968*	Insignificant over entire sample; significant in subsample, adding 0%–15% to salary change.
Freund (1974)	Municipal employees, 1965–1971	Insignificant; adds about 1% to beginning and maximum salaries.
Frey (1975)	Teachers, 1964–1970	Insignificant; adds 0%–1.5% to beginning and maximum salaries.
Hamermesh (1975)	Bus drivers, craftsmen, other	Significant for bus drivers; adds 9%–12% to wage changes. Insignificant for all other; adds −4% to +4% wage changes and/or earnings.
Chambers (1977)	Teachers, 1970–1971*	Significant; adds 8%–17% to teacher salaries and 2%–14% to administrative salaries.
Lewin and Katz (1983)	Municipal building departments, 1970	Significant; adds 10%–14% to annual salaries.
Lewin (1983)	Municipal building and sanitation departments, 1970 and 1974	Significant; adds 6%–21% to minimum and maximum salaries and 9%–25% to annual compensation.

Table 6–3 (continued)

Author(s)	Employee Group and Year(s) of Data	Major Finding(s)
Ichniowski (1980)	Firefighters, 1966 and 1976	Generally significant; adds −1.6% to +3.4% to hourly wage and 7.2%–18.0% to fringe benefits.
Lewin, Horton, and Kuhn (1979)	Seven blue- and white-collar occupations in four municipal governments, 1951–1976	Generally significant; adds 1%–8% to annual salaries.
Lewin and Keith (1976)	Police, 1971–1972	Insignificant; adds −1% to 6% to beginning and maximum salaries.
Fottler (1977)	Hospital employees	Significant; adds 4.0%–5.5% to weekly wages.
Hall and Vanderporten	Police, 1973	Significant in independent (monopsonistic) cities, insignificant elsewhere: adds $250–$1,000 to beginning and maximum salaries.
Shapiro (1978)	Blue- and white-collar government workers at federal, state, and local levels, 1971	Signficiant; adds −20% for white-collar workers and +22% for blue-collar workers.
Victor (1977)	Police and firefighters 1972	Significant; adds 6%–12% to beginning and maximum salaries or average hourly earnings.
Smith (1977)	Individual, federal, state, and local government employees 1975	Significant; adds 0%–17% to annual salaries of individuals employed by governments.
Bartel and Lewin (1981)	Police, 1973	Significant; adds 9%–19% to beginning and average salaries or to average hourly earnings.
Edwards and Edwards (1982)	Sanitation, 1974	Signficiant; adds 9%–11% to hourly wage.
Baugh and Stone (1982)	Teachers, 1974–1975 and 1977–1978*	Signficiant; adds 4%–21% to hourly wages.
Freeman, Ichniowski, and Lauer (1985)	Police, 1965, 1973, and 1978	Significant; adds 3%–18% to average salaries.
Delaney (1985)	Teachers, 1979–1981*	Significant; adds 10%–20% to beginning and average salaries.
Schwochau (1987)	Police, 1983	Significant; adds 2.5%–5.1% to minimum and maximum salaries.

Note: See full citations in references at end of the chapter.

*School year or years.

port for the thesis that public sector bargaining outcomes are diverse rather than singular, varied rather than monolithic.

It is especially unfortunate that there are very few longitudinal studies of the wage impacts of government employee bargaining. In addition, none of the studies summarized in table 6–3 incorporate data more recent than 1983; indeed, relatively few of the studies employ data beyond the mid-1970s. Consequently, we have little evidence about public employee union wage impacts during an era of economic retrenchment (particularly the late 1970s), and virtually no evidence about these impacts during the third generation of public sector bargaining that is developing in the 1980s.

Furthermore, if unionism continues to expand in the public sector—and that is a very big if—the utility of cross-sectional analysis of the type presented in the Bartel-Lewin reading and most of the studies listed in table 6–3 will become more limited. This is because both the size and comparability of the nonunion group will decline, making them subject to potentially larger wage spillovers emanating from the unionized sector. Consequently, future studies of public employee union wage impacts will require a purely longitudinal research design or a pooled (combination) cross-sectional and longitudinal approach. From such research, we believe, will emerge a better understanding of how public sector bargaining affects the wages of government employees.

Moreover, such longitudinal studies should be able to provide more concrete estimates of the impacts of bargaining on fringe benefits in the public sector. Although the available cross-sectional research on this topic has expanded in recent years (just as it has in the private sector), it remains sparse. Yet there is evidence from other sources that fringe benefits, especially pension benefits, are not only substantial in the public sector, but in some respects surpass those in private industry.[13] Thus, it is important for researchers to deal with this issue empirically and thereby broaden their estimates of the monetary impacts of public sector bargaining beyond the wage area.

In sum, it may be concluded that the first generation of public sector bargaining in the United States featured shock effects that produced relative wage (and benefit) gains for organized public employees; the second generation of public sector bargaining resulted in a declining relative wage position of organized public employees; and the nascent third generation of public sector bargaining has witnessed at least a partial restoration of the relative wage position of organized public employees—albeit spread across a proportionately smaller public sector work force than existed in the 1960s or 1970s. Whether these are truly cyclical changes is uncertain. It is especially important, however, that studies of the pay impacts of public employee unions be made during periods of both economic expansion and economic contraction. Only by doing so will we be able to judge whether organized public sector workers are better able than unorganized workers or their private sector counterparts to protect themselves from wage erosion.[14]

Notes

1. H. Gregg Lewis, *Unionism and Relative Wages in the United States* (Chicago: University of Chicago Press, 1963).

2. Albert Rees, *The Economics of Trade Unions,* rev. ed. (Chicago: University of Chicago Press, 1977), pp. 70–75.

3. George E. Johnson, "Economic Analysis of Trade Unionism," *American Economic Review* 65 (May 1975), pp. 23–28. Two other studies that employed data on individual workers to study the wage impacts of public employee unions are Sharon P. Smith, *Equal Pay in the Public Sector: Fact or Fantasy?* (Princeton, N.J.: Princeton University Press, 1977), and David Shapiro, "Relative Wage Effects of Unions in the Public and Private Sectors," *Industrial and Labor Relations Review* 31 (January 1978), pp. 193–204.

4. Richard B. Freeman and James L. Medoff, *What Do Unions Do?* (New York: Basic Books, 1984). Also see Freeman and Medoff, "The Impact of Collective Bargaining: Illusion or Reality," in Jack Steiber, Robert B. McKersie, and Daniel Q. Mills, eds., *U.S. Industrial Relations 1950–1980: A Critical Assessment* (Madison, Wisc.: Industrial Relations Research Association, 1981), pp. 47–97.

5. Freeman and Medoff, *What Do Unions Do?,* p. 77.

6. See, for example, the sources of data used by Smith, *Equal Pay,* and Shapiro, "Relative Wage Effects," and those reported in Richard B. Freeman, "Unionism Comes to the Public Sector," *Journal of Economic Literature* 24 (March 1986), pp. 41–86.

7. A case in point is Ronald G. Ehrenberg, "Municipal Government Structure, Unionization and the Wages of Firefighters," *Industrial and Labor Relations Review* 27 (October 1973), pp. 36–48.

8. Note that we do not discuss in detail here the impact of other institutional forces in public sector wage determination, such as impasse procedures. Refer back to chapter 5 for discussion of this issue. A study that examines the effects of one type of impasse procedure on public sector pay is Craig Olson, "The Impact of Arbitration on the Wages of Firefighters," *Industrial Relations* 19 (Fall 1980), pp. 325–339.

9. See David B. Lipsky and John E. Drotning, "The Influence of Collective Bargaining on Teachers' Salaries in New York State," *Industrial and Labor Relations Review* 27 (October 1973), pp. 18–35; Ronald G. Ehrenberg and Gerald S. Goldstein, "A Model of Public Sector Wage Determination," *Journal of Urban Economics* 2 (July 1975), pp. 223–245; and John T. Delaney, "Unionism, Bargaining Spillovers, and Teacher Compensation," in David B. Lipsky, ed., *Advances in Industrial and Labor Relations,* vol. 2 (Greenwich, Conn.: JAI Press, 1985), pp. 111–142.

10. A similar finding for firefighters is reported in Casey Ichniowski, "Economic Effects of the Firefighters' Union," *Industrial and Labor Relations Review* 33 (January 1980), pp. 198–211.

11. Orley Ashenfelter and George E. Johnson, "Unionism, Relative Wages and Labor Quality in U.S. Manufacturing Industries," *International Economic Review* 13 (October 1972), pp. 488–508; Peter Schmidt and Robert Strauss, "The Effect of Unions on Earnings and Earnings on Unions: A Mixed Logit Approach," *International Economic Review* 17 (February 1976), pp. 204–212; and Freeman, "Unionism Comes to the Public Sector." A private sector study that reaches similar conclusions to those of Bartel and Lewin is Wesley Mellow, "Employer Size, Unionism, and Wages," in Joseph D. Reid, Jr., ed., *New Approaches to Labor Unions, Research in Labor Economics,* Supp. 2 (Greenwich, Conn.: JAI Press, 1983), pp. 253–282.

12. This is an updated version of the summaries contained in David Lewin, "Public Sector Labor Relations: A Review Essay," *Labor History* 18 (Winter 1977), pp. 133–144; David Lewin, Raymond D. Horton, and James W. Kuhn, *Collective Bargaining and Manpower Utilization in Big City Governments* (Montclair, N.J.: Allanheld Osmun, 1979), pp. 84–86; and David Lewin, Peter Feuille, and Thomas A. Kochan, *Public Sector Labor Relations: Analysis and Readings,* 2nd ed. (Sun Lakes, Arizona: Thomas Horton and Daughters, 1981), pp. 401–405. Also see Freeman, "Unionism Comes to the Public Sector," pp. 53–61.

13. See Elizabeth Dickson, Harold A. Hovey, and George E. Peterson, *Public Employee Compensation: A Twelve City Comparison* (Washington, D.C.: Urban Institute, 1980); Linda N. Edwards and Franklin R. Edwards, "The Effects of Unionism on the Money and Fringe Compensation of Public Employees: The Case of Municipal Sanitation Workers," Working Paper, Queens College, City University of New York, 1979); and Freeman, "Unionism Comes to the Public Sector."

14. Note that private sector studies have generally shown that union wage effects are greatest during the early years of a collective bargaining relationship. On this point, see Rees, *The Economics of Trade Unions,* pp. 82–89. The "generational" approach to public sector bargaining discussed here calls this "union wage effect" conclusion into question.

References for Table 6–3

Ashenfelter, Orley. "The Effect of Unionization on Wages in the Public Sector; The Case of Firefighters." *Industrial and Labor Relations Review* 24 (January 1971), pp. 191–202.

Baugh, William H. and Joe A. Stone. "Teachers, Unions, and Wages in the 1970s: Unionism Now Pays." *Industrial and Labor Relations Review* 35 (April 1982), pp. 368–376.

Baird, Robert N., and Landon, John H. "The Effects of Collective Bargaining on Public Teachers' Salaries: Comment." *Industrial and Labor Relations Review* 25 (April 1972), pp. 410–417.

Bartel, Ann P., and David Lewin. "Wages and Unionism in the Public Sector: The Case of Police." *Review of Economics and Statistics* 63 (February 1981), pp. 53–59.

Chambers, Jay G. "The Impact of Collective Bargaining for Teachers on Resource Allocation in Public School Districts." *Journal of Urban Economics* 4 (July 1977), pp. 324–339.

Delaney, John Thomas. "Unionism, Bargaining Spillovers, and Teacher Compensation." In David B. Lipsky, ed., *Advances in Industrial and Labor Relations,* vol. 2 (Greenwich, Conn.: JAI Press, 1985), pp. 111–142.

Edwards, Linda N. and Franklin R. Edwards. "Wellington-Winter Revisited: The Case of Municipal Sanitation Collection." *Industrial and Labor Relations Review* 35 (April 1982), pp. 307–318.

Ehrenberg, Ronald G. "Municipal Government Structure, Unionization and the Wages of Firefighters." *Industrial and Labor Relations Review* 27 (October 1973), pp. 36–48.

Ehrenberg, Ronald G., and Gerald S. Goldstein, "A Model of Public Sector Wage Determination." *Journal of Urban Economics* 2 (July 1975), pp. 223–245.

Fottler, Myron D. "The Union Impact on Hospital Wages," *Industrial and Labor Relations Review* 30 (April 1977), pp. 342–355.

Freeman, Richard B., Casey Ichniowski, and Harrison Lauer. "Collective Bargaining Laws and Threat Effects of Unionism in the Determination of Police Compensation." National Bureau of Economic Research Working Paper no. 1578, 1985.

Freund, James L. "Market and Union Influences on Municipal Employee Wages." *Industrial and Labor Relations Review* 27 (April 1974), pp. 391–404.

Frey, Donald E. "Wage Determination in Public Schools and the Effects of Unionization," in Daniel S. Hamermesh, ed. *Labor in the Public and Nonprofit Sectors* (Princeton, N.J.: Princeton University Press, 1975), pp. 183–219.

Hall, W. Clayton, and Norman E. Carroll, "The Effects of Teachers' Organizations on Salaries and Class Size." *Industrial and Labor Relations Review* 26 (January 1973), pp. 834–841.

Hall, W. Clayton, and John Vanderporten. "Unionization, Monopsony Power, and Police Salaries." *Industrial Relations* 16 (February 1977), pp. 94–100.

Hamermesh, Daniel S. "The Effect of Government Ownership on Union Wages," in Hamermesh, ed. *Labor in the Public and Nonprofit Sectors* (Princeton, N.J.: Princeton University Press, 1975), pp. 227–255.

Ichniowski, Casey. "Economic Effects of the Firefighters' Union." *Industrial and Labor Relations Review* 33 (January 1980), pp. 198–211.

Kasper, Hirschel. "The Effects of Collective Bargaining on Public School Teachers' Salaries." *Industrial and Labor Relations Review* 24 (October 1970), pp. 57–72.

Lewin, David. "The Effects of Civil Service Systems and Unionism on Pay Outcomes in the Public Sector." In David B. Lipsky, ed., *Advances in Industrial and Labor Relations,* vol. 1 (Greenwich, Conn.: JAI Press, 1983), pp. 131–161.

Lewin, David, Raymond D. Horton, and James W. Kuhn, *Collective Bargaining and Manpower Utilization in Big City Governments.* (Montclair, N.J.: Allanheld Osmun, 1979), chap. 4.

Lewin, David, and Katz, Harry C. "Payment Determination in Municipal Building Departments Under Unionism and Civil Service." In Werner Z. Hirsch, ed., *Municipal Labor Markets* (Los Angeles: Institute of Industrial Relations, University of California at Los Angeles, 1983), pp. 90–121.

Lewin, David, and Keith, John J., Jr. "Managerial Responses to Perceived Labor Shortages: The Case of Police." *Criminology* 14 (May 1976), pp. 65–92.

Lipsky, David B., and Drotning, John E. "The Influence of Collective Bargaining on Teachers' Salaries in New York State." *Industrial and Labor Relations Review* 27 (October 1973), pp. 18–35.

Schmenner, Roger W. "The Determination of Municipal Employee Wages." Review of Economies and Statistics 55 (February 1973), pp. 83–90.

Schwochau, Susan. "The Impact of Arbitration Statutes on Police and Municipal Budgets." Final Report to the National Institute of Justice, U.S. Department of Justice, 1987.

Shapiro, David. "Relative Wage Effects of Unions in the Public and Private Sectors." Industrial and Labor Relations Review 31 (January 1978), pp. 193–204.

Smith, Sharon P. Equal Pay in the Public Sector: Fact or Fantasy (Princeton, N.J.: Industrial Relations Section, Princeton University, 1977).

Thornton, Robert J. "The Effects of Collective Negotiations on Teachers' Salaries." The Quarterly Review of Economics and Business 2 (Winter 1971), pp. 37–46.

Victor, Richard B. The Effects of Unionism on the Wage and Employment Levels of Police and Firefighters. (Santa Monica, Calif.: Rand Corporation, 1977).

Wages and Unionism in the Public Sector: The Case of Police

Ann Bartel
David Lewin*

One of the most important developments in government during the last two decades has been the growth of public employee unions. Because personnel expenditures comprise a substantial portion of the cost of providing public services, there has been considerable concern that unionization has severely exacerbated budgetary problems of governments, especially local governments. Consequently, a large literature on the wage effects of public employee unionism has developed in recent years.[1] In general, these studies have found rather modest union wage impacts in the public sector, with unions raising the wages of municipal employees by about 5 percent, on average.

There are several reasons, however, that these estimates may be misleading. First, much public sector union wage impact research has focused on teachers, and the demand for teacher services is considerably more elastic than the demand for other public services such as police protection, fire protection, and medical care. Second, previous studies have treated public employee unionism as an exogenous variable, and studies of private sector unionization have shown that the estimated wage impacts of unions change substantially when unionism is treated as an endogenous variable.[2] Finally,

*Columbia University. Reprinted from The Review of Economics and Statistics, Vol. 63, no. 1 (February 1981), pp. 53–59.

the earlier studies have not considered how public employee unionism has affected fringe benefits, which represent a substantial and growing component of governmental compensation.

This reading attempts to deal with each of these problems. First, we focus on the effects of unionism on the wages of municipal police officers.[3] Because police services are commonly thought to be among the most essential of all public services, organized police should be in an especially powerful position when bargaining with local governments. Second, we estimate a system of equations in which wages and unionism are simultaneously determined and compare these results to the estimated wage impacts from a single equation model. Finally, some estimates of the effects of unionism on police fringe benefits are presented.

A Conceptual Framework

A Model of Police Wages When Unionism Is Exogenous

To model the determinants of police wages, we rely on previous research on the determinants of public sector wages in general,[4] and police wages in particular.[5] In the absence of police unionism, police wages are assumed to be a function of a community's ability to pay and its "tastes" for police services, the form of municipal government, and the opportunity wage for potential applicants for police jobs. Ability to pay is proxied by median family income *(INC)* while a community's tastes for police services can be captured by such variables as city size *(POP)*, population density *(DEN)*, the median value of housing in the community *(HOUSE)*, and a vector of geographic region dummies *(REGION)*. [6] The form of government is generally considered to be an important determinant of the demand for police services, given that city managers have professional training and consequently may be relatively more efficient in "producing" police services.[7] This hypothesis can be tested by using two dichotomous variables in the wage equation: *MAYOR,* which equals 1 if the form of government is mayor-council, 0 otherwise, and *COMM,* which equals 1 if the form of government is commission, 0 otherwise. The opportunity wage can be proxied by the average hourly earnings of manufacturing production workers in the municipality *(OPPW)*.

Now suppose that in some municipalities police officers are unionized. Police unions may be expected to raise the wage above the market clearing wage, thereby creating an excess supply of labor.[8] In attempting to measure this union effect, previous studies have employed such variables as the existence of a police labor organization, the percentage of police organized, or the type and affiliation of the police labor organization.[9] We prefer a different measure, however, namely the presence of collective bargaining among police. This is because the behavioral importance of a workers' organization is not simply its existence but, rather, the joint decision making that it engages in with management through collective bargaining. Thus, a dummy variable *(CONTRACT)*, which equals 1 if the city has a written labor agreement covering wages, hours and conditions of employment for police personnel, 0 if it does not, is used here to measure the impact of collective bargaining on police wages.[10] The superiority of this variable over a dummy measuring the existence of a police labor organization is shown in the next section.

Given the assumption that unionism is exogenous, we can estimate the following equation for police wages:

$$\ln W = \beta_0 + \beta_1 INC + \beta_2 POP + \beta_3 DEN + \beta_4 HOUSE + \beta_5 REGION$$
$$+ \beta_6 MAYOR + \beta_7 COMM + \beta_8 \ln OPPW + \beta_9 CONTRACT$$
$$+ \mu_1 \tag{1}$$

where $\beta_1, \beta_2, \beta_3, \beta_4, \beta_5, \beta_6, \beta_7, \beta_8$, and β_9 are hypothesized to be positive, and μ_1 is the residual.

A Simultaneous Model of Police Wages and Unionism

Equation 1 assumes that police unionism (and collective bargaining) in a municipality is exogenously determined. However, if the level of police wages in a municipality partially determines whether or not police are organized and engage in collective bargaining, then CONTRACT will be correlated with μ_1 and the estimated coefficient on CONTRACT in equation (1) will be biased. The following section suggests how the complete simultaneous model may be specified.

As discussed by Stigler (1971), the "economic theory" of regulation treats regulation or legislation as the result of the interplay of demand and supply forces such that individuals who presumably would benefit from the legislation determine demand, and individuals who stand to lose from the legislation determine supply.[11] Within the context of this theory, the level of police wages that prevails in the absence of a union could positively or negatively affect the probability that police will unionize. First, the lower the wage, the greater will be the increase in taxes necessary to finance the increased labor costs resulting from collective bargaining and, thus, the greater should be a community's opposition to unionism and collective bargaining by police. Another way of interpreting such a positive relationship is that legislation sanctioning unionism and collective bargaining by police may merely codify existing behavior. In other words, it is in those municipalities where police are already paid relatively high wages that there will be less opposition to unionization.[12] An alternative argument is that the lower the wage, the greater will be the benefits to the police from unionizing and hence the greater the demand for unionization.[13] Although we cannot predict a priori the sign of the wage variable in the police unionization equation, we can at least conclude that it is an important determinant of the costs and/or the benefits of police unionism.

Other variables can also be suggested as empirical measures of the costs and benefits of police unionism. For example, in their organizing efforts police presumably would be aided by other organized workers, or at least would encounter less opposition to their goals in areas that are heavily unionized; in other words, the supply of public sector unionism would be greater in these areas. In the absence of data on local work force unionization, we use the percentage of private sector workers organized in the state *(PSU)* to measure this variable. Second, the form of government can also influence the ease with which police gain collective bargaining rights. The relatively greater direct personal control that city managers have over municipal services as well as their professional training should make it easier for them to prevent police officers from gaining enough political support to organize and to engage in collective bargaining; therefore, *MAYOR* and *COMM* should have positive signs in the police unionization equation. Third, it can be argued that the higher the median family income in a municipality *(INC)*, the less reluctant will be the city's population to finance the increased wage costs which may result from police collective bargaining. In addition, holding *INC* constant, police may find it more difficult to bargain collectively in municipalities with a relatively highly educated population to the extent that a more educated citizenry has greater awareness of the costs that police collective bargaining may impose on them. Median education in the municipality *(EDUC)* should therefore have a negative effect in the unionism equation. Finally, a vector of geographic region dummies *(REGION)* can be added to the equation to capture unmeasured "tastes" for police unionism.

In summary, the following equation (with μ_2 as the error term) is used to explain variations across cities in police collective bargaining activity:[14]

$$CONTRACT = \alpha_0 + \alpha_1 \ln W^* + \alpha_2 PSU + \alpha_3 MAYOR + \alpha_4 COMM$$
$$\alpha_5 INC - \alpha_6 EDUC + \alpha_7 REGION + \mu_2 \qquad (2)$$

Note that the wage that is included in this equation is W^*—that is, the wage that prevails in the municipality in the absence of police unionism, or, from equation 1, $\ln W^* = \ln W - \beta_9 CONTRACT$. By estimating the simultaneous system represented in equations 1 and 2, we obtain unbiased estimates of the parameters in both equations.[15] The specifications insure that both equations are identified.[16]

Empirical Analysis

Data

Equations 1 and 2 are estimated for a sample of cities that responded to the 1973 Survey of Personnel Policies in Municipal Police Departments conducted by the International City Management Association. These cities had populations of at least 25,000. The survey elicited information on size of the police force, structure of police salaries, total police labor costs, whether or not the city had a written labor contract with police officers, the form of government in the municipality, the city's total budget, and training, retirement and pension provisions for police. From the 1972 County and City Data Book we obtained information on the economic and demographic characteristics of the municipalities. Information on private sector unionization in the state was obtained from the U.S. Bureau of Labor Statistics (1975). Deletion of the cities that did not report the information necessary to estimate equations 1 and 2 resulted in a sample of 215 municipalities.[17]

The Impact of Unionism on Police Wages

Table 1 presents the coefficients on CONTRACT from wage equations that were estimated alternatively by ordinary least squares (OLS) and two stage least squares (TSLS) techniques. To conserve space, the coefficients on the other variables in the wage equation are not presented. With the exception of form of government, the coefficients on all of these variables had the hypothesized signs and were significant at the 5 percent level. Several different measures of the police wage were used in the equation: the minimum (entry) salary for police privates *(MINSAL)*, the "hourly" minimum wage for police privates *(MINHW)*, calculated by dividing *MINSAL* by the average weekly hours for police privates times 52,[18] the maximum (base) salary for police privates *(MAXSAL)*, and the average salary for all police officers *(AVGSAL)*, calculated by dividing the city's annual cost for salaries for full-time uniformed police by the number of full-time uniformed police.[19]

The results in table 1 show that when the wage equation was estimated under the assumption that unionism is exogenous, CONTRACT was positive and significant in three of the four equations. Annual minimum and maximum salaries were found to be about 6 percent higher in cities with contracts; controlling for the labor supply of police privates in column 2 raised the union effect slightly, indicating that policemen work fewer hours, on average, in cities with a contract.[20] In addition, the average salary of all uniformed policemen was 3.9 percent higher in municipalities with a written labor contract, but this effect was not statistically significant. Before turning to the results of the simultaneous model, it should be noted that we examined

Table 1
Coefficient on CONTRACT from Police Wage Equations
(*t-values are given in parentheses*)

Dependent Variable[a]	(1) MINSAL	(2) MINHW	(3) MAXSAL	(4) AVGSAL
A. OLS Results[b]	0.0590	0.0640	0.0639	0.0393
	(3.90)	(3.72)	(3,86)	(1.34)
B. TSLS Results				
1. Collective bargaining law	(0.1505	0.2070	0.0998	0.0917
excluded from *CONTRACT*	(3.71)	(4.02)	(2.33)	(1.32)
equation				
2. Collective bargaining law	0.1336	0.1722	0.1190	0.1190
included in CONTRACT	(4.57)	(4.81)	(3.80)	(2.24)
equation				

Note: All the other variables shown in equation 1 in the text are included in the wage equation.
[a]See text for definitions.
[b]In columns 1, 2, and 3, the R^2 is approximately 0.65. In column 4, it is 0.47.

the suitability of an alternative measure of unionism, the existence of a police labor organization, by creating two dummy variables to replace *CONTRACT*: (1) *ORGC = 1* if the municipality has a police labor organization *and* a written labor contract, and (2) *ORGNC = 1* if the municipality has an organization but no contract. The superiority of the *CONTRACT* variable is shown by the fact that in the case of the dependent variable MINSAL, the coefficient on *ORGC* is 0.0769 and is significant, while the coefficient on *ORGNC* is 0.0316 and is not significant. Further, the difference in these coefficients is statistically significant.

If we relax the assumption that unionism is exogenous and assume that the police wages and police unionism are simultaneously determined, the estimated union wage impact increases considerably.[21] As can be seen in table 1, we now estimate that municipalities with a *CONTRACT* have annual minimum salaries that are about 14 percent higher than annual minimum salaries in cities without a *CONTRACT*. This effect is more than twice the size of the union impact estimated from the single-equation model. Hourly starting wages are now estimated to be between 17 percent and 21 percent higher in contract than in noncontract cities, while annual maximum (base) salaries and average annual salaries are about 10 percent higher. These results support the hypothesis that the demand for unionization is greater in low-wage municipalities; therefore, single-equation estimates understate the impact of police unionism on police wages.

The Impact of Wages on Police Unionism

To demonstrate further the need for a simultaneous model of police wages and unionism, we present in table 2 the coefficients on the police wage from

Table 2
Coefficients on ln (WAGE) from CONTRACT Equation
(t-values are given in parentheses)

	Wage Measure[a]			
Wage Measure	*(1)* MINSAL	*(2)* MINHW	*(3)* MAXSAL	*(4)* AVGSAL
A. OLS Results[b]				
1. Collective bargaining law	0.3975	0.3289	0.4814	0.0512
excluded from equation	(1.50)	(1.31)	(2.02)	(0.31)
2. Collective bargaining law	0.0492	−0.0026	0.1695	−0.1162
included in equation	(0.19)	(−0.01)	(0.73)	(−0.73)
B. TSLS Results				
1. Collective bargaining law	−0.8242	−0.8079	−0.6474	−0.6491
excluded from equation	(−1.40)	(−1.33)	(−1.27)	(−1.31)
2. Collective bargaining law	−1.443	−1.619	−1.091	−1.130
included in equation	(−2.35)	(−2.38)	(−2.08)	(−2.13)

Note: All of the other variables shown in equation 2 are included in the CONTRACT equation. In some cases, as indicated, the presence of a state collective bargaining law variable is added to the equation.

[a]See text for definition.

[b]The R^2 in each of these equations is approximately 0.30 when the collective bargaining law is excluded and increases to 0.38 when this variable is included.

unionism equations (equation 2) that were estimated alternatively by OLS and TSLS. Again, to conserve space, we do not report the coefficients on the other variables in the equation but discuss them briefly here. The predictions about private sector unionization and a state's collective bargaining law were borne out; in addition, the coefficients on median family income and median education had the predicted signs but were not significant.[22] The only unexpected result in the unionism equation was the finding that police collective bargaining was more likely to occur in municipalities with a city manager form of government. Perhaps city managers are more willing to accept unions because they are better able to obtain productivity gains to offset relatively higher police salaries.[23]

The wage coefficients in table 2 demonstrate the need for a simultaneous model of wages and unionism in order to understand the determinants of municipal variations in police unions. When the wage is treated as exogenous, the wage coefficient is either zero or positive. Allowing for the endogeneity of wages results in a negative wage coefficient that is significant in some of the specifications. Thus the simultaneity bias present in the single-equation estimate of the determinants of police unionism would have prevented us from reaching the important conclusion that a CONTRACT is more likely to be present in a low-wage than in a high-wage city. This finding supports the hypothesis that the demand for police unionization is greater the lower the police wage.

The Impact of Police Unionism on Fringe Benefits

Our analysis has focused on the impact of unionism on police salaries via the collective bargaining process. It is well known, however, that fringe benefits account for a large proportion of total compensation for public employees generally and for police in particular. In this section we consider the role of unionism through collective bargaining in the determination of police fringe benefits. Since the data set we are using contains rather limited information on fringes, the results in this section should be interpreted cautiously.

In panel A of table 3 we attempt to gauge the impact of collective bargaining on total fringe benefits. This is done by defining two variables: *LGACOST,* which equals the logarithm of the municipality's annual expenditures for personnel costs for full-time uniformed police divided by the number of full-time police; and *LGASAL,* which is the logarithm of the municipality's annual expenditures for salaries for full-time uniformed police divided by the number of full-time police.[24] We believe that the first variable includes salary expenditures plus expenditures for all fringe benefits. If this assumption is correct, then we can compare the impacts of unionism on salaries and fringe benefits by estimating equation 1 for each of the two variables we have defined.[25] Since the dependent variables are in logarithmic form, we can compare the estimated *CONTRACT* coefficients and thereby

Table 3
Effects of CONTRACT on Police Fringe Benefits*
(t-values are given in parentheses)

Dependent Variable[b]	OLS	TSLS	Sample Size
A. All Fringe Benefits			
LGACOST	0.0891	0.1723	121
	(1.77)	(1.83)	
LGASAL	0.0575	0.1241	121
	(1.43)	(1.65)	
B. Retirement Benefits			
AGE	−1.750		180
	(−1.69)		
YEARS	−1.234		198
	(−1.30)		
EXPEND	3.457		161
	(1.89)		
ECONT	0.9892		161
	(0.82)		
PCSAL	0.8423		164
	(0.43)		

[a]HOUSE POP.INC.DEN.OPPW.MAYOR.COMM and *REGION* are included as independent variables in these regressions.
[b]See text for definitions.

determine whether unionism has a larger impact on salaries or on fringes.[26] The results in panel A of table 3 show that *CONTRACT* has a larger coefficient in the *LGACOST* equation than in the *LGASAL* equation. This indicates that collective bargaining has had a greater impact on the fringe benefits than on the salaries received by police.

In panel B of table 3 we focus on police retirement benefits and use five variables to measure these benefits: *AGE* = the minimum regular retirement age, *YEARS* = the minimum number of years of service needed to receive a pension for regular retirement, *EXPEND* = the annual employer expenditure for retirement benefits as a percentage of payroll, *ECONT* = the employee contribution to the retirement system as a percentage of annual salary, and *PCSAL* = the percentage of salary received for minimum regular retirement. The results show that unionism has significantly reduced the age at which policemen retire and has significantly increased employer expenditures for retirement benefits as a percentage of payroll.

Admittedly, much better data are required in order to sort out the role of collective bargaining in the determination of police fringe benefits. But it appears that, even with these fragmentary data, we have documented a significant impact of unionism on the nonwage benefits received by police.

Summary

This study has examined the determinants of police wages and police unionism in U.S. cities, with unionism measured by the presence of a collective bargaining *CONTRACT* rather than simply by the existence of a police labor organization. Ordinary least squares estimates of union impacts on police wages range between 3.9 percent and 6.4 percent, which are consistent with the findings of other investigators.[27] However, the impact more than doubles to around 14 percent (in the case of minimum salaries) when police unionism is treated as an endogenous variable. Our results also show that the demand for unionization is greater in low wage cities and that, consequently, an analysis that ignores the simultaneous determination of wages and unionism seriously underestimates the effect of police unionism on police wages.

When the analysis was extended to incorporate fringe benefits, we calculated that unionism has had a greater impact on fringes than on salaries. Further, unionism appears to have significantly improved the retirement benefits attained by police. However, better data are needed before we can draw firm conclusions about the nonwage impacts of police unionism.

In conclusion, it appears that the wage impacts of police unionism are larger than previously thoughts and large compared to the wage increases achieved by other organized public employees; so too may be the nonwage impacts of police unionism. But in order to gauge the true impact of police unionism on municipalities, we must know how police productivity is affected by police unionism and bargaining activity. Brown and Medoff (1978) have shown that unionization has had a substantial positive effect on output per worker in U.S. manufacturing industries. Perhaps police unionism analogously serves to improve the productivity of police so as to fully offset (or even exceed) the increased costs that result from unionism and collective bargaining. Testing this hypothesis is beyond the scope of the present reading, but provides an important topic for further research.

Notes

1. This literature is summarized in Lewin (1977).

2. See Ashenfelter and Johnson (1972) and Schmidt and Strass (1976).

3. Schmenner (1973), Ehrenberg and Goldstein (1975), Lewin and Keith (1976) and Hall and Vanderporten (1977) have examined the impact of unionism on police wages. None of these studies considered the simultaneity problem or the fringe benefit issue that we discuss here.

4. See Lewin (1977).

5. See the sources cited in note 3.

6. Since variations across municipalities in *INC, POP, DEN,* and *HOUSE* will capture much of the variation in the crime rate, it is not necessary to include a variable for the crime rate.

7. See, for example, Ehrenberg and Goldstein (1975).

8. For a discussion of the excess supply of police labor, see Wolitz (1974).

9. See the review in Lewin (1977).

10. By doing this we are implicitly assuming that the percentage wage increase is the same in all unionized cities and that nonunionized cities are unaffected by the existence of these unions.

11. Edwards (1978) used this theory to specify a simultaneous model of school enrollment rates and compulsory schooling laws.

12. In their private sector interindustry analysis, Ashenfelter and Johnson (1972) predicted a positive relationship between wages and unionism on the grounds that unionism is a normal good and that, holding constant the cost of union membership, higher wages will increase the worker's desire to join a union. Their empirical results supported the hypothesized relationship, as did the later findings of Schmidt and Strauss (1976).

13. This is consistent with the work of Moore (1978) who found a negative relationship between teacher income and teacher unionism in a model that treated income as exogenous.

14. It can be argued that the existence of a state collective bargaining law *(CBL)* also belongs in equation 2. However, this variable could be considered as endogenous. In our empirical work, we estimate equation 2 with and without this variable.

15. Note that this simultaneous model implicitly assumes that variations in the variables over time within a city are small relative to variations across cities at a point

in time. We would therefore expect wages to be highly correlated over time within a city. In fact, the simple correlation of 1963 police salaries (when few cities had contracts) and 1973 salaries (when 50 percent of the cities had contracts) is 0.85. This result testifies to the consistent role of the demand-supply variables in the wage determination process. Given this framework, our model enables us to estimate the effect of W^* (not W) on $CONTRACT$ in a simultaneous system. It must be stressed that ordinary least squares estimation of equation 2 could not provide us with this parameter. Heckman (1978) discusses the statistical properties of this type of model given in equations 1 and 2.

16. As our empirical results show, the wage equation is identified simply because of the strong role of PSU in the $CONTRACT$ equation. We believe it is reasonable to argue that PSU belongs only in the union equation. Although private sector unionists could be expected to favor the expansion of unionism in the public sector, it is not at all obvious that their activities would increase the demand for police services, holding the other demand variables constant. In some of our work we did include PSU in both equations, using the state collective bargaining law to identify the wage equation; the results showed that PSU had a significant effect only in the contract equation.

17. It was not possible to perform this analysis for years after 1973 because, unlike police salary and fringe benefit data, police unionism and bargaining data have not been published since then. Obviously, this also prevents us from conducting a time-series analysis of police wages and police unionism.

18. This is the only information on labor supply that was available to us. The assumption of zero unemployment implicit in this calculation is perhaps unrealistic, but far less so than it would be in the case of private sector employees.

19. Note that the salary variables as well as all the other variables that are measured in money terms were deflated by a city cost-of-living index. Data on the cost of living were available for one-third of the municipalities. Using these data, we estimated an equation in which the cost of living was a function of the region of the country and the size of the municipality. A cost-of-living index was then predicted for the remaining municipalities. The results using the deflated variables were very similar to those that used the undeflated variables. The undeflated results are available from the authors.

20. Although $CONTRACT$ has a significant effect on average weekly hours, the actual reduction in hours is only about 1 percent.

21. Equations 1 and 2 were estimated using a standard two stage least squares technique. Heckman (1978) shows that this approach gives consistent estimates even though one of the endogenous variables is dichotomous. Note, however, that the estimates of the variances of the coefficients in the $CONTRACT$ equation will be biased unless this equation is estimated by $PROBIT$ or $LOGIT$. Since we are primarily concerned with the way in which the estimated union wage impact changes when a simultaneous model is specified and less concerned about the significance levels of coefficients in the $CONTRACT$ equation, we chose not to incur the high costs of estimating a simultaneous model using $PROBIT$.

22. The fact that the political variables are significant whereas the economic ones are not may indicate that the taxpayer's political identification with a unionized police force is the motivating factor behind a community's willingness to let its police bargain collectively.

23. Since the available data do not contain productivity measures, we are unable to test this hypothesis directly.

24. Note that only 121 cities provided the information necessary to construct both of these variables.

25. Professor Martin Segal of Dartmouth University and an anonymous referee pointed out that the fringe benefit data used in this analysis are unlikely to include the employers' unfunded pension liabilities, thereby making our fringe benefit estimates imperfect measures of the true value.

26. This is because the union elasticity in the *LGACOST* equation will be a weighted average of the union elasticities on salaries and fringes, with the weights being the shares of salaries and fringes in total personnel costs.

27. For example, Ehrenberg and Goldstein (1975) and Victor (1977).

References

Ashenfelter, Orley, and George E. Johnson, "Unionism, Relative Wages and Labor Quality in U.S. Manufacturing Industries," *International Economic Review* 13 (Oct. 1972), 488–508.

Brown, Charles, and James Medoff, "Trade Unions in the Production Process," *Journal of Political Economy* 86 (June 1978), 355–378.

Edwards, Linda N., "An Empirical Analysis of Compulsory Schooling Legislation, 1940–1960," *Journal of Law and Economics* 21 (Apr. 1978), 203–222.

Ehrenberg, Ronald G., and Gerald S. Goldstein, "A Model of Public Sector Wage Determination," *Journal of Urban Economics* 2 (July 1975), 223–245.

Hall, W. Clayton, and Bruce Vanderporten, "Unionization, Monopsony Power and Police Salaries," *Industrial Relations* 16 (Feb. 1977), 94–100.

Heckman, James J., "Dummy Endogenous Variables in a Simultaneous Equation System," *Econometrica* 46 (July 1978), 931–959.

Lewin, David, "Public Sector Labor Relations: A Review Essay," *Labor History* 18 (Winter 1977), 133–144.

Lewin, David, and John H. Keith, Jr., "Managerial Responses to Perceived Labor Shortages: The Case of Police," *Criminology* 14 (May 1976), 65–92.

Moore, William J., "An Analysis of Teacher Union Growth," *Industrial Relations* 17 (May 1978), 204–215.

Schmenner, Roger W., "The Determination of Municipal Employee Wages," *Review of Economics and Statistics* 55 (Feb. 1973), 83–90.

Schmidt, Peter, and Robert Strauss, "The Effect of Unions on Earnings and Earnings on Unions: A Mixed Logit Approach," *Industrial Economic Review* 17 (Feb. 1976), 204–212.

Stigler, George J., "The Theory of Economic Regulation," *Bell Journal of Economics and Management Science* 2 (Spring 1971), 3–21.

U.S. Bureau of the Census, *County and City Data Book,* 1972, 1977.

U.S. Department of Labor, Bureau of Labor Statistics, *Directory of National Unions and Employee Associations,* Washington, D.C., 1975.

Victor, Richard B., "The Effects of Unionism on the Wage and Employment Levels of Police and Firefighters," Rand Corporation Report, August 1977.

Wolitz, Louise B., "An Analysis of the Labor Market for Policemen," unpublished doctoral dissertation, University of California at Berkeley, 1974.

7
Nonwage Impacts of Unionism

Public employee unions, like their private sector counterparts, have long sought to influence their members' nonwage employment conditions and wages. Public sector contracts reflect this concern for nonwage items. For example, one study has reported that in 1981 the average union contract covering police officers in U.S. cities contained sixty provisions governing issues other than wages.[1] Moreover, research has suggested that the nonwage content of public sector contracts has grown over time.[2] These findings illustrate the importance of devoting attention to the nonwage impacts of unions in order to gain a better understanding of government employee unionism. Thus, this chapter examines the determinants of nonwage bargaining outcomes, the important role that the legislated scope of bargaining plays in nonwage negotiations, the impact of collective bargaining on the management of the public sector work force, and some approaches used by public employers and unions to cope with changes in their environments.

Determinants of Bargaining Outcomes

The first reading in this chapter presents a conceptual framework for analyzing public sector bargaining outcomes and an empirical test of the underlying model. In addition, John Anderson's study of the determinants of bargaining outcomes in Canadian municipalities employs a methodology that was first used in studies of nonwage outcomes in U.S. municipalities.[3] This methodology and its application are instructive for several reasons. First, it measures quantitatively the wide range of issues, in addition to wages, that are included in bargaining agreements. Further, it shows that nonwage issues are systematically related to characteristics of the environment, structure, and process of bargaining, and to the organizational characteristics of the union and the employer. Anderson's results illustrate the importance of considering nonwage contract provisions in assessing the relative power of the bargaining parties in the public sector.

Second, a comparison of the results of Anderson's Canadian study and other U.S. studies suggests that the sources of power that drive the bargaining process and influence its outcomes can vary across political settings and over time. Investigations have suggested that bargaining outcomes in U.S. cities are heavily influenced by the legal environments (collective bargaining laws and impasse procedures) across states and by the political effectiveness of local unions. The Canadian data, drawn from older bargaining relationships and among jurisdictions with more homogeneous laws, suggest that nonwage outcomes are most strongly influenced by the economic and political environments and the managerial responses to collective bargaining. Thus, if the maturation of union–management relationships and changing political and economic environments cause different union and management responses in the U.S. public sector, then both the sources of power and the configuration of bargaining outcomes in this country may change.

Indeed, evidence has accumulated that suggests that the relative power of the bargaining parties and the factors affecting bargaining outcomes change over time. Intensive case studies of school districts[4] and local governments,[5] and empirical examinations of municipal police departments,[6] have documented the evolution of U.S. public sector bargaining relationships. Taken together, these studies suggest somewhat different but converging implications.

In a follow-up to an earlier study, Charles Perry conducted a careful analysis of the bargaining relationships in nine diverse school districts that had been bargaining for at least a decade in the late 1970s.[7] From his comparison of these districts' earlier and later experiences, he concluded that:

1. Management resistance to union demands had stiffened.

2. The strike had become less effective as a source of union power.

3. Unions had achieved some wage gains through direct increases and changes in salary structures, but these gains tapered off in later years and the magnitude of the union impact over time did not suggest that unions had developed excessive power relative to employers.

4. Unions had made incremental gains in contract language reducing managerial discretion, but they had not exercised their contractual rights in ways that seriously constrained managerial policy development.

5. Fiscal conditions appeared to exert a substantial impact on the relative power of the parties, whereas political and community characteristics had only minor effects on bargaining power.

Douglas Mitchell and his colleagues drew somewhat different but compatible conclusions from an intensive year-long study of eight unionized California and Illinois school districts in the late 1970s.[8] First, they suggested that bargaining in public schools is driven primarily by political considerations: politics was more of a barrier than economics to management's accepting that the union had a legitimate role in school governance. As a result, both school officials and teachers made efforts to encourage the election of school board members sympathetic to their respective positions. Second, and in contrast to Perry's findings, they reported that bargaining had an impact on school policy and that the *unintended* consequences of various contract provisions had a substantial effect on the delivery of educational services. For instance, they found that bargaining altered the definitions of teachers' work responsibilities, changed the mechanisms controlling how teachers performed their jobs, and reduced the authority of principals to manage teachers' professional activities. Third, they argued that the combination of direct and unanticipated bargaining effects were causing school management to place more emphasis on the conduct of negotiations than on the delivery of educational services. Finally, they concluded that management resistance to teachers' demands increases over time, as contracts come to be viewed as "a powerful management tool."

The Derber and Wagner study and that of Feuille et al. also provide important insights into the changing patterns of bargaining outcomes over time.[9] Derber and Wagner conducted interviews in twenty-seven Illinois local government units in the late 1970s to determine the impact of fiscal problems on collective bargaining. Among other things, they found that fiscal adversity imposed discipline on the bargaining process; effective restrictions on bargaining outcomes occurred when budgets were tight. Feuille and his colleagues' longitudinal analysis of police nonwage bargaining outcomes in a national sample of 161 U.S. cities over the years 1976–1981 also revealed some interesting trends. Contracts became more favorable to the union over time because of the negotiation of new provisions and changes in contract language favoring labor. Further, other things being equal, certain features of the legal environment had substantial effects on nonwage bargaining outcomes over time.

Although these studies, in combination with Anderson's Canadian analysis, are not completely consistent, they do suggest some complementary inferences. First, the benefits of combining quantitative and institutional analysis are apparent, as each approach offers somewhat different insights into the nonwage impacts of unionism. Second, the research shows that unions can have a substantial impact on nonwage outcomes in the public sector. Further, the unintended or indirect consequences of nonwage contract provisions may amplify any direct effects. The research also illustrates that an analysis solely of contract language cannot capture the complete impact of that language on unionized governmental units.

Third, as we have emphasized throughout this book, the political aspects of public sector bargaining are very important. Politics have not restricted union bargaining success, in part because unions have actively sought to elect sympathetic policymakers to positions having influence over management negotiation strategies. Although this has probably influenced the outcome patterns reported in research, it should be remembered that the influence of competing interest groups in the political process serves as a barrier to excessive union power along this dimension. Fourth, investigations show that fiscal conditions have a major effect on bargaining outcomes and also limit unions' ability to achieve excessive outcomes. Finally, although the studies show that the sources of power affecting bargaining outcomes vary over time and across jurisdictions, the impact of the legal environment in the United States appears to be so persistent and substantial that it deserves closer attention.

The Legislated Scope of Bargaining

The subjects that may be bargained collectively are stipulated by law: state laws govern the bargaining scope for nonfederal public employees, and the Civil Service Reform Act of 1978 regulates the scope of federal sector bargaining. In this section we will focus on bargaining scope differences across the states. This emphasis is appropriate because earlier studies have reported that the variance in the legislated scope of bargaining across the states has a substantial effect on bargaining outcomes. Further, the scope of bargaining in the federal sector is so truncated that meaningful comparisons may not be made between state and federal employee collective bargaining activities.[10]

States have adopted different legislative language to regulate the content of collective bargaining agreements. All states prohibit bargaining over some issues, such as the purpose of government agencies. Bargaining scope differences arise because some states exclude more subjects from bargaining than others. For example, some states have made the determination of pensions an exclusive right of management and thus not subject to bargaining. Research has shown that these state scope-of-bargaining rules, unsurprisingly, have a significant impact on both the favorableness of public employee contracts to the union overall, and the existence of certain provisions in contracts.[11] Scope-of-bargaining provisions also reduce the variance in the types of contract provisions negotiated across governmental units within states. Moreover, Woodbury's recent investigation has presented evidence that the legal treatment of the issue of class size in state teacher bargaining statutes has a significant impact on the student/teacher ratio in school districts across states.[12] Thus, to our knowledge, all the existing evidence suggests that these bargaining scope regulations shape the bargaining outcomes negotiated in the public sector.

Given the wide variety of state bargaining scope regulations and the unlikelihood of a federal law regulating all public sector bargaining in the near future, the substantial variation in nonwage bargaining outcomes across states is likely to continue. Other sources of power may change and cause a different pattern of outcome determinants to emerge over time, but differences in nonwage outcomes will persist as long as variance exists in the legislated scope of bargaining across states.

An additional insight arises from the research on the scope of bargaining. Although it is clear that the stipulated scope of bargaining shapes union contracts, it is unclear that any "most appropriate" bargaining scope exists. States have adopted, maintained, and adjusted particular bargaining scope regulations in order to balance appropriately the interests of unionized workers, the government, and the public.[13] Changing environmental conditions, however, may suggest from time to time the need to strike a new balance of interests. But it may be difficult to alter an obsolete scope of bargaining, especially if the parties are required to drop specific contract language. In short, it is possible that the establishment of any specific bargaining scope may cause bargaining to lose some of its flexibility in adjusting to individual bargaining unit circumstances. Research on this issue is needed to determine more precisely the impact of the bargaining scope on the alteration and adjustment of contract language over time and under different external conditions. As will be seen, research is also needed on the impact of law and other forces on the management of the public sector work force.

The Impact of Bargaining on Management

Although investigators have conducted many studies of the impact of collective bargaining on public employees' wages, and the importance of the nonwage impact of unions has been widely acknowledged, comparatively few studies of the nonwage effects of public sector unions have been conducted.[14] Until recently, most of the nonwage impact research involved intensive study of a small number of cases. Although that research produced important and generally consistent insights, its authors urged cautious interpretation in light of the limited number of governmental units studied. In some areas that research still stands alone in analyzing specific nonwage impacts of bargaining. Recent systematic empirical studies, however, have expanded on the early insights in some areas and have improved the level of confidence with which some conclusions may be stated. Later in this chapter we address selected studies in some of the research streams.

What effects do unions have on the organizational human resource management (HRM) function? The classic private sector study conducted by Slichter, Healy, and Livernash represented one of the first systematic efforts to answer this question,[15] and that work has served as a model for several early intensive institutional analyses of public sector union impacts. Further, just as Slichter, Healy, and Livernash found unions to cause private sector management to implement changes in personnel policies, the public sector studies have discovered similar effects.

For example, David Stanley studied nineteen cities and counties in the late 1960s and early 1970s and reported differences in union impacts across issues.[16] Unions (and collective bargaining) seemed to have little impact in areas traditionally governed by civil service rules (such as selection or promotions), but had caused the implementation of various provisions for job security (such as seniority) and individual security (such as grievance procedure). With a few exceptions, such as New York City, Stanley observed that unions had not successfully negotiated provisions restricting subcontracting, manning, or work load.

Juris and Feuille's study of police departments in twenty-two cities during the early 1970s arrived at remarkably similar conclusions.[17] Further, Juris and Feuille suggested that some of the variance in negotiated outcomes across cities was due to the extent of unions' access to, and exploitation of, the local political process. A selection from Juris and Feuille's study is included in this chapter to illustrate these points and to describe the impact of unions on the formulation of law enforcement policy. Although their analysis suggests that some police unions have much more influence on management policy than others, bargaining overall has reduced management's discretion, encouraged "management by policy," and decreased the instances of arbitrary treatment of employees. Also, the fact that Juris and Feuille show political action to have a substantial impact on working conditions supports our contention that the political power achieved by unions is very important.

Several other researchers have presented findings consistent with those of Stanley and of Juris and Feuille.[18] The consistent findings, however, have been interpreted to mean different things. For instance, Goldschmidt and Stuart's analysis of teacher contracts in force over the 1981–1982 academic year concludes that bargaining has had a much greater impact on educational policy than researchers have acknowledged.[19] Those 1981–1982 contracts contained many provisions dealing with educational policy issues, and field interviews suggested that those policy provisions were uniformly followed. As a result, Goldschmidt and Stuart argued that collective bargaining had reduced the ability of public schools to adapt to changing circumstances or situations.

In our opinion, the Goldschmidt and Stuart study illustrates two interrelated points that should be considered when drawing inferences about the impact of bargaining in the public sector. First, the existence of a contract provision that could affect some aspect of management policy does not demonstrate an impact on such policy. Because management and the union could jointly choose to ignore the contract language, it was necessary for

Goldschmidt and Stuart to determine the extent to which the parties followed the contract provisions. Where contract provisions are followed consistently, it is necessary to pay careful attention to the specific requirements imposed by the contract language. In this regard, the generality of the contract clauses examined by Goldschmidt and Stuart reduces the persuasiveness of their conclusions. For example, provisions covering the implementation of layoffs were studied, but the authors failed to note that contract language governing how layoffs will be conducted may not restrict management's authority to order a reduction in force. Further, the authors studied only unionized schools and thus could not determine whether bargaining and nonbargaining districts follow similar policies. Consequently, both the generality of the language of the provisions affecting educational policy, and sample selectivity problems suggest that Goldschmidt and Stuart's findings should be interpreted cautiously.

Second, different investigators may infer divergent conclusions from the same or similar data. In the context of the impact of impasse procedures, Feuille has argued that the personal preferences or predilections of researchers can have an impact on their conclusions.[20] In this case, on the basis of the data presented, it is possible to conclude that, contrary to what Goldschmidt and Stuart have suggested, bargaining does not substantially reduce the adaptability of schools. Such a conclusion, correct or incorrect, could logically be derived from a researcher's normative assumptions regarding the value of collective bargaining and the adaptability of nonbargaining school districts. Our point is that investigations of the impact of bargaining must be interpreted with caution. Further, there is a need for systematic empirical examinations of the nonwage impacts of bargaining. Although such studies are not necessarily free of bias,[21] they often summarize the impact of bargaining in a large number of local governments. Thus, in evaluating the nonwage impact of bargaining, we will compare the findings of some recent empirical studies with those of institutional analyses.

Table 7–1 presents a summary of the findings of selected recent empirical studies of the nonwage impact of bargaining.[22] It is interesting that, in many respects, the findings reported in the table are generally consistent with the conclusions of earlier investigations, and the empirical studies seem to support several long-standing inferences about the impact of bargaining. Although we do not provide a comprehensive research review here, the results presented are a representative summary of the literature.

Work Rules

Very few studies have empirically examined the impact of public sector bargaining on work rules or working conditions. Further, the relevant research has tended to examine very specific outcome measures, such as class

Table 7 . 1
A Summary of Studies of Public Sector Union Impacts on Nonwage Bargaining Outcomes

Issue and Finding	*Representative Studies*
Work rules:	
Study of federal government supervisors suggests that bargaining affects supervisor's awareness and use of federal alcoholism and EEO policies.	Beyer, Trice and Hunt (1980)
The scope of bargaining in state teacher bargaining laws affects the size of classes in U.S. public schools.	Woodbury (1985)
The scope of bargaining in police bargaining laws affects the grievance procedures included in police contracts.	Delaney, Feuille, and Hendricks (1984)
Wage–nonwage trade-offs:	
A study of teachers reports the existence of compensating differentials between wages and various nonwage outcomes (leaves and fringes). Other studies had suggested wages to be uncorrelated or positively correlated with nonwage outcomes.	Eberts and Stone (1985) Anderson (1979) Delaney, Feuille, and Hendricks (1986)
Management policy and practices:	
Studies suggest that educational policy bargaining is extensive, that such bargaining affects teachers' daily activities, and that unintended consequences frequently arise from such bargaining.	Goldschmidt and Stuart (1986) McDonnell and Pascal (1979) Mitchell, Kerchner, Erck, and Pryor (1981)
Nonwage provisions in police contracts generally impose costs on various management practices instead of restricting practices.	Delaney, Feuille, and Hendricks (1986)
Productivity:	
Studies of workers in libraries, police and fire departments, and school districts show mixed results. Overall, the findings do not indicate that bargaining has reduced public employee productivity.	Coulter (1979) Delaney, Feuille, and Hendricks (1986) Eberts (1984) Ehrenberg, Sherman and Schwarz (1983)
One study suggests that standardized test scores of average students are 7 percent higher in unionized districts than in nonunion districts.	Eberts and Stone (1987)
Budgeting, finance, and taxation:	
Studies show some mixed results; early studies suggest that bargaining is associated with an expansion of the budget, disemployment effects, and increased user fees for using municipal services. The effects vary depending on the size of the city.	Baderschneider (1979) Benecki (1978) Gallagher (1978)

Table 7–1 (continued)

Issue and Finding	Representative Studies
Budgeting, finance, and taxation (continued)	
Later studies suggest that contract provisions individually and in combination affect budget allocation; over time it appears that bargaining leads to reallocations of budget resources.	Eberts (1983) Schwochau, Feuille, and Delaney (1987)
Limited evidence implies that bargaining is associated with higher school tax rates.	Gallagher (1978, 1979)

size in public schools, and thus may not be applicable across all public sector occupations or services. The findings of the research uniformly suggest that bargaining affects various working conditions and personnel policies. Given the outcome measures used, the findings support the conclusions of earlier research, where it was persuasively argued that unions emphasize class size and grievance procedure issues. In fact, recent empirical research suggests a larger bargaining effect than earlier studies reported. Further, recent research confirms that the legal environment regulating bargaining, particularly the scope of bargaining, has a substantial impact on work rules. This is consistent with our beliefs about bargaining scope rules and also suggests that states may have some control over the potential impact of bargaining through the manipulation of certain legal requirements.

Wage–Nonwage Trade-offs

If unions are forced to reduce their demands in one area in order to achieve higher wages, then the total impact of bargaining on outcomes may be lower than separate analyses of wages or nonwage employment conditions suggest. Little research has addressed this topic. Although available evidence is mixed, one recent analysis of school district data has reported the existence of such trade-offs. Until other studies confirm this finding, however, the existence of such trade-offs should not be assumed.

Management Policy and Practices

Much of the research on the impact of bargaining on management policy has focused on school districts and has followed institutional methods. Nevertheless, the available studies have concluded that bargaining has direct, indirect, and unintended effects on policies and practices. It is uncertain from the studies, however, whether these effects occur simultaneously. Some of the school district studies imply that bargaining negatively affects the delivery of educational services; these conclusions are somewhat at odds with earlier institutional analyses of other government functions. The Juris and Feuille reading in this chapter, for instance, reports that police unions have had some, mostly indirect, impacts on law enforcement policy in some cities. Further, a recent study of police contracts in effect in nearly 500 cities above 25,000 population generally confirms Juris and Feuille's inferences.[23] That analysis suggested that although police officers have negotiated contract provisions in many policy-related areas, the provisions generally specify the extra compensation that will be paid to officers in certain situations (for example, when assigned to a one-person patrol car) rather than the policies that the department will follow. Thus, research indicates that police management establishes law enforcement policy, whereas police unions influence how much various policies will cost. Because the studies of police have yielded different conclusions than the studies of teachers, future research is needed in this area. Moreover, in some cases unions have probably achieved influence over management policy; research should study whether such influence is or is not appropriate. Regardless of the findings of future research, the debate about union impacts on policy will likely continue because of the divergent assumptions that individuals make about the propriety of union involvement in this area.

Productivity

Several studies have investigated the impact of bargaining on productivity in the public sector. This research, covering most major categories of government workers, has reached mixed conclusions. No consistent impact of bargaining on employees' productivity can be discerned, but the results do not suggest that bargaining lowers the productivity of public workers. Even this weak generalization, however, must be viewed with caution. Problems exist in many of the past investigations, and it is inherently difficult to obtain accurate output measures in the public sector. Indeed, the existence of these measurement problems suggests that better insight into the impact of bargaining on productivity is a long way off.

Table 7–2 illustrates these problems by presenting Randall Eberts's summary of the impact of collective bargaining on various measures of teachers' productivity and the impact of those measures on school productivity (as measured by standardized student achievement test scores.) The combination of effects portrayed in the table suggests an uncertain union impact on school productivity. Although Eberts's findings are generally consistent with earlier institutional research, his summary demonstrates the complexity of the educational service delivery process, the difficulties associated with the measurement of productivity, and the problems arising in efforts to predict the net effect of collective bargaining on the delivery of public services.

In a subsequent study, Eberts and Stone addressed these issues and calculated estimates of the impact of collective bargaining on school productiv-

Table 7–2

Summary of the Effects of Collective Bargaining on Selected Variables and the Effect of These Variables on Student Achievement

	Effects of Collective Bargaining on the Variable	Effect of the Variable on Student Achievement	Direction of Net Effect
Time teachers spend in instruction	−	+	−
Time teachers spend in preparation	+	+	+
Experience level of teachers	+	+	+
Education level of teachers	+	−	−
Teacher/student ratio	+	+	+
Administrator/student ratio	+	−	−

Source: Reprinted, with permission, from Eberts (1984), p. 358.

Note: The table contains only those variables considered in the analysis whose effects on student achievement have been estimated by the author or supported by other studies. Signs in the second column are taken from the studies listed in footnotes 5 and 6 of Eberts (1984).

ity; that study is reprinted herein. The analysis is especially noteworthy because it reveals that union effects on school productivity vary across student ability levels. The *average* student performs significantly better in a unionized district than in a nonunion district. Students significantly above and below average in ability, however, display significantly greater performance in nonunion than in union schools. Eberts and Stone's findings are consistent with contentions that unions cause a standardization of the production process. On balance, Eberts and Stone report that, other things being equal, student achievement scores are about 3 percent higher in unionized than nonunion districts. This is the first careful public sector analysis to document such positive union effects on service delivery.

In short, both empirical and case studies generally suggest that unions have not negotiated rules or practices that, on average, adversely affect productivity. The findings may indicate that union political power, which Juris and Feuille found to affect negotiations over management practices, is not pervasive. On the other hand, because the productivity studies have not included direct measures of union political power in their equations, future empirical research could yield different results.

Budgeting, Finances, and Taxes

Because evidence suggests that bargaining affects wage and nonwage outcomes, it likely also has an impact on public sector budgets. The magnitude of such a bottom-line effect is important because it indicates how much bargaining costs the taxpayers. Despite the importance of the topic, very little research has investigated the impact of bargaining on municipal finance. Further, the existing studies report inconsistent results, though a pattern may be emerging over time.

Conceptually, bargaining may affect municipal budgeting in a number of ways. First, it could be associated with an expansion of the budget. Public sector unions have long been active in state capitals and Washington, D.C., seeking to obtain increased state and federal support of local governments. Second, bargaining could be associated with disemployment effects, as governmental units attempt to provide a given level of service with fewer employees. Also, governmental units may attempt to replace some comparatively high paid employees with comparatively low paid employees; for instance, civilian police employees could assume certain routine duties from officers to cut costs. Third, municipalities could cut some public services (for example, by reducing the hours that some public facilities are open) or contract out services to the private sector. Fourth, bargaining could lead to budget reallocation, as governmental units shift funds from nonbargaining departments to bargaining departments or from nonsalary budget categories to salary categories. In reality, different combinations of these approaches may occur. For instance, a government unit may institute user fees for some public services, such as drivers' education classes, while maintaining a hiring freeze or raising taxes. The fact that so many possible combinations exist and so little research has been conducted in this area illustrates the need to view the available research cautiously.

Existing studies suggest an evolution of the impact of bargaining on budgets over time. Early studies, using data from the late 1960s or early 1970s, suggested that bargaining was associated with budget expansion.[24] Additional revenues seemed to come from intergovernmental transfer payments, the imposition of user fees, and tax increases. The budget patterns differed across large and small cities, however, and there was some evidence of fiscal stress and layoffs in very large cities. Research also provided little evidence of budget reallocation.[25]

Studies relying on more recent data have reported more substantial bargaining impacts on budgets. Eberts's study of New York State school districts has suggested that individual union contract provisions, both separately and in combination, significantly affect school district budgets.[26] Moreover, evidence has begun to appear that suggests that both budget reallocation and disemployment are occurring.[27] This new evidence is not surprising in light of the taxpayer rebellions of the recent past, the exodus of industry (and tax base) from highly unionized Frostbelt states to generally nonunion Sunbelt states, and the stagnation and decline of federal government funding. More than ever before, fiscal pressure may be forcing local governments to use local revenues to pay for bargaining settlements. Disemployment and reallocation become more prominent, given the legal restraints on the taxing and debt abilities of local governments. Thus, the trend across the research in this area is not surprising. Nevertheless, much more research is needed in this area before a complete picture of bargaining's impact on budgeting is available.

If the observed trend in the impact of bargaining on municipal finances continues, then an interesting possibility arises. Labor relations in the public sector could become much more conflictual as unions attempt to improve their members' lot in the light of stagnating, or decreasing, government revenues. On the other hand, public employers and unions could stress cooperative arrangements in order to benefit affected parties. Although it is not possible to predict accurately what actions unions may take, it is clear that some actions will be necessary. Municipal financing has a powerful impact on bargaining power, and trends suggest that such financing may become tighter in the foreseeable future. This could lead to a new generation of union–management relations in the public sector. The possibility also makes it necessary to examine approaches that are available to bring about change in public sector bargaining relationships.

Introducing Change in Bargaining Relationships

Given our belief that fiscal problems will cause stress and strain in bargaining relationships, the question of how changes may be brought about under bargaining becomes important. Change does not come easily in collective bargaining, particularly when it involves threats to job security or to other vital economic and organizational interests of the parties. Yet we have pointed out throughout this book the fact that external forces will continue to exert pressure for change. One strategy for implementing change is to do so through a joint union–management committee. Such an approach has special potential for success because both labor and management have input into strategies for change. In this regard, the final reading of this chapter—by Robert McKersie, Leonard Greenhalgh, and Todd Jick on the Continuity of Employment Committee in New York State—provides an insightful description of the benefits that can be derived from cooperation. The authors' story of how the committee helped search for effective ways of managing major work force reductions speaks for itself.

Cooperation, however, is not always possible, as other strategies may offer comparatively more benefits to unions or employers at different points in time. For instance, unions may undertake political activities to achieve beneficial outcomes. Ample evidence exists of public sector unions employing political muscle to achieve favorable outcomes.[28] The record suggests, however, that unions do not always win political battles, and this may explain why federal employee unions—which depend on Congress for pay and benefits—have attempted to increase their bargaining opportunities.[29] Further, the pressure applied by competing interest groups makes union political activity a risky activity.

In some cases, the external environment may impinge on public sector labor–management relationships. For example, court orders regarding affirmative action or school desegregation may conflict with negotiated contract arrangements. In such cases, evidence suggests that the parties offer substantial, though sometimes subtle, resistance to the imposed changes.[30] Although court-ordered changes are less common than jointly negotiated changes, the potential for the imposition of a court order is one factor that influences the parties' joint decision making.

In this chapter we have suggested that public sector bargaining has substantially influenced union members' working conditions. Hidden beneath this success, however, is a problem for public sector unions. Union gains and union resistance to change in some areas have exacerbated external pressures affecting governmental units. Fiscal crises, taxpayer revolts, and governmental and judicial intervention have forced public employers to change various policies. The success of public sector unions over the past two decades, in the face of these external pressures, may intensify the pressure for voluntarily negotiated change or, instead, may spur even more externally compelled changes in bargaining relationships. Thus, the stability that has come about in public sector bargaining could begin to erode as pressures for change grow.

Notes

1. John Delaney and Peter Feuille, "Police," in David B. Lipsky and Clifford B. Donn, eds. *Collective Bargaining in American Industry.* (Lexington, Mass.: D.C. Heath, 1987), pp. 265–306.

2. See, for instance, Thomas A. Kochan and Hoyt N. Wheeler, "Municipal Collective Bargaining: A Model and Analysis of Bargaining Outcomes," *Industrial and Labor Relations Review* 29, no. 1 (October 1975), pp. 46–66 (firefighters); Paul F. Gerhart, "Determinants of Bargaining Outcomes in Local Government Negotiations," *Industrial and Labor Relations Review* 29, no. 3 (April 1976), pp. 331–351 (municipal employees); Morris M. Kleiner and Charles E. Krider, "Determinants of Negotiated Agreements for Public School Teachers," *Educational Administration Quarterly* 15, no. 3 (Fall 1979), pp. 66–82; and John Thomas Delaney, "Impasses and Teacher Contract Outcomes," *Industrial Relations* 25, no. 1 (Winter 1986), pp. 45–55 (teachers).

3. See Kochan and Wheeler, "Municipal Collective Bargaining," and Gerhart, "Determinants of Bargaining Outcomes."

4. See Charles R. Perry, "Teacher Bargaining: The Experience in Nine Systems," *Industrial and Labor Relations Review* 33, no. 1 (October 1979), pp. 3–17; Douglas E. Mitchell, Charles T. Kerchner, Wayne Erck, and Gabrielle Pryor,

"The Impact of Collective Bargaining on School Management and Policy," *American Journal of Education* 89, no. 2 (February 1981), pp. 147–188.

5. Milton Derber and Martin Wagner, "Public Sector Bargaining and Budget Making under Fiscal Adversity," *Industrial and Labor Relations Review* 33, no. 1 (October 1979), pp. 18–23.

6. Peter Feuille, John Thomas Delaney, and Wallace Hendricks, "The Impact of Interest Arbitration on Police Contracts," *Industrial Relations* 24, no. 2 (Spring 1985), pp. 161–181.

7. Perry, "Teacher Bargaining." The initial study is reported in Charles R. Perry and Wesley A. Wildman, *The Impact of Negotiations in Public Education: The Evidence from the Schools* (Worthington, Ohio: Jones Publishing Company, 1970).

8. Mitchell et al., "The Impact of Collective Bargaining."

9. Derber and Wagner, "Public Sector Bargaining," note 5, and Feuille et al., "The Impact of Interest Arbitration."

10. For a discussion of bargaining and political action in the federal sector, see Marick F. Masters, "Federal-Employee Unions and Political Action," *Industrial and Labor Relations Review* 38, no. 4 (July 1985), pp. 612–628.

11. See Feuille et al., "The Impact of Interest Arbitration"; John Thomas Delaney, Peter Feuille, and Wallace Hendricks, "Interest Arbitration and Grievance Arbitration: The Twain Do Meet," in Industrial Relations Research Association, *Proceedings of the Thirty-sixth Annual Meeting* (Madison, Wisc.: IRRA, 1984), pp. 313–320.

12. Stephen A. Woodbury, "The Scope of Bargaining and Bargaining Outcomes in the Public Schools," *Industrial and Labor Relations Review* 38, no. 2 (January 1985), pp. 195–210.

13. See Robert G. Valletta and Richard B. Freeman, "Presentation of NBER State Public Sector Collective Bargaining Law Data Set," unpublished manuscript, 1985.

14. Recent reviews of the public sector union impact literature include Richard B. Freeman, "Unionism Comes to the Public Sector," *Journal of Economic Literature* 24, no. 1 (March 1986), pp. 41–86, and David T. Methe and James L. Perry, "The Impacts of Collective Bargaining on Local Government Services: A Review of Research," *Public Administration Review* 40, no. 4 (July–August 1980), pp. 359–371.

15. Sumner Slichter, James J. Healy, and E. Robert Livernash, *The Impact of Collective Bargaining on Management.* (Washington, D.C.: Brookings Institution, 1960).

16. David T. Stanley, with Carole L. Cooper, *Managing Local Government under Union Pressure.* (Washington, D.C.: Brookings Institution, 1972).

17. Hervey Juris and Peter Feuille, *Police Unionism.* (Lexington, Mass.: D.C. Heath, 1973).

18. See, for instance, Lorraine McDonnell and Anthony Pascal, *Organized Teachers in American Schools.* (Santa Monica, Calif.: Rand, 1979); Sar Levitan and Alexandra B. Noden, *Working for the Sovereign: Employee Relations in the Federal Government.* (Baltimore: Johns Hopkins University Press, 1983).

19. Steven M. Goldschmidt and Leland E. Stuart, "The Extent and Impact of

Educational Policy Bargaining," *Industrial and Labor Relations Review* 39, no. 3 (April 1986), pp. 350–360.

20. Peter Feuille, "Analyzing Compulsory Arbitration Experiences: The Role of Personal Preferences—Comment," *Industrial and Labor Relations Review* 28, no. 3 (April 1975), pp. 432–438.

21. For an example of the problems noted here in the context of empirical studies, compare Julius G. Getman, Stephen B. Goldberg, and Jeanne M. Herman, *Union Representation Elections: Law and Reality* (New York: Russell Sage, 1976), and William T. Dickens, "The Effect of Company Campaigns on Certification Elections: *Law and Reality* Once Again," *Industrial and Labor Relations Review* 36, no. 4 (July 1983), pp. 560–575.

22. A careful review of this literature has been conducted by Freeman, "Unionism Comes to the Public Sector."

23. Delaney et al., "Interest Arbitration and Grievance Arbitration."

24. See Daniel G. Gallagher, "Teacher Bargaining and School District Expenditures," *Industrial Relations* 17, no. 2 (May 1978), pp. 231–237.

25. See Stanley Benecki, "Municipal Expenditure Levels and Collective Bargaining," *Industrial Relations* 17, no. 2 (May 1978), pp. 216–230.

26. See Randall W. Eberts, "How Unions Affect Management Decisions: Evidence from Public Schools," *Journal of Labor Research* 4, no. 3 (Summer 1983), pp. 239–247.

27. See Susan Schwochau, Peter Feuille, and John Delaney, "The Resource Allocation Effects of Mandated Relationships," unpublished manuscript, 1987.

28. See, for instance, David Stephens, "President Carter, the Congress and NEA: Creating the Department of Education," *Political Science Quarterly* 98, no. 4 (Winter 1983–1984), pp. 641–663. Note, however, that the Hatch Act and similar state laws impose restrictions on government employee political activity; see Marick F. Masters and Leonard Bierman, "The Hatch Act and the Political Activities of Federal Employee Unions: A Need for Policy Reform," *Public Administration Review* 45, no. 4 (July–August 1985), pp. 518–526.

29. See Masters, "Federal-Employee Unions."

30. For an insightful analysis of one case, see Harry Katz, "The Boston Teachers Union and the Desegregation Process," in David Lewin, Peter Feuille, and Thomas A. Kochan, *Public Sector Labor Relations: Analysis and Readings* 2nd ed. (Sun Lakes, Ariz.: Thomas Horton and Daughters, 1981), pp. 490–500.

References to Table 7–1

Anderson, John C. "Bargaining Outcomes: An IR System Approach." *Industrial Relations* 18, no. 2 (Spring 1979), pp. 127–143.

Baderschneider, Jean. "Collective Bargaining Pressure on Municipal Fiscal Capacity and Fiscal Effort." Unpublished manuscript, 1979.

Benecki, Stanley. "Municipal Expenditure Levels and Collective Bargaining." *Industrial Relations* 17, no. 2 (May 1978), pp. 216–230.

Beyer, Janice M., Harrison M. Trice, and Richard E. Hunt. "The Impact of Federal Sector Unions on Supervisors' Use of Personnel Policies." *Industrial and Labor Relations Review* 33, no. 2 (January 1980), pp. 212–231.

Coulter, Philip B. "Organizational Effectiveness in the Public Sector: The Example of Municipal Fire Protection." *Administrative Science Quarterly* 24, no. 1 (March 1979), pp. 65–81.

Delaney, John, Peter Feuille, and Wallace Hendricks. "Interest Arbitration and Grievance Arbitration: The Twain Do Meet." In Industrial Relations Research Association, *Proceedings of the Thirty-sixth Annual Meeting*. Madison, Wisc.: IRRA, 1984, pp. 313–320.

———. "The Regulation of Bargaining Disputes: A Cost–Benefit Analysis of Interest Arbitration in the Public Sector." In David B. Lipsky and David Lewin, eds., *Advances in Industrial and Labor Relations*, vol. 3. Greenwich, Conn.: JAI Press, 1986, pp. 83–118.

Eberts, Randall W. "How Unions Affect Management Decisions: Evidence from Public Schools." *Journal of Labor Research* 4, no. 3 (Summer 1983), pp. 239–247.

———. "Union Effects on Teacher Productivity." *Industrial and Labor Relations Review* 37, no. 3 (April 1984), pp. 346–358.

Eberts, Randall W., and Joe A. Stone. "Wages, Fringe Benefits, and Working Conditions: An Analysis of Compensating Differentials." *Southern Economic Journal* 52, no. 2 (July 1985), pp. 274–280.

———. "The Effect of Teacher Unions on Student Achievement," *Industrial and Labor Relations Review* 40, no. 3 (April 1987), pp. 354–363.

Ehrenberg, Ronald G., Daniel R. Sherman, and Joshua L. Schwarz. "Unions and Productivity in the Public Sector: A Study of Municipal Libraries," *Industrial and Labor Relations Review* 36, no. 2 (January 1983), pp. 199–213.

Gallagher, Daniel G. "Teacher Bargaining and School District Expenditures," *Industrial Relations* 17, no. 2 (May 1978), pp. 231–237.

———. "Teacher Negotiations, School District Expenditures, and Taxation Levels." *Educational Administration Quarterly* 15, no. 1 (Winter 1979), pp. 67–82.

Goldschmidt, Steven M., and Leland E. Stuart. "The Extent and Impact of Educational Policy Bargaining." *Industrial and Labor Relations Review* 39, no. 3 (April 1986), pp. 350–360.

McDonnell, Lorraine, and Anthony Pascal. *Organized Teachers in American Schools*. Santa Monica, Calif.: Rand, 1979.

Mitchell, Douglas E., Charles T. Kerchner, Wayne Erck, and Gabrielle Pryor. "The Impact of Collective Bargaining on School Management and Policy." *American Journal of Education* 89, no. 2 (February 1981), pp. 147–188.

Schwochau, Susan, Peter Feuille, and John Delaney. "The Resource Allocation Effects of Mandated Relationships." Unpublished manuscript, 1987.

Woodbury, Stephen A. "The Scope of Bargaining and Bargaining Outcomes in the Public Schools." *Industrial and Labor Relations Review* 38, no. 2 (January 1985), pp. 195–210.

Bargaining Outcomes:
An IR System Approach

*John C. Anderson**

Substantial debate still exists about the relevance of the private sector collective bargaining model to the public sector. For example, it has been argued that the inelasticity of demand for public services, the predominance of political rather than economic power, the diffuse nature of management (resulting in intraorganizational conflict), and the existence of multilateral rather than bilateral negotiations combine to produce a set of influences on the wage and benefit determination process that is unique to the public sector. Nevertheless, most wage determination research has not yet gone beyond economic models of bargaining power to explain the outcomes of the bargaining process. Typically, conditions of the labor market (such as unemployment, monopsony, demand for labor); inflation; and private sector wage comparisons are used as the primary predictors of public sector wages. Those studies going beyond these environmental context variables are typically limited to dummy variable measures of the impasse procedures available, the existence of a union contract, or the form of government. Thus, whereas public sector bargaining *theory* identifies a number of critical characteristics of the noneconomic context, the management and union organizations, and the bargaining process that may have an impact on wage and benefit levels, *research* has remained generally limited to economic explanations.[1]

Recent studies, however, evince a new interest in developing empirically testable models of the bargaining process that identify a wide range of potential sources of bargaining power that may affect the outcomes of collective bargaining in the public sector.[2] Moreover, these studies have gone beyond wages to examine the determinants of the contents of collective agreements. The present study extends this nascent trend first by using an industrial relations system conceptual framework to identify the characteristics of the environment, management and union organizations, and bargaining process which may act as sources of union bargaining power affecting bargaining outcomes.[3] Second, both wage and nonwage bargaining outcomes are examined separately as dependent variables. Finally, propositions relating the components of the industrial relations system to bargaining outcomes are developed and tested with a cross-sectional analysis of the outcomes of bargaining between Canadian municipal governments and 95 local unions. The

*UNICEF. Reprinted from *Industrial Relations* 18, no. 2 (Spring 1979), pp. 127–143.

results generally confirm findings in recent research and imply the need for several new directions in future research.

The Conceptual Framework

To develop a more comprehensive approach to the determinants of bargaining outcomes in the public sector, it is first necessary to select a conceptual framework to aid in the choice of independent variables. Perhaps the best known theoretical perspective is Dunlop's industrial relations system, which he defined as "an analytic subsystem of an industrial society on the same logical plane as an economic system."[4] The system comprises three actors— government, employers and their associations, and workers and their associations—bound together by an ideology, with an output of a "web of rules" of the workplace and the work community. The technical, power, and market contexts of the system are viewed as determinants of the web of rules, with each context having a selective impact on the subset of rules (for example, market context affects compensation).

Unfortunately, Dunlop's theory failed to provide a satisfactory unifying framework for the field of industrial relations. The model has been criticized as being a taxonomy that fosters descriptive rather than explanatory research. This is due in part to the failure of the industrial relations system model to present testable hypotheses. In addition, the failure to distinguish between procedures for establishing rules and the established rules themselves has created problems for researchers. Obviously, the nature of the bargaining or grievance process has an impact on the outcomes; but lumping both process and result into the web of rules obscures these distinctions. Second, by examining only the market, technological, and power contexts of the industrial relations system, Dunlop did not delineate possible influences from the wider economic, political, legal, and social systems on the industrial relations system and its web of rules. Of course, some aspects of these wider systems are subsumed into the three contexts, but a vast array of other factors influencing the outcomes of the industrial relations system are not. Third, it is never clear what characteristics of the actors in the system are important or unimportant and how they influence the outcomes of the system. Finally, it is not apparent at which level of analysis the industrial relations system applies—firms, industry, or society—or which actor's perspective is to be taken in examining the system—labor, management, government, the public, or some combination of these.[5] Each of these questions is vital to the researcher who is attempting to operationalize and test the industrial relations system model.

Still, despite its drawbacks as a formal theory, the industrial relations system framework is a potentially useful working perspective. With several minor modifications, this approach can be helpful in identifying the important influences on the outcomes of the industrial relations system. Specifically, if a broader set of environmental variables is assessed, the important characteristics of the actors are delineated, and the outcomes or rules of the system are separated from the procedures for establishing them, researchers will be able to identify the variables of interest within each part of the framework and then test the hypothesized relationships.

The present study uses four conceptual categories from the industrial relations system framework: (1) the environment or context; (2) the actors; (3) the mechanisms for converting inputs into outputs or the procedures for establishing rules; and (4) the outcomes of the industrial relations system. Each of the first three sets of factors may act as a source of bargaining power for union and management, shaping the outcomes of the system. That is, the characteristics of the economic, political, legal, and social environments; the organizational characteristics and expertise of union and management; and the nature of the bargaining process all are likely to influence the costs of agreement or disagreement between negotiating parties and hence to affect the outcomes of collective bargaining. Consequently, in the present research, all these factors are identified and measured as sources of union bargaining power. The hypothesized relationships between these sets of characteristics and wage and nonwage bargaining outcomes are presented with the results.

Research Design

Sample

The sample population consists of police officers, firefighters, clerical employees, and manual workers in twenty-six major Canadian municipalities. All cities over 100,000 people were included and then supplemented so that at least the largest two cities in each of the ten provinces are represented. Personal interviews were conducted with representatives of each of the ninety-five local unions selected and with the negotiator acting for each of the municipalities. In the majority of cases, separate bargaining units are certified for each of the four occupational groups examined. Manual and clerical employees, and in several provinces police and firefighters, are under the jurisdiction of private sector labor legislation.

Dependent Variables

Both wages and an index of nonwage collective bargaining outcomes are included as dependent variables. Similar to the approaches of Kochan and

Wheeler, Gerhart, and Perry and Levine, provisions in collective agreements are identified and assigned values according to their favorability to the union.[6] Categories representing the degree of favorability of the provisions are developed from a comprehensive list of contract provisions, with the least favorable provision being assigned the lowest value and the most favorable one the highest. For example, union security provisions have the following values: no reference (0), maintenance of membership (1), agency shop (2), modified union shop (3), and union shop (4). A total score is calculated for each contract by adding the scores on each of the forty-five provisions included in the particular contract.[7] The base wage rate for each occupational group (local union) is used as the wage dependent variable. Because it is the base wage that is altered directly through negotiations (the higher steps in the wage scale being adjusted accordingly) and because of its comparability across bargaining units, the base wage rate is preferable to the average or maximum rate.

As both wages and the nature of issues demanded in collective bargaining vary systematically by occupational group, two forms of each dependent variable are examined: the raw score and the normalized score. Wages and bargaining outcomes scores are normalized within a particular occupation (police, firefighters, clerical, manual) to a mean value of 0 and a standard deviation of 1. This allows direct comparisons on bargaining outcome measures across occupations.[8]

Independent Variables

The independent variables are characteristics that the industrial relations system framework and previous public sector collective bargaining research suggest might enhance the union's ability to attain favorable outcomes. Measures of the characteristics of the environment, union, management, and bargaining process are taken from published data sources and interviews with union and management representatives. Most measures are specifically developed or adapted for this study and have acceptable estimates of reliability. The definitions of the independent variables and the data sources are presented in table 1.[9]

Hypotheses and Zero-Order Correlation Results

Environmental Sources of Union Power

Environmental characteristics may be classified into economic, political, legal, social, and task categories. As previous research on the public sector wage and benefit determination process has emphasized, the objective conditions of the environment have a substantial impact on the costs of agreement

Table 1
Correlations of Sources Bargaining Power with Bargaining Outcomes

Independent Variables	Hypothesis	Wages	Bargaining Outcomes
Economic environment			
Inflation rate[a]	+	.27***	.05
Unemployment rate[b]	–	– .44***	– .08
City's ability to pay[c]	+	– .08	– .22***
Demand for city services[d]	+	.37***	.20**
Private sector wage rate[e]	+	.33***	.19**
Political environment			
Percentage voting NDP[f]	+	.31***	.34**
Municipal election year[g]	+	.23***	– .17**
Legal environment			
Comprehensiveness of the law[h]	+	– .27***	– .23**
Social environment			
Percentage of labor force unionized[i]	+	.22***	.04
Rate of strikes in the city[j]	+	.24***	– .22**
Percentage of labor force in manufacturing[d]	+	.16*	.51***
Task environment			
Support from task environment[g]	+	– .32***	.13*
Management structure			
Negotiator authority to bargain[g]	–	.17**	.17**
Internal management conflict[k]	+	– .19**	– .15*
Elected official on bargaining team[k]	+	.12	.14*
Form of city government (manager)[m]	–	– .33***	.12
Departmental representatives on bargaining team	–	.02	– .15*
Management preparation for collective bargaining			
Negotiator skill and experience[g]	–	.12	.05
Professional negotiator training[k]	–	– .19**	– .22***
Management commitment to industrial relations[k]	–	.10	.39***
Union structure[l]			
Specialization of labor	+	.04	.22***
Standardization of activities	+	.09	.01
Formalization of activities	+	.21**	.23***
Centralization of decision making	+	.07	.13**
Vertical differentiation	+	.15*	– .02
Professional staff/members	+	.10	– .02
Internal union processes			
Leadership competence[k]	+	.07	.15*
Union democracy[g]	+	.09	– .01
Union tactics[g]			
Militant tactics	+	.07	– .09
Public relations tactics	+	– .05	– .17**
Political pressure tactics	+	– .07	– .13*
Overall index	+	– .03	– .17**

Table 1 (continued)

Independent Variables	Hypothesis	Wages	Bargaining Outcomes
Bargaining process			
Multilateral collective bargaining[g]	+	.10	.10
Joint collective bargaining[k]	+	.05	−.04
Stage of impasse resolution[k]	+	.01	−.02
Control variables			
Age of bargaining relationship[k]	+	.28***	−.06
Union–management hostility[k]	−	.11	.14*
Union size[k]	+	.21**	−.00

Sources:

[a]Statistics Canada. *Prices and Price Index* (Ottawa: Information Canada, 1975, 1976).

[b]Statistics Canada. *The Labor Force,* monthly (Ottawa: Information Canada, 1974–1976).

[c]Statistics Canada, *Municipal Revenue and Expenditures* (Ottawa: Information Canada, 1973).

[d]Statistics Canada, 1971 *Canada Census* (Ottawa: Information Canada, 1973).

[e]Labour Canada, *Wage Rates, Salaries and Hours of Labour, Volume 1 — Community Rates* (Ottawa: Information Canada, 1973).

[f]Election Canada, *Twenty-ninth General Election, 1972 — Report of the Chief Electoral Officer* (Ottawa: Information Canada, 1974).

[g]These data were obtained in union interviews.

[h]This index was developed by classifying provincial bargaining laws into 12 categories and assigning a value to each category according to the degree to which it provides for a more formalized bargaining relationship. For a description of the coding scheme see Thomas A. Kochan. "Correlates of State Public Employee Bargaining Laws." *Industrial Relations,* (October, 1973), pp. 322–337.

[i]Labour Canada, *Corporations and Labor Unions Returns Act* (Ottawa: Information Canada, 1975).

[j]Labour Canada, *Strikes and Lockouts in Canada* (Ottawa: Information Canada, 1970, 1971, 1972).

[k]Management interviews.

[l]The approach to organizational structure of unions used in this research is based on the Aston studies and adapted for local unions. See Lex Donaldson and Marcolm Warner, "Structure of Organizations in Occupational Interest Associations," *Human Relations* (August, 1974), pp. 721–738.

[m]ICMA, *Municipal Year Book* (Washington, D.C.: ICMA, 1974).

or disagreement both for the union and management. Specifically, it has been hypothesized that the greater the employers' ability to pay for wage and benefit increases; the greater the demand for city services; the greater the municipality's demand for labor; the greater the comparable private sector wages; the greater the erosion of wages by inflation; and the lower the level of unemployment, the higher the ratio of costs of disagreement to costs of agreement for the employers, and thus the greater the bargaining power of the union.[10] The results presented in table 1 generally support these hypothesized relationships, especially with respect to the wage dependent variable. Only the measure of the city's ability to pay does not appear to be significant. On the other hand, only demand for city services and high private sector wages increased the favorability of nonwage bargaining outcomes to the union. Interestingly, the greater the city's ability to pay, as measured by per capita revenues, the lower the level of nonwage bargaining outcomes.

A favorable political environment may also increase union bargaining power. Political support in the form of a greater level of citizen vote for Canada's labor party (the New Democratic party) is associated with increased levels of both wages and nonwage bargaining outcomes. However, bargaining in a municipal election year has opposite effects on wages and bargaining outcomes. This result possibly indicates the existence of trade-offs, such that during an election year the union may be willing to push for increased wages at the expense of fringe benefits.

The favorableness of labor and other related legislation to the position of unions also may be a significant source of power for the union. The comprehensiveness of the law would be expected to reduce employer resistance, increasing union bargaining outcomes. Kochan and Wheeler found measures of the legal environment to have the strongest impact on bargaining outcomes.[11] The most surprising result of this research is the consistent negative impact of a comprehensive labor relations statute on the dependent variables. This may be due to the relatively standardized nature of labor legislation across Canadian provinces and to the fact that some of the most comprehensive statutes are in less industrialized provinces (such as Saskatchewan), which also have lower wages.

The more favorable the characteristics of the community and community sentiment toward industrial relations and unions, the more power the union would be expected to have in the bargaining process.[12] Thus, it could be hypothesized that bargaining outcomes would be generally more favorable to public sector unions where a greater proportion of the labor force is unionized and concentrated in highly unionized industries, and where the labor force is generally militant. Each of these conditions raises the probability of support for public sector unions and thus increases the potential costs to the employer of disagreement.

As table 1 indicates, unionization, militancy, and a more industrial base in the city are all positively related to wage levels. The relationships are not as clear for nonwage outcomes. For example, the city strike rate has a negative effect on nonwage outcomes. Again, it is possible that the results suggest the existence of a trade-off between wages and benefits. The percentage of the city's labor force in manufacturing is strongly correlated with the nonwage variable. Industrial communities are more likely to have comprehensive collective agreements governing the work force; therefore, this independent variable may represent a private sector comparability measure for nonwage outcomes.

The union's environment comprises not only the economic, political, legal, and social setting but also a network of other organizations with which the union interacts.[13] Support from these outside organizations may have a significant impact on the employers' perception of unions' ability to impose costs; hence, where support exists, the outcomes are likely to be more favorable to the union. This contention receives some support in nonwage outcomes, but the results suggest that unions with lower wages are more likely to seek help from other organizations.

Management Characteristics as Sources of Power

The manner in which management is organized and the extent to which it is prepared for collective bargaining may be reflected in the ability to impose costs on the union. Several authors have identified the problems of dispersion of authority among management officials in the public sector as a source of internal conflict. The existence of conflict within management increases the probability of union success through multilateral bargaining. Thus, the union's ability to impose costs on management should be increased when: authority is not delegated to the negotiator; internal conflict is present; an elected official is on the bargaining team; the city does not have a city manager form of government; and only a few city departments are represented in collective bargaining.[14]

The relationships appear to be weaker for this set of characteristics than for the environmental variables (see table 1). Moreover, several of the associations are not in the expected direction. Contrary to the hypothesis, the delegation of authority to the management negotiator increases the favorability of the settlement to the union. Kochan and Wheeler discovered the same relationship and suggested that delegation of power may be a result rather than a cause of union success. Alternatively, experienced negotiators may be more willing to negotiate a broad range of issues since they accept the value of a comprehensive contract. The results of the present study also strongly refute the hypothesis that internal management conflict aids the union because it allows use of a divide and conquer strategy. However, a qualitative analysis of the situations where internal conflict occurred reveals that, in most cases, the conflict involved an individual powerful enough both to resist union demands and to have those demands rejected at the political level.

The remaining variables assessing management structure are consistent with the hypotheses, although only for one of the two dependent variables. Furthermore, they support multilateral bargaining theory. That is, having an elected official and only a few departmental representatives on the bargaining teams are positively related to nonwage bargaining outcomes; and having a mayor-council form of government positively affects wage outcomes.

Management's preparation for collective bargaining is also important.

Where the city's negotiator is trained, skillful, and has greater expertise in collective bargaining, and where management is committed to the industrial relations function, it might be expected that management would be better able to manipulate the costs of agreement and disagreement as perceived by the union representatives.[15] The data presented here indicate that having a professionally trained negotiator on the management team limits the ability of the union to obtain greater bargaining outcomes. A management committed to the importance of industrial relations functions is also likely to be able to halt union demands. The skill and expertise of the negotiator are not related to bargaining outcomes.

Union Characteristics as Sources of Power

Previous research on the determinants of bargaining outcomes has been more concerned with the existence of a union or contract than with the actual characteristics of the union organization. It could be hypothesized, however, that the manner in which the union is organized would have an impact on its ability to achieve its goals through the collective bargaining process. For instance, Bok and Dunlop view the lack of coordination, supervision, and specialization; the failure to develop goals and strategies; the failure to ensure that leaders are administratively competent through planned selection and promotion procedures; and the reliance on part-time officers as causes of ineffective union performance.[16] Similarly, Barbash argues that rationalization, "making of union decisions through rules, organization and expertness rather than through trial by struggle, ideology, and hit-or-miss,"[17] is a requirement for the continued effectiveness of unions. The use of staff experts has also been identified as a criterion of effectiveness.[18] These arguments suggest that the development of an administrative bureaucracy is not only inevitable in unions, but also needed to enhance their effectiveness. Thus, it is possible to hypothesize that increased specialization of functions, formalization and standardization of activities, centralization of decision making, and differentiation of structure will enhance union effectiveness in collective bargaining. The results of testing this hypothesis are generally disappointing (see table 1). Only five associations are significant, and only a single variable is correlated with both wage and nonwage outcomes. It appears that specialization, formalization, and centralization are positively associated with nonwage outcomes. This implies that the development of an administrative structure may increase the ability of the union to prepare demands and rationales for nonwage components of the collective agreement. Only formalization of activities and a taller union hierarchy are correlated with better wages.

Internal union processes such as leadership and democracy have received a substantial amount of attention in the literature. A competent, well-trained leader can manipulate the employer's perceptions of the costs of agreement and disagreement in such a way as to increase the level of bargaining out-comes.[19] The extent of union democracy, though a popular topic of debate, has rarely been included in discussions of the outcomes of collective bargain-ing, possibly because predictions have ranged from negative, through no effect, to positive.[20] The present results indicate that leadership competence is only related to increased nonwage bargaining outcomes; union democracy is not significantly correlated with either dependent variable.

The third set of union characteristics examined is the extent to which the union used militant, public relations, and political pressure tactics to place extra pressure on management to accede to union demands.[21] None of the union tactics is significantly correlated with wages, but both public relations and political pressure tactics reduced the level of nonwage outcomes. It appears that bargaining tactics are not necessarily relevant within the Cana-dian system, and that, in fact, the use of political means to obtain benefits may be harmful to the union's position.

Characteristics of the Bargaining Process as a Source of Power

Because unions are able to strategically select the government official or body with which they will deal, the existence of multilateral collective bargaining is likely to raise bargaining outcomes.[22] Furthermore, when two or more muni-cipal unions jointly negotiate with an employer, they are likely to be able to inflict a greater cost, and, therefore should be able to negotiate more favor-able outcomes. Finally, pushing the dispute further into the impasse proce-dure will increase the costs of agreement for unions, and, therefore, they are unlikely to settle without substantial increases in bargaining outcomes.[23]

Testing these propositions results in none of the relationships being sig-nificantly different from zero. Because of the theoretical importance of the multilateral bargaining concept to public sector research, the index was broken down into its five component items and the correlations with bargain-ing outcomes were examined. Three of the five items are significantly corre-lated with both wage and nonwage outcomes:

1. Bargaining leverage of management is jeopardized by actions of other management officials (wages, $r + .13$, outcomes, $r + .18$).
2. Union representatives discuss their demands with city officials who are not on the formal negotiating team (wages, $r + .18$, outcomes, $r + .18$).
3. Elected officials intervene when an impasse occurs to mediate the dispute (wages, $r + .18$, outcomes, $r + .15$).

The associations are only significant at the 10 percent level, however.

Control Variables

Theory and research indicate that bargaining outcomes more favorable to the union are more likely to exist under certain conditions which are not directly related to the power of the parties. The older the collective bargaining relationship, the less hostility in the union–management relationship, and the larger the union, the more likely the union is to have favorable bargaining outcomes. These variables are therefore included as controls. The age of the bargaining relationship is correlated positively with the level of wages but not nonwage outcomes. The degree of union-management hostility is only slightly related to nonwage outcomes (negative). Finally, larger unions tend to have higher wage levels.

Regression Results

In order to examine the relative importance and combined effect of the independent variables and sets of characteristics as sources of union power on bargaining outcomes, a series of regression equations were estimated. The first equation for each dependent variable in table 2 uses the unstandardized form of the variable and dummy variables to estimate union effects. Equations 2 and 3 use the normalized form of the dependent variables, with the results in equation 3 representing a reduced model of the second. All variables that attained a significant correlation at the 10 percent level were entered into equation 2. Overall, these variables explain approximately two-thirds of the variance in both wage and nonwage outcomes. Past research has typically explained less than 50 percent, which suggests that there is some efficacy to the model presented.

The results of the regression analyses are generally consistent with the correlational findings. For both wage and nonwage outcomes, only the environmental and management characteristics make unique contributions to the variance explained.[24] Union characteristics and characteristics of the bargaining process are not significant in either of the regression equations. Age of the bargaining relationship alone exhibited a significant beta coefficient in the control variables. That is, as the relationship matures, management may become more generous with its wage concessions.

Unions appear to be more effective in obtaining higher wages when (1) unemployment is low, (2) the demand for city services is high, (3) it is a municipal election year (4), the city has greater per capita man-days lost because of strikes, (5) the local union is autonomous of task environment support, (6) a mayor-council form of government exists, (7) a professionally trained negotiator does not exist, (8) internal conflict is low, and (9) the parties have been bargaining for some time. Nonwage bargaining outcomes are higher, on the other hand, when (1) ability to pay is low, (2), demand for city services is high, (3) the base of the city is manufacturing, (4) strike activity is low, (5) there is support from the task environment, (6) commitment to the industrial relations function is low, and (7) a professionally trained negotiator is not present. Thus, there is only minimal overlap between the determinants of wage and nonwage outcomes. In fact, in several cases the signs on the variables change direction across outcomes.

Although Kochan and Wheeler discovered the comprehensiveness of the law to be the strongest predictor of bargaining outcomes, it is insignificant in this analysis. Two explanations are possible. First, the characteristics of public sector bargaining laws in Canada, unlike those in the United States, are relatively standard across jurisdiction. Thus, a lack of variance may explain the results. Alternatively, it seems possible that the law is an important source of union power in the initial stages of collective bargaining, when the parameters of the union–management relationship are not well defined. Subsequently, however, when the units have been negotiating for thirty years, as is the case in Canada, neither the comprehensiveness of the law nor the type of impasse procedures may be particularly important.

An examination of the relationship between union dummy variables and bargaining outcomes (equation 1) demonstrates the relative impact of the four occupational groups represented by municipal unions. In the wage-level equation, as a result of the distribution of wages among occupations, the dummy variables increase the variance explained to over 90 percent. The results indicate that clerical workers have the lowest wages, followed by manual employees, fire fighters, and, finally, police officers. Although the differences are less dramatic with nonwage outcomes, the same pattern is apparent. Police and firefighters have significantly less comprehensive collective agreements than clerical or manual workers. These results point out that the nature of the work may result in different types of union demands. The findings also support the use of dependent variables normalized by occupation.

Conclusions

The results presented here are generally consistent with previous research. The findings also include several implications for future research on public sector labor relations. First, it is clear from investigating wages and benefits as separate dependent variables that different factors influence the wage level than affect the nonwage package. While the pattern of results does not instantly reveal any underlying dimensions to these differences, it is apparent that we need better theorizing about the determinants of each. In several cases, the relationship of a given independent variable was positive for one of the dependent variables and negative for the other. Despite the fact that the

Table 2

Regression of Bargaining Outcomes on Characteristics of the Environment, Management and Union Organizations, and Bargaining Process

Independent Variables	Wages			Nonwage Outcomes		
	1	2	3	1	2	3
Environment:						
Inflation rate	.06	.02	—	—	—	—
Unemployment rate	-.22***	-.48***	-.48***	-.42***	-.43***	-.44***
City's ability to pay	.13	.14	.17*	.32**	.36***	.37***
Demand for city services	.04	-.11	—	.04	.04	—
Private sector wage rate	-.03	.04	.15**	-.01	.03	—
Percentage voting NDP	.10***	.16*	—	-.001	-.03	—
Municipal election year	-.10	-.08	—	.10	.02	—
Comprehensiveness of the law	—	—	—	—	—	—
Percentage of labor force in manufacturing	.003	.07	—	.57***	.47***	.52***
Percentage of labor force unionized	.11	.07	—	-.07	-.18*	-.17**
Rate of strikes in the city	.20***	.33***	.31***	.31***	.30***	.32***
Support from task environment	-.13**	-.24***	-.26***	—	—	—
Management:						
Management commitment to IR	-.17***	—	—	-.31***	-.42***	-.43***
Form of city government (manager)	-.07	-.27***	-.25***	-.03	-.21*	—
Professional negotiator training	-.03	-.21**	-.21***	-.02	.04	-.23**
Negotiator authority to bargain	-.08	.01	—	-.02	.04	—
Internal management conflict	—	-.15	-.18**	-.08	-.04	—
Elected official on bargaining team	—	—	—	-.002	-.04	—
Departmental representatives on bargaining team	—	—	—	-.02	-.01	—
Union:						
Specialization of labor	-.001	—	—	.02	.02	—
Formalization of activities	—	-.15	-.13	.02	.07	—
Centralization of decision making	—	—	—	-.02	-.05	-.06
Vertical differentiation	-.06	-.02	—	-.01	-.001	—
Leadership competence	—	—	—	-.01	-.05	—
Union tactics	—	—	—	-.02	-.05	—

Process:						
Union discusses with elected officials (multilateral collective bargaining)	-.01	—	—	.31**	.20*	.15
Control:						
Age of bargaining relationship	.07	.15	.17**	—	—	—
Union size	-.12*	-.14	-.13	—	—	—
Union–management hostility	—	—	—	-.02	.12	.15
Manual workers	.28***	—	—	.001	—	—
Firefighters	.64***	—	—	-.48***	—	—
Police officers	.78***	—	—	-.27*	—	—
R^2 $(\bar{R}^2)$	.92(.88)	.66(.55)	.64(.59)	.75(.62)	.64(.51)	.63(.58)
Overall F-value	23.59***	6.38***	11.67***	5.73***	4.88***	12.25***
Unique contribution:						
R^2 – Environment $(\bar{R}^2)$	—	—	.18***(.11)	—	—	.26***(.21)
R^2 – Management $(\bar{R}^2)$	—	—	.50**(.44)	—	—	.50*(.44)
R^2 – Union $(\bar{R}^2)$	—	—	.60(.56)	—	—	.63(.58)
R^2 – Process $(\bar{R}^2)$	—	—	—	—	—	.62(.57)
R^2 – Control $(\bar{R}^2)$	—	—	—	—	—	.62(.57)

Note: Equation 1 uses the unstandardized dependent variable; Equation 2 uses the standardized dependent variable; Equation 3 is a reduced model. — indicates that the variable was not entered into the equation.

$*p < .10$

$**p < .05$

$***p < .01$.

two dependent variables were uncorrelated ($r = -.02$), the results suggest that we need to consider the possibility of trade-offs between wages and benefits. Although industrial relations theorists have emphasized the give and take of the collective bargaining process, research has not formally pursued this issue. Furthermore, these results reiterate the need for longitudinal rather than cross-sectional research designs, which are better able to capture the dynamic nature of the bargaining process.

The findings also raise concerns about the ability of the union to affect the outcomes of collective bargaining, as environmental and management characteristics were of prime importance. It may be that the measures of union structure, process, and tactics were not designed with a specific enough reference to collective bargaining, weakening the results. On the other hand, the unions interviewed relied heavily on changes in environmental conditions as a basis for demands; hence, the results may to some extent reflect the ability of the union to use that information in the bargaining process. Although we have relatively good economic models of bargaining outcomes, our conceptualization and empirical measures of other characteristics continue to be sorely lacking.

Public sector collective bargaining theory is based in large measure on a rather limited set of experiences in the United States. Most states have only enacted public sector labor legislation during the past decade.[25] Prior to that, political processes rather than collective bargaining were the norm. Thus, in a relatively new, experimental, and unstable context, the role of the law, political pressure, and other union tactics are stressed. Conversely, in Canada municipal employees have enjoyed the full right to collective bargaining since the 1940s, and many had formal negotiations prior to that time. This suggests that stability in the system and the maturity of the relationship between the parties may change the nature of the process. Over time, bargaining may tend to move from a reliance on hard-core tactics and political pressure to an emphasis on more rationalized and professional negotiations. If this is true (qualitative findings do provide some support), it would help to explain several of the present findings that conflict with previous research: (1) the unimportance of the comprehensiveness of the law, (2) the negative impact of union pressure tactics, (3) the negative sign on internal management conflict, (4) the insignificance of the multilateral bargaining index, and (5) the relative importance of the age of the bargaining relationship as an independent predictor.

An emphasis on the difference between public and private sector labor relations[26] may be misguided if we are only experiencing a reflection of the maturity of the system and the relationships between the parties within the system. Moreover, it is possible that the application of different standards of evaluation to public sector policies could lead to inappropriate policy decisions. Therefore, in addition to improved specification of the characteristics of unions, management, and the bargaining process, future research should also consider the maturity of the industrial relations system.

Notes

1. For a review of public sector wage determination literature, see Daniel J.B. Mitchell, "The Impact of Collective Bargaining on Compensation in the Public Sector," in B. Aaron, J.R. Grodin, and J.L. Stern, eds., *Public Sector Collective Bargaining* (Madison, Wisc.: Industrial Relations Research Association, forthcoming).

2. For the most complete study of the determinants of bargaining outcomes to date, see Thomas A. Kochan and Hoyt N. Wheeler, "Municipal Collective Bargaining: A Model and Analysis of Bargaining Outcomes," *Industrial and Labor Relations Review* 29 (October 1975), pp. 46–66.

3. This research was supported by grants from the University Research Committee–Labour Canada and the New York State School of Industrial and Labor Relations, Cornell University. I would like to thank my doctoral dissertation committee, Lawrence K. Williams, Thomas A. Kochan, and Robert N. Stern for their support and assistance throughout the research from which this reading is taken.

4. John T. Dunlop, *The Industrial Relations System* (New York: Holt, 1958), p. 5.

5. For the main critiques, see Alan Flanders, *Industrial Relations: What Is Wrong with the System?* (London: Faber and Faber, 1965); R. Singh, "Systems Theory in the Study of Industrial Relations: Time for a Reappraisal?" *Industrial Relations Journal* 7 (Autumn 1976), pp. 59–71; A.N.J. Blain and J. Gennard, "Industrial Relations Theory: A Critical Review," *British Journal of Industrial Relations* 8 (November 1970), pp. 389–407; S.J. Wood, A. Wagner, E.G.A. Armstrong, J.F.B. Goodman, and J.E. Davis, "The 'Industrial Relations System' Concept as a Basis for Theory in Industrial Relations," *British Journal of Industrial Relations* 13 (November 1975), pp. 291–308; and J. Goodman, E.G.A. Armstrong, A. Wagner, J.E. Davis, and S.J. Wood, "Rules in Industrial Relations Theory: A Discussion," *Industrial Relations Journal* 6 (Spring 1975), pp. 14–30.

6. See Kochan and Wheeler, "Municipal Collective Bargaining," appendix I; Paul F. Gerhart, "Determinants of Bargaining Outcomes in Local Government Negotiations," *Industrial and Labor Relations Review* 29 (April 1976), appendix I; and James L. Perry and Charles Levine, "An Interorganizational Analysis of Power, Conflict, and Settlements in Public Sector Collective Bargaining," *American Political Science Review* 70 (December 1976), pp. 1185–1201.

7. A list of the specific contract provisions included in this research is available from the author.

8. To check on the normalization procedure, two analyses were performed. The normalized and unnormalized bargaining outcomes were correlated with the occupational dummy variables (that is, police, firefighter, manual, and clerical unions). Although each correlation between unstandardized dependent variables and occupation was significant, none of the correlations with the normalized measures exceeded 0.02. Second, the correlations between the normalized and raw measures

ranged between 0.52 and 1.0, with all except the wage level being in excess of 0.90. For these reasons, the correlational results presented are based on the normalized bargaining outcomes measures.

9. A full description of the independent variables, means, standard deviations, and reliability estimates is available from the author on request.

10. Examples of studies focusing on the economic determinants of bargaining outcomes include the following: David B. Lipsky and John E. Drotning, "The Influence of Collective Bargaining on Teachers' Salaries in New York State," *Industrial and Labor Relations Review* 27 (October 1973), pp. 18–35; Roger Schmenner, "The Determination of Municipal Employee Wages," *Review of Economics and Statistics* 55 (January 1973), pp. 83–90; James L. Freund, "Market and Union Influences on Municipal Employee Wages," *Industrial and Labor Relations Review* 27 (April 1974), pp. 391–404; and W. Clayton Hall and Bruce Vanderporten, "Unionization, Monopsony Power, and Police Salaries," *Industrial Relations* 16 (February 1977), pp. 94–100.

11. Kochan and Wheeler, "Municipal Collective Bargaining," p. 54.

12. For a review of this theory, see Delbert Miller and William Form, *Industry, Labor and Community* (New York: Harper, 1960). For the actual results, see Kochan and Wheeler, "Municipal Collective Bargaining," p. 52; Gerhart, "Determinants of Bargaining Outcomes in Local Government Negotiations," p. 348; and Alan Balfour, "More Evidence That Unions Do Not Achieve Higher Salaries for Teachers," *Journal of Collective Negotiations in the Public Sector* 3 (Fall 1974), pp. 289–303.

13. The union–management relationship itself has been classified as a special type of interorganizational linkage. See Myron Joseph, "Approaches to Collective Bargaining in Industrial Relations Theory," in Gerald Somers, ed., *Essays in Industrial Relations Theory* (Ames: Iowa State University Press, 1969), p. 89. For a more theoretical discussion of the notion of task environment, see James D. Thompson, *Organizations in Action* (New York: McGraw-Hill, 1967.

14. For discussions of public sector management, see, for example, John Burton, "Local Government Bargaining and Management Structure," *Industrial Relations* 11 (May 1972), pp. 123–139; Fred Helburn and N. Bennett, "Public Employee Bargaining and the Merit Principle," *Labor Law Journal* 23 (October 1972), pp. 618–629; and Thomas A. Kochan, "A Theory of Multilateral Collective Bargaining in City Governments," *Industrial and Labor Relations Review* 27 (July 1974), pp. 525–542. For empirical tests of the impact of these factors on outcomes, see Ronald Ehrenberg, "Municipal Structure, Unionization, and the Wages of Fire Fighters," *Industrial and Labor Relations Review* 27 (October 1973), pp. 36–48; Ronald Ehrenberg and Gerald Goldstein, "A Model of Public Wage Determination," *Journal of Urban Economics* 2 (May 1975), pp. 223–245; and Gerhart, "Determinants of Bargaining Outcomes in Local Government Negotiations."

15. For a test of these hypotheses, see Thomas A. Kochan, Mordehai Mironi, Ronald Ehrenberg, Jean Baderschneider, and Todd Jick, *Dispute Resolution under Factfinding and Arbitration: An Empirical Study* (New York: American Arbitration Association, 1978).

16. Derek Bok and John Dunlop, *Labor in the American Community* (New York: Simon and Schuster, 1970), pp. 138–188.

17. Jack Barbash, "Relationalization in the American Union," in Somers, *Essays in Industrial Relations Theory*, p. 147.

18. For example, see Arie Shirom, "Union Use of Staff Experts: The Case of the

Histadrut," *Industrial and Labor Relations Review* 29 (October 1975), pp. 107–120. Unfortunately, the author did not provide an empirical assessment of the validity of the assumption that the use of experts is related to effectiveness.

19. See W.E. Chalmers, E.K. Chandler, L.L. McQuitty, R. Stagner, D.E. Wray, and M. Derber, *Labor–Management Relations in Illini City,* Experiments in Comparative Analysis, vol 2 (Champaign-Urbana: Institute of Labor and Industrial Relations, University of Illinois, 1954), p. 326.

20. Seymour Lipset, Martin Trow, and James Coleman, *Union Democracy* (Garden City, N.J.: Anchor, 1956), present a strong case for a democratic union being more effective. In contrast, Richard Lester, *As Unions Mature* (Princeton, N.J.: Princeton University Press, 1966), argues that centralization is necessary for effectiveness, as does Barbash, "Relationalization in the American Union," Others have pointed to contract rejections as an indication of how democracy limits effectiveness. See Donald Burke and Lester Rubin, "Is Contract Rejection a Major Collective Bargaining Problem?" *Industrial and Labor Relations Review* 26 (January 1973), pp. 820–833.

21. For a discussion of tactics, see James Craft, "Fire Fighter Strategy in Wage Negotiations," *Quarterly Review of Economics and Business* 11 (Autumn 1971), pp. 65–75. These tactics and their impact on bargaining outcomes were examined by Kochan and Wheeler, "Municipal Collective Bargaining," p. 54.

22. For a discussion of multilateral collective bargaining, see Kenneth McLennan and Michael Moskow, "Multilateral Bargaining in the Public Sector," *Proceedings of the Twenty-first Annual Meeting of the Industrial Relations Research Association* (Madison, Wisc: IRRA, 1968), pp. 34–41; George Hildebrand, "The Public Sector," in John T. Dunlop and Neil W. Chamberlain, eds., *Frontiers of Collective Bargaining* (New York: Harper and Row, 1967), pp. 125–154; and Kochan, "Multilateral Collective Bargaining."

23. David B. Lipsky and John E. Drotning examine the impasse procedure usage on wages in "The Relation between Teacher Salaries and the Use of Impasse Procedures under New York's Taylor Law," paper presented at the 1976 Annual Meetings of the Society of Professionals in Dispute Resolution, October 25, 1976.

24. In order to determine the relative contribution of each *set* of independent variables (environmental, managerial, union, bargaining process, control), after computing a regression equation with the full model, partial solutions were computed by removing each set of characteristics one at a time. This permits the calculation of the unique variance in the dependent variable attributable to each set of characteristics. The significance in addition to explained variance was then calculated for each set. The results are available from the author upon request. For the formula used, see Fred N. Kerlinger and E. Pedhazer, *Multiple Regression in Behavioral Research* (New York: Holt, Rinehart and Winston, 1973). Prior to the regression analysis, the intercorrelation matrix was examined for evidence of multicolinearity. Only one correlation exceeded 0.45, and that was less than 0.60, so that multicollinarity does not appear to be a problem.

25. Thomas A. Kochan, "Correlates of State Public Employee Bargaining Laws," *Industrial Relations* 12 (October 1973), pp. 322.337.

26. These differences are discussed in Hildebrand, "The Public Sector," and Harry Wellington and Ralph Winter, *The Unions and the Cities* (Washington, D.C.: Brookings Institution, 1971), chap. 1.

Police Union Impact on the Formulation of Law Enforcement Policy

Hervey Juris
Peter Feuille[*]

What constitutes the formulation of law enforcement policy can be a difficult question. A department has many policies: a policy concerning prostitution, a policy concerning the use of sick leave, even a policy concerning the frequency with which squad cars will be washed. In this list it is easy to distinguish the first, which is a law enforcement policy issue, from the other two, which are administrative policies. However, how does one classify policies coming under the broad rubric of "manning"? We discussed "manning" under the heading "ability to manage," but the use of civilians, the number of men in a squad car, and the number of cars on the street are also an important part of law enforcement policy. Conversely, the question of the type and number of weapons carried by policemen and the conditions under which they may be used are discussed under "law enforcement policy," but they are clearly germane to the chief's ability to manage.

Other law enforcement policy issues are not as easily discerned because they are discussed in contexts that draw attention away from the underlying law enforcement policy implications. Thus, earlier we discussed the question of entry standards and minority recruitment in the context of the professionalization issue. We might also have discussed these in the context of their impact on law enforcement policy — the extent to which the minority community perceives efforts to exclude blacks from the department as an unobtrusive measure of the department's hostility toward them. In short, while public attention is focused on particular disputes, each of which involves some aspect of control and authority, the broader policy issues tend not to get raised. In this next section we attempt to point up some of these broader policy questions.

Law Enforcement Policy Issues

How Will the Law Be Enforced?

Police services are delivered within the context of broad policy guidelines.[1] The precise policies to be followed are subject to a great deal of discretion.

[*]Northwestern University and University of Illinois, respectively. Reprinted from Hervey Juris and Peter Feuille. *Police Unionism* (Lexington, Mass.: D.C. Heath, 1973), pp. 151–163.

The basic thrust of union efforts has been to place limits on managerial discretion.

In the case of civil disturbance, for example, management may choose to follow a policy of containment rather than risking life on both sides by attempting to extinguish the disturbance. In several cities where this policy was pursued the unions objected strenuously. In New York City, PBA President John Cassesse's call for "100 percent enforcement of the law" in August 1968 was issued in the context of police dissatisfaction with the containment policies of city officials established during the riots following Martin Luther King's assassination in April 1968 and continued into the following summer,[2] as was a similar statement by former Boston Police Patrolmen's Association President Richard MacEachern a few days later.[3] Similarly, a group of Baltimore policemen, through a publicized letter to their AFSCME local, criticized the department's preparedness for, and handling of, the King riots,[4] and during the riots the Police Wives Association publicly castigated the "weak-kneed" policy used in containing the disturbances.

The most explicit union activity in this area occurred in Pittsburgh, where the Fraternal Order of Police (FOP) lodge published formal investigatory reports after two civil disturbances. The first followed the King riot, and strongly criticized the department's lack of preparedness and the containment nature of the city's response.[5] The second report dealt with a June 1970 disturbance which followed the slaying of a black youth by an elderly white woman. In this report the union severely criticized the city's permissiveness and appeasement of the "hoodlum element."[6]

Sometimes law enforcement policy can be affected by benefits secured strictly for bread-and-butter reasons. In the previous chapter, for example, we mentioned that unions in many cities have secured financial compensation for off-duty court appearances, some of it at premium rates. Thus, at the time of our field visit, Boston patrolmen earned approximately $22.50 for each off-duty court appearance (time-and-one-half pay with a three-hour minimum). One conceivable law enforcement impact of this benefit is that officers, especially those on evening and night duty, may see a financial incentive to make arrests that necessitate a court appearance the next day. This phenomenon has been given a name—"bounty hunting," making arrests primarily to increase earnings. We pursued this issue in three cities, where management interviewees admitted that when premium pay for court appearances was first established there may have been a few bounty hunters, but said that such men were transferred to other positions. Management interviewees minimized the phenomenon, saying that aggregate arrest figures (which we did not examine) showed no significant increase in arrests after court time premium pay was established. However, street patrolmen in two of the cities were emphatic that bounty hunters did exist.

Another factor that can be quite important is the union's stance on residency. The question of whether a police officer need reside in the city of his employment is an important law enforcement policy issue with emotional overtones. The men argue that, given their middle-income economic status, they should be free to live in the suburbs, where the streets are safe and the schools sound. Cities, on the other hand, argue, that residing implies a commitment to the city and to its improvement; that public employees should reside in the tax district; and that the men should be available for call-in, call-back, and standby. Norton Long raises another interesting perspective: with the center-city population becoming more dependent over time, the nonresident police, teachers, and other civil servants come to represent emissaries from the mother country to the colony or from the government to the Indians on the reservation.[7] This latter perspective is often overlooked.

Whenever the residency issue arose in our sample, it was usually because of union attempts to eliminate it. For example, the New York City PBA has lobbied extensively in Albany for the right to live outside the city, and successive pieces of state legislation now give city policemen the right to live in several suburban counties. Cleveland officers removed the residency requirement through a charter amendment. In contrast, unions in several other cities were unsuccessful in attempts to eliminate residency requirements. Police organizations in Chicago lost a lawsuit, and the Milwaukee union failed with a lawsuit and at the bargaining table. Cincinnati tried a city council resolution and a lawsuit and lost both times.[8] In Detroit the patrolmen's union fought a lengthy court battle against the requirement, but lost. The Seattle union objected to the mayor's decree that new policemen must live within the city limits (although those already on the force could maintain their suburban residency), but at the time of our visit had not been able to change the situation. In one city the union actually did oppose the elimination of a residency requirement.[9]

In summary, a few unions have been able to eliminate residency requirments, and a few unions may have contributed to the phenomenon of bounty hunting through securing a premium for off-duty court appearances. Several unions have objected to management's containment policies for handling civil disturbances, but nowhere did we find that management had changed its riot policies in response to union criticisms. However, these union demands for a "hard line" are a clear statement to the community of how the rank and file views its law enforcement duties, and they are a clear statement to police and city officials who may be considering adopting other policies or techniques that deemphasize the use of force.

The Use of Force

The armament carried by officers and the conditions under which weapons or physical force is used are an important element of the law enforcement policy of the community and, like the issue of how the law is to be enforced, has an impact on the way in which the community perceives the department's intentions toward them. Among the issues raised are the number of weapons carried, the use of private weapons, the presence of long guns, the conditions under which an officer may fire his weapon, and whether the rifles and shotguns should be carried in the trunk, carried in the front of the car, or taken from the car routinely.

Consistent with their hard line on the handling of civil disorders, police unions have pressed for heavy armaments and minimal restrictions on the police right to use force, especially fatal force. In seven cities in this sample the use of force was an overt issue, usually with the police unions opposing actual or proposed restrictions on their coercive license. The Cleveland unions, for example, were successful after the 1968 Glenville shootout in pressuring the department for new armaments. Interviewees in two other midwestern cities told of men on patrol carrying unauthorized long guns in addition to their authorized sidearms. In Hartford, the union's hard bargaining (not to be confused with collective bargaining), lobbying, and display of public support was instrumental in persuading the city council to vote against the adoption of gun use restrictions. The San Francisco union was able to persuade the chief and the police commission to change a proposed set of gun guidelines so that an officer involved in an on-duty homicide is not automatically suspended pending an investigation.[10] In Seattle the union negotiated a contract clause providing that no officer can be required over his objection to work without a gun.

In contrast the Oakland union has protested in vain against the chief's gun use restrictions (which are much tighter than the "fleeing felon" standard in the state law). A union in a western city pressed unsuccessfully for the right of each officer to carry the weapon of his choice. In an eastern city the union lobbied the city council for the right to carry shotguns in squad cars, but the chief was able to muster sufficient opposition to have the union voted down. In a midwestern city the union unsuccessfully made public demands for, and lobbied with the chief for, a shotgun for each man in a squad car (instead of the existing one per car) and for the reinstitution of a formerly eliminated dog patrol. Finally, after the 1971 murders of two New York City patrolmen, the PBA called for shotguns in every patrol car. Although this demand was rejected, the department did begin training in shotgun handling for many members of the force. The union again raised the issue in 1973.[11]

Many of the police demands for increased armaments and the authority to use them can be traced to their belief that patrol conditions in many central cities are tantamount to wartime. Support for this belief comes from the increasing rate of assaults on police officers and the increasing numbers of policemen killed during the 1960s and early 1970s. For instance, in 1960, 28 police officers were killed in the line of duty as a result of felonious assault; in 1970, 100 officers were killed; and in 1971 the figure increased to 126.[12]

Many of the rank and file see the use of heavier force as a self-protection issue.

The direct impact of union efforts in some departments has been to minimize the restrictions placed on an officer's use of firearms and to help obtain increased armaments. In other departments the unions have pushed in the same directions but have no observable impact. Successful or not, the union's demands for heavier armaments and minimal restrictions on their use are additional statements to the community, especially the minority segments of the community, of police intentions toward them.

Civilian Review of Police Behavior

The topic that has attracted the most publicity in the area of law enforcement policy is union opposition to civilian review of citizen complaints against individual officers or groups of officers. The most celebrated instances are the Philadelphia and New York cases: in both cities the unions successfully thwarted civilian review. In New York City the defeat of Mayor Lindsay's proposal came as a result of a referendum in which the union succeeded in killing civilian review but actually increased the volume of complaints to the departmental review board as a result of its publicity campaign broadcasting the existence of such a board. In Philadelphia the civilian review board was dropped by the mayor even after a favorable state supreme court verdict reversing two lower courts who had sustained a union challenge to the legitimacy of the board. The Rochester union's court battle against the review board in that city contributed to the board's demise.

In Boston in 1968 the patrolmen's union worked with several city council members to scrap the police portion of Mayer Kevin White's proposed Model Cities program, including a civilian complaint board. In Buffalo the union lobbied vigorously against a proposal before the city council to give that city's Commission on Human Relations subpoena power when investigating charges of police misconduct, and the council defeated the proposal. In Baltimore in 1970 the two unions campaigned vigorously against a Baltimore Urban Coalition proposal for a civilian review board, and the issue was abandoned by its proponents in the face of this opposition.[13] After the Pittsburgh Commission on Human Relations investigated and recommended that several policemen be disciplined for their behavior in a series of incidents, the Pittsburgh FOP lodge castigated the commission, announced that policemen would refuse to cooperate with it, and asked the mayor to investigate it.[14]

The direct impact of union activities in many of these cities seems clear: civilian review boards that existed have been defeated, and new proposals to establish review boards have been stopped before they were implemented. In other cities the impact may have been more indirect. Union condemnation of human relations and civil rights commissions may not have produced any structural changes, but the expressions of police opposition to any kind of civilian review of police behavior have informed community leaders of the difficulties of instituting formalized review procedures. In all, civilian review was an issue in eleven of our twenty-two cities.

Citizen Complaints and the Identification of Police Officers

Like civilian review of complaints against officer behavior, facilitation of complaints and identification are a manifestation of an adversary relationship between police and the community.[15] The policy issue raised is the extent to which the department will facilitate the taking of complaints and the identification of officers.

In an eastern city the union objected to a department plan to have officers earn community goodwill by interviewing five citizens each week, with a key portion of the interview consisting of the officer explaining to the citizen how to file a complaint against the police. The union dropped its objection when the interview program produced evidence of substantial public support for the police. In Omaha the union criticized the department's new citizen complaint procedure, which the chief said was adopted at the request of a local citizen's committee. The union objected to the fact that complaints could be made by telephone, saying that all complaints should be made in person and the officer being complained about should have the opportunity to confront the citizen as he made the complaint.[16]

In Boston, Detroit, and Seattle the identification question surfaced as a name tag issue. In Seattle the union agreed to name tags on shirts and identifying numbers on riot helmets and overalls, the latter after many citizens complained of police brutality and the inability to identify police offenders during campus and antigovernment demonstrations. The Detroit patrolmen's union used the grievance arbitration procedure to stall but not prevent the introduction of name tags, and the Boston patrolmen's union was able to prevent name tags via the judicious combination of picketing police headquarters, using the grievance arbitration procedure, lobbying with the state legislature and governor's office, and lobbying with the city council.

In Buffalo the identification issue surfaced as an identification lineup of all the police on a particular shift in order that the black victims of alleged excessive police zeal be afforded an opportunity to identify the assailants. The unions used a federal court suit to delay for more than a year the implementation of the lineups, thus reducing the chances for accurate identification.

These specific issues again point up the distinction between the direct and indirect impact of union efforts. Only in Boston did the union score a total victory, although in Buffalo and Detroit the unions were able to delay implementation of identification mechanisms. However, the union position in these cases conveyed to the community a clear picture of rank-and-file police attitudes toward the handling of citizen complaints and identification of police misconduct.

The Functioning of the Criminal Justice System

In theory, the various aspects of the criminal justice system function independently: the police effect arrests, the prosecutor decides if a formal charge is warranted and prosecutes the case, the judge presides over the trial and passes sentence, the legislature defines criminal activity and determines a range of penalties, and a parole board may determine what portion of a particular sentence will actually be served. Although in practice these are not necessarily independent events, still the question arises as to whether such interdependence as does exist should be formalized through police union activities such as court-watching; union endorsements in campaigns for prosecutor and judge; or union endorsements in campaigns for mayor and governor where the candidates go on record as to the types of individuals who will be nominated to civilian review boards, parole boards, and other agencies having jurisdiction in the criminal justice area.

Police unions in our sample were quite concerned about judicial handling and disposition of criminal cases. Police unions in five cities threatened to engage in court-watching (stationing an observer in court to record the disposition of criminal cases), and these statements were invariably couched in coercive language castigating judicial leniency. The Detroit patrolmen's union, through its wives' auxiliary, actually engaged in court-watching for six months. The Seattle union publicly threatened to implement a court-watching program but backed off after receiving substantial adverse criticism. One midwestern union collected data for six months but never used it. The Seattle and Baltimore unions endorsed judicial candidates because of their ideological sympathy with the police.[17] In Pittsburgh the police delayed the appointment of a black magistrate in whom the union had taken a vote of no confidence, and the union publicly castigated some magistrates for releasing on own recognizance and nominal bonds certain categories of criminal suspects. The union president warned that the union will watch all magistrates to see if they follow the magisterial code section on bail-setting and will charge them with misconduct if they violate the code.[18]

Union spokesmen in four cities said their organizations have lobbied to influence the substance of criminal statutes or changes in the penal code. For example, the Baltimore unions successfully lobbied against a city proposal to increase the upper age limit for juvenile offenders from sixteen to eighteen. The former president of the union in another city said he actively lobbied on behalf of certain criminal statutes in the state capital. Electoral processes may also be used to influence law enforcement matters. The California supreme court declared the state's death penalty unconstitutional in early 1972; the response among several police groups (and others) was to launch an initiative effort that resulted in a death penalty constitutional amendment on the November 1972 ballot. In Pittsburgh in 1971 a law-and-order district attorney who enjoyed good relations with the police and who was up for reelection refused to prosecute thirty-four policemen who fraudulently collected $41,000 in witness fees.[19] In an example from outside our sample, the Eugene (Oregon) Police Patrolmen's Association endorsed and gave a large contribution to the successful challenger to the incumbent district attorney in the November 1972 election.

It is difficult to pinpoint any direct impact of union efforts to influence the operation of the criminal justice system. One may feel, as we do, that the independence of the components of the criminal justice system is reduced when judges and district attorneys are elected with the aid of police union support or when the police lobby to influence criminal statutes, but we cannot accurately describe the effects of this alleged reduced independence on the handling and disposition of criminal cases. Similarly, several police unions have made threatening noises about "judicial leniency," but it is difficult to show how these union statements and activities have affected judicial handling of criminal cases.

In contrast, we can discern some indirect impact. By their statements and activities, the police organizations have informed the community that the police favor strict bonding, prosecuting, and sentencing practices and in general a "get tough" approach to the handling of criminal cases. On the one hand, these postures are supported by those segments of the community who are concerned about "law and order" and "crime in the streets." On the other hand, other segments of the community may see these police postures as being directed against them.

Other Issues

We encountered a host of other law enforcement–related issues and police union involvement in them. In New York City the PBA opposed the creation, funding, and subpoena powers of the Knapp Commission and its investigations into police corruption. In Seattle the union went to court to block a new chief's use of polygraphs (lie detectors) in internal investigations of police corruption. The Seattle union also informally negotiated changes in the coroner's inquest system used when a civilian is killed by a police officer. The Boston patrolmen's union lobbied in the city council and state legislature to block a mayoral proposal to give traffic control duties to civilians, and the Buffalo union was instrumental in convincing city officials to abandon a 1968 plan to upgrade 475 civil defense auxiliary policemen to limited-duty status (that is, they would carry radios and nightsticks but would not have firearms or arrest powers).[20] The Buffalo union also opposed the establishment of a minority-oriented, community peace officer plan and stalled (but did not prevent) the introduction of a program whereby sixty-one officers would have off-duty use of squad cars in exchange for answering calls in their vicinity. In Rochester the union established a "truth squad" to monitor police-related news in the city papers (this effort was abandoned after one month),[21] attempted unsuccessfully to convince the state conference of police unions that officers should stop informing arrestees of their Miranda rights,[22] and attempted unsuccessfully to have a children's book that pictured police officers as pigs in blue uniforms removed from the public library.[23]

Police unions have also engaged directly in electoral politics on behalf of local candidates whom they perceived as ideologically compatible with rank-and-file law enforcement interests. Some of the more publicized examples include police union endorsement of or sympathy with such mayoral candidates as Sam Yorty in Los Angeles, Charles Stenvig in Minneapolis, Roman Gibbs in Detroit, Frank Rizzo in Philadelphia, and Louise Day Hicks in Boston. Police unions have also opposed candidates from whom they felt ideologically estranged: in Cleveland the unions were bitterly opposed to Mayor Carl Stokes; the New York City PBA was one of the few municipal unions that did not support Mayor John Lindsay's reelection efforts in 1969. Police unions have also supported city councilmen with whom they are ideologically compatible, including former police union president Wayne Larkin's successful bid for a seat on the Seattle city council. It is difficult to discern any direct impacts of these union electoral involvements, but an important indirect impact has been to increase the saliency of the law-and-order issue.

Summary

Because the individual issues over which conflict occurs in the area of law enforcement policy tend to be viewed in isolation as single occurrences, often the underlying issues of control and authority are not articulated. In this section, we have attempted to relate the specific incidents to the larger policy context in which they might be viewed. Two major themes have emerged from this investigation. First, although the unions may not have been particularly successful in their frontal attacks on various aspects of law enforcement policy, we should not overlook the impact of their actions on the minority communities and on the willingness of political officials to act in future situations. Second, as the reader reviews mentally the types of actions undertaken by the unions, it becomes obvious that it was not the collective bargaining process but rather the political arena that the unions exploited in their attempts to influence law enforcement policy. We consider each of these themes briefly.

Direct versus Indirect Impact

As one considers the direct victories by unions in the law enforcement policy area, one is struck by the fact that they revolve around either one issue (civilian review) or two cities (Seattle and Boston). The list of unsuccessful efforts is much more impressive: the handling of civil disturbances, the judicial disposition of criminal cases, greater armament and more freedom to use it, the election of law-and-order politicians on any grand scale, influence on hiring standards, and so forth. For example, consider the efforts of the Detroit patrolmen's union: through its wives' auxiliary it engaged in court-watching for six months; it attempted but failed to impeach a local black judge; it stalled the introduction of name tags (and flap holsters) until arbitrators ruled in support of the city's right to require them; it filed a lawsuit against a civil rights commission to force it to change its method of operation involving citizen complaints against the police; it spoke out against civilian review, including political candidates who supported the concept; it pressed for heavier armaments for street patrolmen; and it repeatedly espoused a hard line on law enforcement issues. Although the union scored no direct victories, the totality of its statements and actions created a clear picture about where it stood on civilian control, citizen identification, judicial disposition of criminal cases, and the use of force. Similar examples could be cited from other cities.

It is the overall impression left by the union's totality of behavior from which we draw our concern about the indirect impact of the union's efforts to influence the formulation of law-enforcement policy. Although we cannot measure these results, we are concerned with the potential impact of overall union activity in causing city and police executives not to undertake certain programs and policies in anticipation of the union's reaction and the political costs attendant to the struggle—even if management believes it will ultimately prevail.

Second, we are concerned with the impact of the union's totality of behavior on police–community relations. Union positions on law enforcement policy issues are frequently "hard line" or "get tough"—remove restrictions on the use of force, crack down on offenders, extinguish riots rather than contain them—and oriented toward maximizing rank-and-file discretion in the performance of their duties and insulating on-the-job behavior from civilian review, complaint systems, and identification.[24] Although unions may have valid reasons for opposing civilian review and while each officer accused of a departmental or civilian indiscretion deserves a vigorous defense, the fact is that these union positions are perceived as hostile signs in the black community. Although the measurement of citizen attitudes toward police union law enforcement efforts was not within the scope of this study, our data (newspaper files and interview comments, especially from black officer association representatives) suggest that these union efforts had some negative impact on police–minority community relations in at least eleven cities: Boston, Buffalo, Cleveland, Detroit, Hartford, New York City, Omaha, Philadelphia, Pittsburgh, Rochester, and Seattle.

We caution strongly against ignoring these secondary consequences of union actions in the policy area, and we especially caution against underestimating the impact of a union on law enforcement policy because the union has had few direct successes.

Collective Bargaining and Political Action

Police union concern with proposals for civilian review boards and gun guidelines, with citizen complaint procedures and identification lineups, with judicial disposition of criminal cases, with managerial handling of civil disturbances, and with investigations of police corruption reflects very real rank-and-file police concern with actual or proposed changes in police working conditions. However, this concern usually cannot be translated into specific bargaining demands because these issues are not decided at the bargaining table. In contrast to the issues examined elsewhere in this study, most of which were resolved at the bargaining table, the resolution of the issues discussed here will remain political issues to be fought out in various political arenas.

In fact, the major factor that distinguishes the impact of police unions on law enforcement policy formulation from their impact on the ability to manage is that the former would have occurred in the absence of collective bargaining rights whereas much of the latter would not. Moreover, the changing constitutional climate with respect to the First Amendment rights of public employees, including free speech and participation in elective politics, has created an environment in which the already politicized police employee organizations have extended the range of their activities.[25]

Thus the testimonial dinner for a criminal court judge in Milwaukee, the New York City campaign against the civilian review board, and the visit of Vice-President Agnew to the prayer breakfast of a New York City police employee organization to praise the police and condemn opponents of law and order all would have occurred in the absence of collective bargaining. Similarly the activities of the line organizations in New York City in their attempts to block the Knapp Commission hearings into corruption (the attempts to block creation, funding, and subpoena power) all took place in the courts and the press outside the context of collective bargaining.

Public policy with respect to free speech and political action is unclear. For years, the celebrated dictum of Mr. Justice Holmes had been predominant: "The petitioner may have a constitutional right to talk politics, but he has no constitutional right to be a policeman."[26] This has been interpreted as limiting the rights of police officers to make critical public statements on policy issues and as limiting their participation in elective politics—the latter because of possible misuse of their unique power and station in the society. However, this position has recently been modified with respect to public policy statements.

The ambivalence of public policy with respect to political participation is best seen in the sometimes tacit, sometimes overt encouragement by police executives of participation by employee organizations in legislative and elective political activity concerning larger appropriations for city government, salaries, retirement systems, and welfare benefits. Given this unofficial sanction and a functioning political organization, and given the leverage inherent in the public concern with law and order, it is not surprising that police employee organizations took advantage of their new constituency to move into elective political action and public statements on issues of law enforcement policy even though local regulations may have prohibited both.

This expanded activity with respect to public statements was reinforced by the changing constitutional climate during the 1960s. In a line of cases from *New York Times Co. v. Sullivan* [376 U.S. 254 (1964)], through *Pickering v. Board of Education* [88 S.Ct. 1731 (1968)], the Court moved from a virtual prohibition of public employee rights to the exercise of critical speech to a standard that has been interpreted as allowing critical statements so long as they do not include knowing falsity, disclosure of confidential information, falsehood that would impair the operation of the agency, destruction of an effective superior–subordinate relationship, or adversely affect work relationships in the agency.[27]

An example of the extent to which we have moved from the Holmes' statement can be seen in the Maryland case, *Eugene C. Brukiewa v. Police Commissioner of Baltimore City* [257 Maryland 36, 263 A. 2d 210 (1970)]. Brukiewa, the president of the Baltimore police union, had made comments critical of the department and the commissioner on a local television program. He was suspended by the department's disciplinary board, which ruled that he had violated two departmental regulations relating to discussion of departmental business in public and criticism of superiors. A Baltimore city court upheld the suspension on the grounds that the regulations cited were clear and unambiguous. The state appeals court overruled the city court on the grounds that the state did not show that the appellant's statements hurt or imperiled the discipline or operation of the police department and were, therefore, within his right to make under the First Amendment and the decisions of the Supreme Court.

Most of the activities we have discussed were a function of the unions' exercise of their political prerogatives. Whether these activities were legal or illegal is irrelevant; the fact that the unions are free to engage in such activities and the concomitant lack of official sanctions levied against them must be viewed as tacit approval consistent with the evolving climate just discussed.

Finally, because of the numerous actors who participate in law enforcement policy debates and the formulation of policy (judges, prosecutors, human rights commissions, leaders from various segments of the community, elected officials, police management, police rank and file, and the like) and the fact that law enforcement issues are decided in a variety of forums (the state legislature, the city council, the mayor's office, courtrooms and judicial chambers, the prosecutor's office, the station house, and so forth), we suggest that most of the issues discussed in this section will remain political issues to be fought out in the political arena and are not likely to become included within the scope of collective bargaining in the short run.

Notes

1. We are indebted to Herman Goldstein for his discussions with us on the policy generally and especially for his comments on earlier drafts of this chapter.

2. *New York Times,* August 13, 1968, p. 1. It also represented an attempt by Cassesse to co-opt the conservative dissatisfaction in the PBA.

3. *Boston Globe,* August 15, 1968.

4. *Baltimore Sun,* April 17, 1968.

5. The union was bitterly critical of city officials' use of "red vest" patrols of ghetto youths used to help calm the situation, for the police maintained that many of these youths also engaged in lawless behavior.

6. Fraternal Order of Police, Fort Pitt Lodge no. 1, *A Report: The Manchester Incident, June 21, 1970* (Pittsburgh: Fraternal Order of Police, 1970), esp. pp. 86–91.

7. Norton Long, "The City as Reservation," *The Public Interest* (Fall 1971), pp. 22–38.

8. The court found in favor of the police officer who resided outside the city but decided the case on such narrow grounds that did not establish precedent.

9. This occurred in Pittsburgh in 1968 when the city was having some difficulty finding qualified applicants. The union president proposed raising police pay instead. See *Pittsburgh Press,* June 5, 1968. A union leader in another city, which had a residency requirement, which, however, interviewees said was about to be eliminated, was ambivalent about the requirement's expected demise. On the one hand, his members are strongly in favor of its elimination, so he was not in a position to push for its retention. On the other hand, he believed the union would have reduced municipal political clout if substantial numbers of policemen moved out of the city, thus making his job more difficult.

10. See the *San Francisco Chronicle,* January 6 1972, p. 1.

11. For a presentation of the PBA's position, ses the statement by PBA President Robert McKiernan on the Op-Ed page of the *New York Times,* February 7, 1973, p. 39.

12. Figures on the assaults on police officers and the number of officers killed are available in the annual Federal Bureau of Investigation, *Crime in the United States, Uniform Crime Reports* (Washington, D.C.: U.S. Government Printing Office).

13. For a more detailed account of union efforts in Buffalo, Baltimore, and Philadelphia, see Stephen Halpern. "The Role of Police Employee Organizations in the Determination of Police Accountability Procedures in Baltimore, Philadelphia, and Buffalo," mimeo, State University of New York at Buffalo, 1972.

14. See the *Pittsburgh Press,* June 6, 10, 11, 1969.

15. For two examinations of relations between the police and the civilian community, see Skolnick, *Justice without Trial,* chap. 3; and Reiss, *The Police and the Public.*

16. *Omaha World-Herald,* July 25, 1971.

17. In 1970 the Seattle union endorsed a state supreme court candidate and a local superior court candidate, and in 1970 the Baltimore AFSCME local endorsed a municipal court candidate. Of these three, only the Seattle superior court candidate won at the polls.

18. Descriptions of these Pittsburgh efforts can be found in Ralph Hallow, "The Mayor is 'Nobody's Boy,'" *Nation,* April 19, 1971, pp. 492–496; *Pittsburgh Post-Gazette,* October, 1, 22 and 26, 1970.

19. See the *Pittsburgh Post-Gazette,* March 13 and September 22, 1971. These policemen were disciplined by departmental trial boards for receiving the money.

20. *Buffalo Evening News,* January 6 and February 19, 1968.

21. *Rochester Democrat and Chronicle,* September 12, 1970.

22. *Rochester Democrat and Chronicle,* April 18, 1968.

23. *Rochester Democrat and Chronicle,* January 18 and May 28, 1971. The book in question was *Sylvester and the Magic Pebble* by William Steig.

24. What we referred to earlier as the quest for professional status.

25. For a discussion of the political activities of social and fraternal organizations who were the predecessors of the current employee organizations, see chapter 2 of the authors' orginal work [editors].

26. *McAuliffe v. City of New Bedford,* 155 Mass. 216, 220, 29 N.E. 519 (1892).

27. From a legal point of view: "The First Amendment and Public Employees: *Time* Marches On," 57 *Georgetown Law Review* 134 (1968). From an operational point of view: Anthony Mondello, "The Federal Employee's Right to Speak," *Civil Service Journal* (January–March 1970), pp. 16–21.

Teacher Unions and the Productivity of Public Schools

Randall W. Eberts
*Joe A. Stone**

The public controversy over how teacher unions have affected public schools is not surprising: public schools are a prominent part of almost every community and absorb a major share of local public expenditures. What is surpris-

*Reprinted from *Industrial and Labor Relations Review* 40, no. 3 (April 1987), pp. 354–363.

ing, however, is that after more than two decades of experience with unions in public schools, almost nothing is known about their effect on student achievement. We know that teacher unions increase salaries (Baugh and Stone, 1982) and costs (Eberts and Stone, 1986), alter the allocation of resources and the time teachers spend in the classroom (Eberts, 1984), and influence district educational policies (Goldschmidt and Stuart, 1986; Woodbury 1985), but we do not know whether union schools are more or less productive than nonunion schools in teaching students. McDonnell and Pascal, (1979), for example, acknowledge the absence of systematic research on this question, arguing that "what is available is a collection of untested assertions and anecdotal evidence." Cresswell and Spargo (1980) draw a similar conclusion.

In this reading, we examine the effect of teacher unions on the productivity of public schools, as measured by achievement gains of individual students in a national sample of school districts. To accomplish this task, we first estimate separate production technologies for students in union and nonunion schools and then calculate the difference between union and nonunion productivity.

Freeman and Medoff (1979) and others have suggested that unions may increase productivity by reducing worker turnover, expanding training opportunities, and improving communication between workers and management. There is evidence in support of this hypothesis for the private sector (Brown and Medoff, 1978; Clark, 1980; Allen, 1984), but not for the public sector. A study of municipal libraries by Ehrenberg, Sherman, and Schwarz (1983), for example, found that unions do not significantly affect productivity. Baumol (1967) offers one explanation for why productivity gains might be more difficult to achieve in the public sector than in the private sector. His "unbalanced growth" hypothesis asserts that productivity increases for public services lag behind increases for the rest of the economy because they are relatively labor intensive, which may limit the opportunity for technological innovation.

Education Production Functions

To establish a link between collective bargaining and student achievement, one must begin with an individual student in a particular classroom. The productivity effect of teacher unions is measured in two steps: first, by estimating an education production function, which relates student outcomes to various types of educational inputs; and second, by using these estimates to calculate differences in productivity between union and nonunion schools. This method enables us to answer the question: Do teacher unions affect the level of student achievement at given levels of educational inputs?

Education production functions (as presented by Brown and Saks, 1975, and Summers and Wolfe, 1977, for example) differ from typical production functions in two ways. First, studies of the educational process have concentrated almost entirely on detailed differences in student, teacher, and principal characteristics, since physical capital explains little of the variation in student outcomes (Hanushek, 1978). Second, because of the considerable attention to detailed inputs, the number of variables entered into the production function is relatively large and little attention has been given to the properties of the functional form. Most studies use a simple linear form.

For this study, we adopt a model of achievement in which student outcomes at the end of one school year (as measured by standardized tests) are related to student outcomes at the beginning of the school year; to stocks of student, family, community, teacher, and other school characteristics at the beginning of the year; and to flows of school-based inputs received by the student during the year.

The model can be presented more formally as:

$$A_{it} = f[A_{it}^*, I_i, B_{it}^*, S(t - t^*)] \tag{1}$$

where $f(.)$ is a general implicit function; A_{it} = achievement of the ith student at time t, the end of the school year (or at time t^*, the beginning of the school year); I_i = vector of innate abilities of the ith student; B_i = vector of family background influences of the ith student; and $S_i(t - t^*)$ = vector of school inputs of the ith student, measured as both quantitative flows during the period $(t - t^*)$ and as qualitative stocks.

This model incorporates a number of essential aspects of the educational process. First, inputs are those relevant to the individual student. Second, the inputs reflect a cumulative process, since schooling and other experiences in past years have a bearing on student outcomes in the present period. Third, school-based inputs include purchased inputs (for example, teachers, administrators, and other staff) as well as nonpecuniary inputs related to instructional modes, supervision activities, and the like. Fourth, the allocation of educational resources is predetermined in the context of the production function.

The union–nonunion productivity differential is obtained by estimating separate education production functions for union and nonunion districts and using these estimates to calculate the difference in output at given levels of inputs.

Data and Empirical Specification

Our data were collected under the Sustaining Effects Study (SES) conducted during the late 1970s under a grant from the Office of Education (now the

Department of Education). The data base contains information on educational programs for a stratified sample of about 14,000 fourth-graders in 328 elementary schools nationwide. A description of the study and detailed definitions of the data collected are presented in Hemenway (1978). Means of the variables used in our analysis are presented in table 1.

The achievement measures (A in equation 1) are based on two test results. An achievement test was given at the beginning of each school year (a "pretest") to assess the student's mastery of various skills. At the end of the school year, a similar "posttest," asking questions with the same level of difficulty, was administered to determine the gain in skills over the school year. Test scores in mathematics are used as our measure of student achievement. School-based inputs are relatively more important in determining achievement in mathematics than in reading, which is more a function of family background (Madaus, 1979).[1]

There is still the question of whether standardized test scores are an appropriate measure of student outcomes. A number of other measures have been used, including student attitudes (Levin, 1970; Michelson 1970), atten-

Table 1
Means of Variables by Union Status

Variable	Union	Nonunion	Pooled
Posttest score—student	39.68	37.84	39.01
Pretest score—student	29.08	27.96	28.67
Pretest score squared—student	942.20	869.78	915.86
Sex (male = 1)—student	0.50	0.51	0.50
Race (white = 1)—student	0.73	0.74	0.73
Childhood experience—student	1.05	1.06	1.05
Parental involvement—student	1.96	1.74	1.88
Economic status—student	228.99	217.94	224.97
Teacher/student ratio	0.06	0.05	0.06
Administrator/student ratio	0.01	0.01	0.01
Clerical staff/student ratio	0.02	0.02	0.02
Highest degree—teacher	2.48	2.44	2.47
Years in teaching—teacher	12.36	11.33	11.99
College math courses—teacher	0.63	0.57	0.61
Math in-service—teacher	6.15	9.49	7.36
Instruction time—teacher	4.83	4.99	4.89
Preparation time—teacher	1.43	1.37	1.41
Administrative time—teacher	0.80	0.78	0.79
Highest degree—principal	2.99	3.02	3.00
Years in teaching—principal	10.60	9.47	10.19
Years in administration—principal	9.13	8.41	8.87
Instructional leadership—principal	53.48	53.62	53.53
Number of students	9,468	5,411	14,879

Source: Sustaining Effects Survey (U.S. Department of Education). See text for description of variables.

dance rates (Katzman, 1971), and college continuation and dropout rates (Burkhead, Fox, and Holland, 1967).[2] Even so, virtually all other previous studies use cognitive test scores, not only because they are the best available measure of cognitive achievement, but also because they are positively correlated with other dimensions of student achievement. Kiesling (1977–1978), for example, finds that standardized achievement tests appear to produce the same results as broader based measures of output in judging input effectiveness. Despite the considerable controversy over standardized tests, most school districts administer them; most states require them; and most educators, parents, and employers believe that they are important. Performance on tests is used to advance students through the educational system, to evaluate programs, and even to allocate funds.

Student-background measures (I and B in equation 1) are entered into the production function to account for a variety of family and other nonschool factors. These measures include gender, race, and indices of early childhood educational experience (a cumulative index ranging from 0 to 5 for exposure to kindergarten, Head Start, summer school, nursery school, day care, or preschool), parental involvement (a cumulative index ranging from 0 to 12 for parent participation in twelve categories of school activities), and economic status (the Orshandsky Poverty Index, with a range from 46 to 427).

School-based resources (S in equation 1) include school-level variables measuring the ratios of administrators, teachers, and clerical staff to students, as well as variables describing each student's mathematics teacher and school principal. The teacher/student ratio, a proxy for class size, has been used by other researchers to measure the intensity of the flow of teacher services. Although we have a direct measure of the time spent in instruction, class size affects the intensity of instructional time with individual students. The numbers of administrators and clerical personnel per student are included to capture certain supervisory, organizational, and resource features of the school.

The variables related to each student's mathematics teacher are divided into stock and flow measures. Years of teaching experience, highest degree earned (with less than a bachelors degree equal to 1, bachelors degree equal to 2, masters degree [or the hours equivalent] equal to 3, and Ph.D. equal to 4), number of college mathematics courses taken in the last three years, and hours of formal on-the-job mathematics training (in-service training) in the last three years are all measures of the teacher's stock of human capital.[3] These attributes are expected to increase the effectiveness of the teacher's interaction with students. It should be noted, however, that most studies find negative effects for the teacher's highest degree. These perverse effects are presumably due either to the matching of more highly trained teachers with students who are more difficult to teach (Hedrick, 1984) or to an auxiliary correlation between degrees and some unobserved negative attribute. Murnane (1981), for example, argues that higher degrees may be sought more to obtain salary increases than to achieve substantive improvements in teaching capabilities.

Three categories of teacher time are also included to reflect the flow of teacher services: time spent in instruction and time spent in preparation are expected to increase student achievement, and time spent performing administrative duties is expected to have a negative effect. All three categories are measured as average hours per school day, and together they account for about 90 percent of the time a teacher spends in school-related activities. Although total time spent in all types of instruction is not the same as time spent in mathematics instruction, the two activities are highly correlated and yield similar results.

The final set of variables refers to each student's school principal: highest degree (measured the same as for teachers), total number of years as a teacher, total number of years as an administrator, and hours devoted during the year to instructional leadership activities (curriculum development and program planning, monitoring, and evaluation). All three principal variables are presumed to have positive effects on student achievement, although most studies also find negative effects for the principal's highest degree (see, for example, Murnane, 1981).

Consistent with previous formulations of education production functions (Brown and Saks, 1975; Hanushek, 1978; and Summers and Wolfe, 1977, for example), we use a linear functional form, although results are similar using a semilogarithmic function. The pretest score is entered in quadratic form to allow for possible nonlinear effects. Such effects might occur, for example, because each test has a finite number of questions, and students who began the school year with high test scores might be less likely to make significant gains because of the truncated measurement of achievement. In addition, the effect of unionization may not be the same for all students—that is, the effect may be nonlinear across students with different initial achievement levels.

Estimates

The union–nonunion productivity differential is measured using separate estimates of union and nonunion production functions, where unionization is indicated by the presence of a district contract negotiated by a recognized bargaining unit. Differences in the technical coefficients in production are then evaluated at common input levels to obtain an estimate of the union–nonunion difference in output. Thus, evaluating the differences in coefficients between the two samples (using a common value for each variable as the weight) measures the union-induced shift in the production function. A similar estimate of the union–nonunion productivity differential is obtained using only an intercept shift for the union effect, but this approach constrains other union and nonunion coefficients to be the same. These constraints are rejected by an *F*-test for quality of the coefficients. Because many of the coefficients differ, we are able to identify important components of the overall productivity differential.

Separate estimates of the education production functions for union and nonunion districts are presented in table 2, along with the differences in coefficients. In general, our estimates are consistent with those of past studies that have not distinguished between union and nonunion districts (most recently, for example, Murnane, 1981). Traditional variables, such as the pretest score, student background variables, class size and teacher experience, are positively related to student achievement in at least one of the two sets of districts. Less traditional variables, such as teacher instruction time and teacher preparation time, however, are equally important determinants of student achievement. Consistent with previous studies, teachers and principals with more formal education appear to be less effective, at least in union districts.

Equality of the union and nonunion coefficients in table 2 is rejected by an *F*-test at the 1 percent level. Furthermore, about half the individual coefficients differ significantly, including those for the pretest score, teachers per student, clerical staff per student, teacher degree, college mathematics courses taken by the teacher, teacher inservice training in mathematics, teacher instructional time, principal degree, principal teaching experience, and instructional leadership by the principal. The most significant difference in coefficients is for instructional leadership.

Union–Nonunion Productivity Differential

To measure the union–nonunion productivity differential, we use the values of the independent variables for each student to calculate the difference between that student's predicted achievement if he or she were placed in a union school with the same student's predicted achievement in a nonunion school. For a particular student, a union–nonunion productivity differential will arise only from differences in the union and nonunion production functions, since the variables for that student are held constant.

The calculated productivity differential can vary from student to student, however, because of variations in the independent variables across students. In particular, the productivity differential will vary with the initial ability of a particular student because the union–nonunion pretest score coefficients differ significantly. The coefficients for the pretest score and its square, respectively, are 0.97 and -0.00165 for union districts and 0.71 and 0.0027 for nonunion districts. To see how the average union-nonunion differential varies by pretest scores, we calculate the difference in predicted posttest

Table 2
Estimates of Production Functions by Union Status
(dependent variable: math posttest score)

Variable	Union	Nonunion	Difference
Intercept	11.23*	9.98*	1.25
	(5.58)	(4.01)	(0.31)
Pretest score—student	0.97*	0.71*	0.28*
	(21.56)	(11.18)	(3.45)
Pretest score squared—student	−0.002*	0.003*	−0.005*
	(−2.43)	(2.89)	(−3.82)
Sex (male = 1)—student	−1.86*	−2.03*	0.167
	(−10.43)	(−8.44)	(0.56)
Race (white = 1)—student	1.80*	1.07*	0.73
	(7.62)	(3.49)	(1.89)
Childhood experience—student	−0.13	0.10	−0.23
	(−1.37)	(1.18)	(−1.81)
Parental involvement—student	0.14*	0.02	0.12
	(2.38)	(0.28)	(1.26)
Economic status—student	0.02*	0.02*	0.001
	(13.49)	(9.37)	(0.50)
Teacher/student ratio	11.38	39.09*	−27.71*
	(1.40)	(3.55)	(−2.03)
Administrator/student ratio	−198.24*	−13.25	−185.00
	(−3.66)	(−0.14)	(−1.67)
Clerical staff/student ratio	3.07	−25.13*	28.21*
	(0.35)	(−2.77)	(2.24)
Highest degree—teacher	−0.86*	−0.19	−0.66*
	(−4.82)	(−0.77)	(−3.26)
Years in teaching—teacher	0.01	0.03*	−0.02
	(0.87)	(1.89)	(−0.99)
College math courses—teacher	0.19*	−0.21	0.40*
	(2.19)	(−1.74)	(2.70)
Math in-service—teacher	0.001	−0.04*	0.05*
	(0.11)	(−5.58)	(4.15)
Instruction time—teacher	0.38*	0.79*	−0.41*
	(2.95)	(4.96)	(−2.03)
Preparation time—teacher	0.34*	0.57*	−0.23
	(2.59)	(3.08)	(−1.01)
Administrative time—teacher	0.05	−0.31	0.36
	(0.34)	(−1.60)	(1.45)
Highest degree—principal	−2.09*	0.09	−2.18*
	(−4.53)	(0.17)	(−3.14)
Years in teaching—principal	0.09*	0.02	0.07*
	(5.01)	(0.83)	(2.61)
Years in admin.—principal	0.11*	0.13*	−0.02
	(4.91)	(4.47)	(−0.45)
Instruction leadership—principal	0.03*	−0.08*	0.11*
	(2.06)	(−4.65)	(4.92)
R^2	.558	.539	

Note: The t-statistics for coefficients are in parentheses. See text and Table 1 for a description of variables and the SES data.

*Significant at the 5 percent level (one- or two-tailed test, as appropriate).

scores for each student in our sample and average them for each pretest score. These differences (and the corresponding 5 percent confidence interval) are displayed in figure 1.[4]

The results show a pronounced nonlinear relationship between the union–nonunion productivity differential and initial student ability (as measured by the pretest score). For students with pretest scores at the sample mean (about 29), the average union–nonunion difference in posttest scores is 0.67, or about 7 percent of the average gain in achievement (and statistically significant at the 5 percent level).[5] For students extremely above or below average, however, nonunion schools are more productive by about the same margin, with the difference statistically significant at pretest scores below 8 and above 48.

Measured across the entire sample of students, the average union–nonunion productivity differential remains positive at 0.33, just over 3 percent of the average gain in achievement (also statistically significant at the 5 percent level). Thus, we find evidence of a modestly positive productivity effect for teacher unions, although it is quantitatively smaller than the productivity effect typically found for unions in the private sector. Estimates for the private sector average about 15 percent, but vary from slightly negative to nearly 40 percent (Freeman and Medoff, 1984, p. 166).

This method of evaluating the union–nonunion differential at each pretest score has at least two possible difficulties. First, the sample of students for each pretest score is relatively thin, resulting in a large confidence interval. Second, the production technology is assumed to be the same for students in the tails of the sample distribution as for average students (varying only by the coefficients on the quadratic term for the pretest score).

The first problem can be addressed by averaging union–nonunion differentials in posttest scores across students in various ranges of pretest scores. We do this for three ranges: 6 to 14, 26 to 34, and 46 to 54. The estimated differentials are quite similar to those given here, but with smaller confidence intervals. The two extreme groups are roughly the same size and together equal roughly 20 percent of the middle group.

We deal with the second problem by estimating separate equations for students in each of the three ranges of pretest scores (instead of using the same coefficients for all ranges of pretest scores). Based on this method, the union–nonunion differentials for each range of pretest scores are virtually identical in size to those in figure 1, but with smaller confidence intervals.[6]

Discussion

Although we lack the data that would be needed to explain fully why the impact of collective bargaining appears to vary for different students, we speculate that this effect results from the standardization of the work force, work rules, and production techniques associated with collective bargaining in most industries. Previous analysis reported in Eberts and Stone (1984,

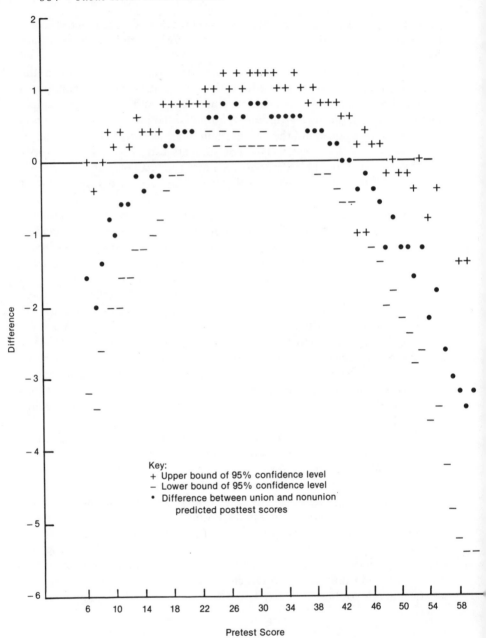

Figure 1. Differences between Union and Nonunion Predicted Posttest Scores

p. 149), in particular, indicates that organized districts rely to a greater degree than nonunion districts on standard classroom instruction as a uniform teaching mode, reducing the use of specialized techniques and resources. Standard classroom instruction is tailored to the abilities and problems of the majority of students and, not surprisingly, works best for average students (Michelson, 1970).

To pursue this point further, we also calculate differences for union and nonunion districts in the use of special instructional modes and resources, as reported in the national SES data. These differences are presented in table 3, along with the separate union and nonunion means. Three of the four instructional modes in table 3 represent the use of nonstandard, specialized instruction in groups smaller than the normal class size. The fourth, independent study, represents individual study using programmed instructional materials. As revealed in table 3, students in union districts clearly have less exposure to specialized instructional techniques than do students in nonunion districts. Since specialized techniques are those typically associated with students whose achievement is well above or below average, these differences may explain why union districts work less well for these atypical students.

Finally, instructional leadership appears to play a key role in the overall union advantage. As noted earlier, instructional leadership on the part of the principal—the time he or she spends in curriculum development; program needs assessment; and program planning, monitoring, and evaluation—is the most significant difference in the union and nonunion functions. Table 2 shows that these activities by the school principal are associated with significantly higher achievement in union districts, but with significantly lower achievement in nonunion districts. Note, however, that the mean values of

Table 3
Use of Specialized Instructional Mode

Instructional Mode	Union	Nonunion	Difference
Student hours spent with mathematics specialist	2.12	3.63	− 1.51* (− 6.78)
Student hours spent with mathematics aide	1.97	5.24	− 3.27* (− 15.57)
Student hours spent with mathematics tutor	0.96	1.29	− 0.33* (− 3.76)
Student hours spent in independent programmed study	3.37	5.65	− 2.28* (− 8.69)

Note: The t-statistics for the differences in the union and nonunion means are in parentheses. See text for a description of the variables and the Sustaining Effects Survey (U.S. Department of Education).

*Significant at the 5 percent level.

the time devoted to instructional leadership are quite similar for the two sets of districts (see table 1).[7]

The surprising fact that instructional leadership has opposite effects in union and nonunion districts may be explained by the "voice" function of unions emphasized by Freeman and Medoff and others. In organized districts, for example, individual teachers have formal mechanisms for expressing their views to school and district supervisors. In this context, instructional leadership by school principals may be much more effective than otherwise, both because specific principal actions are conditioned by teacher opinion and because the effectiveness of particular actions is enhanced by improved communication and coordination. The difference is so stark in our results that strong leadership activities by principals in nonunion districts are not just ineffective, but even counterproductive. The importance of instructional leadership, in fact, appears to be strong direct evidence in support of the voice role of unions.

Conclusion

In this study we have estimated the union-nonunion productivity differential for public schools, the largest local public sector activity. Estimating separate union and nonunion education production functions for over 14,000 fourth-graders, we have found that students in union districts have 3 percent higher scores on standardized achievement tests than students in nonunion districts, holding input levels constant. Although modest in size, this productivity effect suggests that union productivity gains are not unique to the private sector, although they may be quantitatively smaller in the public sector.

The union productivity advantage arises from two major factors. First, union districts rely to a greater degree than nonunion districts on standard classroom instructional techniques, which work best for the majority of students. Thus, average students perform 7 percent better in union than in nonunion districts. Students whose achievement is significantly below or above average, however, appear to perform better in nonunion districts, where there is significantly greater use of specialized programs and instructional techniques than in union districts. The finding of standardization of instructional techniques in union districts is consistent with familiar evidence from other industries that unions tend to standardize the workplace. A second major source of the union productivity advantage is the greater effectiveness of instructional leadership activities by school principals in union districts. This difference may be explained by the communication and coordination fostered by the "voice" function of unions, as argued by Freeman and Medoff and others.

Notes

1. Auxiliary results from our data based on reading scores support the view that schooling inputs are relatively less important for reading achievement, but they also yield estimates of the union–nonunion productivity differential similar to those based on mathematics scores. These results are available to interested readers on request.

2. Of these, only attendance rates are relevant for elementary school students. Moreover, we regard attendance rates as an input rather than an output.

3. Coding highest degree as separate binary variables for each degree level would permit greater precision in measuring the relative effects of degree levels, but the differences would be trivial in our data.

4. The procedure for calculating confidence intervals for predictions away from the sample mean is outlined in Johnston (1984, pp. 196–198).

5. The achievement base for the percentage change is the average achievement gain, not the average posttest score. Average gain is the standard measure because it represents achievement beyond the initial level of the pretest score.

6. These auxiliary results are available to interested readers on request.

7. Eberts and Stone (1985) provide a more detailed analysis of the role of the principal in student achievement. They, too, find that instructional leadership by the principal is a significant factor in student achievement.

References

Allen, Steven G. 1984. "Unionized Construction Workers Are More Productive." *Quarterly Journal of Economics* 99, no. 2: pp. 251–275.

Baugh, William H., and Joe A Stone. 1982. "Teachers, Unions and Wages in the 1970s: Unionism Now Pays." *Industrial and Labor Relations Review* 35, no. 3, pp. 368–376.

Baumol, William J. 1967. "Macroeconomics of Unbalanced Growth: The Anatomy of Urban Crisis." *American Economic Review* 57, no. 3, pp. 414–426.

Brown, Byron W., and Daniel M. Saks. 1975. "The Production and Distribution of Cognitive Skills within Schools." *Journal of Political Economy* 83, no. 3, pp. 571–595.

Brown, Charles, and James Medoff. 1978. "Trade Unions in the Production Process." *Journal of Political Economy* 86, no. 3 (June), pp. 355–378.

Burkhead, J., T.G. Fox, and J.W. Holland. 1967. *Input and Output in Large-City High Schools.* Syracuse, N.Y.: Syracuse University Press.

Clark, Kim B. 1980. "Unionization and Productivity: Micro-Econometric Evidence." *Quarterly Journal of Economics* 95, no. 4, pp. 613–639.

Cresswell, Anthony, and F. Spargo. 1980. "Impacts of Collective Bargaining in Elementary and Secondary Education: A Review of Research." Denver, Colo.: Education Commission of the States.

Eberts, Randall W. 1984. "Union Effects on Teacher Productivity." *Industrial and Labor Relations Review* 37, no. 3, pp. 346–348.

Eberts, Randall W., and Joe A. Stone. 1984. *Unions and Public Schools: The Effect of Collective Bargaining on American Education.* Lexington, Mass.: Lexington Books.

———. 1985. "Determinants of Principal Effectiveness: Assessing the Findings of Case Studies." Center for Educational Policy and Management, University of Oregon, mimeo.

———. 1986. "Teacher Unions and the Cost of Public Education." *Economic Inquiry* 24, no. 4, pp. 631–644.

Ehrenberg, Ronald G., Daniel R. Sherman, and Joshua L. Schwarz. 1983. "Unions and Productivity in the Public Sector: A Study of Municipal Libraries." *Industrial and Labor Relations Review* 36, no. 2, pp. 199–213.

Freeman, Richard, and James Medoff. 1979. "Two Faces of Unionism." *The Public Interest* 57, no. 4, pp. 69–93.

———. 1984. *What Do Unions Do?* New York: Basic Books.

Gall, Meredith D. 1983. "Using Staff Development to Improve Scholarship." In Center for Educational Policy and Management, *R&D Perspectives.* Eugene: University of Oregon (Winter).

Goldschmidt, Steven M., and Leland E. Stuart. 1986. "The Extent and Impact of Educational Policy Bargaining." *Industrial and Labor Relations Review* 39, no. 3, pp. 350–360.

Hanushek, Eric A. 1978. "Conceptual and Empirical Issues in the Estimation of Educational Production Functions." *Journal of Human Resources* 14, no. 3, pp. 351–388.

Hedrick, David W. 1984. "Student Achievement and Institutional Time: A Simultaneous Equations Approach." Ph.D. dissertation, University of Oregon.

Hemenway, Judith A. 1978. "Report #9: The Measures and Variables in the Sustaining Effects Study." Santa Monica, Calif.: Systems Development Corporation (December).

Johnston, J. 1984. *Econometric Methods,* 3rd ed. New York: McGraw-Hill.

Katzman, Martin. 1971. *The Political Economy of Urban Schools.* Cambridge, Mass.: Harvard University Press.

Kiesling, Herbert. 1977–1978. "Productivity of Instructional Time by Mode of Instruction for Students at Varying Levels of Reading Skill." *Reading Research Quarterly* 13, no. 4, pp. 554–582.

Levin, Henry M. 1970. "A Cost-Effectiveness Analysis of Teacher Selection." *Journal of Human Resources* 5, no. 1, pp. 24–33.

Madaus, G.F., et al. 1979. "The Sensitivity of Measures of School Effectiveness." *Harvard Educational Review* 2, pp. 207–230.

McDonnell, Lorraine, and Anthony Pascal. 1979. "Organized Teachers in American Schools." R-2407-NIE. Santa Monica, Calif.: Rand Corporation.

Michelson, S. 1970. "The Association of Teacher Resources with Children's Characteristics." In Office of Education, *How Do Teachers Make a Difference?* Washington, D.C.: Office of Education, OE-58042, pp. 55–75.

Murnane, Richard J. 1981. "Interpreting the Evidence of School Effectiveness." *Teachers College Record* 83, no. 1, pp. 19–35.

Summers, Anita, and Barbara Wolfe. 1977. "Do Schools Make a Difference?" *American Economic Review* 67, no. 4, pp. 639–652.

Woodbury, Stephen. 1985. "The Scope of Bargaining and Bargaining Outcomes in Public Schools." *Industrial and Labor Relations Review* 38, no. 2, pp. 195–210.

Change and Continuity: The Role of a Labor–Management Committee in Facilitating Work Force Change During Retrenchment

Robert B. McKersie
Leonard Greenhalgh
*Todd Jick**

The tension between change and continuity is likely to be the central dilemma in labor–management relations in the 1980s. Change is required if organizations are to prosper in increasingly competitive world markets, take advantage of new technology, or streamline operations in a declining niche. At the same time, continuity of employment is a goal that workers and their union representatives are embracing with increasing vigor: the old maxim that job loss is "one of the breaks of the game" is no longer acceptable (McKersie, Greenhalgh, and Jick 1980).

The purpose of this reading is to outline the experience of one program that reconciled the tension so that change and continuity could occur in a mutually reinforcing way. The change occurred as the state of New York phased out some of its programs and, in response to fiscal constraints, cut back some others. As a result of these changes, continuity of employment was at stake for the state's more than 150,000 workers. The reconciliation was accomplished through the innovative work of a joint labor–management committee. The committee conducted research to assess impacts, needs, and pilot programs; developed and implemented reemployment programs for workers displaced prior to formation of the committee; and evolved policies and procedures for handling program shifts in ways that avoid the dysfunctions that arise when employment changes are poorly executed.

Origin of the Committee

The state of New York had been a stable employer from the 1930s through the 1960s. The early 1970s, however, saw a reversal of this trend whereby

*Massachusetts Institute of Technology, Dartmouth College and York University, respectively. Reprinted from *Industrial Relations* 20, no. 2 (Spring 1981), pp. 212–220.

more than 10,000 employees had been laid off by 1976. The history of stability was a double-edged sword. First, the cuts suddenly and dramatically violated expectations of job security held by state workers, many of whom had self-selected into state employment because of the security it traditionally offered (Hall and Schneider, 1972; Hanlon, 1979; Schuster, 1974). Second, the years of stability had provided state decision makers with little experience in reducing its work force, so that when the cuts came, they were handled with little consideration of the impact on employees.

As a result of these factors, membership pressure on the unions grew dramatically. The major public sector union, the Civil Service Employees Association (CSEA)[1] entered the 1976 negotiations willing to fight hard for a prohibition of future layoffs.[2] The chief negotiator for the state, Donald Wollett, was familiar with the work of the Armour Automation Committee, which had experienced some success in cushioning the impact of major change in the meat-packing industry (see Schultz and Weber, 1966). He advanced a counterproposal involving six months' advance notice and establishment of a Continuity of Employment Committee, to which the union eventually agreed. The committee's three-year mandate, provided in the 1976 contract, was to:

1. Study worker displacement problems arising from economy reductions in force, programmatic reductions and curtailments, closedowns, relocations, consolidations, technological changes, and contracting out.

2. Make recommendations for the solution of these problems, including but not limited to the use of normal and induced attrition (for example, early retirements), sharing of available state job opportunities (for example, transfers), indemnification (for example, severance pay), and transition to work in the labor market beyond state employment (for example, retraining).

To indicate that it meant business, the state agreed to appropriate $1 million for the work of the committee. As will be seen, this money became a key factor for success, for it enabled the committee to buy its way into demonstration projects and provided seed money for the establishment of special programs within existing agencies. Since the rank and file quickly dubbed the committee "the million dollar operation," the money also put pressure on the committee to develop programs that would benefit workers who had been on layoff and to initiate visible preventive programs for those who might be subject to layoff in the future.

Formation of the Committee

The committee began operations in the fall of 1976, with the appointment of representatives. The president of CSEA nominated five vice-presidents, representing different regions. These individuals brought status from the union side as well as an independence, since each of them was an elected official in his region. Management representatives were drawn from the middle ranks: the civil service department, the office of employee relations, the division of the budget, one of the mental health agencies, and the department of education.[3]

Early in its operation, the committee agreed on a number of ground rules, which stood the test of time over the three-year period. First, all decisions would be taken only after full discussion and consensus by all members of the committee. This meant that each member was in a position to stop a decision until he or she felt comfortable with the proposal. Second, the work of the committee was viewed as parallel to the adversary process of collective bargaining. Recommendations were to be submitted to the principals—that is, the director of the office of employee relations and the president of the CSEA—and through their roles brought to the bargaining table or implemented by executive orders.

The most important ground rule involved what the committee members came to call the black box understanding—namely, that the committee would concern itself with the impact of a specific program change on workers and not with the rationale for the program change itself. For example, the union strongly opposed the state's deinstitutionalization program[4] in other forums—yet the committee agreed that the union's concern with the policy itself would not affect the design and implementation of contingent programs to help mental health care workers who would be displaced by deinstitutionalization. At times it became difficult to hold to this separation of the policy rationale from the consequences of the policy, since it appeared to some rank and file that, by dealing with the consequences, the committee was assenting to the policy itself. Nevertheless, this principle made it possible for the committee to move ahead with its program of assistance and protection and shielded it from the conflict that would have been inherent in discussing the appropriateness of the changes sought by the state.

Finally, the committee agreed that it would try to utilize existing state agencies and incorporate its ideas and programs within the existing agencies of the state rather than using its funds to establish a new and separate office.

Impact of Layoffs

The first task undertaken by the committee's research staff was an analysis of the layoffs that had occurred over the preceding six years to determine the extent and nature of needs to be addressed. The general picture that emerged indicated that about 10,000 individuals had been laid off, with heavy concentrations occurring in the drug abuse agency and in the several mental health agencies. The heaviest hit area of the state was New York City. Females were underrepresented in the layoff group; whereas they comprised 44 percent of state employment, they accounted for 32 percent of those laid off. The reverse was true of minorities; whereas they represented approximately 10 percent of state employment, they accounted for almost 20 percent of those laid off. This pattern is explained largely by the sharp cutback in the state's drug abuse program; drug abuse officers were predominantly minority males.

For individual workers, the severity of the layoff experience ranged over the spectrum. Approximately 35 percent of those affected experienced a "technical layoff" that involved virtually no unemployment; these employees left one agency or title of work to be quickly reemployed by the state in another position. Another 45 percent were soon recalled to state employment, usually to the same or better pay grade than they had prior to the layoff. The remaining 20 percent were unemployed for an average of 24 weeks.

The research work also assessed noneconomic consequences of layoff for state workers. Through questionnaires and a large number of face-to-face interviews, it became clear that many individuals had experienced considerable stress as a result of the layoff experience. Particularly hard hit was a group of semiprofessional employees in the drug abuse agency. This agency had come into being in the 1960s and had expanded rapidly, making it possible for individuals with associate degrees in counseling and narcotic control to advance rapidly into important positions of responsibility. Many of these individuals had salaries in the range of $15,000 to $20,000 and had bought homes and had been enjoying the other appurtenances of middle-class living when the cutbacks occurred. Having assumed—like so many state employees—that their jobs were secure, they were unprepared for the shock of job loss and the ensuing uncertainty of finding alternative employment. The result was widespread stress-induced illness (Greenhalgh and Jick, 1978) and alcohol abuse; two suicides also occurred.

State agencies as well as individuals experienced adverse effects arising from layoffs—specifically, in the form of impaired organizational effectiveness. This phenomenon occurred with sufficient regularity that the general pattern can be described as follows. The shock of actual or rumored layoffs generates a ripple effect that diffuses throughout the organization. Insecure employees react by engaging in dysfunctional behaviors. For example, there is a rise in the turnover rate that is correlated with impaired job security. Worse, it is the higher-quality and harder-to-replace workers who are the first to leave (Greenhalgh and Jick, 1979). Subsequent understaffing leads to greater costs of overtime and disrupted teamwork. Those that remain behind are often withdrawn and demoralized, and tend to put in the least effort that is acceptable.

The prospect of reduced effectiveness of state service delivery was recognized by the committee and its staff as a persuasive point, one that could be used in overcoming the resistance of the state system to adopting the committee's policies and programs. More specifically, since initial field research suggested that layoffs created costs for the state that might offset much of the presumed savings, systematic research was undertaken to estimate these costs (see Greenhalgh, 1978; Greenhalgh and McKersie, in press). The research was designed to enable state decisionmakers to draw conclusions about the relative cost effectiveness of the two principal alternatives for reducing a work force—layoff versus attrition.

As a result, it was ascertained that attrition could be a practical alternative to layoff. Since the typical layoff had involved only a small reduction relative to the size of the work force in a particular agency, an attrition program—for example, imposing a selective hiring freeze—could accomplish the same overall reduction after a transition period of less than a year in all but a few cases. Beyond the transition period, the savings from the reduced payroll size would be equal whichever strategy is chosen.

There are several costs that arise when the layoff strategy is chosen over the attrition strategy. The layoff strategy incurs the substantial costs of unemployment insurance chargebacks. These do not accrue to an employer using the attrition approach, wherein workers leave voluntarily; the costs accrue only when workers are laid off. Other incremental costs of the layoff strategy result from the effects of job insecurity that pervades an organization for a long time following the first rumors of layoffs. The drop in productivity noted earlier can be measured in cost terms, as can increased turnover and its multiple consequences. Furthermore, agencies experience increased alcoholism, grievances, and lawsuits contesting layoffs. Perhaps worst of all, job insecurity can engender resistance to change; thus, ironically, the planned reorganizations that gave rise to the layoffs become much more difficult to introduce successfully.

When dollar amounts are attached to these factors, the cost-effectiveness of layoff and attrition can be compared. For the typical work force reduction situation, layoffs do not prove to be cost-effective. In fact, there is a difference in favor of attrition sufficiently large to justify an investment of almost $1,000 per surplus worker for programs to induce redeployment through retraining and relocation. In sum, the cost-effectiveness study indicated a need for the committee to develop policies, guidelines, and legislation so that the layoff strategy would be used as a last resort rather than as standard operating procedure.

Readjustment Programs

The research had identified a group of 1,200 individuals as potentially in need of the committee's assistance. Approximately 500 (5 percent of the total of 10,000) had been laid off in the early 1970s and never recalled to state service. The other 700 had regained employment, but at lower salary levels.

This combined group became a target clientele for the development of a number of readjustment programs operated by the committee during the first year of its work.

The first step was establishment of a special Continuity of Employment Center to provide counseling and referral service to the target group. Most laid off employees had expressed a strong desire to return to work with the state (primarily because of fringe benefits, especially pensions). Thus, it was natural to locate the center in the state's civil service department, which had the best information about employment opportunities throughout the state system.

Next, all members of the target group were contacted and asked to complete a skills inventory profile. The existing civil service recall procedure had used only past state job titles to determine skills to be matched to openings. The profile was designed to broaden possibilities for matching by considering skills acquired through training programs and nonstate jobs.

Members of the target group were then contacted by circulars when openings developed, and many came to the center to be interviewed and counseled about opportunities for reinstatement. In addition, several retraining programs were instituted to allow for reemployment into new careers. To give one example, with funds from the committee, a training program was established to retrain a group of laid-off meat inspectors to become fruit inspectors. Half a dozen such programs serving about 100 individuals were implemented on a pilot basis by the center, with development, funding, and evaluation provided by the committee and its staff.

The committee also instituted, in cooperation with the state department of labor, an outplacement program, which sought to open up opportunities in the private sector for those still unemployed. Money was allocated on a pilot basis to enable individuals to enroll in training programs, to search for employment elsewhere within or even outside of the state, and to subsidize private industry for wages paid during the break-in period for the new workers. Only a handful availed themselves of the program, however, confirming the point revealed in interviews that very few individuals were interested in working in the private sector. Indeed, out of the original 10,000 affected, only about 5 percent moved to employment in the private sector. On the basis of this experience, the efforts of the readjustment center were subsequently refocused almost exclusively on finding employment for the job losers within the state system.

Overall, the work of the center and the readjustment activities more generally must be viewed as only minimally effective. Only about 10 percent of the target group benefited in any measurable way. One reason for the low yield involved the fact that the target group, after all, was "residual" in the sense that they had been passed up by potential state hiring agencies because of their unwanted skills or perhaps their marginal performance records.

Policy Development and Recommendations

Having gone about as far as it could in reemploying those who continued to be disadvantaged as a result of layoffs, the committee turned its attention to formulating proposals for achieving program changes without layoffs. The union representatives on the committee advocated a guarantee of no layoffs for state employees, but the management representatives resisted it, knowing that such a policy would not be acceptable to top state officials because it would be too constraining in certain situations.

The compromise that developed involved the principle of "one employment alternative." The concept involved offering each surplus employee a reasonable alternative for remaining employed with the state. An alternative would be "reasonable" if it were in the same general pay range and commuting area. Access to a retraining program would constitute an offer. The worker would be free to refuse the offer and be laid off without losing any of the layoff/recall rights provided by state law, and without prejudicing eligibility to draw unemployment compensation.

Since the fall of 1978, when the committee submitted its unanimous recommendation for the avoidance of layoffs through the employment alternative concept, the state has laid off only a handful of employees on an involuntary basis. Although the state has not adopted the policy in any formal sense (the executive branch has said that it did not want to tie its hands to the commitment of providing an employment alternative in all cases), this guideline has nevertheless been followed in the closing down of a number of programs and establishments involving several thousand workers.

The committee also advanced several accompanying recommendations that would be needed in the successful implementation of an employment alternative program. First, it would be essential for work force planning to take place on a centralized basis so that workers who were scheduled for displacement could be matched to openings that were available or projected. Consequently, the committee recommended that human resource planning be institutionalized in parallel with financial and program planning conducted by the division of the budget.

Another recommendation involved the provision of lead time. On the basis of several research studies, the committee recommended that the state provide advance notice of three months before individuals would be displaced. Three months would allow sufficient time for arranging the employment alternative but would not be excessively long, as was the case with the six months' advance notice. The latter had been instituted for a one-year experimental period, and then not renewed. It had been found that six months' notice created so much slack that pilferage and other counterproductive behavior developed.

The Gouverneur Demonstration Project

The committee had made the case that the layoff strategy was not cost-effective and that an array of viable techniques was available for managing work force reductions. A task remaining was to show by a demonstration project that, with sufficient lead time, cooperation of the potential employing agencies, and resolution of local labor–management conflict, it should be possible to close down a facility and redeploy all the workers involved to other positions within state employment. The site that was chosen for the test was the Gouverneur Unit, operated by the Office of Mental Retardation in lower Manhattan. This small facility had been slated to close for some time: as part of its overall program of deinstitutionalization, the state desired to move the patients to other care arrangements; furthermore, the building had been condemned. The union, however, opposed in principle to deinstitutionalization, had publicly indicated that it would fight the decision to close the facility with every means at its disposal. Into this bitter conflict walked the committee.

Starting first at the level of the statewide committee, meetings were held with key representatives from the agency, the governor's office, the top staff of CSEA, and the Division of the Budget. A document was prepared by the committee that outlined the principles mentioned earlier for continuity of employment, and commitment was secured that the various parties would cooperate with the demonstration project. For the Division of the Budget, this meant agreeing to a phase-out timetable that would incur additional labor ("holding") costs. For the Office of Mental Retardation, it meant exerting influence on the administrators of other units within the agency to accept displaced employees on a transfer basis. For the union, it meant holding its fire on the short-term question of deinstitutionalization and giving the project a chance—in order to see if it would be possible for the workers involved to continue employment without being subjected to layoff, thus providing potential long-term benefits for union members.

To summarize a complex stream of events, the project succeeded. All 300 workers were redeployed, many of them to other units in Manhattan operated by the Office of Mental Retardation. A local-level labor–management committee functioned very effectively in settling the individual problems that inevitably arise in establishing seniority lists and transfer opportunities. A staff member from the statewide committee chaired the local committee and provided the impetus for moving the project ahead.

Two previously laid-off employees who had worked as counselors for the drug abuse agency were recalled to serve as counselors for the project. In effect, they were the outreach arm for the Continuity of Employment Center. They performed the invaluable function of meeting regularly with the displaced workers, outlining options and helping them make intelligent choices.

In an effort to evaluate the effectiveness of the Gouverneur redeployment program, the staff conducted research to determine whether the program had successfully avoided the dysfunctional consequences of job insecurity that had been measured at agencies where the layoff strategy had been used. The results were very encouraging. Job security itself was significantly higher among Gouverneur employees who were provided opportunities for continued employment. In addition, their productivity was higher and their propensity to quit the organization lower. Since the effects on productivity and turnover were the major costs associated with layoff-induced job insecurity, the Gouverneur redeployment program was judged a success (see Greenhalgh, 1980).

Work Force Planning

Although the Gouverneur demonstration project showed that a workable technology did exist for achieving a work force reduction without layoffs, it involved the closing of only a small organizational subunit. A question remained as to the applicability of this approach to large-scale program change. Thus, the committee welcomed the opportunity that arose with a request from the state legislature to examine work force changes in the state's mental health agencies. At this point in the history of deinstitutionalization, CSEA found itself ready to modify its opposition if it could be assured that program changes would take place without forcing its members out of the state system. The study, therefore, was undertaken by the committee's staff.

The study concluded that over a projected five-year period, depending on the rate at which deinstitutionalization took place, anywhere from 5,000 to 15,000 state workers might be displaced. However, with the institution of an attrition program, the number of workers who would be in excess could be reduced to well under 1,000; if a geographical transfer program were utilized, all displaced workers could be accommodated. Although the overall conclusion was encouraging, a number of practical problems remained. For example, attrition rates in the Adirondack counties were far lower than those in the New York City metropolitan area. Consequently, to achieve overall system balance, it would be necessary to induce some employees from upstate counties to transfer to downstate counties, which would meet with resistance. Further, the attrition program, with its attendant hiring freeze, would have to be modified for some occupations where turnover would be higher than required and where it would be impossible to retrain people within the system to fill these openings: doctors and other high-demand occupations would be the examples. Although a number of ramifications remained to be worked out in implementing program changes without layoffs, the work force planning exercise demonstrated to the legislature and to the executive branch that, with sufficient lead time and proper staff work, it should be possible to achieve even major program changes as well as a successful redeployment of the personnel involved.

Overall Results

From the inception of the committee in 1976 through the end of its first phase of work in the summer of 1979, no massive layoffs of New York State employees took place. Moreover, the state subsequently adopted attrition programs as standard operating procedure for work force reductions.[5] Thus, in a very important sense, the work and thinking of the committee had been adopted by the decision makers within the executive branch of the state.

At the level of individual agencies, the concept of bringing about change without layoff had also been institutionalized to some extent. For example, during the summer of 1979, the remaining institutions of the drug abuse agency were phased out with virtually no involuntary layoffs. Moreover, this redeployment of personnel took place under the auspices of the industrial relations personnel in the agency, without the assistance of the committee. The transition program did not run as smoothly as Gouverneur, where a local labor–management committee solved implementation issues. Nevertheless, the agency did consult with the representatives of the union, and the handling of the phaseout emphasized a concern for the job security of the workers involved that was far different from that present in the early and mid-1970s.

During the period 1976–1979, at least half a dozen other program changes took place within state agencies that involved the redeployment of several hundred personnel. For most of these program changes the Continuity of Employment Center within the civil service department provided important support services. Staff counselors were dispatched to the sites to assist in the readjustment efforts. In addition, the data bank capabilities of the central office in Albany were used to help match individuals to openings in other state agencies.

In the longer run, the center will house two separate functional units.[6] First, intraorganizational transfer will be facilitated by a computerized information system programmed to match available personnel to position openings. Second, an expanded range of services will be provided. These services will include employee assessment assistance in the form of career counseling, resume preparation, and development of interview skills; increased employability through retraining, job search grants, relocation allowances, on-the-job training wage reimbursement; and outplacement assistance with public and private sector employers. In practice, these units will be tightly integrated so as to facilitate the systematic progression of employees toward reemployment.

Lessons from the Continuity of Employment Committee

Several points stand out in retrospect. First, it is extemely important in bringing about a fundamental change in the thinking and approach of any large organization for the intervention entity to have "buying power." Part of this was supplied by the $1 million allocation, which enabled the committee to encourage agencies to undertake new functions by supplementing budgets with seed money. All changes require start-up funds, and the presumption was that after the test period the agency would be able to carry forward on its own out of existing funds or seek additional funds from the legislature for new levels of activity.

Support from the executive branch also became extremely important in securing the cooperation of agencies with a program of employment continuity for state workers. This was illustrated during the Gouverneur project, when it became necessary to invoke the prestige of the governor's office to encourage various agencies to accept displaced employees.

Another lesson learned was that civil service departments do not think of themselves as personnel agencies—on the contrary, they emphasize almost exclusively the standard functions of classification and appeal. Hence, it took considerable time and effort to reorient the thinking of key people in the state to the need for a hands-on personnel function that would view the work force as more than a static factor—that is, would view it as a human resource to be developed and effectively redeployed.

Finally, this project illustrates the important positive interaction between labor–management cooperation, demonstration projects, research analyses, policy recommendations, and basic changes in the thinking and practice of governmental agencies.

Notes

1. At the time of the 1976 negotiations, CSEA was an independent union. In April 1978 it affiliated with the American Federation of State, County, and Municipal Employees Union (AFSCME).

2. A minority of the state's work force was represented by AFSCME during this period, but no arrangement similar to the state–CSEA Continuity of Employment Committee existed for those workers.

3. The first author of this article was selected as neutral chairman of the committee. The other two authors directed the committee's full-time professional staff.

4. The deinstitutionalization program involved a change in patient care from residential, institution-based to outpatient, community-based services.

5. The state experienced some operational difficulties in its early experience with attrition programs. In some cases, a straight hiring freeze resulted in the work force shrinking faster than was projected. Some administrators compensated for this with overtime, which was costly and further increased the attrition rate.

References

DeAngelo, Charles. Developing an Employment Readjustment System in Response to Layoffs in New York State Government: A Case Study. Unpublished M.S. thesis, Cornell University, 1978.

Greenhalgh, Leonard, *A Cost–Benefit Balance Sheet for Evaluating Layoffs as a Policy Strategy.* Ithaca, N.Y.: New York State School of Industrial and Labor Relations, Cornell University, 1978.

———. "Maintaining Organizational Effectiveness During Organizational Retrenchment." Working paper, Amos Tuck School of Business Administration, Dartmouth College, 1980.

———. "The Relationship between Job Security and Turnover, and Its Differential Effect on Employee Quality Level." Paper presented at the Annual Meeting of the Academy of Management, Atlanta, August 1979.

Greenhalgh, Leonard, and Todd Jick. *The Closing of Urban State Agencies: Impact on Employee Attitudes.* Ithaca, N.Y.: Continuity of Employment Research, New York School of Industrial and Labor Relations, Cornell University, 1978.

Greenhalgh, Leonard, and Robert McKersie. "Cost Effectiveness of Alternative Strategies for Cutback Management." *Public Administration Review,* in press.

Hall, Douglas, and Benjamin Schneider. "Correlates of Organizational Identification as a Function of Career Pattern and Organizational Type." *Administrative Science Quarterly* 17 (September 1972), pp. 340–350.

Hanlon, Martin, *Primary Groups and Unemployment.* Ph.D. dissertation, Columbia University, 1979.

McKersie, Robert, Leonard Greenhalgh, and Todd Jick. "Economic Progress and Economic Dislocation." Working paper, Sloan School of Management, MIT, 1980.

Schultz, George, and Arnold Weber, *Strategies for Displaced Workers.* New York: Harper and Row, 1966.

Schuster, Jay. "Management-Compensation Policy and the Public Interest." *Public Personnel Management* 3 (November–December 1974), pp. 510–523.

8
Conclusions and Future Issues

I t is customary for authors of a book like this one to use the final chapter to speculate about the course of future events. But since one of the arguments made throughout this book is that predictions about the future should be based less on armchair prognostication and more on an empirically grounded understanding of past and present events, we will follow a cautious course. We continue to believe that more research on public sector labor relations is needed and we recognize the hazards of making statements about the future in environments as dynamic and diverse as the ones in which public sector bargaining operates. We also believe, however, that it is time to make some summary statements about what has been learned from completed research and what unanswered questions or practical problems are likely to pose the greatest challenges to professionals in this field in the immediate future.

The reader should, however, be cognizant of the dubious track record of industrial relations researchers as crystal ball gazers. Suffice it to say that no one we know of writing in this field in the 1950s predicted or anticipated the sudden rise of public sector bargaining in the 1960s. It is not surprising, therefore, that one of the more articulate and honest practitioners in the field for years published a monthly newsletter entitled "The Cloudy Crystal Ball."[1]

What, then, have we learned from the accumulated research and experiences of the past two decades? We will organize our summary comments according to the framework used throughout the book—that is, by beginning with a discussion of the environment and working our way through to the outcomes and impacts of bargaining during its evolution in the public sector.

The Environmental Contexts

Much of the early debate over the long-run consequences of unionism and collective bargaining in the public sector was predicated on some assumptions about the nature of the economic and political environments in which bargaining takes place. Those who initially opposed providing bargaining rights and/or the right to strike to public employees assumed that the absence of clear market constraints and the presumed vulnerability of elected officials to citizen pressure to avoid disruption in services would give undue power to unionized employees. These early predictions, however, underestimated both the diversity of the economic and political environments in which bargaining takes place, and the changes experienced in bargaining environments in response to economic and political developments. The evidence to date simply does not support the hypothesis that collective bargaining inevitably and permanently alters the balance of power in favor of public employees. Rather, public employees gained an initial bargaining advantage in those environments where the economy was strong and the political context was supportive of labor. As the economic constraints tightened, however, the political climate turned against public employees, management resistance to union bargaining demands stiffened, and the economic and substantive bargaining gains of employees moderated. More recently these gains have increased, but they have benefited a comparatively shrinking public sector work force.

Still, there is some validity to the essence of the argument advanced by Wellington and Winter—namely, that the nature of the political process is altered through collective bargaining. What they failed to anticipate, however, is that not only would unions become more politically active and astute at the local level, but that collective bargaining would also stimulate the formation of more active school boards and school board associations, parent associations, taxpayer groups, minority group coalitions, management labor relations professional groups, and so forth. Whether an "appropriate" balance of power among these interested parties has evolved is still an open question (no interest group ever believes it has enough power) and one worth constant attention and analysis in the years ahead. Indeed, there are certain forces on the horizon that portend a period of heightened interest group conflict in public sector labor relations.

In particular, two developments at the federal level suggest that states and localities may have to pick up a greater share of the tab for the provision of various public services. First, and as noted earlier, congressional actions aimed at reducing the federal deficit threaten to reduce and even eliminate various programs that now provide aid to state and local governments. Second, changes in the federal tax law may affect the cost of state and local government borrowing and may change the amount of state tax revenue generated. These forces may compel states and localities to cut public services and institute "revenue–enhancement" programs. States and localities may end up caught between the rock of unionized public employees demanding better bargaining outcomes, and the hard place of taxpayers organized to prevent tax increases. Thus, economic and financial forces may interact with public sector bargaining in a way that produces instability.

The financial pressure facing cities may be further exacerbated by three important public sector developments. First, gender-based pay discrimination has pushed the issue of comparable worth—equal pay for work of comparable value—into the political spotlight during the 1980s. For various reasons, such as occupational segregation, full-time female employees earn less than what full-time male employees earn in the U.S. public sector.[2] This male–female pay discrepancy, combined with the large female share of the government work force and the political appeal of a fairness issue, have resulted in an array of comparable worth lawsuits, lobbying efforts, and bargaining demands by public employee unions across the country. Although it is unclear what outcome will result from these comparable worth actions, the attention given to this issue is likely to cause public employers to raise the relative pay of their female employees, at least by a token amount.[3] Thus, in an era of scarce resources, concern about comparable worth may reduce public employers' flexibility in allocating revenues. This, in turn, may cause or contribute to an increase in fiscal stress.

Second, cities have recently experienced drastic increases in insurance premiums.[4] For example, Dallas, Texas, was forced to drop its insurance coverage and self-insure when its liability insurance premium was increased by 900 percent in 1986. Hartford, Connecticut, the nation's insurance capital, saw its liability insurance premium increase by 20 percent, to $1.9 million, at the same time that its insurance carrier decreased its maximum coverage from $31 million to $4 million. Across the nation, municipal insurance premiums have reached unaffordable levels, thereby creating or contributing to labor relations difficulties. For example, in 1986, Jersey City, New Jersey, was forced to lay off essential service workers (police and firefighters) ostensibly in order to afford its insurance premium. These employees were reinstated only after their unions made labor cost concessions sufficient to offset the increased insurance costs.

Third, demographics dictate that large numbers of public employees will reach retirement age early in the twenty-first century. Public employers will then be legally required to pay out billions of dollars in pensions. Yet, on and off over the past decade, concern has been expressed about the serious underfunding of public sector pension systems.[6] For example, in 1975, less than 25 percent of a sample of 44 Pennsylvania cities had adequately funded their pension plans, and over $1 billion in unfunded pension liabilities existed across the other cities.[6] Moreover, the Pennsylvania experience seemed representative of the situation existing across U.S. cities generally.[7] Absent high pension fund investment returns or reforms of public employee pension systems, or both, this issue also threatens to increase fiscal stress in the public sector. As a result, pension underfunding may also cause future labor relations instability in the public sector.

As noted in chapter 2, financial difficulties for cities have gone hand in hand with an increased demand for public services. Further, the greatest demanders have often been those groups of people least able to provide additional revenue. This situation is unlikely to change in the future. If our observations regarding the potential effects of current trends are correct, then we foresee a crisis in public sector labor relations in the 1990s, with a volatile environment resulting from the combination of unionized employees' demands, declining federal government aid, taxpayer resistance, greater non-labor operating costs (such as insurance premiums), and high public service demands.

What are the implications of such an environment for public sector unionization and bargaining legislation? Consider that although the rate of passage of state and local government employee bargaining laws slowed in the 1980s, most states have enacted a legislative framework regulating bargaining. These laws have made collective bargaining an accepted practice and have given public employee unions a legitimate role in society. In turn, the percentage of employees represented by unions is much larger in the public than in the private sector (about 43 percent versus 16 percent in 1985).[8] Although the extent of public sector unionism has declined slightly since the mid-1970s, stagnating or contracting levels of public employment are partly responsible for the change. These facts suggest that collective bargaining has become accepted and that employees have embraced unions in the public sector.

Further, the bulk of the evidence suggests that unionization and favorable legislative environments have translated into higher pay and better working conditions for public employees.[9] This has led to increases in and reallocations (favoring unionized employees) of public sector budgets. Because unionism has made public employees better off, it has probably also increased their expectations regarding future negotiated settlements.

Yet, in a newly volatile economic-financial environment, public sector unions are likely to be severely buffeted by taxpayer-generated demands for both improved public services and a smaller public sector — developments that have already emerged in the third generation of public sector bargaining. To the extent that this implies further shrinkage of the public sector work force and the substitution of part-time for some full-time personnel, it is likely also to result in a lower incidence of public sector unionization.

As to the regulation of public sector bargaining, it is quite unlikely that a new wave of economic-financial volatility will bring about the repeal of bargaining laws. A stringent economic environment will more likely weaken whatever pressures have developed for the extension of bargaining rights to public employees in the South, while strengthening the forces favoring the removal of bargaining rights for public sector supervisory (and some management) personnel. In states with heavily unionized public sector work forces, public sector bargaining laws may even be amended or enacted to regulate more closely unions' internal governance and financial affairs.

Whatever legislative developments do emerge in this regard during the remainder of the 1980s and in the 1990s, it is useful to remind ourselves that the diversity of public sector bargaining laws continues to provide a laboratory for researchers who can compare wages, benefits, impasse procedures, union influence, and management decision-making processes, among other things, across states with differing regulatory frameworks. What has been neglected in this regard is a research focus on those states that lack public sector bargaining laws. We continue to know very little about conditions of employment, employee organizations, and employer practices in the unorganized public sector. Whether or not economic-financial volatility comes to characterize state and local government in the near future, research attention needs to shift to the unorganized and unregulated portion of the public sector if we are to learn more about the effects of an absence of bargaining laws in environments not normally conducive to unionism.

The Structure of Bargaining

Despite periodic calls for greater consolidation of bargaining units and structures, the decentralized and relatively narrow structure of bargaining units has continued in most public sector jurisdictions. The main exceptions to this characterization are to be found in some state governments and in very large cities, where unit consolidation and experiments with coalition bargaining have taken place. The latter experiments have occurred mainly in response to severe financial crises, such as in New York City.

There are two primary reasons that public sector bargaining has remained decentralized—one economic, the other political. The economic reason is that tax and revenue generation and allocation decisions are still made primarily at the local level. Even as large cities became increasingly dependent on state and federal sources of revenue, external funding agents did not attempt to constrain the wages paid to public employees, including those in New York City, Boston, Cleveland, and other cities where fiscal adversity had reached severe proportions. The political reason for this is that local authorities judiciously guard their autonomy on all issues, including decision making over collective bargaining. Thus, they are unlikely to be receptive to arrangements that require the sharing of authority or the coordination of decisions and policies with other political units. The same has historically been true on the union side. Consolidation of units or more temporary experiments in coalition bargaining require union leaders to overcome traditional rivalries and to coordinate decision making across two or more independent constituencies. For these reasons, bargaining has remained quite decentralized in local governments and school districts.

Although we do not foresee major changes in the structure of public sector collective bargaining, federal initiatives to reduce the budget deficit may have the effect of strengthening the role of state governments and weakening the role of local governments in both fiscal relations and labor relations matters. From this perspective, it will be primarily the state governments that must confront federal revenue shortfalls and decide how to make up those shortfalls, in part or in whole. Whether state governments focus their efforts on policies concerning sales taxes, income taxes, user fees, or revenue transfers, they are likely to hear from numerous local government officials who will argue in one way or another for state replacement of revenues previously derived from the federal government. In some cases, local government officials may be joined by local union officials, such as those from protective service and teacher unions, who generally are quite experienced at dealing with state legislatures on such issues as pension benefits and state aid to local education.

All this activity may culminate in a few experiments in regional or statewide collective bargaining. Although such initiatives are not expected to become permanent or to presage wholesale alterations in the structure of public sector bargaining, their possible emergence is nevertheless consistent with empirical studies showing that major changes in the economic-financial environment, and fiscal stress in particular, can have significant, if short-term, effects on bargaining structure.[10] In sum, it is possible that, in some parts of public sector, the structure of bargaining will become somewhat more centralized.

The Bargaining Process

Has the process of public sector bargaining continued to operate in multilateral fashion, or is it becoming more bilateral? Has public sector bargaining blocked other groups from participating in the political process on issues where their vital interests are at stake? Because there are no clear or readily agreed on benchmarks to use in answering these questions, we rely on our own value judgments in offering some conclusions.

First, where public sector labor agreements are reached routinely through negotiations—that is, where they are settled short of a declaration of impasse—bargaining appears to take on some characteristics of a bilateral process. Even in these cases, however, there is the potential for multiple management actors to negotiate with one or more public sector unions. Second, when negotiating impasses do take place, one or another third party almost always becomes involved. The fact that interest arbitration in the United States occurs almost entirely in the public sector adds to the multilateral character of bargaining in this sector and sharpens the contrast with bilateral negotiations in the private sector.

Third, some critical terms and conditions of employment in local govern-ment remain determined at the state government level, so that local govern-ment officials, especially local union officials, negotiate not only among themselves but also with state legislatures and state-level executives. Pension benefits are a common subject of such state-level negotiations. Thus, in a developed public sector bargaining system, such as exists among govern-mental units in the state of New York, local police, firefighter, and teacher unions continue to bargain over wages at the local level and over pensions at the state level. In the state of New Jersey, protective service unions have recently "negotiated" with state officials, notably the governor, to introduce new police and firefighter pension arrangements into local governments.[11] In Illinois and Ohio, public unionists have recently "negotiated" successfully for the enactment of statewide public sector bargaining laws, even though some of them were able to negotiate local labor agreements in the absence of sup-portive legislation. Further, these unionists can be counted on to engage in local-level negotiations over wages and other conditions of employment, and in state-level negotiations over pension benefits and retirement system contri-butions.

Fourth, the onset of a climate of economic-financial volatility in the pub-lic sector generally, and the development of an insurance crisis in some units of government particularly, seem likely to deepen the multilateral nature of public sector bargaining. Although in some cases this may result in local-level union–management coalitions to "negotiate" with county- or state-level rep-resentatives, in other cases it may pit state and local government management officials against local union representatives. In any case, such predicted sce-narios are more consistent with a multilateral rather than a bilateral concep-tualization of the public sector bargaining process. In a nutshell, we think that multilateralism will endure as a central feature of public sector bar-gaining.

Strikes and Dispute Resolution

No set of issues has provided more controversy and research than the role of the strike and alternative dispute resolution procedures. More than most others, these issues have provided us with a laboratory for experimentation and research. In return for these laboratory conditions, do we have some firm conclusions and advice to give to policymakers? We think we do, even though each of us has been critical of the quality of research conducted on these topics.

Based largely on the material presented in chapter 5, the following may be concluded:

1. The average duration of strikes is shorter in the public than in the private sector.

2. State bargaining laws that contain strong strike penalties and highly structured impasse procedures, such as New York's Taylor Law, have reduced the number of strikes that might otherwise have occurred. For example, strikes by teachers in New York under that state's procedures and penalties have been less frequent than in (a) a state like Pennsylvania, where the right to strike exists; (b) states like Illinois and Ohio (prior to 1983), where bargaining occurs in the absence of a specific bargaining law or impasse procedures; and (c) states like Michigan, where a bargaining law exists and strikes are illegal, but penalties for striking are weak and uncertain.

3. The number of strikes by units of essential service employees has been lower in states with interest arbitration laws than in states where these units bargain under a fact-finding procedure or without a law.

4. The occurrence of strikes does not uniformly result in more favorable bargaining settlements for employees than occur in nonstrike situations or as a result of interest arbitration.

5. The occurrence of strikes does not uniformly endanger the public interest. Rather, the public welfare consequences of public employee strikes vary from nonexistent to very large.

Even these statements should be interpreted and used cautiously. Recall that we are reporting only on the experiences under state laws passed in the United States during the 1960–1985 period. Whether jurisdictions in different environments with differing bargaining histories will experience these effects by passing laws similar to any of those discussed in this book is an open question. Again, we are more proficient in interpreting past experiences than in projecting these experiences into the future. In this regard, consider that few students of industrial relations predicted that private sector work stoppages would drop to record low levels in the 1980s or that the federal government would actually fire striking air traffic controllers and decertify the controllers' union.

What can be concluded about the performance of alternative impasse procedures in the public sector? The best that can be said, perhaps, is that researchers have become more sophisticated about this matter. There are very few evangelical zealots who still believe that there is one best way to resolve all bargaining disputes. Apparently and thankfully, we seem to have gone beyond arguing for a single fixed system of dispute resolution in all circumstances and at all times. Instead, there is growing recognition that a wide range of workable options are available to policymakers depending on the importance they place on alternative policy objectives.

If, for example, the most important objective is to avoid public employee strikes, then some form of arbitration appears to be the preferred option. If two objectives—avoiding strikes and avoiding dependence on arbitration—are both given great weight, then a form of final offer arbitration or perhaps a tripartite mediation and screening committee prior to invoking arbitration are options that, to date, have proved most likely to serve these goals. If the main concern is to limit the discretion of the arbitrator and maintain as much control as possible in the hands of the interested parties, then a tripartite arbitration structure may be built into the dispute resolution system. For those willing to relax somewhat their concern with avoiding strikes, a wide variety of additional options is available, ranging from the choice of procedures (for example, the right to strike or arbitration) to the right to strike itself. Those who remain philosophically opposed to both the right to strike and arbitration can turn to fact-finding with recommendations. The number of strikes that will actually occur under these alternative systems appears to turn on the severity and certainty of the strike penalties built into the law, the political contexts of the negotiations, the militancy of the parties to bargaining, and the role of third-party experts. Again, however, the validity of these predictions depends on the extent to which past experience can serve as a guide to future events.

The Outcomes and Impacts of Bargaining

The more the results and impacts of public sector bargaining are examined, the more they appear to parallel the effects of unions and bargaining in the private sector. Unions have had a positive impact on wages in the public sector. The magnitude appears to fall in the range between 5 and 15 percent—not very different from private sector estimates. Further, emerging evidence suggests that public sector unions have had a somewhat larger impact on fringe benefit expenditures than on wages, again paralleling the experience in the private sector. Finally, there is even some qualitative evidence suggesting that public sector unions have exerted a shock effect on public sector management—forcing managers to formalize policies, professionalize their service delivery and administration, and search for ways to recoup increases in labor costs.

These general statements cover an impressive range and diversity of union effects across bargaining units and organizations. Indeed, both in research and in practice, the next step regarding the effects of public sector bargaining is to examine variations in the impacts of collective bargaining on the key economic and behavioral goals of individual workers, employers, and public policy objectives, and to use these variations to point out ways that managers and unions can improve the effectiveness of their bargaining relationships by making them more responsive to these diverse needs and goals. We expect that pressures from the taxpaying public and from other sources external to the parties to public sector negotiations will mean that more will be demanded from collective bargaining in the years ahead, just as more is being demanded from all of our governmental institutions. Thus, we need to shift the attention of both researchers and practitioners from their traditional focus on procedural and institutional aspects of the bargaining relationship as ends in themselves to the question of how we can use and/or adapt these structures, policies, procedures, and practices in ways that will improve the performance of the bargaining relationship. In operational terms, this implies giving greater attention to the administration of the bargaining relationship during the life of a contract, and experimenting with and improving the performance of joint labor–management structures to address problems of productivity, safety and health, equal employment opportunity, quality of service, quality of working life, and so on. We know that these experiments do not always work and are not suited to all bargaining relationships. However, we need to break out of the inertia that characterizes bargaining relationships—relationships that are constantly preoccupied with questions of short-run procedural advantage at the expense of analysis of the long-run substantive impacts on the constituents served by the parties to bargaining.

Indeed, this charge may become all the more important if, as some evidence suggests, the public sector comes to dominate the private sector with respect to labor relations. Consider that the incidence of unionism is now far greater in government than in industry, that public sector bargaining agreements seem to be constituting a growing portion of all labor agreements, that some large industrial states have enacted new public sector bargaining laws, that the incidence of public sector interest arbitration is rising while the incidence of private sector strike activity is falling, and that bargained wage settlements currently are far larger in government than in industry. Whether or not these characteristics are peculiar to the third generation of public sector bargaining in the United States is problematic (as is the assertion that we are in a third generation), and it may be that the 1990s will parallel the 1970s in the sense that a period of public sector retrenchment and consolidation may occur. Even if this were to come about, however, the present size, scope, and importance of government generally, and of public sector labor relations in particular, supports the view that researchers should devote relatively more attention to the outcomes of public sector bargaining and to the impacts of those outcomes on the constituents of public enterprises.

Will the Public Sector Survive?

In our judgment, the public sector will certainly survive, but this is a bit like saying that capitalism will survive. The more pressing questions concern what form, scope, and structure the public sector will take on, and what impacts it will have on the larger society. To attempt to answer these questions would take us far beyond our area of expertise. But believing that the public sector will survive and recognizing the key role that labor relations have come to play in that sector, we close the text of this book by reiterating that it is crucial for researchers to analyze the environments, structures, processes, and outcomes that characterize public sector collective bargaining if greater understanding of such bargaining is to be achieved. Industrial relations researchers have been studying the private sector for decades, but most public sector research has been conducted only since the early 1970s. We believe that the public sector will continue to offer major research opportunities for industrial relations scholars, and that the application of these researchers' creative and analytical abilities will advance our knowledge of bargaining generally. If this book stimulates researchers' attention to these issues and problems and to the development of better theoretical and empirical studies, our collaborative authorship efforts will have been more than repaid.

Notes

1. "Harold Newman's Cloudy Crystal Ball," *PERB BULLETIN* (a monthly newsletter for mediators and fact-finders published by the New York State Public Employment Relations Board).

2. See Janet Norwood, "Perspectives on Comparable Worth: An Introduction to the Numbers," *Daily Labor Report,* January 17, 1986, and Marick F. Masters, "The Politics of Comparable Worth: A Case Study," unpublished manuscript, 1986.

3. Since 1980, for example, at least six states (Iowa, Minnesota, New Mexico, New York, Washington, and Wisconsin) have implemented comparable worth policies that have required some pay adjustments. See Marick F. Masters and Deborah Good, "The Effect of Unionization on States' Comparable Worth Policies," unpublished manuscript, 1986.

4. The information in this section is drawn from "Liability Insurance Squeeze Spurs Pleas to Hill for Relief," *Congressional Quarterly Weekly Report,* January 25, 1986, pp. 148–153; Nancy Blodgett, "Premium Hikes Stun Municipalities," *American Bar Association Journal* 72 (July 1, 1986), pp. 48–51; and "Liability Insurance Squeeze," *Editorial Research Reports,* December 6, 1985 (ii), pp. 907–923.

5. See, for example, Michael S. March, "Pensions for Public Employees Present Nationwide Problems," *Public Administration Review* 40, no. 4 (July–August 1980), pp. 382–389.

6. See "City Pension Plans Go Deeper in the Hole," *Business Week,* September 16, 1975, pp. 80–81.

7. Ibid.

8. Courtney Gifford, *Directory of U.S. Labor Organizations,* 1986–1987 edition (Washington, D.C.: Bureau of National Affairs, 1986), p. 67; U.S. Bureau of Labor Statistics, *Employment and Earnings* 33, no. 1 (January 1986), p. 214.

9. This evidence was reviewed in chapter 6.

10. See the Feuille et al. and Lewin-McCormick readings in chapter 3 and the Horton reading in chapter 4.

11. "Kean Urges New Pension Provisions for New Jersey Police and Firefighters," *New York Times,* January 17, 1987, p. B-2.

Part III
Bargaining and
Grievance Exercises

Collective Bargaining Exercise

This exercise was prepared for use as a learning experience in a public sector labor relations course. It is included in this book because it has been a useful teaching tool and has elicited highly favorable student reactions. In particular, students participating in this exercise have enthusiastically involved themselves in their negotiation roles and have commented favorably on what they perceive as the realism of their experience.

The case is best used toward the end of the semester to give students the opportunity to use the substantive knowledge they have acquired during the term. The negotiation portion of the exercise can profitably occupy four class meetings of one and one-half hours' duration, but the number of meetings can be changed to suit the length of the term, the length of the class periods, and instructor or students preferences. Four students per bargaining team is preferable in order to give each student the opportunity to participate fully, but the number can be varied to accommodate class size constraints. To save time and minimize arguments, the instructor may assign students to various negotiating roles (chief negotiator, attorney, and so on). Also to save time, the initial demands of union and management are specified in each case. The ideal physical location of each negotiation arena (one union and one management team) is a seminar room with a table that will accommodate at least four persons on each side, but changes can easily be made to conform to available settings. During the negotiating sessions, the instructor should be available nearby to handle any procedural questions and requests for case information.

The exercise is largely self-contained, with relevant background information, a set of union initial demands, a set of employer initial demands, and a current contract. The students are responsible for the actual conduct of the negotiation and impasse resolution processes. Their goal is to secure a new contract on favorable terms (which terms are defined by each bargaining team). Securing a new contract is easy; securing favorable terms is somewhat more difficult. There should be no bargaining outside the official negotiation sessions, although individual team preparation meetings outside of class hours will be necessary. To increase each team's negotiating incentives, the instructor might establish and use a contest in which prizes are awarded to the teams that bargain the best management contract and/or the best union contract.

From an equity standpoint, it is very difficult to grade the students' participation in this exercise. If a grade is deemed necessary, perhaps the most useful and equitable assignment is a postexercise paper in which each student analyzes (rather than merely narrating) the negotiation experience along several dimensions: how and why the team developed issue priorities, how and why the team resolved internal conflicts, what criteria were used in making bargaining table trade-offs, what kinds of attitudinal structuring activities took place across the table, what forces pushed the participants toward agreement or kept them in a state of disagreement (with a special focus on the role of the arbitration procedures), and so forth.

The instructor may want or need to make a few changes in the setting and substance of the case. For example, the New York location was used to increase the interest of the students in the course where the case was developed, and to use these students' knowledge of New York's Taylor Law. The instructor may find it useful to substitute the public sector legislation from his or her own state. Similarly, pensions were not included as an issue in this case because the New York legislature had removed them from the scope of bargaining. The instructor may want to include a pension demand to make the exercise conform more closely to local practice. In addition, each year the dates and salary figures in each exercise will need to be changed. Finally, if time constraints are tight, the number of issues can be reduced.

Exercise
QUEEN CITY, NEW YORK
and the
QUEEN CITY POLICE ASSOCIATION (Ind.)

[handwritten margin note: urban city]

Background

[handwritten margin note: weak economic condition]

Queen City is an aging central city of about 350,000 (1985 estimate) located in upstate New York, and is the center of a standard metropolitan statistical area (SMSA) of more than one million people. The city's main job base is in heavy manufacturing, but over the years the area has become steadily less attractive to employers because of obsolete plants and equipment, high taxes, high labor costs, and the like. As a result, many of them have moved away, taking thousands of jobs with them. This job decline is reflected in the SMSA's high unemployment rate (9.0 percent in 1987), and the hardest hit part of the area has been Queen City itself. The city has been losing population for years (in 1950 it had 560,000 residents), and it is no secret that most of the city's emigrants are middle-class whites fleeing what they perceive as unsafe streets, poor schools, and high taxes. Over the past two decades there has been an influx of blacks and Puerto Ricans, to the point where blacks currently make up about 25 percent of the city's population and Hispanics about 10 percent. Many members of these two groups are indigent; consequently, welfare costs have increased significantly over the past several years. One result of these population changes is a depletion of the city's tax rolls. In short, Queen City is a classic example of the stagnation and subsequent decline of central cities in the northeastern United States.

[handwritten margin note: declining tax base]

The city government is organized on a strong-mayor basis (that is, the mayor has appointive, budgetary, and veto powers over the city council), with the city council consisting of fifteen seats elected on a ward basis. The mayor and the council members serve four-year terms, with half of the council up for election every two years. The elections are partisan, and the city is solidly Democratic (the mayor and thirteen of the fifteen council incumbents are Democrats). The mayor is not only the dominant elected official but also the local strongman in the Democratic party—the closest thing Queen City has to a political boss. As a result, the council tends to pass what the mayor wants and to reject what he doesn't want. The annual budget approval process provides the best example of the mayor's hegemony.

City finances strongly reflect the city's weak economic situation. The 1988 city budget totals $350 million (the city school district has its own budget, and the school district has been similarly hit by stagnating revenues and increasing costs), and the city expects that its 1989 budget will require even more money. The current budget includes about $175 million in county-

[handwritten margin note: $350 M budget]

and state-collected revenues of various kinds and about $80 million in federal revenue, so the city has become the fiscal handmaiden of higher level governments. City officials have been hit with stagnating local revenues and increasing costs (the city's population decline has not been matched by a similar decline in the demand for city services, especially police and fire services), and each year is a struggle to break even. Next year promises to be tough because of the state's own financial problems and proclaimed inability to increase the amount of aid to local governments. City officials are constantly trying to persuade Queen County to assume various city functions (and, of course, their associated costs); but, given that county government is largely Republican, the usual response is negative. The city has reached the constitutional ceiling on its property tax (taxes equal to 2 percent of the full value of city property), which means that in coming years only minimal additional revenues can be derived from this source. Because of very strong voter resistance to higher taxes (New York citizens on a per capita basis pay among the highest state and local taxes in the nation), city officials are reluctant to increase property taxes and do not dare institute a city sales or income tax (the latter two taxes would need enabling legislation from Albany). For 1989, the city's best estimate is that it will have 2 percent more money to spend on services and functions that it now provides. Labor costs account for about 70 percent of the city budget.

The city government employs about 5,300 people (down from 6,500 in 1970), most of whom are in one of five bargaining units. The independent Queen City Police Association represents the patrol officers and communications operators in the Police Department; the International Association of Fire Fighters, AFL-CIO, represents the uniformed, nonsupervisory employees in the Fire Department; the American Federation of State, County, and Municipal Employees, AFL-CIO, represents most of the city's blue-collar employees (the majority of whom are in the Public Works and Parks departments); the independent Queen City Civil Service Association represents most of the city's white-collar employees (who are scattered across virtually all city departments); and the Queen City Building and Construction Trades Council, AFL-CIO, represents the various craft classifications (electrician, carpenter, plumber, and so on). The city has a reputation as a union town because of the high incidence of unionization in the private sector. Although this union influence contributed to the early and solid organization of the city's employees, and although some private sector union officials play important roles in local politics, it is not entirely clear how this union context has directly resulted in tangible benefits for city employees. Except for special cases, the city has not done any general hiring in the past several years, and municipal employee ranks have been thinned by attrition. Each year city officials contemplate actual layoffs, but in recent years layoffs have not been necessary.

The city's director of labor relations (DLR) heads the city's Office of Labor Relations and is responsible for the negotiation and administration of contracts with all the city unions. He is appointed by and serves at the pleasure of the mayor, and currently enjoys the mayor's complete confidence. He receives policy (that is, maximum dollar limit) guidance from the mayor and has been able to convince the mayor and the council to shut off union end runs on matters within the scope of bargaining. The DLR also maintains good relations with city department heads and works closely with them on contract language questions so that city labor contracts will not unduly limit managerial prerogatives. The city's collective bargaining takes place under the aegis of New York's Taylor Law (except as expressly modified for the purposes of this case) and the state Public Employment Relations Board's (PERB) decisions regarding the interpretation of the Taylor Law.

The Queen City Police Department is one of the most important of the city's departments. The police budget for 1988 totals about $52 million, of which almost 90 percent goes for labor costs (including fringes, which average about 50 percent of salaries). The average 1988 salary (excluding fringes) in the entire department is about $26,500, and the department consists of about 1,050 sworn officers and about 125 civilian employees, with the civilians employed in a wide variety of jobs (clerical, custodial, mechanical, administrative, communications, and so forth). The police bargaining unit consists of 800 patrol officers (including detectives) and 40 communications operators (COs). The COs are civilians, but they wear uniforms and some of them eventually become patrol officers. The department is directed by the police commissioner, who is appointed by and serves at the pleasure of the mayor. The department is divided into ten police precincts, each with its own stationhouse. Patrol officers assigned to regular patrol duty work out of the various station houses. Most patrol officers and COs work rotating shifts, which rotate every three months. The police department has the usual big city problems of crime, police–minority group friction, and political decision-making criteria.

The police union consists of two occupational groups, the patrol officers and the COs. The patrol officers naturally look down on the COs because of the latter's civilian status—they have no arrest powers and carry no weapons. The COs are in the unit, however, because there is some measurable "community of interest" across the two groups and because the union leadership want the COs there in case of a strike so that the police communications processes will be disrupted and there will be fewer personnel available for management to use during the stoppage. The union's membership (which includes 98 percent of the eligibles) is divided along the usual lines: age and seniority (the older officers are interested in pensions, the younger ones in wages and, more recently, job security), duties (the street patrol officers—the "combatants"—sneer at the desk jockeys or "noncombatants" in headquarters), and so on. There is—for a police union—the usual rank-and-file militance to get "more" and get it yesterday.

The parties negotiated approximately 3.25 percent and 3.5 percent pay increases (measured at step D) in the current two-year contract covering 1987–1988. Because these pay raises lagged behind increases in some other New York cities, the union and its members are looking for a nice catch-up increase. In addition, the younger and shorter service officers, concerned over possible layoffs, are looking for job security protection in this year's contract as well as the usual bundle of cash and other benefits.

Currently there is police and fire pay parity—not contractually, but as a result of a long-standing political custom. As a result, pay increases negotiated by one public safety group are given to the other group. In some years the police settle first, and in other years the firefighters are the pacesetters. Neither group has settled yet for 1989, and each group is keeping a sharp eye on the other.

Union Demands

After careful evaluation of membership desires, the police union leadership has formulated the following package of contract demands to be submitted to management. They are listed in no particular order of importance, though the weights attached to them should reflect the facts of the case. To facilitate cost calculations, background information is provided for some of these demands.

1. In light of police salaries elsewhere and increases in inflation, the union wants a 12 percent pay increase at all steps for patrol officers and communications operators.

2. The city will pay the entire cost of the family Blue Cross–Blue Shield–Major Medical coverage. The city already pays the employees' premium and most of the family premium. The current employee-only premium is $1,200 per year; the current family premium is $2,400 per year ($1,200 additional). Blue Cross benefits are the same across all city groups. Premiums have increased about 5 percent annually during the past three years. About 80 percent of the members have family coverage, and about 20 percent have single coverage. The health insurance plan covers all city employees.

3. The city will increase life insurance coverage from $25,000 to $40,000 and will continue to pay the full premium. Premiums currently are $80 per year per employee; the premium for $40,000 coverage would be $120 per year per employee. Police and firefighters receive the same life insurance benefits, but other city employees receive from $5,000 to $10,000 less coverage, depending on the unit.

4. The city will provide a dental insurance plan covering each employee and his or her family; premiums are $125 per year for single coverage and $300 per year ($175 additional) for family coverage. No other city group has dental insurance.

5. The city will provide a 10 percent shift premium for all hours worked between the hours of 6:00 P.M. and 6:00 A.M. No other city group receives such a premium. Approximately 50 percent of all police hours are worked between 6:00 P.M. and 6:00 A.M.

6. The city will increase annual longevity pay for patrol officers as follows: from the present $300 to $600 after 10 years service and $900 after 15 years service; from the present $600 to $1,200 after 20 years service and $1,500 after 25 years service. For COs, increases will be from $150 to $300 after 10 years service, to $450 after 15 years service, to $600 after 20 years service, and to $750 after 25 years service. Firefighters receive the same longevity pay as police; other city employees receive lesser amounts depending on the unit.

7. An increase in sick leave accrual to 18 days per year of service (or one and one-half days per month), including the first year, with the maximum accrual increased to 300 days. Whenever an employee is terminated for any reason, the employee shall receive a cash payment equal to the value of all accrued sick leave.

8. An increase in the uniform allowance to $450 for patrol officers and $225 for COs.

9. Four more paid holidays (Martin Luther King's birthday, Washington's birthday, Lincoln's birthday, and the day after Thanksgiving). Other city employees receive the same number of holidays the police currently receive. All officers are given one day's pay for each holiday. Officers who work on a holiday receive the one day's holiday pay just mentioned plus time-and-one-half for working on that day.

10. An increase in vacation time to 3 weeks after 5 years, 4 weeks after 10 years, 5 weeks after 15 years, and 6 weeks after 20 years. At present all city employees, including police, receive the same amount of vacation.

11. An increase in the standby pay rate as follows: 60 percent of the employee's straight time hourly pay rate for the first 8 hours; $35 for each 12-hour period (or fraction) thereafter. In an average week approximately 15 officers will be required to stand by for one shift (8 hours) each.

12. A new section 2.3 be added to article II that will establish an agency shop. About 98 percent of the unit already belong to the union, but union leaders believe that everyone should help pay for the costs of collective bargaining services.

13. Section 5.6 (Civil Service) be deleted and replaced by a new section: "*Just Cause*. No disciplinary action shall be taken against any member of the bargaining unit except for just cause." In 1987, seven major disciplinary cases

were processed and discipline levied by the police commissioner according to departmental and civil service regulations. Two of these cases involved discharges (for on-the-job misconduct), and both cases have been appealed to court (with the Association's assistance).

14. A no-layoff clause.

15. A requirement that seniority be the determining factor in layoffs, work assignments, transfers, vacation selection, and holiday scheduling. As a result of long-standing custom, seniority is currently used on a de facto basis for vacation selection and holiday scheduling, but this is not a contractual requirement. As in any large city police department, there is the usual griping that many personnel decisions are made according to favoritism and political criteria. Also as usual, there is little hard evidence to support these complaints.

16. A one-year contract expiring on December 31, 1989.

Again, these demands are not listed in any particular order of importance beyond the facts presented in the case. It is the responsibility of the union bargaining team to gather supporting evidence, to put priorities or weights on various items, to develop specific contract language to implement various proposals, to develop justifications for its demands, to decide what compromises to make, and to decide what will constitute a minimum acceptable agreement. The city currently is negotiating with all the other unions, and each is jockeying for position while keeping an eye on what is going on with the other groups. The current contract is enclosed.

Although the number of students to be assigned to each bargaining team will be constrained by the size of the class, experience has suggested that four students per team is preferable. The roles on the union bargaining committee include the union president and chief negotiator, the union attorney, the union secretary-treasurer, and a communications operator. Other roles can be added if necessary.

Employer Demands

In collective bargaining the employer typically spends much time responding to union demands. However, as a result of problems that have arisen during the life of the existing contract and because of the city's fiscal constraints, the city has formulated the following demands:

1. In light of the city's finances and the modest rate of inflation, no increase in pay during 1989, a 2 percent salary increase on January 1, 1990, and another 2 percent on January 1, 1991; and no increase in any fringe benefit at any time. Considering how fringe benefit increases spread to other city bargaining units, the city is especially eager to avoid benefit increases.

2. A reduction in the off-duty court appearance pay minimum guarantee to one hour. About 100 officers per week make off-duty court appearances, and the city estimates that about 50 percent of them complete their appearances in less than three hours.

3. Sick leave accrual to remain the same; however, there shall be no payment to terminated or retired officers.

4. The definition of a grievance be changed such that everything beyond the comma in section 5.1 is deleted. During 1987, about 300 step 1 grievances were filed, and five of these went all the way to arbitration. The Association won three cases (overtime pay, court appearance pay, and standby pay), and the city won two (sick leave pay at termination, Association representation at a step 1 grievance meeting). All five of the arbitration cases involved contractual interpretation disputes, but about one-quarter of the step 1 grievances did not. The city does not want to process city or department rules complaints through the grievance procedure, and it notes that these matters can be processed through the existing civil service appeals procedure.

5. Deletion of the phrase "or at least reasonably close to these time limits" in the second sentence of section 5.4.

6. Insertion of the following sentence into article VI such that it is the second sentence in that article: "The Association agrees that if any such activity occurs the Association and its officers and agents shall work as speedily and diligently as possible for the complete cessation of any such activity." There have been no strikes in the department's history, but at contract negotiation time there are periodic rumblings from some officers about "showing the city we mean business."

7. The elimination of communications operators from the bargaining unit so that the unit will be limited to police patrol officers.

8. A three-year contract expiring on December 31, 1991.

These demands are not presented in any particular order of importance. It is the responsibility of the management bargaining team to gather supporting evidence, to put priorities or weights on various items, to develop specific contract language to implement various proposals, to develop justifications for its proposals, to respond to union demands, to decide what compromises to make, and to decide what will constitute a minimum acceptable agreement. The city currently is negotiating with all the other unions, and each is jockeying for position while keeping an eye on what is going on at the other bargaining tables. The current contract is enclosed.

Again, four-member student teams are recommended. The roles on the management bargaining team include the director of labor relations and chief negotiator, an assistant city attorney, an assistant budget director, and a deputy police commissioner. More roles may be added if necessary.

Impasse Resolution

If no agreement is reached by the end of the time set aside for direct negotiations, there are a variety of methods for resolving the impasse: mediation, fact-finding, some form of arbitration, or strike. In light of the increasing use of compulsory arbitration to resolve police and firefighter bargaining impasses, it would be useful and instructive to have any impasse in this case be resolved by the following arbitration procedures. If two or more negotiation arenas exist, it may be particularly instructive to use two or three of the following methods in order to see what impact the different procedures have on the bargaining process.

Final Offer Arbitration with Package Selection

If the two sides do not reach full and complete agreement by the end of the time set aside for negotiations, then all unresolved items shall be submitted directly to final offer arbitration. Specifically, at the next class session, each party shall submit to the arbitrator (the instructor or the instructor's designee) and to the other party a written list of all unresolved items and its final offer on each of those items. Each party shall concurrently submit a list of all items, if any, that have been agreed on in direct negotiations. The arbitration hearing shall commence promptly at the beginning of the class period and shall be heard by the single arbitrator with full powers to issue a binding decision. Each side shall have twenty minutes to present its case and an additional five minutes for rebuttal, and each side shall be responsible for developing and presenting justifications of its final offer. The arbitrator's decision shall be final and binding upon the parties. The decision, together with accompanying explanation, shall be delivered orally to the parties before the end of the class period.

The arbitrator shall be limited in his or her decision to choosing the most reasonable final offer. The arbitrator shall not compromise or alter *in any way* the final offer he selects. The arbitrator shall make his selection decision on an entire package basis (that is, he shall *not* make separate selection decisions on each issue), and his selection, together with any previously agreed-on items, shall constitute the new collective bargaining agreement between the parties. In making his determination of the most reasonable offer, the arbitrator shall be guided by the arbitration criteria listed at the end of this section.

Nothing in the foregoing shall preclude the parties from requesting a recess during the arbitration hearing in order to resume direct negotiations, nor shall it preclude the arbitrator from recessing the hearing and ordering the parties to resume direct negotiations if the arbitrator believes that such resumption of negotiations may be helpful in resolving the impasse. Similarly, nothing in the foregoing shall limit the arbitrator from rendering any mediation assistance to the parties if the arbitrator believes such assistance will be helpful in resolving the impasse. (Time constraints, however, will limit the amount of additional negotiation or mediation activities during the arbitration session.)

Final Offer Arbitration with Issue-by-Issue Selection

Everything is the same as stated in the preceding section, with the important exception that the arbitrator will make a separate "most reasonable" selection decision on each issue in dispute.

Conventional Arbitration

Many of the details are the same as stated in the first section, with the important exception that the arbitrator can fashion the award he or she deems appropriate and hence is not limited to selecting either party's final offer.

Arbitration Criteria

In reaching a decision, the arbitrator shall take into consideration the following:

1. Comparisons of the wages, hours, and conditions of employment of the employees involved in the arbitration proceeding with the wages, hours, and conditions of employment of other employees performing similar services or requiring similar skills under similar working conditions in public employment in comparable communities
2. The interests and welfare of the public and the financial ability of the public employer to pay
3. The average consumer prices for goods and services in the area, commonly known as the cost of living
4. The overall compensation currently received by the employees, including direct wages, vacations, holidays and other excused time, insurance and pensions, medical and hospitalization benefits, the continuity and stability of employment, and all other benefits received
5. Changes in any of the foregoing circumstances during the preceding negotiations or during the arbitration proceedings
6. Such other factors, not confined to the foregoing, that are normally or traditionally taken into consideration in the determination of wages,

hours, and conditions of employment through collective bargaining, fact-finding, or arbitration in public employment

Postexercise Analysis

The instructor and the students will find it profitable to spend all or most of a class period analyzing the negotiation and impasse resolution experiences of the various bargaining teams (whether or not they go to arbitration). The students probably will have numerous questions about various facts of the negotiation and impasse processes, and the instructor should have a variety of constructively critical comments to make about how the students tried to obtain a favorable contract.

Background Information

Tables 1-5 provide background information for this exercise.

Table 1
Queen City Budget, 1988

Revenues

Local:	
Property taxes	$79,025,000
Licenses and permits	2,705,000
Parking meters	2,400,000
Fines and forfeitures	3,550,000
Interest	1,300,000
Other local	5,480,000
County and state distributions:	
Sales taxes	70,600,000
Gasoline taxes	4,700,000
State aid	100,115,000
Federal revenues:	
Shared revenue	17,900,000
Housing and community development	50,880,000
Other federal	12,045,000
Total revenues	$350,700,000

Appropriations

Police department	$52,150,000
Fire department	41,610,000
Public works and sanitation department	65,750,000
Parks and recreation department	11,675,000
Finance and accounting department	5,005,000
City auditor	1,480,000
Total departments	$177,670,000
City's share of special districts:	
School	$8,680,000
Sewers	15,865,000
Public health	6,175,000
Public housing	80,500,000
General administration	61,090,000
Reserve	720,000
Total appropriations	$350,700,000

Table 2
New York Comparability Information for Patrol Officers, 1988

City (Pop.)	Longevity Pay			Health Insurance (Percentage paid by employer)		Dental Insurance (Percentage paid by employer)	
	Maximum Salary	Maximum Amount	Years to Max.	Employee	Family	Employee	Family
Rockville (250,000)	$25,700	$1,000	25	100%	100%	100%	50%
Swinton (180,000)	25,000	800	20	100	90	100	0
York (200,000)	24,900	1,200	30	100	100	75	0
Albert (110,000)	24,300	750	25	100	95	Not provided	
Queen View (50,000)	23,700	600	20	100	80	Not provided	
Queen Woods (60,000)	24,900	600	20	100	90	Not provided	
Queen Falls (85,000)	24,600	900	25	100	100	100	0

City	Annual Clothing Allowance	Term Life Insurance Coverage	Sick Leave		Night Shift Premium	Number of Paid Holidays
			Days per Year	Maximum Accrual		
Rockville	$400	$30,000	12	180	None	12
Swinton	325	20,000	12	150	25¢/hr.	11
York	350	25,000	12	120	3%	12
Albert	400	20,000	15	200	None	11
Queen View	300	15,000	10	125	None	11
Queen Woods	325	20,000	12	140	None	10
Queen Falls	350	20,000	12	160	None	10

Note: Over the years the City and the Association have relied heavily on these New York cities for comparison purposes. Queen View, Queen Woods, and Queen Falls are suburbs of Queen City; the other cities are located in upstate New York. None of these cities have negotiated or arbitrated their 1989 contracts. From time to time the City and the Association also look at similar size cities in other states.

Table 3
Queen City Police Salary History

Year	Step D Patrol Officer	Step D Communication Operator
1980	$18,000[a]	$13,800[a]
1981	18,900[a]	14,700[a]
1982	20,100[a]	15,800[a]
1983	20,900[a]	16,500[a]
1984	21,600	17,000
1985	22,300	17,600
1986	23,000	18,200
1987	23,750	18,800
1988	24,600	19,450

[a](Salaries set by an arbitrator; salaries in other years determined in collective bargaining. The city and the Association negotiated a two-year contract for 1987–1988; the arbitrator issued a two-year award in 1980–1981; all other contracts and awards were for one year each.

Table 4
Police Bargaining Unit Seniority Distribution

Years of Service	Number of Employees
25 or more	90
20–24	160
15–19	230
10–14	225
5–9	100
4	12
3	10
2	8
1	5
Probationary	0

Note: Within each years-of-service category, employees are distributed on a linear basis.

Table 5
Queen City, New York Salary Schedule, Effective January 1, 1987, through December 31, 1987
(annual salaries)

Step	Patrol Officer	Communications Operators
A (Probationary)	$20,000	$15,200
B	21,200	16,400
C	22,400	17,600
D	23,750	18,800

Salary Schedule Effective January 1, 1988, through December 31, 1988
(annual salaries)

Step	Patrol Officer	Communications Operators
A (Probationary)	20,200	$15,400
B	21,500	16,700
C	22,800	17,900
D	24,600	19,450

On the annual anniversary date of his or her employment, each employee shall advance one step until Step D is reached.

Longevity Pay, Effective January 1, 1987, through December 31, 1988
(annual salaries)

After completing the specified years of service, each eligible employee shall receive an annual longevity stipend, as follows:

	Patrol Officer	Communications Operators
After 10 years	$300	$150
After 20 years	600	300

AGREEMENT
between
QUEEN CITY, NEW YORK
and
QUEEN CITY POLICE ASSOCATION
January 1, 1987
through
December 31, 1988

AGREEMENT

This Agreement is entered into by and between Queen City, New York (hereinafter called the "City"), and the Queen City Police Association (hereinafter called the "Association").

ARTICLE I
Recognition and Representation

The City recognizes the Association as the sole and exclusive bargaining agent with respect to wages, hours, and other conditions of employment for employees classified as Police Patrol Officer and Communications Operator.

ARTICLE II
Check-off

Section 2.1. Check-off Association Dues. Upon receipt of a signed authorization from an employee in the form set forth by the City, the City agrees for the duration of this Agreement to deduct from such employee's pay uniform monthly Association dues. The Association will notify the City in writing of the amount of the uniform dues to be deducted. Deductions shall be made on the second City payday of each month and shall be remitted, together with an itemized statement, to the Treasurer of the Association by the 15th day of the month following the month in which the deduction is made.

Section 2.2. Indemnification. The Association shall indemnify the City and hold it harmless against any and all claims, demands, suits, or other forms of liability that may arise out of, or by reason of, any action taken by the City for the purpose of complying with the provisions of this Article.

ARTICLE III
No Discrimination

Section 3.1. General. Neither the City nor the Association shall discriminate against any employee because of race, creed, color, national origin, sex, or Association activity.

Section 3.2. Job Transfer. The City will not use job transfer as a form of disciplinary action. Violations of this section will be subject to the grievance procedure.

ARTICLE IV
Management Rights

The City shall retain the sole right and authority to operate and direct the affairs of the City and the Police Department in all its various aspects, including, but not limited to, all rights and authority exercised by the City prior to the execution of this Agreement. Among the rights retained is the City's right to determine its mission and set standards of service offered to the public; to direct the working forces; to plan, direct, control and determine the operations or services to be conducted in or at the Police Department or by employees of the City; to assign or transfer employees; to hire, promote, demote, suspend, discipline or discharge for cause, or relieve employees due to lack of work or for other legitimate reasons; to make and enforce reasonable rules and regulations; to change methods, equipment, or facilities; provided, however, that the exercise of any of the above rights shall not conflict with any of the provisions of this Agreement.

ARTICLE V
Grievance Procedures

Section 5.1. Definition of Grievance. A grievance is a difference of opinion between an employee or the Association and the City with respect to the meaning or application of the express terms of this Agreement, or with respect to inequitable application of the Personnel Rules of the City or with respect to inequitable application of the Rules of the Police Department.

Section 5.2. Association Representation. The Association shall appoint an Employee Committee of not more than three members to attend grievance meetings scheduled pursuant to Steps 3 and 4. The Association may appoint three Stewards, one from each shift (who may be the same persons selected for the Employee Committee), to participate in the grievance procedure to the extent set forth in Step 1 and Step 2 of the grievance procedure. The Association shall notify the Director of Labor Relations in writing of the names of employees serving on the Employee Committee and as Stewards. One representative of the Executive Board of the Association and/or the Association's legal counsel shall have the right to participate in Steps 3, 4, and 5 of the grievance procedure.

Section 5.3. Grievance Procedure. Recognizing that grievances should be raised and settled promptly, a grievance must be raised within seven (7) calendar days of the occurrence of the event giving rise to the grievance. A grievance shall be processed as follows:

Step 1. Verbal to Immediate Supervisor. By discussion between the employee, accompanied by his Steward, if he so desires, and his immediate supervisor. The immediate supervisor shall answer verbally within seven (7) calendar days of this discussion.

Step 2. Appeal to Captain. If the grievance is not settled in Step 1, the Association may, within seven (7) calendar days following receipt of the immediate supervisor's answer, file a written grievance signed by the employee and his Steward on a form provided by the City setting forth the nature of the grievance and the contract provision(s) involved. The Captain shall give a written answer in seven (7) calendar days after receipt of the written grievance.

Step 3. Appeal to Police Commissioner. If the grievance is not settled in Step 2 and the Association decides to appeal, the Association shall, within seven (7) calendar days from receipt of the Step 2 answer, appeal in writing to the Police Commissioner. The Employer Committee and the Commissioner will discuss the grievance at a mutually agreeable time. If no agreement is reached in such discussion, the Commissioner will give his answer in writing within seven (7) days of the discussion. The City may join the Step 3 and Step 4 meetings if it so desires, by having in attendance both the Commissioner and the Director of Labor Relations or his designee.

Step 4. Appeal to Director of Labor Relations. If the grievance is not settled in Step 3 and the Association decides to appeal, the Association shall, within seven (7) calendar days after receipt of the Step 3 answer, file a written appeal to the Director of Labor Relations. A meeting between the Director, or his designee, and the Employee Committee will be held at a mutually agreeable time. If no settlement is reached at such meeting, the Director, or his designee, shall give his answer in writing within ten (10) calendar days of the meeting.

Step 5. Arbitration. If the grievance is not settled in accordance with the foregoing procedure, the Association may refer the grievance to arbitration by giving written notice to the Director of Labor Relations within twenty-one (21) calendar days after receipt of the City's answer in Step 4. The parties shall attempt to agree upon an arbitrator promptly. In the event the parties are unable to agree upon an arbitrator, they shall jointly request the Federal Mediation and Conciliation Service to submit a panel of five arbitrators. The Association shall strike one name and the City shall strike one name; then the Association shall strike another name, and the City shall strike another name, and the person whose name remains shall be the arbitrator; provided that either party, before striking any names, shall have the right to reject one panel of arbitrators. The arbitrator shall be notified of his selection by a joint letter from the City and the Association requesting that he set a time and a place for hearing, subject to the availability of the city and Association representative. The arbitrator shall have no right to amend, modify, nullify, ignore, add to, or subtract from the provisions of this Agreement. He shall consider and decide only the specific issue submitted to him, and his decision shall be based solely upon his interpretation of the meaning or application of the terms of this Agreement to the facts of the grievance presented. The decision of the arbitrator shall be final and binding. The costs of the arbitration, including the fee and expenses of the arbitrator, shall be divided equally between the City and the Association.

Section 5.4. Time Limits. No grievance shall be entertained or processed unless it is filed within the time limits set forth in Section 5.3. If a grievance is not appealed within the time limits for appeal set forth above, or at least reasonably close to the time limits, it shall be deemed settled on the basis of the last answer of the City, provided that the parties may agree to extend any time limits. If the City fails to provide an answer within the time limits so provided, the Association may immediately appeal to the next Step.

Section 5.5. Investigation and Discussion. All grievance discussions and investigations shall take place in a manner that does not interfere with City operations.

Section 5.6. Civil Service. It is understood that matters subject to Civil Service, such as promotion, discharge, and disciplinary suspension of seven days or more, are not subject to this grievance procedure. However, in the event a permanent employee is discharged or suspended for seven days or more, the Association may request a meeting to discuss said discharge or suspension prior to institution of a Civil Service appeal. Upon receipt of such request, the City will meet promptly at Step 3 or Step 4 for this purpose.

ARTICLE VI
No Strikes-No Lockouts

The Association, its officers and agents, and the employees covered by this Agreement agree not to instigate, promote, sponsor, engage in, or condone any strike, slowdown, concerted stoppage of work, or any other intentional interruption of operations. Any or all employees who violate any of the provisions of this Article may be discharged or otherwise disciplined by the City. The city will not lock out any employees during the term of this Agreement as a result of a labor dispute with the Association.

ARTICLE VII
Wages and Benefits

Section 7.1. Salary Schedules. The salary schedule and longevity pay effective from January 1, 1987, through December 31, 1987, and from January 1, 1988, through December 31, 1988, is attached hereto.

Section 7.2. Fringe Benefits. The fringe benefits in effect during the term of this Agreement shall be as follows:
a. *Holidays* shall be as follows:

New Year's Day	Veteran's Day
Good Friday	Thanksgiving
Memorial Day	Christmas Eve
Fourth of July	Christmas
Labor Day	New Year's Eve

b. *Vacation* shall be accrued at the following rates:

Recruitment through sixth year	2 weeks
Seventh through fourteenth year	3 weeks
Fifteenth and later years	4 weeks

Uniform Allowance. The City shall provide annual uniform allowances as follows:

Patrol Officers:	$350
Communications Operators:	$175

In the administration of the foregoing uniform allowance, the City will not set any dollar limit on any authorized item.

d. *Group Insurance.* The City's term life insurance program ($25,000 coverage per employee) shall be continued in effect for the term of this Agreement, and the City's 100 percent contribution shall continue. The City's Blue Cross–Blue Shield–Major Medical program (single and family coverage) shall be continued in effect for the term of this Agreement. For the term of this Agreement, the City shall pay the entire cost of "employee only" Blue Cross–Blue Shield–Major Medical coverage. As of January 1, 1987, the employee's monthly contribution for "family" Blue Cross–Blue Shield–Major Medical coverage shall be $8.00.

e. *Retiree Blue Cross–Blue Shield–Major Medical Coverage.* An employee who retires on or after January 1, 1987, and is eligible for an immediate pension under the New York Police pension fund, may elect "employee only" or "family" coverage under the City's Blue Cross–Blue Shield–Major Medical program by paying the entire group premium cost, which may increase from time to time, by means of deduction from the pensioner's pension check.

f. *Sick Leave.* The City's sick leave plan shall be continued in effect for the term of this Agreement (accrual of 6 days for the first full year of employment and 12 days for subsequent full years of employment), with the maximum accrual increased to 150 days. Whenever an employee with ten years or more of service is terminated for any reason, the employee shall receive one of the following, whichever is greater: (1) payment of all sick days accrued in excess of 50 days (to a maximum of 25 days' pay), or (2) the current four-week special retirement allowance for employees who retire with eligibility for current pension benefits.

Section 7.3. Overtime Pay for Emergency Duty. A Patrol Officer shall receive time and one-half his regular straight-time hourly rate when ordered to report for overtime emergency duty or when ordered to remain on the job for overtime emergency duty. A Patrol Officer will not receive overtime pay for any work during his regular working hours.

Section 7.4. Off-Duty Court Appearance Pay. A Patrol Officer shall receive time and one-half his regular straight-time hourly rate for required court appearances during his off-duty hours. Patrol Officers shall be guaranteed three hours at the time and one-half rate for each separate off-duty court appearance or actual time spent, whichever is greater.

Section 7.5. Emergency Standby Pay. Whenever the City places an employee on emergency standby, the employee shall receive standby pay as follows: (1) for the first four hours, 30 percent of the employee's straight-time hourly rate, and (2) for each twelve-hour period thereafter, or fraction thereof, $15.00.

ARTICLE VIII
Termination and Legality Clauses

Section 8.1. Savings. If any provision of this Agreement is subsequently declared by legislative or judicial authority to be unlawful, unenforceable, or not in accordance with applicable statutes or ordinances, all other provisions of this Agreement shall remain in full force and effect for the duration of this Agreement.

Section 8.2. Entire Agreement. This Agreement constitutes the entire agreement between the parties and concludes collective bargaining on any subject, whether included in this Agreement or not, for the term of this Agreement.

Section 8.3. Term. This Agreement shall become effective January 1, 1987, and shall terminate at 11:59 P.M. on December 31, 1988. Not earlier than July 1, 1988, and not later than August 1, 1988, either the City or the Association may give written notice to the other party by registered or certified mail of its desire to negotiate modifications to this Agreement, said modifications to be effective January 1, 1989.

Queen City   Queen City Police Association

Public Sector Grievance Arbitration Exercise

T he following grievance arbitration exercise illustrates some of the issues that public employers and unions present to grievance arbitrators. This exercise is based on an actual case heard by one of the authors (the names of the organizations and individuals involved have been changed). Of the three issues presented to the arbitrator, one is most pertinent to teacher unions and school boards; the other two are applicable to all public unions and employers. Specifically, the key issue that generated this arbitration was a dispute over a teacher's placement on the school district's salary schedule. The handling of this matter generated two procedural disputes: whether or not the salary placement grievance was timely referred to arbitration by the teachers' union, and whether or not the district was justified in charging employees 15 cents per page for copying materials in their personnel files in conjunction with the processing of the salary placement grievance.

The reader is presented with the pertinent background facts, the contentions of the teachers' union and the school board, and the relevant contract provisions. Armed with this information (which is a summarized version of the evidence presented to the arbitrator), the reader is asked to render a decision and supporting opinion on each of the three disputed issues as if the reader were the arbitrator. To increase the value of this decision-making exercise, the actual award in this matter is *not* printed here.

PRAIRIELAND COMMUNITY UNIT SCHOOL DISTRICT
and
PRAIRIELAND EDUCATION ASSOCIATION

The Prairieland Community School District ("District") employs 200 teachers to educate its 3,400 students in grades K–12. Prairieland is on the edge of a small metropolitan area in central Illinois, and its population (20,000 in 1987) has been slowly expanding. As a result, the District's enrollment and number of teachers have also been increasing, in contrast to declines in many other districts. The Prairieland Education Association ("Association"), which is an affiliate of the Illinois Education Association–National Education Association, is the exclusive bargaining representative of all the District's teachers. About 90 percent of the District's teachers are Association members (that is, the contract does not contain an agency shop clause).

On September 2, 1987 (the school year started on August 25), teacher Judy Arlington ("Grievant") filed a grievance protesting the fact that she was placed in the MS column of the teachers' salary schedule. She believed that she should be placed in the MS + 16 column (see the reprinted contractual salary schedule) because of the additional graduate credit hours she had completed. In accordance with the contractual grievance procedure (see the reprinted grievance procedure), the Grievant and Association Grievance Chair Joan Edwards informally discussed the grievance with Assistant Superintendent Douglas Collings on September 10. The parties were unable to resolve the matter at this meeting. After additional discussion of the matter between Ms. Edwards and Superintendent Lee Wilson, the District and the Association agreed to bypass Steps 1 and 2 in the grievance procedure. Ms. Edwards indicated that the Association needed time to investigate the matter fully before making a decision to take the grievance to arbitration (which is Step 3 in the grievance procedure). As a result, on September 16 she and the Superintendent agreed in writing that the Association had until October 24 to file a "demand for arbitration" with the District. On October 22 Ms. Edwards indicated that she needed more time to investigate the matter, and the two of them agreed in writing to extend the Association's arbitration filing deadline to December 5. By December 5, however, the Association had not given any indication to the District regarding arbitration of this grievance.

In the meantime, the Association filed another grievance on behalf of eight teachers who copied numerous pages from their personnel files in connection with the salary placement grievance. The District charged them 15 cents per page for this copying, and the Association grieved on October 31 that this copying charge violated the contract. The parties were unable to resolve this matter during their grievance procedure discussions in subsequent weeks.

On January 8, 1988, Ms. Edwards met with Superintendent Wilson and suggested that the salary placement grievance and the copying cost grievance be consolidated and referred to arbitration together. The Superintendent demurred and indicated that the salary placement grievance was dead because the Association had failed to meet the December 5 arbitration filing deadline; therefore, he said, only the copying grievance could be arbitrated. Ms. Edwards strenuously disagreed, but on January 15, 1988, Grievant Judy Arlington refiled her salary placement grievance. Thereafter the Superintendent refused to discuss the merits of the salary placement dispute on the grounds that the matter was procedurally dead.

After additional discussion, the parties agreed to consolidate the following three issues in a single arbitration proceeding:

1. Did the District violate Article 23 by charging employees more than the District's actual cost of duplication for duplicated materials? If so, what is the appropriate remedy?

2. Were the September 2, 1987, and/or January 15, 1988, grievances regarding the salary schedule placement of Grievant Judy Arlington timely filed and processed within the meaning of Article 6 and hence arbitrable?

3. If the matter in issue number 2 is ruled to be arbitrable (and the District continues to insist that it is not), did the District violate Article 21 or Appendix A by the manner in which the District placed Grievant Judy Arlington on the salary schedule? If so, what is the appropriate remedy?

The arbitration hearing occurred on April 24, 1988.

POSITION OF THE ASSOCIATION

Copying Grievance

The Association says there is no justification for the District's charge of 15 cents per page for duplicated material. The Association says that this excessive charge clearly violates the Section 23.F contractual requirement that payment for copying "shall be based on the District's actual cost of duplication." The Association says that the District's standardized 17.5 cents per page cost calculation clearly is not based on the District's actual cost of duplication. The Association says that the District's itemized costs are excessive, especially the costs for paper and clerical staff time; further, the Association says that the assumptions involved in the District's calculations do not use actual costs. The Association estimates that the District's actual costs are 3 cents per page: 1 cent for depreciation of the copying machine, 1 cent for toner, and 1 cent for staff time. The Association says that eight teachers copied a total of 380 pages of material from their personnel files at a total cost of $57. As a remedy, the Association requests that the District be ordered to charge its estimated actual cost of 3 cents per page and that the District be ordered to reimburse the employees charged the 15 cent rate the difference between 3 cents and 15 cents.

Arbitrability of the Salary Placement Grievance

The Association agrees that the September 2, 1987, salary placement grievance was not referred to arbitration by the December 5 deadline, but the
Association says that there is a reasonable excuse for this. The Association
says that the lengthy period between September 16 and December 5, including the extension of the original October 24 arbitration filing deadline to
December 5, gave a clear signal to the Association that the District was willing to interpret loosely the December 5 arbitration filing deadline. As a result,
the Association says it had good reason to believe that it could file for arbitration after the December 5 deadline. Further, the Association says it had difficulty in acquiring all the information it needed to make an arbitration filing
decision by December 5 because of the controversy created over the excessive
copying charge.

In addition, the Association says that if the September 2 grievance is
ruled nonarbitrable, the January 15 refiled grievance clearly is arbitrable.
The Association points out that the ongoing nature of the claimed salary
placement error makes this grievance continuously timely (that is, every
month that the Grievant continues to be paid in the MS column rather than
the MS + 16 column constitutes a new violation). Further, the Association
says that Section 6.13 allows the September 2 grievance to be considered
withdrawn "without precedent," which means that the grievance clearly can
be refiled on January 15. Moreover, the Association says that the District
refused to discuss the merits of the refiled January 15 grievance, and thus the
Association was unable to process the refiled grievance through the prearbitration steps of the grievance procedure. Also, the Association says it is ironic
that the District was quite willing to skip these lower steps with the September 2 grievance, but that the District now insists that the January 15 grievance must be processed through these steps. The Association requests that the
September 2 grievance be ruled to be timely filed and processed and hence
arbitrable and, failing that, that the January 15 grievance be ruled to be
timely filed and processed and hence arbitrable.

Merits of the Salary Placement Grievance

The Grievant teaches junior and senior English, which is a mixture of composition and English and American literature, at the District's high school. Her
classes are aimed at preparing students for college; almost all of her students
go on to college. She is in her ninth year in the District, so she is on experience
Step 9 on the salary schedule. She is widely regarded as an excellent teacher.
She has a B.A. in English (with a minor in French) and an M.A. in Education,
both from the University of Illinois, and she is certified by the state as a sec-

ondary English teacher. During the past three years she has completed 18 additional graduate credit hours of coursework at the nearby University of Illinois. All six of these courses have been in French literature, and she has performed well in all of them.

The Association argues that these additional graduate credit hours entitle the Grievant to be placed in the MS + 16 salary column. The Association says there is no question that these additional credits were earned from an accredited university, or that all of these credits were earned and reported to the District prior to the start of the 1987–1988 academic year (Ms. Arlington completed the most recent courses during the 1987 summer session).

In response to the District's contention that these credit hours were not earned in the Grievant's teaching subject areas, the Association makes two points. First, the Association notes that during the 1986–1987 and 1987–1988 years the Grievant incorporated a few French literature reading assignments (translated into English) into the literature portions of her English classes. The Association notes that this improved the quality of the course by enabling students to compare English and American writers with French writers. Second, the Association points out that the District has allowed other teachers credit for salary placement purposes for courses they took that were outside their teaching subject areas. Specifically, math teachers Barbara Kinney and William Goldman, chemistry teacher Christine Garcia, and physics teacher Ben Browder were given salary placement credit for courses in computer science that they completed. None of these teachers teaches computer science, but they nevertheless were given credit for these courses because of the computer applications in their courses. The Association says that the Grievant's application in her course of her recently acquired knowledge of French literature is very similar to the situations of these other four teachers. The Association adds that it is just as important to reward teachers for additional education in the liberal arts and humanities as it is in such currently fashionable areas as computer science. As a result, the Association says it is inconsistent and hence an unreasonable exercise of managerial discretion for the District to deny salary placement credit to the Grievant.

In response to the District's claim that the Grievant did not obtain advance approval from the administration for her additional coursework, the Association says that there is no requirement anywhere in Article 23 or in Appendix A that such advance approval is necessary. In addition, the Association says there are at least three instances during the past four years where teachers received salary placement credit for courses they completed without advance approval.

In sum, the Association says that the District's denial of salary placement credit to the Grievant for her completed coursework is an inconsistent, inequitable, and hence unreasonable exercise of managerial discretion, and thus the District violated Article 23 and Appendix A. As a remedy, the Association asks that the Arbitrator order the District to place the Grievant in the MS + 16 column retroactive to the start of the 1987–1988 school year, pay her the difference between the salary she earned and the salary she would have earned had she been properly placed, and place her in the MS + 16 in future years.

POSITION OF THE DISTRICT

Copying Grievance

The District says that it has carefully calculated its "actual cost of duplication" to justify the 15 cents per page charge. Amortizing the cost of the copying machine in the District's administrative office over its expected five-year life, assuming 60,000 copies produced annually on the machine (which is the number of pages specified in the maintenance contract for the machine); assuming one minute of clerical staff time for each copied page; and using approximate cost figures for maintenance, paper, and toner and developer, the district calculates its actual cost of duplication as 17.5 cents per page. This figure is arrived at by adding 1 cent per page for machine depreciation, 1 cent for maintenance, 1 cent for toner and developer, 0.5 cent for paper, and 14 cents per page for clerical staff time. The District notes that by far the largest share of the duplicating cost comes from charging for the time of the clerical staff who perform or administer the actual copying. The District says that the clerical staff must retrieve the documents to be copied, copy them, return the documents to the files, collect payment, and in general oversee the copying. While this copying work is being done the clerical employee essentially is precluded from performing other duties, and the District insists that it is entitled to be compensated for this staff time. The district points to Secretary Donna Garrett's testimony that it took her 45 minutes to copy 50 pages of requested material from one teacher's personnel file, and that single-page copying requests often require more than one minute to complete, as justification for the one minute per copied page assumption. The average hourly pay rate of the five clerical employees who perform this copying is $8.38 per hour (the range is $6.25 to $9.60 per hour), and the District has used this average rate to calculate the cost of staff time.

The District says it is entitled under Section 23.L to charge the full amount of its actual cost of duplication, and that the full amount includes all the relevant operating costs plus attendant labor costs. The District agrees that specific copying requests may take more or less time than the one minute per page assumption used in its calculation, but the evidence indicates that this is a reasonable assumption. The District says that it is highly impractical and hence unreasonable to require the District to time each copying request with a stopwatch and perform a separate calculation for the cost of clerical time devoted to each request. In general, the District says it has used reasonable assumptions in performing these copying cost calculations, and that it does not charge employees for the complete amount of its final copying costs. The District notes that it specified its cost calculation in a multipage written exhibit replete with various receipts for copying equipment and supplies, but that the Association offered no evidence whatsoever to support its 3 cents per page estimate. In addition, the District says that its 15 cents charge is consistent with the charges levied by other school districts in Prairie County, which range from 5 to 25 cents per page. Further, the District charges 15 cents per page to members of the public who request copies, so it is not discriminating against the teachers. Accordingly, the District says that no contract violation has occurred, and thus the grievance should be denied.

Arbitrability of the Salary Placement Grievance

The District says that the salary placement grievance is dead. The Association had a clear and unambiguous obligation, expressed in writing, to inform the District by December 5, 1987, if the Association was going to take the September 2 grievance to arbitration. The Association clearly did not do this, and the Association has acknowledged that it did not do so. There is no reasonable excuse for missing this deadline, according to the District. The fact that the District agreed to extend the original October 24 arbitration filing deadline to December 5 cannot be interpreted to mean that December 5 is a meaningless date, which can be unilaterally extended by the Association. In particular, the extension of the deadline to December 5 does not constitute a signal from the District that the arbitration filing deadline would be loosely interpreted. Instead, the District agreed to this extension only as a professional courtesy to Ms. Edwards, this extension was expressed in writing so that there would be no disagreement later about the extended deadline, and there never was any subsequent discussion about extending the December 5 deadline. In addition, the copying cost dispute arose in October and is completely irrelevant to this missed December 5 deadline. Consequently, the District insists that the September 2 grievance has been "deemed withdrawn" under Section 6.7 and hence is no longer arbitrable.

Regarding the January 15, 1988, refiled salary placement grievance, the District agrees that the matter in dispute involves an alleged ongoing contractual violation. However, the District points to the final sentence in Section 6.1 and says that this "bars future appeal" language makes the refiled grievance also nonarbitrable. The District says that this language should be interpreted to prevent the kind of grievance refiling that occurred here. In addition, the District says that the refiled grievance was never processed through the prearbitration steps of the grievance procedure. As a result, this January 15 grievance is not properly before the Arbitrator, and thus its merits should not be addressed. The District says that a decision that this refiled grievance is arbitrable will send a message to the Association that it can file a grievance and then immediately take it to arbitration. The District says that the Arbitrator should not allow the parties to bypass the prearbitration steps, for such a bypass eliminates the possibility of a bilateral resolution of the grievance prior to arbitration. For these reasons, the District says that the January 15 grievance is not arbitrable.

Merits of the Salary Placement Grievance

If either salary placement grievance is ruled to be arbitrable, the District says that it correctly placed Grievant Judy Arlington on the salary schedule and thus no contractual violation occurred.

The District points out that there is no language in Article 23 or Appendix A that provides any teacher with a guarantee that all graduate credits would be applied to horizontal advancement across the salary schedule. Instead, this District has had a lengthy, well-developed, and fully understood past practice regarding horizontal salary schedule advancement, and the Grievant's situation is not consistent with this past practice.

First, the District says that the Grievant never sought advance approval for her coursework beyond the MA degree. The District agrees that there is no contractual requirement that this approval be obtained, but the District says that the Superintendent or Assistant Superintendent have met with several teachers each year to discuss teacher plans for additional graduate coursework. The District says that these discussions have been crucially important in those instances where there is some doubt whether the proposed coursework falls within the teacher's subject area. The District says that the Grievant never had such a discussion with the administration at any time, and thus she undertook this additional study at her own risk. The District agrees that at least three teachers had coursework credited without advance approval during the past four years, but the District says that in each of these three cases the teacher's coursework was clearly and directly relevant to the teacher's subject area.

Second, the District says it has had a clear policy for at least the past ten years of only allowing salary schedule placement credit for additional coursework in the teacher's subject area. Because the Grievant is a state-certified English teacher, her advanced coursework in French literature is clearly outside her teaching area, and thus this coursework has not been applied to her placement on the salary schedule. As an English teacher, the Grievant teaches a mixture of composition and English/American literature. French literature has nothing to do with these subject areas. The District has no objection to the Grievant's recent incorporation of a very modest amount of French literature into her classes (as long as the amount remains modest), but the District notes that this new subject matter is neither a necessary nor an integral part of her classes, was not requested by the administration, and was done by the Grievant on her own initiative. Consequently, her French literature coursework is too far afield from her teaching area to warrant salary schedule credit.

The District also says that the Grievant's situation is different from the situation involving the four teachers mentioned by the Association (Kinney, Goldman, Garcia, and Browder). Four years ago the Board of Education decided to enhance computer education, especially at the high school. This decision included not only the purchase of numerous personal computers and the development of computer science courses, but also the development of computer applications in other courses, especially math and science courses. These four teachers were willing to develop such applications in their courses, and they were willing to pursue advanced education to acquire the necessary expertise. To provide a monetary incentive for these (and other) teachers to pursue such education, the administration agreed that such coursework would be credited for salary placement purposes. In addition, these four teachers obtained advance approval for this coursework. As a result, the District says that the Grievant's situation clearly is not comparable to the situation involving these four teachers.

In general, the District agrees with the concept of continuing advanced education for incumbent teachers. However, the District insists that such education must be directly relevant to the teacher's subject content or instructional methods for such advanced education to merit a monetary reward. The District insists that it is extremely unwise to expend its scarce dollars to reward teachers for taking additional coursework that is not relevant, or only tangentially relevant, to their teaching duties, and the District points out that it has never done so in the past—even for excellent teachers such as the Grievant. As a result, the District says that the Association is using this grievance to establish a precedent that will enable other teachers to obtain unjustified salary rewards. The District notes that there is no contract language or past practice evidence that supports this grievance, and therefore it should be denied.

RELEVANT CONTRACT PROVISIONS

Article 6—Professional Grievance Procedure

Section 6.1. Grievance Defined. Any claim by the Association, a group of teachers, or a teacher that there has been a violation, misinterpretation, or misapplication of the terms of this Agreement, or that the teacher's rights under this Agreement have been impaired, must be brought to the attention of the immediate supervisor within twenty (20) days of the date of occurrence of the matter or the date the situation ceased to exist. Failure to act within this time limit bars future appeal.

Section 6.4. Informal Step. The parties hereto acknowledge that it is usually most desirable for a teacher and the supervisor immediately involved to resolve problems through free and informal communications. When requested by the grievant, the building representative may accompany the grievant to assist in the informal resolution of the grievance. If however, such aforementioned informal processes fail to resolve the grievance, it may then be processed as follows:

Section 6.5. Step 1. The Grievant may present the grievance in writing to the supervisor immediately involved who will arrange for a meeting to take place within four (4) days after receipt of the grievance. The grievant and the immediately involved supervisor shall be present for the meeting. The supervisor shall provide a written answer to the grievant within two (2) days after the meeting. The answer shall include the reasons for the decision.

Section 6.6. Step 2. If the grievance is not resolved at Step 1, then the grievant shall refer the grievance to the Superintendent or his official designee within six (6) days after receipt of the Step 1 answer or within eight (8) days after the Step 1 meeting, whichever is the later. The Superintendent shall arrange for a meeting with the grievant to take place within five (5) days of his receipt of the appeal. Each party shall have the right to include in its representation such witnesses as it deems necessary to develop facts pertinent to the grievance. Upon conclusion of the hearing, the Superintendent shall have three (3) days in which to provide a written decision with reasons to the grievant.

Section 6.7. Step 3. If the Association is not satisfied with the disposition of the grievance at Step 2, the Association may submit the grievance to final and binding arbitration. If a demand for arbitration is not filed with the District within fifteen (15) days of the date of the Step 2 answer, then the grievance shall be deemed withdrawn. If after seven (7) days of the filing of the demand with the District the parties cannot agree on an arbitrator, the demand shall be submitted to the American Arbitration Association, which shall act as the administrator of the proceedings.

The fees and expenses of the arbitrator and the court reporter (if requested) shall be shared equally by both parties. If either party requests a postponement of the arbitration meeting, all costs related to the postponement shall be the responsibility of the requesting party. Expedited arbitration may be used when mutually agreed upon by both parties. It is further agreed that no new information shall be submitted during arbitration proceedings.

Section 6.8. Bypass. If the grievant and the Superintendent agree, Step 1 and/or Step 2 of the grievance procedure may be bypassed and the grievance brought directly to the next step.

. . .

Section 6.13. Withdrawal of Grievance. A grievance may be withdrawn at any level without establishing precedent.

Article 21 — Professional Compensation and Related Provisions

Section 21.1. Credit for Teaching Experience. The teacher shall be awarded full credit for teaching experience outside of the District. Fractions of years earned outside of the District will not count.

Section 21.2. Salary Schedule Placement. For the purpose of placement on the Salary Schedule, a teacher who has had at least one previous contract within the District, and who had completed a fraction of a year, greater than one-half, shall be given credit for one full year of teaching for that fraction.

Section 21.3. Salary Schedule. The salary schedule shall be added as Appendix A for 1987–1988.

. . .

Article 23 — Personnel Files

. . .

F. The teacher may copy material maintained in his/her personnel record. Payment for record copying shall be based on the District's actual cost of duplication.

Table 1 shows the salary schedule for 1987–1988.

Table 1
Salary Schedule, 1987–1988
(in dollars)

Years	BS	BS + 16	MS	MS + 16	MS + 30	MS + 45
1	15,800	16,300	16,800	17,300	17,800	18,300
2	16,300	16,825	17,405	17,915	18,425	18,935
3	16,800	17,350	18,010	18,530	19,050	18,570
4	17,300	17,875	18,615	19,145	19,675	20,205
5	17,800	18,400	19,220	19,760	20,300	29,840
6	18,300	18,925	19,825	20,375	20,925	21,475
7	18,800	19,450	20,430	20,990	21,550	22,110
8	19,300	19,975	21,035	21,605	22,175	22,745
9	19,800	20,500	21,640	22,220	22,800	23,380
10	20,300	21,025	22,245	22,835	23,425	24,015
11	20,800	21,550	22,850	23,450	24,050	24,650
12	21,300	22,075	23,455	24,065	24,675	25,285
13	21,800	22,600	24,060	24,680	25,300	25,920
14		23,125	24,665	25,295	25,925	26,555
15			25,270	25,910	26,550	27,190
16			25,875	26,525	27,175	27,825
17				27,140	27,800	28,460
L[a]	22,100	23,525	26,425	27,740	28,500	29,260

[a]L = Longevity.

Questions

1. How would you decide the copying cost grievance, and why? How many separate copying cost elements may properly be included in "the District's actual cost of duplication"?

2. Is the September 2, 1987, salary placement grievance arbitrable? Why? If not, is the January 15, 1988, grievance arbitrable? Why?

3. If you ruled that the salary placement matter is not arbitrable, then the merits of the grievance are beyond the jurisdiction of the Arbitrator and hence are moot. If you ruled that this matter is arbitrable, how did you rule on the merits of the grievance? Why? If you ruled for the District and denied the grievance, there is no need for a remedy to be awarded. If you ruled for the Association and affirmed the grievance, what remedy did you award?

Index

About the Editors

David Lewin is professor of business, director of the Industrial Relations Research Center, and director of the Ph.D. program at the Columbia University Graduate School of Business. He has published seven books and many scholarly and professional journal articles on collective bargaining, wage determination, and human resource management. He serves as a consultant to business, labor, and government, is a member of the mediation-fact-finding panel of the New York State Public Employment Relations board, and serves on the executive board and program committee of the Industrial Relations Research Association. He holds M.B.A. and Ph.D. degrees from UCLA.

Peter Feuille is professor of labor and industrial relations at the University of Illinois School of Labor and Industrial Relations. He has published widely on public sector unionism, bargaining, and dispute resolution, with special emphasis on interest arbitration. The coauthor of *Police Unionism,* Professor Feuille has frequently served as an arbitrator of public sector bargaining disputes in several states. He was elected to the executive board of the Industrial Relations Research Association in 1984 and is a member of the Academy of Management. He holds a Ph.D. degree from the University of California, Berkeley, and has taught industrial relations at the University of Oregon and the State University of New York at Buffalo.

Thomas A. Kochan is professor of industrial relations at the Sloan School of Management, Massachusetts Institute of Technology. He has published many books and articles on both public and private sector labor-management relations, including *The Transformation of American Industrial Relations.* He is a member of the Industrial Relations Research Association, the Society for Professionals in Dispute Resolution, and the Academy of Management. Professor Kochan often serves as a consultant to business, labor, and government, including the U.S. Department of Labor. He holds a Ph.D. degree from the University of Wisconsin and formerly taught at Cornell University.

John Thomas Delaney is associate professor of business and research associate with the Industrial Relations Research Center at Columbia University Graduate School of Business. He has published many articles on public sector bargaining, unions and politics, and the regulation of industrial relations in such journals as *Industrial Relations, Industrial and Labor Relations Review, Journal of Labor Research, American Journal of Political Science,* and *The Arbitration Journal.* A member of the Industrial Relations Research Association, Academy of Management, and American Economic Association, Professor Delaney holds a Ph.D. degree from the University of Illinois.